A CENTURY OF JEWISH LIFE

by

ISMAR ELBOGEN

PHILADELPHIA
THE JEWISH PUBLICATION SOCIETY OF AMERICA
5704–1944

Copyright, 1944, by

THE JEWISH PUBLICATION SOCIETY OF AMERICA

All rights reserved. No part of this book may be reproduced in any form without permission in writing from the publisher: except by a reviewer who may quote brief passages in a review to be printed in a magazine or newspaper.

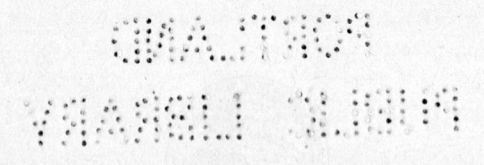

PRINTED IN THE UNITED STATES OF AMERICA
PRESS OF THE JEWISH PUBLICATION SOCIETY
PHILADELPHIA, PENNA.

Dedicated to

THE DROPSIE COLLEGE
FOR HEBREW AND COGNATE LEARNING

◆

THE HEBREW UNION COLLEGE

◆

THE JEWISH INSTITUTE OF RELIGION

◆

THE JEWISH THEOLOGICAL SEMINARY OF AMERICA

PREFACE

THE American edition of Graetz's *History of the Jews* has enjoyed an undiminished popularity for more than a generation. For this reason the Jewish Publication Society thought it desirable to supplement Graetz's monumental work with an equally authoritative and attractive account of the stirring, profound and significant events of the past fifty years. This presentation was to begin where Graetz left off.

The problem of authorship for the proposed volume was happily solved by the arrival in the United States of Professor Ismar Elbogen. On his part, he recognized here an opportunity to summarize his own lifetime of wide reading and study, as well as active participation in the making of Jewish history. He, therefore, undertook the task enthusiastically.

Professor Elbogen wisely interpreted his purpose to be not only the presentation of the events of the past half century, but also the re-interpretation, in the light of their consequences, of those movements which originated during the second half of the 19th century and which furnished the foundations of our contemporary world. Graetz himself, because of his proximity to the scene, had overlooked some of those events and failed properly to evaluate others. This volume, therefore, records the history of the Jews, not from where Graetz left off, but rather from the generation before that time, thus encompassing *A Century of Jewish Life*.

Untimely death robbed Professor Elbogen of the earthly joy of seeing the publication of this volume. Fortunately, however, his manuscript was completed and its translation from the German finished in time for the author to give it his considered approval. His friend, Professor Alexander Marx, who serves as Chairman of our Committee on Jewish History and Literature, has contributed an especially written Appreciation of Professor Elbogen, in which he makes clear how great is the loss suffered by Jewish scholarship in the learned historian's death. We are deeply grateful to Professor Marx for this labor of love and tribute.

During the preparation of the manuscript for the press, Professor Elbogen mentioned to the Editor various institutions and individuals whom he desired to thank for their assistance. He was most grateful to the Dropsie College, the Hebrew Union College, the Jewish Institute of Religion and the Jewish Theological Seminary of America for providing him with the leisure needed for his scholarly research and the preparation of this volume. Cherishing high hope for the future of Jewish life in the United States, Professor Elbogen expressed the wish that the volume be dedicated to these four institutions of higher learning as token of his faith in the happy future of American Jewish scholarship.

He also wished to thank the American Jewish Historical Society and Rabbi Isidore S. Meyer, its Librarian, for the many kindnesses and courtesies he received and Professor Moses Hadas for the exacting pains he took in translating the manuscript.

And, finally, Professor Elbogen spoke of the aid given him in the preparation of the manuscript by his wife, Mrs. Regi Elbogen. To the gratitude which he would undoubtedly have expressed to her, had he written this Preface, the Editor wishes to add the thanks of the Jewish Publication Society, as well as his own, for her valuable assistance in seeing the book through the press; no small part of that labor lay in reading the proofs. There may be others whom Professor Elbogen would have

PREFACE

desired to thank here; but the Editor is aware only of those mentioned.

For the helpful assistance given him during these labors, the Editor conveys his personal appreciation to Professor Moses Hadas for aid in the proof-reading and for making the Index; to Doctor Joshua Bloch, Chief of the Jewish Division of the New York Public Library; to Professor Jacob R. Marcus of the Hebrew Union College; and again to Professor Alexander Marx.

It is a high privilege, indeed, to have been associated with the lovable and learned author of this volume, whose achievements have enriched the literature of Israel and whose memory will prove a blessing to the Jewish people and all mankind.

SOLOMON GRAYZEL, *Editor*

THE JEWISH PUBLICATION SOCIETY OF AMERICA

Ismar Elbogen: An Appreciation

By Alexander Marx

IT IS a sad privilege to introduce to the public the last work of my distinguished colleague and dear friend, Professor Ismar Elbogen. In 1938, shortly after his arrival in this country, I approached him on behalf of the Publication Committee of the Jewish Publication Society with the proposal to add a volume to Graetz's *History of the Jews*, bringing it down to the present. He took up the suggestion with enthusiasm, and with his unusual energy he threw himself into the new task for which he was prepared as few others. A few days before his untimely death, on August 1, 1943, one month before completing his sixty-ninth year, he revised the epilogue of the book to which he had dedicated the last five years of his life.

To a future historian Professor Elbogen's activity will be part of the history of the Jews of the past hundred years to which this volume is devoted, for during the last four decades he played a conspicuous role in various aspects of this history in the country of his birth. To enable us to appreciate his place in Jewish life I have endeavored in these pages to give a brief outline of his activities as educator, scholar and servant of his people.

Born on September 1, 1874, in Schildberg, a city of the former German province of Posen, the son of a learned teacher, Ismar Elbogen received his education in Breslau under the supervision of his uncle, Professor Jacob Levy (1819-1892), the famous lexicographer. His early teachers of Talmud were Hayyim Bloch, a talmudic scholar, and Mr. Tiktin, a grandson of Rabbi Abraham Tiktin. After completing the course at the Breslau *Gymnasium*, he entered, in 1893, the Jewish Theological Seminary founded in that city by Zacharias Frankel. There Elbogen studied under David Rosin, Saul Horowitz, Marcus Brann and the eminent Talmud critic, Israel Lewy, who, among all his teachers, exerted the greatest influence on him and whose favorite pupil he became.

In 1898 Elbogen received the diploma of Doctor of Philosophy from the Breslau University for a thesis on one of Spinoza's philosophical treatises (*Der 'Tractatus de intellectus emendatione' und seine Stellung innerhalb der Philosophie Spinozas*). In the following year he graduated from the Seminary and shortly thereafter was called to the *Collegio Rabbinico Italiano* at Florence as teacher of Jewish History and Bible. Here he laid the foundation for his thorough knowledge of Italian Jewish history and literature with which many of his articles are concerned.

After three years of successful activity at Florence he accepted a call from the Berlin *Lehranstalt* (1922–1933, *Hochschule*) *für die Wissenschaft des Judentums*. To this institution Elbogen devoted the greater part of his life up to the time when conditions compelled him to give up his fruitful activity and leave the now inhospitable fatherland. He interrupted his work in Berlin only twice: once for the winter of 1922–1923 when he accepted the invitation of the Jewish Institute of Religion at New York to become a guest-lecturer, and again in October 1928 to deliver a series of lectures at the Hebrew University in Jerusalem.

At the *Lehranstalt* Elbogen taught Jewish history, literature, liturgy and cognate subjects, and, in addition, during the entire period, he taught a class in Talmud.

The chairmanship of the faculty rotated among its members, but the actual direction gradually was turned over to Elbogen because of his great talent for organization and his readiness to give service. He was deeply concerned with the welfare of the students, who always came to him with their troubles and needs, certain to find a ready ear and a helpful suggestion. He provided for their physical as well as for their spiritual well-being.

When Hitler's "new order" excluded the Jewish students from the German universities, the *Lehranstalt* enlarged its scope to include philosophy and other indispensable general subjects. It devolved upon Elbogen to plan these additional courses.

His service to the cause of Judaism, however, was not limited to teaching and administrative activity in that institution. With his gifts as an organizer, his encyclopedic learning, his wisdom, his lovable personality, and his ability to get along with people, it was natural that he should occupy a leading position in all the organizations and causes which enlisted his interest. Learned institutions and those which aimed at propagating Jewish knowledge in wider circles primarily appealed to him. Thus he became a leading member of the board of the Collected Archives (*Gesamtarchiv*) of the German Jews, of the Academy for the Science of Judaism at Berlin, of the Society for Furthering the Science of Judaism (*Gesellschaft zur Förderung der Wissenschaft des Judentums*), of the Society for Jewish History and Literature which he served as president for nearly three decades, of the Committee for the Publication of Jewish Youth Literature (*Jugendschriften Kommission*) of the Order B'nai B'rith of Germany, of which latter he was also president at one time, of the University Extension (*Volkshochschule*), and of other organizations too numerous to mention. He also served on the board of the Judaistic Institute of the Hebrew University, Jerusalem.

German Jewry, moreover, turned to Elbogen not only in his capacity of expert on questions of scholarship and education; he was also called upon to help them solve their practical problems. When the Union of Prussian Communities (*Landesverband Preussischer Gemeinden*) was founded in 1925 he became a member of its Council and, some years later, was elected to the executive board, from which he resigned after three years for reasons of health. He was prominently concerned with the cultural activities which originated with that body: he became chairman of the Committee for the Preservation of Monuments of Jewish Art and a member of the Committee of Education which arranged for the training of teachers and the establishment of extension courses. He joined the examining board of the preparatory training school for teachers and the liberal Committee of Worship, under whose auspices he produced the Union Prayer Book for the liberal German Jewish communities (*Einheitsgebetbuch*).

Though overloaded with public duties, he gave freely of his time and his best efforts to all the tasks entrusted to him. At the same time he was one of the editors of the Doctrines of Judaism (*Lehren des Judentums*, 1920–1929), of the *Jüdisches Lexikon* (1927–1930), of the *Encyclopedia Judaica* (1928–1934), of the comprehensive edition of Moses Mendelssohn's Collected Works (1929 seq.), of the *Zeitschrift für die Geschichte der Juden in Deutschland* (1929–1937), which he re-established in cooperation with A. Freimann and M. Freudenthal and which was particularly close to his heart, and of the Jubilee volumes for several prominent Jewish scholars such as Heinrich Brody, Hermann Cohen, Simon Dubnow, and others.

When, under the impact of the Hitler regime, the whole of German Jewry at last united to form the *Reichsvertretung der deutschen Juden*, he became chairman of its Committee on Education, which was given the task of organizing parochial schools and preparing their curricula. As a member of the Editorial Committee his advice was sought in the selection and revision of textbooks.

When Dr. Elbogen finally felt constrained to leave Germany, his outstanding position in the Jewish scholarly world found unique recognition in this country. Four of the important institutions of higher Jewish learning—the Dropsie College, the Hebrew Union College, the Jewish Institute of Religion, and the Jewish Theological Seminary of America—combined to invite him as a research professor on their faculties. He thus was enabled to spend the last years of his life free from official duties and could devote himself completely to scholarly work of his own choosing. Elbogen adapted himself with great ease to the new conditions and felt happy in the surroundings already familiar to him from his former visit.

It is almost unbelievable that, with all the demands on his time as teacher and as leader of German Jewry, Elbogen was able to make most valuable original contributions to Jewish learning—an astounding evidence of his amazing capacity for work. The bibliography of his writings up to 1934 enumerates over three hundred publications: fifteen books and pamphlets, two hundred and twenty-five articles, and sixty-three reviews; besides some two hundred and seventy contributions to various encyclopedias, some of the latter forming extensive and important treatises.

Elbogen's interests were so varied and his great learning so embracing that hardly any branch of Jewish knowledge was foreign to him. Jewish liturgy and history, however, were the fields to which he devoted the greatest part of his literary work.

An accident seems to have turned him to the study of liturgy. A prize had been announced at the Breslau Seminary in 1898 for tracing the history of the Eighteen Benedictions. The subject attracted the young scholar, who received the award. Publication had been made the condition for this particular prize contest, and thus his *Geschichte des Achtzehngebetes* appeared in 1902. In his preface the author expresses in the warmest terms his indebtedness to his revered teacher, Professor Israel Lewy, a tribute paid again a decade later in his comprehensive work on the liturgy. One might suspect that it was the influence of Israel Lewy which had lead Elbogen to this branch of Jewish literature. In the following years he wrote several further studies on liturgical subjects, one of them inaugurating the series of publications of the institution at which he was teaching. His activity in this field culminated after a decade in his book on Jewish worship in its historical development (*Der jüdische Gottesdienst in seiner historischen Entwicklung*) which appeared in 1912 and was reprinted with additional notes in 1924 and 1931. The author continued to do considerable work on this subject, which had a great attraction for him and to which many of his articles in various encyclopedias are devoted. During his last years he planned to rewrite and enlarge the book that had established his pre-eminence in the field for which Zunz had laid the scientific foundation. Elbogen felt that, after thirty years, a mere revision was not sufficient, but that a complete recasting was required. It is a matter of deep regret that it was not granted him to accomplish this task.

Elbogen's book is mainly concerned with the ancient prayers, medieval religious poetry taking a secondary place in his account. Although he was conservative in his inclinations and belonged to the middle party, his interest in the religious life of his own time prompted him not to limit himself to the past but to pay considerable attention to the liturgical reforms of the last century. His book was quickly accepted as the standard work in its field and gave its author a place in the forefront of Jewish scholars.

In the early years of the present century the biased characterization of Pharisaism on the part of the famous theologians Harnack and Bousset had spread in wide circles a false, one-sided picture of rabbinic Judaism. Their presentation was based on a complete ignorance of the true source, that is the old tannaitic literature, which was inaccessible to them except insofar as it was translated. There was a general feeling in Jewish circles that an authoritative account of the teachings of the Pharisees should be available to the public. It was this need which induced Elbogen, a year after he came to Berlin, to deliver a series of public lectures on The Religion of the Pharisees.

Part of these lectures was published in 1904 as *The Religious Views of the Pharisees* (*Die Religionsanschauungen der Pharisaeer*). Therein the author revealed himself as an apologist whose chief care was to present a correct picture of Pharisaic Judaism as contained in the sources. He let the facts speak for themselves rather than write a polemic essay refuting false statements in detail.

His first important contribution to the study of Jewish history, the other branch of Jewish scholarship which attracted Elbogen from the outset of his career, appeared in 1902. His *The Latest Construction of Jewish History* (*Die neueste Construction der jüdischen Geschichte*) is a lively criticism of a learned work by Isaac Halevy which deals with the end of the talmudic and the geonic periods. Elbogen proves that a partisan approach and a lack of scientific method vitiate the conclusions of this one-sided book, which is full of bitter attacks against the German Jewish scholars.

An excellent, brief *History of the Jews after the Fall of the Jewish State* was published in a general series of short, comprehensive, popular booklets on subjects of general interest (*Aus Natur und Geisteswelt*, vol. 748, 1919). In accordance with his method, Elbogen aimed to deal with the fate of the Jews in connection with general history, to show the driving forces of the historical development and to present a graphic and objective picture of Jewish history. Originally intended for the Jewish soldiers, it appeared after the end of the first World War. The author hoped it would contribute to a better understanding between the Jew and his neighbors. A second edition appeared in 1920, a Swedish translation in 1922 and an English one, revised and somewhat enlarged by the author, in 1926.

When the absolute failure of assimilation had become evident and a new interest in their past had been awakened among the German Jews, Elbogen followed up his general Jewish history with a more extensive, equally popular *History of the Jews in Germany* (1935). Both these books are devoid of footnotes and all dry scientific accessory material, but they are based on researches extending over decades. Offering in attractive form the mature result of Elbogen's studies, they show the hand of the master. Every statement had been carefully weighed and all controversial questions had been examined, so that the books present thoroughly reliable information in brief compass.

A carefully documented outline of the history of the Jews in Germany up to 1238 forms the introductory essay of the first and only volume of the *Germania Judaica* of which he was one of the editors (1934). In this connection the popular volume, *Personalities and Events of Jewish history* (*Gestalten und Momente aus der jüdischen Geschichte*, 1927), may be mentioned.

Most of Elbogen's writings treat of specific topics or single branches of Jewish research. In one of his papers, however, he dealt with the whole complex of the subject. In the jubilee volume published on the fiftieth anniversary of the *Lehranstalt*, in 1922, he drew an outline of "A Century of The Science of Judaism" (*Ein Jahrhundert Wissenschaft des Judentums*) showing sovereign mastery of the entire field combined with sound judgement. He pointed to the difference between the former study of the traditional literature and the modern investigation of all aspects of Jewish life and its manifestations. In rapid survey he characterized the important contributions to the various fields and drew attention to the numerous desiderata in all of them. From the individual scholar he turned to the institutions dedicated to the propagation of Jewish learning in the European countries and the United States and to the periodical publications devoted to it. He expressed regret that the lack of prospects for economic security makes it impossible to train a generation of young scholars who might in time replace the older men. Finally Elbogen discussed the definition of the Science of Judaism which, according to him, is "the science of living Judaism standing in the midst of evolution as a sociological and historical unit."

This definition was taken up again by him ten years later, on the sixtieth anniversary of the *Lehranstalt* (1932), and here he examined the influence of the present and its demands on the Science of Judaism and the institutions dedicated to it.

The progress in the field of Jewish history since the time of Graetz is the subject of Elbogen's contribution to the jubilee volume for Simon Dubnow (1930): "From Graetz to Dubnow, Fifty Years of Jewish Historical Research." In this paper he showed how much the aims of Jewish historiography had changed during the period under discussion. Examination of the archives in various countries as well as the discovery of the Genizah had added greatly to the source material and, together with a more methodical and philological treatment of the sources on the part of trained scholars, had pushed subjective hypotheses into the background. The limits of research had been extended by including careful consideration of the legal, social, economic, and cultural elements and by attention to the close connection between Jewish and general history.

It is from this point of view that Elbogen approached his task in the present work, the maturest fruit of his scholarly activity. All these aspects are given due consideration in his treatment. The present volume is by far the best and most adequate discussion that we have of modern Jewish history. Meant as a supplement to the master-work of Graetz, it shows the same warmth of tone, though it is much more objective. Eastern Jewry and that of the United States are dealt with on a par with the Jewries of Western Europe. The development in Palestine evokes the writer's sympathy and admiration to the same degree to which the cruel fate of European Jewry under the heel of Hitler arouses his burning indignation. It is a vivid and, at the same time, authoritative account of the development of the last hundred years of Jewish history in all its aspects. And in this work the author's statements are amply documented in the copious references at the back of the volume. It is the end of an important epoch in Jewish history, delineated on the basis of careful study of the sources by the hand of an eminent scholar who could speak from personal knowledge of the more recent events, and who, with all his sympathy, does not lose his well-balanced judgment.

This posthumously published book will greatly contribute to the knowledge and understanding of modern Jewish history and will preserve the memory of a man whom we esteemed for his scholarship as well as for his human qualities.

CONTENTS

	PAGE
Editor's Preface	vii
Ismar Elbogen: An Appreciation, by Alexander Marx	xi
Introduction	xxv

BOOK ONE
THE ERA OF LIBERALISM

CHAPTER I

EMANCIPATION IN CENTRAL AND WESTERN EUROPE.................... 3
The Constitutional Struggle in Germany, 3–17; The Constitutional Struggle in Austria-Hungary, 17–29; Emancipation in Italy, 29–32; Emancipation in Switzerland, 32–33; France and the *Alliance*, 33–36; Emancipation in Other European States, 36–37; The Attainment of Equality in England, 37–40.

CHAPTER II

THE JEWS IN EASTERN EUROPE AND THE NEAR EAST.................. 41
The Policy of Russification, 41–48; Moses Montefiore's Intervention, 48–57; Liberalism and Reaction under Alexander II, 57–64; Jews and the Polish Insurrection of 1863, 64–66; The Jews in the Balkans, 66–75; The Jews under Mohammedan Rule, 75–80.

CHAPTER III

INNER DEVELOPMENT (1850–1880).................................... 81
Jews in European Civilization, 81–92; Religion and Culture in Western Europe, 92–103; Religion and Culture in Eastern Europe, 103–113.

CHAPTER IV

THE JEWS IN THE NEW WORLD....................................... 114
Growth and Organization in the United States, 114–120; Judaism in the United States, 121–131; Jews in the English Colonies, 131–138.

BOOK TWO
THE INTERNATIONAL OF HATE

CHAPTER I

ANTISEMITISM AS A POLITICAL MOVEMENT............................ 141
New Bases for Anti-Jewishness, 141–152; The Talmud on Trial, 152–154; Ritual Murder Falsehoods, 155–159.

CHAPTER II

ANTISEMITISM IN WESTERN EUROPE 160
   The Anti-Social Movement in Germany, 160–168; Nationalism and Antisemitism in the Austrian Empire, 168–181; The Dreyfus Case, 181–190; The Response to Antisemitism, 190–199.

CHAPTER III

THE JEWS OF RUSSIA UNDER ALEXANDER III 200
   Violence as a Policy, 200–210; The May Laws, 210–220; Inner Life under Czarist Oppression, 220–223.

CHAPTER IV

THE EXODUS: BARON MAURICE DE HIRSCH 224
   Problems of the New Exodus, 224–231; Baron de Hirsch and the ICA, 232–237; The Immigrants in Their New Homes, 238–241.

BOOK THREE

THE JEWISH RENAISSANCE

CHAPTER I

THE LOVERS OF ZION: AHAD HA'AM. 245
   Jews in Palestine in the 19th century, 245–252; Christian and Jewish *Hoveve Zion*, 252–263; Ahad Ha'am, 263–272.

CHAPTER II

THEODOR HERZL AND POLITICAL ZIONISM. 273
   The *Judenstaat* and Its Reception, 273–281; The Organization of the Zionist Movement, 281–288; Herzl's Diplomatic Journeys, 288–294; Zionist Congresses and Debates, 294–300; Consequences of Herzl's Death, 300–303; Progress in Palestine, 303–308.

CHAPTER III

THE JEWS IN THE BRITISH EMPIRE: EFFECTS OF IMMIGRATION 309
   The Immigrants as a Problem, 309–314; Problems of Religion and Culture, 314–320; The Jews in the Empire, 320–325.

CHAPTER IV

THE JEWS IN AMERICA AND THE IMMIGRANTS 326
   Problems of Adjustment, 326–336; Immigrants' Progress, 336–342; Religious and Cultural Organization, 343–352.

CONTENTS

BOOK FOUR
THE WORLD UNREST

CHAPTER I

The Terror in Rumania and Russia.................................. 355
  The Rumanian Policy of Deception, 355–366; International Political Crises and the Jews, 366–371; Stirrings in Russian Jewry under the Last Czar, 371–376; Pogroms as Czarist Policy, 376–389; The Constitutional Movement and Czarist Reaction, 389–404; Life in the Pale, 404–407.

CHAPTER II

The Jews of Western Europe Before the First World War........ 408
  Economic and Social Progress, 408–412; Defense Organizations and Philosophical Literature, 413–418; New Religious Currents, 418–423; The Deep-Rooted Prejudice, 423–426.

CHAPTER III

The Jews of America at the Beginning of the Twentieth Century. 427
  The Process of Americanization, 427–432; Defending Jewish Honor and Rights, 432–438; Community, Religion and Culture, 438–449.

BOOK FIVE
THE FIRST WORLD WAR AND ITS CONSEQUENCES

CHAPTER I

The World War... 453
  The War and the Jews of Europe, 453–460; Jews in the War Zones, 460–465; American Jewry's Sense of Responsibility, 466–469; Revolution and Civil War in Russia, 469–473; The Balfour Declaration, 473–479; British and Jews in Palestine, 479–484.

CHAPTER II

The End of the War: Pogroms and Treaties of Peace............. 485
  The Heritage of War, 485–492; Polish and Ukrainian Terror, 492–502; Minority Rights, 502–509.

CHAPTER III

The Jews of Europe in the Post-War Era........................ 510
  Antisemitism and Reconstruction, 510–519; Spiritual Reconstruction, 519–524; The Struggle for Survival in the Succession States, 525–539;

The Balkan States, 539–544; The Jews in Italy and Liberal Europe, 544–547; Jewish Life in Soviet Russia, 547–556; The Re-Discovered Marranos, 556–558.

CHAPTER IV

THE JEWS IN THE UNITED STATES (1919–1933).......................... 559
Racism in America, 559–570; Zionism and the Jewish Agency, 570–573; Cultural and Religious Progress, 573–584; Business, Philanthropy, and Effects of Economic Depression, 584–588.

CHAPTER V

THE JEWISH NATIONAL HOME IN PALESTINE........................... 589
Foundations of British Policy, 589–601; Foundations of Jewish Policy, 601–616; Conflict and Investigations, 616–624; Progress in an Era of Conflict, 624–632; The Arab Revolt against England, 632–635.

CHAPTER VI

HITLER'S TOTAL WAR AGAINST THE JEWS............................. 636
Hitler's Policy, 636–644; The Response to Nazism, 644–648; Life in the Land of the Nazis, 648–657; The Intensification of Nazism, 657–663; Pogroms and the Last Flight, 663–668; Nazism for Export, 668–674.

EPILOGUE.. 675
NOTES... 683
BIBLIOGRAPHY... 771
INDEX... 787

Introduction

A FULL century has been added to the past from the point at which Graetz closed his account of Jewish history, a century as eventful, revolutionary and explosive as any in human annals. Never before has the world undergone such profound alteration in so short a span. Not only have great technical changes transformed human life, but the unchaining of cultural revolutions and nationalist passions have been factors even more potent. In politics and economics, in religion and society, no institution has remained unaffected by upheaval.

Jews had always been exposed to the storms of world history, and now they were tossed about by the buffeting of the age with particular violence. They were wrenched out of their isolation and drawn into Western civilization. More markedly than in any previous period their lives were bound up with those of the people among whom they lived. World history forms the background against which the particular episode of Jewish fate is enacted. The drama is one of a peculiar struggle for self-assertion, amongst the Jews themselves and in relation to the world at large.

Emancipation, the main Jewish problem during the first half of the 19th century, was not achieved by a single revolutionary act but was the outcome of a historic evolution. Capitalist economy from the 17th century on had brought Jewish industrialists into touch with leading Christian entrepreneurs or administrators, and their cooperation had created a friendly atmosphere. The individual Jew whom the Christians now met was not the bogey they had imagined. The Enlightenment created a fellowship of culture between the educated classes regardless of national or religious affiliation. The conviction spread that all men were good by nature and perfectible. A noble example of this new attitude was the friendship between Moses Mendelssohn and Lessing. Very soon it was evident that Jews in general were open-minded people, estranged from general culture by social circumstances, not by innate dislike.

Contacts between Jews and non-Jews had thus existed before the French National Assembly began to discuss the problem whether or not Jews should be granted "human rights." In the United States the Bill of Rights knew of no discrimination, and George Washington, in his letter to the Hebrew Congregation of Newport, R. I., wrote: "All possess alike liberty of conscience and immunities of citizenship. It is now no more that toleration is spoken of, as if it was by the indulgence of one class of people, that another enjoyed the exercise of their inherent natural rights." But to the French legislators only the Sephardic and the Parisian Jews were acceptable; those of Alsace-Lorraine, by far the majority of France's Jewry, they rejected. The latter were living under all the restrictive measures of medieval legislation and by reason of their occupations enjoyed little favor among their neighbors. In keeping with the feudal system they possessed autonomous administration and jurisdiction in their communities. This made them appear a "nation within a nation" and provoked the oft-quoted dictum of the liberal deputy Clermont-Tonnere: "To the individual Jew everything; to the Jews as nation nothing!"

Such were the tensions, not to speak of those who opposed the new order on principle and were not at a loss to find a thousand arguments for their attitude. At last, on September 27, 1791, the Jews were declared French citizens with equal rights. It was the first time since the Roman Empire that Jews had obtained full citizenship. French arms carried the principles of the Revolution to all countries they occupied: to Italy, Belgium and Holland, Western and Central Germany and even to the Grand Duchy of Warsaw.

Legislation could not, by a single stroke, remove the consequences of century-old practices and prejudices; the buoyant revolutionary period could not smooth conditions and human relations. Alsace remained tense; and, when the great Napoleon visited it, he was showered with complaints that the Jews were ruining the country. He considered his abilities as a ruler impugned and was so deeply offended that he decided to force the Jews to his will by special legislation. That such a procedure contradicted the principles of the Revolution did not matter to the Emperor, who asserted that the period of Revolution was over. Just as he had imposed his will on the Catholic Church so he wanted an absolute guarantee that no rabbi, no Jewish court, would teach or decide anything repugnant to existing French law and that, on the contrary, they would instruct their flocks to abide by the state law exactly as they did by religious law. He convened the famous Grand Sanhedrin to formulate legislation binding on the whole of Israel. An allurement to many Jews and a brilliant spectacle to the outside world, transmitted to posterity through an impressive picture, it was, in reality, an empty gesture, because the answers to be elicited from the Sanhedrin were dictated by the Emperor. The members faced a dilemma: they must either agree or risk the loss of citizenship for all Jews.

Most of the questions were harmless and without bearing on the Jewish way of life. The question whether the Jews considered France as their home country and Frenchmen as their brothers seemed puzzling. The answer was in the affirmative. This position became the pattern for similar declarations in other countries and split the

Jewish community into French Jews, German Jews, Polish Jews, or into Frenchmen, Germans or Poles of the Mosaic persuasion. How such a declaration could be made to harmonize with the feeling of Jewish solidarity was no concern of those generations which lived in glowing optimism and did not foresee the conflicts to come.

On one point the Sanhedrin was obdurate. Napoleon conceived the ludicrous idea of eradicating the Jewish national character by enforced mixed marriages, and desired the Sanhedrin to sanction such marriages. He did not succeed. He could obtain no more than a declaration that intermarriage, if legalized by the civil authorities, would be respected by the Jewish community and not be considered as concubinage.

Here a crucial problem was touched upon, namely, the inviolability of Jewish law. Could it stand as it had developed during centuries of isolation, or was it subject to changes when Jews joined the fellowship of the nations? Irresponsible observers behind the scene suggested all kinds of reforms in the Jewish way of life; but the rabbis belonging to the Sanhedrin had no outlook beyond the blueprint drafted by the Emperor. They did not see the dangers involved in the encounter with a world so different from the ghetto and so full of temptations. It was tragic that, at this unprecedented turn in their history, the Jewish people had no leader who combined loyalty to the past with vision into the future, that rabbis were immersed in unworldly ideas and activities and that leadership passed into the hands of laymen whose foremost concern was the accumulation of worldly goods and worldly honors.

Notwithstanding the loyalty of the Sanhedrin, Napoleon continued on his road of insincerity and enacted against the Jewish people discriminatory legislation in the form of his "Infamous Decree." He created supervising organizations in the district consistories, which were subordinated to a Central Consistory in Paris. Their main task was to educate the Jewish community to yield to military conscription and to commercial honesty — two functions which had no meaning to the average Jew, because these duties were self-evident to him and his behavior was so blameless that the restrictive laws hardly survived the Empire. The French people restored itself and remained a stronghold of liberty in Europe. The consistories, superseded in their original function as beadles of the police, were as little effective as religious guides.

Of a different type were the problems which resulted from the developments in Germany and especially its largest territory, the realm of the enlightened King Frederick the Great. Any change in the status of the Jews had to be granted by the rulers, almost all of whom objected to the Jews as a nuisance to the country. As early as 1745, Frederick's finance administrator had found it unfair "that men reproached the Jews for being useless when these same men prevent them from being useful." A generation later, Christian Wilhelm Dohm made it the thesis of a book that Jews were harmful citizens because they were prevented from being useful citizens. He proposed that Jews be granted freedom of movement and occupation and thus be enabled to contribute to the welfare of their countries. One major issue was whether Jews would be fit for military service. Very soon large numbers of them served in the armies of France, Westphalia and Austria, and proved not inferior to their Christian comrades in arms.

But the rulers in Germany and Austria moved slowly and insisted on having the Jews pass through an educational purgatory. Where the French invaded and established their rule, from the Rhine to the Elbe, the emancipation of the Jews followed automatically. Austria rested where the decrees of Emperor Joseph II, of 1782, brought her. In Prussia, where the atmosphere seemed so promising and Jews enjoyed high social respect, any move toward emancipation was halted by a pedantic bureaucracy. The improvements offered were so abhorrent that self-respecting Jews rejected them. But these petty concessions were sufficient to provoke the contemporary Hamans to a frontal attack on the Jews as a group and to blame them for all the diseases of the time. These pamphleteers were lavish with quotations from the Talmud, as if all of them were learned rabbis, while in reality none was able to read a single line of Hebrew. Some pro-Jewish writings and the ban of the Prussian government on the circulation of the anti-Jewish rubbish notwithstanding, it was evident that the clock had been turned back and that the good-will of twenty years ago had disappeared.

The old Prussian state collapsed in the campaigns of 1806–7. A rebirth was not possible unless the population was granted a share in the administration. When the municipalities were being organized, the importance of the Jews for the welfare of the cities could not be overlooked, and they were included in the franchise. A revision of their whole status was inevitable. The representatives of the old system tried to withhold a prompt guarantee of full civic rights, but the chancellor, Hardenberg, uncompromisingly insisted on legislation which exacted equality of duties and granted equality of rights. On March 11, 1812, the Jews of the Prussian monarchy were declared natives and citizens, possessed of all rights. Only appointment to judicial and administrative offices was for the time being denied them. They had to adopt and register family names — a step urged in other countries also — they had to be able to sign their names in a readable alphabet and they had to keep their business records in a European language, that is, not in

INTRODUCTION

Yiddish or Hebrew. Their existing communities, based on political and fiscal foundations, were dissolved and rabbinical jurisdiction eliminated. A new regulation of the status of the communities was to be established. But thirty-five years were required for the government to find a new pattern for Jewish community life.

A year after the emancipation, the War of Liberation began, and the Jewish soldiers, according to the most competent judges, did their full duty and won the confidence of their superiors. The French were hardly driven out of the country, when some of the restored governments renewed all the discriminations against Jews which had existed before the French occupation. The Congress of Vienna, called upon to reorganize Central Europe, was approached by numerous German citizens with petitions to provide democratic constitutions for their countries. The Jews, too, sent representatives and asked that they be not forgotten in the framing of democratic constitutions. The Congress recognized that the conditions of the Jews had to be revised. As in most matters, the delegates could not reach a definite decision. The Assembly of the Confederated States was assigned the task of regulating the civil status of the Jews as uniformly as possible and of guaranteeing them equal rights. Since complete equality had not yet been granted in every State, the Assembly decided that "until then the rights already granted to them *in* the Confederated States shall remain in force." A shrewd delegate replaced the word "in" with "by." The leading statesmen did not notice this forgery and so the Jews were cheated of their freedom, because as a rule their full rights had been accorded by the occupation army and not by the States.

Prussia was one of the states *by* which full citizenship had been granted, but after the War of Liberation she manifested a tendency to limit the validity of the Edict of 1812 as much as possible and to reduce the Jews to their former status. Almost thirty different statutes regulated the life of Prussian Jewry, and removal from one section to another was not allowed. The same held good for Bavaria. The hundreds of regulations established by the former territorial rulers (*Standesherren*) remained valid; the Royal Bavarian government confessed expressly that its policy tended to diminish, not to increase, the number of Jews. One of the curbs used was a *numerus clausus* for Jews, which did not permit a Jewish family to establish itself in Bavaria unless one of the numbers on the list had become vacant. When, from 1818 on, Bavaria, Baden and Württemberg were given constitutions, some deputies insisted on justice for Jews; but the majorities were far from agreeing, and the governments pretended that their educational experiments needed still more time. Many young and efficient men, despairing of an improvement of their living conditions, emigrated to the United States, where these despised citizens became an asset to the flourishing new country.

The trend of the general European policy was reactionary. Already at the Congress of Vienna attempts had been made to abolish the "revolutionary" principle of democracy and to support the principle of the old "divine order." The Holy Alliance between the great European powers was a dam against all free movements. In Germany, furthermore, public opinion was dominated by romanticism and Teutomania. What was characteristic of Teutonism was to be exalted; what was connected with the French oppressor was to be extirpated. The Jews had obtained human rights from the French and therefore were to be hated, to be branded as a foreign element, to be eliminated from a German commonwealth if not entirely annihilated. All privileges were to be abolished in the modern state. The only privilege people insisted on retaining was that of Jew-baiting. The German people were deluged with a flood of lampoons and bungling pamphlets of the basest and vilest character. The most contradictory charges were brought against the Jews. But they had their advocates, too. To cite only one instance, Lips, the Professor of Philosophy, wrote: "Let us be different towards the Jews, and they, too, will change." None of those who fought the Jewish cause was more effective than Ludwig Börne or Heinrich Heine, who ridiculed all Teutomania and Judaeophobia and whose words resounded through the world. To be sure, both had deserted Judaism, as did many from among the intelligentsia; much as the Jewish race was being abused and hated, the baptized Jew was everywhere welcome. It was a depressing period. German Jews saw their hopes for a proper place in modern society buried.

Not before the successful July Revolution of 1830 did the Liberals in Germany dare to rally against reaction. They fought for the freedom of the individual and for constitutional rights — to be shared by all citizens without exception. Liberalism was the battle cry of the cultured classes and of the rising generation. So it was among Jews. They no longer begged for rights and privileges, but asked for "right and freedom." Their spokesman became Gabriel Riesser (Graetz, V, 598 ff.), who had himself experienced all the Jewish disabilities, but was not prompted to fight for his personal interests or the interests of his people alone. He fought for the unalterable and indivisible right innate to every human being and not to be forfeited except by crime. The State was bound to grant right and freedom to all its inhabitants, regardless of birth or religious belief, who were willing to assume or who were actually performing all the duties of citizens. He refused to accept the crumbs generously thrown by some would-be liberals. "Human Rights" of the citizen had to be political rights. Jews could not be denied their claims on German citizenship; they had no other fatherland; they knew of no other loyalty; and, if declared foreigners, they were outlawed. He rejected the pretext that their religious observances were symbols of a different nationality. Like his contemporary, T. B. Macaulay, he emphasized that whether a man worshiped in a church or a synagogue may be decisive for his election as bishop or rabbi, but not for his value as citizen. Whatever views his coreligionists had about the observance of the Sabbath or the dietary laws, he warned them not to sacrifice their religious freedom to concessions of a political nature, because there was no freedom where freedom of conscience was denied. He admonished his fellow-Jews to organize themselves and to fight for their right, to fight under the name "Jew," which he gave to the monthly dedicated to their cause. Riesser was fascinating in his pathos and brilliant in his polemic. With irresistible logic he analyzed the absurdity of the arguments against the emancipation of the Jews proferred in parliamentary debates, governmental decrees, or political essays of the period. Hard fighting was needed to capture bastion after bastion behind which the foe took shelter. Step by step the enemy was pushed to the wall; public opinion was won over; the press and the strengthened bourgeoisie supported liberalism vigorously. About 1870 there was no doubt that democracy had been achieved.

The long struggle and the bitter opposition caused a serious internal Jewish problem. It had been acute since the days of Moses Mendelssohn and concerned the compatibility of Judaism and modern thought. Mendelssohn found for himself the solution that Judaism was a revealed law, not a revealed belief, its basic doctrines being identical with those of "natural religion." His children and some of his disciples identified "natural religion" with enlightened Christendom and rejected the Jewish Law which was an obstacle on their way. They admitted the great merit of Mosaic teaching, but had little appreciation for the doctrines of the Talmud and the rabbis. The splendor of the outside world attracted them; the Synagogue appeared to them dark and gloomy. This mood was not prevalent everywhere in Germany; but local variations notwithstanding, the general trend was identical. The well-to-do classes, who had the better opportunities for education and culture, were indifferent, not to say hostile, toward all things Jewish, and, when the temptation came, were willing to pay "the admission ticket to European civilization," as Heinrich Heine styled conversion. The masses of the Jews were scattered in tiny congregations and lived in direst poverty. They needed guidance and support if they were to be educated — as everybody demanded and they themselves wanted to be. But who could help them? Certainly not those who did not believe in the future of Judaism. When they turned to the rabbis, on the other hand, they heard warnings against the rampant apostasy, but never any adequate instruction on the way to be loyal. Later experience taught that the apprehensions of the rabbis were not unjustified; but these religious guides never overcame their worries long enough to propose a positive program of education. Thus they could denounce but not stem apostasy. At least one or two generations were lost to Judaism during this period of disintegration.

But a moment came when prominent Jews assumed the responsibility for constructive work. Israel Jacobson, head of the Cassel Consistory, laid stress on the education of the youth and on the dignity of worship. He loved Judaism warmly and was deeply affected by the fact that Jewish worship had no attraction for Jews and was even ridiculed by Christians. He wanted to help through an aesthetic reform of the Synagogue. He introduced trained choirs, in some places even an organ, regular sermons in German, and the recitation of some prayers in the vernacular. In Hesse and Hanover, where a genuine piety prevailed, this education was effective for a long time. But Jacobson was not concerned about theology; he could not give new impulses to Judaism. After the Napoleonic era he made an attempt to establish a "German Synagogue" in Berlin; the same idea found favor in distant Karlsruhe. In Sachse-Weimar the government imposed on the Jewish communities a liturgy in the German language. None of these experiments lasted for any considerable time.

In 1818, however, the New Israelitish Temple in Hamburg organized a permanent service with the accompaniment of vocal and instrumental music, and published a prayerbook where basic Hebrew prayers were replaced by German texts and where all prayers for the restitution of the sacrificial cult, for the return to Zion and for a personal Messiah were changed or eliminated. Such innovations provoked a protest by the local rabbis, who sought the support of foreign colleagues. Their collected opinions were the swan-song of the dying old-fashioned rabbinate. They contain nothing but abuse of the rebels. With a single exception, no rabbi was concerned to search into the causes of the rebellion, of so widespread a dissatisfaction with the traditional form of worship. The old Hamburg community tried to check the movement by calling a new chief rabbi in the person of *Haham* Isaac Bernays, who had carried on philosophical studies at a university and had become the first orthodox rabbi to preach regularly in German, the first to reinterpret traditional Judaism for the modern world. The Temple soon lost its revolutionary ardor; its members were not born for religious heroism. Heinrich Heine mocked at the Temple and its preachers, and many a later critic, who had as little use as Heine for the traditional synagogue, followed him. Nevertheless, the institution endured; its influence reached as far as London and even Charleston, S. C.

Another attempt at constructiveness was made by a group of university students in Berlin, under the leadership of Leopold Zunz and Eduard Gans. As a response to the "Hep Hep" riots in 1819, they organized the *Verein für Kultur und Wissenschaft der Juden*. Their program aimed at a thorough education of all Jewish groups and the whole Jewish personality on the basis of a new self-assertion of Jewishness. They were the first to appreciate Judaism's indigenous culture and to realize that in a partnership with modern culture Judaism would not only have to take but would also be able to give of its own treasures. The organization was premature and not successful, but it created what Zunz called the "Science of Judaism" and what he considered the safeguard of the Jewish future. And though it never became popular like the study of the Talmud in former ages, the movement stirred the blood circulation within Judaism and became an agent of continuous rejuvenation. No Jewish movement of any worth has originated during the last 120 years which was not directly or indirectly indebted to the scientific and systematic study of Judaism.

The younger generation of rabbis, who had obtained a university education, now found inspiration for a deeper penetration into Judaism and very soon approached the Jewish problem from a new angle. Samson Raphael Hirsch and Abraham Geiger gave new meaning to the call for Reform, that of a thoroughgoing transformation. Both theologians recognized that Judaism had entered a new period and needed a new orientation. Both emphasized the ethical and universal goal of the Jewish religion and the fervor of the prophetic spirit. Both waged war against a mechanical, meaningless recital of prayer or performance of ceremonial and claimed that "the difficult as well as the simple, the whole as well as the part, must have sense and meaning, must elevate the spirit, warm the heart, so that it may influence the entire life of the individual." As for the "pilgrim's progress," the two theologians differed widely. Hirsch stressed revelation and its implications in contrast to the utilitarian spirit of the epoch. He saw the "Israel-man" bound to the task of re-establishing communion with God by fulfilling the duties prescribed in the "Torah," that is in the entire body of biblical and rabbinical laws. "The reform needed by Judaism is education of the present generation in the Torah, and not levelling the Torah to the need and spirit of present times." To Geiger revelation was not centered in the unique original act, but was an organic power inherent in the Jewish spirit. The first duty of the theologian, according to him, was a historic-critical study of the evolution of Judaism; it was to discover and distinguish between the essence and the accretion and to harmonize life with doctrine. Geiger regarded the dispersion of the Jews as the means of carrying out their messianic mission, and the emancipation as an advance in this direction. He broke entirely with the national aspect of the Jewish religion, while Hirsch upheld the peculiar character of the God-dedicated Jewish people and considered the dispersion as a process of purification by God.

Revelation and rationalism, loyalty to the law and critical adjustment of it — these were two platforms about which parties could group themselves. At times it looked as if a schism could be expected like that then occurring in the Christian churches of Germany. But things within Judaism moved slowly and became confused through the continuing struggle for emancipation and the pressure exerted from the outside to change Jewish religious practices. In the midst of this crisis Sigismund Stern of Berlin launched the idea of a "German-Jewish Church," in which religion was to acquire a universal appeal through the abolition of all points of separation, and in which all those religious regulations which were in contradiction to the present problems of life or which had no moral significance for present-day existence were to be eliminated. He found dialectical support in the works of Samuel Holdheim who distinguished "the Mosaic religion" from the Mosaic state, rejected all those ordinances which belonged or could be ascribed to the latter, and retained from this legislation one point only, namely "the religious belief in the holiness of the actual political state as a divine institution." On the basis of these principles the Jewish Reform Community in Berlin was established. It introduced Sunday services, a liturgy which, apart from a few biblical quotations and the *Kaddish*, was throughout German and fundamentally different from tradition; men appeared bareheaded, women were seated in the same room with them. These radical deviations resulted in a splendid isolation as far as Europe was concerned, but exerted an influence on American Reform Judaism.

Such an extreme had an immediate effect. The Berlin mother-community, which for a generation had had no authoritative rabbi, called Michael Sachs, a poetic mind, a fascinating personality, a captivating preacher of conservative Judaism. Zacharias Frankel also entered the arena. He launched the platform of moderate conservatism, which did not reject the idea of reform, but insisted on historic continuity and the maintenance of the links with the general Jewish community. Industrialization and mechanization were still in their beginnings, religion was still a strong power in Jewish life, and all these discussions excited the communities mightily. They were not large (Frankfort had about 5,000 souls in 1840, Hamburg, Berlin, Posen about 6,500 each), and their communal life was intense. Alarming extremism confused Jews as well as their Christian neighbors.

Common ground had to be sought. Rabbinical conferences were planned for the discussion of problems in which Jews of all wings were interested. The blood-accusation raised in Damascus (1840), so preposterous in the 19th century, was a warning signal not to rely too firmly on the enlightenment of the age. In 1844 Ludwig Philippson succeeded in summoning a rabbinical conference at Brunswick. He prepared an absolutely neutral program, but some of the radicals in attendance insisted on discussing controversial matters. The next conference, which met in Frankfort in 1845, was attended by Frankel who expected to exercise a moderating influence. Instead, there was a clash because a majority vote resolved that there was no need for the Hebrew language in Jewish worship. Frankel left ostentatiously, and the fate of the conference was sealed. There was one more conference in Breslau (1846) which continued on the way of radicalism without satisfying the radicals, and this was the end of a promising experiment.

To this point Graetz brought his *History*. Born in 1817, Graetz had grown up in an age which had fought for democratic principles and had been ready to make the supreme sacrifice for democracy, an age which looked upon the State as a community of rights and of culture based upon the consent and the devotion of its citizens. This optimistic idealism Graetz retained in his old age, so that he closed his *History* with an epilogue whose mood is one of boundless faith in the progress of humanity.

Pessimism had meanwhile begun to cast its shadow. Nationalism based upon community of blood and race already had conquered the continent of Europe. As outsiders, nationalism granted the Jews neither the space nor the right to pursue their own lives. Few as were their numbers, they were still too many. Assimilated though they were, they were still alien. Racial doctrine knew no patience. Not since the days of Torquemada had the Jewish people been subjected to so concentrated an attack upon their very existence as that which they had to endure at the beginning of the twentieth century.

To its foe's will to destroy, Judaism opposed its own will to survive. It did not accept its suffering with passive resignation, but made strenuous efforts to fashion its own fate. It bethought itself of its spiritual heritage, which it had esteemed lightly in the age of cosmopolitanism, and sought clarification of the status of the Jews among the nations. It bethought itself of its slumbering energies, and directed them to countries where they would not have to lie fallow. A migration without parallel in history brought five million Jews into new homes, new environments, new mores. This migration was managed by the Jews' own energy, and their own energy prevented their moral collapse — a supreme cultural achievement. The locale of Jewish history was infinitely expanded in this period; its center of gravity, and concomitantly its sphere of cultural interests and its ideals of education underwent repeated change.

It was to the new world that migration was chiefly directed, and the United States which received the largest numbers of immigrants. The United States became a new factor in Jewish life, not only because it willingly and generously provided scope for a large settlement of Jews, but because, in keeping with the principles of the founding fathers, it defended the Jews' right to live "on grounds of humanity" even when its own political interests were not immediately involved. In addition to the comprehensive westward migration, there was a smaller movement towards the East. High moral force was displayed in the settlement of *Eretz Yisrael*. There the will of the Jewish people worked enthusiastically to transform the swampy soil of their ancestral land into a fertile country and to shape it into a new National Home and a nursery for new Jewish values.

The nineteenth century had been dominated by a rational view of life and education which conceived its duty in exact scientific research and in a secularizing liberation from the rabbinic world. But at the end of the century, without a complete rejection of positivism, an irrational ideal was formulated, the awakening and the idealization of an unspeculative Jewish folk life. Hasidism, rabbinic tradition, and above all the love of Zion were celebrated in story, verse and song. Yiddish, which had been ridiculed at the beginning of the century, became a spiritual power at its end. In quantity as in quality its achievements demanded respect. Hebrew was again raised to the level of a living tongue and made the vehicle for expressing a full national life. The renaissance of Hebrew and its literary proliferation surpassed the most sanguine expectations.

For the history of the past hundred years sources and studies are more numerous than for any earlier period. Never before has so much been published. Not only advances in techniques but also the abolition of censorship have contributed to the increase of printed materials. Even the limitations upon the freedom of the press, lately imposed in certain large states, still allow a considerable flow of material. National archives and records generally make not only drafts of legislation and administrative measures available for public information, but as a rule also supply the memoranda upon which such laws are based and the arguments that had been offered for and against them. More men in public life have published their memoirs, and so preserved important events and moods; many have become the subject of biographies which illuminate characters and their modes of thought.

The historian is confronted by an abundance of material

embarrassing in its richness. He must sort out, choose, appraise; that is to say, he must apply a subjective criterion. Danger of straying from scientific objectivity grows when the requisite detachment is lacking, when the thoughts and the feelings of the judge are inextricably involved in the stream of events, and where the reader expects not only a factual account but an attitude. The historian cannot be confronted with a more difficult task than writing contemporary history. The grace which is vouchsafed him as a prophet of past events forsakes him when his gaze is directed towards the future. Proper detachment and scale are difficult to attain, and only the closest self-discipline can prevent impossible distortions.

Yet the attempt must be ventured, with the optimism which characterizes Jewish history and which dominates the first section of the period we are about to survey. Optimism, idealism, and liberalism built up a world and made space for the Jews (1848–1880). Pessimism, materialism, and nationalism undermined that world (1880–1914) and headed Europe along with its Jews to destruction (1914–1939). We are now standing at a turning point which is to determine whether the world is be delivered wholly to the powers of destruction or to be built up anew upon a foundation of justice.

BOOK ONE
THE ERA OF LIBERALISM
1848-1880

CHAPTER I

Emancipation in Central and Western Europe

THE CONSTITUTIONAL STRUGGLE IN GERMANY

THE popular movement of 1848 spread irresistibly. Moving with speed and power, it swept away in a short while prejudices whose abolition had been vainly urged on grounds of reason for decades. Not all the gains of the spring tide of popular exuberance were retained, but certain fundamental principles which were then established have remained the inalienable possession of all peoples. Such are the abolition of privileged classes and the equality of all men before the law. Even politicians whose conduct is at open variance with these principles feel constrained to render them at least lip service.

The foundations of Europe, when the spring storm of 1848 struck, were neither deep nor plumb. The old pillars of government — bureaucracy, police, censorship — had fallen into decay and were no longer able to support the restless weight of burgeoning economic and cultural progress, of mature and independent thought. Dissatisfaction was intensified by economic distress, by crop failures and a consequent rise in the cost of living. And so the storm which broke in Paris could seize unopposed upon almost all the capitals of Europe and everywhere overthrow existing governmental forms. And even though reaction quickly consolidated its forces and looked towards the restoration of its power, its day was definitely over. The new order could be shaken for the moment, but it could no longer be thrust aside. Even the Jews retained their gains though reaction inveighed against them.

In Germany the struggle for unity and freedom had raged for more than a generation; but its progress had been slow. The popular movement of 1848[1] was ushered in by a flood of petitions issuing from various class organizations, from representatives of the cities, and from citizen associations, all seeking guarantees of civic and political freedom. Almost without exception they demanded freedom of religion along with freedom of speech and freedom of the press. Many specifically stated that this freedom would be extended also to their Jewish fellow-citizens, and even where such a stipulation was not made it was clearly implied by the context. An upsurge of the spirit gave wings to the people; whole populations were imbued with the prevailing mood of idealism and humanism. It was not that all hatefulness and baseness were silenced; economic distress frequently found expression in disturbances among peasants, which might eventuate in the destruction and plunder of Jewish property. But these were the exceptions; the dominant mood was one of brotherhood. Public opinion favored the demand that all political rights should be granted to the Jews, who had fulfilled their obligations to the state with no diminution and with the fullest devotion. The will of the people was carried out. The Federal Council, hitherto ineffective, summoned a National Assembly which was to be elected by a general and equal suffrage in all the territory of the German Confederation, including the former Polish provinces, and was to determine the form of the constitution for the greater German empire. Under no constraint, but at the free decision of this Assembly, common rights were proclaimed for a people hitherto divided into disparate fragments. In this surge of democratic sentiment there was not a moment's doubt that Jews were to share in the right to elect and to be elected, and to cooperate in the formulation of the constitution. Two Jewish deputies[2] each from Germany and Austria were elected to the German National Assembly: Moritz Veit from Berlin and Gabriel Riesser for Lauenburg, where Riesser, being a Jew, would even have been debarred from residence; and Moritz Hartmann and Ignatz Kuranda from Bohemia, where the rights of the Jews had also been sharply limited. The choice German spirits of the time were members of this Assembly, and among them Riesser enjoyed high regard. For a time he was honored with the office of vice president.

The Assembly first established the democratic "Fundamental Rights of the German People," and its draft of the constitution contained a provision that "enjoyment of civic and citizen rights will not be conditioned or limited by religious faith." This significant principle was carried over into almost all constitutions of German states. There was an attempt to make "the peculiar conditions of the Israelitish race" the object of special legislation, but Riesser opposed this attempt on high moral grounds. He pointed to the implicit contradiction. Now that all disabilities based on religion had been abolished, new disabilities were to be based on difference of nationality; the Jews were not conscious of a national difference, whereas the nationality of many alien peoples, consciously hostile to Germany, such as Danes, Poles, and Czechs, was expressly recognized as not constituting a disability. Riesser also warned that any legalized exception would introduce a disruptive cleavage into the whole body of freedom. The Assembly felt the force of Riesser's arguments; they rejected the proposal and recognized the full legal rights of the Jews.

This constitution never became an actuality, but it set a tangible goal in the struggle for freedom. The Frankfort National Assembly and its idealist dreamers had to yield to rising reaction, which left none of the newly won liberties intact. Disillusion and disappointment led to rebellion in Baden and the Palatinate. A number of Jews participated, and the revolution cost many their lives. Some, like Ludwig Bamberger,[3] were able to escape by flight abroad; some migrated to the United States, where liberty was in flower.

The storm of revolution touched the individual states also, and everywhere it effected an extension of popular rights. In Prussia the constitution[4] which had long been denied was finally obtained. The liberal movement constantly increased in power. It was particularly successful in the regions which had been under French domination and had possessed free citizen rights under that rule. The revolutionary explosion in Berlin was ascribed to intransigent Poles and revolutionary emissaries from France. A later fabrication named the Jews along with the Poles and the French as instigators of revolution. But this is an impossible exaggeration of the political activity of the Jews, of which contemporaries say nothing. On the afternoon of March 18, 1848, fighting unexpectedly broke out between the military and the citizenry, and no fewer than twenty-one Jews lost their lives. The 180 victims of the revolution were interred in a common grave, and, after the Christian clergymen had spoken, Michael Sachs, the preacher of the Jewish congregation (Graetz, V, 687 ff.) pronounced a prayer. In his *Word of Comfort*, addressed to the survivors of those who had fallen in the March fighting, Leopold Zunz[5] gave expression to the feelings of thoughtful men and women:

Great will be the honor which will be paid to your dead and to ours. For the dominion of Freedom will arise: law founded upon the will of the people, order comprised in voluntary obedience, recognition of Man unshaded by distinctions of sect or class, the rule of love as witness to faith in God.

The draft of the constitution had declared all Prussians equal before the law and had recognized no differences of class or birth. This basic principle was retained in all the revisions which the pressure of reaction compelled, and was received into the definitive Prussian constitution of 1850. The Jews thereupon received the right to elect and be elected — a number of Jews were immediately elected to both chambers of the *Landtag* — and the right to hold state offices. In addition, the constitution guaranteed freedom of worship and freedom to form Jewish religious congregations.

The advance over previous attempts to regulate the condition of the Jews was enormous. As late as 1847[6] the government had wished to place petty restrictions upon the rights of all Jews and to set special disabilities upon the Jews of Posen, who constituted 40% of all the Jews of Prussia. The government had felt constrained to acknowledge the advances brought about by the cultural and moral naturalization of the Jews since the Edict of 1812, but it was manifestly concerned to depreciate the usefulness of the Jews to the state. The memorandum which the government submitted came to the remarkable conclusion that Jews were wanting in sense of honor, in gentleness, and in the philanthropic impulse, and sought to explain this condition by reference to the Jews' business activities, their poverty, and their lack of schooling. Statistics specially prepared and arranged were cited in proof. The remarks of the government representatives and of the deputies who discussed the question reveal an abysmal ignorance of the character and history of the Jews. The spread of education had done nothing to alter fixed opinions; even representatives of liberalism clung to old prejudices and unjustifiable generalizations.

While the cumbersome bureaucracy sought to block any fundamental change, the representatives of the people, the true spokesmen of public opinion, expressed themselves as favoring the full equality of the Jews. The deputies of the province of Posen in particular, whose Jews the government alleged were backward and harmful to the state, almost without exception advocated full civil rights for the Jews. The Jews also found warm advocates among the advanced middle class and in the ranks of the nobility. Even the opposition refrained from such irrelevant and hateful attacks as were customarily heard at discussions upon Jews.

The chief argument against granting Jews equal rights was the notion of a Christian State. The government benches supported this concept energetically. What the term "Christian State" could mean, none of the advocates of the principle could define with either logic or consistency. Actually the modern State came into being in opposition to the Church. The State's insistence upon its paramount rights in taxation, justice, and particularly in military matters constituted a plain rejection of the lessons of the Sermon on the Mount. Prince von Lynar and others declared that a State founded upon the teachings of Christianity must practice love and forbearance and dare not injure and degrade men willing to bear all their obligations, and actually bearing them, by withholding their rights. The replies which the champions of the Christian State offered to such arguments were shabby and threadbare. The most gifted of their number, Otto von Bismarck, later to become chancellor, frankly admitted that he was unable to free himself from old prejudices and long cherished hatreds.

The specter of the Christian State made its appearance at diverse times in all countries. It is an irony of history that the exponent of this theory was born a Jew; he was Friedrich Julius Stahl,[7] prominent in the field of the philosophy of law.

> The essence of the Christian State [he wrote] is comprised in the subjection of all authoritative regulation and administration to the commandments and ordinances of God, and therewithal to discipline and morality. Similarly the citizen body must show the obedience of subjects, and this can only be secured by the consciousness of the presence of the true and living God and by the religious faith of the people.

Any believing Jew might readily have subscribed to such a concept of the State; it contains nothing of specific Christian dogma. The point at issue is the question whether or not the State and its rights should remain the exclusive property of a special group. "The political equality of all men," Stahl continued, "does not in itself imply the destruction of the Christian State; but it does constitute a disturbance of its principles and a peril to its existence." Now the various Christian sects and the free thinkers were assured full freedom of conscience and equality of citizen rights; it was only the Jews to whom they were to be denied — to those Jews who clung to their traditions unaltered, because they were allegedly alien or even hostile; to those Jews who had reformed their traditions, because they were "unbelieving." With naive self-deception, the Christian could look away from the breakdown in Christian faith effected by contemporary philosophy; but of the Jews the complete credulity of the olden days was demanded.

At this time the Jews of Posen were faced with a difficult trial. The restoration of Poland was one of the aims of all friends of freedom, that is to say of all those who worked for equalizing the rights of the Jews. Not only the Poles in Posen sought to persuade the Jews to join their struggle for national resurgence, but the Jews of Cracow directed a moving appeal to their brethren in Posen to follow the Polish banner. With few exceptions the Jews remained faithful to the German cause. During the Polish uprising the Jews suffered from Polish acts of violence, but they had the satisfaction of closer sympathy on the part of the German population. If their favorable development be compared with that of the Polish Jews under Austrian or Russian domination, the Jews of Posen could only be grateful for the Prussian educational and administrative measures, even though they sometimes felt the heavy hand of bureaucracy.

The basic rights of the German people were recognized by practically every German state; even the grand duke of Mecklenburg-Schwerin gave his country a liberal constitution, which, however, was withdrawn after a short period. In Württemberg[8] the government expressly stated that special legislation concerning Jews, insofar as it affected citizen rights, was void. When, in 1852, a succeeding reactionary government withdrew the constitution and demanded the abrogation of the equality that had been granted to the Jews, both Chambers refused their consent. The conflict was closed only in 1861. The government gave the Jews a testimonial to the effect

that they were good citizens and respected the laws, and that, furthermore, their equality with other citizens was to the interest of the national economy, because their activity contributed considerably to the promotion of commerce and their brisk trade in produce and cattle was of particular advantage to agriculture; nor could any one deny that their efforts had been advantageous in many branches in the field of industry.

A law was passed declaring that citizen rights were not dependent on religious faith. Some few economic restrictions remained; but in 1864 these remaining inequalities were also abolished.

The situation in Baden[9] developed in a peculiar manner. In Karlsruhe, in the beginning of March, 1848, political equality of all citizens without distinction of religion was demanded by the people and the Chamber and was promised by the grand duke. But several days later rioting and excesses began in the open countryside against "officials, landowners, and Jews." In many small localities houses of Jews were damaged, their property plundered, and even their lives threatened. In Heidelberg members of the custom-tailors' guild, who believed their livelihood was threatened by the introduction of occupational freedom, stormed the shops of Jewish clothing merchants. In Odenwald broadsides incited to

CENTRAL AND WESTERN EUROPE

a general Jewish persecution. The government drew its conclusions from this attitude and granted Jews full equality only in the domain of *state* rights, and allowed the old regulations to govern the question of local civic rights. This was in keeping with the wishes of many Jews in small localities, who feared any change in the law would endanger their lives. The communes, in fact, were obstinate in maintaining their privileges. Baden-Baden, for example, refused civic rights to Baron Meier Carl von Rothschild of Frankfort as late as 1861, although the government had endorsed his request. With the granting of freedom of vocation and of movement the last inequalities were removed, and in 1862, after a long struggle, the right of the Jews to settle freely in all parts of the country and to be accepted as citizens was secured. Subsequently Baden became one of the most liberal states of Germany. It carried out the equalization of the Jews faithfully, and was the first German state to call a Jew to the position of Minister of State.

In Bavaria[10] the government declared in 1846 that "ripe reflection" was necessary before proposals for the improvement of the legal position of the Jews could be made. In one respect the Jews made the attainment of clarity rather difficult for the government: in regard to the formulation of the religious provisions they submitted recommendations that were quite contradictory. The magistrates of the large cities, Munich, Nuremberg Würzburg, Bamberg, in their expressions of opinion to the Ministry and in their petitions to the king, declared themselves unconditionally in favor of the Jews. When the popular movement of 1848 brought the fall of the reactionary ministry of Abel, the king promised, among other reforms, a measure for improving the citizen status of the Jews.

In Bavaria also there were hostile excesses against the Jews in the rural districts. The people, on the other hand, promptly elected two Jews to the *Landtag* in 1848; and this not only in Fürth where the Jewish element in the population was numerous, but also in the constituency where no Jews resided. When, in 1850, the government proposed equality for the Jews, the deputies agreed but the Upper House (*Reichsrat*) rejected the proposal. However, laws relating to trades and property and small business were removed by decree. There were dozens of old special regulations of local authorities which put stumbling blocks in the way of Jews following any trade or profession. Most of the limitations on Jews practicing the various callings were now eliminated, though many a perversity remained on the books. For example, Jews might acquire and convey equities in breweries, taprooms, and taverns, but they could not manage such businesses upon their own account. Moreover, the severest disability of all, the registration requirement (*Matrikel*), remained. As before, Jews were prohibited from establishing an independent household, if there was no free place in the register. For many young people it was impossible to acquire the right to domicile and to establish a family. The consequence of this Pharaonic rigor was that a vigorous emigration to the United States set in. There many of these young people distinguished themselves by their intelligence, industry, and creative ideas, and became highly respected citizens. The prohibition came to be relaxed tacitly; so, for example, Nuremberg opened its doors to the Jews and very soon was able to record an unexpected rise in the hops trade. But another decade of exertion was required until, in 1861, both Chambers determined upon the abolition of the registration requirement, and the government approved their proposal.

It was the fate of revolution in Germany that the powers it cast down quickly recovered and gathered their strength for a counter-blow. Reaction made prompt use of the freedom of the press and of speech, which it had so long opposed, for the purpose of robbing of their rights a people that had grown indolent after their first successes. In Prussia the Conservative Party made itself the representative of political and clerical reaction. Its organ, the *Kreuzzeitung* (*Neue Preussische Zeitung*), was outspoken in its hostility to Jews during its entire history. Its publisher, Hermann Wagener,[11] proposed, in 1856, that the provision making citizen rights independent of religious faith be stricken from the constitution; such a symbol of the Godless State must not be tolerated in the constitution of a Christian monarchy. Even though the proposal was made in general terms, it was clearly directed against the Jews. As a result of Ludwig Philippson's efforts the Jewish side submitted three hundred petitions to the House of Deputies, asking for the rejection of the proposal. When it came up for action, a motion was made and passed to proceed to the regular order of the day. Wagener did not even dare to ask for the floor. But it was only a Pyrrhic victory. For the reactionary Minister of the Interior declared that there was no need to amend the constitution: its provision, that in all religious matters Christianity should be regarded as basic, was sufficient to exclude non-Christians from judicial, administrative, and other offices which were connected with the Christian character of the state. In practice the government took the absurd point of view that the constitution controlled future legislation but did not void the laws of the past.

Even in the liberal era (after 1859), when the Minister of the Interior expressed the conviction that this problem would be settled in future upon the basis of constitutional principle, the Minister of Justice declared that Jews could not become judges because they could not administer a Christian oath nor sit upon the Sabbath.

The Minister of Instruction added that the Christian character of the schools made it impossible to engage Jewish teachers. Both ministers acted accordingly and so would not permit Jews to enter even the preparatory services of their departments. In 1862, when the Chamber of Deputies again criticized this practice, the Minister of Instruction had discovered a new basis for it: "Christianity alone was tolerant of other beliefs; atheism, like Judaism, was bent on persecution." It could hardly be said that such an utterance showed tolerance; nor is evidence of tolerance to be found in the fact that baptism removed at a single stroke all obstacles to the employment of Jews. Neither can tolerance be perceived in the government's hesitation to accede to the Jews' request for a change in the wording of the oath, though there was no substantial reason for retaining the old form. So stubbornly did the bureaucratic cabal resist every forward move!

Gabriel Riesser's[12] masterful speech in favor of Prussian hegemony — a speech as lucid as it was moving — had carried the National Assembly at Frankfort to a pitch of general enthusiasm. The man whose faith cut him off from every civic career was appointed to the committee which offered King Frederick William IV of Prussia the crown of the Emperor of Germany. The committee met with a refusal, for the legitimist king would accept the crown only from the princes, not from the representatives of the people. Among the younger generation spirits so diverse as Moritz Lazarus and Ferdinand Lassalle entered the literary lists in behalf of a unified Germany under the strong leadership of Prussia. Lassalle[13] sought and found his way to Bismarck after it had become apparent that Bismarck's policy also tended to the unification of Germany. The country squire recognized in the labor leader a most gifted and amiable man, outspoken in his nationalist and monarchist convictions. Lassalle tried to win Bismarck for general suffrage, equal and direct. For Prussia the great statesman rejected such suffrage, but he introduced it in the North German Confederation and later in the German Empire, to the great surprise of all concerned.

Among those who were reconciled to the government by Bismarck's German policy was Eduard Lasker,[14] who was convinced that a liberalism without a national orientation was an impossibility. Thus Lasker became one of the pioneers of the National Liberal Party, the Party which advocated the establishment of the Empire. As a member of the Reichstag of the North German Confederation he was foremost among those who drafted the constitution and the new codes, always with a view towards the later extension of the Confederation into an Empire. By his advocacy, the liberal partisan won many hearts in South Germany to union with the North. It was he, too, who proposed proferring an address to the Prussian king when the North German Confederation assumed the designation "German Empire," and he was the author of the address presented to the new Emperor by the first German Reichstag (March 30, 1871), which expressed the significance of the founding of the Empire to the German people.

Among the men who early grasped Bismarck's genius and advocated his policies was Ludwig Bamberger, who returned to Germany in 1866 from his exile and by the written and spoken word attempted to arouse the enthusiasm of his South German countrymen in favor of Bismarck and of union with Prussia. In 1870 Bismarck invited Bamberger to the headquarters of the army, where he functioned as liaison official for the German press. He was one of the parliamentarians[15] whom Bismarck valued most highly, and his counsel did much for the currency and banking laws of Germany.

By the war of 1866 the realm of Prussia was considerably increased. The new provinces[16] of Hanover and Hesse-Kassel, with which Frankfort was incorporated, had a not inconsiderable Jewish population. The extension of the Prussian constitution over these regions, as also over Schleswig-Holstein, abolished the legal limitations upon the Jews which still existed there. Furthermore, the laws of the North German Confederation provided freedom of movement and of occupation without distinction within the entire compass of the Confederation. This included Saxony and Mecklenburg, which had hitherto resisted any change in their backward economic laws. When the government hesitated to propose a contemplated law on the full emancipation of the Jews, the Liberal Party seized the initiative[17] and proposed the passage of a law to the following effect:

All limitations of civic and citizen rights deriving from differences of religion which are still in force shall hereby be abolished. In particular, competence to act as communal and provincial representatives and occupy public positions shall be independent of religious faith.

The government declared its agreement and there was scarcely any debate. The law was promulgated on July 3, 1869. And when the constitution of the Confederation was extended over the entire Empire (April 16, 1871) this statute became imperial law.

And now all relegation of Jews to a lower legal status had become impossible, at least on paper.[18] The same Otto von Bismarck who had spoken decisively against the equal rights of Jews in 1847 had now, as Imperial Chancellor, established those rights legally. Small wonder that the Jews were jubilant over this advance attained at long last, that they dreamed of a new era of peace and humanity. What was still wanting was the legal recognition of Judaism as a religion. For Alsace-Lorraine, the newly acquired imperial province, such recognition was taken over along with the French regulations on the churches, but in the rest of Germany it was practically ignored.

THE CONSTITUTIONAL STRUGGLE IN AUSTRIA-HUNGARY

In Austria,[19] that great mixture of nationalities in the heart of Europe, conditions were much more difficult for the population as a whole as well as for the Jews. Nobility and Church held dominion in the land, which was the nursery of reaction; its leading statesman, Prince Metternich, would not suffer a single stone in the structure of absolutism to be stirred. The poet, Moritz Hartmann called pre-revolutionary Austria "a slave-galley laden with unfortunate nations who could free themselves only if the ship struck a rock." Politically and economically the country was convulsed, and the first attack of the revolution sufficed to shatter Metternich's dominance. That statesman intervened warmly for the rights of Jews in other states, but in Austria he would not permit even the harshest injustices to be removed. The old Field Marshal Radetzky declared it was a patriotic duty "to win over the class which, by reason of its intelligence and wealth, exerts so great an influence;" but Metternich resisted any change in the laws as being a part of the revolutionary system.

The distribution of Jews in greater Austria was very uneven. In the Alpine provinces, and also in some localities in Moravia and Bohemia, they were forbidden to reside altogether; in Galicia they constituted 8% of the population. Their cultural attainments, despite the school laws of Emperor Joseph II, also differed widely in the eastern and western parts of the monarchy. In Prague, where the Jews had lived longest and where their numbers were largest, the Czech populace began the revolution with an attack on the Jewish quarter.

In Vienna there were only a few "tolerated" Jews with an assured existence; there were many more who lived there without possessing the right of residence. The Damocles sword of expulsion constantly hovered over their heads. Among them were many university graduates who could find no sort of employment after the completion of their studies and became, perforce, willing fellow-travelers of every revolutionary movement, particularly of those movements which had a social as well as a political character. The majority of Viennese Jews were not really at home there. They had grown up with none of the existing institutions and had no stake in the city; they had nothing to lose and could only gain by an overturn. And so it came about that the participation of Jewish university men in the Viennese revolution carried on by students was relatively large and obvious; some even took leading positions in the movement. Certainly Adolf Fischhof[20] could have no inkling, when he left his room on the morning of March 13, 1848, that by midday he would be raised aloft upon the shield of the students and citizenry, and would soon become one of the most influential personalities in the empire. He was a man of sound political instinct and spotless idealism; for the purity of his motives even so rabid an antisemitic leader as Lueger (see p. 170, below) gave testimony. He tried always to exert a moderating influence upon the excited crowds, especially upon the students. He enjoyed the full confidence of the people, and they sent him as their delegate to the Reichstag which was to formulate the constitution. Later, when the military group in control determined to exact vengeance from the leaders of the popular movement, he courageously faced the court-martial, though flight was easy; his conscience was clear, and even the reactionaries could only acquit him. By his side Dr. Josef Goldmark, another physician, worked tirelessly.[21] Goldmark had greater understanding of the realities of life and a keener perception of detail. At the very beginning of the intrigue of the court party and their efforts to engineer a counter-revolution, he saw through their schemes and used all his persuasiveness and his patience in an effort to prevent bloodshed. Time and again he faced great danger; in the battle of October 6 he imperilled his life to protect Count Latour, the Minister of War. But when Latour was murdered, Goldmark was accused of complicity in the plot. He saved himself by flight to the United States, and returned to Austria in 1882 in order to work for rehabilitation, which he eventually succeeded in effecting completely.

Another of the champions of liberty was Ludwig August Frankl,[22] the publisher of the widely read literary *Sonntagsblaetter*. The first night that Frankl had to stand watch as citizen-guard, he composed his poem *Die Universität* which became the Marseillaise of the Viennese populace, attained a circulation of no fewer than a quarter of a million copies, and was set to music twenty-seven times. These and other leaders were moderates; there were some radically minded Jews, like Dr. Adolf Chaizes, who inflamed the impoverished proletariat, especially those of the outskirts of Vienna, to class-consciousness and to participation in the struggle.

At the first clash between students and military five fell dead, and of these two were Jews. All were buried in a common grave, and at the funeral Mannheimer,[23] the Jewish preacher (Graetz, V, 578 ff.), was allowed to speak *before* the Christian clergy: "You have wished," he said, "that these dead Jews should rest with you in your earth, in the same earth. Do not begrudge it that those who have fought the same battle with you, a hard battle, should live with you upon the same earth, free and untroubled as yourselves."

On March 15, Emperor Ferdinand promised a constitution. In a sermon Mannheimer warned the Jews against making special demands:

What must now be done for us? For us, nothing! Everything for people and country, as you have done in these latter days! Now nothing for us! No petitions, no supplications, no prayers and laments for our rights! . . . First the right to live as a man — to breathe, to think, to speak, first the right of the citizen — the Jew comes afterwards! Let men not charge that always and everywhere we think first of ourselves! Do nothing! Our time, too, will come; it shall not fail!

But his words were not heeded. A petition was put into circulation, and immediately evoked the reaction to be expected of hate-mongering publications. Even the Viennese shoemakers' corporation declared they would be in danger of certain destruction if the Jews should obtain equal rights.

The draft of the constitution recognized the equality of all citizens without distinction of faith; but it reversed the abolition of special legislation affecting Jews for the constitutional Reichstag.[24] In this Assembly, in addition to Fischhof and Goldmark, who represented the people of Vienna, there sat Mannheimer and Rabbi Meisels of Cracow, who represented Galicia. When the government proposed the abolition of the special taxes which the Jews had to pay, the proposal encountered opposition. The deputies were not aware of the burden which the Jews had to bear; Mannheimer set forth the crass injustice of these special taxes, and by the clarity and decisiveness of his conclusions he won a vote of confirmation for the proposal.

One day after this vote new revolutionary disturbances broke out in Vienna. The hope of help from Hungary collapsed. At the end of October the capital was conquered by the troops of Prince Windisch-Graetz and martial law was decreed. Among the victims of the soldiery was Dr. Hermann Jellinek, who had indeed written radical pieces for the press but who was not the man to make himself understood by the people or to incite them. No one could explain this judicial murder. The poet Bauernfeld suggested that vengeance against the hated class of journalists was the motive: a Catholic and a Protestant had been apprehended and now a Jew was sought, and, for want of another, Jellinek was seized. Such was the first application of equality for all the faiths.

In consequence of the new situation the Reichstag was dissolved and the king abdicated. His nephew took over the government under the title Francis Joseph I, and on March 4, 1849, he issued the constitution which finally brought the Austrian peoples those basic rights to which, among others, Ignaz Kuranda (see p. 5, above) had devoted himself in Frankfort and the Jewish champions of the revolution in their own country. The constitution guaranteed full freedom of conscience and provided that all citizens of the Austrian Empire, and therefore the Jews also, should enjoy equal civic and political rights. Citizens of the Empire possessed freedom of movement in all lands controlled by the Crown. Local residence laws had to be revised accordingly, and as citizens of the Empire Jews could claim the right to exercise suffrage in communes. The institution of a "Jewish city" in the older sense, with separate communal administration, such as existed in many places in Moravia, was now discontinued. All citizens of the state, furthermore, were granted the right to hold state offices, including judicial posts. Similarly, insofar as trades were free generally, all citizens secured full freedom of occupation.

The benefits which the constitution brought to Austria cannot be exaggerated. But to the Jews it brought far more: nothing less than the beginning of a new existence. One of them[25] put it feelingly and cleverly: "I was born in 1828, I saw the light of day in 1848." The most obvious relief for the Jews was the freedom of movement. They could settle anywhere in the Empire. Places which had formerly barred them now had to permit their sojourn. In Vienna they no longer needed to cower and be plundered by the police. In his reception of a deputation the Emperor had used the expression "Israelitish community," and this became the basis of a hope that a true community, not permitted by the old regulations, might now be formed; another forty years were to pass before such a community, in the full legal sense, could be established. Acquisition of landed property was also permitted. No other limitations on trades and professions applied to Jews than to Christians. The old regulations governing the limitations on marriages became void; similarly, the general schools were opened to Jewish children. All these were steps forward which the government retained even after the constitution was abolished.

The resentment of the forces that had been curbed made itself felt much more sharply in Austria than in Germany. Church, nobility, and cities could not abide the loss of dominion, and sought to turn the clock back. They had not the vision to recognize the possibilities which the new development brought. All blame for objectionable phenomena they thrust upon the Jews. The great advantages which the freedom of trade brought to the general economy was obvious; but as soon as inconveniences appeared or reverses came, fingers were pointed at the Jews as the only ones responsible. Whenever newspapers, which had sprung up like mushrooms with the granting of freedom of the press,[26] took on radical coloring, the small handful published by Jews were seized upon out of the whole number and the "Jewish press" was made to serve as scapegoat. All political radicalism was said to derive from Jews, behind every attack upon the Church their weapon was descried, and they were pilloried as "freethinkers."

When the constitution was abolished on December 31, 1851, the government emphasized that the Jews were citizens of community and Empire, and as such to be put upon the same footing as other citizens. But this interpretation was vigorously disputed, and the communities and the courts frequently declared against the Jews. The Jews saw themselves rudely set back in their forward advance. In Galicia they were not only excluded from owning land and from employing Christian workers on estates which they leased, but some cities even wished to restrict their places of residence to a ghetto and others to forbid them the right of residence altogether. A Viennese lawyer, Dr. Heinrich Jacques,[27] set forth the situation of the Jews in a widely-read memorial and showed the disadvantages which the perverse policy of the ruling class brought to the state as a whole:

By excluding its Jews from the rights of freedom of enterprise, the ownership of property, and the attainment of civil and political offices, Austria allows a substantial part of its material and spiritual national capital to lie idle. It makes of its Jews unproductive consumers instead of generally useful producers. Austria harms itself by driving the material capital of the Jews into cosmopolitan trade instead of identifying it with the fate of the Fatherland. Instead, it ought to do all it can to draw them in the direction in which their own nature and their own interests lead them, toward patriotic activity in the development of property, agriculture, mining and manufacture. Austria permits the spiritual wealth of the Jews to evaporate aimlessly and ineffectually, when by its own laws it forces them to devote their energies to a quest for possessions and riches.

It was only after the unsuccessful conclusion of the Italian war in 1859 that a more liberal era set in. First the situation with reference to trades and professions was ameliorated, and subsequently the acquisition of landed property was permitted. When the guild requirements were abolished and Jewish journeymen were permitted to qualify as master artisans, the clerical party declared that this step constituted a threat to the Catholic religion, and again the shoemakers' corporation of Vienna seized the opportunity of declaring itself against the Jews. The constitution which was issued in 1861 was again voided in 1865. Only after Austria had suffered severe losses in Germany, Italy, and Hungary, was a liberal constitution finally issued, on December 21, 1867. This constitution[28] established the equality of all citizens before the law and freedom of settlement and of occupation. The right to hold public office and full freedom of religion and of teaching were also vouchsafed. The attempts of Polish politicians to limit the rights of the numerous Jews in autonomous Galicia were defeated; the basic rights had to be introduced in Galicia also. Austria thus took its place among the modern constitutional states. In the liberal era which followed, the central government carried out the constitution without injury to the rights of the Jews. Not the least part of the credit is due to Emperor Francis Joseph I, who was firm in opposing any sort of intolerance. The Jewish electorate and the Jewish deputies were among the most faithful constituents of the constitutional party and of liberal German centralization.

In Hungary[29] the reform party strove for the economic improvement of the country, and therefore could not neglect so active an element as were the 200,000 Jews. The difficulty lay in the Jews' preponderance in commerce — a situation that was, indeed, forced upon them, by the existing law — and also in the fact that the great mass of Jews constituted an alien element as compared with the native population. Rabbi Moses Sofer of Pressburg (Graetz, V, 567 ff.) had declared that the Jews could have no fatherland other than Palestine; but the advanced communities in Budapest, Arad, Papa, and other places, thought otherwise. They sought every opportunity to Magyarize their coreligionists and to turn them towards handicrafts and agriculture. There were warm advocates of Jewish rights among the deputies of the *Landtag* (Diet), but the Crown refused even the lesser rights which the nobility were willing to grant. To all native and naturalized Jews of irreproachable reputation they granted the right of residence; but they made an exception of the "mountain cities." They granted freedom of trades and permitted the acquisition of estates that had belonged to the nobility — "the small result of big words," as Louis Kossuth termed it. The abolition of the Residence Tax came only on June 24, 1846, after the Jews had obligated themselves to pay a capital sum, 1,200,000 florins, for release from this preposterous levy. In the meanwhile the sentiment of the populace towards the Jews had undergone another change; the demand for full equality of rights called forth much opposition. "Our population," so one author argued, "does not yet possess sufficient education to compete with the Jews, is more averse to commerce than attracted to it, loves idleness rather than diligence." Because the Jew was inventive, industrious, and diligent, he was to be penalized and remain without rights.

The struggle for freedom in 1848 was utilized by the citizens of Pressburg[30] for an attack upon that part of the Jewish population which had settled outside the ghetto. What meaning could this whole business of freedom have, these heroes argued, if one might not even indulge in a raid upon the Jews? Houses and property of Jews were destroyed and their lives were threatened. Similar occurrences took place in Pest also and in other localities. In Steinamanger the synagogue was stormed and scrolls of the Torah were cut to bits and thrown into the water. In the Diet also harsh words were spoken against the Jews. Many among them despaired and began to organize emigration to the United States.

But the majority joined the fight[31] not only for a democratic constitution but also for independence from Austria.

Many a Jew joined the national guard, but was forced to leave because of the double dealing of the Kossuth-Batthyany government. Despite the readiness of the Jews to die for their country, the Reichstag, called to draft a constitution, denied them equal rights. The Hungarian patriots did not perceive that freedom is indivisible and must be applied to all alike. It was only in the hour of danger, when the Slavic part of the population separated itself from Hungary, and the Croatians advanced against the capital with the support of the Vienna government, that Jews were permitted to enter the armed forces, the national guard and the *Honved*. The recorded number of 20,000 Jewish campaigners may be exaggerated, but the enthusiasm for the struggle was widespread among the Jews. Respected rabbis, like Schwab in Ofen and Loew in Papa, enrolled in the ranks of volunteers. Jewish congregations devoted considerable sums of money to the insurrection; many sacrificed their silver utensils. Since Kossuth insisted upon full Magyarization of the Jews, a reform congregation was formed in Budapest with a radical program: sermons and prayers were to be in Hungarian. The Reichstag, which had fled to Széged, finally adopted a unanimous resolution by the terms of which native Hungarians or naturalized Jews might enjoy equal civic and political rights with those who professed other religions. An assembly of representatives of Jewish communities was to be convoked for the purpose of reforming the principles of Judaism to conform to the spirit of the new age (June 28, 1849). The joy was short-lived. Only two weeks later the Russians, whose help had been summoned by the Austrians, moved into Hungary and crushed the Hungarian movement for freedom along with its resolutions for the benefit of the Jews.

Even before this, the Jews had suffered sharply from repressive measures. The Slovaks and Serbs exacted vengeance from the Hungarian communities and even struck down a number of rabbis. When Prince Windisch-Graetz, the hangman of Vienna, conquered Budapest in February 1849, he laid the congregation there under heavy contribution. But General Haynau, who brought with him from Italy the reputation of being the "hyena of Brescia," brought more serious suffering. His abuse of the population in Hungary was so barbarous that he was recalled after a year. Of the Jews as a whole he demanded a cash contribution of 2,300,000 florins, a sum till then unheard of. He wished to make an exception in favor of those congregations or individuals who could prove their loyalty, that is to say, to any who would denounce those who had fought for liberty. Such alleviation was promptly rejected.

The king commuted the contribution to a million florins and provided that the sum be made into a cultural fund. The principal was to remain intact, and the income used for establishing a Hungarian rabbinical college, for founding model schools and a teachers' seminary, for supporting needy Jewish elementary schools and, finally, to provide for needy Jewish blind or deaf-mute children. In the decade after 1850 there came a pause in political activity, and the Jews had leisure to devote their energies to problems of education and adjustment. After 1859 a milder atmosphere pervaded Hungary. But it was not till the end of 1867 that the questions of constitution and of the equal rights of the Jews were legally fixed, when the relations with Austria were adjusted and Emperor Francis Joseph was crowned King of Hungary. The emancipation law was accepted unanimously and without debate:

> The Israelitish inhabitants of the country are declared to possess equal rights with the Christian inhabitants in the exercise of all civic and political functions. All laws, usages, and ordinances contravening this principle are hereby rescinded.

For several decades Hungary remained a stronghold of the liberal spirit and of the fullest freedom of conscience.

But along with the emancipation law the government raised its old demand for regulation of the internal affairs of the Jews. The liberal minister Oetvoes summoned delegates to draft a statute for Jewish congregations and schools, and to submit its draft for final formulation and adoption to a Congress[32] which was to assemble at the end of December 1868. But Oetvoes underestimated the cleavage between the two elements in Hungarian Jewry. The intransigent orthodox mass, extending from Burgenland through Slovakia to Siebenbürgen, fanatically opposed even the slightest deviation from "tradition," and stubbornly rejected all educational reforms. The middle class element in Hungary proper had for a generation shown itself inclined towards moderate progressiveness and towards Magyarization. No uniform platform could be formed which would embrace these diverse tendencies. The party of the Pressburg rabbinate rejected even so strict a traditionalist as Esriel Hildesheimer of Eisenstadt, to say nothing of a reformer like Leopold Loew of Papa. In the Congress the opposition was embittered and passionate, and it ended with the withdrawal of the orthodox delegates. These rejected the proposed constitution and for their own part submitted another draft. In order not to invade freedom of conscience, the government allowed two organizations to exist side by side, the *Israelitische Landessekretariat* of the orthodox, and the *Israelitische Landeskanzlei* of the great "neologist" majority. In addition there were congregations who retained their old status and styled themselves *status quo*, as well as the Hasidim who designated themselves "Sephardic" congregations. Thus, with the consent of the government, the Jews were split into several "Churches." The principal task which had been set the Congress, the establishment of a national rabbinical school, required almost a decade for its performance;[33] it was carried out against the opposition of the orthodox with the assistance of the *Landeskanzlei*.

Emancipation in Italy

In Italy, as in Germany, the question of equal rights for Jews was bound up with the liberation and unification of the many divisions of the country. The champions of the *Risorgimento*[34] were also champions of a democratic popular commonwealth. Pope Pius IX, at the beginning of his pontificate, when he was sympathetic to the party of unification, extended the rights of the Jews in the Papal State and set up a commission to study their situation. He even intended to abolish the ghetto of Rome completely. But before his decree was issued the citizens of Rome, who were favorably disposed to the Jews, took matters into their own hands. Under the direction of the popular leader Ciceruacchio, they pulled down the gates of the ghetto on April 17, 1848. It was the night of Passover and the Jews trembled for fear of one of the customary attacks. This time they discovered that the crowd had pressed into the ghetto to liberate them and to proclaim their common brotherhood. In other places also, where there still were ghettos, the best citizens pulled down their gates. Popular opinion was predominantly in favor of the Jews. They had resided in the country for a very long time, had fulfilled all the obligations of citizens, were aglow with the idea of the *Risorgimento*, and had promoted its progress with a readiness to sacrifice and with a courage which did not stop short of death. The poet and statesman, Massimo d'Azeglio, became spokesman for popular opinion; he contended that equality for the Jews was a precept of Christian love. His brother, Roberto, was minister of the King of Sardinia, and two weeks after Piedmont received its constitution the equality of the Jews was proclaimed there (November 19, 1848). This was particularly important, for with the victorious advance of Piedmontese arms this constitution was spread over ever wider reaches and eventually was extended over the entire kingdom of Italy. Camillo Cavour employed Jews as his closest co-workers.

In the Papal State, to be sure, the Pope was able, with French help, to restore the old conditions and to punish the Jews for their share of responsibility in the Revolution. The old regulations were put back into force, so that Jews everywhere were compelled to return to the gloomy ghetto. In Rome the ghetto was searched, on the pretext that church vessels had been secreted there, and though nothing was found the ghetto was thoroughly plundered. The ghetto of Rome was situated in a marshy and miserable section of the city; it was overcrowded and unwholesome, and its denizens were degraded to a low cultural level by occupational restrictions. Conversionist sermons had been discontinued by the Pope, but Christian domestics who were employed in Jewish homes frequently exerted themselves to save the souls of children entrusted to their care, and so were the occasion of a great evil.

The case of Edgar Mortara,[35] a child from Bologna, is world-famous. During an alleged illness a housemaid had secretly undertaken to give him private baptism. Several years later, on June 26, 1858, a military detachment appeared by night at Mortara's house and demanded the delivery of the boy, who was now six years old, at the instance of the church authorities. The stunned parents could only look on helplessly while their son was taken from them. All of Europe seethed with indignation at this act of violence. Catholic monarchs like the Emperor Francis Joseph and Napoleon III intervened personally with the Pope and besought him not to antagonize the public opinion of Europe. The Jewish congregations of the kingdom of Sardinia invoked the assistance of their government; a number of German rabbis directed a petition to the Pope; the Prince Regent of Prussia, being a Protestant, would not involve himself in the affair but gave assurances of his sympathy. In England there were public meetings of protest; Sir Moses Montefiore hastened to Rome in person, but was not received by the Pope. On the other hand, at the customary New Year's reception, the Pope threatened the leaders of the Jewish community with retaliatory measures for having made the affair a concern to all of Europe. It was on this occasion that he is reported to have said that he snapped his fingers at the whole world. But the world snapped back. There can be no question that this throwback to the Middle Ages dangerously sharpened the already keen opposition to the existence of the Papal State. The Church was anxiously concerned to keep young Mortara safe from the advancing Italian troops. Later he himself rejected attempts to free him because he was unwilling to leave the Catholic faith. But he remained loyal to his Jewish relatives.

The days of the Papal State were numbered. Giuseppe Garibaldi tried to conquer Rome, but his way was barred by a French army. Among the many Jews[36] who served as volunteers with Garibaldi was the rabbinical student Adolf Moses, who died in 1902 in Louisville, Kentucky, where he was rabbi. After Napoleon's defeat, the Italians were able to enter Rome, September 20, 1870, and the Eternal City became the capital of the kingdom of Italy. In a matter of days, on October 13, 1870, the Jews of Rome were declared to possess equal rights, and the Roman ghetto, the oldest and cruelest of all, was abolished. There was no country in Europe where government was more liberalized in the course of a decade. "The Tiber waves have overthrown and sunk the unhappy past so that on the Tiber shores olive branches are now blossoming out" — so did Pope Pius XII recently (1939) summarize the change of eras.

Emancipation in Switzerland

The Swiss Confederation[37] furnishes an example of how remote a freedom-minded people can be from making universal freedom an actuality. Except for the canton of Aargau, where Jews had lived for centuries and endured medieval humiliation, they were forbidden to live in the country. In 1843, Geneva was the first canton to naturalize a number of Jews and permit them to conduct worship in the capital. Berne was generous in calling Jewish scholars to its university; so, for example, the twenty-six-year-old physician and physiologist, Gabriel Gustav Valentin of Breslau (died 1883). But the few remaining Jews of the canton were subjected to laws governing aliens. Basle was stubbornly exclusive; the canton went so far as to antagonize its great neighbor, France. It had guaranteed by treaty to allow French citizens freedom of settlement and of acquiring landed property, but it refused to honor its guarantee if the citizens in question were Jews. As the basis for the exclusion of foreign Jews it was alleged that Jews of Alsace, who inclined towards usury, might work injury to the country. The French officials were firm in their denial of the accusation. The new constitution of the Swiss Confederation, promulgated in September 1848, guaranteed democratic rights, but made their possession depend on Christian faith; though several cantons, and those, indeed, with a Jewish population, had advocated full equality for the Jews.

The decade which followed saw a twofold conflict. Foreign powers, such as France, England, Holland and the United States, which had concluded mutual agreements with the Swiss Confederation, insisted that their citizens should not suffer disabilities because of their religious faith. In the United States especially there was lively dissatisfaction among the Jews and among the public generally; people could not understand how an American president could sign an agreement which made any sort of discrimination on grounds of religion possible. There was pressure to recall the trade agreement or to call for a change in the Swiss constitution; a suggestion which the Swiss interpreted as an unfriendly intervention in their internal affairs. The Federal Council gave the problem its full attention and was pleased to be able to report a change in public opinion favorable to the Jews.

Within the Confederation there was a struggle between centralization and federalism, and it was only in 1866 that a decision was made in favor of centralization. Beginning with 1860, several cantons voluntarily abolished their restrictions upon Jews. In 1862 a Cultural Association of Israelites was formed, and worked for closer relations with the Swiss population. A plebiscite, on January 15, 1866, sanctioned a law which granted civic equality to all Swiss without reference to their faith, and permitted the free exercise of all religious cults. The federal constitution of 1873 removed the last remains of inequality. Such was the obstinacy shown by a freedom-loving people towards a group mostly native, which did not comprise more than a seven-hundredth part of the whole population. Freedom of residence, indeed, combined with persecutions of Jews in other countries doubled the population in the course of a generation.

France and the *Alliance*

In France[38] the Revolution of 1848 could bring the Jews no new rights, for with the abolition of the Jew's Oath in 1846 the last legal inequality had been removed. In French society clerical influence was widely prevalent, and this influence furthered prejudice against the Jews. Since the clerical party desired to subject the schools to the Church, it put obstacles in the way of Jews being engaged for service in the schools. But in the political sphere equality was observed. Jews participated actively in the work of all political parties; after 1848 some became ministers and as such belonged to governments of the most diverse tendencies. Jews enjoyed the opportunity of working in the universities and in the fine arts, and they found posts in the courts and in the army.

The France of the period regarded herself as the conscience of the world, and wherever men were unjustly persecuted France let her voice be heard. It was in France that Jews first felt an obligation to unite for the protection of their oppressed coreligionists in all the world and to intercede for them, well aware that they could count on public opinion and the help of the government. The experience of Damascus (Graetz, V, 636 ff.) was not forgotten; and the case of Mortara (see p. 30 f., above) precipitated the decision to establish an organization to carry out their purposes. After the model of the *Alliance Protestante Universelle* it called itself[39] *Alliance Israélite Universelle* (1860). The brilliant presidency of Adolphe Crémieux lent it special distinction. But what was perfectly intelligible in the case of the Protestants was misinterpreted in the case of Jews. On the basis of the name it was supposed that Jews strove for world dominion — a matter which will occupy us time and again in the sequel. The actual goals of the *Alliance* were exclusively humanitarian in character, to wit: "to work everywhere for the emancipation and moral progress of the Jews; to give effectual support to those who are suffering persecution because they are Jews; to encourage all publications calculated to promote these ends." The *Alliance* wished to sharpen the conscience of the emancipated Jew, to impress upon it the *noblesse oblige* of solidarity; it wished to restore his human dignity to the oppressed Jew and to help him attain political and economic standing; to the Jew who had strayed morally it wished to point out the true path. Of the achievements of the *Alliance* in fulfilling these tasks, and of the imposing school system which it erected, we shall have to speak at various relevant points.

While world-famous Christians like Alexandre Dumas and Jules Simon hailed the new institution warmly, in wide Jewish circles there was anxiety and fear of political misinterpretations and complications. Especially after the Franco-German War of 1870-1871 there was a tendency to partition the universal *Alliance* into national alliances, and this served to invalidate its original design.

When Alsace-Lorraine went to Germany (1871), Jews were, for the first time after they had obtained civil rights, in the position of taking up a new citizen affiliation. A considerable number exercised their option in favor of France and removed thither — later they were to be represented by "real" Frenchmen as a "Prussian invasion." Those that remained, like the rest of the population, showed a negative attitude towards German rule, although that rule had allowed them to keep all their rights undiminished, including their consistorial organization. There was always tension between them and the Jews who immigrated from the German Empire.

In the French colony of Algiers,[40] Jews, like other natives, could be naturalized individually, but in that case they lost their civil standing, for they were then no longer members of the political Jewish community. A change in this situation, which had led to various difficulties, was concluded towards the end of the old Empire. On October 24, 1870, the *Délégation du Gouvernement de la Défense Nationale* presented the Jews of Algiers generally with the right of French citizenship. Crémieux, who was the presiding officer of the body, was severely blamed for expediting such a law in an hour when his country was in dire need. His skillful defense in the Chamber brought confirmation with slight alterations, but the political sting remained. The precipitate exemption caused antagonism between the Jews and their countrymen and repeatedly found expression in bloody excesses.

Emancipation in Other European States

Even in Spain[41] the spirit of the new age was stirring. General Prim, who had brought about the fall of Queen Isabella in 1869, rescinded the decree of 1492 which forbade Jews to live in Spain. Jews did not make any great use of this invitation to return, nor would it have been wise to urge such a return after the centuries-old indoctrination of the Spanish people. Nevertheless, a small congregation was formed in the capital, Madrid; this congregation conducted regular services and built a modest synagogue with the help of Jews in the outer world.

In Belgium[42] and in Holland the equality which had been guaranteed was faithfully observed. In both countries Church and State were separated, and consideration was therefore given to the religious requirements of all faiths without prejudice. In 1850 the Dutch Jews were united in the *Maatschappij tot Nyt van Israeliten in Nederland*. The distinguished jurist, M. H. Godefroi, who as deputy had successfully opposed the ratification of the trade agreement with Switzerland until such time as commercial rights should be granted to Dutch Jews, was repeatedly invited to assume a post in the Ministry. He yielded only in 1860, when the king applied to him personally. Among the many illustrious Jewish jurists of Holland he was the first to occupy a ministerial post; he was also the president of the Israelitish consistory.

Of the northern countries,[43] Denmark received a constitution on June 5, 1849. Although the constitution made the Lutheran Church the official State Church, it also provided that no one could be debarred from full political and civic rights by reason of his faith, any more than he could abstain from his civic and political obligations for that reason. "Thereafter the Jews of Denmark were set upon a footing with their environment in every respect, not only on paper but actually in life."

In Sweden the citizen rights of the Jews were impeded both by the Lutheran Church and by the artisan restrictions. When freedom of trades won the day, the occupational distinctions and the clash of economic interests between the "adherents of the Mosaic faith" and the population generally disappeared. Liberal views led gradually to an extension of the rights of the Jews. In 1860 they were allowed to acquire real estate in the country, and after 1863 marriages between Jews and non-Jews were recognized but the children of such marriages had to be brought up in the Lutheran faith. Along with the Catholics, the Jews received further political rights, and since 1878 they have possessed all citizen rights except such as are expressly reserved for members of the State Church.

Norway was entirely closed to the Jews. Beginning in 1839, the poet Henrik Wergeland, a peasant deputy, campaigned warmly for the abolition of this severity, but his efforts came to fruition only a few years after his early death (1851). Not many Jews took advantage of permission to settle in Norway. Since 1891 they have been in full possession of all civil rights.

The Attainment of Equality in England

In England the question of equalizing the rights of the Jews took a form quite different from that in other countries. England[44] possessed the oldest democracy in Europe, but no one could have a share in its constitutional rights who was not a member of the Church of

England. When the emancipation of the dissenters and the Catholics was carried out in 1829, the grant of similar rights to the Jews seemed to be a matter of logic and of justice. The Tories, however, and with them the majority of the Upper House, clung to the concept of the Christian character of the State. All oaths of members of Parliament, of public officials, and of doctors of the universities retained the formula of Christian faith. The Liberals fought with tenacious stubbornness for the admission of Jews. In his *Civil Disabilities of the Jews* the great historian Macaulay showed the inconsistency of the political situation with unparalleled clarity and logic. Public opinion declared itself unmistakably in favor of the Jews, and Queen Victoria left her own favorable attitude in no doubt. Jews were elected to civic posts, but they could not assume such posts until the formula of the oath of office was altered by law. In 1855, David Salomons entered office as the first Jewish Lord Mayor in the City of London. The City elected Lionel Rothschild its member of Parliament, but because he was unable to take the customary oath, he could not take his seat. David Salomons was punished for having ventured to participate in the voting. Five times thereafter Commons voted for a change in the oath of office, but each time the change was rejected by the Lords. Finally, in 1858, the ridiculous aspects of this procedure were recognized, and a compromise proposal was carried, by which each House was permitted to formulate the oath according to its own decision.

Thereafter Jewish representatives were to be found in the ranks of both parties. As member of Parliament, Sir Francis Goldsmid (1808-1818) fought for the alleviation of Jewish suffering in the East. In 1885, Lionel Rothschild's son, Nathaniel, was able to enter the House of Lords, and many other Jews followed him. The changes in the university oath were also several times rejected by the Upper House and became effective only in 1871. Thus all legal obstacles were gradually removed, not only in England, but also in its colonies; and with the straightforwardness of political thought in Great Britain, the equalization of Jewish rights was soon achieved.

Freed from civil disabilities the English Jews could look after their internal affairs. Dr. Nathan Adler, the first Ashkenazic Chief Rabbi with an academic background, inducted in 1843, modernized the system of Jewish education, crowning it with a "Training College for the Jewish Ministry" (afterwards called "Jews' College"). In his efforts completely to reorganize the machinery for the relief of the poor, Lionel Louis Cohen became his right hand. He was most active in the establishment of the Board of Guardians. The cooperation of the various synagogues in the field of relief provided the common ground for a union of the congregations which led to the creation of the United Synagogue. The new organization was subsequently endorsed by an act of Parliament and extended to the United Kingdom. The conflict with the Reform Congregation fell into oblivion. Their leaders cooperated with the United Synagogue in common affairs; and so did the Sephardim, although they remained in their isolation. In this way the community won that strength and unity which was badly needed if it would weather the storm to come.[45]

Thus, in the course of a single generation, the civic and legal disabilities of the Jews were removed in Central and Western Europe. But social ostracism could be done away with, not by laws, but only by good will — and good will was not everywhere to be found. Even liberal politicians who, in accordance with their concepts of justice, advocated the rights of Jews to election, shuddered at the possibility of a member of the Jewish faith occupying the seat beside them in Parliament. Man clings to nothing so tenaciously as to his prejudices. Even the emancipated Jew was regarded by his countrymen, humanly and socially, not as their peer but as a pariah. It is told of a German-Polish count that he visited, from time to time, the salon of a Jewish financial grandee with whom he had business relations, but that he never removed his gloves because he did not wish to contaminate his aristocratic fingers by the touch of a lower caste. This man's socially immaculate fingers were, however, notoriously tainted with the touch of gold.[46]

CHAPTER II

The Jews in Eastern Europe and the Near East

THE POLICY OF RUSSIFICATION

DEVELOPMENTS in the East of Europe took a turn quite different from that in the West. In culture and education the peoples were backward, and the governments did little or nothing to raise the intellectual level, although such countries as Rumania and Serbia prided themselves in passing for "advanced" and in aping the political structures of Western Europe. None of these countries possessed the broad middle class upon which constitutionalism rested in other parts of Europe. The people were not yet ready for constitutional government, and so were susceptible to every sort of demagoguery.

The Jewish population[1] was numerous. This was true also of Galicia and Hungary. Broadly considered, these two countries, with Russia and Rumania, constituted a single large realm of migration, within which flight from one country to another, as occasioned by persecution or catastrophe, was constant. This fact was frequently employed by the rulers as a pretext for treating the Jews as aliens. It was undeniable that small groups were constantly in motion, but their wanderings were insignificant in view of the millions of settled Jewish inhabitants.

These countries were at best impoverished, and their Jews lived in incredible wretchedness and misery. They were excluded from so many occupations and were so densely crowded that despite willingness and capacity to work — in all of these countries they were the most skillful artisans — it was impossible for them to sustain themselves and their large families. One occupation widely followed was trade in alcoholic beverages and the keeping of taverns where liquor was served. This was a concession leased by the nobility to the Jews in order to draw the largest possible profits from their distilleries. The occupation proved to be the reverse of a blessing and was made the occasion for constant charges against the Jews. The drunkenness of the peasants was laid at the door of the Jewish innkeeper. But alcohol was the only solace of peasants who were kept in serfdom; drunkenness was widespread, and was no less prevalent in regions where Jewish innkeepers were unknown.

The Jewish population lived mostly in the cities, and quite apart from the Christians. There were two disparate worlds which existed side by side. The peoples did not know one another and had no social relationships one with the other. What economic connections there were, were not always pleasant; when money was borrowed of a Jew or goods received on credit, the Jew was always complained of as grasping when payment had to be made. Even officialdom knew the Jews only from the outside and proceeded upon the conviction that the Jew could only be the object of arbitrary power and exploitation. Anything that might form a common ground between the two parties was eschewed by both. The suspicions of the Greek Orthodox Church were no less a barrier than the aversion of the hasidic or the antagonism of the orthodox rabbinic Jews.

The ruling class was hostile to the Jews; they attempted to impute to the Jews blame for all the undeniable shortcomings in their countries, and to direct against them the dissatisfaction which such shortcomings occasioned. They believed, or professed to believe, that if the Jews were granted any rights at all they would soon come to dominate the country. They saw only the prosperity of the very few Jewish entrepreneurs, not the grim misery of the hungry Jewish masses. They saw only the outer appearances, frequently repulsive, of hounded and hunted Jews; they did not see the evils, far worse, in the ranks of their own native proletariat. The hostility of the ruling class, which quickly roused the credulous populace to violence, brought cruel martyrdom upon the Jewish masses of Eastern Europe. Their treatment was frequently so horrifying that the nations and governments of Western Europe felt constrained to express their misgivings. But such intervention injured the *amour propre* of the governments in question, and actually did more harm than good.

The pitch for Jewish persecution was set by Czarist Russia.[2] By the partition of Poland many provinces with dense Jewish populations had fallen to Russia's lot, but it wished to keep old Russia free of Jews, as it had been in the past, and so forced all Jews to reside in the Pale of Settlement, in the western and southern provinces of former Poland. The cities of these provinces were overcrowded with a greatly increased Jewish population; trade in them was sparse and offered scant profits; many eked out an anxious and insufficient livelihood as middlemen. Artisans were too numerous for the need, and so were little employed and poorly paid. Many thousands heeded Czar Alexander I's call to settle on the land. Their settlement, insofar as it was not sabotaged by Russian officials, was successful. The entire western region of the empire, where most Jews lived, was a problem for the government, for it failed to make use of the region's natural capacity as a bridge to the West; similarly the Jewish population was a special problem, for the government assumed a hostile attitude towards it and refused to recognize or use its constructive capacities.

In his youth Czar Nicholas I[3] (1825–1855) was not untouched by ideas of enlightenment. But he had never reckoned with the prospect of his succession, and his extreme despotism was frequently only an over-compensation for certain enlightened tendencies. The motto, "For Russian Nationalism, for the Orthodox Church, and for Autocracy," was suggested to him in the middle of his reign by flatterers who did not themselves believe in it. What he called autocracy was dependence on an administration which was no administration but only a conglomerate of bureaucrats, frequently ignorant, unreliable, and easily corruptible. He faced the problem of the Jews, as he did many others, with helpless perplexity. He regarded them as an alien body, and hesitated whether to eliminate or assimilate them—which meant, for him, convert them.

The latter tendency was apparent in his regulations concerning military service for Jews. In all other countries acceptance of Jews into the army was the first step towards receiving them into the body-politic, the first indication that the State regarded them as citizens. But Nicholas I was very far from granting the Jews any rights in their fatherland. His decree concerning their obligation for military service,[4] dated 1827, was special legislation for the express purpose of wrenching them from their environment for a period of twenty-five years and subjecting them to Christianizing influences. The army in Russia was not a citizen-army, as it was in other states. Merchants, university graduates, nobles were not required to serve but only to pay a commutation fee. It was the dregs of the people that were forcibly thrust into the army by the noble landowners or court officials; and after a long term of service they were colonized and continued to work for the army. It was with this class that the Jews were now to be incorporated.

Parents looked upon sons that were conscripted as lost. They had no prospect of seeing them again for twenty-five years; and, if they did eventually return, they were quite alienated from their parents. Such soldiers as were concentrated in considerable numbers in fortresses like St.

Petersburg kept up worship and had an opportunity to follow Jewish traditions. But the preponderant majority found themselves deep in the interior of the country, in regions where, ordinarily, the law forbade them to set foot, in an utterly alien environment, which enticed or compelled their assimilation. Even in their isolation most remained true to their faith. One cannot but be moved by the accounts of some of those who returned, by their descriptions of their long religious struggles, their first reunion with their parents, their first visit to the synagogue in which they had been reared.

In order to provide more tractable victims for the Moloch of conversion, a truly wicked plan was conceived. The period of service, which normally began in the eighteenth year, was made to begin some years earlier in the case of Jews, so that boys of twelve and even of nine and eight were recruited into the service. These boys were called "cantonists," as were the children of married Russian soldiers who were consequently required to enroll their sons in the army. The difference was that the Russians were prepared for front-line service and so had prospects of advancement and subsequent appointments to government posts, whereas Jewish soldiers, as a rule, were not prepared for military service, but were made to serve as officers' orderlies, drummers, and musicians.

In the name of Russification, national as well as religious, tender children were recruited. The eighteen-year-old conscripts had already had some little experience of life and their character was in some degree formed. But these helpless and inexperienced children, it was believed, could be moulded like wax and directed at will. It was a frightful human tragedy that was here enacted. Children were kidnaped or violently torn from their mothers' arms; they were dragged off to an environment in which the human and physical elements were alike alien to them, in which they were exposed to brutal treatment and were made to toil at slave labor without regard for limitations of their strength. How many thousands of these poor victims never reached their destination but succumbed to the hardships of the road or to forcible conversion? How many fell victim to cruel treatment? It was a dear price that the Church paid for the few souls it won. Not the least item of cost was the anguish which engulfed all Jewry, which preserved the memory of this wretched period in stories and memoirs, in songs and in proverbs.

Such were the bolts of horror which the Jews had constantly to expect during the reign of Nicholas. Royal commissions for investigating the Jewish question were in almost constant session, but no conclusion was ever reached, for their members had no competence in the problems involved, and so were repeatedly making false starts. Memoranda were continually being submitted which were calculated to solve the Jewish question, but not one had aught to suggest beyond the customary restraint and repression, and so nothing was accomplished. The shortsighted Russian statesmen did direct their gaze to the West where Jews were far advanced. They overlooked the fact that these Jews too had been backward only two generations before, that they had been improved by wise governmental regulations, that the Russian Jews were indeed more numerous and poorer but no less capable of being educated, and that profitable returns would be realized if only the state would take up their cause with good will. Among the Jews themselves there was no unanimity in evaluating such "progress;" what one group regarded as a remedy the other looked upon as the greatest misfortune.[5]

The wisdom of Russian councils of state could devise nothing more profound than proposals for Jewish expulsions, particularly from villages, though such expulsions had clearly proved mistaken in White Russia and the lot of the peasants had not been improved in the slightest, and although the governors of the provinces concerned frequently emphasized the dangers with which such expulsions threatened their territory. Because of the dislocations which expulsions would cause, the ukases of the Emperor were not always carried out; but though their execution was deferred they caused unrest in the Jewish communities nevertheless, for the sword of Damocles hovered always over their heads. The interpretation of the decrees, which were often vague, lay in the hands of a corrupt body of officials, who used the emergency to enforce exorbitant demands. The consequences of all these ill-considered measures were greater impoverishment of the Jews, aggravated crowding of unemployed in the cities, and a greater strain on the national economy.

In 1835 a Jews' statute[6] was issued which was to remain effective for decades. It contained some few wholesome regulations, as for example the prohibition of child marriages and the admission of Jews to public schools with the express assurance that no constraint would be put upon religious beliefs. But the beneficial elements were lost in a mass of medieval legislation which was exhumed, furbished up and sharpened. The Pale of Settlement was further reduced, and the number of forbidden rural communities was thus further increased. Synagogues might not be erected in the vicinity of churches. In business communications the hereditary language of the Jews was forbidden; Christian workers might not be employed permanently, and when employed temporarily must be kept separated from their Jewish fellow-workers.

For the execution of all legal prescriptions and the accurate collection of taxes the Kahal[7] was responsible. To this body and to the municipal Duma only such as could speak and write Russian might be elected. But in 1844 there appeared a ukase concerning "the abolition of the Kahal and the subjection of the Jews resident in city and country to the general administration." This took from the Jews the remainder of their self-administration and delivered them to a power that was hostile to them. They could no longer be represented as a body, and their participation in the civic governing bodies was limited to a maximum of a third of the whole number, even where Jews comprised a majority of the population. Even the administration of special Jewish taxes was put into the hands of the communes. To the Kahal was left only the burdensome obligation of providing the prescribed contingent of recruits. Simultaneously a decree was issued which forbade the traditional Jewish garb for men and women and imposed a penalty for its retention. It was to no purpose that pioneers hailed this measure, which was calculated to modify the separateness of the Jews, and that they took the historically correct position that this garb had nothing whatever to do with the Jewish religion; the masses looked upon this very externality as an inviolable part of Jewish life, and they were ready to sacrifice themselves to retain it. So strong was the resistance that the government postponed the enforcement of the measure for several years, and even later did not insist upon its execution to the letter.

Moses Montefiore's Intervention

In view of the confused character of the legislation and the difficulty of achieving a view of the whole situation and of its component details, it may be useful, in order to clarify matters, to see how the situation presented itself to a foreign observer. In 1846 Moses Montefiore[8] accepted an invitation of the Russian government, which anticipated that the visit of so distinguished a personality would make a salutary impression upon the public opinion of Europe and upon the attitude of the Jewish masses.

For his part, Montefiore was sincerely concerned to learn of the situation of his oppressed brethren at first hand, and to attempt to influence the government in their favor. He was received in court society with princely honors, and the impressive personality of this faithful Jew left a vivid impression. The emperor and the ministers concerned assured him of their good will towards the Jews, but they were not backward in laying accusations against them. They charged them in particular with being unwilling to work, with plundering the peasants, with engaging in smuggling in the border provinces, and with being opposed to education out of superstitious fanaticism.

Montefiore accepted these charges perforce, for he was not familiar with the circumstances; but at the recommendation of the government he traveled about in the Jewish centers. Especially in Wilna he had the opportunity of speaking with the representatives of the Jews who had gathered from far and near to greet the famous philanthropist and to make him acquainted with their needs. Out of regard for his character and position the mutually hostile parties of the traditionalists and the enlightened effected a truce and appeared before him with a united front. The material of which he came into possession in this way he elaborated in two memoranda which he despatched to St. Petersburg after his return to London. Without injuring the self-esteem of the Russian state dignitaries, and more explicitly than any Russian citizen might dare do, the English baronet could point out to the ministers how badly they were informed on the Jewish question, and where the real difficulties lay.

Count Kisselev, the Minister of Dominions (Interior), had given Montefiore a sketch of the extent of the Pale of Settlement and of the civic rights which the Jews in the Pale enjoyed. Now Montefiore could point out to the Count the limitations within the Pale, the recent expulsions from Kiev, Nikolaev, Swartopol, from the villages of

White Russia, from a stretch thirty miles wide extending along the long border facing Austria and Prussia, where Jews were even reported to be forbidden to take rooms in houses where liquor was served. He could point to the devastating effects which might be expected for hundreds of thousands of Jews. He could point to the fact that Jewish merchants could travel in the interior of the country only in exceptional cases, and that this was an obstacle to their enterprise and served to increase their expenses.

The overwhelming majority of Jews were not merchants, but artisans and unskilled laborers. They were not inclined to idleness, but sought every chance of employment they could find as tailors, shoemakers, furriers, glaziers, smiths, stonemasons, carpenters, and the like, and were happy indeed when they obtained permission to work at low pay in crushing stones for highway construction. In all trades they were hampered by lack of work and restrictions on their movements, whereas in their own Pale outside workers could come in as competitors. They had offered themselves also for agricultural work and they had journeyed to remote Siberia (1835) under indescribable difficulties; but upon their arrival they were informed that the land was not to be cultivated by Jews. In 1840 a large number of families accepted an invitation to practice agriculture in the region of Kherson; but there too the plans were not carried out. They were sent farther and exposed to untold difficulties, only to find, upon their arrival at their destination, nothing of what the government had held out in prospect. It was small wonder that agricultural colonies could not thrive under such conditions; and surely there was no basis for charging that Jews were disinclined to agriculture.

There was as little truth in the charge that the Jews were the ruin of the peasants as there was in the accusation that they were disinclined to work. It was even proven that the peasants of White Russia were worse off after the expulsion of the Jews from the villages than they had been before, that seed-grain was no longer available as it had been before the Jews were expelled. The Jews were only lease-holders of Christian proprietors, and it was not to be supposed that they would be retained if their presence led to the ruin of the peasants. That the peasants did not hate the Jews was proven by their peaceful attitude towards them, and that the Jews had accumulated no wealth by the fact that they had come into the cities poor and bare.

The defense against the charge of smuggling is the weakest, for proof to the contrary was difficult to adduce. Montefiore contented himself with pointing out that such deception was forbidden by the Jewish religion and that he would not have any transgressor released of his penalty. To designate the Jews as rebellious, disobedient, and shiftless and to declare that they required special coercive measures, indicated insufficient and misleading information. The Commission on Jews wished to have them registered in one of three classes; merchants of one of the three guilds, urban property holders, and artisans; and those who did not associate themselves with one of these groups by 1850 were threatened with severe punishment. Montefiore assented with qualifications, which had already been expressed in the State Council. He remarked that four-fifths of the Jewish population would thus fall into the class of undesirables, and that large groups of useful persons, such as workers and employees of all sorts, wagoners, clergy, and teachers, were subsumed in none of the classes.

After the recent dissolution of the Kahal the Jews lacked common representation and therewith a natural protection. They were exposed to degradation, for the management of their own financial affairs and of their charitable institutions had been transferred to the municipal Duma, in which the Jews, despite their preponderance in the population, were represented insufficiently or not at all. Their character must not be judged by external appearances; these were conditioned by their wretchedness, and could be brought to a wholesome state by improvement in their situation. Poverty, legal restrictions, and disproportionately high taxation had been hindrances to attaining a higher level. Then Montefiore brought his considerations together in a petition that the Jews be really granted what, according to the information of the ministers, had been held in prospect for them, namely "equal rights with all other subjects of the Empire;" and he showed in detail what the advantages of such a grant would be.

A second memorandum was directed to Uvaroff, the Minister of Public Instruction, and concerned the educational system of the Jews. The minister was inclined to enlightenment, and was convinced that the Jews could be incorporated into the Russian people and made useful to the state not by tormenting them but by raising their cultural level. Now the Jews possessed a very extensive system of instruction, which they had maintained with much love and at considerable sacrifice. In contrast to the Russian population, they tolerated no illiteracy in their midst. Their teaching was indeed one-sided and antiquated, and was carried out by ill-trained and uninformed teachers following faulty methods. But attempts towards improvement were initiated by the Jews themselves.[9] As early as 1828 Isaac Baer Levinsohn of Kremenez (1788–1860), in his *Te'udah b'Yisrael* ("Testimony in Israel"), had addressed himself earnestly to his brethren on the subject, as N. H. Wessely (Graetz, V, 368 f.) had done forty years earlier. They were to change their entire educational system. Hebrew must be taught methodically, but the vernacular and secular knowledge must also be cultivated. Occupational training must be provided, trades and agriculture being specially recommended. Levinson used many citations from biblical and rabbinic literature to prove that Jewish tradition did not oppose these innovations but on the contrary encouraged them.

Obscurantists, who were in the great majority, railed at Levinson's book, but enlightened men everywhere, particularly in Lithuania, the center of talmudic study, greeted it joyfully. To strengthen their feeble influence they sought the support of the government, and agreed with the government's condemnation of talmudic study. Certain commercial cities which had foreign connections, like Uman, Odessa, and Kishinev in the south and Riga in the north, succeeded in establishing modern schools which proved to be brilliantly successful. It was such a process that the government wished to promote and accelerate.

After the emperor had been won over to the plan, Uvaroff summoned Dr. Max Lilienthal, the successful director of the school at Riga, for a confidential conference regarding his plans. Lilienthal was only twenty-five years old and had newly arrived from abroad, but he had an amazingly clear and sure perception of the enormous responsibility of the task and of the difficulty of winning the confidence of the Jews without trifling away the favor of the government. A journey through the capitals of the Pale of Settlement showed the presence of a concern, which indeed he had himself also felt, that these new measures were connected with conversionist attempts and that education without improvement in their legal position could only be a disaster for the Jews. But neither he nor Uvaroff were disheartened. A commission meeting in St. Petersburg, to which rabbinic leaders such as Rabbi Isaac of Wolozhin and Rabbi Mendel of Lyubavicz belonged, approved of the plans of instruction and selected the text books.

On November 13, 1844, the enactment on "the education of the Jewish youth" was issued. It provided for the establishment of elementary and secondary schools for Jews and for the training of future leaders by means of two higher schools (for rabbis) at Wilna and Zhitomir. Jews as well as Christians would be acceptable as teachers; the inspectors could be only Christians. Similarly, Christians as well as Jews were to be represented in the local administration of the schools. The charges for the schools were to be borne by the Jews themselves, by means of a tax; and the pupils were given the prospect of exemption from military service. The government permitted instruction in Talmud during the period of transition, but it looked forward to its eventual abolition; it planned, similarly, to check the teaching activity of *melammedim* if they had not prepared themselves for teaching by a general education.

But the confidence of the Jewish populace in the effectiveness of these schools was dissipated even before they were opened, when other governmental offices chose that particular juncture to issue new special legislation. It was fully destroyed when Lilienthal, who had been openly approached with conversionist proposals, unexpectedly laid down his post and left the country in great haste (1845). It is understandable, then, that Uvaroff should have expressed his disappointment to Montefiore.

But the impressions which Montefiore had gained on his journeys were quite different from Uvaroff's. He found[10] the Jews of Russia as little hostile to education as they had ever been during their long history, and he found that their religious teaching was neither unsocial nor unethical. In government circles the Jews' belief in the Messiah and the talmudic teachings upon men's relations to their country and to their fellow men were regarded as the root of all evil. Montefiore therefore undertook to set forth clearly and comprehensively the significance of the Messianic belief and the content of the social ethics as he had heard them expounded in the schools. In the schools which he had inspected he found a great deal more secular knowledge than he had expected. Secular subjects were not taught in the Talmud Torahs because the means for engaging suitable teachers were wanting. He was pleasantly surprised by the educational aims and the standards of the schools. He asked only that the government discontinue its attitude of distrust and leave the administration of Jewish schools to the Jews. They should not be subjected to such humiliation as had occurred at Warsaw, where one of the teachers of the rabbinical school was named director of the school after he had been baptized.

The government paid no heed to these admonitions. Uvaroff retired in 1848. His entire Jewish school system was a mistake,[11] involving enormous useless expense. The most obvious shortcoming was the lack of adequate teachers. In Russia none was to be found; the original plan of recruiting them abroad was given up; but there was no effort to train proper teachers at home. Conditions in the rabbinical school which was opened in Wilna in 1848 were scandalous. The teachers were incompetent, and the pupils were drawn from the dregs of the population. They sought only to get a diploma by blackmail or wheedling, and the people whom they were to educate despised them. By their conduct they brought enlightenment into discredit. The Jewish communities would have nothing to do with rabbis and teachers who came from this school. Even the school at Zhitomir in the southeast, which was conducted in a Jewish spirit and had teachers and pupils of high spiritual worth, was not able to strike root. The government schools had extremely small enrollments and very irregular attendance. The exact reverse of the consequence for which the officials had looked came about; the number of old fashioned *Hadarim* grew, for the people had more confidence in them than in the schools which had been thrust upon them.

But Montefiore's advocacy was not entirely in vain. In 1851[12] the division of Jews into classes was carried out (*Rasryaden law*), and the government heeded Montefiore's suggestion by forming an additional class of those who were neither merchants nor landowners nor artisans and yet performed useful functions. In other respects it followed the path it had plotted out. The law concerning dress[13] was put into effect, and lower police functionaries took their pleasure in mocking or blackmailing Jews. Despite the ruthlessness with which the law was administered, resistance was very great. The masses were ready to suffer martyrdom for the sake of the garb which had grown dear to them. But the government was unwilling to let matters go so far, and allowed the law to fall into disuse. Time did its work, and in due course the garb was altered without pressure.

At the same time the regulations for military service were made more severe for the Jews.[14] Whereas the rest of the population were called up for service every second year, the Jews were required to provide a contingent each year. This was set at the rate of ten men per thousand of population, whereas the remaining population were required to provide only five or at most seven men per thousand. Beginning with the Crimean War in 1853, recruits were taken up twice each year. The Jewish communities were required to provide recruits in lieu of their arrears in taxation. They were responsible for the number of recruits precisely as the noble gentry were responsible for their contingents of peasants. For the Jewish population military service constituted the most horrible of all horrors. They used every means to maim themselves, as did the peasants; many a mother preferred to mutilate her own son so that he should not be subject to conscription. At the season of conscription there was a general exodus out of the cities into the forests and across the borders. The directors of the community, for whom this grim function was the only relic of their former autonomy, were forced to use the most detestable measures. They employed informers whose cruel duty it was to hunt down victims. Naturally the poorest and most unfortunate were the first to fall into their nets. From these humble classes they would capture their quarry, preferably at a tender age, and deliver them mercilessly to the military authorities. According to the law, homeless men who were not in possession of a passport were drafted for service without further ado. Refugees who crept about the cities were therefore hunted down, and men were cozened of their passports so that they might then be apprehended for military service. Criminals might also be delivered over to the military, and men were frequently written down as criminals by forged endorsements in order to increase the number of recruits. Frightful confusion and demoralization invaded the Pale of Settlement; the poorer classes were filled with anger against the more prosperous and with bitter hatred against the leaders of the community.

Liberalism and Reaction under Alexander II

Remarkably enough it was during the Crimean War itself, in 1854 and 1855, that the conscription regulations were ameliorated for the Jews. The Emperor Nicholas had died in the meanwhile and had left his realm in serious difficulties. His son, Alexander II,[15] wished to employ every possible means for reconstruction, and so gave some attention to the Jews also. In his Coronation Manifesto he proclaimed the abolition of the earlier recruiting regulations and made the Jews equal with the other inhabitants of Russia in regard to the number, age, and character of those to be drawn into military service. The Crimean War saw the complete collapse of the Russian Army and for a time there were no conscriptions at all. Later the government, which had undertaken enormous obligations in the care of war victims, allowed redemption from military service by the purchase of bonds. The defense law of 1874 established the requirement of personal service for rich and poor without distinction, and limited the length of such service to a maximum of six years.

At the very beginning of the new regime Count Kisselev, the chairman of the Commission on the Jews, proposed an extension of the Pale of Settlement. He was moved, not by affection for the Jews, but by a desire to add to the economic resources of the country.[16] How the proposition was broached to the Emperor is evident from the decree which the liberal-minded Czar subsequently issued:

All regulations at present governing the Jews are to be subjected to a revision in order to harmonize them with the ultimate aim of fusing this people with the native population insofar as the moral condition of the Jews allows of such fusion.

This formulation exudes an odious savor; the bureaucracy was very shrewd in reacting to such hints. Some of the provincial governors promptly expressed their apprehensions that the Jews would flood the entire realm and dominate it.

But such misgivings were disregarded. The Crimean War had demonstrated the need for improved highways and railroads, and the government welcomed Jewish entrepreneurs and financiers who would promote their construction, and who would establish industries and distribute their products. After long consideration the right of residence was extended, first for those merchants who for a number of years had been paying the high taxes of the first guild in the Pale of Settlement. They were allowed to remove into the interior of the Empire, or into any of the capital cities, with their families and with a limited number of employees and servants. A second forward step was taken when unlimited right of residence for the entire Empire was granted to those Jews who were distinguished by some academic degree; these were even promised employment in the service of the state. It was 1867 before all veterans who had completed their term of service were also granted a free right of residence in the whole Empire. For the "Nicholas soldiers" this privilege was made hereditary.

Influential governors had pointed to the lack of skilled artisans in the interior of Russia, whereas the Jewish regions were overcrowded with them and the consequent competition worked general hardship. Yet it was 1865 before the right of free sojourn in the entire realm was granted to artisans, apprentices, mechanics and distillers; the combination shows what ends the government had in mind. Besides, the privilege was limited by so many qualifications that the local police had it in their power to grant passes and to extend their term, and they used this power for purposes of blackmail. Completely at their mercy were those who were not themselves artisans but were engaged in trade with artisan products and so had come to use artisan privileges. They were subject to the caprice of the police, and furthermore they brought discredit upon the whole class of Jewish workers.

The consequence of the new regulations was a noticeable reclassification within the Jewish population.[17] In both capitals and in many places in the interior of Russia new communities were formed composed principally of wholesale merchants, industrialists, financiers and their employees, of academicians, artisans, and discharged veterans. All of these elements were susceptible to assimilation; they quickly took up the Russian language and Russian habits; they willingly sent their children to Russian schools and brought them up in the Russian manner. Their attitude corresponded with the intentions of the financial circles in St. Petersburg. By reason of their economic success they claimed the right to assume the role of educators for all Jews. They suggested that the government make a selection: those Jews who sought to rise above the level of the masses by dint of education, skill, and ability, should be encouraged by an extension of their rights; and the prospect of this reward should be used to spur the others on to imitate them. They established a Society for the Diffusion of Culture among the Jews,[18] with headquarters in St. Petersburg and local branches in all suitable communities. Their aim was to spread enlightenment by means of literary works and to encourage young men who wished to dedicate themselves to handicrafts or to the sciences. Their principles may be summarized in the succinct formula of their executive director, the poet Judah Leib Gordon: "Be a human being upon the street; a Jew in your home." The implication was that the Jews must give up all external marks of differentiation and be set off from their environment only by their religious beliefs.

When Moses Montefiore came to St. Petersburg again in 1872 he was no little surprised to find there a community which was advanced by centuries beyond that which had greeted him in Wilna (p. 54, above). He wrote in his *Diary*:

I conversed with Jewish merchants, literary men, editors of Russian periodicals, artisans and persons who had formerly served in the imperial army, all of whom alluded to their present position in the most satisfactory terms. All blessed the Emperor, and words seemed wanting in which adequately to praise his benevolent character. The Jews now dress like ordinary gentlemen in England, France, or Germany. Their schools are well attended, and they are foremost in every honorable enterprise destined to promote the prosperity of their community and the country at large.

What the casual visitor could not see was the alienation from Judaism which proceeded apace in this class and quickly reached the proportions of a fundamental cleavage. There was no transition; assimilation came at an even more rapid pace than it had done in Mendelssohn's age. It had no guidance, but rushed blindly into the new life, carrying with it the seeds of a hidden danger. Jewish values were lightly surrendered and other values were not received in exchange. A spiritual void was created. The older generation looked upon this development with horror. They took it as inevitable that, as surely as they themselves would live and die as Jews, their grandchildren were destined to live as Jews no longer.

It is hard to understand how Montefiore could fail to see, beyond the glitter of the new communities, the increasing poverty[19] of the great masses in the Pale of Settlement. The economic transformations under Alexander II had seriously affected the livelihood of many Jews. Improvement in communications had made callings widely followed, such as innkeepers and wagoners, unnecessary; and the easing of credit eliminated the small moneylender. The unguided emancipation of the peasants proved to be economically disastrous and was followed by a number of agrarian crises; it hurt those Jews who had business dealings with the peasants. Myriads lost the scanty livelihood they possessed. To earn anything at all, large numbers became what Mendele (p. 112, below) called "lick-and-smell" or "walking-stick" businessmen. Change was imperative, but was blocked alike by the inertia of nature and the law of the state.

And so poverty increased. Pestilences, such as the typhus brought on by starvation, which raged in Lithuania in 1869, revealed the situation to the world at large. The *Alliance Israélite Universelle*[20] summoned a relief conference to meet in Berlin. It suggested, besides the maintenance of orphans and students in Germany, the organization of large-scale emigration to the United States. But no confidence could be placed in the stability of Czarist policies, and there was a prevalent fear that the bureaucracy might sabotage such plans. In America the demand was for farmers; these were available only in very small numbers, and so the American committee rejected the plan for emigration. But the *Alliance* undertook the risk notwithstanding. It made its selections carefully and, in the decade 1870–1880, it assisted no fewer than 41,057 Jews from Russia to the United States.

This large-scale planning was very wise, for the honeymoon of emancipation and of closer relations was in fact over. Nationalist literature and political passions combined to disturb its harmony. The old Russian prejudice that the Jews were required by their religion to regard country and environment as alien and hostile received apparently authentic confirmation through the revelations of a convert, Jacob Brafmann.[21] Brafmann had been dragged off and delivered to the soldiers as a child, and now he wished to avenge himself upon the Jewish communities and their leaders. He was a teacher in the seminary for Russian preachers in Minsk. He published periodical articles and later an entire *Book of the Kahal*, in which he alleged, on the basis of reports of negotiations and decisions of the Kahal, that this organization, disregarding the decree of dissolution of 1844, continued to work in secret, that it instigated and confirmed the hostility of the Jews to the state, that it did not stand alone but together with similar organizations elsewhere constituted a world Kahal which was embodied in the *Alliance Israélite Universelle* in Paris. He even charged that the members of the Society for the Diffusion of Culture, in St. Petersburg, were fellow conspirators. What could be more welcome than to have a born Jew proclaim to the world what all the enemies of the Jews had long suspected? It was to no avail that proof was promptly brought by the Jewish authorities showing that the allegedly official notations were forged or invented. The government circulated the imposture among its higher officials; the Czar and the Crown Prince were strongly impressed by it.

The Commission on the Jews also pricked up its ears; it resumed its sessions to devise schemes for transforming the life of the Jews. Its deliberations continued for a decade; but no voice of reason, no proof of the productive work contributed by Jews or of the use which the government made of their capacities in time of need, was ever allowed to affect its counsels. The bureaucracy had been aroused by other causes. Radicalism[22] was making gains, especially among the youth, and was proceeding from theoretical opposition to the existing political and spiritual subjugation, to active propaganda and even to acts of terror. Some Jews appeared among the Activists, and this fact was used by the Pan-Slavic press to brand the Jews as a body as enemies of the Russian state and the Russian people. It followed the same technique when a rats'-nest of fraud and deception was discovered after the Russo-Turkish War. The implication of princes, generals and high officials was passed over in silence and the culprits were spared. But a barrage of slander was directed against those few Jews who had served the exalted personages as accomplices. To the heir apparent, who had followed events attentively, the Jews were represented as the carriers of corruption.

But agitation was not limited to journalistic polemic; it reached the stage of violence. In 1871[23] occurred the first cruel attack upon the Jews of Odessa, which exhibited all the concomitant phenomena of the later pogroms. Incited by Greek competitors of the Jews, a mob attacked the latter on Easter Sunday, maltreated them and looted their homes and shops. The authorities permitted rioting to continue for four days before they decided to intervene and restore order. It is characteristic of the bureaucratic method that these excesses were interpreted as a "crude protest of the masses" against the exploitation of the Jews. Among the Jews panic ensued. They recognized a definite deterioration of their position. Thousands of them fled abroad, seeking, along with their comrades in suffering, to reach the United States.

Jews and the Polish Insurrection of 1863

Until its last insurrection Poland[24] retained its own laws. The Jews had to live according to the decrees of the Saxon rulers of 1808; the only change was the requirement of military service, which was imposed in 1842. The structure of Polish society and of its Jewry was different from that of Russia. The spirit of Western Europe had penetrated far more deeply. The Poles considered themselves part of western civilization; and among the Jews, particularly those who had become acquainted with assimilation in Germany, there was a widespread tendency to adopt the Polish language and Polish culture. The advocates of enlightenment, who were styled "Berliner," were opposed by the great mass of the orthodox and the Hasidim, who wished nothing in the existing order changed. Alexander II desired to introduce seasonable reforms into Poland also, but here again his officials got no further than the composition of memoranda. The Jews were hampered by limitations of residence and occupation and by increased taxation.

After they had been disillusioned by the Jewish policy of the Russians, the party of enlightenment attempted to draw closer to the Poles. They established a synagogue in Warsaw in which sermons were preached in Polish, and a Jewish weekly to popularize their ideas, especially those relating to occupational changes. At the end of the 50's the Poles were preparing their insurrection against Russian rule, and they took care not to antagonize the Jews, as they had done in their pride in 1830, but to win them to the cause of national liberation. This was urged especially by the leaders of the Polish émigrés in Paris and Brussels; they called for the suppression of the Jew-baiting which was a favorite Polish pastime, and for inviting the active cooperation of the Jews. On the Jewish side, beside representatives of the financial world, the chief rabbi of Warsaw, Dov-Baer Meisels, advocated close union with the Poles. Meisels had previously functioned in Cracow. Always eager for the restoration of an independent Poland, he had been sent to the Austrian Parliament (*Reichsrat*) as the representative of the Poles. At the burial of the first victim of the insurrection in Warsaw (1861), Meisels walked arm in arm with the Catholic bishop at the head of the procession. Along with the Christian clergy there followed the preachers Moritz Jastrow and Emil Kramstück; the brotherhood of Jews and Christians seemed to have been attained. By sermons and proclamations the rabbis of Warsaw attempted to convey this attitude to the Jewish masses, and leading Polish circles made every effort to demonstrate their change of heart by deeds. When the government ordered the closing of Christian churches, on the ground that they were constantly misused for political demonstrations, Meisels had the synagogues closed also; the rabbis of Warsaw and some from the province were taken into custody, and a number of young revolutionary Jews were exiled to Siberia. The Marquis Wielopolski, who had been appointed governor by the Czar, determined to take the wind out of the sails of the revolution by a policy of reconciliation. He revoked various laws which were oppressive to the Jews, and gave them all the rights of citizenship (end of 1862); he also worked for the organization of the Jews on the basis of a consistory — probably the most beneficial legislation which was ever planned for Jews by a Pole.

His mission failed. Insurrection broke out in 1863,

but because of inadequate preparation and leadership it collapsed quickly. It flickered up again briefly under the influence of Napoleon III, but to no avail. In a short while the Russians were masters of the situation. Among the Jews the great masses had kept away from the insurrection because they feared assimilation with the Poles and their national church; but the intelligentsia which had been influenced by Meisels, and especially the youth, supported the insurrection, some with weapons and others by providing weapons and managing the finances of the war. The enthusiasm of the Poles, as of the Jews, left much to be desired. The Polish national committee increased its efforts to win the Jews by protestations of their good intentions. It sought the support of the Jews of Galicia; but this did not prevent the Polish populace there from making hostile attacks upon the Jews.

Needless to say, the victorious Russians exacted vengeance of the rebels who fell into their hands. Poland became part of the Russian Empire, and the laws of Russia were applied to the Jews. In Lithuania, Count Nicolai Muravyev, called "the Hangman" by the people, was charged with suppressing the uprising and Russifying the population. He gloated over the spectacle of Jews being beaten by Cossacks. A brutal despot, he tormented the Jews by his mischievous whims.

The Jews in the Balkans

The Balkan countries underwent a complete transformation. Turkey retained Mohammedanism as its state religion, but it acknowledged the equal rights of all citizens without distinction of religion and granted full freedom of conscience to all. The Christian states, Bulgaria, Serbia, and Rumania, kept to the model of their protector, Nicholas I. They overlooked the important distinction that the Czar was an autocrat determined to preserve medievalism, whereas they juggled with the phraseology of modern democracy, had given themselves a constitutional regime, and had obligated themselves to the European powers, from whom they had obtained liberation from religious cleavage, in their turn to grant equal rights without distinction of religion to all their citizens. But the population of these countries was far too backward to raise itself to the democratic viewpoint, and ambitious politicians, instead of educating them, strove only to confirm them in their passions. These countries prided themselves upon their religious tolerance, but the fact that they withheld equal rights from non-orthodox Christians, to say nothing of Jews,[25] that they baptized Jewish children against the will of their parents, that they destroyed synagogues, burned Torah scrolls, desecrated cemeteries, does not speak well for their religious toleration. It is true that hatred for all things foreign was deep-rooted in these countries, and the mainsprings for each of the excesses probably lay in economic competition and jealousy.

In Serbia and Bulgaria there were relatively few Jews; no one denied that they had been in the country for centuries, and the fact was confirmed by the language and customs which they had brought with them from Spain (Graetz, IV, 268). There excesses were fewer and less serious. The energetic position taken by the European powers prevailed over the intrigues of ambitious parliamentarians. Before the Congress of Berlin (1878) recognized the independence of Bulgaria (including Eastern Rumelia) and Serbia, it imposed upon the new sovereign states the obligation of granting all citizens, of whatever religion, full equality of rights and freedom of religion, and of not excluding anyone from office or positions of honor on the grounds of religion. Both states carried these obligations out faithfully.

Things were quite different in Rumania,[26] as the combined princedoms of Moldavia and Wallachia have been called since 1861. Here there lived a considerable number of Jews, particularly in Moldavia; moderate estimates placed their numbers at 6% of the whole population, some made it as high as 10%. They had lived in the country for generations, and had themselves settled many villages; but there had been some immigration from Russia and Galicia, and so the Rumanians declared them one and all aliens. Rumania was a battleground for parliamentary campaigns; cabinets followed one another in quick succession, and elections were warmly contested by numerous candidates. The electorate had to be offered inducements, and a common bait was incitement against the Jews, who were hated as economic competitors. "Competitors" is not quite the correct expression, for the Rumanians refused to demean themselves by the work which was necessary in order to exploit the potential wealth of their country. They preferred comfortable political posts, and envied Greeks, Germans and Jews the wealth they drew from agriculture, mining and commerce. "Repression of the Germans and of the Jews who are everywhere their advance guard" was the program of the Rumanian minister Bratianu. He advocated Rumanian solidarity which was to be achieved by boycotting the foreigners.

In reality only a small number of the Jews were wealthy. Most lived in crushing poverty; in the cities they occupied miserable sections, which agitators declared were dangerous centers for pestilential infection. Very many of the Jews followed trades of every sort. Peter Carp, the Young-Conservative statesman, once related the following experience to the Rumanian Chamber:

One day at the Club we had a lively discussion of the Jewish question which lasted until three o'clock in the morning, without coming to any conclusion. On our way out we noticed a poor Jewish workman toiling busily at that hour, while three Rumanian workers, drunk and singing patriotic songs, were coming out of a neighboring tavern. I pointed out the contrast to my opponent and said, "There you have the Jewish question!" If you wish to prevail against the Jews, be industrious, sober, and frugal as they are, and you will have nothing to fear.

That was not only Carp's conviction, but also that of other realistic statesmen.

But to incite the populace against the Jews or to undermine the security of the Jews by violent means was more convenient than to work, though such conduct was contrary to treaty obligations. In the Paris Convention of 1858[27] it had been established beyond cavil that under certain conditions non-Christians might receive political rights in the princedoms, and that they were to receive all personal rights automatically. But the Rumanian statesmen boldly declared that the Jews were not natives but aliens; they created a category otherwise unknown to modern state law, that of native aliens not under the protection of a foreign power. They justified themselves by the claim that the Jews lived apart, in language and in customs; but they did little to bring them nearer. When the requirement of universal education was introduced in 1865 and the Jews were urged to attend the general schools instead of their own Jewish ones, they obeyed willingly and accommodated themselves to Rumanian education. They were also drawn into military service, as Rumanians or as foreigners according to the whim of the politicians in power. But even this did not serve to bind the peoples together. The middle class voter must be appeased and it was expedient to make the Jew the victim.

The Rumanian politicians, particularly those from Moldavia, were stubborn and crafty in their campaigns against equalizing the rights of the Jews. Adolph Crémieux[28] was received by parliamentary circles in Bucharest with high honors in 1866, and when he expressed the hope that equal rights would be provided for the Jews in the new constitution, his views were greeted with cheers. But when the chamber was in session, immediately thereafter, a fanatical mob was let loose against the parliament building; the session was disturbed by threats until the frightened members yielded and voted against the freedom of religion which had been proposed by the government. Fired by this triumph, the mob then attacked the handsome synagogue which had just been completed and destroyed it. They rifled one of the older synagogues thoroughly, trod upon the Torah scrolls, tore them, and threw them into the dirt; the silver vessels and ornaments they stole. Some weeks later, when Carol von Hohenzollern, the new regent, entered Jassy, he could see the Jews being hunted down because they had placed an inscription in Rumanian upon the triumphal arch erected in honor of the prince. The government lacked the courage to condemn such excesses, but drew back timidly and declared that the granting of equal rights to the Jews was remote from its thoughts.

In 1867 an old decree dating from the Russian occupation (before 1834) was exhumed, and upon its provisions, with no legal grounds, Jews were forbidden to live in villages and to possess inns and taverns. Hundreds of Jewish families were robbed of their hard won rights with a single stroke of the pen and were driven from their possessions. Even Rumanians were astonished and asked the government for the justification of this act of violence. But the officials extended their grim procedure to embrace the cities too. In Jassy the overcrowded Jewish quarter was declared a dangerous focus of infection, and, following the Russian model, the Jews were driven out as penniless vagabonds, although a considerable proportion of them possessed real estate and others followed sanctioned trades. A kind of Vigilance Committee was formed, and undertook further arbitrary arrests and maltreatment.

The Minister of the Interior, who was present in Jassy, attributed everything to the misunderstanding of his subordinates and promised relief; his promises were denied, as were the entire proceedings. A whole series of highly esteemed personages, senators, superior judges, former ministers, protested to Prince Carol against "the inhuman, illegal deeds which were committed in disregard of justice and amounted to a flagrant violation of the constitution and the laws."

The concern of the whole world[29] was answered by the ministry with a number of mendacious distortions. The consequence was that the police and the military continued to beat and maltreat Jews, even in the presence of the prince, who visited Jassy again and expressly voiced his displeasure with the proceedings. But these abuses were exceeded by cruelties which took place at Galatz a week later. There the Rumanians wished to thrust a number of Jews onto Turkish territory across the Danube. The Turks would not receive the foreigners and drove them back. This grim game was repeated for several days, until the Rumanian soldiers mercilessly drove the victims into the Danube at the point of bayonets. The consuls of the European powers at Jassy protested loudly against this barbarous proceeding and clearly established the responsibility of the prefect and his superiors before the whole world. The retirement of the cabinet was possibly the result of this crime, but the persecutions continued. The new ministers found new excuses and new lies with which they believed they could appease the guaranteeing powers.

And so it continued, year after year. Consistently the Rumanians committed new horrors, and as consistently denied them; it was the worst political hypocrisy Europe had ever known. Napoleon III and the public opinion of France, which was the protectress of Rumania, were roused by this barbarism. The English government declared that "the peculiar position of the Jews places them under the protection of the civilized world." The vigilance of Europe, which in those days still reacted to invasion of human rights, was able to ward off the worst. The United States[30] also protested. In 1870, President Grant named the Jewish jurist, Benjamin Franklin Peixotto (1834–1900), Consul General in Bucharest, and designedly declared at his nomination:

> The United States, knowing no difference between her citizens on account of religion or nativity, naturally believes in a civilization the world over which will secure the same universal views.

Even though Peixotto was not able to prevent disturbances, the very presence of a Jew among the diplomatic representatives served as an admonition to the Rumanian officials and as an encouragement to the Jews, whose efforts to accommodate themselves to the customs of the country he promoted. His eye-witness accounts of the Rumanian persecutions made his participation in the Brussels Conference very valuable. Jewish organizations under the leadership of the *Alliance Israélite Universelle* and the Anglo-Jewish Association, which had always interceded on behalf of the Jews in Rumania, had called this Conference (1872) so that they might be able to represent the rights of the Jews effectively when the prospective regulation of the political situation of Rumania should take place.

The great powers were in fact won over to demand equal rights for the Jews at the Congress of Berlin[31] because Jews had shed their blood in the Turkish War. Prince Gortschakov, indeed, the Russian representative, opposed the proposal with the threadbare argument that the Jews of Rumania must not be set on a level with those of Western Europe (as if the Christians of Rumania could be set on a level with those of Western Europe); but Bismarck and Disraeli espoused the French proposal vigorously. The Rumanian delegates were constrained to accept:[32]

> that absolute freedom of worship should be granted to all persons in Rumania; that no religious beliefs should be a bar to the enjoyment of any political rights; and, further, that the subjects of all the powers should be treated in Rumania on a footing of perfect equality (Article 44 of the Berlin Convention of July 13, 1878).

No one could imagine that this plain and solemn obligation could be broken.

When the European powers supposed that Rumania would be willing to make concessions in return for the recognition of its independence, and would accept this "principle of all civilized states," as Bismarck called it, they underestimated the intensity of the passions that dominated Rumania. Even the enforced cession of Bessarabia did not move men as deeply as did the Jewish question. Article 44 of the treaty involved a change in the constitution and delivered the government into the hands of Parliament, which had a tendency to exaggerate the principle of nationalism and grant foreigners only a minimum of rights. In Moldavia all the evil passions of men were whipped up, not only by politicians who saw an opportunity to fish in troubled waters and to make difficulties for the government and the prince, but also by the Metropolitan of Jassy, who declared that Christian Moldavia must not be turned over to the Jews, and proclaimed anathema upon all who should speak for the Jews.

The guaranteeing powers became impatient and pressed for the fulfillment of Article 44 as an indispensable prerequisite to their recognition of Rumania. The government found itself between the hammer and the anvil; the foreign powers charged them with making too few concessions to the Jews, their opponents within the country with making too many. Their proposal to naturalize at least those Jews who had fulfilled their military service since 1864 or who had fought in the last war met with rejection and forced their retirement. The Chamber took the factitious position that there were no Rumanian Israelites and that there never had been. When the French Foreign Minister made a compromise proposal, that all Jews who had been born in Rumania, had been brought up there until their majority, and had never been under foreign rule, should be naturalized at once, the new ministers were horror stricken. They estimated the number involved as at least a hundred thousand — a drastic concession in view of the lies which propaganda had spread.

The tentacles of this propaganda reached into the European capitals and subtly and by degrees broke down the opposition of the powers. Austria-Hungary recognized Rumania before Article 44 was implemented. The other great powers waited for some solution which would make it unnecessary for them to break with a rich and developing country. After months of struggle with the parliament the government carried through, in 1879, a revision of Article 7 of the constitution, whereby religion would henceforward not constitute a bar to the acquisition and possession of political rights. The letter of Article 44 of the Berlin Convention was satisfied. The catch was that this provision applied only to the various Christian denominations. The Jews were still declared foreigners and remained shut off from all political rights. Only individuals could be naturalized, and only under the most difficult conditions. A special law passed by a two-thirds majority was required for each case; and those who passed through this purgatory still did not receive the right of acquiring landed property. An exception was made in the case of 883 war veterans, who were granted naturalization *en bloc*. All other Jews continued in the status of "foreigners who are not subject to another power." They were liable to all obligations, excluded from all rights. Only very few Jews received naturalization in the course of decades — eighty-seven before 1900. The powers were relieved of an uncomfortable burden. Even the English government, which had signified that the change of the constitution did not comply with the spirit of the Berlin Convention, comforted itself with the expectation that a more tolerant practice later would meet the wishes of Europe.

The Jews under Mohammedan Rule

One of the problem children of the Jews of Europe was the Jewry of Morocco,[33] which suffered severely under fanatical special regulations. Such lawlessness prevailed in the country that a Jew might be murdered with impunity; among the Moslems there was a saying that up to seven Jews might be killed without punishment being exacted. According to the statistics of the *Alliance Israélite Universelle* no fewer than 307 Jews were murdered between 1864 and 1880 without punishment for the murderers. Every political catastrophe, furthermore, worked harm to the Jews. In 1844 the French bombarded Mogador, and the Jews were subjected to special suffering by the populace. Moses Montefiore intervened with the reigning sultan and received his assurances that the Jews would not be treated differently than his other subjects. In 1859, on the occasion of the attacks of the Spaniards, the Moors fell upon the Jews of Tetuan, plundered their houses and killed 400 persons. The remainder saved themselves by flight, many going to Gibraltar.

This brought about a change, in that it put the Jews of Morocco into touch with the Jews of Europe. The *Alliance Israélite Universelle*, which had just been founded, opened its first school in Tetuan and continued to expand its school work throughout the country, in the expectation that the abolition of ignorance among the Jews would bring an improvement in their condition. A year later

English Jews received word of a judicial murder in Saffee. Under pressure from the Spanish consul two Jews were condemned on the suspicion of poisoning, and others were thrown into prison. Despite his 79 years, Sir Moses Montefiore, who had just returned from the Orient, went to Morocco without delay and procured an edict from the sultan which proclaimed the full equality of the Jews before the law and strict justice for them and their property before all courts of justice. The sultan's son and successor carried the edict out solemnly and, at the instance of the Pope, the Madrid Conference of 1880 extended it to cover all non-Moslems.[34] The sultan may have been earnestly concerned for the fulfillment of his edict, but the pashas did not respect his ordinance.

What the situation was really like we can learn from the notes of the Italian poet, Edmondo de Amicis. In connection with the remark that the Jews might not wear sandals outside their own quarter (*mellah*) and had to traverse the murderous pavements barefoot, he pictures their condition as follows:

> They cannot bear witness before a judge, and must prostrate themselves on the ground before any tribunal; they cannot possess lands or houses outside their own quarter; they must not raise their hands against a Mussulman, even in self defense, except in the case of being assaulted under their own roofs; they can only wear dark colors; they must carry their dead to the cemetery at a run; they must ask the sultan's leave to marry; they must be within their own quarter at sunset; they must pay the Moorish guard who stands sentinel at the gates of the Mellah; and they must present rich gifts to the sultan on the four great festivals of Islam, and on every occasion of birth or matrimony in the imperial family.

Even if they wished, the sultans[35] could not change the position of these unfortunate people essentially without exposing them to worse evils than this frightful slavery, so fanatic and violent was the hatred of the Moorish population. Still the government was convinced of the usefulness of the Jews for the welfare of the country and recognized the advantages of retaining them as middlemen. Insurmountable obstacles were therefore put in the way of emigration; women, for example, were forbidden to travel abroad at all.

Merchants who acted as intermediaries for the trade with Europe and whose function as interpreters was also frequently indispensable, enjoyed the advantage of being placed under the special protection of the European powers and had access to the consular courts. Their special position was the point of departure for the conference in Madrid. Although the English delegates protested vigorously, the position of the exempted was fully confirmed. Their number, however, was insignificant in relation to the total Jewish population.

A Mohammedan country in which the Jews were similarly subjected to discriminatory legislation and to the fanaticism of priests and populace was Persia.[36] From time to time frightful reports of occurrences there reached the Jews of the outer world. In 1848 a messenger came as far as Montreal, Canada, with the difficult task of raising an enormous sum of money which was demanded as ransom, the alternative being that, in the event of failure, the entire Jewish population would be put to death or forcibly converted to Islam. The traveler Benjamin the Second reports that about 1840 there were approximately 3,000 Jews in Shiraz and nine synagogues, and that within twenty years 2,500 of them had been forced to accept Islam. A kind of Marrano existence came into being, and those discovered were punished as severely as such cases formerly had been in Spain and Portugal. Pretexts for penalties and persecutions were quickly found; the state of public security was very low. Crimes against Jews could be punished only if two credible witnesses appeared, and one can readily imagine how difficult it would be to find Mohammedan witnesses who were willing to imperil their lives. In Persia the intolerant sect of

Shiites was dominant; they behaved towards Christians and Jews alike with merciless cruelty. Everywhere that Benjamin traveled — in Ispahan, Hamadan, Kermansha, Kashan, Meshed — he found the Jews oppressed and constantly imperilled. Only the five hundred families of the capital, Teheran, enjoyed somewhat greater security, because of the presence of the officials and the court.

The regulations for the Jews in Persia were somewhat similar to those in Morocco. Their basis was a thorough disdain of all infidels, who were regarded as unclean and treated with the greatest cruelty. The Jews might not live outside their quarter, and even within their quarter they might not keep open shops but must content themselves with selling spices and jewels. When they let themselves be seen in streets where Mohammedans lived, they were stoned, beaten and spat upon. According to the belief of the Shiites, their prophet Ali had been killed by a Jew. During the days of mourning for Ali (*Katel*), Jews might not show themselves upon the streets at all without the risk of being beaten. In the bazaars they might neither enter a booth nor touch the merchandise. They could only state their wants and pay what was demanded. Any slight difference of opinion, even in the games of children, might lead to serious excesses and to corporal punishment of the Jews. The most improbable pretexts were devised to justify pillaging, blackmailing, or beating the Jews. At the same time the Jews enjoyed the greatest confidence as merchants, particularly as jewelers; and the commercial courts were ready to afford them protection. Many also attained considerable esteem as physicians. For the rest, the Jews mostly followed various trades, skilled and otherwise. Their callings were not the same in all provinces, and therefore the reports of travelers are frequently contradictory.

The Jews of Europe were able to extend direct assistance to their unfortunate coreligionists only when the

Persian government sought connections with the West and the Shah visited the capitals of Europe. When, in 1865, reports of horrors and persecutions reached London and petitions for intervention were to be submitted to the Shah Nazr ed Din, Moses Montefiore, who never denied an appeal for help, at once made ready to go East. He was advised by the Foreign Office not to burden his old age with the distant journey but to allow his representations to be submitted by the British envoy to the Shah and to petition him for an edict similar to that of the Sultan of Constantinople (Graetz, V, 662) or of Morocco (p. 76, above). The petition was successful; the Shah forbade further acts of injustice.

In 1871 famine followed by epidemic broke out in the region of Shiraz and Ispahan. In London collections were made immediately for the regions affected; Sir Moses made a considerable contribution which was to be distributed among Mohammedans, Christians and Jews. Requests for further assistance were accompanied by a complaint that a converted official had received the right to confiscate the estates of Jews. When new complaints of starvation and oppression were received, Montefiore again wished to set out despite his eighty-eight years, but the Foreign Office restrained him because of guerrilla warfare in the country. In 1873 a deputation from Ispahan brought more precise information on the deplorable situation.

In June 1873 the Shah visited London. A memorandum on the situation of the Jews was submitted to him, and he replied with both oral and written assurances. In Paris the representatives of the *Alliance* also called upon him; they requested permission to establish schools in the country in order to raise the level of the Jewish population. The Shah again gave assurances that the injustices would be rectified and himself did whatever he could towards that end. But the officials did not always adhere to his regulations and continued to commit frequent acts of cruelty. Finally, in 1878, the Shah determined upon a decisive measure. He set up a separate commission for the protection of the Jews and placed it under the Foreign Office from which he expected a fuller understanding of justice and humanity.

In Syria and Mesopotamia which were parts of the Turkish Empire, Jews lived as they had lived for centuries. Occasional excesses against them were the consequence of the general lack of security. Aleppo and Smyrna, Mosul and Bagdad continued in their patriarchal conditions. World traffic, of course, began to affect them too. Merchants from Bagdad, above all the Sassoon family, settled in Bombay (India) and took care of the old Jewish tribes, the brown Beni-Israel and the black Jews in Cochin, who vegetated in terrible poverty. About Ceylon the governor reported that no capitalists in the colony have contributed more to its advancement than the brothers Worms of London.

CHAPTER III

Inner Development (1850-1880)

Jews in European Civilization

THE miraculous had come about. Early in the century Lord Byron had lamented (Graetz, IV, 127) that Israel possessed but the grave. Now it possessed a home in which it could live, work, and develop its potentialities; it had found, to use Graetz's expression, "not only justice and liberty, but a certain recognition." It was an age of optimism, an age in which men believed that the guarantee of democratic rights had solved all problems, and no one dreamed that the structure was founded on crumbling ground, that it would totter under the impact of the first storm. Not all Jews realized the magnitude of the miracle that had befallen them. They saw that the road lay open before them, but they did not perceive the forces that had laid it open. They looked not backward, but only forward; they measured the stretch that still lay ahead and thought they must negotiate it in rapid strides. They thought, mistakenly, that they must free themselves straightway of the baggage under which their ancestors had toiled for centuries, and they realized too late the greatness and the worth of what they surrendered. Men thought they had reached the threshold of the Messianic Age; they looked upon the world through a haze of idealism. With the happy optimism of a liberal philosophy, they anticipated a bright and cloudless future. Day by day men's mastery of the forces of nature increased; day by day new victories of the spirit were scored up. When liberty was spreading, why should brotherhood fall short; what problem could not be solved in a spirit of reconciliation!

Emancipation entailed the right of free settlement, and a lively migratory movement was the consequence most immediately apparent. The development of industry had brought with it increased restlessness among the population generally. People drifted from village to town, from town to metropolis, from poorer places to richer, from agricultural regions to industrial centers; and the Jewish population also sought new places to live.[1] They migrated in larger numbers, because, generally speaking, their ties to their places of residence were not so strong, and they had no ties to the callings which had been forced upon them. Furthermore, they were anxious to provide better education for their children. The process did not everywhere maintain the same lively tempo, but everywhere it followed the same course, whether in countries with a very small Jewish population like Denmark, France, Italy, or with a medium Jewish population like Germany, or a large Jewish population like Austria-Hungary. Paris and London were points of attraction for the West, just as Vienna was for Eastern Europe and Berlin for Eastern Germany. Between 1850 and 1864 the Jewish population of Paris rose from 20,000 to 30,000 souls. That of Turin amounted to 5,700 at the end of the century, and had grown at the expense of the numerous communities of the Piedmont. In 1840 there were only 6,456 Jews in Berlin, or 2% of the entire population; in 1871 there were 36,015, or 3⅓% of the whole. Cologne grew from 615 (.89%) to 3,172 (2.45%). At the same time the province of Posen, which in 1843 still had 79,575 Jews, had only 61,982 in 1871, and only 56,609 in 1880, a reduction of 30%. Before 1848 Jews were practically forbidden to remain in Brünn (Moravia); by 1880 there were 5,500 Jews there. Vienna grew very rapidly (1846, 3,739; 1850, 9,731; 1854, more than 14,000), and the communities from which it drew, such as Pressburg or Prosnitz, were not emptied, but recruited their numbers in turn from the smaller places in their own hinterland. In 1849 Budapest had only about 19,000 Jews; in 1880 it contained about 72,000 (19.4% of the population) and the tendency was in the direction of further expansion. In 1825 Lemberg counted only 4,265 Jewish souls; in 1869 there were 26,694. Lemberg rapidly grew to be one of the two chief communities of Galicia; the other was Cracow, whose growth was very slow. In the realm of the Czar, as in Rumania, Jews were forcibly driven into the cities. The Rumanian government claimed that their aspiring country received constant accessions from lands in which the Jews were even worse treated; their statistics were entirely unreliable.

The removal of guild restrictions and the admission to open competition reacted favorably upon the Jews who were eager to work, and made the full use of their powers possible. Jews had not become hawkers and hucksters (and this petty trade had given great annoyance to governments) because of innate endowment or inclination, but under duress; they were ready to change their form of livelihood at any moment if only opportunity were given. Freedom to pursue trades, ease of communications, the change from a closed to an open economy, from artisan handwork to machine operation, opened undreamed of possibilities of employment, for the Jews as for the population generally. They need no longer bridle their energies; they found favorable fields for employing their intelligence and their capacities for organization. They had always been accustomed to pioneer their paths, and now they seized with sure instinct upon the immense possibilities which were offered by the undreamed of expansion of production and of demand.[2]

In great part they could remain in the callings with which they were familiar. They needed only to adapt them to the requirements of a capitalist economy and to expand the scale of their activity. Their former trade in raw produce enabled them to assume commanding positions in grain, wool, hides and metals. Formerly they had been forced to deal in old clothes, and now the range of their activity embraced all branches of the clothing trade and industry, from head to foot, from raw material to the finished product and its distribution. Clothing fashions and habits underwent revolutionary change, and Jewish enterprise and industry were largely responsible for the satisfaction of the enormously expanded requirements. Jews opened up new fields, such as the manufacture of furniture and wooden ware. They recognized the opportunities of export trade and made efforts to develop it. A new occupation that was favored was the book and publishing trade, which combined business with intellectual activity.

In all countries Jews also participated in marked degree in real estate development and building. New residential quarters and their necessary communications owed their origin to Jewish initiative. They prompted the construction of railroads by providing the necessary capital, at a time when countless objections, on economic and hygienic grounds, were being levelled at the new means of transportation. The Rothschilds of Vienna and Paris, the Oppenheims of Cologne, the Warschawskis and Poliakoffs of St. Petersburg, and last but not least, Maurice de Hirsch of Brussels, may be named among the Jewish pioneers of railroad construction. When later the advantages of the railroad were universally recognized, their bold enterprise was repaid with ingratitude and their names were showered with abuse.

In finance,[3] the Jews' traditional experience in money affairs stood them in good stead. They grasped the requirements of the new age — to gather capital dispersed in many hands and to make it available for industry, commerce or national requirements. After 1848 the House of Rothschild had to surrender its practical monopoly in the money market, and many smaller banks, individual and corporate, entered into competition with them. Jews were as ruthless as others in this competition. The brothers Pereire, imbued with the doctrines of Saint-Simon, established the Crédit Mobilier in Paris, in order to advance the cause of socialism. It became the model for numerous similar undertakings by Jews and non-Jews alike, and proved to be a force in promoting growing industries everywhere. Not only in regions poor in capital, such as Hungary and Upper Silesia, did Jewish bankers prove to be the supports of the process of industrialization; they served the same purpose in richer regions also, such as the Rhine province, Belgium, and Flanders.

The number and influence of Jewish bankers, especially in such financial centers as Paris and Vienna, might sometimes give the impression that they were actually in control of the money market. The impression is incorrect; for aside from a very few houses of the first rank, their liquid capital, not secure against the exigencies of financial crises, was insignificant when compared to properties based on holdings of land and forest, of smelters and mines. The fact that such enterprises entrusted their holdings to Jewish bankers is a shining proof of their soundness and reliability. Unfortunately among these bankers there intruded some who sought easy profits in market speculation and the unwholesome manipulation which this made possible. Often they controlled large capital over short periods of time, but they inflicted signal injury upon the honor of the banking profession and of the entire Jewish community. It was their conduct which was generally represented as typically Jewish. But services to the common interest — such as Bleichröder's grant of credit which enabled Bismarck to declare war in 1870, or that of the London Rothschilds which enabled Disraeli to purchase the shares of the Suez

Canal, both grants consummated without the delay involved in first consulting parliament — were soon forgotten.

The number of Jewish artisans[4] increased sharply until 1850; but, despite the activity of associations and foundations for teaching and promoting handicrafts, the rate of increase did not continue constant in Western Europe. It was then that industrialization cast doubt upon the old maxim that a trade has a golden foundation. Artisans changed their ways in keeping with the advances of the period. They refined methods of production and increased volume; wherever possible, they introduced the use of machinery. Tailors turned into clothing manufacturers, tanners into leather manufacturers, malt-makers into brewers, tinkers into building contractors. Occupations of women changed also. Women had always been employed as seamstresses, milliners, and domestics of all sorts. They had helped husbands and fathers in running small businesses. Now they went to the big cities and found work in shops and factories. Some few took up professions in teaching, the fine arts, or acting. Feminism was not yet a burning question in Jewish circles, but it had already become noticeable.

In Eastern Europe the number of Jewish artisans continued large. There they constituted at least one half, and occasionally a larger proportion, of the employable Jewish population. In Posen, which was formerly a Polish province, the number of Jewish artisans was greater than in the rest of Germany. In the Russian Pale of Settlement there was a disproportionate number of artisans, compared with the numbers in the interior of the country, where access was difficult for Jews. In the closed economy there prevalent opportunities for advancement were exceedingly slight. Nevertheless out of the artisan class there developed so outstanding a sculptor as Mark Antokolski (1843–1902). In Rumania also even observers who were extremely hostile towards the Jews acknowledged and approved of their wide distribution in all branches of skilled labor. The trade schools founded in the Near East by the *Alliance Israélite Universelle* aroused a love for skilled workmanship in boys and girls, and turned them from primitive methods. Their new accomplishments frequently won them higher esteem among their neighbors.

At a time when exodus from the land was general, a great increase in agricultural[5] activity was not to be expected. Nevertheless, some advantage was taken of the new possibility of acquiring or leasing landed property and a number of Jews went into farming. In Germany, Bohemia or Russia they frequently operated small farms along with other employment; in agricultural regions like Hungary and Rumania they themselves worked farms which they had bought or leased. None of the governments which deplored Jewish indifference to agriculture provided land for Jewish settlement. In Russia and Rumania space and means for a large scale settlement were available, but in those countries the prevalent tendency was to keep Jews away from the land. The Russian government did make certain lands available, little cultivated and unproductive, but its efforts were sabotaged by administrative officials precisely as these officials sabotaged other efforts at settlement. The lively commercial relations of the Jews with the peasants through trade in cattle and land seldom led to satisfactory results. The peasants were eager for gain at the moment, but were susceptible to the hateful agitation which pictured the Jews as exploiters.

The most obvious change was that which brought the Jews into the learned professions, a step easy for them because of their traditionally intellectual character. Formerly the charge had been made that Jews were only concerned with trade and had no interest in science and fine arts; now the complaint was made that the Jews were overcrowding the learned professions. Service to the State or in the army was for the most part closed to them and so it was natural to turn to the free professions.[6] The Viennese physicians, as the Viennese shoemakers had done earlier, feared they would be ruined if Jews should be admitted to their calling. No one could deny that many Jewish physicians in all countries won affectionate esteem in homes ranging from peasants' cottages to princely palaces and served their patients well and faithfully as friends in need. Their early contributions to the science of medicine are demonstrated by such names as those of the surgeons Michelangelo Asson of Venice (1802–1877) and Leopold von Dittel of Vienna (1815–1898), the anatomist Jacob Herz of Erlangen (1816–1871) who was honored by his city with a public monument, the brilliant researcher Valentin of Berne (see p. 32, above), and Robert Remak (1815–1865) and Ludwig Traube (1816–1876), both of Berlin.

Admission to the legal profession depended on the degree of civil rights. At first, generally speaking, Jews could progress only as far as becoming advocates, and as such they won high esteem. But even the first generation produced judges of international reputation. In London Sir George Jessel (1824–1883), after 1875 member of the Supreme Court of Judicature, enjoyed the highest reputation as scholar and practitioner in the law and as jurist. Tobias Michael Carel Asser (1838–1913) of Amsterdam established the *Institut du Droit International* in 1873. Levin Goldschmidt (1829–1897) of Berlin was the author of the code for international arbitration adopted by the *Institut*.

A number of Jews distinguished themselves in mathematics. Moritz Abraham Stern of Göttingen (1807–1894), a friend of Abraham Geiger and Gabriel Riesser, was

INNER DEVELOPMENT (1850–1880)

outstanding in algebra. James Joseph Silvester (1814–1897) at first could find no professorship in England because he was a Jew. After a long and distinguished career in the United States he was called to Oxford in 1883 as a geometrician. Like Silvester a number of Jews in Europe established and published periodicals for their special disciplines and so contributed greatly to the organization and promotion of their several sciences. Peter A. Riess of Berlin (1805–1883) won such distinction by his physical experiments and discoveries that Alexander von Humboldt urged the Prussian Academy of Sciences to accept him as member though he was not converted. The Prussian king was more tolerant in the case of Giacomo Meyerbeer (1791–1864), whom he appointed general music director of the Berlin Royal Opera in 1843. The brilliant composer had won his laurels in Paris, then the focus of all cultural activity. There he had a rival in Jacques François Fromental Halévy (1798–1862) whose opera, *La Juive*, ranks among the masterpieces of French music of the 19th century. A little later Jacques Offenbach (1819–1880) dominated the society of the Second Empire with his comic operettas. The history of music has stripped these composers of their crowns, but in their lifetime the whole world applauded their musical works.

In the fine arts, Josef Israëls (1824–1911) and Camille Pissarro (1830–1903) laid the foundations for their later fame as great masters and leaders in the new impressionistic way of painting. Mark Antokolski (1842–1903) of Wilna displayed such unusual talent in the workshop of a woodcarver, in which he was an apprentice, that he was granted free education at the Academy of St. Petersburg and became one of the greatest Russian sculptors. Joseph Engel (1815–1901), whose inclination towards sculpture his orthodox father tried in vain to curb, distinguished himself in the artistic circles of London and Rome, and at last settled in his native Hungary where he created one of Budapest's famous monuments.

Two institutions rose on the social ladder after 1848: the theater and the press. Both professions attracted many a Jewish talent although they promised no material security. Both of them demanded a quick mind, a keen adaptability, a poetic creativeness. Jews were soon to be found in all genres of the theatrical profession, but the remarkable phenomenon is that the very first generation produced some first rank stars. Elisa Félix Rachel (1820–1858) of Paris was recognized as the greatest actress of her day and played the leading roles in many classic plays. She was acclaimed with enthusiasm all over the world. In the Vienna *Burg*, the leading German language theater, Bogumil Dawison's (1818–1872) theatrical genius and tragic pathos struck his audiences with awe and admiration. His triumphs attracted young Adolf Sonnenthal (1832–1909), then a tailor's apprentice (he himself later became godfather of Ludwig Barnay), who for a long time was the outstanding actor in the German language and such a favorite of the population that the 25th anniversary of his stage activity was celebrated by all Vienna. In the Vienna Opera, Pauline Lucca (1841–1908) electrified large audiences with her extraordinary vocal gifts as well as with her personal charm and dramatic talents. These stars made guest appearances in the world's capitals where the audiences became aware of the genius and the charm of these Jewish personalities.

Many Jews had been active in the press even before 1848; and now that the fetters of censorship were struck off, the press attracted fresh energies. Jews attained distinction in various fields of journalism, occasionally pioneered in new directions, and brought international reputation to the journals they served. It is significant that the two important telegraphic agencies, Reuter's in London and Wolff's in Berlin, were both established by

INNER DEVELOPMENT (1850–1880)

Jews. It is also significant that the evil habit soon spread of referring to whatever part of the press that seemed unpleasant as "the Jewish Press."[7] "The whole European press is in the hands of Jewish capitalists," Karl Anton von Hohenzollern wrote his son in 1868 when the Paris papers took exception to the cruelties of the Rumanian government. It was not long before Rumanian emissaries changed the opinion of these papers and so incidentally proved the charges concerning their control baseless. Nevertheless prejudice kept the earlier designation alive.

In these decades of expanding capitalism huge fortunes were created. The general welfare was improved, and the income and possessions of the Jews grew[8] according as they participated in the new economy. In Western Europe, and here and there in Eastern Europe also, their standard of living was raised and their social position improved. They took advantage of available opportunities for education and for extended travel, and so their tastes were refined, their horizons expanded, their cultural inclinations broadened. For new strivings in literature, art, or science one could always find Jewish Maecenases. At the time Jews controlled considerable fortunes and frequently devoted large sums to general welfare. In keeping with the humanitarian spirit of the time and of Jewish ethics, they did not limit themselves to Jewish interests, but spread their benefactions abroad. They willingly put their business skill and experience at the service of municipal administrations and other self-governing bodies.[9] Their services in these honorary posts were recognized as remarkable and were honored as such by their fellow citizens without distinction of creed.

They were not an unsocial element; they understood the art of living and letting live, and maintained intercourse with their fellow citizens on a social footing. They participated in their festivals, insofar as religious considerations were not involved, and Christians participated in Jewish celebrations also. In hamlets and villages Christians were familiar with Jewish practices and festivals. Domestics who were expert in Jewish religious usages and in the Hebrew prayers of the children entrusted to their care were no rarity.

Many were ambitious to rise too quickly, and the parvenu became the butt of the caricaturist. But this type was not the rule. Over against it are to be set the numerous cultivated families who made their houses centers of literary, cultural and social refinement. In many cases social mingling led to marriages[10] with heirs of noble families or with representatives of the cultural and artistic élite. The attraction was not only the power of wealth but also the charm of Jewish young women. Even so thoroughgoing a Junker as Bismarck declared with characteristically forthright imagery that the coupling of a German stallion with a Jewish mare was altogether desirable; his own son married the daughter of a Jewess. Through frequent intermarriages in the upper social levels, Judaism suffered serious losses. It was not, as Zangwill later explained, that bad Christians and bad Jews combined; the social standing of the Christian party was the factor which made him retain his faith and caused the Jewish party to surrender his or her religious affiliation, formally or in practice.

Religion and Culture in Western Jewry

The efforts of the prosperous and cultured levels were directed outward; the Jewish community was no longer the center of their activity. Profession, politics, society occupied the center of attention; it was no longer religion that controlled their lives. The road was open and they wished to press onward; free citizens of the enlightened nineteenth century felt they had no need of external ties with an age that was departed. It was of small concern

INNER DEVELOPMENT (1850-1880)

to them whether Judaism could survive with such an attitude. If it had survived centuries of persecution, why should it not persist in an age of freedom? And why lament if it should become amalgamated with the larger world of the cosmopolis?[11] That seemed to some only a fulfillment of the universal Messianic dream, whose realization was believed to be near. Jewish congregations now had to meet the test of continuing their existence without political pressure or legal coercion in a world that was rapidly becoming secularized.

The question was whether Judaism could, following its own nature and its past, turn into a religious communion.[12] The opposition to the change was insignificant; it was limited to a few intransigents, like Rabbi Moses Sofer (see p. 24, above), who were scarcely able to justify their position on theoretic grounds. Eventually their adherents refused to give up the advantages of a modern constitutional state and modern economy. All the rabbis had yielded to the necessity of surrendering Jewish civil jurisdiction. What remained of marriage and inheritance law could be put into practice insofar as it was subordinated to the law of the state. The unfortunate thing was that the change of Judaism into a synagogal and congregational form fell precisely in a period of religious crisis, during which the synagogue no longer exercised its old power of attraction. The movement towards big cities, the propensity towards comfortable living, and the attraction of a positivistic philosophy did nothing to help the position of the synagogue. The Christian churches suffered similarly from these severe handicaps. Jews were sharply differentiated according to their environment, education and calling; there was no longer a uniform type of Jew who wished to appear as nothing other than Jewish. There were many variant types, each differing from the others in its relations to the Jewish community. Not group affiliation, but the individual's sense of responsibility now determined the intensity of his reaction and the direction of his energy. When Moses Hess or, with much deeper feeling, S. D. Luzzatto wrote of a Jewish national sentiment, they found no understanding for their particular note.

In France, Great Britain, and Italy membership in the congregation depended on the free choice of the individual; and it is remarkable that the congregations continued to exist notwithstanding. In Holland, Germany, and Austria-Hungary membership was made obligatory, and the congregation was empowered to exact a tax of all Jews. In Poland and Russia, after the abolition of the old Kahal (see p. 51, above), there existed no legalized communal administration at all for decades; in Poland the "prayer-houses" (*Bet-Stuben*) served as a feeble substitute. The government of all countries supervised the administration, but did not interfere in matters of religion and left such questions to the autonomous regulation of the Jews themselves. The congregations voluntarily built up an imposing charitable activity, and their achievement in ordinary relief, in foundations for the poor and sick, for the deaf and the blind, for orphans and the aged, were nothing short of marvelous. They were supported by numerous associations and by individual generosity. They erected numerous stately synagogues, not only in the larger cities where the increase in population made the need pressing, but also in smaller places where greater sacrifice was required. By the splendid outward appurtenances of the synagogues and the dignified forms of the service they showed their desire to serve God worthily.

The flaw was in the leadership,[13] which shifted from the hands of the rabbis into those of the laymen. Israel Zangwill's criticism of the organization of the United Synagogue in England, "so that they could be run as a joint-stock company for the sake of dividends," was echoed in the complaint of Martin Philippson in regard to the communal administration in Germany, and the criticism might be applied with equal justice to all countries. Those who managed the congregations were men of proven integrity, men with practical experience who had attained success economically. But they possessed no strong Jewish consciousness and were not particularly concerned with creating or preserving one. Vision and the sense of eternity were luxuries to be dispensed with. In the synagogues the peace of the churchyard prevailed; there was no public opinion, there was no leaven of criticism.

There was some feeling of Jewish solidarity in case of actual calamities, but the appeal of the *Alliance Israélite Universelle* found a poor response; the *Alliance* remained far from being universal; the membership amounted to no more than 13,370 in 1870.

The failure of that generation rested not on wickedness or incompetence; it was due to lack of preparation for the tasks of the new age. The education of the ghetto sufficed as long as life within the group was undisturbed; but it did not equip the individual with resolution for the dangerous struggle in the world without. If we scan the considerable list of Jewish families[14] from Pressburg or Kittsee (in Hungary) who, when they had grown sufficiently wealthy in Vienna, sought and found their way to the church, we can appreciate with what slight powers of resistance these people had been fitted for their path through life. In other centers also there was a quick revolution from the totalitarian practice of the ghetto to a radical denial of everything. One can then readily imagine how easy was the fall of those who had grown up in a less exclusively Jewish atmosphere and had been exposed even longer to the temptations of their environment.

Many Jews became willing captives of the materialism which had grown rampant as a result of the great progress in natural science. On the Jewish side there was no considerable counter-stream; no attention was paid to such a philosophy as Steinheim's *Religion of Revelation*.[15] Attempts to counter the propaganda, which was more alarming than profound, by means of sermons and periodical articles were ineffectual and late, and never reached the people to whom they were directed. Cosmopolitanism and the free spirit were parts of the baggage of the cultivated Jews, whether in Berlin or Manchester, in Copenhagen or Livorno, in Kovno or in Lyons. Many retained their pious memories and clung to the house of their fathers, but even these took no thought for their children's probable attitude to Judaism.

Problems of faith did not seem very pressing. Men rested comfortably upon the proposition that Judaism was a rationalist religion which permitted great latitude in faith. Traditionalist as well as "enlightened" circles were imbued with this simple rationalism.[16] Not questions of faith but the practical execution of Jewish precepts and of a Jewish form of life were the objects of passionate concern. In Hungary and Galicia battles over such questions as the position of the *Almemar* in the synagogue or the hair-dress of women were waged without restraint and might even lead to the drawing of knives. But nothing could prevent the relaxation of the forms and institutions. In Russia itself a truce had intervened in the struggle between the Hasidim and the Mitnaggedim, and farther west struggles of this character were unknown. It was only in a refined form which recognized the realities of life, such as that taught, for example, by S. R. Hirsch, that orthodoxy could attract recruits. Rabbis of the old school could not understand Hirsch's motto "Torah with *Derek Eretz*." His enthusiastic affirmation of contemporary culture, his devotion to Schiller, would

INNER DEVELOPMENT (1850–1880)

surely have caused his excommunication in another age and another environment.

Zeal for reform of Judaism was gone. The inner storm and stress which had driven the older generation upon the road to freedom no longer animated the younger people. Their efforts took a preponderantly aesthetic direction. Instead of Reform they were content with a number of small reforms. The most important was the introduction of the organ to accompany the synagogue service. To this innovation large and ancient congregations in Italy as well as the French Consistory had agreed without calling forth active opposition; but in Germany the organ became the shibboleth of a party struggle. Nevertheless the organ was introduced in almost all the larger synagogues. The prevailing direction was that of Zacharias Frankel's conservatism, which retained a firm hold upon historic Judaism and yet did not reject certain concessions to the age. Frankel was the first director of the Jewish Theological Seminary at Breslau (1854) which had upon its staff such distinguished teachers as Heinrich Graetz and Jacob Bernays. In the Seminary he created an institution with a high standard of scholarship, whose alumni occupied pulpits in congregations in many lands and spread far and wide the moderate spirit of the party of the center. In the same spirit the *Istituto Rabbinico* in Padua and the *Landesrabbinerschule* in Budapest worked in their own countries.

From time to time attempts were made, especially in Germany, to carry Reform further, but they were without substance.[17] In 1869 a synod of rabbis and laymen met at Leipzig under the presidency of the folk-psychologist Moritz Lazarus (1824–1903). It was attended by many representatives from continental and overseas countries, but its voice found no echo. On individual questions of Jewish practice there dealt with, the average man took a positive or negative position without deep reflection, but in the theoretic discussions and the determination of fundamental principles he was simply not interested. He could understand that prayers for the restoration of sacrifice should not be used, but the struggle over a new expression for the ancient imagery of the Messianic future left him cold. One thing lay close to his heart, that his faith and his prayer should not come into conflict with his position in his fatherland attained with such difficulty, and that the service should somehow express this feeling. In 1870 Abraham Geiger[18] was called as rabbi to the community in Berlin, which had expanded greatly. There he was enabled to carry out the dream of his youth. In the newly established *Hochschule für die Wissenschaft des Judentums* (1872) his activity in teaching and research bloomed and flourished, but he proceeded no further on the path of Reform. He exerted a greater influence in the United States than in his own country. His early death left a great void in his circle.

But none of these attitudes, whatever the degree of their emphasis upon tradition, was capable of reconciling the opposition which had entered as a wedge between life and doctrine. Most obvious of all was the disappearance of the Sabbath,[19] which more and more became a day of labor. The neglect of the Sabbath began in the large cities and large establishments, and spread to the smaller places. The first surrender was made shamefacedly and behind closed doors, and then work was done with doors opened wide. Fathers who themselves observed the Sabbath strictly took it as a decree of fate that their sons would give it up when they went to the cities. Israel Zangwill has portrayed with delightful humor the excitement of a community over a Sabbath breaker and their self-sacrificing efforts to prevail over him, and how, when he refuses to be won over, they themselves yield and give up the Sabbath.

The drive for success, the pressure of competition, dominated all other urges. It set the pace for the conduct of Judaism in all its aspects. Men had to scurry to their work, and so the daily prayers at home ceased; men had to hurry in their errands, and observance of dietary regulations ceased. This revolution in habit, this drive towards efficiency, did not everywhere maintain the same rapid pace; it progressed in stages, but its drive was irresistible.

In the course of time, though gradually, there developed forces to oppose these tendencies. A new orthodoxy[20] arrived at a consciousness of its obligations. Its spread was due to the organizing talent of Esriel Hildesheimer (1820–1899), who continued the movement of S. R. Hirsch. Unlike Hirsch, Hildesheimer did not isolate himself, but kept in contact with people; he understood their troubles and was always helpful, and so he was able to influence them. In the Rabbinical Seminary for Orthodox Judaism, which he founded in 1873, he created a seed-bed from which disciples spread over the whole world to devote their energies to the maintenance of Jewish tradition in an altered world. A similar program had been undertaken by Jews' College in London (1856).

One of the most meritorious provisions of Hirsch's system was the establishment of schools to provide Jewish education; but for the time being it found little regard. There were a number of Jewish elementary schools in Central Europe, but the subject matter of instruction and the goal of the educational process was humanism and preparation for active life; there was no concern for the strengthening of Judaism. The preponderant majority of children did not attend Jewish schools and came under Jewish influence only in their religious education.

Education was the paramount problem, and the goal

education set for itself was of decisive importance. The old method had been to teach children Bible and Talmud and to rely for the rest upon the example afforded in the home and in the congregation. But such a method was no longer practicable, for suitable examples were rarer and rarer and their general schooling preoccupied the major portion of the children's energies. Intensive instruction in Hebrew literature was made difficult. The older ideal of prosperous families had been to make the first requisite in the selection of a son-in-law his competence as a talmudic student; this was no longer the case; a physician or a lawyer would have better prospects. To say nothing of western countries, even in Galicia and Hungary talmudic studies[21] declined rapidly, despite such outstanding masters as Salomo Kluger (1783–1869) of Brody, Joseph Saul Nathansohn (1808–1875) of Lemberg, or Abraham Samuel Benjamin Schreiber (1815–1875) of Pressburg. In Germany torsos of *yeshibot* existed in Fürth and Altona until about 1865. In France the *yeshibah* at Metz was transformed into an *École Rabbinique;* and in London the *Beth Hamidrash* was incorporated into Jews' College.

The need was for rabbis and teachers with a general cultural background, familiar with the methods and problems of modern education, able to reach people by preaching and instruction and to arouse them to an appreciation of Jewish values. The seminaries had the thankless task of educating men for a profession whose ministrations would not be gratefully received. Parents responsible for education were concerned lest too much Jewish knowledge should serve to isolate their children, burden them with a heavy load, render them unfit for the struggle of life; and so they hindered rather than promoted intensive Jewish education for their children. The age did have a certain appreciation for factual knowledge, but none for the emotional content of religion. Preaching and instruction, even when administered by the most gifted preachers and teachers, could be fruitful and suggestive only if they were met in a receptive mood.

Congregations or associations for the preservation of Judaism, in order to be effective, had to swim against the current. Their own energy, the strength of their hearts and their bodies, determined the measure of their success, and it is little wonder that in a time of transition there were many failures. A contribution of great significance was the translation of the Bible[22] into the various vernaculars — German, French, English, Italian, Polish, and, at first only partially complete, into Hungarian and Russian. Translations of prayers had already become usual and were widely circulated, as were newly composed devotional books. Sermons of favorite preachers, such as Jellinek of Vienna, Joel of Breslau, and later Zadoc Kahn of Paris, found willing readers. In all countries textbooks for elementary instruction were prepared; these presented the substance of Jewish thought in a form easily comprehensible. Literary associations set as their task the diffusion of Jewish knowledge. The most successful work was done by the Institute for the Promotion of Jewish Literature[23] founded by Ludwig Philippson, if only because knowledge of German was widespread among the Jews of all countries.

Among other achievements this Institute made the completion of Heinrich Graetz's monumental *History*[24] possible. By the thoroughness of its comprehension, and the vividness and warmth of its exposition Graetz's *History* won widespread success. Quite apart from its significance in scientific research, it became an educational factor of the first importance in Judaism, and translation into all cosmopolitan languages assured it a lasting effectiveness. No other work of contemporary Jewish scholarship penetrated so deeply into Jewish popular consciousness. Much as a scholar's erudition, acumen, and versatility were admired, knowledge of his work remained limited to specialists and seldom reached wide circles. Even so great a master as Leopold Zunz[25] did not find it easy to secure publication of his monumental work on synagogal poetry. The prodigious learning of Salomon Munk or of Moritz Steinschneider (1816–1907) remained unknown to ordinary readers. Modern Jewish scholarship could not win for itself the popularity which had formerly attached to talmudic study.

Popular literature, on the other hand, enjoyed great favor.[26] A new literary genre arose, the novel of the Jewish ghetto. Deep insights into a friendly world that has disappeared are afforded by Aron Bernstein's (1812–1884) idyllic sketches of the life of the Jews in West Prussia. This gifted and versatile man was a radical in his time. In politics he was the founder of the *Berliner Volkszeitung;* in the field of religion he was one of the leading spirits in the Jewish Reform Congregation in Berlin. His popular books on natural science (21 volumes published in several editions) became, because of their lucidity, favorite and widely diffused adjuncts to popular education. They were translated into Hebrew and so exerted a considerable influence upon the Jewish masses of Eastern Europe. But uncontested primacy in the ghetto novel of that early period was held by Leopold Kompert (1822–1886). Under the influence of Berthold Auerbach's village stories, he portrayed the Jewish life of his own Bohemian country in a series of sentimental stories with love and devotion, with faithfulness and truth, and his life-like figures made an enormous impression. In a more realistic age Kompert was displaced by Karl Emil Franzos (1840–1904), whose *Sketches from Half Asia* were composed with consummate art, but were hard and unfeeling. Grace Aguilar (1816–1847) was warm-hearted and devoted to Judaism. She glorified the martyrdom of the Marranos and in *The Jewish Faith* attempted to prove the superiority of Judaism over other religions. Her early death prevented the further unfolding of her talents as author.

The Jewish press became an important factor in education. Its expansion and growth were very rapid. In 1842 an attempt was made to found a Jewish periodical in far-off Australia. Under Ludwig Philippson's editorship, the *Allgemeine Zeitung des Judentums* (1837–1921) was epoch making.[27] It deserved its name, for it was not only read in all countries where Jews lived, but its contents embraced all phases of Jewish life, and it strove to represent all interests. The publisher was able to maintain his paper at a level which would keep the interest of all strata, educated and uneducated alike. He established the practice of offering news reports, entertainment, and instruction, and of observing or advocating political changes. His example was followed in all countries. In Paris the *Archives Israélites de France* was started in 1840, and the *Univers Israélite* in 1844. In London the *Jewish Chronicle* was started in 1841, and in Mainz the *Israelit* in 1860. These have survived to our own days. The number of short-lived publications of slighter importance is beyond computation. Mention should be made of the various[28] yearbooks, or almanacs, which provided, in connection with the calendar, great quantities of information and entertainment. Upon all sides efforts were made to meet the crisis in Jewish consciousness, but their power and penetration was insufficient, and they had not the strength to counteract the dominant centrifugal force.

Religion and Culture in Eastern Europe

In Eastern Europe the development differed not in kind but in pace: as in politics and economics, progress was two generations delayed. Mass and immobility made the pressure of the group much more clearly perceptible, and in consequence of rigid exclusiveness the general atmosphere was more densely impregnated with the Jewish element. Externally the structure seemed firm, but it was crumbling within. Talmudic learning, rabbinic rigor, and hasidic exclusiveness controlled the field, but the circle of *Maskilim* grew steadily even if slowly. Every *bahur* who strayed from home brought back tales of his experiences; every merchant who traveled abroad returned with new impressions and new reports of Jewish life. It was no accident that the great trading centers which maintained relations with Vienna and Berlin became the chief seats of the *Haskalah*. Inasmuch as these were ultimately related to Mendelssohn and his school, these seats were popularly styled "Berlinerisch." In Wilna, which was the metropolis of the rational study of Talmud, rational *Haskalah* also found its chief center. School teachers in particular became the bearers of enlightenment as well as the creators of a belletristic literature.[29]

The word "enlightenment" is not sufficiently descriptive. The real objective was social revolution, a complete transformation in education and habits of life, a revolt of youth against elders, of congregations against their leaders. Sympathy was aroused for the lamentable young people who were the victims of misguided education, who had spent the best years of their youth in dark and squalid rooms over books and over minute and vexatious problems which, so far from opening the road to life, blocked it. This unnatural phenomenon is described in gripping imagery in Bialik's poem called *Ha-Matmid*. Out of this sympathy there arose a demand that youth be not robbed of its proper joys, that it be brought up in contact with life and familiarity with nature, that the sun be permitted to illuminate its eyes as well as its souls, that a race healthy in body and soul alike be nurtured. The *Maskilim* regarded aberrations in education as the work of unworldly rabbis; but they believed that the mission of rabbinism was to promote the welfare of the people, and appealed from the rabbis who were misled to those who were better informed. They cried the alarm because they saw the house in flames, and they expected that those responsible for the house would help in the work of rescue. But they were undeceived when their calls for aid remained unanswered. The rabbis betook themselves to the stiff-necked communal leaders, and they persecuted the agitators exactly as the hasidic miracle workers were doing. The party of enlightenment then committed the fateful blunder of urging a government which was hostile to Jews to press for haste in making reforms.

Not all religious leaders were inexorable opponents of enlightenment. Rabbi Isaac, the leader of the famous *Yeshibah* of Wolozhyn, admonished Lilienthal to be patient and to yield. He trusted that time and toleration would heal all wounds. Rabbi Israel Lipkin (Salanter, 1810–1883) was a more active nature.[30] His goal was to spread knowledge of the Talmud over the widest possible area without alienating its students from the pursuit of some trade or calling. He therefore wished to improve the method of study so as to attain greater results with less expenditure of energy. But he was also eager to make rabbinism fructify Jewish life again, and so he placed self-discipline and ethical conduct in the foreground. He taught *Musar* (Ethics) and consistently urged that Jewish moral literature be included in the curriculum of *heder* and *yeshibah*. He did not, to be sure, achieve immediate success, but later his attitude did exert significant influence on the study of Talmud and on Jewish life in general in Lithuania.

Whatever attitude various groups assumed towards these questions, the world proceeded apace, and neither

Russia nor its ghettos were enclosed by a Chinese wall. The stimulating association with a Jewish educator of broad general culture like Lilienthal's (see p. 53, above) left a very great impression upon younger men. He had brought them, in a manner of speaking, the fruit of the tree of knowledge, and they reached for it eagerly. With a zeal peculiarly theirs they studied languages and literatures. They began to open their eyes, to observe nature and its marvels; and their new interests astonished and shocked their staid environment. At first parents counted their children lost when they discovered them following such paths of iniquity. But life was grim, and among other things constrained the realization that this outlawed kind of knowledge could be quite useful in the world outside or in dealing with Russian officialdom. The more families reached the higher station of entrepreneurs, the more young people fell into the temptation of backsliding in these mundane matters. For the daughters of the well-to-do knowledge of German and French was regarded as obligatory. It is not to be wondered that they grew restive under traditional usages. They rebelled against the old manner of betrothal and demanded the right to see the person chosen by their parents, and eventually to reject unsympathetic suitors before an engagement was undertaken.

The worldliness which was allowable for daughters was still tabu for sons, but what was outlawed in public young men managed to procure for themselves in private. Forbidden fruits are sweet, and students were ingenious in their eager pursuit of forbidden literature. They read in secret corners or kept books hidden in their Talmud folios, and frequently they buried themselves in these illicit books instead of mulling over problems in the Talmud. They not only read the classics of world literature, history and natural science, but political pamphlets also came into their ken. This reading brought them nearer to life, opened new horizons, introduced them to the search for a new ideal.

The new curiosity created a spiritual craving which cried aloud for satisfaction. Works produced in the traditional manner, as for example Rabbi Naftali Zevi Judah Berlin's learned commentary on the *She'eltot*, attracted only the disputatious band of older Talmudists. The new generation sought different pabulum, and this was provided by the new secular literature which was just then coming into being in Yiddish and Hebrew and which was also nurturing a Russian seedling. The leaders of the *Haskalah* created a new belletristic literature in Hebrew. The pioneers were almost all teachers. They were incredibly poor and hard pressed; practically all of them had had to bear the yoke of matrimony from their thirteenth or fourteenth years. Lacking proper models, they were forced to create their own Hebrew style, one which should be related to contemporary life and capable of giving expression to contemporary thoughts. They took up their task in the first instance as an educational enterprise[31] and cultivated history chiefly, the field of knowledge which occupied the foremost place in contemporary Russian literature also.

Mordecai Aron Günzburg (1795–1846) was chiefly concerned with spreading the knowledge of world history. He offered translations or adaptations of standard works in unadorned and straightforward language. When he touched upon the abuses of the time, he avoided outspoken or sharp criticism and left it to the reader to surmise what lay behind his delicate irony. Similarly Kalman Schulmann (1819–1893) was occupied principally in popularizing historical works in translations or adaptations, but he ventured also upon Eugene Sue's *Secrets of Paris*, and wafted the innocent citizen of the Russian village to that thrilling mixture of fantasy and reality.

The poetry of Abraham Baer Lebensohn (1794–1878) struggled under the weight of pedantic language unsuitable to his simple and natural themes, but it did succeed in lifting its readers from their commonplace world into a more exalted level. His precocious son, Micha Joseph (1808–1852), found more natural tones. He had had a European education, and he built bridges between the new Hebrew poetry and the masterpieces of world literature. His translations of Schiller, Goethe, and other Olympians pointed the direction which almost all succeeding Hebrew writers of significance followed, fertilizing the Hebrew spirit with the towering geniuses of other cultures.

Abraham Mapu (1808–1867) gave Hebrew literature its first original novel. It was a historical romance, following famous models. Despite objections which may be taken by modern literary criticism to *Ahavat Zion v'Yerushalaim*, Mapu's influence on his contemporaries cannot be rated too highly. To them his book was fascinating reading. With the magic of poetry it reproduced the splendor of ancient Israel, the majesty of its capital and the glory of its leaders; and at the same time the reader enslaved in his ghetto was exalted by the awareness that his people too at one time possessed national independence and greatness. The rabbinic group had nothing so charming to offer, and Mapu was firmly convinced that his was the correct approach and that it had the support of youth. He therefore ventured upon an open attack. In his '*Ayit Zabu'a* he tore the mask from the faces of the Tartuffes of his day and showed how their hypocritical sanctimoniousness poisoned the life of the community as well as that of the family.

These revolutionary tendencies dominated the Hebrew publications and the Jewish life of the next generation. The problem of Fathers and Sons[32] was a burning question in the Jewish street long before Turgeniev wrote his famous novel. On the one side stood obscurantist parents who rejected their sons because they had learned a living language or because they possessed "dangerous" books such as the Bible with Moses Mendelssohn's commentary, parents who surrendered themselves to the machinations of deceiving hypocrites and so lost their peace of mind and their property alike. On the other side stood children who desired nothing more than to lead normal lives, to take advantage of existing opportunities for education, and thereby to increase their usefulness and their enjoyment in life.

The spokesman of the young generation was Judah Loeb Gordon (1830–1892), the most gifted and the best beloved Hebrew writer of the century. Along with the culture of the West he had imbibed its anticlericalism, and he transferred this hostility to rabbinic and even to prophetic Judaism. Its spiritual leaders had, according to his view, cast Judaism into fetters, hindered its natural development, and forced it into a no less difficult situation than its external enemies had done. He laid his finger upon the sore spots in the body politic of Judaism and assailed rabbinism bitterly because it might have healed the woe but had rather aggravated it by its stubbornness and by the tyranny of literalism. Education according to rabbinical methods seemed to him perverse in all its parts, a device to cripple people and make them unfit for life; he himself saw the remedy in healthy physical activity — it was the period of Alexander II's reforms (see p. 58, above) — in manual work, and in participation in the social life of the environment. Gordon's poem, *Awake, My People*, set the old and the new ways of life in sharp opposition to one another: it came to be looked upon as the Jewish *Marseillaise*, and like the *Marseillaise* it served as a rousing battle-call. In comparison with Gordon, Mosheh Loeb Lilienblum (1843–

1910) seems gentle and mild. From a scholarly and factual study of rabbinism in his early period, Lilienblum arrived at the conviction that the existing system was indefensible and thorough reform inevitable.

How deeply such thoughts as these penetrated into the people it is impossible to determine statistically. But certain it is that the intelligent portion of the Jewish population, those with eyes turned towards the culture of the West and those destined for leadership, were among the admirers of the new ideas. The evolution amounted to a transformation in Jewish life, and its basis was in Judaism. And now the reform legislation of Alexander II brought the eagerly longed for ameliorations. But reality assumed an aspect different from that anticipated by the *Maskilim*; the Jewish elements of the enlightenment were overrun by the Russian. When limitations on residence were relaxed, the Jews experienced a shift in space; they experienced an economic shift in consequence of rapid railroad construction and industrialization. With the release from the ghetto came an astoundingly rapid alienation from religious life. As in the west of Europe, indifference to traditional institutions and forms was the rule.[33]

Children were enrolled in Russian schools, and even if the father persisted in his adherence to *Haskalah*, the ear of the child belonged to the masters of Russian language and culture. Leadership passed from bourgeois Lithuanian teachers to cosmopolites from southern Russia, men like the gifted jurist Ilya Orschansky (1846–1875) and the skillful storyteller Ossip Rabbinowicz (1817–1869). They fought for the rights of the Jews, but they demanded reforms in Jewish life, especially acceptance of Russianism. Unfortunately the catastrophe of the Mendelssohnian period was here repeated. A number of leaders left Judaism and drew with them a large part of the youth. Even if they did not apostasize, their interests

INNER DEVELOPMENT (1850–1880)

lay outside Judaism. They were captivated by Russian socialism with its cry of "Out to the land;" they saw their duty in improving the lot of the Russian peasant, in campaigning for the grant of a constitution. A great many among them found their way into the camp of the radicals and took part in agitation and incitement. For Judaism and its struggle for existence they were lost.

Hebrew as a language receded into the background. It maintained a precarious existence in the popular books subsidized by the Society for the Diffusion of Enlightenment among the Jews. Such a champion of culture as Judah Loeb Gordon looked towards the future with despondency and saw himself as the last singer of Zion, who must reckon with a fast dwindling circle of readers. His entire life-work seemed on the point of collapse. The hardest blow which the enlightenment suffered was the outbreak of pogroms in Russia, which proved that all attempts to draw nearer the dominant race were futile. The orthodox groups thought they could triumph when the enlightenment which they had deprecated and opposed suffered its fiasco.[34] But neither before this fiasco nor afterwards had they any general prescription for effectively educating and retaining the mass of youth. Even though the *Haskalah* also finally gave the task up, it had at least succeeded in arousing the spirit and in producing a generation capable of a new life and receptive to new ideas.

That such was actually the case and that a genuine popular need existed is proven by the fact that the striving for enlightenment was not limited to the educated classes or those who could use Hebrew. On the contrary, the demand for secularization was also urged in the broad masses of the downtrodden. The problems remained identical. Among the Yiddish[35] speaking masses the stirrings and struggles already dealt with were repeated, if in a slower tempo. Here, too, periodicals and translations of the classics were used. Here, too, satire was employed in combating Hasidism, the Kahal, the traditional usages in arranging marriages. A sweeping success was won by Salomo Ettinger's (1803–1856) comedy, *Serkele*, which depicted the opposition between the old Jewish manner of life and the new. For a long period *Serkele* had something of the standing of a basic work of the enlightenment. Abraham Baer Gottlober (1811–1899), who was also known as a Hebrew writer, showed far greater keenness in portraying the depression, human and social, of Ukrainian Jewry and in his constant mockery of the doings of the hasidic masses. Eisik Meir Dick (1814–1893) was inexhaustible in his invention of ever fresh matter which he worked up into short stories. These possessed little literary merit, but they were eagerly devoured by the women of the market-place and influenced their manner of thinking. Later Shaikev-Shomer and Oser Blostein flooded the market with their stories of love and adventure. They provided new reading matter and opened new perspectives. Traveling minstrels, such as Wolf Ehrenkranz (1820–1883), who arose in Galicia, also traveled about in Russia-Poland. They produced collections of songs, and these induced Abraham Goldfaden (1840–1908) to establish a Yiddish theater — a sketchy enterprise, but rich in promise.

Literature, in its artistic sense, was first created by Shalom Jacob Abramowitch (1835–1917). He wrote under the pseudonym Mendele Mocher Seforim and produced realistic descriptions based on his own observations of Jewish types drawn from the entire Pale of Settlement. He was already a respected writer in Hebrew, a recognized representative of realism, but he felt himself closely bound to his people, to the great amorphous mass whose sighs, under the heavy yoke of political and economic oppression, he heard, and whose lot he desired to improve by instructing them, by cultivating them, by making them happier. The life, the language, the psychology of the people seemed to him to be the basis of a people's art. He observed his people with great accuracy and became an excellent interpreter. It irked him that Yiddish should be despised as the language of the lowly, of the ignorant and of women; to him it was a sacred patrimony of his people. He listened to the people's speech and found in it their true life and character, their thoughts and their feelings. He became a master of the folk art, and his stories became part of the common folk legacy. Keen satire guided his pen, but the folk recognized a loving hand which yearned for their improvement. Mendele's style — realism in content, in language, in expression — became the model for most of his successors, in Hebrew as well as Yiddish, and they honored him as the *Zayde* ("Grandfather").

Undifferentiated as the mass then seemed, the literary development of two generations had completely changed the substance of its education and had greatly influenced its outlook on life. It was from its literature that it drew strength for the wanderings upon which it now had to enter.

CHAPTER IV

The Jews in the New World

Growth and Organization in the United States

IT WAS to be expected that overseas countries, in which a new world was in the building without the prejudices of the old, would exert profound influence upon the development of Jewish life. Brightest hopes were centered in the United States[1] where the founding fathers had "brought forth a new nation conceived in liberty and dedicated to the proposition that all men are created equal." The new country, whose development in the south and west was proceeding apace, needed people. In his message to Congress, June 1, 1841, President John Tyler extended "to the people of other countries an invitation to come and settle among us as members of our rapidly growing family." The invitation did not go unheeded. In the next decade the number of immigrants grew to an average of 100,000 annually, and in the succeeding decades of increasing industrialization the rate was accelerated. In the years between 1841 and 1881 immigration amounted to approximately ten million persons.

Among those who heeded the call there were Jews from all parts of Central Europe who were oppressed in their homeland and had no opportunity for advancement. This wave is generally referred to as the German immigration. Particularly striking was the large number of Bavarians, who despaired of the possibility of settlement in their own country because of the retention of the registration requirement (see p. 12, above). But there were many immigrants from other parts of Germany also, and from

Bohemia and Poland. In his invitation, the President had continued:

> For the blessing which we offer them, we require of them to look upon our country as their country, and unite with us in the great task of preserving our institutions and thereby perpetuating our liberties.

No other group yearned to fulfill this requirement with greater zeal than did the Jews.

Out of an environment heavy with malice they came into a land of good-will, where freedom rested not upon concessions wrung from individual princes, but upon the free will of the people and the conviction of the dignity of man. Here was a country that recognized no State Church; Church and State were separated, not so that religion might be oppressed, but, on the contrary, to guarantee to each faith the possibility of developing its own spiritual and religious values. The piety characteristic of the country was based upon old Puritan traditions, and so had a marked biblical coloring which was sympathetic to the Jews. "Hebrew mortar cemented the foundations of American democracy" (Lecky). The Liberty Bell in Independence Hall in Philadelphia was inscribed with a verse out of the Torah, "Ye shall proclaim liberty throughout the land unto all the inhabitants thereof," and its peal found a deep echo in the hearts of the Jews. In this land they could quickly make themselves at home, could quickly grow into its faith and its future.

The immigrants did not linger in the ports of their arrival,[2] New York, Philadelphia, or Baltimore, but traveled on, north to Boston, south to St. Louis and Galveston and west to Cincinnati, Chicago, San Francisco. They shared the growing pains of these new cities and assisted their rapid rise by promoting trade and industry. The number of immigrants grew; they were joined by relatives; they founded families and multiplied, so that in 1858 the number of Jews was estimated at 200,000.[3] The country afforded them the fullest freedom of movement and, since it was newly opened, undreamed of possibilities for the future. Upon their arrival, the immigrants were for the most part poor, but they were young and used to hard work, and they were willing to continue to work hard. Their industry and perseverance, their sobriety and frugality, stood them in good stead. As many artisans as there were among them found their skill in great demand. The few physicians quickly found remunerative employment. Others began very modestly as peddlers.[4] They traveled out to the country with baskets of goods bought on credit, and found a ready welcome in farmhouses which were distant from one another and from the city and accessible only by bad roads. In the period when mail and rail service were lacking, they carried out, in a measure, the economic function later largely taken over by the mail-order houses. They prospered, increased their stock, obtained horse and wagon, and eventually opened stores in the cities or engaged in industry and left peddling to others. By 1858 many already belonged among the respectable representatives of commerce and finance. Not all were successful. Journeys lasting for months required large expenditures and so reduced their income that they had to leave the care of their families at home to their co-religionists or risk having them yield to the insistent patronage of church missions. Gradually, and more speedily in the newly opened West than in the settled East, they attained to wealth and to a better social position. Some entered the political life of the country and gained success and respect.

It was not always easy for the individual, to maintain his spiritual integrity, especially where Jews were isolated or their numbers few and where they had no leaders.

The best of laws cannot straightway abolish deep-rooted convictions. Even if the native Americans were all filled with the spirit of Jefferson and Jackson, the great number of immigrants brought with them the inbred prejudices of their various countries of origin and were not immediately assimilated to their new environment. The Church[5] was not indifferent to the loss of its power. It was distressed to see its influence upon men's thoughts wane, and it exerted every effort to make the State Christian, to equate Protestantism and Americanism. Attacks were directed particularly against the "Godless" schools, and long and earnest struggles were waged over the maintenance of the "barriers against the horrors of spiritual tyranny and every species of religious persecution" which had been proclaimed by George Washington. Attempts to introduce religious instruction or scriptural reading in the public schools are still disturbing to the leaders of Judaism because they fear that these may lead to incitement to hatred and to persecution. All too many had experience enough of instances of a narrow intolerance. Many had also been subjected to more or less insistent attempts at conversion.

It appeared necessary to defend the rights of the Jews, and, in 1859, the Board of Delegates of American Israelites[6] in New York formed "a national organization for the purpose of securing and maintaining civil and religious rights at home and abroad." The aims of the Board were broad. Besides the protection of civic and religious rights, it proposed to promote Jewish education, to set up a union of all Jews in the United States and to keep statistical records of them. The Board was established at about the same time as the *Alliance Israélite Universelle*, and sought to work in close cooperation with it in protecting the rights of oppressed Jews. The government recognized the Board's right to function, and listened to its representative, who always resided in Washington, whenever he brought complaints or petitions. It was due to the Board that the government of the United States was informed of the frequent oppressions of Jews in other countries and that it allowed its voice to be heard, in consequence, on behalf of humanity and justice towards the oppressed. This was a new turn in the life of nations.

The grave crisis which confronted the Union before and during the Civil War had profound significance for the Jews. It is not to be assumed that the great mass of new immigrants, completely unschooled in the political sense, had any deep understanding of the highly complex problems which underlay the conflict. The question of slavery[7] was concrete. But even those Jews who possessed slaves were not concerned to preserve the institution, for in reports written long before the outbreak of the struggle we read of "some Jews who have refused to have any right of property in man or even to have any slaves about them." Very unfavorable comment was aroused by a sermon of a New York rabbi, Dr. Morris J. Raphall, printed under the title *Bible View of Slavery*. Raphall maintained that slavery could not be regarded as a violation of biblical law. He was sharply refuted by Rabbi David Einhorn of Baltimore who had already emphatically shown that slavery was contrary to the spirit of biblical religion, if not to its letter. Einhorn was outspoken in his conviction, although he endangered his life thereby, and was forced to flee Baltimore secretly in order to escape being lynched. When his congregation forbade his speaking upon the subject, he showed sufficient spirit to offer his resignation. Other rabbis who vigorously opposed slavery, such as Sabato Morais in Philadelphia and Bernhard Felsenthal in Chicago, were prevented from speaking out by the timid leaders of their congregations. Of Jewish laymen, Michael Heilprin and Moritz Pinner were outstanding in the literary warfare against slavery.

But a great many Jews stood on the side of the South and sacrificed political and civic positions in order to join the Confederacy. Judah Philip Benjamin (1811-1884), one of the most gifted orators and outstanding jurists of his time,[8] was a convinced proponent of slavery and secession. He became Jefferson Davis' Secretary of War, and later Secretary of State. He was called "the brains of the Confederacy" and it wanted but little for his diplomatic skill to win the intervention of Napoleon III and the French power against the Union. General Butler made Benjamin's activity a cause for blaming all Jews. The fact is that numerous volunteers served on both sides, that many Jews from the southern states enlisted in the Union army, and that many distinguished themselves for bravery. The sculptor Moses Ezekiel was one of the volunteers in the Confederate army. The figures that are cited for the number of Jewish participants in the war rest on estimate, but 8,000 are known by name, among them nine generals, eighteen colonels, and many officers of lower rank. Cases are noted of "brothers in the army," that is to say, several sons of a single family who volunteered to serve in the same regiment.[9]

One of the strongest weapons of the Union was the blockade, and it was an important object of the Confederacy to break the blockade. Among those who ran the blockade were a number of Jews. In December 1862, an order was issued by General Ulysses S. Grant, commander of the Department of Tennessee, "to expel the Jews as a class." This unconstitutional order met with vigorous disapproval and was quickly recalled by President Lincoln. Grant himself later showed how remote Jew-hatred was from his thoughts by his attitude towards the Rumanian Jews (see p. 72, above); after his election to the Presidency (1869) he explained that one of his subordinates had used a blank form with his signature and that the order had been directed, not against Jews in general, but only against those who violated the rules of war. Another incident was occasioned by General Butler, who thought fit to mention expressly in one of his army reports that his troops had taken captive "among others sixty contrabands and four Jews." Judge M. S. Isaacs, who was the representative of the Board of Delegates at the time, regarded it as his duty to ask the General for an explanation.[10] The exchange of letters that ensued provides melancholy proof of how slight a knowledge of Jews a man in so responsible a post could have and how he could nevertheless not hesitate to generalize on the basis of a few unfavorable impressions and make them the criterion for official action.

These cases may appear insignificant enough, but they show a sharp discrepancy between the Jews' own concept of their rights and the position to which their environment assigned them. They show that even in the New World men of high position — to say nothing of lesser persons — were frequently imbued with the prejudices of the old continent. They are the forerunners of certain unlovely manifestations of social life which later found expression in the exclusive attitude of American society[11] towards Jews and other presumed outsiders.

The devotion of the Jewish immigrants to their new home had been shown by their readiness to sacrifice themselves in military service. It was shown also in their mourning for Abraham Lincoln.[12] History offers but few examples of a statesman who in so short and fateful a period had won the unqualified love of his fellow citizens and who was so universally and so feelingly mourned. By his life and his sad death Lincoln had contributed more than any one man to the unification of the American nation, and by their heartfelt participation in the national grief the Jews proved their ardent wish to become part of the nation of the martyred president.

Judaism in the United States

It was only in religion that the Jews of the United States desired to be different from their fellow citizens. It was for them to show what power religion had in them and over them, and it may be said that they stood up to the test and proved the power of their religious consciousness. With no exercise of force, without the intervention of a hierarchy, the immigrants formed congregations on an entirely voluntary basis. In those few places where there were already congregations (usually these were Sephardic, as in Charleston, S. C.; Savannah, Ga.; New Orleans, La.) they regularly joined them. Many indeed lived in isolation, two or three families in a place; but as their numbers grew and they found it possible to do so, they united for common worship, founded a congregation, purchased burial ground, and erected a synagogue. When means for such structures were wanting, collections were taken up in other communities, and help was never denied. Judah Touro[13] of New Orleans was a generous benefactor who dedicated his entire and considerable fortune to the common welfare. In his last will (1854) he made most of the synagogues of the country beneficiaries, in particular that of his birthplace, Newport, R. I.

Soon each community had one or more charitable organizations[14] and gave assistance not only to new arrivals but also to the needy in their own communities. Wherever it was possible to do so, a hospital and an orphanage were established. New York and Philadelphia provided the pattern and other communities followed suit. Most communities provided for Jewish schools, not only for religious training, but also, since the public school system did not come into being till about the middle of the century, for complete secular education; parents in remote places often sent their children to such schools. The first Sunday School was established in Philadelphia in 1838 by Rebecca Gratz,[15] who is presumed to be the model for the gentle Rebecca in Scott's *Ivanhoe*, and her example was followed by all congregations.

The communities also fostered social life, necessary to retain the interest of the youth; to this end Young Men's and Women's Hebrew Associations were founded (1874). One of the most effective organizations for promoting union among Jews was the Independent Order B'nai B'rith,[16] founded in 1843 by Henry Jones and several of his friends:

having for their objective the true amelioration of our race by elevating the mind, and harmonizing those conflicting sentiments and prejudices, nurtured in ignorance and engendered by the persecutions of the despotic governments of Europe.

That the Order answered a real need was proven by its rapid growth, which enabled it to establish many social institutions. It not only created social organizations, but it also directed its attention to the legal rights of the Jews. It was due to the spirit of service shown by members of the Order that B. F. Peixotto could be sent as United States Consul to Bucharest (see p. 72).

Congregational politics were always lively. Men of diverse origin, frequently of limited outlook and experience, clung obstinately to the minor usages of their home countries, and so fell into disagreement with one another.[17] They were very ready to be guided by the individualism which was the prevalent note in American life. Where the number of members sufficed, a group would secede and the strain would be relieved by the establishment of a new congregation. In this way the first Ashkenazic congregations, Rodeph Shalom in Philadelphia (1802) and B'nai Jeshurun in New York (1825), were formed by cleavage from the old Sephardic congregations, and in the course of their own growth they produced other offshoots which after their separation maintained peaceful and harmonious relations with the original bodies.

The most serious problem was the lack of spiritual leadership. The existing Sephardic congregations had not provided for the rabbinic succession. The need was so great that Philadelphia's old and proud Sephardic congregation, Mikveh Israel (founded 1740), called Isaac Leeser[18] (1816–1868), a native of Neuenkirchen in Westphalia, as its *Hazzan*. Leeser had had no rabbinic training and had worked for several years in a business establishment at Richmond, Va. But the choice was excellent. Acknowledging the predominance of the English environment, Leeser made it his task to anglicize American Judaism. He introduced the English sermon as a regular feature of the service; he translated the prayer book, according to both the Sephardic and Ashkenazic ritual, into English; he translated the Bible into English. He replied publicly to attacks on Judaism, and for spiritual direction as well as to represent Jewish interests he established a monthly, *The Occident and American Jewish Advocate*, the first Jewish periodical in the United States (1843–1869). Leeser was truly a self-made man, a type common in America at the time. He instinctively felt the needs of the day and worked for the strengthening of a Jewish sense of responsibility in the new environment; "his name is connected with the inception of nearly every charitable and educational institution of his time." Samuel Myer Isaacs (1804–1878) and Morris J. Raphall (1798–1868) cooperated in these efforts. Both were educated in England and introduced the English sermon in Ashkenazic congregations. Both also understood the use of journalism for reaching larger circles. Dr. Raphall enjoyed a considerable reputation as preacher and lecturer. He was the first Jewish minister to be invited to open the House of Representatives in Washington with prayer and was so designated "to introduce the equal rights of Israelitic prayer in the halls of Congress."

These men were surpassed in creative gifts and organizing skill by a man of action who set as his goal the creation of an "American Israel" and saw its attainment after twenty-five years of devoted and persistent effort.[19] Isaac Mayer Wise (born at Steingrub, Bohemia, in 1819; died at Cincinnati, Ohio, in 1900) came to the United States in 1846. Wise had hardly arrived and got his first impressions before he recognized, as by sure instinct, what was needed to secure the future of Judaism in this country. He saw a great readiness to make material sacrifices, much good-will, but little circumspection, no plan, no leadership. "We are," as he later expressed it, "the sons of different countries and the disciples of different schools; we had too many different educators; our dear mother, the religion of Israel, and the freedom of our country, could not at once overcome all the difficulties, dissensions and inherited notions which did necessarily cling to us." Into this chaos he strove to bring order, into this solipsism a communal consciousness and a sense of responsibility for the future. As early as 1848, when he was rabbi in Albany, New York, he called, in the columns of The *Occident*, for

the association of Israelitish congregations in North America to produce one sublime and grand end, to defend and maintain our sacred faith. . . . We have no system for our worship, nor for our ministry and schools, and we are therefore divided in as many fragments as there are congregations in North America. It is lamentable, but true, that if we do not unite ourselves betimes to devise a practicable system for the ministry and religious education at large, if we do not take care that better educated men fill the pulpit and the school-master's chair, if we do not stimulate all the congregations to establish good schools and to institute a reform in their synagogues on modern Jewish principles, the house of the Lord will be desolate or nearly so in less than ten years.

Leeser, who opposed Wise in so many other respects, did not hesitate "to second earnestly his ideas about the necessity of a thorough union of Israelites residing on this continent." But the call failed of success. In New York, which possessed far the largest Jewish community, it found no response.

Wise had hardly accepted the call to Congregation B'nai Jeshurun in Cincinnati, after h's hard struggle in Albany, and had just founded his weekly, *The Israelite* (1854), before he resumed his admonitions. All the difficulties which threatened the future of Judaism in the United States, he maintained, cou'd be removed by a Union of American Judaic Congregations. He declared it essential to found a college at once in which the future spiritual leaders of American Judaism could be trained. He called upon rabbis and communal representatives to meet in Cleveland in the autumn of 1855; the principal agendum was to be the consideration of Articles of Union of American Israel on Theory and Practice. Wise put himself under severe limitations in order to attain unity with Leeser. A common resolution declared:

> The Bible is of immediate Divine Origin; the Talmud contains the Traditional, Legal and Logical Exposition of the Biblical Laws which must be expounded and practiced according to the Comments of the Talmud; the Resolutions of the Synod in accordance with the above Principles are Legally Valid; Statutes and Ordinances Contrary to the Laws of the Land are Invalid.

The meetings went off harmoniously, but the resolution stirred David Einhorn, of Sinai Congregation, Baltimore, into action; together with his congregation he protested in the most vigorous terms against the decision on the Talmud. Wise enjoyed the unqualified support and vigorous cooperation of Max Lilienthal, who also worked in Cincinnati at the time and shared Wise's efforts to find sound middle ground between uncompromising Reform and uncompromising Orthodoxy.

There was no further conference. In the difficult times of Civil War and Reconstruction, it was not to be expected that the community would be receptive to such projects. Despite their recent experiences the blessings of union had not yet reached the Jewish communities even after that period; among them the spirit of secession and anarchy prevailed. But Wise continued the indomitable struggle for his ideas. The number of congregations was increasing constantly, and it was Wise's hope that the union he conceived might banish ignorance and support seats of learning whose disciples would make the congregations independent of the chance of immigrant rabbis. A number of rabbis supported his ideas, but his old opponents in the East sought to sabotage them. Even the efforts of the Board of Delegates to effect a union miscarried.

In this desperate conjuncture Wise's own congregation leaped into the breach and summoned a meeting of rabbis and congregations of the West and South. On July 8, 1873, in Cincinnati, this assembly founded the Union of American Hebrew Congregations,[20] whose aims were:

to establish and maintain institutions for instruction in the higher branches of Hebrew Literature and Jewish Theology; to provide means for the relief of Jews from political oppression and unjust discrimination, and for rendering them aid for their intellectual elevation; to promote religious instruction and encourage the study of the Scriptures and of the tenets and history of Judaism — all this, however, without interfering in any manner whatsoever with the worship, the schools, or any other of the congregational institutions.

Every clause of this document reveals the spirit of Wise, particularly the sharp emphasis upon the spiritual tasks of the Union and the provision against interfering in the internal affairs of the congregations, which made it possible for all congregations without exception to join the Union. It is significant that, after the founding of the Union, Wise called his weekly *The American Israelite*; he was now convinced that he had created a really unified American Judaism. And in fact, four years later the congregations of the East were also won over to the Union. The Board of Delegates worked for unification, as it had long done; and when unification was achieved, it continued its own work in protecting the civil and religious rights of Jews as a committee of the Union. Simon Wolf

(1838–1923) labored for decades with devoted zeal and extraordinary skill as the common representative of the Union and of the Board in Washington.

One of the first acts of the Union was the founding of the Hebrew Union College[21] and the assumption of responsibility for its maintenance. Previous attempts to establish similar institutions in Philadelphia and New York had only ephemeral significance. When the Hebrew Union College was opened in Cincinnati, on October 3, 1875, with the rabbinic motto, "The study of the Torah is equivalent to all other duties," it became the first seat of higher Jewish learning in the New World which was destined to endure. In the Hebrew Union College, Wise saw the capstone of his life work, and to its upbuilding and expansion he devoted the last twenty-five years of his life. It was obvious to the founders that the management of the institution should be entrusted to Wise: no one could give the new-born infant truer love and more devoted care than he. In conjunction with Wise, instruction was given by Max Lilienthal and others at hand. Gradually Wise assembled a faculty of high standard. His unwearied efforts and the affection and esteem which he himself enjoyed brought the College new means; despite continuous attacks on the part of extremists in the East, its development continued favorable.

It was Wise's wish to make the College serve all the various tendencies in Judaism; he invited authorities of the conservative wing, such as Sabato Morais, to participate in the examinations, in order to win their confidence. But unity could not be maintained permanently, for Reform tended to diverge more and more sharply from the traditional norm.

For Wise, American Israel implied not only external unity, but also the breaking down of distinctions from within.[22] To him the experience of the new freedom was overwhelming. Freedom he regarded as the Messiah. In the land of freedom he looked for the soaring rhythm of the Messianic Age, the striving for perfection. It seemed to him intolerable that the New World should be dominated by antiquated forms; the narrowness of ghetto life seemed incompatible with the breadth of cosmopolitanism. America and all it implied cried aloud for an American Judaism. In such a Judaism the petty forms of rabbinism were to yield to the lofty ideas of the prophets; ethics had to become the predominant influence. The tenor of this program went far beyond the expressions of the moderate reformers in Germany. Leeser would hear nothing of the very word Reform, and attacked its advocates, and above all Wise, as teachers of unbelief, godlessness, and rebellion, and their doctrines as a "fierce and relentless onslaught on Judaism." Yet with all his earnestness Leeser had to admit the existence of abuses, of follies and superstitions, and to confess that he was "not opposed to rational religious reforms based on Scriptures and Tradition." Wise and Lilienthal, too, sought to retain a similar criterion, but it was difficult (as it had proved to be in Germany) to draw a line of demarcation where Reform ceased to be legitimate and became illegitimate. In Albany, Wise was charged with "preaching a God of reason while the congregation believed in the God of Abraham, Isaac and Jacob." The expression of this conflict was naive, and it was more naive to subject such a conflict to a vote of a meeting of the congregation. But with all its naiveté the statement covered the point at issue. Eventually the controversy centered upon this question: Should a purified faith (Wise advocated that of Moses Maimonides) be taught, or one that reflected the views of Bavarian and Hessian villagers? Neither the learned rabbis, the traditionalists included, nor the majority of the laity could be content with the faith of their childhood.

Matters went farther than theoretical disputations. Many synagogues introduced innovations in the services, such as organ accompaniments (when the first organ was introduced in Charleston, South Carolina, in 1841, some members of the congregation called for a judicial decision against it), mixed choirs, family pews, bared heads, abolition of the second day of festivals, abbreviation and alteration of the traditional prayers and, last but not least, omission of all references to Zion or to a personal Messiah. The new concept of Messianism became a shibboleth between the Reformers and those opposed to them. The rift was widened when men like David Einhorn, Samuel Adler, and Samuel Hirsch, who had participated in the rabbinic assemblies in Germany (Graetz, V, 677 ff.), transplanted the radicalism there prevalent in the New World. Success, which was denied the Berlin Reform Congregation in its own country, was attained in the United States. Einhorn[23] became the ardent and enthusiastic champion of the idea of the Messianic task and priestly mission of Israel, "as people of religion, as the bearers of the highest ideals of humanity." Next to the doctrine of God this constituted for him the central point of Judaism, as "the hope of both earthly and heavenly salvation." These thoughts formed the basis of his prayer book, *Olat Tamid*, printed in German in 1856, whose composition was radically different from that of the traditional prayer books. Wise retained his Hebrew *Minhag America*, while others, like Benjamin Szold (in Baltimore, Md., after 1859), sought for a more moderate transition.

Leadership of the Reform movement went over to the radical German rabbis and congregations of the East. They dominated the rabbinical assembly in Philadelphia,[24] which was the first in the New World to make a declaration of faith. This declaration was, indeed, negative rather than positive; its strength lay in its departures from the traditional body of doctrine, not in the creation of a new body. Judaism, according to Einhorn, had certain dogmas but exercised no coercion for their acceptance. One of these dogmas, the assembly declared, was the Messianic mission of Israel: "the unity of all the children of God in the confession of the unity of God, so as to realize the unity of all rational creatures and their call to moral sanctification." The dispersion of Israel they declared an act of the divine will, "for the realization of their high priestly mission, to lead the nations to the true knowledge and worship of God." The assembly declared that faith in bodily resurrection is baseless; they rejected all mention of sacrifices in the prayers, as well as all special recognition of Aaronides. They recommended that Hebrew as the language of prayer be minimized as far as practicable. In their consideration of the traditional marriage laws, they urged a new concept and a new significance for the ceremony of betrothal; actual marriage and the release of a wife from the marriage bond on grounds of desertion they left in the province of civil law. How little the imminent realization of the Messianic Age could be made a point of departure for a philosophy of life was shown by the events which transpired a few years later and which pointed clearly to a completely new tendency within the surrounding world.

It was a very small quorum which voted the Philadelphia platform. Their sharp attack upon Jewish tradition did not encounter open opposition. The progressive rabbis who held moderate views, like Benjamin Szold, Marcus Jastrow, Adolph Hübsch, had no leader, and the orthodox rabbinate had no standing. The Orthodox[25] of the time spent their energies in petty quarrels concerning ritual practices and in minor jealousies. They were ineffective and unable to cooperate in any constructive enterprise. They had no well-defined course and therefore did not profit by the weight of their increased numbers.

Immigration from Germany ceased for a time, and the first victims of persecution began to arrive from Russia and Rumania. Although their numbers were at first relatively small, they did constitute the first Jewish mass immigration, and the Board of Delegates, which was pessimistic concerning the possibility of settling them, made strong representations to their emissaries in Europe, as we saw above, on the necessity of the careful selection of prospective immigrants. The committees which received the immigrants on landing were pleasantly surprised to find that they did not expect alms but were eager to work; and after no long while the greater part were able to stand upon their own feet. They were the forerunners of the congregations of East European Jews which became a leaven within American Judaism. The powers that lay slumbering within their midst may be illustrated by the case of Jacob Epstein. He was born in the New York ghetto in 1880, went to Europe, and became one of the most famous sculptors of his age.

Jews in the English Colonies

In the English colonies[26] Jews enjoyed equal rights sooner than they did in the mother country. The old and honorable communities in the West Indies had indeed fallen into decline and had suffered by the brilliant development on the continent of North America, and their numbers fell off sharply. All the congregations in the English colonies were hampered in their development by the fact that they were placed under the patronage of the Chief Rabbi, whose seat was in far-distant London. He had no real concept of local conditions, and, when he did interfere, he usually worked more harm than good.

One of the most significant Jewish settlements in the Antilles, at the beginning of the nineteenth century, was Jamaica, most of whose Jews lived in the capital, Kingston. As early as 1831 Jamaica became the first British colony to abolish all inequality of rights for the Jews. Equality was faithfully observed, and in 1838 Sir Francis H. Goldsmid was able to present in London a long list of Jews who had occupied civil and military positions in Jamaica and so to illustrate the beneficial results of equality. In 1849 the population elected eight Jews among the forty-seven members of its parliament; Dr. C. M. Morales was chosen speaker. A number of Jews occupied outstanding positions in the banks and commercial enterprises of the island. Here, too, the first Jewish settlers were Sephardim, and their congregation continued to be the most important. But an "English and German Synagogue" was founded before 1880, and its rabbi, M. N. Nathan, even published a Jewish monthly, *First Fruits of the West* (1845).

In Barbados the local parliament abolished all political inequality as early as 1820. The Jews even enjoyed a certain autonomy in that their tax was assessed and collected by their own commission, chosen from their own numbers. But the Jewish community of Barbados did not attain the development that might have been expected. Natural catastrophes brought destruction upon the island and caused a dislocation in its entire economy. A current of immigration to the United States set in, and its numbers steadily declined. The decline in Dutch Curaçao was not so marked; there the Jews continued to be numbered among the leading citizens. Curaçao was the only congregation in the West Indies in which the Reform movement found an early footing (1859); the result was that even the old Sephardic congregation was not able to reject all reforms.

The development in those British colonies which were destined to become great dominions was quite different. Jewish life in Canada[27] took the same forms as it had done in the United States; as was the case with the Dominion as a whole, the Jewish settlement did not approach that of the United States in extent or fruitfulness. Even in the French colonial period certain Jewish families, like the Solomons and the Harts, had attained distinguished positions. Ezekiel Hart was elected to parliament in 1807, and thereby the people recognized the *de facto* equality of the Jews. But Hart was unable to make use of his privilege, for the oath required of him contained the Christian formula, as was the case in England (p. 38, above). The conflict on this point lasted for a quarter of a century; finally a change in the formula was established by law and the bill was authorized by the king's signature in 1832. Since that time Jews have frequently been distinguished by election to parliament or to civic posts of honor. As in the world at large, individual Jews made great strides socially; in commerce and navigation and in the professions they achieved high standing. During the rebellion of 1837 many Jews fought as volunteers on the side of the government, and their courage and loyalty were expressly recognized. Individual Jews likewise made considerable contributions to the industrial development of the country.

In the early period the Sephardic congregation in Montreal, called Shearith Israel like its elder sister in New York, was the only Jewish organization. Its rabbi, Abraham de Sola (1825–1882), was at the same time professor of Semitic languages at McGill University and also had a deep interest in natural science. He effected the transition into the modern period; but, in contrast to the Reform tendencies in the United States, he supported the unconditional maintenance of tradition. Immigration proceeded slowly; in many places it began with individual Jews and in the course of time communities were formed. In 1845 the first synagogue was established in Toronto. In 1846 Jews from Poland attempted to organize in Montreal; but despite the assistance of the Sephardic congregation an independent Ashkenazic synagogue was not established until 1858. Communities were established in other places also, such as Quebec, Hamilton, Victoria, and elsewhere; but the Jewry of Canada as a whole was without significance before 1880. In 1863 the Young Men's Hebrew Benevolent Society was established in Montreal "with the object of assisting their needy or unfortunate coreligionists." In order to make sure that the management would devote its full attention to the affairs of the association it was provided that the association should remain "under the entire supervision and control of the young unmarried men of the city." This association did in fact become the nucleus for all Jewish social institutions in Canada and undertook important tasks as their need became apparent.

South Africa[28] is the British colony in the pioneering of which individual Jews cooperated actively, as the Sephardim of the sixteenth and seventeenth centuries had done in Brazil and the West Indies. What the English lacked in initiative was frequently supplied by the Jews. Details cannot here be given of the contributions of outstanding men of Jewish blood to the development of the Dominion, nor can their names be listed. But mention must be made, at all events, of Nathaniel Isaac, who was a very unusual phenomenon in Jewish life. In 1825, as a lad of seventeen, he ventured, as one of the "knights errant of Natal," into the realm of Tchaka, King and Protector of the Zulus, the cannibal Attila of South Africa. To save his life he was forced to fight for Tchaka and, in recognition of his success, he received the honorary title of *Tamboosa* ("the Brave Warrior"). In the course of his manifold adventures he investigated the country up and down and across, and his *Travels and Adventures in Eastern Africa* (1836) was long regarded a basic work. In 1828 he was solemnly named *Induna Incola*, or Principal Chief, of Natal by Tchaka and was granted valuable privileges and extensive land-holdings for himself and his heirs; Tchaka's successor, Dingaan, confirmed these grants without qualification. Isaac's petition to the British government to annex the territory was heeded only in 1843 after the author had despaired of British interest, had taken up new adventures, and had removed to the Gambia region in West Africa.

Jonas Bergtheil did pioneer work in establishing cotton plantations in Natal; he too could not persuade the British government to provide settlers. His plan to settle Jewish planters from his German homeland also miscarried, and he finally brought peasants from northwest Germany to cultivate the plantations. His memory survives as a colonizer and benefactor of the colony. He was deeply rooted in Judaism and was one of the founders and promoters of the Jewish community in Cape Town.

After 1820 several dozens of Jewish merchants gradually settled in the Cape Colony from Holland and Germany; they became pioneers of industrialization. The most outstanding were the brothers De Pass who had been settled in Cape Town since 1846. They were active in shipping, built docks, and controlled all coastwise shipping in the east and west of South Africa. They established the sealing and whaling industries as well as the fishing industry generally, and they built the first refrigerating plants in the country. They took up the cultivation of guano and the exploitation of the Panona copper mines. Later they laid out the sugar plantations in Natal, and a younger generation participated in the first gold mining in Kimberley. The brothers Mosenthal opened up gigantic possibilities for cattle breeding in Cape Colony and the Orange Free State. They settled their relatives, whom they brought from Hesse-Cassel, at various points in the country and put them in charge of collecting agencies for purchasing hides, which had brought the farmers no income until then. They promoted ostrich breeding and were the first to supply South African ostrich feathers to Europe. They were pioneers in the wool trade, and introduced Angora goats into the country. Enormous efforts and investments were required, but they did not give up until they had brought the first shipload of genuine Angora goats and had thereby given the farmer a prime animal for breeding purposes and the country an important article for export.

In religious matters, the Jews experienced all the diseases of infancy incident to colonial life. They lost many valuable people to the Christian missions; it was a rare exception that the distinguished jurist Simeon Jacobs (died 1883), who became judge of the Supreme Court, remained loyal to Judaism. Their numbers were few and they were without leaders, but most had a strong determination to remain loyal to Judaism. They wished to maintain public worship, and they united for prayer in private houses until they were in position to build synagogues. The first Jewish congregation, Tikvath Israel, was established in Cape Town in 1841 and acquired its own synagogue in 1849; it formed a focus for all the Jews scattered over the country. It was due to the energy of its leader, Benjamin Norden, that this congregation did not disintegrate because of internal and external difficulties. The Jews of Cape Colony and of the Orange Free State found their religious organizer in Rabbi Joel Rabinowitz (1859–1892), who established personal relations with them in difficult journeys over the broad land and gave them religious and humanitarian care. The diamond mines had scarcely begun to be worked and Jews to be attracted to Kimberley, when public worship was held on the High Holy Days, in 1869. In 1873 a congregation was formed and a synagogue erected in Kimberley.

In the Orange Free State, in Bloemfontain, it was Isaak Baumann, also from Hesse-Cassel, who, after 1871, gathered the Jews into his own house for worship. Baumann was a merchant, had won general esteem, and was elected mayor of his city. Transvaal was opened up and settled by Jews relatively late; the first public worship was held in Pretoria in 1876. The Barberton gold fields had attracted Jews as Kimberley had done, and after 1883 regular worship was held there also. Despite the contributions of the Jews and despite the biblical background of the Boers, the latter were bigoted and biased against the Jews.

In the development of Australia[29] also the Jews made their contribution. Montefiore, at the confluence of the Bell and McQuarrie Rivers in Wellington Valley, and Montefiore Hill in Adelaide (southern Australia) are reminders of the two brothers Jacob (1801–1895) and Joseph Barrow (1803–1893) Montefiore, who were among the pioneers in the settlement of the newest continent. Jacob, a member of the South Australian Colonization Association, submitted plans for systematic settlement and self-government to the government, and became a member of the first Board of Commissioners. He finally settled in Adelaide and there became one of the founders of the Jewish congregation (1840); he built a synagogue for this congregation, as he had built many churches for the Christian settlers. Joseph remained in New South Wales, where the brothers had started several very successful enterprises, among others extensive sheep breeding. Joseph was one of the founders of the Jewish congregation in Sydney (1833), where, indeed, Jews had settled long before and had laid out a cemetery. In 1837 Jacob Israel Levi (1819-1885), who called himself Montefiore also, after his mother, settled in Sydney. He was among the leading merchants, was director of the Bank of Australia for a long while, and, after 1857, member of the first Legislative Council of New South Wales. Even after his return to England (1876) he continued his connection with economic undertakings in Queensland.

Jews contributed to the development of the sugar and the lumber industry of the country in a smaller degree. They went to Ballarat (Victoria) with the gold miners. In 1853 public worship was held at the gold fields on the High Holy Days, and in 1855 a small synagogue was dedicated in Ballarat. In the uprising of the gold miners against the unjust distribution of concessions, the Jew, Charles Dyte, was among the leaders of the rebels; later he was mayor of Ballarat.

Pioneer work of a different character was done by Barnett Levy in Sydney. In 1828 he established the first theatrical company in Australia, and in 1833 built the Theatre Royal for it. At that time there still was little provision for the spiritual requirements of the Jews, there was as yet no synagogue, and worship was held at the invitation of private citizens in their own homes. Aaron Levi, who immigrated from England in 1831, became the first rabbi in Sydney. He, and later A. T. Boas (after 1871), who served as rabbi in Adelaide for fifty years, did much for the organization of Jewish life in Australia. An attempt to found a Jewish periodical, in 1842, was premature and failed. The settlers came mostly from the Ashkenazic synagogues of London, and that gave the Australian synagogues their character. The number of the Jewish inhabitants of Australia was always small; in 1881 there were 8,815 Jews, .4% of the population. About a fourth lived in Sydney,[30] where an active community life developed.

BOOK TWO

THE INTERNATIONAL OF HATE

CHAPTER I

Antisemitism[1] as a Political Movement

New Bases for Anti-Jewishness

TO most of the peoples of Europe democratic rights had come as a gift. They had done little to acquire the rights they possessed. They accommodated themselves to the outward forms of democracy, but had no real appreciation of its true character. They did not realize that only that people is worthy of freedom which strives to secure freedom for others. The Jews were the first to feel this anomaly, and they felt it most keenly. They had scarcely been granted equal rights when these same rights were put into question. As long as good-will, democracy, and humanity prevailed in Europe, everything seemed orderly and correct. But when ill-will, nationalism, and egoism gained dominion and baser instincts were aroused, men began to cry over the rights that had been granted the Jews as over spilt milk. Particularly if any toes were trodden on, the cry arose: *cherchez le Juif!* — no further cause need be sought. The Jews were a community without protection and so a convenient target for any attack.

When Pope Pius IX was irked by the diminishing prestige of the Catholic Church by reason of its loss of temporal power and by the opposition which the Vatican Council had met, he looked about for the opportunity for a counter-stroke. His rage fell upon Jewish journalists whose publications, he alleged, were obscene and slanderous and who gave currency to lies and reproaches against the Church. When the Protestant Pope, Richard Wagner,[2] sought an outlet for his resentment against

Meyerbeer, he shaped it into a campaign against "Judaism in Music," to which he charged corruption of culture, art and higher morality. When Bismarck's internal policies did not suit the reactionaries in Germany, they clamored that all of Germany's commercial and financial legislation had been devised by Jews for the benefit of Jews. Even William Ewart Gladstone, the English liberal parliamentary leader, could not refrain from connecting Disraeli's Turkish policy with his Jewish ancestry. Disraeli was different, and being different was an unpardonable crime even for the Earl of Beaconsfield who had created an empire for England!

The Jews were different:[3] different in appearance and in figure, different in habits and traditions. They were noticeable in their environment and excited more attention in the anonymity of a metropolis than in the intimacy of a village. They were different in their occupations; many callings were altogether without Jews, while Jews were very strongly represented in others, and particularly in such as had been newly developed and the importance of whose function remained a puzzle to the masses. They were different in their religious beliefs and institutions; they attended different houses of worship, celebrated different festivals, and prayed in a different language. They were different in their mental faculties and in their temperament; they lacked the calm security which permanence, privilege, and possession bestow. The law had indeed granted them equality such as they were, but the man in the street found their non-conformity striking and regarded them as aliens and inferiors. However much they assimilated themselves to their environment, however much they surrendered their identity or changed their faith, a certain otherness remained, and because of this quality they were looked upon as people deserving inferior rights.

After the Franco-German War of 1870–1871 nationalism[4] was raised to a guiding principle in European politics. In countries with mixed populations, particularly in those inhabited by Teutons, Magyars and Slavs, politics and economics were infused with a militant nationalism which excluded everyone who was different in blood, descent, or language. The very presence of the Jew was a disturbing element, and he was kept out of the national ranks even though he yearned to join them and was ready to offer supreme sacrifices for the national cause. His economic success was begrudged, even though he put his capacities fully at the service of the national economy; the merits of the stranger could never be recognized. Nationalism was held in check when retaliatory measures might be anticipated. But the Jews — being a scattered minority — were without the resource of a compact minority or the protection of a foreign power; and so no retaliatory measures need be feared when they were made the object of discrimination.

For periods of time the opposition might become dormant, but it was always latent and might be roused into action whenever opportunity offered. In Germany such opportunities did offer, as a result of religious conflicts and economic disillusionment. Bismarck's *Kulturkampf*, the age-old conflict between Church and State, was countered by the Catholics with a press campaign against the Jews.[5] The movement was represented as a Jewish attack upon the Christian religion, a subtle attempt thus being made to draw the Protestants into the lists. How misguided this agitation was became manifest some years later when the Catholic party of the Center gained certain successes in church politics and dropped the campaign against the Jews on the ground that Catholics, being themselves a religious minority, should not countenance religious hatred. The economic disillusionment was the result of the collapse of wild speculation which had infected German exchanges during the years of expanding industry;[6] countless people who had no legitimate business on the stock market were financially ruined. A number of Jewish names occurred among the financiers responsible for over-expansion; and so it was easy to represent the phenomenon as "the victory of Judaism over Germanism" — as if the poor, innocent Germans had not come to grief because they had skated on thin ice in an attempt to get rich quick!

These skirmishes would have had no serious consequences had not political propaganda[7] seized upon hatred of the Jews as a welcome weapon. The economic crisis which originated in international commerce spread gradually to agriculture, the trades and industry, and showed the necessity for some change in the economic policies of the German Empire. The Liberals refused their support, and so the new protective policy had to be carried through in opposition to liberalism. In order to draw voters from the Liberal ranks that party was discredited as being the exclusive domain of Jews and slaves of Jews. The masses could be won over by attacks upon Jews and so the campaign against liberalism was transformed into a campaign against the Jews. A "Jewish question" was created and made the object of popular agitation. Its spokesman was the court-preacher, Adolf Stöcker[8] of Berlin, a spellbinder with all the tricks of demagogy at his command. He desired to win the populace of Berlin back to Christianity; he desired particularly to reconcile workers to the State and to the Church. He founded the Christian Social Workers Party, but he used the party's mass meetings for base attacks against the Jews who were alleged to have become too influential and too arrogant.

Agitation against the Jews finally became an end in itself. In 1879 Stöcker's disciples formed The League of Antisemites,[9] which set as its task "the liberation of the German Fatherland from complete Judaization and the preservation of tolerable existence for the descendants of the original inhabitants." This formulation reveals an inferiority complex justified neither by the facts nor by the proportion of Jewish population. The example of Germany found imitators in other countries, where similar associations were formed.

Receptivity to the seed of hatred exceeded all expectations. It spread over most of the countries of Europe with the irresistible force of an epidemic. No one could have believed that these same regions had recently echoed with jubilant cries of liberty and equality. Emphasis upon the foreignness of Jews facilitated the spread of hatred. To lay too great weight upon differences in belief was not in accord with the spirit of the times, which demanded enlightenment and freedom of conscience. But the same end was attained by a circuitous route; the Jew, it was said, could not acquire a proper feeling of nationality as long as he remained a Jew: the old religious hatred was after all the decisive factor. Hatred was supported also by the doctrine of the racial[10] differentiation of the Jew as a Semite. Eugen Dühring, a turgid thinker, constructed a philosophy of racial hatred which did not spare Christianity, the offspring of Judaism. He postulated that the Jews were an inferior and depraved race, incapable of any creative work, but eager to share in corruption and destruction. Only total social ostracism could cope with the situation, according to Dühring; right and law were to be replaced by the natural instincts and lusts of gangsterism. Dühring's writings inspired Hitler's slogans.

But neither religious nor racial theories were adequate to incite the masses. The desired pitch of hysteria could be attained only by concrete arguments, and such were found in the economic situation. In the midst of a serious depression which created manifold dissatisfactions among farmers, artisans, workers, industrialists, small and middle-class merchants and officials, it was possible to point to the wealth of the Jews. Their large business establishments, their handsome houses, their elegantly clothed women, were undeniable and obvious facts well calculated to fan envy and to activate the masses. To represent Jewish prosperity as the exploitation of frugal people and as acquired by cunning and fraud, led to the inference that it was a public duty to protect the simple Aryans against the cleverer Jews.

Such demagoguery won numerous adherents. The antisemitic party's platform was a concoction of any kind of religious, racial, economic, social, political and other poisonous ingredients. It found fellow travelers among those who had had unfortunate experiences with individual Jews and found satisfaction for their resentment or vengefulness in agitation against all Jews. The Jewish question pervaded all spheres of life, not only politics and administration but also economics and society. Hatred of Jews poisoned public opinion; the antisemitic press constantly incited its readers against the Jews, and all who did not straightway submit to this agitation were branded as Jews or companions of Jews or slaves on the payroll of Jews. Even jurisprudence was not spared this influence. Though there were not many judges, at first, who accepted antisemitic assumptions and evaluations uncritically, it was nevertheless inevitable that the persistent rooting should confuse men's ideas.

And so there was formed a political party whose only program was to sow hatred and schism, to pursue with the means of democracy the completely undemocratic end of setting one part of a nation against another. Towards the solution of the pressing questions of the time, such as agriculture, capitalism, socialism, or imperialism, the antisemites had nothing to contribute. The diverse groups of which they were composed were frequently poles apart in their opinions on these basic problems, but they thrust their heads into the sands and looked upon the Jewish question as *the* social question;[11] they fought not against capitalism generally, but only against Jewish capitalism. Antisemitism was not a social but an antisocial movement, a demagogic attempt to ensnare those who might be concerned with social questions and to direct their attention away from actual, existing needs. Antisemitism has justly been called the socialism of the stupid.[12] By their Christian gestures and the impression they gave of drawing workers away from socialism and towards Throne and Altar, the antisemites secured the approbation of the parties of the Right who called themselves conservative. Politically-minded men were not seriously concerned about the antisemites, for though they alleged that their struggle was against revolution, their goal could be attained only by revolution and their agitation was inciting the greed of the masses. The antisemites, they knew, were playing with fire, but it was only the Jews that would be singed. Even among liberal-minded men there were only few who recognized that this agitation denied the very bases of constitutional life. The world required sixty years and the manifestation of mass brutality before it realized the power of destruction which its acquiescence had fostered.

To be sure, as a group and as individuals, the Jews offered points of attack.[13] They had their weaknesses and their failings. Their painful history had left marked traces on their bodies and in their souls, and the short breathing space of a few decades was not sufficient to efface these traces. But what group could dare proclaim its innocence and cast the first stone? Surely not the antisemites, for the level of morality upon which they stood was low indeed. They struggled, they said, on behalf of Christianity, but little Christian virtue was to be found among them, neither love, nor humility, nor truth.

They were heroes of falsification and self-righteousness, quick to perceive the mote in the eye of their neighbors — the slanders which the antisemites hurled at dissenting comrades were at least as strong as those against the Jews[14] — and blind to the beam in their own eye.

Never had a political party in any country possessed so many leaders whose actions were flagrant violations of the penal law. It was not merely that the exuberance of a political campaign carried them beyond the bounds of fairness; their proceedings were actually criminal and included such violations as perjury, embezzlement, assault, rape and the like. Lawlessness began with Stöcker[15] of whom the Superior Council of the Evangelical Church, as well as the courts, confirmed the charge that he had dealt cavalierly with the truth, and who was finally forced to retire from the arena because of an infamous political intrigue. It continued with Jules Guérin, the Don Quixote of Paris, whose frauds and cheats covered every crime in the calendar. It reached its climax with Ernest Schneider of Vienna, a true criminal type, the chiefs of whose party suspected that he was a paid *agent provocateur* and stool pigeon. The frauds perpetrated by this shadowy gentleman cannot be enumerated here. He occupies a unique place in the history of parliamentary procedure. As a member of Parliament he falsified the ballots under the very eyes of the presiding officer, and was consequently exposed in a public session. This same individual was able to misuse the parliamentary tribunal for many years for vicious attacks against the Jews and for instigating charges of ritual murder. It was no doubt because of the exemplary conduct of his life and his model educational techniques — he had to warn the public against his own son — that he was named school inspector for Lower Austria by the Christian Social Party. So little did antisemitism heed moral decency in the face of unscrupulous demagoguery.

Antisemitism became a business, and frequently a quite profitable one. One could establish a publishing house, issue a periodical, brochures, or picture-books, and find a rich profit in revelations about the Jews if only they were sensational enough; and inasmuch as defamation of a group is a crime rarely prosecuted, one could count on carrying on with impunity. If a man were successful and attained a seat in parliament, he could utter any slander he liked under the protection of parliamentary immunity, and use the printed report for exploitation; or he might be rewarded with some official post. Small wonder that adventurers found their way into the party, with the hope of mending their fortunes. Things came to such a pass that Wilhelm Marr, the father of the movement in Germany, turned from the "crew" with a "loathing amounting to nausea." "Modern antisemitism," he wrote in 1891, "manufactured and packaged antisemitism of bogus quality, has become, for me, utterly futile. It deceives itself, only to deceive and swindle others."

Although the antisemites styled themselves the advance guard of nationalism, their hearts were quickly united with those of their comrades-in-hatred in other countries. In September 1882, they were able to hold the first International Anti-Jewish Congress in Dresden;[16] it was presided over by Stöcker, and the demagoguery of the Hungarian deputy, Géza von Onody, set the tone. This gentleman exploited the murder case of Tisza-Eszlár (see p. 155, below), which had been instigated under his aegis. His countryman, Victor von Istoczy, offered a proclamation to governments and peoples, warning them against the Jewish peril. The Congress was careful not to publish its conclusions; it was learned only that the Jews were to retain their rights as citizens, but were not to have access to state, judicial, or teaching positions, and that their activities on the money markets were to be limited.

There was also an appeal for a boycott against the Jews. The sum of the conclusions was an appeal for the restoration of the "Christian State."

The weapons which antisemitism employed were chiefly lies and defamation. No other movement ever perpetrated so many falsifications or circulated them so unscrupulously. Fantastic fables[17] on the proportion of Jews in the population and their rate of increase and on their influence on the press and the money market were given circulation. The misuse of criminal statistics to prove that the Jews were an asocial element was an old device. Exaggerations were followed by generalizations.[18] The Jews were regarded not as individuals, but collectively. The antisemites refused to see that Jews differed among themselves, that they varied according to their origin and temper, according to their education and culture. Objectionable utterances or actions of individual Jews were generalized, and all Jews, present and past, were held responsible. There was no need to investigate; "in any case," the old saying had it, "the Jew will be burned." If the consequences had not been so deplorable, the Jews might have prided themselves upon being the only community in the world of whom absolute perfection was expected — a peculiar application of the notion of the Chosen People, otherwise so objectionable to non-Jews. Any offense, let alone crime, committed by one of their number was followed by relentless vengeance upon all the Jews. Even in circles whose attitude to the Jews was not one of hatred, the oddest notions concerning what the Jews did and aimed to do, concerning their solidarity and their financial power, prevailed. The prejudices which had been handed down for centuries were deeply rooted and were strengthened by constant repetition.

An annoying phenomenon paralleling antisemitism was a patronizing "philosemitism." The philosemites chose individual Jews or groups of Jews as objects of their esteem, and sang their praises loudly; in doing so they showed how far they were from recognizing the fundamental equality of the Jews as a whole. After the outbreak of antisemitism, his Christian friends sought to comfort Berthold Auerbach by saying, "If only all the Jews were like you!" Auerbach would reply, "Are all Christians like me?" But self-knowledge was rare; every Christian believed himself the superior of the Jew and entitled to pass judgment upon him. The Jewish question was a Christian question, a question of justice, truth, and good faith of the Christians.

Antisemitism created an elaborate Jewish myth,[19] for which, consciously or unconsciously, it falsified the facts. Everything pertaining to Jews, from their physical appearance to their thoughts and conduct, was represented as being repulsive and unwholesome. Not only individual Jews but their entire body were represented as bent solely upon injuring non-Jews. Whatever was disagreeable or distressing in the contemporary world, in art, literature, economics, politics, was debited to the account of the Jews, as if there would have been neither materialism nor positivism nor naturalism but for the Jews, as if, but for the Jews, the world would have been in a blessed state of uncorrupted innocence. All the dangerous thoughts which the diseased and criminal brains of the antisemites could invent were ascribed to the Jews, although not one of them had uttered such thoughts.[20] Antisemitism made no conscience of bribing false witnesses, or suborning perjury, or of forging documents to prove alleged Jewish crimes before courts of law. A favorite theme was the world-conspiracy of the Jews, of which the *Alliance Israélite Universelle* was supposed to be the embodiment. The activities of the *Alliance* were carried on openly before the eyes of the whole world; their reports were printed; their financial weakness was common knowledge; but why should an antisemite trouble about the truth? Such forgeries as supposititious appeals and circular letters of the *Alliance*, addresses of its president Crémieux or admonitions of rabbis were fabricated and circulated. Even when the deception was revealed, the masses who had been excited by such slander never learned the truth, and for decades these forgeries could be made to pass current, first in one country and then in another. "A bold lie, if big enough, is likely to gain credence by its very bigness," so wrote, at a later date, the great master of the antisemitic lie, and no one has understood the psychology of the masses better than he.

The Talmud on Trial

As star witness for its assumptions regarding the moral teachings of Judaism, antisemitism called the Talmud[21] into the witness box. Alleged quotations from the Talmud and other rabbinic writings were tossed off in edition after edition, circulated in the periodical press, read out in courts of law and from parliamentary tribunals, as if their accuracy were demonstrated beyond question. The quotations were all derived from a book called *Der Talmudjude*, written in 1871 by Dr. August Rohling, Professor of Theology at Münster. Tens of thousands of copies were distributed gratis at the time of the Catholic incitements (see p. 143, above), and the pamphlet was repeatedly reprinted. To be sure, not only Jews but also Christian scholars, such as the distinguished Lutheran theologian, Franz Delitzsch, demonstrated clearly that Rohling was totally ignorant of his subject matter, that his citations were plagiarisms which he had frequently misunderstood or misrepresented. But in the meantime Rohling had been called as Professor of Hebrew Antiquities to the University of Prague; and when he repeated his charges he made reference to his oath of office to increase his credit. Things went so far that passages out of Rohling were read in courts of justice as authentic citations out of the Talmud; and even Jews declared openly that they were ashamed of being Jews if ethical teachings of such a character were contained in a basic book of Judaism. "After Rohling's appearance the Talmud became a common subject of conversation, in cafés, at bars, in public houses, at club meetings, and at popular gatherings; numberless broadsides and brochures about the Talmud or against the Talmud flooded the book market and were disseminated gratis in the humblest laborer's cottage." So reported Josef Samuel Bloch, rabbi at the time in Florisdorf near Vienna, the man who won the distinction of unmasking Rohling.

In an article which appeared in a widely read Viennese newspaper, Bloch showed that Rohling was equipped neither morally nor in scholarship to engage in criticism of the Talmud. By examples which were clear even to the man in the street Bloch proved that Rohling lacked the slightest basis of knowledge to justify him in pronouncing expert opinions upon the Talmud. When Rohling made bold to reply, Bloch offered a forfeit if Rohling showed that he could read correctly any page in the Talmud that he might choose and translate it accurately. With so little actual knowledge did he credit the bumptious "scholar."

This polemic made a deep impression in the scholarly world and in the public mind; but it did not prevent Rohling from offering his testimony in three cases involving ritual murder[22] which were in the air at the time (see p. 170, below). He offered to confirm upon oath that the use of Christian blood was not only allowed to the Jews by their religious writings but even commanded. But this time Rohling's fate overtook him. Franz Delitzsch branded his conjectures a clumsy fabrication, compact of ignorance and malice. "The man," he wrote, "is in a diseased condition of delirium and subject to its delusions." The Roman Catholic Bishop of Leitmeritz stigmatized his calumnies as infamous lies and audacious deceptions.

Rohling again found his master in Bloch, who wrote in a Viennese daily that Rohling practiced lying as a trade and that he had offered to perjure himself. Rohling was a professor and thus an official of the imperial and royal state; he could not allow the charge to stand unchallenged. On August 10, 1883, he entered a charge of defamation against Bloch at the district court in Vienna. Bloch had meanwhile been elected deputy to the Austrian Parliament (*Reichsrat*), but he insisted that parliament rescind his immunity and permit the investigation of the charge. He desired an opportunity to demonstrate Rohling's total ignorance and his moral insanity in the public procedure of a court of law. In association with a well known Christian lawyer, Bloch had been preparing his material for a year, and he submitted the opinions of recognized Christian scholars to the court. The whole world waited for the sensational public trial, which was to begin November 19, 1885, last for two weeks, and bring complete clarity to a universally vexatious question. But the world received an even greater sensation. One month before the date fixed for the trial Rohling withdrew his complaint. This priest and censor of morality, who had given opinions upon the Talmud under oath and had offered to furnish new testimony hostile to the Jews, did not dare attempt even the slightest judicial defense of his honor; he accepted the imputation of perjury and remained silent! Before the bar of public opinion of Europe he stood condemned; it was he that had condemned himself. But antisemites are concerned with neither morality nor truth. Rohling's cowardly retreat does not prevent them from using his fraudulent material as established truth to this day.

Ritual Murder Falsehoods

The most powerful weapon in the arsenal of antisemitism was the accusation of ritual murder.[23] The charge was connected with similar fabrications in the Middle Ages, and alleged that the Jewish religion required that Christian boys be slain and their blood used in baking *mazzot*. The myth could be altered according to need. Thus Rohling had offered to swear that the Jewish religion required the slaughter of a pure Christian virgin as pleasing to God; on another occasion he made it a grown young man. As for the purpose of this crime, various versions, alike insane, were in circulation. In culturally backward regions the Jews were in terror each spring at the Easter season, even where there was no organized antisemitism, lest the charge of a child murder be raised against them. Antisemitism prosecuted this agitation as a piece of political business. In the two decades between 1880 and 1900 it staged a number of sensational charges in Austria-Hungary and Germany; their purpose was to make it impossible for the Jews to live as a group in modern society.

In Tisza-Eszlár,[24] a small Hungarian village on the Theiss, on the Sabbath before Easter, April 1, 1882, a fourteen-year-old girl, Esther Solymosi by name, disappeared. No trace of her could be discovered, but it was the Easter season and she had last been seen in the vicinity of the synagogue, and that was sufficient to spread the rumor that she had been done to death in the synagogue by several slaughterers from another place who were there present, that her blood had been drained, that the body had then been dismembered and buried. Local police and court officers conducted the investigation with this in mind, but could not find the slightest basis for establishing guilt. The support of the charge was the twelve-year-old son of the janitor of the synagogue, Scharf. He recounted all the details of the procedure with the greatest minuteness: peeping through the keyhole of the locked synagogue he claimed to have seen the gruesome business of the binding, the slaughter, the draining of the blood, and the disposition of the members of the body.

The excitement against the Jews which raged in all the villages of Central Europe when the papers reported the news is scarcely imaginable today. Hungary was a country which had granted the Jews full equality, whose government was well disposed towards them, whose population generally lived amicably with them; and now they had committed so horrifying a crime that a son gave testimony of it against his own father, against his whole religious communion. The fact, not immediately known, was that the boy had had his story crammed into him by certain criminal officials whose "favorite" he was, by blows and threats, later by promises and hopes; he recited his story parrot fashion, but upon cross-examination lost the thread and involved himself in contradictions. Cross-examined on the spot he clearly proved himself to be completely false. His testimony dominated the investigation. New witnesses turned up, and from one hearing to the next they had more to tell; but they had nothing to contribute towards clarifying the case or discovering the remains of the body.

Seventy-nine days after the disappearance of Esther Solymosi the current of the Theiss deposited a corpse upon the shore. The body was in an advanced state of decay, but everything indicated its identity with the missing girl, particularly the fact that the clothing was proven to be that which the missing girl had worn. But public opinion was now so poisoned that the medical experts on the spot bluntly declared that the corpse was a stranger's and that it had been dressed in the clothing of Esther Solymosi. And now a new act of the tragedy began. Jewish river men were accused of body snatching, and, to further a miscarriage of justice, a whole web of lies was constructed to prove their guilt. But despite brutality and torture no confession could be wrung from the principal defendant. The others had made confessions under torture but had later revoked them and had involved themselves in contradictions of a character which made it impossible to maintain the charge. Finally the experts of the University of Budapest declared that the whole theory of body snatching was untenable from the medical point of view. Nevertheless the investigation was dragged on for fourteen months; evidence was sought by means of brutal coercion. About eighty Jews, the greater number of whom were later released as innocent, were imprisoned. Finally the case was called, and for six weeks (June 19—August 3, 1883) it was tried, with the greatest thoroughness and under the terror of antisemitic agitators. At the end the state's attorney declared that the charges could not be maintained, and the court pronounced an unqualified acquittal.

The trial of Tisza-Eszlár showed with frightening clarity the abysmal depths to which antisemitic agitation could lead a democratic state. No trace of a body could be found, no drop of blood, no tangible basis for suspicion. Yet someone had mentioned the blood-myth, "that absurd abortion of medieval superstition," as the state's attorney called it in his pleading, and this sufficed to direct the entire investigation along that dismal track. The delays, perversities, illegalities of the officials conducting the investigation were beyond number. They were completely under the control of irresponsible, cunning and unscrupulous stage-managers, who presented a drama of evil and guilt and organized a regime of terror. From month to month the number of those allegedly informed on the matter grew; from month to month the extent of their knowledge likewise grew. The witnesses cannot even be charged with conscious perjury, for they stood under the twofold domination of suggestion and terror. But those that pulled the wires, the antisemitic journalists and deputies, were perfectly conscious of their wicked means and criminal goal. They not only controlled the preliminary investigation and attempted to reduce the defense to silence, but they exercised their terror in the trial and made every effort to bend the judges to their will and to destroy all Jewry along with those who happened to be incriminated. They made the whole proceedings, as their spokesman tastefully expressed it, a struggle of "the slaughterer's knife against the cross." Their enterprise was a crusade against Judaism, and in such a crusade no regard need be had for justice and truth; false testimony might be given without fear of sin. How different was the attitude of Friedmann, the Jewish advocate! After their acquittal he admonished the defendants, who had suffered grievously despite their innocence, to cherish anger or vengeance against no one.

The case at Tisza-Eszlár is typical for all later trials for ritual murder. Later trials differed chiefly in that the discovery of a body was usually the occasion for the charge. Scarcely would a body be found under strange circumstances than irresponsible elements would rush in, seize the threads of the investigation, fan agitation among the populace, and by mobilizing public opinion exert pressure upon justice. Every such case was a martyrdom for the professional guardians of the law, for even though they might be susceptible to the suggestion of antisemitism, they yet retained a remnant of the consciousness of legality which rebelled at the complete prostitution of justice. They were exposed to a drumfire of attack and a variety of evidence.

In these cases excitement and consequently suggestibility reach their highest level; passions are whipped up as they never are in quiet periods. Suggestion is expressed in far-reaching and dangerous symptoms. The trials for ritual murder become a special category in criminal psychology.[25]

Fantasies derived from popular superstition and propaganda determined the character of the testimony; their outlines became firmer and more distinctly visible, and in the course of time acquired many new details. Months after the event, witnesses would appear who wished to testify, under oath, upon decisive points which they had, strangely enough, never before reported, and whose truth, indeed, they could never maintain under any sort of cross-examination.

It is impossible to gauge the moral damage which was done by the ritual murder lie. The chief sufferers were the Jews, who were put into the prisoner's box as a people, and were baselessly heaped with the gravest reproaches. The regions in which the agitators had roosted were poisoned with the bane of hatred. The Jews who had enjoyed amicable relations with their neighbors were intimidated, and threats and actual attacks made it necessary for many of them to leave their homes. Their lives were imperilled, their security as human beings was shattered. But they were not the only sufferers. The foundations of justice, of order, and of security were undermined in those communities. Every such trial was accompanied by violence against the Jews and destruction of their property. Loyalty and faith suffered lasting injury, for the populace had been trained to testify to untruth and to confirm it under oath.

CHAPTER II

Antisemitism in Western Europe

The Anti-Social Movement in Germany

IT HAS been said that every country has the Jews it deserves. It may be said with equal truth that every country has the antisemites it deserves. Or more precisely, in every country antisemitism has taken on a special form, corresponding to the cultural, economic and political structure of the country.

In Germany, where organized antisemitism first appeared, the government was so strong that the movement could not have arisen without its connivance, and Stöcker's agitation came very opportunely for the ministry of the reaction after 1878. Bismarck[1] was too shrewd a tactician not to take advantage of an ally who was also eager to break the power of the parties of the left; but at the same time he was too far-seeing a statesman not to recognize the inconsistency of the antisemitic agitation and the incompatibility of antisemitic demands with constitutional government. He expressed his views on the subject repeatedly, directly and indirectly. He made no response to the formal demands of the antisemites, and the more rabid among them made him feel the full force of their hatred. Kaiser William I, though he did not go as far as the crown prince, later Frederick III, who designated antisemitism the disgrace of the age, nevertheless did conform to the old Prussian tradition, and would brook no disturbance of the established order. In Stöcker's demagoguery, in his incendiary attacks on the wealth of individual Jews, the Kaiser saw a danger to public security and the possibility of incitement to violence.

Disturbances[2] did in fact take place. Stöcker's henchmen proceeded with their irresponsible Jew-baiting and appealed to the base instincts of the people. "The Philistine," said Bismarck, "is troubled by phrases and falsehoods;" he found himself suddenly concerned with all manner of problems relating to Jews, whose existence he had previously not noticed or had taken for granted. In the larger cities Jews were mobbed on the street or in taverns and when they showed resentment they sometimes met with actual violence. In provincial towns, where the crowd was more inflammable, the stage of violence was reached more quickly. In Ostelbien excesses were perpetrated against several of the small Jewish communities. Neustettin[3] in Pomerania attained a deplorable distinction. Its antisemitic champions not only produced a regular pogrom, but hired an incendiary to set the synagogue on fire and then charged the Jews with the crime.

The decent part of the population had their eyes opened by these brutalities. In Berlin, immediately after Stöcker's first appearance, seventy-five of the most respected citizens[4] voiced a sharp protest against this reversion to barbarism, and notables of other large cities joined with them. Now men could see to what dismal consequences the new movement might lead, and the Russian pogroms (see p. 202, below) furnished a further sample of their eventual results. Lawlessness of this kind was abhorrent to temperate citizens. The police took vigorous measures at all points, and maintained general calm and security. The assault of antisemitism was repulsed and the movement collapsed by its own disruptive force.

But this did not mean that militant hatred of Jews was crushed. The young German Empire was subject to all the diseases of infancy, and the "better citizens" quickly arrived at a diagnosis of the infection which caused all social unrest. "The Jews are our misfortune:" such was the verdict spread abroad by the historian Heinrich von Treitschke,[5] one of their most respected spokesmen. Jew-baiting he explained as a "natural reaction of the German folk-feeling against an alien element." He belonged, indeed, to the older liberals and declared that "the abrogation or limitation of complete emancipation is manifestly unjust," but he demanded that the Jews earn their equal rights, that they become Germans. Every last man of them must prove his worth.

This in itself constituted a limitation on the principle of equal rights. The governments of various German states[6] put Treitschke's maxims into practice by barring Jews from appointments as judges, state officials, and teachers of all grades, by excluding them completely from the active officers corps and admitting them as reserve officers only in the most exceptional cases. Even such posts as those of honorary magistrates and jurors and the like were denied them. Immigration of foreign Jews was limited, and special legislation of a rigorous character was applied to foreign Jews resident in Germany. The protection granted to the Christian religion, its doctrines, symbols, and scriptures, was denied to the Jewish religion. Those in charge permitted a coarsening of tone in the schools, allowed textbooks which propagated hatred against Jews, but granted to the antisemites the right of examining the moral content of textbooks used for instruction in Jewish religion. In general the Jews were made to feel that they were regarded as an inferior estate.

Equality of rights was not abrogated, but administrative procedure nullified the principle. The proof of their worth which the Jews were expected to demonstrate turned out to be mainly conversion[7] undergone for this specific purpose, and therefore essentially unworthy. The consequence of the policy was continual disquiet punctuated by constant pin-pricks. The nervous stability of the Jews was sorely tried.

The test of worth was applied also by "society," which excluded Jews from social organizations and from social intercourse generally. In the forefront of this exclusive attitude were the associations of German students,[8] which accepted members only of pure Aryan extraction and German mother-tongue; and these associations set the mark for other organizations which were unwilling to appear less concerned for German nationalism. In the universities the theory of the inferiority of Semites was presented in the various disciplines and was made to refer especially to contemporary Jews. The domestic bible of the young students was the *Deutsche Schriften* of the famous linguist Paul de Laguarde,[9] whose ideal was the creation of a German Christianity. This led him to sharp attacks on Jewish monotheism, and this led him, in turn, to deny any originality and genius to the Jewish spirit, any profound religious or moral striving to the Jewish soul. This was the spirit in which future judges and teachers, state officials and officers, bank managers and manufacturers were trained, and one can easily imagine how such education influenced their subsequent conduct of affairs.

We can see then how the state officials lent a certain countenance to the manifestations of antisemitism in social and business life, so that it spread over the entire Empire. Numerous periodicals, broadsides, and brochures, crammed with insults and slander, proclaimed the inferiority of the Jews and Judaism, of Jewish morality and Jewish writings, and stressed their danger to the state. On one pretext or another, judges[10] refused to call the authors to account. The Jews were humbled, dishonored, and defenseless. No wonder that young Jews were attracted by the parties of the opposition. When they joined the Social Democrats, at that time everywhere in Europe considered a subversive group, this act of self-defense aroused new indignation.[11]

And so the antisemites saw their aim attained even though their party was in eclipse. Stöcker[12] had high hopes for the young and impulsive Emperor, William II, who as prince had shown interest in his social work; but a declaration of the monarch in 1889 quickly undeceived him. Among the general population also there were strong groups who deplored Jew-baiting. The Catholic authorities were quick to point out whither religious intolerance might lead. Similarly the Social Democratic Party, whose thunder antisemitism had tried to steal, declared itself against all forms of racial and religious hatred. Thanks to these two groups the antisemites were unsuccessful in making pogroms or securing the parliamentary measures they desired. The Conservative Party, which had the strongest influence in the administration, did countenance suppression of the Jews, but was opposed to the excesses of antisemitism. And finally, the liberals were not all extinct; some remained even in the ranks of the Right who were anxious for the future of justice and political morality if the Jew-baiting should continue unrestrained. "When bad men combine, the good must unite." In 1891, five hundred Christian representatives of the élite of every rank and profession combined to establish an Association for Warding off Antisemitism.[13] By publishing a periodical and by issuing a *Mirror of Antisemites*, it threw light into the dark corners of the movement. It did not reach the masses, but men of good will could inform themselves if they so desired. Needless to say, the opponents of antisemitism were stigmatized as slaves of the Jews.

How great was the need for such a defensive movement was shown in the summer of 1891, when the antisemites resurrected the myth of ritual murder. In Xanten[14] on the Lower Rhine, where Jews had resided from time immemorial, a five-year-old child was found dead with his throat cut, and the slaughterer, Buschhoff, who had been a beloved figure in the city, was accused of the murder. Investigation brought to light no slightest evidence of his guilt, and he and his family were released from imprisonment. But now press, public meetings and parliament resounded with tom-toms against Prussian justice, and under the pressure of public opinion Buschhoff was again arrested and formally charged with ritual murder. After thoroughgoing investigation and detailed examination the prosecuting attorney himself recommended the release of the defendant, for no evidence of any kind could be found against him. But the fury of the people had been whipped up to such a pitch that the Jewish inhabitants of the surrounding countryside had to leave. A measure of calm was restored only when Bishop (later Cardinal) Fischer of Cologne stirred the people's conscience.

The period was characterized by social unrest generally, and furnished a favorable field for demagogues. In 1893 the antisemites elected sixteen representatives to the Reichstag, mostly from Saxony, where there were almost no Jews, and Hesse, where the peasants thought they had cause for complaint. It is needless to indicate what shining opportunities their office provided to travel up and down the country gratis, to deliver incendiary speeches from the floor of the House under the protection of parliamentary immunity, and to make their sweeping demands. But their new hero, Hermann Ahlwardt, so degraded the level of agitation, that even party members felt uneasy and the people became disgusted with his coarseness. A kind of substitute was provided by the influential Farmer's League (*Bund der Landwirte*), which blamed the Jews for the depression in agriculture and advocated a boycott against them. The principal sufferers from these activities were the middle-class Jews in the towns and villages. They were unable to maintain their position and were forced to migrate to the larger cities, where they surrendered their economic independence and swelled the ranks of the proletariat. The Jewish wholesale merchant or banker, against whom the antisemites professed to direct their campaign, was not deeply affected; the social position of the Jews in the big cities remained almost untouched.

The feverish heat of political passion cooled gradually. The German people turned to fortifying its position in world politics, and the Jewish problem retired into the background. In the conquests of world markets[15] Jewish representatives of trade and industry participated to an outstanding degree: one need think only of the far-seeing vision of Emil Rathenau and Albert Ballin. As the prosperity of the German people increased, that of the Jews increased with it. The Jewish merchant and the Jewish scholar enjoyed the high esteem of his colleagues. His ready cooperation could always be counted on in the support of cultural plans. The struggle of creative spirits to find new expression in poetry and fine arts, or in a new philosophy of life, met with a lively response and willing help in Jewish circles. Inevitably they assisted some decadent artists, too; but many a promising poet or painter, at first rejected by public opinion, found a Jewish Maecenas who supported him during crucial times. Max Liebermann (1847–1935) became one of the pioneers and, for almost two generations, the leader of impressionist painting in Germany. Otto Brahm (1856–1912), the ardent champion of social naturalism in drama, inaugurated a new period in Germany's theatrical production. Only when the Jew knocked at the gates of the state did he find the doors shut — or rather he was shown to a back door, the baptismal font, through which he might gain entry. Liberal Protestantism[16] at the end of the century regarded dogmatic differences as trivial; it emphasized the ethical loftiness of Christianity and its superiority over Judaism. There were plenty of Jews, and some of considerable spiritual stature, who allowed themselves to be lured by the prospects of a brilliant career, without realizing what a frivolous mockery of religion and ethics was involved. A considerable part of the theologic and philosophic literature of the day had a decided anti-Jewish tendency, while the Jews lacked any competent champion of adequate proportions.

Church and state sought to draw the Jews by gentle bonds and to bring the children, at least, if not the adults, to baptism. But the nationalistic movement severed all relationships with Judaism. Houston Stewart Chamberlain, Richard Wagner's son-in-law, in his *Foundation of the Nineteenth Century*, carried Gobineau's race theory to the extreme. He emphatically claimed that the Nordic peoples, and especially the Germans, were the master race of the world, the creative initiators of everything which is perfect in the realm of the great, the good and the beautiful. He gave credit to that part of Christian culture which he claimed as Aryan, while he proclaimed a crusade against all Jews whom he cast out as the bitterest enemies of the Germanic and the Christian spirit. The book is so biased that even the champions of racialism declared it dilettantish. But the façade was so attractive, the role ascribed to the German race so flattering that William II hailed it as a classic. For several years it was a best seller and spread the virus of racialist contagion among the cultured classes.

This narrow intolerance expressed itself not only in the printed word but occasionally even in violence. In 1900, in Konitz, West Prussia, the mangled body of a sixteen-year-old high school student was found. Evidence led to a definite clue, later corroborated by the opinion of the highest medical authorities. But the clue was not followed up, for the secret justice of the antisemites under the leadership of its boldest agitators worked up a feverish activity to create the suspicion of a Jewish ritual murder. The attempt failed because no evidence was available, but it did succeed in setting the populace in commotion so that martial law was proclaimed and the military had to be called in to restore order. The energy of the Prussian ministry showed the antisemites that the time for their orgies was past.

NATIONALISM AND ANTISEMITISM IN THE AUSTRIAN EMPIRE

Austrian politics were completely controlled by the struggle of the various nationalities. The Jewish delegates and the Jewish electorate, with decreasing exceptions, adhered to the constitutional party,[17] which advocated centralization and the hegemony of the Germans. When Count Taaffe attempted to rule on federalist principles, the reactionary part of his program was rejected and the nationalist part regarded as a personal affront. The tragedy of it was that the Slavic nationalities hated the Jews because they would not join them, and the Germans hated them because they *wished* to join them. The wavering of the government resulted in the crystallization of the German national movement. Its program was outlined by two Jews, but it was immediately so extended that it preached a clear-cut race hatred and stopped neither at popular incitement nor actual violence. The Christian Social Party, led by the clergy, vied with the German nationalists for popular favor. In the beginning the episcopacy rejected antisemitism and declared it contrary to the teaching of the Church; but this rejection was later withdrawn when the secular leaders of the party received support directly from Rome. And now the party adopted an outspoken and unscrupulous antisemitism[18] everywhere in Austria, but especially in Vienna. The once liberal capital fell victim to clerical antisemitism.

In the east of Europe Vienna occupied the position that Paris occupied in the west. It was the center of science and art, of theater and music, of culture and refinement. In this life of the spirit the Jews took a considerable part,[19] far greater than their relative numbers would lead one to expect. This was one aspect of Vienna, the aristocratic aspect. There was another, that of the little man, troubled and burdened. And here, too, the Jews had their full share, not less deplorable than the Aryans' who were being incited against them. The antisemitic agitators represented their campaign as directed against the "powerful" Jews who were alleged to control the entire Austrian economy; but it was the small and poor Jews who had to pay the score. In the beginning of the movement it might have been possible to obtain governmental protection. But Jews of position refused to negotiate with Count Taaffe, and the government acted as if it were completely oblivious to the situation, even when Emperor Francis Joseph repeatedly expressed his sharp dissatisfaction with "Vienna's disgrace."

Viennese antisemitism was from its inception disorderly, brawling, unreasoning, and dependent chiefly on mob agitation; the demagogues understood how crowds were to be swayed. The movement hesitated at neither slander nor filth. Their texture of lies and deceptions, woven by the clergy no less than by the laity, form a dreary volume in human history. Of the noisier antisemites most might have occupied a distinguished place in any rogue's gallery; one need only read the abuse which they dealt out to one another to be convinced of the quality of their human mercy. But the masses were carried away by the torrent of their unscrupulous assaults and followed them through thick and thin. In the Austrian parliament, which had lost much of its dignity in consequence of the struggles between the nationalities, the level was further reduced by the antisemites to that of the street and the public house.[20] In the parliament, to be sure, a fighter against antisemitism was found in the person of Dr. Joseph Samuel Bloch, who had passed from defensive to offensive and who uncovered the abysmal ignorance and moral insensibility of the antisemites. The august assemblage tittered with pleasure when his head and body blows found their mark. But the masses heard nothing of the discomfiture of their chieftains. The amiable atmosphere of Vienna was soon tainted by an element of crudeness which stopped at nothing. The deputy Schneider went so far as to propose a prize for hunting Jews.

Hatred of Jews was prevalent everywhere, in offices and shops, in taverns and theaters. Churches and schools were breeding-stations of this hatred. School children were guilty of coarse cruelties against their Jewish fellows, and university students believed they possessed a license for such exercises. Forged "citations" from the Talmud were brought into play as alleged "secret lore," and docile disciples, male and female, from the lower classes concocted astounding charges against their Jewish employers. A Viennese pastor even fabricated a letter in which a Jewish convert gave an eye-witness account of a ritual murder in which he had himself allegedly participated; at a trial he was absolutely unable to offer any exculpation of his action.

These tactics seemed justified by their success. The impoverished middle classes joined the Christian Socialist Party in great numbers, and so helped them attain a majority in the Vienna Communal Council and in the Austrian *Landtag*. The party possessed a remarkably clever leader in Dr. Karl Lueger[21] who began his political career with the aid of democrats and of Jewish friends. Lueger quickly scented "the dawn" and put his talents at the disposal of the rising sun of the opposition. He had no convictions, not even hatred of the Jews; he had a single goal, and that was to become mayor of Vienna; and any means that brought him nearer his goal were to him justifiable. He had the completest understanding of the psyche of the little man. He himself remained a little man even after he had attained the pedestal for which he had yearned. His speeches were filled with commonplaces, but of whatever he spoke he always returned to the Jews — and always carried his listeners with him. It was from him that Adolf Hitler as a youth learned the demagogic art of handling crowds. Personally he was not self-seeking, but he knew of the knaveries of his followers and allowed and even excused them. When he finally did attain his heart's desire and was elected mayor of Vienna, the Emperor refused to confirm the demagogue in this office. The populace insisted upon its choice and even threatened disturbances; and after the fifth election, in 1897, confirmation could no longer be withheld. As mayor Lueger was concerned with administration, and he attempted to moderate the cruder aspects of the movement. That the new regime in the Viennese town hall had evil consequences for the Jews need hardly be emphasized. Appointments of Jews and business contracts with them were rescinded. Police regulation of tradesmen and peddlers were manipulated to the disadvantage of Jews, and it was the less prosperous and the quite poor Jews who suffered. In the school administration also, which was in any case retrograde, efforts were made to impose disabilities, and there was an inclination to bar Jewish pupils from the general schools altogether.

This policy was a symptom of a tendency prevalent in the monarchy.[22] The parliament (*Reichsrat*) worked towards an increasing limitation of freedom of trade and for the restoration of the old guild regulations. The aim was the improvement of the middle classes, but it could not be achieved by such measures, for the new economy could no longer tolerate their antiquated regulations. The attitude of the officials was such that there could be no question of carrying out the principle of Jewish equality. In public administration and in judicial posts Jews seldom reached beyond the lowest rung unless they had been baptized. It was different in the army,[23] where the decision on advancement lay with the Emperor. His strong sense of justice took care that no Jew was passed over merely because he was a Jew, and so in the Austrian army and navy some few Jews advanced to the rank of general or admiral. Another field in which Jews attained high position was that of scholarly research. The University of Vienna[24] had Jews of world-wide reputation in all its faculties. They were especially numerous in the Faculty of Medicine; and indeed cretins of the Christian Socialist Party kept up an incessant howl against these distinguished scientists. The memorial tablets and monuments in the court of honor of the University are sufficiently eloquent.

The Sudeten[25] people could not be less enlightened than the Austrians, though they owed no small part of their economic upsurge to Jewish initiative. From time to time the charge of ritual murder bobbed up, and in one district after another led to such excesses against the Jews that the officials were forced to intervene to restore order. The struggle between the component nationalities also tended to crush the Jews between the upper and nether millstones. The Czechs, particularly the militant Young-Czechs, could not forgive the Jews their association with the Germans, although by the end of the century 58% of the Jews in Bohemia designated themselves as Czechs, and there was an active Association for Czech-Jewish Understanding. The Germans, on the other hand, regarded it as part of their national obligation to attack the Jews, although the most active and influential section of the Jewish population supported their demands.

Czechs and Germans combined forces in 1899 to frame a charge of ritual murder against Leopold Hilsner,[26] a half-witted cobbler's helper of Polna, on the Bohemian-Moravian border. The responsible Jewish circles refused to engage a Czech lawyer to defend Hilsner because they regarded such a move as anti-national. The Czech jurists, for their part, regarded it as a patriotic duty to give the Jews a reckoning to be remembered. They operated with the belief in the calumny of ritual murder and succeeded in procuring a "verdict of complicity" against Hilsner and in obtaining his condemnation to death by hanging. The sentence of the court excluded the presumption of a religious motive in the fact, but antisemitic propaganda proclaimed that the existence of a Jewish association to murder their Christian fellow citizens for the purpose of using their blood had been demonstrated in a court of law. It was in vain that the Czech sociologist, T. G. Masaryk, later to become the first president of the Czech state, issued a brochure on *The Necessity of a Retrial of the Polna Case*. His brochure was sequestered. Hilsner was indeed tried again, but with the result that he was found guilty of another murder and again sentenced to death. His sentence was commuted to life imprisonment, and later (1916) he was pardoned. A re-examination of the trial was not granted, but scholarly investigation demonstrated the monstrosity of both actions. The agitation was accompanied by wild excesses in many localities in Bohemia and Moravia. Advocates of an understanding between Czechs and Jews stood resigned at the grave of their hopes.

Galicia, the eastern province of Austria, was a hotbed of anti-Jewish commotion.[27] The country offers a significant example of conditions in Austria. Galicia was left to the rule of the nobility and clergy and survived as a relic of the Middle Ages. According to the constitution, Jews could claim freedom of movement, but they were in fact under pressure wherever they turned. The country was poor, and, although its potential resources were considerable, it remained undeveloped; the mineral resources were not worked and only a feeble start had been made towards industrialization. Its 800,000 Jews[28] constituted roughly a tenth of the whole population and formed a balance between the Poles and the Ruthenians. Their higher birth rate and relatively low infant mortality accelerated their rate of increase; at the same time their scope of subsistence decreased. Though they lived apart from the Christian population and spoke their own language, Austrian law did not recognize them as a nationality. Politically they were claimed by the Poles, in order to maintain their predominance over the Ruthenians. Economically, especially in Eastern Galicia, they were grouped with the Ruthenians, but were alienated from them by the policies of the Poles. But the Poles were concerned only with the votes of the Jews and had no thought of allowing them to participate in their national economy. Here they claimed every opportunity and every farthing for their racial kindred and for their growing middle class. Whether or not the nature of this nationalistic Polish bias was antisemitic, the Jews in any case had to pay the piper. The peasants were organized in cooperatives, and this was tantamount to the exclusion of the Jewish middlemen. A Polish merchant class was maintained by a propaganda whose cry was "Buy of Poles," the corollary of which, even if not expressed, was "Do not buy of Jews." It was self-evident that Jews were employed as little as possible in the civil service of the state and community, in railways, or in military offices. The attempt was even made to keep them from teaching positions in Jewish schools. Jews were not admitted to professional schools, so that occupations which required professional training were closed to them. Everything conspired to trouble their lot.

On the part of the Jews, on the other hand, little or nothing was done to meet this comfortless lot. The intelligentsia and the well-to-do were almost without exception subservient to the Poles. The rabbinate, Hasidim and Mitnaggedim alike, conspired with the Polish *Schlachta* in the expectation that they could thus keep the monster of western culture away from the country. In Kolomea-Buczaz the Jews constituted the majority of the electorate.[29] When in 1883 a deputy was to be elected and J. S. Bloch (see p. 170, above) offered himself as candidate in order to defend the honor of the Jews from the floor of Parliament, he obtained no support from the authorities of the Jewish community. This was given to a nonentity who had not the slightest interest in Judaism but who spent money freely on the election, as was the Galician custom. Bloch was the only Jewish member of the Polish bloc to maintain his independence; the others were domesticated "tame" Jews. This attitude lost Bloch his nomination in 1895, when the Poles collaborated with the Christian Socialists and would have no more patience with an outspoken representative of Jewish rights.

The victim of this policy was the mass of Jews who found themselves without a leader at a time when their position as middlemen had become superfluous and a new economic direction was essential. They could only be ground between the wheels. Technical innovations had made it impossible for most of them to earn a livelihood in their old callings, and they had not the education and energy necessary for learning new techniques and new trades. The land grew poorer, the Jews more wretched. "These people are so poor," said von Gniewosz, a Polish deputy in the Imperial Parliament (*Reichsrat*) in 1893, "they are so crowded in their living quarters, that they take turns in using their beds, shifting places on the hour. Their only sustenance is frequently an onion and a crust of black bread." According to the computations of a statistician, not fewer than 5,000 Jews died of starvation annually.

Emigration to Vienna and, after about 1890, to England and America did not balance the natural increase, and the spread of wretchedness and poverty grew to threatening proportions. The evil could only be attacked at its root. The Jews had to be helped in their own homes. The *Israelitische Allianz*[30] in Vienna was founded in 1873 with the same program as the *Alliance Israélite Universelle*. The task it set for itself was to make the Jews of Galicia adequate to the struggle for existence, to provide schooling, to train competent artisans, to prepare suitable young men for a career in farming. The *Allianz* met with vigorous opposition on the part of the very powerful hasidic leaders, who would not suffer boys to receive worldly education. But the *Allianz* courageously persisted, fought a new battle for each school, and carried out its policy of education. Through Adolf Jellinek the attention of Maurice de Hirsch in Paris was drawn to this philanthropic enterprise, and since it fell in line with his own philanthropic endeavors he gave it his support. On the occasion of the fortieth anniversary of the rule of Emperor Francis Joseph (1888), the Baron provided for the work by the establishment of the Baron de Hirsch Foundation for Galicia and Bukovina,[31] with a capital of twelve million francs ($2,500,000). The purpose of the foundation was

the establishment of nursery and primary schools and of children's recreation-grounds and their maintenance through granting of subsidies to teachers and providing of school-books as well as of clothes and food for pupils; the establishment of commercial, technical and agricultural schools; the granting of assistance to Jewish pupils at commercial and professional schools; the apprenticing of Jewish youths to handicraftsmen and agriculturists; the granting of loans, free of interest, to artisans and agriculturists.

The schools were open to Christian pupils also, a remarkable fact, for in this same period the antisemites of Vienna wished to exclude Jewish pupils from the general schools which were supported in part by taxes paid by Jews.

Until George Peabody's foundations, funds of this size had never before been put at the service of educational enterprises. But this did not prevent German and Polish nationalists alike from attacking the founder and his intentions and delaying the confirmation of the Foundation by the Austrian government. More deplorable was the attitude of certain Jewish circles which did not appreciate the blessing to be anticipated from the Foundation. Some used its ample means in their own ambitions for power; others wished to frustrate its effectiveness for fear of the enlightenment it might spread. It was then that the forty-year struggle over the organization of the Jewish communities in Austria reached its height. The question was whether the rabbis alone should direct the communities or whether laymen should also receive a voice in administration. The government rejected hierarchical aspirations in other cases but made an exception in Galicia; rabbis there were not required to demonstrate the measure of worldly education regularly required of others.

If the Baron de Hirsch Foundation had done nothing else than remove the boys from the unhygienic and chaotic *Heder* and give them a normal education, that alone would have justified it. But its primary purpose went much farther. It sought to increase the usefulness of the Jew for artisan employment. Its efforts, indeed, did not suffice to remove misery among the Jews. "One must have nerves of steel," wrote a traveler at the turn of the century,[32] "to remain calm at the sight of the unmitigated misery here." Laborers and artisans received starvation wages, and the Poles begrudged them even such scant earnings. Despite their toil and diligence they were forcibly excluded from industry. Home life had so degenerated that there could be no thought of proper housekeeping. Baroness Clara de Hirsch extended the educational work with a new foundation for establishing housekeeping schools for girls. The impossibility of earning even a bare crust of bread drove many Jews to emigration, many Jewesses to prostitution. Apart from migration to Vienna, to western Austria, and to Germany, the number of emigrants to the United States[33] grew to 83,720 in the decade between 1891 and 1900; in the preceding decade the number had been 44,619. But in view of the persistent and fearful oppression on the part of the Poles emigration brought no amelioration.

When in 1897, at the first parliamentary elections in which general suffrage obtained, the Jewish proletarian masses had ventured to vote for Polish Social Democrats, the Poles determined upon bloody revenge. All at once many antisemitic newspapers were established in the country. These papers agitated against the Jews and carried through merciless repressive measures. Agitation did not stop with such measures but went on to frightfulness and violence. The *Schlachta* had made its peace with Father Stojalowski, who had conducted demagogic agitation against large landholders during the elections; now, aided and abetted by the *Schlachta*, he initiated a crusade of the peasants against the Jews. "Either we or the Jews," "Out with the Jews," were his slogans. Following the Russian formula, the peasants were told that the Emperor and Crown Prince Rudolph, the latter through letters from America where it was alleged he was still alive, had granted them permission to do with the Jews as they wished for a period of three years. In March 1898 rioting[34] began in Cracow and its vicinity, and in the course of the summer spread to central and eastern Galicia. Ten thousand Jews were killed and many more wounded; how much of their poor possessions were destroyed is unknown. If the peasants, who had now grown quite wild, had not come to threaten the ownership of large estates, they would have been allowed further excesses. As it was, the governor was forced willy-nilly to take vigorous measures and to restore order by calling out the military. An inquiry which followed had no positive results, for the ruling Polish society sabotaged all measures for the economic improvement of the Jews. One of the advocates of understanding with the Poles complained in tones of resignation: "We are again in the midst of an exclusive, noble, caste society which ruthlessly stamps the Jews as an alien, hostile element and bars them from all paths to honorable livelihood." A gleam of hope was brought into the lives of these despairing people by Zionism.

The Hungarian parliament possessed the first deputy with a Jew-complex. As early as 1875, Victor von Istóczy,[35] who counted himself a member of the Liberal Party, delivered speeches in which he called for the emancipation of active Hungarians and for the liberation of Hungary from the rapacity of the Jews. Emboldened by Stöcker's agitation, von Istóczy together with several friends founded a Union of Non-Jews, for the purpose of protecting the Christians in the monarchy. These men caused disturbances everywhere, and when Russian refugees began arriving (see p. 224, below) they deluged the government and parliament with petitions not to admit the Jews. On grounds of humanity the ministers refused to hound innocent victims of persecution, and they also energetically banned the circulation of antisemitic propaganda publications. The Liberal Party read Istóczy and his friends out of their ranks. He countered with the declaration that the emancipation of the Jews in Europe was a disgrace and that Russia's Jewish policy should serve as a model. Mention has already been made of the efforts of these advocates of pogrom in the trial of Tisza-Eszlár and of their incitement to similar heroic deeds in Hungary, and also how they peddled their packs of lies even so far afield as Germany (see p. 149, above). When their attempt miscarried, the reaction from their disappointment took the form of further threats against the Jews. Under the motto "Self-Protection of the Christian Population," they caused excesses in numerous localities. Many Jews were forced to flee for their lives. Even in the capital, Budapest, the stage of violence was reached. At this point the government, which in the beginning had looked on unconcerned, intervened with energy and caused the local officials to suppress tumults and agitation. The princes of the Church also made efforts to restore calm, and, last but not least, the bearer of the Holy Crown of Stephen gave public expression of his disapproval and particularly deplored the fact that even the clergy had participated in the spread of hatred. The agitation had been so far effective that in 1884 not fewer than seventeen antisemites were elected to the Chamber of Deputies — not as many, indeed, as their opponents had feared, but too many not to commit the movement to action.

The Liberal Party, under the leadership of Kolomon Tisza, had guaranteed the Jews their protection and full participation in the economic development of Hungary. Rich as it was in natural resources, Hungary was equally rich in highly gifted Jews. No country can boast of more prominent Jews, who won fame in all sectors of scientific and artistic culture, at home and abroad. The isolation caused by the Hungarian language had the effect of limiting the appreciation of their achievements. In the economic field, too, Jews, and not Magyars, became the pioneers of modern industrialization and commercialization. But the interests of the Magyars in the Jews was conditioned by the willingness of the Jews to become

Magyarized. The Jews did in fact become Magyarized; in a short space of time three-fourths of all the Jews declared that Hungarian, not German, was their mother-tongue, and they took a considerable part in the spread of Hungarian culture.[36] The Magyars triumphed, and the non-Magyar peoples held it against the Jews that they had contributed to the maintenance of the dominant position of the Magyars who were actually in the minority. As opposition to the Liberals there was formed, as in other countries, the Catholic People's Party (1890), which recognized that the Jews were the Achilles heel of the opposition and so directed their attacks against them. They undermined their economic position by means of consumers' cooperatives in small localities. The Liberals remained strong, and introduced a policy of religious parity. Judaism[37] was declared a legally recognized religion on a footing with the Christian faiths; conversion to it and marriages with its adherents were recognized as legal. The clergy employed every device but could succeed only in postponing the Law on the Churches but not in preventing its passage.

Antisemitism contributed to the uneasy relations with Austria. The party of Lueger employed a provocative tone in all its dealings with "Judapest," as they styled the capital, because 25% of its population were Jewish.

The Dreyfus Case

Even in France,[38] the home of the Rights of Man, men had not ceased to emphasize the alien character of the Jew. Those who bore foreign-sounding names were numerous. Most of them were Alsatians who had opted for France, but many a persecuted Jew from Central or Eastern Europe had found an asylum in the hospitable country. Among them were first rank scholars like the astronomer Maurice Loewy or the linguist Jules Oppert, but also adventurers who sought their lot in all kinds of ill-famed financial transactions. The Third Republic was embarrassed by a plethora of problems and contradictions. Its determined opponents, the royalists and the clerical party, channeled popular passions against the Jews.[39] Léon Gambetta had said, *le cléricalisme voilà l'enemi*; and they parried neatly by declaring that Gambetta was a Jew, and that the anticlerical legislation was the Talmud's revenge against the Gospel. The lurid flare of Jew-hatred brought about a crash in France. Banks owned by Jews were numerous and successful in Paris and, in order to beat them down, clerical groups founded the *Union Générale*. In consequence of ill-judged speculations, mistakes and ineptitude, this bank failed and took with it the fortunes of large numbers of the nobility and of Catholic congregations. The crash was represented as the result of Jewish maneuvers on the exchange and the populace was incited against the Jews.

In the torrent of clerical resentment, Edouard Drumont[40] wrote his *La France Juive*, in two volumes (1886). This is not really a book, but a heap of sweepings brought together from many places and then flung at the head of all who do not fit into the author's scheme: Jews, Freemasons, Protestants, financiers, republicans, even politicians of the Right who had at one time taken a position other than that desiderated by the malignancy of the author. The true Christian Frenchmen, that is to say, the members of the clerical party, were pictured as immaculate and angelic: their paradise would have continued untroubled but for the incursions of "Prussian-German" Jews. The book, with its innumerable digressions and endless citations, lacked structure, insight, force; yet it became one of the most widely read books of its time and spread the virus of Jew-hatred over the remotest villages which had never seen a Jew and had heard of Jews only as monsters. Such a reply as the anonymous *La France n'est pas Juive* was hardly noticed. Drumont and his patrons took care that Rohling's *Talmud-Jew* should be circulated in a French translation and that the calumny of ritual murder should be aired. In 1889 public opinion in France was ready for the establishment of a *Ligue Nationale Antisémite en France*.[41] Two years later thirty-two deputies of the French Chamber proposed a law for the expulsion of all Jews from France on the ground that they were exploiting the country and making themselves its masters.

With the favor and protection of the Jesuits, Drumont founded a daily, called *Libre Parole* (April 20, 1892).[42] This paper, which lived on scandal-mongering, started a campaign of baiting Jewish officers in the French army and accused them of shamelessly delivering to the enemy secrets of national defense. A number of duels and the specific rejection of antiquated class prejudices on the part of the Minister of War brought the matter to a close. But the baiting went on, and on November 1, 1894, *Libre Parole* could triumphantly report the arrest of Captain Alfred Dreyfus, the first Jewish officer to have been assigned to the general staff. Dreyfus was accused of high treason.

It is superfluous at this date to enter into the details of the web of intrigues, lies and forgeries which were spun by the French general staff in order to cover their original falsifications. The registers of the Dreyfus case[43] are closed, and there can be no intelligent person who is not convinced of the utter baselessness of the charges against him. It has been demonstrated beyond a shadow of a doubt that the traitor was Esterházy, whose friend, Lieutenant Colonel Henri, was the first to direct suspicion to Dreyfus, that he caused Dreyfus' conviction by means of forged documents, that he continued to forge incriminating material to prevent a retrial, that he had begun to admit his disgraceful procedure and then forestalled further revelations by suicide. The Dreyfus case belongs to the history of the French general staff. Its code of honor, upon which it so prided itself, did not prevent it from heaping lie upon lie and bringing France to the abyss of revolution.

The aspect of the Dreyfus case which belongs to Jewish history is the element of malignity in the inception and prosecution of the affair which was due solely to Dreyfus' being a Jew.[44] Alfred Dreyfus had no inner bond with Judaism, but became a martyr of Judaism nevertheless. He was subjected to suffering and his suffering was intensified because he was a Jew; he endured his torments heroically because he was convinced of his innocence and wished to free his name and his children's name from the taint which had befouled it. He succeeded in doing so because his family life had been pure, because his wife and his brothers never lost faith in his innocence and staked their all upon his rehabilitation.

If the suspicion that fell upon Dreyfus and his arrest were due to his being a Jew, the goal of his enemies was made clear by the fact that they reported the matter to the antisemitic press. At a time when the Ministry of War had commanded Madame Dreyfus to keep absolute silence in the matter, Henri furnished the *Libre Parole* with a report of the high treason of the General Staff Officer Alfred Dreyfus, of his alleged complete confession, and of the danger, because he was a Jew, of allowing him to cross the border and so to forestall the investigation. *Tout Israel est en mouvement.* The antisemitic and clerical newspapers embroidered the gravity of the offense and magnified the danger to the Republic; they aroused a storm of discontent. The purpose was to bring the Minister of War, who was still wavering, into line and to force him to prosecute the "traitor," and, secondly, to arouse public opinion not so much against Captain Dreyfus as against the Jew Dreyfus, and so to bring all Jewry to the bar of justice along with Dreyfus. *Le juif, voilà l'ennemi*: during the whole decade in which the struggle over Dreyfus' fate was fought, this cry crippled all the mental processes of the military and nationalist circles. Succeeding ministries and Chambers of Deputies continued under its terror until 1900.

In order to deport Dreyfus to Devil's Island a special law was voted. A specially rigorous guard and stringent limitations were decreed for him in order to foil an alleged Jewish plot to deliver him. The Chamber of Deputies echoed with insulting expressions against Jewish and Protestant treachery. When Major (later Colonel and General) Picquart offered the first proof of Esterházy's guilt to Bertillon, the handwriting expert, and Bertillon found himself unable to deny the identity with Esterházy's handwriting, the only solution he could give was that "the Jews have, for the past year, been training someone to imitate the writing; he has succeeded in making a perfect reproduction." When the same courageous officer received more light on the subject and laid further evidence of Dreyfus' innocence before his superior, General Gonse, he was told, "What can it matter to you whether the Jew remains at Devil's Isle or not?" As for the question of justice, it simply did not exist for this "man of honor." He could not conceive that he was facing a true man of honor who was determined to struggle heroically and suffer all that might be necessary in order to restore truth and justice to their proper position. Dreyfus' opponents thought they had scored a point when they suggested that the "Jewish syndicate had engineered a plot and had bought a man of straw to exculpate Dreyfus and disgrace the army." Even the deputies of the Left allowed themselves to be pushed onto the thin ice, for they feared for the safety of the country and, in the general confusion, wished to preserve the honor of the army; and so they too joined in the hue and cry against Jewish traitors.

Gradually odd facts began to leak out;[45] the Right, out of fear of exposure, revealed one ugly spot as it tried to hide another. Attempts to cover each suspicious falsehood with a fresh fabrication resulted in a labyrinth in which its very makers could not find their way. Truth, as Émile Zola proclaimed, was on the march. That celebrated writer entered vigorously into the lists, and raised the conflict into a fundamental opposition between the clerical-monarchist reaction and republican-democratic progress. The first response to his angry *J'accuse*, "a cry of the conscience of humanity," was his judicial persecution for slander and the onset of pogroms in Nantes, Nancy, Bordeaux, Lyons and other localities in the *départements* where Jews were to be found in some numbers. Jews were railed at, beaten, plundered, and robbed after the Russian manner.[46] The police prevented the excesses from becoming too violent, but could not prevent boycott slogans and printed lists of Jewish businessmen from being distributed all over France.

In Algiers[47] reaction celebrated a veritable orgy. Hatred of Jews was deep-rooted in any case, and now it experienced a tremendous upsurge. Nationalism was a secondary theme, emphasized not so much by the French and Moslems as by immigrant Spaniards and Italians, among whom Max Régis took a leading part. For several days the police looked upon the agitation in the suburbs passively, and the result was that the mob broke into the Jewish homes on the two main streets of the capital and plundered them. When the Jews turned to self-defense and killed one of the pillagers, the crowd replied with an attack which cost the lives of three Jews. The disturbances spread to the neighboring area, and in four days 158 shops were plundered, burned or destroyed. Similar scenes were enacted in other colonial *départements* also. The antisemitic leaders congratulated themselves and rendered thanks to Christ for the grace with which He had protected their undertakings. When the government brought the ringleader, Régis, to trial, the populace countered with a direct uprising. Régis was acquitted by a jury, though he later boasted in Paris that he had broken into cash-boxes, thrown looted gold into the sea, and burned accounts. He exhorted the Parisian populace to water the tree of liberty with the blood of the Jews. Together with Drumont he toured the country in triumph in order to prepare it for the elections to the Chamber. He succeeded in having almost exclusively antisemitic deputies elected in Algiers.

In Paris[48] the vigilance of the police prevented pogroms, but antisemitic agitation raged in the streets and, during the trial of Zola, around the halls of the court of justice also. Men did not stop short of violence; the cry "Death to the Jews" sounded in the ears of the judges. The general staff threatened to resign, and pressure on the jury was so intense that they sentenced Zola, the defender of justice, to the highest penalty permitted by law. The mood of the populace had been roused to such a pitch, witnesses have declared, that Zola's acquittal would have led to a coup d'état and to the St. Bartholomew's Eve massacre that the antisemites had long been threatening. The government was at a loss. It condemned the wild threats and excesses against the Jews, but declared that the Jews were themselves responsible for antisemitism and that they had provoked hostility by their intervention on behalf of Dreyfus. The government had only one desire, to bury the affair in silence and restore calm to the troubled land.

Liquidation of the Dreyfus affair was the platform in the elections to the Chamber of May 1898; no Dreyfusards but a number of ardent antisemites were elected.

Although they did not control a majority, the Right gave no rest. They demanded new measures against Picquart, Zola, and the "Jewish Syndicate." Cavaignac, the new Minister of War, in order to cut off all debate, gathered all the material known to him, in order to demonstrate Dreyfus' guilt.

The Chamber[49] was carried away and in its enthusiasm determined to post Cavaignac's speech. This seemed to strike a decisive blow at all attempts to revise the case, but it was in fact the first step in that direction. For now, for the first time, relevant documents were made publicly accessible and so subject to examination. Criticism did in fact raise its voice, and it disturbed the conscience of the man who, in complete trust of the official material, had publicly asserted Dreyfus' treachery. Cavaignac instituted a re-examination whose effects were like a landslide. They brought on the confession and the subsequent suicide of Colonel Henri and the flight of Esterházy to London.

Recognizing instinctively that this dramatic turn had utterly shattered their house of cards, the antisemites turned to a stroke of violence.[50] Their leader, Guérin,[51] was an adventurer. He conspired with the Orléanists for the overthrow of the Republic. Several months later, when the president died unexpectedly and was being carried to his burial, Guérin actually attempted to storm the Elysée. But the Republic had been warned. It was even more alarmed when the royalists, under the protection of Guérin's bands, openly attacked the newly-elected president because the Court of Appeals had declared the verdict against Dreyfus void, despite the desperate opposition of the military clique. It had once been feared that revolution would be precipitated by the Dreyfusards: it now actually came about that their opponents were using revolutionary tactics. When the government discovered that another coup was planned during the proceedings of the court-martial at Rennes, it intervened quickly and arrested Deroulède, one of the royalist leaders. Guérin barricaded himself in the printing office of *L'Antijuif* and stood a forty-day siege, which did not pass without bloody incident. At Rennes,[52] the generals again left no stone unturned, and reached the absurd decision that Dreyfus was guilty of high treason, but that he merited milder treatment. He was recommended to the President of the Republic for mercy (September 9, 1899). Such half measures satisfied no one, but made it possible for the government to pardon Dreyfus and to restore calm to the country by an amnesty and by cancelling all pending criminal procedures.

It was the purpose of Waldeck-Rousseau, the presiding minister, to purify "the atmosphere of threats, slanders, secret inquisitions which pervaded all things." That was the reason he excepted the nationalist conspirators from the amnesty and brought them to the bar of justice.[53] A thoroughgoing investigation threw light upon the antisemitic machinations; and their goal of overthrowing the Republic with the help of the royalists was proven beyond a shadow of a doubt. This battle they lost completely, although the strong forces that had been summoned to the conspiracy from various camps yielded neither easily nor quickly. The preponderant majority of the people recognized that they had been deceived and brought to the brink of revolution by a combination of royalists, nationalists, clericalists, and antisemites.

The year 1902 produced a new fact[54] which made possible the re-examination of the extraordinary trial at Rennes and led, when it was discovered that the trial was based on error, to its being declared void. The cabinet led by Georges Clémenceau, an old campaigner on behalf of Dreyfus' honor, not only conclusively rehabilitated the honor of Dreyfus and Picquart (July 12, 1906), but also, in order to prevent recurrence of similar dangers, curtailed the rights of the Catholic congregations.[55] And when these measures led to conflicts with the Church, the severance of State and Church was effected. France again acknowledged the principles of liberty and equality.

THE RESPONSE TO ANTISEMITISM

How did the Jews react to the antisemitic storm? At first they were paralyzed, incapable of all movement. What they were then experiencing contradicted all they had imagined of the spirit of the time.[56] When they sought an explanation, they found it in a diagnosis such as that of Gustav Freytag, that what they were faced with was a deep-rooted disease in the German folk spirit, and they hoped for a quick recovery. The appeal to the Court and the Ministers by the Jewish community of Berlin proved to be a mistake. No one had a positive program. Many preferred to hide themselves; many determined to escape persecution by submitting to baptism.[57] From 1872 to 1879 an annual average of sixty-six Jews had been baptized in Prussia; in 1880 the figure suddenly increased to 120, and in 1888 there were 348. In the same year 781 Jews were baptized in Vienna, and 141 in the rest of Austria.

The general press ignored the agitation and the Jewish press was weak. The will to struggle, such as was developed by Hirsch Hildesheimer's *Jüdische Presse* or later by J. S. Bloch's *Oesterreichische Wochenschrift*, was rare and not popular in Jewish circles who had their fill of struggle. Jews were alarmed but not panic-stricken. The "Retrospect" added by H. Graetz to the English translation of his *History*, was thoroughly optimistic and showed no sadness over the shocking experiences of the eighties; he had full confidence in the vitality of the Jewish people and in the strength of democratic institutions. No less characteristic was the remark made by one of the finest spirits among the Jews of the time, the philosopher H. Steinthal:

> I deeply deplore antisemitism, but it does not trouble me. Untroubled by antisemitism, the Jews will continue to spread good among Jews and Christians according to their power.

The first Jew of standing who was articulate in rebuttal was the philosopher Moritz Lazarus.[58] In a lecture entitled *On the Meaning of 'National'*, he demonstrated that nationality was a matter of historical experience and of the will to maintain a certain culture, and that language was its criterion. This principle established that the Jews belonged to the nationality of their home countries. Not much later a student organization called *Kadimah* was formed in Vienna, whose program was based upon a totally different concept of Jewish nationalism.

All else that was published, as for example the replies to Treitschke,[59] was mostly in the nature of self-accusations. The Jews, who had shortly before carried their heads high, behaved like scolded children and were often oppressed by the sense of inferiority. The explanations given by the German rabbis[60] of the Talmud and of the system of Jewish ethics based upon it (1884, repeated 1893), also smacked of self-accusation. They were paralleled by similar publications of the rabbinate and the faculty of the Rabbinical Seminary in Budapest. These were supplemented by an illuminating exposition of the *Shulhan Aruk* by the famous talmudic scholar, David Hoffmann (1885).

In daily life Jews had to defend their traditional way of slaughtering (*Shehitah*), which was denounced as cruelty to animals. The agitation[61] started as early as 1871 in Bavaria and quickly passed to the Swiss border of the Bodensee. The attacks grew more systematic and more violent with the rising tide of antisemitism. Petitions to the German legislators to forbid *Shehita* were not granted, because this would have violated the freedom of religion. The opinions of the best known specialists in physiology and veterinary medicine, collected from the Jewish side, acknowledged that the ritual slaughtering was one of the mildest forms of killing animals. Within Germany the kingdom of Saxony ordered stunning of animals before killing them, and thus made the Jewish method impossible; in Switzerland a referendum resulted in almost 60% of the votes against *Shehitah* (both in 1892). Drumont cynically confessed that the motive for this agitation was antisemitism and by no means protection of animals against cruelty.

The value of the apologetic publications must not be overestimated. They never penetrated to the mass of the people, and the antisemites took no notice of them. But neither must they be underestimated. It was not a matter of indifference, in the view of the great majority of educated people, that the Jews did not accept the charge of religious barbarism in silence but refuted it by authoritative expositions.

It was in the middle classes that defeatism was mastered in the social realm. In this class were found those who first realized that they were not wanted and had the courage to withdraw. Julius Fenchel[62] of Berlin, a small merchant but a man of vision, courage and tenacity, along with several friends who like him had been excluded from the order of Odd Fellows by an antisemitic crowd, invited the Independent Order B'nai B'rith of the United States to expand its activities to include Germany. The representative of the Order sent to Berlin was disappointed not to find such notables as Lasker, Lazarus, Bleichröder among those who desired to be enrolled. He did not realize that these ordinary people were pioneers with a will-power as yet untapped. They provided the Order with centers for expansion in Germany and in the neighboring countries, and their achievements within the

Jewish communities won general recognition and eventually drew the notables into the work. The Order performed valuable Jewish educational work. Shutting out all controversial questions of politics and religion, it united men of varying points of view and bridged over the conflict of religious attitudes. It supplemented the antiquated patriarchal type of charity with the application of modern social principles, and gave a strong impulse to Jewish enterprise in the field of welfare work. It provided a bond for Jews of the world, and awoke understanding for the Jewish fate.

In the political realm also, the younger generation sought for group consciousness and union for the purpose of representing its own rights. Vienna[63] took the lead with the establishment of the Austrian Israelitish Union (1885) which accepted as the basis of its program community of race, not of religious faith, and declared its aims:

to promote a love for Jewish learning among the Jews of Austria and to further their interests; to oppose and dispel the widespread errors in regard to the Jews and the prejudice against them; and to combat the efforts to increase the severity of the religious and racial opposition to them.

In pursuit of this program the Union offered lectures on Judaism. Later it established a legal aid bureau which assisted Jews, particularly those outside Vienna, in maintaining their legal rights. It was the Union also which, in 1898, founded the Relief Association for ameliorating the frightful poverty among the Jews of Galicia and devoted its efforts to the improvement of this entire Jewry.

A year after the founding of the Union, the student association[64] called *Viadrina* was formed in Breslau and became the model for later similar associations at other German universities. The task it set itself was to combat antisemitism in the universities. At the same time its purpose was to educate the Jewish student to a consciousness of his Judaism: he must not despair of his position in the fatherland but must maintain the struggle for full political and social equality. Like other student associations, they wore colors which made them known as Jews, and, according to the custom of German students of the time, they answered insults with weapons. Young men of the standing of university students who publicly admitted their Jewishness with no reticence and would suffer neither insult nor injustice were a new phenomenon in the Jewish life of the time. It could not fail to arouse interest nor to strengthen the backbone of many young Jews, even if they were not affiliated with the association, nor to gain the respect of even antisemitic students by its courage and openness. At about the same time students at Berlin, mostly of foreign origin, tried to prepare the ground for a nationalist outlook and the diffusion of the Hebrew language. But their success was ephemeral; it was only in 1892 that a student association with Jewish national principles, the *Verein Jüdischer Studenten*, was formed.

The process of growing Jewish consciousness had always had as its basis the strengthening of Jewish learning. In all countries the growing youth[65] became estranged from Judaism and knew nothing of it. They strove, indeed, to make an aristocratic showing, but the possession which constituted their own patent of nobility had become an alien thing. When they were made aware of it, it seemed to them anachronistic and clerical. The Bible was the common possession of all the civilized world; it was only the Jew that knew so little of it. Even the orthodox Jew generally knew only so much as was read in the synagogue. When Zadoc Kahn,[66] the rabbi of Paris, tried to establish a *Société des Études Juives* and to found a scholarly journal, he had to give binding assurances to Jewish doctrinaires that no matter tending to religious conviction would be included. Not even the Dreyfus fury awoke in French Jewry the spirit of solidarity. In England an opposition group of younger men demanded a program "of deeper understanding of Judaism, of will for an historical faith." They met together under the name of *The Wanderers*,[67] and each of their members later became an ornament to Judaism. The Anglo-Jewish Historical Exhibition showed the wealth of interesting Jewish monuments available and created a strong sentiment for preserving them. The lectures delivered at the Exhibition evoked an understanding of the Jewish past.

Gustav Karpeles[68] was the first to find the way to the rank and file of the people when, at Berlin in 1892, he founded an Association for Jewish History and Literature. He was able to arouse interest in his project throughout Germany, so that in the space of twenty years more than 200 such associations were functioning in all parts of the Empire. By lectures, forums, libraries and reading rooms, as well as by the publication of a *Yearbook* (beginning with 1898) these associations sought to promote knowledge of the Jewish past, of Jewish literature, of current Jewish events, among Jews and non-Jews alike. It was not a resurrection of the old *Bet ha-Midrash*, for these audiences had no such great perseverance; but it was an attempt to bring the people of the time nearer to Jewish lore. The scientific research of Judaism had continued to bear rich fruits, but they were not the dainties of the cultured Jew. "Judaism is rich," wrote H. Steinthal, "but the individual Jew remains a spiritual beggar." Bible and Talmud, Jewish philosophy and poetry, and above all Jewish history, were in the process of thorough investigation. Men like Wilhelm Bacher, Jacob Barth, Abraham Berliner, Pinkus F. Frankl, Jacob Freudenthal, Ignaz Goldziher, Jacob Guttmann, David Hoffmann, Israel Levy, Isidore Loeb — to mention a few — had their reputation among scholars, but the Jewish public took little notice of their work. Nobody could expect that

Hebrew writers like Meir Friedmann and Isaac H. Weiss would find many readers, but even the fascinating German books of Moritz Güdemann and David Kaufmann reached only a small circle. In England, where Christian people were interested in religious problems, Israel Abrahams and Solomon Schechter had a wider public. In general these were lean years for Jewish literature, not because these studies were so dry and uninspiring as Ahad Ha'am (below, p. 318) accused them of being, but because they found little response. The new literary unions, quickly imitated in many countries, contributed to the popularization of such research. Gustav Karpeles' *History of Jewish Literature* was not an original work but a well written and attractive survey of this immense field.[69]

Finally the realization began to take form that antisemitism, being a political movement, could only be combatted by political means. It was not enough for unprejudiced Christians to take the defense against antisemitism into their hands. An obligation rested upon the Jews to defend themselves; to stake their own persons in the struggle was a point of honor. It was not enough for a group of notables to work quietly as a Committee for Defense against Antisemitic Attacks:[70] the ordinary Jewish man must become aware of the magnitude of the danger, must recognize that it was his own interest, his own right, his honor that was in jeopardy. Not to beg for another's protection but to fight for one's own right — that was the new slogan. Mustering all Jewish forces for self protection was the goal which the founders of the *Zentralverein deutscher Staatsbürger jüdischen Glaubens*[71] ("Central Association of German Citizens of Jewish Faith," May 1893) set for themselves. They wished

by means of the spoken word and the written, by open meetings and lectures, to arm the individual with the weapons that would enable him to maintain in a spirit of truth the struggle that was forced upon him, so that all who, out of the need of the time, had recognized the duty of self-defense should strive for improvement, within and without, in the bright light of public knowledge.

The *Zentralverein* conceived the Jewish problem as a question not of party but of rights. It therefore purposed to unite all Jews, regardless of their convictions in individual details in politics or religion. It desired to make them one in their loyalty to Germany and in their common determination not to allow their love of the fatherland to grow embittered. It wished to develop in the Jews an *esprit de corps*, to convince them that antisemitism concerned each and every one, even if he were not being personally singled out, that attacks were directed not against individual, unworthy Jews, but against all, without exception. It was not their purpose to shield the guilty because they were Jews, but to protect those who, being innocent, were traduced and persecuted because they were Jews. Foremost among the defenseless was Judaism itself, the Jewish writings, Jewish religion and ethics; against unjustified attacks upon these things Jews as individuals and as a group were obliged to protest. That the discrepancy between the constitutional rights of the Jews and the practice of the state could be discussed freely and openly, marked a break with the pussy-footing of the earlier generation and impressed both Jews and non-Jews deeply. The Association, furthermore, gave the Jew courage, hope and an incentive, and from its very inception it enjoyed the large following it merited.

The Association did not abolish antisemitism, but it did tame it at the time, and made its more vocal representatives watch their steps. They learned that they could not slander at will, but would have to give an account of their calumnies before a court of law. The Association took a hand in issues that were too large for an individual or a single community, as, for example, the murder case of Konitz, the question of *Shehitah*, or the charge that Jewish butchers polluted meat sold to Christians (a peculiar phantasm of the diseased antisemitic imagination); in such cases the Association employed its collective resources. When legislation was being prepared on such questions as public schools or Sunday observance, the Association would inform governments and parliaments on the special conditions and requirements of Jewish life, and frequently obtain consideration for these requirements.

Gabriel Riesser had once suggested founding associations for winning emancipation; now a great association had arisen to protect emancipation. It regarded itself as Riesser's spiritual heir, and it employed Riesser's arguments. To be sure, the religious impulse, the understanding of the positive value of Judaism was wanting; it was a sort of defiant Judaism that was in the making. In the early years of its work the Association was so occupied with the organization of defense and with the protection of rights that the question of ideology remained in the background. But in the course of time ideology became central. Out of German Jews the Association desired to make Jewish Germans; as nationalist ideas became paramount the Association rejected anything that suggested Jewish nationalism. This led to a conflict within Judaism, which was fought out in Germany with systematic thoroughness and was carried thence to neighboring countries and to England. When Solomon Schechter[72] entered the lists against "Englishmen of the Jewish persuasion," he found much opposition, even in the ranks of conservative Jews; even so strong a nationalist as Israel Zangwill could not see eye to eye with Schechter on the subject. The fact was that the problem was a very intricate one which could be solved, if at all, only in a calm and clarified atmosphere; at a time of constant excesses against the Jews it was inevitable that arguments should be weighted, on one side or the other.

A typical product of the period is Moritz Lazarus' *Ethics of Judaism*[73]— typical in that it was composed not out of didactic but out of apologetic motives. It is typical also in that it is developed not upon systematic philosophic bases but according to the dicta of rabbinic literature on actual questions of practical ethics. But the author could not deny his philosophic past, and so he sought for the basic principle which informed his individual ethical precepts and measured this principle by the gauge of ethical absolutes. As the norm of religious conviction, Lazarus argued, Jewish ethics require the fulfillment of the revealed moral law out of pure love of God and out of striving to emulate the divine. This moral law is perfectly known to the inward consciousness which resides in the thoughts of the morally good man. Religion idealizes the moral imbued with the highest ideals of love and communion, and so may be spoken of as an autonomous morality. Typical also, finally, was the enthusiasm with which the book was received. The educated public was famished, and the dry specialized publications of Jewish scholars had nothing to offer except to a very restricted few. But Lazarus charmed by the attractiveness of his presentation as well as by the warmth of his feeling, and so, although it was not completed, his book went through several editions and was several times translated.

CHAPTER III

The Jews of Russia under Alexander III

Violence as a Policy

IN RUSSIA[1] antisemitism revealed a will to destroy utterly. Hatred of Jews was there transformed into violence against Jews, and the word "pogrom" gained popular currency. Pan-Slavic[2] ideology and the professional jealousy of artisans, merchants and intelligentsia alike combined to create a phantom danger; to permit Jews to work in the interior of Russia would, it was argued, inevitably lead to the enslavement of the Slavic masses. The gravity of the "Jewish peril" was set forth by certain periodicals[3] in a tireless stream of incendiary articles, unrestrained and unhampered by the strict regulation which the government ordinarily exercised over periodical publications. They inveighed against German *Kultur*, and at the same time imported wholesale the poisonous fungi of the antisemitic pamphlets which spored there. If the land of poets and thinkers led the way towards antisemitism, why should Russia not follow? And so the tinder was laid. The explosion came with the criminal attempt upon the life of Alexander II, who was struck by a bomb on March 3 (13), 1881; it had been his intention, despite all opposition, to give Russia a constitution. The officials of the central government were in a quandary, and were relieved to discover a solution of their own difficulties when the newspapers,[4] especially those in Moscow, Kiev, and Odessa, inaugurated a campaign against the Jews and so directed attention away from the general situation.

This was the prelude. The drama itself followed shortly, at Easter, April 16 (27). A brutal attack was made upon the Jewish population in Elisavethgrad. Although excesses had been threatening for some time and officials had been approached for protection, the mob was able to destroy and plunder the Jewish quarter with brutal vandalism for two days under the very eyes of the military. From Elisavethgrad the terror spread in waves during the next few months through the provinces of Kiev, Chernigov, Poltava, Kherson, and Ekatrinoslav; some 160 cities and villages were the scenes of raging violence. Accounts of the devastation fill the reader with horror even to this day. The intent was chiefly to destroy and plunder Jewish property, but there were many instances of savage murder, cruel mutilation, especially of children, brutal rape of women and girls. It is hard to believe that human beings could be capable of such paroxysms of fury.

A disgraceful series of disorders [reported the American Ambassador at St. Petersburg to the Secretary of State in Washington[5]] have occurred during the past month in the Southwestern provinces of Russia, directed against the Jewish residents, resulting in the loss of a number of lives and the destruction of an enormous amount of property. The scenes of these riots have been at and in the vicinity of Elisavethgrad and Kief with less serious demonstrations at Odessa and other places. The participants have been almost exclusively of the lowest and most ignorant classes in the towns and cities, joined by the peasants, and the demonstrations in the two localities first named appear to have been so powerful that for days the authorities were paralyzed, and the rioters were able to give full sway to their work of bigotry and destruction. In Kief the work was so thorough, it is stated, that not a single Jewish house escaped, the inmates being driven out, beaten, and stoned, and some of them killed and the contents plundered or thrown into the streets. The damage there is estimated at several millions of roubles, and business has been seriously affected thereby.... Massacre and destruction of property have become so threatening in other localities, where no actual outbreaks have taken place, that the Jews in large numbers have fled from their homes and taken refuge across the frontier in Austria or in Moscow, where the military force is sufficient to guarantee safety. In some instances the railroad officials have refused to run the trains by which the Jews were seeking to escape, for fear of attack from the infuriated mobs debauched with liquor and plunder. Indiscriminate pillage became so much feared, that Christians chalked their houses with crosses or exhibited holy images with lighted lamps before them to save themselves from the fury of the rabble. The acts which have been committed are more worthy of the Dark Ages than of the present century.

This dispassionate report of a detached observer reveals only part of the story. The attacks were not spontaneous outbursts of popular rage; they were carefully planned beforehand. They all started in the same way, and everywhere they took the same course. It cannot be proved that these pogroms were directed from a government office, as later pogroms certainly were; it is not even probable that they were so directed. But it may be assumed with certainty that there was a central group of malefactors which kept control in its own hands. The disturbances began in the larger cities and from them fanned out in rays. The mob leaders were not local people, but old Russians from the north. The railroads from Kursk, Moscow, Kharkov were filled with bands of these red-shirts whose transportation and maintenance had been paid for. Their assignment was to organize and lead the disturbances in Elisavethgrad and Kiev. As soon as this duty had been performed they changed their location in order to prosecute their pious work elsewhere. No two of the larger places were ever attacked upon the same day. This did happen later, when the disturbances had spread to the low country.

The procedure employed was always the same.[6] Placards were posted "accusing the Jews of fomenting nihilism and charging them with the assassination of the Emperor." Then newspaper articles making similar charges were read to the illiterate masses and proclamation was made that an imperial ukase "gave three days to plunder the Jews." If anyone inquired where this ukase might be read he was craftily answered that the Jews had prevented its publication by bribing the officials: a truly lofty concept of the moral standards of their country's officers. This alleged order of the Emperor had the effect of a magic formula uttered by some sacred authority against which no exception could be taken. There were peasants who had not the slightest intention of harming the Jews, but out of fear of appearing disobedient they were ready to yield at least token compliance with the imperial decree or to appear to accept it with good-will. When the passions of the mob had been whipped up to the boiling point, a quarrel would be picked with some Jewish shopkeeper, preferably a liquor merchant. Excitement seethed, the mob fell upon the liquor and drank itself into unconsciousness. In this state the mob proceeded to pillage, like so many wild beasts. If the police and military, of whom there were sufficient numbers available on the spot, had taken hold at once they could easily have controlled the situation. A single word would have sufficed to restrain the excesses; but that word was never spoken. Police and military looked on calmly, and so undermined the authority of the government. Occasionally they did take a hand, but then it was *against* the Jews, whenever these ventured to defend themselves. In Balta, the majority of whose inhabitants were Jews, the storm broke as late as the spring of 1882. The city "was given up to pillage through thirty-six hours, like a place taken by assault, in time of war. Out of over one thousand houses belonging to Israelites, not forty remained intact."

The horrible scenes of devastation are described in the following account, which rests upon official reports:

The houses which were not marked with a cross were invaded by the mob. Doors were beaten in, show-windows demolished, window-frames torn out. Furniture was thrown out of windows, crockery smashed, house-linen torn up, with a joy in destruction both child-like and savage. The mob took untold delight in ripping open feather-beds and down-quilts, and sending the contents drifting in the air like a fall of snow. In several places the pleasure the mob took in sheer destruction overcame their rapacious instincts. Peasants who came from their villages with wagons to take away their share of booty, were repeatedly driven away by the rioters. For in certain boroughs, after the house-gear was destroyed, the houses went — floors and roofs being carried away, and nothing left standing but the bare stone walls. Not even the synagogues and cemeteries were spared by popular fury. The tombs were desecrated and the rolls of the *Torah* defiled. The mob naturally made first for the taverns and tap-rooms. Barrels were staved in; whiskey ran down the streets; men lay down in the gutters flat on their stomachs, to gorge themselves with the stuff. In several localities, women, crazed with drink, gave pure spirits to swallow to infants two or three years old, that they might forever after remember these glorious days. Others brought their small children to the ruins of Jewish houses, there to bid them "remember the judgment they had seen overtake the Jews."

Newspapers[7] were filled with reports of these occurrences, some because the news was sensational, some out of hatred, and some out of genuine sympathy with the victims.

What I have seen and heard this day [writes a non-Jewish lawyer in a Kiev newspaper] beggars all description. My pen cannot reproduce the heavy, crushing impression made upon me by the sight of thousands of persons with no food or shelter, humbled, insulted, and beaten.... it is grievously painful to have to say that this multitude could come to such a pass in a civilized country with established institutions and with laws which guarantee social and personal security.

The writer tells how he made his way to a barn in which many of those saved had taken shelter, and he describes "the truly heartrending scene" which met his eyes.

The whole gloomy barn and the space about it resembled an ant-heap; at the latest counting the persons of more than 1,800 ruined Jews with their wives and children and nurslings had crowded together there. Their number increased each moment. All of these sufferers are in rags, most are barefoot, many bear marks of mutilation upon their faces, their heads bound up, their expressions blanched and glazed... I went into the barn; it was indescribable, like some inferno filled with sinners struggling in their torture... The hardest heart could but be softened by the spectacle, involuntary tears sprang from every eye.

Simultaneously with the wave of pogroms an unusually large number of great fires[8] broke out in the Pale of Settlement. Thousands of houses were reduced to rubble and ashes, tens of thousands of Jews were made homeless and lost their all. Many of the fires had been threatened beforehand, and broke out chiefly in those places in which the authorities would not allow pogrom agitation. They were intended to give the Jews a memorandum after another fashion.

These pogroms constitute a turning point in Jewish history. For the Jews of the Czar's realm, which is to say for the greater number in the whole world, they ushered in a period of indescribable suffering. They uprooted masses of people and occasioned migrations on a scale never before known. The sense of being at home had been shattered, and a new national ideology was brought into being, which spread far beyond the confines of Russia and came to affect Jews everywhere. These various aspects of the problem will occupy us later in some detail.

A thrill of horror shook the civilized world when these barbarities became known. Humanitarian considerations were still potent enough for crimes against human beings, even against Jews, to call forth a feeling of revulsion. Even the government in St. Petersburg was horrified that such deeds of violence could take place in Holy Russia, and even more, that they should become known abroad. Count Ignatiev[9] who had shortly before been named Minister of the Interior, was amazed and dismayed, for he knew that Czar Alexander III disapproved of illegality in any form. But this master of intrigue, who was generally styled "Lier-Pasha," recovered his composure quickly and looked about for an alibi. He set into motion a vast piece of hypocrisy calculated to restore the reputation of the ministry, but not the security of his country. Criminal procedures were instituted, 3,675 persons were apprehended, and 2,350 of them brought up on charges. These figures indicate the extent to which the lawlessness had gone; nevertheless penalties were extremely mild.

Ignatiev's party quickly concluded where it should seek for the instigators of the evil. The Terrorists, already objects of hatred, were blamed for these misdeeds also; the Czar himself expressed such a conviction to a Jewish deputation[10] which he assured of his own feelings of revulsion at the excesses. Now, Nihilists may have used the opportunity to fish in troubled waters, but no well-founded evidence of their complicity came to light. Promptly then another scapegoat was found, none other than the Jews themselves. By their callings as tavern-keepers, money-changers and moneylenders, in a word as exploiters, they were said to have dug their own graves. But the explanation was utterly false. The mobs had raged most furiously in the agricultural colonies, where there were neither Jewish capitalists nor Jewish tavern-keepers. They had been instigated by outsiders. The relations between the native population and the Jews in South Russia were entirely satisfactory. This is proven by the attitude of many peasants mentioned above, who would never have dreamed of attacking the Jews were it not for the alleged ukase of the Czar. It is proven also by the conduct of many of the clergy,[11] high and low, some of whom opposed the pogrom-makers at the peril of their own lives, or saved the lives of those imperilled by receiving them into their own homes. Thirty-two priests and other clergy received decorations from the Czar on account of their services in connection with the suppression of rioting against the Jews. Good relations are proven also by the memorials of gratitude which filled the periodicals during those months, addressed by Jews to their local officials who had prevented them from being misused and plundered or who had provided aid and comfort to the victims.

The baselessness of the diagnosis is further indicated by the fact that in the northwest provinces, where Jews were thickly settled and in control of the innkeeping and moneylending trades, there were no pogroms; one must except Warsaw where Russian provocateurs instigated a pogrom on Christmas day in 1881 in order to pillage the Jews and compromise the Poles. In these provinces the governors, many in extremely sharp language, had threatened those responsible with rigorous penalties and so had prevented any excesses. But in South Russia, as the commissioner dispatched by the Czar reported, the officials, and in particular the governors themselves, were lamentably deficient in their duty, some even fraternizing with the plunderers.

Instead of quieting the country, where excesses were still taking place, Ignatiev, by placing the blame on the Jews, poured oil onto the fire. The Russian population perceived quite clearly on what side the government stood, and behaved accordingly. It was only after full reports of these events had been received abroad, and after protests were heard in all capitals — the most impressive being that of the London Guild Hall Meeting of February 1, 1882[12]— that the minister found it necessary to issue vigorous orders for the suppression of disturbances and to forbid specifically the recurrence of similar lawlessness. His successor, Count Dimitri Aleksandrovitsch Tolstoi, who was anything but a Judaeophile, succeeded in preventing further pogroms straightway. It was indeed high time that these disturbances should be brought to an end if the spread of serious economic crises or even of complete anarchy in the affected areas was to be avoided.

If these pogroms were symptoms of a disease, of the "anomalous relationships between the autochthonous population and the Jews," the problem then was how to locate the germ and consider how to prevent the recurrence of the disease. "If these events lead to a serious consideration of the wisdom of abolishing all the Jewish disabilities, and of placing Russian legislation on this subject alongside of that of the other enlightened nations, the loss of life and property will not have been in vain." These are the words with which the United States Ambassador closed his report, and all impartial observers thought as he did. In his memoirs Sergei Witte,[13] who later became Minister of Finance, tells of a conversation with the Czar. The Czar once asked him what he thought of the Jews. He replied that the Jews must either be thrown into the sea, or, if they were to continue alive, tolerable living conditions must be provided for them.

But arguments such as these could not affect the court circles of St. Petersburg. The crown, to be sure, was Alexander III's, but the dominant opinion in the government was that of his former teacher, Konstantin Petrovich Pobiedonostzev,[14] the Procurator of the Holy Synod. Pobiedonostzev regarded it as his mission to guard unhappy Russia from the fearful pollutions which were being released against it out of Europe. Any different conception of what might be regarded as Russian or Christian, such as that of Leo Tolstoi's, Pobiedonostzev looked upon as rebellion which it was his inexorable duty to suppress in order to support absolutism. He was a modern Torquemada. His goal was the unification of the State and the Orthodox Church, and he advocated the Russification of all alien peoples and suppression of all faiths other than the Russian Orthodox, including Protestantism and Roman Catholicism. Towards other nationalities he was forced to exercise a measure of restraint, but against the Jews he could carry out his will unhampered. To him is to be ascribed the authorship of the notorious prescription for the solution of the Jewish problem: one-third of the Russian Jews should emigrate, one-third must be baptized, and the remaining third starved. His Christian conscience was in no wise disturbed by the prospect of delivering some millions of human beings to starvation; what did annoy him was that the Jews did not recognize the blessings of his Christianity and did not flock to baptism.

This totalitarian belief in Pan-Slavism was the faith of Ignatiev[15] also, one of the most cunning representatives of the Russian bureaucracy which was smitten with blindness and which drove the Empire to the abyss. Instead of establishing facts they prosecuted theses; instead of searching for reality they pursued phantoms. Ignatiev's attitude involved double-dealing from the start. He was resolved to persist in his policy even before he had read a single report. His investigation was not directed towards understanding the acts of violence, that cried to heaven, and finding means for averting them in the future. For him a single question occupied the foreground, the question "of ascertaining the sad condition of the Christian inhabitants, brought about by the conduct of the Jews in business matters." In his view, then, the Jews had already been tried and proved guilty, and though he declared that he wished to do his best "to deliver the Jews from oppression and slaughter," he nevertheless regarded it "a matter of urgency and justice to adopt stringent measures in order to put an end to the oppression practiced by the Jews on the inhabitants and to free the country from their malpractices which were, as is known, the cause of the agitation." On top of the blows to which they had been subjected the Jews now received an official scolding.

When the Minister instituted separate commissions for investigating the Jewish question, their decisions were prejudiced from the start; the direction their findings were to take was clearly indicated by the questions to which they were to find the answers: What economic activities of the Jews were particularly harmful? What were the obstacles in enforcing the laws regarding the possession or the leasing and use of land, regarding trade in alcoholic beverages or in moneylending? What changes were necessary in order to prevent circumvention of these laws on the part of the Jews? And, finally, what legislative or administrative measures would be appropriate for making such injuries as the present impossible? And as if the decisions anticipated were not enough, discretion was left to the commissions to include further matter injurious to the Jews. The commissions did not disappoint expectations; their reports abounded in accusations and in suggestions for repressive measures. In order to create the impression of impartiality each commission was required to have two Jewish representatives;[16] but their position in the midst of the scornful and contemptuous gathering was so excruciating that their voices were not heard at all; and the written memoranda and minority votes which they submitted seldom received attention.

The May Laws

The real aim of the inquiry was revealed by the government newspaper, *Novoye Vremye*,[17] which declared, with complete cynicism, that Jew-baiting was indeed desirable, but that repressive measures well considered by the government could deliver far more effective blows than could the blindly raging populace. The blow which Ignatiev devised was his *Temporary Orders Concerning the Jews*. The word "Temporary" in the title was a cunning trick, for its inclusion made it unnecessary for the orders to obtain the approval of the State Council where Ignatiev feared opposition; temporary orders required only the acquiescence of the cabinet and the signature of the Czar. But the orders were never regarded by their author as temporary, and indeed they remained in effect until the collapse of Russia in 1917. To be sure, Ignatiev himself was swept out of office only a few months after the publication of these orders by the storm of indignation which had been evoked by his administration and particularly by the bribery which had attained heights unusual even in Russia. But Ignatiev's successors continued to brood over the cuckoo egg which he had left behind in the nest.

The May Laws,[18] as these regulations were subsequently called, after the month in which they were published (May 3 [16], 1882), constituted a permanent administrative pogrom against the Jews. They were valid only for the Pale of Settlement, but their spirit made itself felt over the whole Russian Empire. For one thing, they prohibited Jews from engaging in any business activity on Sundays and Christian holidays. This worked an economic hardship upon the Jews, for it not only forced a day of idleness upon poor Jews who had already observed their own Sabbath, but it excluded them from doing business with the peasant population which visited the towns on Sundays.

But this measure was far less serious in its ultimate implications than were the other two. It was enacted "to suspend temporarily the completion of instruments of purchase of real property and mortgages in the name of Jews; as also the registration of Jews as lessees of landed estates situated outside the precincts of towns and hamlets, and also the issuance of powers of attorney to enable Jews to manage and dispose of such property." The intent of this enactment was to make it completely impossible for Jews to have anything to do with land or to reside in the arable districts. Jews were blamed for not engaging in agriculture, but here the legislative machinery itself was employed to prevent any connection with farm lands. Indeed, the legislation went so far as to make the extension of an existing lease a forbidden transaction in real estate. Count Ignatiev himself is reported to have prudently arranged for the extension of leases on his family estates in good season.

The preamble of the regulation was deceptive; it only went so far as "to forbid the Jews henceforth to settle outside the towns and hamlets, the only exceptions admitted being in those Jewish colonies that have existed before, and whose inhabitants are agriculturists." But the deeper intent of the law was to set up a pale within the Pale, to limit further the Jews' right of domicile and freedom of motion. How vile the act really was can only be seen in its interpretation and application. The Russian bureaucracy had always been crafty, and now that malice and business were in league its cunning reached its highest pitch. The interpretation of the law was in the hands of petty officials whose slave souls reveled in the consciousness that they were in position to trample upon other people. Furthermore, a large proportion of the official class was corrupt. The Jews were delivered into their hands with no means of defense and proved a favorite object for constant extortion. It is hard to imagine the subtleties and pretexts which were devised to embitter the life of the Jews and fill the pockets of the officials.

Before the May Laws, Jews had been permitted to move from one village in the Pale to another. Now any change of place was regarded as a new immigration and so not allowed. If a Jew worked in a neighboring village and spent a single night there, if he visited parents or relatives in another village, even if he was an army conscript who wished to spend his furlough in his home village — all such sojourns were declared to be new settlements and as such forbidden. If a man lived in a dilapidated hovel and the landlord offered him the use of another while his own was being repaired, this too was regarded as a new settlement and not permitted. Many of these senseless interpretations were declared illegal and abolished by the

Senate in St. Petersburg, the court of highest instance for questions of this sort; but in the meanwhile the gendarmery intervened and frequently drove people from hearth and home with brutal want of consideration. Furthermore, these vetoes were made only during the early years; later, conditions deteriorated sharply.

Only those whose names had been recorded in local registers before May 3, 1882 were regarded as possessing the right of domicile. But if anyone, for any reason whatsoever, had not been registered, if the register had been badly kept, or if it had disappeared altogether, those affected might be driven from the city mercilessly though they could produce a hundred witnesses to declare that they had been born and brought up in that same town. Designations of places were also suddenly altered. Suburbs and market crossroads were styled villages. In 1890 such changes occurred by the hundreds, and, since these new villages had no registers, the Jews became liable to expulsion. The same fate befell them when places which had previously belonged in the Pale of Settlement were assigned to a different province in which Jews were not permitted to live without special permission. At first the dominion of Poland was excepted from these regulations, but in 1891 the Imperial Council extended them to cover Poland also. Now Poland too was open to raids, and this refuge was closed to those who had been expelled from the Pale of Settlement. According to the law, former soldiers had the right of domicile anywhere in the Empire, but in 1892 they too were subjected to the May Laws. Here, as in other cases, the principle prevailed that where Jews were involved everything which the law did not specifically permit was understood to be forbidden. By these devices tens of thousands were driven from their villages, uprooted, and deprived of their small possessions. They were driven into the cities where they made the overcrowded ghettos even more intolerable, where their sharp competition further limited the scanty possibilities of earning a livelihood, where they were degraded to the level of *Luftmenschen*.

Even before the pogroms, raids on Jews had taken place in a number of places where Jews had no right of domicile. As late as 1880 a ukase was circulated instructing the authorities to overlook transgressions of this kind and not to molest the culprits. But Alexander II was no sooner dead than sojourn-licenses began to be investigated and illegalities searched for and found. From Kiev alone, whose governor distinguished himself by his venom against Jews, 4,400 families, or 20,000 souls, were expelled in the course of a single year. It wanted only administrative manipulation for horrors of this sort to be repeated anywhere. Security, enterprise, satisfaction in work were undermined. The sadism of the officials extended even to those whose right of domicile was irreproachable, namely the Jewish artisans. Artisans had been expressly invited to settle in eastern Russia, since that region suffered from a great lack of such craftsmen. They had heeded the call, and had advanced themselves by industry and sobriety, and the population as a whole profited from their presence. Their competitors, however, were not pleased, and the police were always ready for some piece of trickery. The law had granted the right of domicile to "trained artisans." But the decision as to what constituted a trained worker and who fulfilled the conditions stipulated, lay with the masters of the artisan guilds. One can easily imagine with what eagerness these masters set about ridding themselves of their Jewish competitors. It was at once declared that certain trades, such as baking, glazing, tailoring, should not be included in the classification of artisans, for these were light trades and did not require skilled handicraftsmen. Another time a Jew committed the crime of using machines for certain work, and that sufficed to give him the classification of manufacturer and deprived him of his standing as artisan. Or it was shown that a watchmaker sold watch-chains which he had not himself made, or that a pastry-cook served coffee with his pastry, or the like, and at once these artisans were stamped as merchants and their right of domicile was declared forfeit. A favorite device was to inspect Jewish workshops on the Sabbath or holidays when they were not in use, and then to declare that the trade was not being practiced so that the privilege could be cancelled. The Jewish trade school at Zhitomir was closed on the ground that there were already too many Jewish artisans. And all this was done by the same people who complained that the Jews were unwilling to engage in productive work and who knew very well how badly skillful and industrious workmen were wanted in the wide regions of the Russian interior.

But chicanery was not enough.[19] The privilege of veterans to reside anywhere was limited to the "soldiers of Nicholas" and withdrawn from all who had been impressed into military service since the introduction of universal conscription. After 1882 certified instructors in artisanship no longer possessed the right of domicile outside the Pale. Midwives possessed the right for themselves but not for their families. Pharmacists might reside but not practice their profession outside the Pale. The number of Jewish military surgeons was limited to 5%. Until death reduced those in service to the stipulated number, no new ones were to be appointed. In the military academies for medical officers, accordingly, the Jewish candidates were limited to 5%. This was the beginning of the percentage norm for students in higher schools and universities which affected Jews most severely. The aim was to keep Jews from education, and particularly to see to it that an academic diploma should not secure for them a general right of domicile. Diplomas obtained abroad were not recognized after 1887. In

1889 a series of special ministerial permissions were required for admission to the practice of law, with the result that no Jew was admitted to the bar for fifteen years.

There can be little doubt that the system was malice incarnate. There can be equally little doubt that the need of persecuting 200,000 artisans, midwives, and professional men gave the lie to the thesis of the government that all Jews were exploiters. These groups were certainly not the ones who encroached upon the monopoly of exploitation enjoyed by the *Kulaks* and officials. On the contrary, as the writer V. G. Korolenko[20] has established on the basis of his own investigations, it was the Jew that alleviated the lot of the population by providing a degree of competition for the exploiters. The official statistics laid before the Commission for Resolving the Jewish Problem[21] (convened 1883–1887 and usually styled "the von Pahlen Commission," after the name of its presiding officer) revealed figures quite different from those assumed by the May Laws, and it became known that the majority of those who were in touch with the situation advocated alleviating the limitations set upon the Jews.

But in St. Petersburg the spirit of Pobiedonostzev still stalked abroad and sought new disabilities for the Jews. So an old law of 1858 was unearthed, which forbade Jews to reside within fifty versts (thirty-five miles) of the German or Austrian border. Finance ministers had on several occasions called for the abolition of the law on the ground that it was useless and ineffective, and had fallen into desuetude. But now it was exhumed and rigorously enforced even against people who had acquired land long before the passage of the law. It was even extended to apply to the western boundary of Bessarabia, which had come into the possession of Russia twenty years after the passage of that law. That the area in which Jews might live might not be too spacious, they were expelled from the Baltic provinces in 1884 and from Finland in 1887. Later the period permitted for residence was shortened for Siberia and limited even in Turkestan, where the Muscovites themselves surely possessed no more real home right than the Jews.

The privileges of merchants of the first guild remained undisturbed, but in the course of years every effort was made to nibble them away and to make their acquisition and use perceptibly more difficult. A Jewish percentage norm was introduced for the exchanges and chambers of commerce; rights of Jewish stockholders in corporations were limited so that they might not come into control of landed property through the roundabout route of corporate management. They were completely excluded from the naphtha industry. Every conceivable chicanery was brought forth and put to use. Even in military service, to which they were conscripted perforce, they suffered endless obstacles and annoyances. From all quarters fuel was assembled to heat the inferno of the Pale in which the Jews were to be consumed.

In a memorandum addressed to the Czar on December 10, 1890, the Lord Mayor of London summarized the sufferings of the Russian Jews as follows:

Pent up in narrow bounds within your Majesty's wide Empire, and even within those bounds forced to reside chiefly in towns that reek and overflow with every form of poverty and wretchedness; forbidden all free movement, hedged in every enterprise by restrictive laws; forbidden tenure of land or all concern in land, their means of livelihood have become so cramped as to render life for them well-nigh impossible. Nor are they cramped alone in space and action. The higher education is denied them, except in limits far below the due proportion of their needs and aspirations. They may not freely exercise professions, like other subjects of your Majesty, nor may they gain promotion in the army, however great their merit and their valour.

As if the chain of brutality was not yet complete, reports spread in 1890 that new blows against the Jews were in preparation. There can be no doubt that such plans had in fact already been made and that it was due only to the energetic protests from England and America that they were abandoned.[22] Upon the suggestion of prominent Christians the Lord Mayor of London called a meeting of "every grade of society, every phase of public opinion, every section of the Christian Church" at the Guild Hall;[23] and that meeting passed a unanimous resolution

that the renewed sufferings of the Jews in Russia from the operation of severe and exceptional edicts and disabilities are deeply to be deplored, and that in this last decade of the nineteenth century religious liberty is a principle which should be recognised by every Christian community as among the natural human rights.

They appealed from the Czar uninformed to the Czar informed "to annul those special laws and disabilities that crush and cow your Hebrew subjects."

The reply of the cabal at St. Petersburg was to have the Czar sign a decree to expel Jewish artisans from the Gouvernement Général and the capital Moscow.[24] The decree was kept secret until negotiations for a foreign loan had been completed, and then, with refined malice, it was published on March 28–29 (April 9–10), 1891, the two first days of the Passover. The Czar's brother, the Grand Duke Sergei, had been named Governor General of Moscow and was to find the city cleansed of Jews. Police and firemen surrounded the Jewish quarter and hunted the Jews down; anyone unable to show proper documents was arrested on the spot, fettered, and forcibly removed to the Pale. An eyewitness compared the affair with an organized hunt to round up wolves or bears. Others, to whose right of domicile no exception could be taken, were sought out individually by the police and made to sign a petition stating that they wished to leave the city of their own accord and besought permission to do so. The terms for departure varied according to the business and the standing of the household. Those who stood well with the police, which is to say, those who paid well, were granted a postponement, but not for long. Even hospitals received an order not to suffer Jews to remain within their walls. Permission to remain was granted only to those who submitted to baptism. Girls, too, might remain, if they enrolled themselves as prostitutes. A Jewess who was a student was reckoned a desecration, one who prostituted herself a gain — and that was Russian morality. In a short while, 14,000 Jewish families were expelled from Moscow, industrious and intelligent people, artisans, industrialists, bank officers, merchants, professional men, people who had contributed not a little to the welfare of the capital and now stood on the brink of ruin. The experience was so ghastly that Pobiedonostzev himself lamented its rigor.

The immigration commissioners from the United States who happened to be in Moscow at the time summarized their impressions as follows:

The pressure is general and forces out the rich as well as the poor — those who have or had the right of residence legally and by invitation, as well as those who presumed upon the toleration of former years, those who because they are Jews are first deprived of their passports, arrested for not having them, confined in prison to be sent in chains *per étape* — as well as soldiers who have been decorated for faithful service to their country and who in their old age, instead of receiving pensions are separated from their children and ordered into the Pale, where only the strongest and most vigorous can hope for existence.

Homes are destroyed, businesses ruined, families separated, all claiming that they are not criminals except that they are charged with being Jews; all expressing a willingness and anxiety to work, begging for the opportunity to begin life somewhere, where they do not know nor do they care.

The year 1891 was the culminating point of the terror under Alexander III. Later trials could not compare with the tribulations already passed. What did the Russian government gain by its brutality? Did it bring closer the solution of any of the numerous political and social problems which troubled the land? Did it alleviate the need of the peasants, did it mollify the dissatisfaction of the workers, did it appease the spirit of rebellion on the part of the intelligentsia? The constant fury against subversiveness and against the universities showed there was something rotten in the state of the Czar. The fault, so the government would have it, lay with the revolutionary spirit of the Jews; and indeed there were among the Jews enemies of the government and champions of subversion, but not so many as to be a decisive factor in the underground movements. How could one expect them to be among the mainstays of the regime?

> How can citizens [wrote Henry Edward Cardinal Manning[25]], who are denied the right of naturalisation, be patriotic? How can men, who are only allowed to breathe the air, but not to own the soil under their feet, to eat only a food that is doubly taxed, to be slain in war, but never to command — how shall such a homeless and exiled race live of the life of the people among whom they are despised, or love the land which disowns them?

Count Witte,[26] too, in his *Memoirs*, lays the responsibility for making revolutionaries and activists out of timid Jews squarely upon the Russian government. He himself was made Minister of Finance because the national finances were in a state of confusion, and the money standard was in danger. As a device for improving the budget he introduced the liquor monopoly, by which the state itself exploited Russia's great scourge, drunkenness (1894). Naturally Jews were excluded from management in the state monopoly; but they welcomed the change nevertheless, for it removed the odium from them although it deprived very many of their livelihood.

Inner Life under Czarist Oppression

How could the ghettos of Russia and Poland endure this uncalculated pressure, this constant inflow of pauperized men, women, and children? They could not have passed without a trace. Many an individual lost his spiritual balance through the constant assault upon his nerves, his physical balance through the vain search for a dry crust, his moral balance through the constant underground struggle with the police. But on the whole they resisted heroically and maintained their spirit. Their courage was strengthened by the sympathy of Jews the world over and by their readiness to help; all made efforts to relieve the emigrants and regulate the emigrations. Emigration did effect some improvement by reducing the number of competitors for the scant food and scant work available. And many of the emigrants sent their small savings to assist those at home, reported the kindliness and expansiveness of the new world, and held up a glimmer of hope that those still suffering in the inferno might yet be able to follow.

But the decisive factor was a kind of inner self-defense, a will to survive. Communities made every exertion to maintain unimpaired their various communal institutions — charity organizations, schools, *yeshibot* — and even to establish new ones. A leader of great stature appeared in the person of R. Isaac Elhanan Spektor (1817–1896), who was rabbi in Kovno[27] for thirty-two years. He was not officially a government appointee, but was nevertheless recognized by Jewry as a whole and by the Russian government as representative and mouthpiece of the Jews. His devotion and selflessness, his reasonableness and eagerness to serve, made him friend, counselor and confidant of all his coreligionists. He was imbued with a spirit of charity and humanity and he was concerned to prevent the ritual law from oppressing the community like a dead weight, but so to interpret it, wherever possible, that it should remain tolerable.

During the earnest deliberations which took place in St. Petersburg after the persecutions, Spektor's utterances gained a general hearing. His goal was always so to guide

Jewish interests that faith and morality should be strengthened. He insisted that only rabbis with traditional training be recognized as religious leaders of the community. But he took no exception to modern secular education in addition, and he worked closely with the Society for Promoting Enlightenment among the Jews of Russia. When the Pahlen commission met and newspapers bombarded it with attacks upon the Talmud, he procured a supporting opinion of S. R. Hirsch entitled, *On the Relations of the Talmud to Judaism and to the Social Attitudes of its Followers*; this treatise exercised a lasting and favorable influence upon the commission. The high regard in which Spektor was held in Western Europe enabled him to alleviate the lot of his enslaved brethren in some particulars. At his side stood Baron Horace Günzburg (1833–1909), the presiding officer of the Jewish community in St. Petersburg, a noble soul, a man of far-reaching influence who was the moving spirit of incessant efforts in behalf of the Jews.[28]

A very important factor in the survival of Russian Jewry was the nationalist movement, which affected the people deeply, and gave them a certain immunity to despair and to inferiority complexes. Perez Smolenskin[29] of Monastyrstchina (1841–1885) was an effective apostle of this nationalism. In the columns of the Hebrew monthly, *Ha-Shahar*, which he published in Vienna, he challenged the ideology of the century. For him Moses Mendelssohn was not the liberator of Judaism but its destroyer, for he made Judaism into a religion and did away with its national content. Judaism must again become national, and even though it possessed no land it must emphasize its character as a folk and cultivate its national language. M. L. Lilienblum rejected the "sins of his youth," as he styled his early religious liberalism (see p. 109, above) and became the advocate of a national consciousness centered in Palestine. Among the rabbis, spirited men[30] like Samuel Mohilever of Radom, later of Bialystok (1824–1898), and the somewhat younger Isaac Jacob Reines of Lida (1839–1915) became stout supporters of the Zionist movement.

CHAPTER IV

The Exodus: Baron Maurice de Hirsch

Problems of the New Exodus

DISMAY and despair was the response of all Russian Jewry to the pogroms.[1] The Jews felt themselves aliens in a hostile land. All faith in a burgeoning humanity, in the possibility of closer accord with their neighbors, had been shattered by the ruthless hostility of their environment. Everyone anxiously awaited the destiny the morrow might bring: over what community would doom come crashing next? "To die is evil," many wrote, "but to feel oneself condemned and to be uncertain when the executioner may call is torment greater far." Life could not go on in a country which denied the most elementary rights of humanity; instinctively the conviction took form that only one solution remained, and that solution was emigration from the land of horror. All that had the means to do so hastened over the borders, with the goal of reaching one of the Anglo-Saxon countries. There one might hope to draw free breath and to move about with freedom, even though the future was otherwise altogether uncertain.

Of the difficulties which a mass exodus of uprooted families entailed, both for themselves and for the land of their refuge, none had an inkling at the time. None would have hearkened had a warning voice been raised. The avalanche was irresistible. Unplanned and desperate flight claimed many victims, necessitated much retracing of steps. When a small number of refugees arrived in England it was still possible to shelter them in certain harbor and industrial cities, where they could find their daily bread. In the United States nothing was yet known of what had transpired in Russia, and when immigrants[2] arrived unexpectedly, still depressed by the shock of the persecutions and wearied by the exhausting voyage, the prevalent attitude was one of despair. No one was prepared to face an assault in force. The Jewish communities were neither numerous nor rich; for ten years they had protested against the immigration requested by the European relief committees, and now they saw themselves confronted with a burden to which they felt themselves entirely inadequate. They underestimated, indeed, the absorptive capacities of the American employment market, and likewise the employability of those who desired admittance. They could not conceive that these people, furrowed with care and tormented by hunger, belonged to the culturally advanced *Am Olam* (Eternal People), and that they had no more passionate longing than to establish a new existence by the work of their hands. That their efforts were not in vain was confirmed ten years later by no less a person than the President of the United States:[3] "The Hebrew is never a beggar; he has always kept the law — lives by toil — often under severe and oppressive civil restrictions." But for the moment the men responsible for the Russian Relief Fund found themselves overwhelmed by the care and responsibility which increased day by day. They could see only a single solution to the problem, and that was to stop the immigration. With this end in view they sent a delegate to Europe, to attend a meeting of the united relief committees called in Berlin in April 1882; his mission was to set forth the difficulties of mass settlement in the United States and the obstacles of the immigration laws.

But the torrent continued its onward rush. The first cofferdam to catch it up was Brody,[4] on the Russo-Austrian frontier. Brody itself was wretchedly hungry and ill-housed, and suddenly thousands of refugees had to be sheltered and fed until they could be enabled to continue their journeyings. This stage, the second act of the tragedy, brought a generally clearer perception of the scope and intensity of the catastrophe. Charles Netter had hurried to Brody as the representative of the *Alliance Israélite Universelle* and had organized the care of the refugees with the greatest devotion and energy; his contacts with the refugees brought him to the realization that millions of Russian Jews stood in need of complete resettlement. The task with which he and his helpers saw themselves confronted was overwhelming; it was a kind of general mobilization, but no general staff had prepared plans years in advance, and there was no government to put transportation and moneys at their disposal. All of these things had to be procured by the committee. The *Alliance* set all its forces in motion. Relief committees were formed everywhere, after the model of the Mansion House Committee in London, and many Christians sent contributions to these committees. But assistance did not arrive with such speed or in such profusion as to eliminate obstructions in the way of emigration.

The period of waiting in Brody, which seemed to many a barrier beyond which lay Paradise, had salutary psychologic consequences. In the general solicitude for their welfare the victims regained their faith in humanity. An imposing demonstration was convoked in the Mansion House[5] in London by the élite of English society, representatives of the highest nobility, of the most distinguished clergy, of the aristocracy of the spirit, men like Charles Darwin and Matthew Arnold, Robert Browning and Alfred Tennyson; its purpose was to emphasize the inalienability of human rights and the spiritual relationship between Judaism and Christianity. Simultaneously demonstrations of the sympathy of their people took place in New York and other cities, British and American.

These manifestations produced a wholesome effect in quickening the spirits of the downtrodden and disinherited. Closer acquaintance with the refugees showed what excellent human material was to be found among them. These were no ordinary paupers who had left home because they could not get bread there. These were men of intelligence and skill, of resourcefulness and discipline, who had been driven forth from their homes by a catastrophe and who sought another home, which they hoped to find in the wide open spaces and inexhaustible resources of the United States. Many dreamed of bringing about a change in Jewish destiny by a return to the soil; and in America, where the West had just been opened, this aspiration met with the fullest sympathy.

Clarification of the problems of emigration came with time, and experience taught that those fit for manual work should be dealt with separately from those unsuited for physical labor. The Berlin conference of the relief committees, the first of such compass to occupy itself with the Jewish fate, united on a common plan of action.[6] At the same time a conference of leaders of Russian Jewish communities took place in St. Petersburg.[7] Its guiding spirits were not at all enthusiastic on the subject of emigration. To be sure, Ignatiev and other state officials had cynically declared that the western border lay open to the Jews; but the Russian law forbade emigration, and the conference was unwilling to become criminally involved in an invitation to lawbreaking. Furthermore, they looked upon emigration as treason and as a surrender of hard-won rights. Jacob Polyakof, the railroad magnate, offered a huge sum to promote settlement of Jews upon the land, but quite apart from the fact that the May Laws immediately rendered all such kindly intentions futile, the delegates from South Russia, where no end of the pogroms seemed to be in sight, would have no part in any such plan. Their alternatives were "equal rights or emigration." The question as to whether Palestine or America should be regarded as the goal for the emigrants was subordinated to this basic position. The Palestine proposal was preferred from the point of view of convictions, but immigration to America had the advantage of offering an immediate solution; and bitter necessity declared for the solution of the moment.

No theory could avail to stem the exodus. A whole people was in motion. The urge to migrate laid hold of those who were declassed economically as well as those who were immediately affected by the political regulations. It was only natural that the migrants should seek out those lands which had long had the reputation of affording asylum to the persecuted. Each year several thousand Russian and Galician Jewish refugees settled in England, especially in London. They lived huddled together in wretched quarters which might easily become foci for epidemics. They worked for starvation wages and so depressed the wage level. These dangers, in part real and in part exaggerated, called a vigorous counter movement into action. The Society for the Prevention of a Destitute Alien Emigration demanded in specific terms "legislation for restricting the immigration of destitute aliens and to prevent pauper Russian Jews from further degrading the East End of London by spreading the sweat system, driving out English workmen and lowering the wages." A parliamentary investigating commission established that no immediate danger to the English worker existed. But the Jewish organizations, who had indeed warned against immigration but who had supported those aliens who arrived in England, insisted that as many as possible continue their migrations overseas. A small number found shelter in the English colonies of South Africa and Canada. Agriculturists were directed by the *Alliance Israélite Universelle* to Argentina.[8] In 1889 some nine hundred souls arrived there from Kamenetz Podolsk, established the agricultural colony of Mosesville, and became the pioneers of Jewish agricultural settlements in Argentina.

By far the largest masses streamed towards the United States. To be sure, the wave which had become enormously swollen under the immediate impact of the persecutions declined sharply in the years after 1882, but the immigration continued[9] greater than it had been previous to the excesses. And each time legislation in Russia became more stringent, as for example after the introduction of the percentage norm for students in 1887, the number of immigrants straightway soared. Indeed, the number of Jewish immigrants to the United States can be regarded as a gauge for the course of Jewish legislation in Russia. The first immigrants had relatives and friends in the old homeland, and as soon as they were able to earn their pittance they regarded it as their duty to redeem their kin who still suffered in the Russian inferno. Whenever new oppressions were reported, steamship passage was sent home, and this brought new refugees into the country. The United States was in the midst of a great economic upsurge and there was no difficulty in assimilating the huge influx of the decade. Of the almost six million aliens who arrived in the country, the Jews constituted barely three per cent; they did not, however, disperse over the entire country, but the preponderant number remained in the large cities of the eastern seaboard, and there they attracted considerable notice.

When the economic situation threatened to deteriorate, efforts were made to arouse public opinion and to represent immigration as unfair pressure against the United States which Europe was exerting by disposing of its useless population. In particular there was a demand for rigorous immigration restrictions for undesirable elements, and for the application of the law which prohibited subsidized immigration. This happened precisely at a time when the threat of new outrages in Russia and draconian expulsions raised the number of immigrants to unprecedented heights; in 1891 and 1892 the number amounted to no fewer than 107,710 persons. The Jewish organizations labored with the State Department to prevent exclusion of Jews who were persecuted on account of their religion. They emphasized the point of view that there was no question of paupers or of destitute persons but of people who had suffered shipwreck, who might with justice claim consideration. They pointed also to the fact that many of the immigrants of the preceding decade had, under the most difficult circumstances, sought for and found employment, and that many, under the beneficent influence of American law, had by their diligence achieved the position of respected and contented citizens. They were further enabled to point to the Baron de Hirsch Foundation of $2,400,000 which had just been established for the purpose of assisting immigrants to find their footing in the new country.

Notwithstanding the satisfactory assurances extended by the Secretary of State, the Jewish Relief Committee considered it part of its duty to lay the pitiful plight of the refugees, who were arriving almost daily, before President Benjamin Harrison[10] and to petition him "to remonstrate to Russia." The President desired to obtain reliable information on the immigration in general and on the Russian Jews in particular, and so despatched an investigating commission to Europe. The report drawn up by J. C. Weber, the Commissioner of Immigration, and Dr. W. Kempster, a neurologist, was the first authentic document of its kind and aroused widespread interest by its completeness and detail. The commissioners arrived in Moscow at the moment that the expulsions were in progress, and made themselves familiar with the character and work of those who were being expelled. They visited towns and villages of the Pale of Settlement as well as the Jewish agricultural colonies in the Ekatrinoslav district. They interviewed men of various professions, Jews and Christians, and gained a profound insight into the extent of the tragedy and the manner of people affected by it. The following is part of their report:

> There was an entire absence of intoxication, and we may say here that the Jew is singularly free from this vice; not a single case of intoxication among Jews was noticed anywhere in Russia. Conversation with some of them disclosed the fact that the principal questions discussed are, "What shall we do, and where shall we go to get bread?" for anticipation of the terrors of approaching winter and the certainty of starvation, which they see no means of averting, aggravate the present misery. Willing and able to work, they are unable to obtain it; forbidden to work outside the city, forbidden to trade in the country, unable to leave the precincts where they now are, excluded from governmental work, it is no wonder they wish to fly somewhere where they can breathe and have an equal chance in the struggle for existence. The only thing which prevents them from going *en masse* to other countries is their poverty.

This gripping report brought about presidential intervention:[11]

> This government has found occasion to express in a friendly spirit, but with much earnestness, to the Government of the Czar its serious concern because of the harsh measures being enforced against the Hebrews in Russia.... The immigration of these people to the United States is largely increasing and is likely to assume proportions which may make it difficult to find homes and employment for them here and to seriously affect the labor market. It is estimated that over one million will be forced from Russia within a few years.... The sudden transfer of such a multitude under conditions that tend to strip them of their small accumulations and to depress their energies and courage is neither good for them nor for us.
>
> The banishment, whether by direct decree or by not less certain indirect methods of so large a number of men and women is not a local question. A decree to leave one country is in the nature of things an order to enter another — some other. This consideration, as well as the suggestion of humanity, furnishes ample ground for the remonstrances which we have presented to Russia, while our historic friendship for that Government cannot fail to give the assurance that our representations are those of a sincere well-wisher.

Baron de Hirsch and the ICA

The fateful year of 1891, which marked the culminating point of the Russian persecutions of the period and the crisis in immigration policy, brought a ray of hope for the Jews of darkest Russia. Baron Maurice de Hirsch,[12] who himself diffused this hopefulness, merits a golden page in Jewish history. He was born in Munich, in 1831, the son and grandson of Bavarian court bankers who exerted themselves in behalf of the emancipation of the Jews in Bavaria. He removed to Brussels early, and there, in 1855, married Clara Bischoffsheim, two years his junior, daughter of a senator and banker. His progressive and energetic spirit seemed too revolutionary for the conservative methods of the Brussels banking house. Hirsch made himself independent and undertook railroad building in Austria, Russia and the Balkans. He entered into arrangements with a Brussels bank which had undertaken the construction of the first railroad to Constantinople and had been unable to fulfill its engagements. Men jested at his venturesomeness, but he was justified by the sequel. His keen insight and his power of judgment gained for him the reputation of a leading financier and industrialist. At the height of his success his fortune rated as one of the greatest of his time. He enjoyed to the full the elegance and luxury of a *grand seigneur*, but at the same time his philanthropies were also on a princely scale, and in these his noble wife supported and encouraged him. He maintained, for example, one of the greatest racing stables of the day, but he gave all his considerable winnings on the turf unreservedly to London hospitals. His wealth he looked upon as a social responsibility. Philanthropy meant for him "to make human beings who are capable of work out of individuals who otherwise must become paupers, and in this way create useful members of society."

"And it came to pass in those days, when Moses was grown up, that he went out unto his brethren and looked on their burdens." With no feeling of condescension or sentimentality he conceived it his immediate obligation to help in the regeneration of his people which had been persecuted for a thousand years. In the Orient he discovered the poverty and the cultural degradation of his Jewish brethren. He secured the cooperation of Immanuel Veneziani (1825–1889), a high-minded humanitarian of Constantinople; Veneziani became his almoner and represented him on the central committee of the *Alliance Israélite Universelle*. Hirsch approved fully of the *Alliance's* school and continuation-school system, for it trained its pupils for productive work. He endowed this work generously, and from 1880 to his death he covered its annual deficit. It was by his generosity also that the *Alliance* was enabled to provide means for the first emigration of Russian Jews. But it was Maurice de Hirsch's wish not merely to give alms; he sought rather for a plan for productive help. When misfortune struck him in the loss of his only son at the beginning of his manhood (1887), he and his wife found consolation in humanitarian work. "My son I have lost, but not my heir; humanity is my heir." The anguish of the unhappy parents released a heroic will to sacrifice which was unexampled at the time and which has scarcely found its equal since. Its first tangible expression was the Foundation for making the Jewish youth of Galicia and Bukovina productive (p. 176, above).

He wished to devote a grant five times as great to a foundation for educating the Russian Jews and training them in handicraft and agriculture, but the Russian government refused its sanction to the proposal. As a result of the negotiations on the subject[13] Hirsch became convinced that only one solution remained to the Jews of Russia — to leave the country; and he was prepared to devote large sums to migration and settlement. He considered it his task to direct the enforced exodus along orderly paths, to transmute the flight into a migration, to coordinate problems of geography and vocation. His travels had convinced him that Jews could become competent agriculturists. He had heard of the devoted and successful work of the Jewish farmers in South Russia. He believed in the moral strength of the Russian Jews and wished to make it possible for them to work as free men for themselves and for mankind, unhindered by hampering legislation. He sought for virgin territory in one of the new and sparsely settled countries, which Jews might build up with full civil rights in compact settlements. His plan involved not only the liberation but the rejuvenation of his people. His intention was to transform the curse into a blessing, to establish an enterprise which should usher in a new epoch of civilization, not only for the Jews, but for mankind as a whole. His attention was directed to Argentina, which with its vast expanses might offer a firm and enduring refuge to all who were persecuted, and to those spirited Jews who strove manfully under discouraging conditions to achieve success in working the land (see p. 229, above). After thorough investigation of the project he determined to purchase land in Argentina and to direct the Jewish emigration thither. It was his wish to remove all Jews out of Russia in the course of a fixed period, in accordance with a plan to be worked out.

But so far-reaching a scheme could not be effected without the sanction of the government. According to Russian law emigration was prohibited; the majority of emigrants had passed the border secretly or by bribery. Hirsch's representatives proposed to the Czar's government that permission be granted for establishing commissions to select the emigrants and to organize and supervise the emigration. They requested also that official emigration permits be granted free of charge, and, finally, that permission be granted to institute instruction in agricultural and technical subjects in order to prepare those without training to be eligible for emigration. The government was obviously pleased at the prospect of being rid of the Jews and declared itself satisfied with the scheme, with the exception of the proposal to establish schools; later it consented on this point also. Hirsch purchased large tracts of land in Argentina, in the provinces of Santa Fé and Buenos Aires, and, when these appeared inadequate, in Entre Rios also; and he arranged that these lands be carefully prepared for colonization.

As a permanent instrument for carrying out his purposes Baron de Hirsch established the Jewish Colonization Association,[14] with its seat in London. He endowed it with a capital of ten million dollars at once, in the hope that his gesture might serve as a model for other Jewish millionaires to follow; and he himself was determined to provide more munificently for the Association in the future. In order to facilitate the activities of the Association he had it incorporated as a business enterprise under English law, its purposes being stated as follows:

To assist and promote the emigration of Jews from any parts of Europe or Asia, and principally from countries in which they may for the time being be subjected to any special taxes or political or other disabilities, to any other parts of the world, and to form and establish colonies in various parts of North and South America and other countries for agricultural, commercial, and other purposes.

To establish and maintain or contribute to the establishment and maintenance in any part of the world of educational and training institutions, model farms, loan-banks, industries, factories, and any other institutions or associations which in the judgement of the council may be calculated to fit Jews for emigration and assist their settlement in various parts of the world, except in Europe, with power to contribute to the funds of any association or society already existing or hereafter formed and having objects which in the opinion of the council may assist or promote the carrying out of the objects of the association.

After questions of organization had been settled, Maurice de Hirsch addressed a personal "Proclamation to his Coreligionists in Russia." He made his intentions known to them and admonished them in a fraternal and cordial spirit to accommodate themselves to the new and carefully thought-out scheme of emigration, not to leave the country in pell-mell flight, and, on the other hand, not to grow despondent if the number of emigrants should be limited while necessary preparatory measures were still under way, but to trust with traditional Jewish faith that more would subsequently be cared for. These "words of comfort and exhortation" met with a stout response in the hearts of the masses; they overcame their despair and emerged with new hope. Baron de Hirsch's portrait hung in many Jewish homes beside that of the other great philanthropist, Moses Montefiore. His name was called blessed; "a touch of kindness from an unseen hand gave fresh courage, new resolution, and new hope."

Even this act of purest philanthropy was not safe from misrepresentation.[15] It was construed to portend the inundation of the western hemisphere with Jewish paupers from the East. But neither hopes nor fears were destined to be fulfilled; all expectations were disappointed. Emigration from Russia followed its own natural laws of motion and disregarded bureaucratic dispositions. Whether organizational difficulties constituted the factor that retarded emigration, or a breathing space in Russia, or the economic crisis in the United States, the fact remained that in the first years of the Jewish Colonization Association's activities emigration lagged far behind the evacuation that had been planned. In consequence of the pressing need, immigration to Argentina was precipitately hastened, contrary to the will of the founder, and met with unfavorable results.[16] Baron de Hirsch knew well enough that miscarriages are inevitable at the beginning of any colonization enterprise and expected real results only from the second generation, but he was irritated nevertheless by the recalcitrant mood of the first colonists and the failure of his representatives to control it. He sought for apostles who should be congenial to him, and it grieved him that none such were to be found. Improvement came sooner than might be expected, but Hirsch did not survive to see it. He died prematurely, on April 21, 1896.

His widow continued his humanitarian benefactions in accordance with his designs. She was open-handed in disbursing funds to the institutions her husband had founded, and she endowed them anew. Her special interest was in helping working girls and women. Three years later she too died, on April 1, 1899. All Israel mourned the loss of these benefactors who had devoted their hearts and their possessions as none other had done to the welfare of their persecuted brethren. One hundred and fifty million dollars is not too high an estimate for the gifts and bequests of the Hirsches for assisting needy Jews. But even nobler than this unique liberality was the intention that lay behind it, to create enduring and healing benefit for downtrodden and suffering Israel.

It cannot be said that the Jewish Colonization Association brought into being the high achievement that might have been expected of it.[17] By the death of its founder it gained a considerable increase in its monetary resources, thirty million dollars, to be exact; but it lost its directing spirit. A select group drawn from the Jewish committees of London, Paris, Brussels, Frankfort on the Main, and Berlin directed the management conscientiously and prudently, but with no guiding principle. They sought to help where it was possible to do so, and we shall meet with their work frequently and in various places. But the Jewish Colonization Association never fully attained the goal set by its founder, it never became an instrument for total emigration.

The Immigrants in Their New Homes

Emigration was indeed a necessity for the emigrants and brought them liberation, yet we can not close our eyes to the hardships it brought in its train. It posed problems for all concerned, for the immigrants no less than for the countries to which they immigrated and for the Jewish communities residing there. The immigrant was torn from his home which, however wretched it might have been, was still home. And now, after a long journey which exhausted his physical strength and his material resources, he was set down in an alien world which did not understand him and of which he had no conception, which was strange to him and in which his own strangeness excited attention. Uncertainty, the need for contacts, habit, all drove him to the existing Jewish quarters with their bad and cheap housing. The requirements of the newcomers were modest indeed, but even so the existing Jewish quarters could not provide sufficient living space and the immigrants spread to neighboring streets. In Whitechapel in London or on the Lower East Side in New York one might feel himself transported to a small town in Poland or White Russia: "foreign sounds, foreign faces, foreign smells."

This phenomenon disturbed the phlegmatic little man in London to no small degree.[18] For decades he had not emerged from his insular calm, and he could not imagine people who differed from his own lifelong habits. The New Yorker had become used to foreign ways earlier, but even the great melting pot could scarcely manage such huge lumps. "They fill whole blocks of model dwellings; they have introduced new trades as well as new habits; and they live and crowd together and work and meet their fate almost independent of the great stream of life surging round them."

Employment for the immigrants was a problem not

only in overpopulated England but also in labor-hungry America, even when the problem was not aggravated by crises which disturbed the normal economic balance. Simply because the distribution of trades among the immigrants was very uneven, at least 60% of the working Jewish population sought and found employment in the needle trades. They worked tirelessly, far beyond the normal length of hours, in unhygienic surroundings and at starvation wages.[19] The introduction of the sweatshop and the consequent lowering of wages caused bad blood between immigrants and workers already established and gave the Jews the reputation of being the enemies of the working class. In reality they were only miserable creatures who (in sharp contrast to the numerous other immigrants of the period) were unwilling to beg and eager to accept any work under any conditions, even when these conditions were injurious to their health. Their standard of living was extremely low, nevertheless they saved some part of their pitiful wages to educate their children or to support their parents or their brothers and sisters. When they finally realized their situation they defended themselves warmly against the exploitation of their labor.[20] They established unions and were not backward in their demands. Their struggle was waged with all the emotion they had imbibed from their socialist and revolutionary preceptors, and in consequence their radicalism aroused opposition. The Jewish worker was no resigned proletarian; an inner compulsion drove him to attain independence. Then as employer he frequently succumbed to the temptation of introducing the sweating system against which he had struggled as an employee.

Not every immigrant had the strength and the will to work; many preferred petty trade, and did not understand that business habits customary in the East are not to be used in the West. Many applied themselves to real estate speculation; they purchased or constructed slum dwellings and rented them at exorbitant rates to the immigrants that kept pressing in. A cloud of distrust spread over the surrounding population. The situation began to be canvassed in an unfriendly temper, and the question was raised whether the right of asylum should not be limited, whether the people concerned were really victims of political or religious persecution, and whether steps should not be taken to dam the stream of destitute aliens. An English labor leader who had passed the stage of fury and had attained a calmer view of the situation gave outspoken utterance to his feeling with reference to the Jewish workers in London: "We sympathize with you, we have a feeling of solidarity with you, but we should have been thankful if you had never come."

Something of the same feeling, albeit with a different undertone, was the basis of the attitude of the Jewish communities in the immigrant countries. *They* had not invited the immigrants, *they* had not demanded immigration; in fact, English and American Jews alike considered it their patriotic duty to keep immigration far from the shores of their own homeland. On the other hand, they regarded it their equally sacred duty not to leave their brethren, who had landed, in the lurch and not to allow them to become charges of the public charities. The burden was a heavy one, and grew heavier with every shipload that arrived; but along with the burden the readiness to sacrifice grew also. Communities learned to realize the Jewish fate from the example of the shipwrecked voyagers stranded on their shores. They could not think of denying their oneness with people of their own kin who had been persecuted for their religion's sake. In no long while the communities were swamped with newcomers.[21] In the course of twenty years London and Manchester received an increment of 10% in their Jewish population; Leeds and Philadelphia more than 200%, and New York fully 400%.

Before 1881, when immigrants came singly, they sought and obtained affiliation with the existing communal bodies. But when they arrived in crowds they clung together and formed their own groups. They clung also to the German-Jewish language in which they had grown up; and lo! a miracle! Yiddish, to be sure with an admixture of new English additions, experienced a renaissance in the lands of freedom and became the language of newspapers, of a literature, of the theater. The newcomers were dissatisfied with existing educational institutions and sent their children to *Heder*, a kind of pedagogical sweatshop in which quantities of time and energy extorted under duress brought small profits. They were dissatisfied with existing congregations, their usages and their rabbis, and they branched off into separatist groups. But the opposite extreme was also to be found. There were Jews who would have nothing to do with religion except to ridicule and oppose it, who rudely violated every pious feeling of the faithful and believed that in so doing they were doing honor to the doctrine of their prophet, Karl Marx.

Frequently the immigrants were the objects of complaint and accusation; they seldom had opportunity to air their own grounds for complaint and accusation. Many experienced bitter disillusion and defeat, suffered deprivation and degradation, were perplexed by the estrangement of their children, and cursed the day on which they had changed Pruth or Njemen for Thames or Hudson. Israel Zangwill has illuminated many of these remarkable figures with the golden rays of his humor; he has sketched their human failings and their strength — and he has done so with the love that reconciles and heals. He has transmuted these strange figures into human beings, so that Jews and Christians alike may understand them.

BOOK THREE
THE JEWISH RENAISSANCE

CHAPTER I

The Lovers of Zion: Ahad Ha'am

JEWS IN PALESTINE IN THE 19TH CENTURY

WHEN the question of emigration from Russia was first broached, a small but energetic group, composed principally of younger men, advocated immigration to Palestine. For half a century the attention of the West had been turned increasingly towards Palestine,[1] and from time to time it had been mentioned as a center for a large Jewish agricultural settlement. The country was in a deplorable state of neglect, as desolate and forsaken as the gloomiest biblical prophecies would suggest. Vegetation and soil conservation were absolutely neglected, roads were impassable and dangerous, the water supply extremely inadequate and unwholesome. Periodic epidemics, crop failures, and earthquakes aggravated the prevailing misery.

After Syria and Palestine had been assigned to the Ottoman Empire (1841) the European powers began to take some interest in the country. Church missions went out, and consulates were set up for their protection. This protection worked to the advantage of the Jews also, who flocked into the country in large numbers and put themselves under the sovereignty of the various European powers. When Moses Montefiore first visited Jerusalem in 1827 he counted fewer than a thousand Jewish souls in the city. On his seventh visit, in 1875, the estimate of the Jewish population was in excess of 12,000; and a decade later Jews constituted more than half of a population estimated at 35,000. Other cities with memorable traditions, such as Safed and Tiberias and even Mohammedan Hebron, received considerable accessions. The commercial cities of Jaffa and Haifa received smaller increments.

At first the immigrants were predominantly Sephardim from Levantine countries; but Ashkenazim from Russia, Poland, Hungary, Bohemia, and Germany came in increasing numbers, and in the course of time attained a majority. The inhabitants of Jerusalem were almost exclusively pietists, who wished to breathe the sacred air of the Holy Land, to pray and think devout thoughts there, and there to be buried. Their principal gathering place was the area in front of the Wailing Wall of the Temple, which took on its present aspect about 1870. The interest of the devout pilgrims was bound up with the ruins of the past; they took no thought for building up a future. Their pious hope was that God number their tears, hearken to their songs of grief, and take thought for the desolate sanctuaries.

Many of the new immigrants brought their small savings with them, which they then consumed; most relied entirely on support from home. They were convinced that their manner of life gave them a just claim for such support, just as the Christian churches supported their own anchorites. A system of distributing alms to the various national groups (*kolelim*), complicated by many ramifications, was elaborated and given the name *Halukkah*.[2] This system was not free of elements of corruption and grew to be a considerable moral evil and an active hindrance to cultural progress.

The sharp rise in Jewish population aggravated the prevalent poverty and affected hygienic conditions particularly. Incoming gifts did not nearly suffice for increasing families. Children and grandchildren desired nothing better than the contemplative life of their fathers and grandfathers, and the elders, for their part, regarded any worldly occupation as a defection from religion, or at least as a dereliction of their chosen profession. The result of this attitude in the upbringing of children was that girls received no education at all and that boys were taught only the traditional Hebrew books, and that by outmoded methods and with no regard to the realities of daily life. Even such modest demands as that the Talmud Torah curriculum be supplemented by instruction in Arabic and arithmetic were denied by the more fanatical, though certain rabbis did approve of these additions. Among the Sephardim there was less hostility to secular knowledge, but they were equally remote from worldly interests. There was no far-seeing and directing personality among the Jews.

The poverty of the Jews and their general fecklessness were narrowly observed by the Christian missions,[3] which employed all means, fair and otherwise, to promote proselytization. To convert the children of Israel upon the very soil on which they had rejected the Saviour seemed the greatest conceivable triumph of Christianity. The first Anglican Bishop of Jerusalem had been born a Jew, and this heightened their hope of success.

The Fairy Prince who aroused the Sleeping Beauty of Palestine from its magic slumber was Moses Montefiore.[4] The name of Jerusalem was blazoned upon his escutcheon and was an outward expression of the profound spiritual bond which united him with the Holy Land and the Holy City. He was devoted to it with the complete fervor of a deep Jewish piety, and his faith saw the desolate countryside in a new splendor as the future home of Jews who would renew its soil with love and devotion. He visited Palestine seven times, and on each occasion, during her lifetime, his loyal wife accompanied him. Each of these journeys involved hardships scarcely imaginable today, if not actual peril; upon each occasion he distributed bountiful largess for the alleviation of immediate needs; and for each visit he contrived some new plan for the permanent improvement of the material and social condition of his coreligionists. As a young man he conceived a large-scale colonization project. Mehemed Ali, the Egyptian pretender, had made certain promises, but was relieved of the embarrassment of having to fulfill them by losing title to the country. The Sublime Porte would hear nothing of ceding or even of leasing any areas, no matter how small, to foreigners, and Montefiore required the support of the British Foreign Office to obtain permission to acquire small plots in cities. The inhabitants of Jerusalem, Jews, Christians, and Mohammedans alike, praised their unique benefactor as heaven-sent; they could rely upon his support for every need, and of needs there was no lack.

Montefiore's immediate objective was the improvement of hygienic conditions. At his own expense he sent the first Jewish physician to Jerusalem. He installed a pharmacy and planned a hospital, which was subsequently built by the Paris branch of the House of Rothschild. His efforts to relieve the overcrowding of the Jewish quarter marked a significant departure. He built a row of houses outside the Jaffa Gate. Under the prevalent conditions of insecurity it was actually dangerous to live outside the city walls, but the new houses with their little gardens attracted tenants and gave a direction to the expansion of the city. Montefiore was also concerned for the improvement of education; but here even his very modest demands met with the opposition of the Ashkenazim, and he did not dare proceed counter to the decision of the rabbis. He did succeed in establishing a sewing school for girls, and some elementary instruction was given there. In general his efforts were directed towards making the population productive; through small industries and work at home they were to be educated to become self-supporting and to reduce the cost of living. He purchased an orange grove near Jaffa, and in Galilee he helped hundreds who were willing to farm to acquire land. But these enterprises, all undertaken with the best motives, unfortunately met with little tangible success. Many blunders were blamed upon Montefiore and those acting in his name, and in the course of time his activities met with sharp criticism.[5]

More significant than Sir Moses' own accomplishments was his instigation of others. His warm advocacy of Palestine gave others faith in his ideals and aroused a spirit of emulation. When Judah Touro, the New Orleans philanthropist (see p. 121, above), died, he bequeathed $50,000 for the Jewish poor of Palestine and made Montefiore joint trustee for the disposition of this sum. The example of constructing new houses was later followed by the Hirsch[6] family of Halberstadt and by other wealthy Jews. For the improvement of education Elise Herz von Lämel of Vienna founded a boys' school in the name of her father, Simon Edler von Lämel. Ludwig August Frankl,[7] the Viennese poet and liberal, was entrusted with the task of establishing the school; he has left us a vivid account of his experiences (1856). Frankl was not deterred by the difficulties which were put in his way, and the school which he established attained great significance in the development of Palestinian Jewish education. The same may be said of the Eveline de Rothschild School for Girls, founded by her London relatives after the premature death of that enthusiastic young woman. This school was later supplemented by the Lionel de Rothschild School (*Institution Israélite pour Instruction et Travail*). The repeated visits of the great scholar Albert Cohn[8] had beneficial results. He was the almoner of the Paris Rothschilds and had an advantage over Montefiore in that he knew Arabic and so could enter into fuller understanding with the natives. It was he that organized the hospital. He also worked for the education of girls and for freeing the Jewish population from the scourge of the *Halukkah*.

Cohn's reports to Paris failed to arouse any hope there for the immediate future of Jewish productive work in the Holy Land. Zevi Hirsch Kalischer,[9] the rabbi of Thorn (1795–1874), called attention to the necessity of settling Palestine from the point of view of Jewish tradition and of contemporary needs. His book, *Derishat Zion*, aroused considerable notice. He urged that a fund be gathered for the purpose of establishing Jewish agricultural colonies in the Holy Land. As a result an *Israelitischer Verein zur Kolonisierung in Palästina* was founded in Frankfort and its efforts were vigorously promoted by Rabbis Esriel Hildesheimer, Isaac Rülf and Adolf Salvendi, who maintained their connection with Palestinian work over a long period. Notwithstanding French interests in the Near East, Paris Jewry, especially the *Alliance*, remained cool. Indeed, when Serbian Jews, who understood agriculture and had suffered persecution in 1865, desired to migrate to Palestine they were met with a direct refusal of the help they requested of the *Alliance*. It was only upon the intercession of Charles Netter that the *Alliance* ventured upon the attempt to train young men in agriculture. In 1870 it set up a gardening and agricultural school, called *Mikveh Israel* ("Hope of Israel"), upon land granted by the Turkish government outside the gates of Jaffa. The institution suffered from the usual ailments of infancy, but Netter never despaired. He devoted every care and every effort to save his child, which gradually developed into a model school and became a nursery for future Palestinian truck gardeners and wine growers.

The reports brought back by eyewitnesses, as for example that of Heinrich Graetz after his visit to Palestine in 1872,[10] were scarcely encouraging. The *Halukkah* used its power to penalize parents who sent their children to the modern schools and to hinder any progress in making them productive. The man who, despite discouragements and obstacles, never lost faith in the willingness of Palestinian Jews to work was Moses Montefiore. He made it the first object of the Montefiore Testimonial Fund, founded in his honor, to settle the Jews of Palestine upon the land. But the collections brought much criticism and little money. The contributions sufficed only for the erection of new dwellings in Jerusalem. Still, the lively discussions on the subject had a beneficial result in that the Jewish population itself came to realize more clearly its own willingness to work. Israel Dob Frumkin[11] and Jehiel Michael Pines (1842–1912) labored to educate and stimulate. Despite their own rigidly orthodox convictions they were unsparing in their denunciations of the *Halukkah*, and consistently advocated the cultivation of trades and especially agriculture.

The time was not yet ripe, and the human material was still as little suited for successful settlement as was the completely exhausted Palestinian soil. Even trained farmers were confronted with grave difficulties for many years, as the Knights Templar of Württemberg had been. In 1878 several Jewish families from Jerusalem ventured to purchase land in the neighborhood of Jaffa and to lay out an agricultural settlement. They named it Petach Tikvah[12] ("Gate of Hope") because in their enthusiasm they expected that their example would open a path of hope for the entire Jewish people. They went out into the desert six miles back of Jaffa, a journey of two and a half hours by horse in the existing state of the roads and completely impassable in the rainy season, with no other equipment than a firm resolve to live by the work of their hands and to make the land fruitful. Fortunately the Arabs of the vicinity were not hostile, but they refused to work for the Jews. The Jews worked with devotion and with every ounce of their strength and were ready to take upon themselves all the toil of making the desert arable and all the self-denials of pioneers. But they were decimated by malaria; provisions for prophylaxis and medical care were negligible, and they could do nothing but abandon their swampy location with deep heartache and wait for more favorable conditions. Whether such would ever come and when, no man knew.

Christian and Jewish *Hoveve Zion*

In the meanwhile a warm interest in the fate of Palestine, and particularly in the return of the Jews to their old national home, was manifested in Christian circles in England. Some were moved by religious considerations; the motive of others was romantic. George Eliot[13] (Mary Ann Evans, 1819–1880) in her novel, *Daniel Deronda*, made Mordecai, a humble, disfigured watchmaker, her spiritual hero, and put into his mouth thoughts which had grown strange to almost all the Jews in the world. Deronda emphasizes the universal power of faith "even when mistaken, expectation even when perpetually disappointed." "I felt the heart of my race beating within me; I counted but as a fool to the divine flame. They say 'he feeds himself on visions' and I denied not, for visions are the creators and the feeders of the world." One of these visions is the resurrection of the Jewish nation on the soil of its ancient home, where they could lead their own life, independent and free. The suggestions of the famous novelist impressed the Anglo-Saxon world enormously, and in many Jewish circles they were looked upon as a new revelation. "She did most among the artists of our day," wrote Emma Lazarus, "toward elevating and ennobling the spirit of Jewish nationality."

Others were more concerned with the political aspects of the problem. "The Sick Man at the Golden Horn," as the Turkish Sultan was then referred to, seemed doomed to a chronic ailment. Recovery — and here England was vitally interested — could only be attained by a complete cure in the Sultan's non-European possessions. As in its earlier history, Palestine might serve as the bridge between Asia and Europe; it might be developed into a productive country by Jews, who would thus attain a rebirth and provide the Sultan with a population devoted to himself. Such were the directions taken by the speculations of Laurence Oliphant,[14] who was an expert in the affairs of the Ottoman Empire, had traveled up and down and across Palestine, and had suggested to the Sultan that Jews be settled in the fertile and depopulated area across the Jordan. Never had a non-Jew devoted such energetic and such selfless efforts to the welfare of Jews. But the Jews of the West, whose moral and material support Oliphant had expected, remained cool to the proposition and hesitated, and so gave Constantinople time to alter its originally receptive attitude. Oliphant did find warm support among his Christian friends who wished to help oppressed Jews everywhere out of humanitarian considerations and were ready to contribute materially to that end. But the only tangible result was the settlement of forty-five Russian families near Aleppo in Syria. One of the rare opportunities for large-scale action was lost.

The Christian friends of Palestine assumed that the Jews would be moved by the same vital interest by which they were themselves actuated. They expected that the considerable fortunes in Jewish hands — greater than such fortunes had ever been before or were ever to be again — would be readily put at the disposal of a historic movement to rebuild a Jewish Palestine. But they were deceived on both counts. A large portion of Jews was hostile to any thoughts of Palestine. They looked back with misgivings on the struggles in which loyalty to Palestine had been used as an argument against emancipation. And even those who had not abolished the Palestine hope from their thoughts and their prayers looked upon this hope as an unsubstantial dream, a symbol for whose actualization there was no place in a modern life which tended to transcend nationalist concepts and think realistically. There were indeed some rabbis,[15] like Jehiel Brill or Samuel Mohilewer, with a complete and simple faith, who looked upon the dream as capable of realization and did not wish to await a supramundane and millenary intervention. They declared it the duty of the Jewish people really to work for a return to its homeland. It was the desire of some to provide the opportunity for a full and complete observance of the ancient law; others merely wished for the reconstruction of a Jewish homeland. For both groups, their ideals were bound up with the philanthropic motive of helping Jews to a place of rest and security.

Into this mixed chorus a new voice was introduced by a young Paris student of medicine named Eliezer Perlmann, who attained fame under the name of Eliezer ben Yehuda.[16] Ben Yehuda emphasized the nationalist aspects of the question. The Jews, he insisted, are a nation, and must regain their national language as well as their national homeland. He threw his studies aside in order to live for his people in Palestine. With unyielding persistence and a determination that was often repellent, he forced everyone with whom he came into contact to converse with him only in Hebrew, and he became a potent factor in the resurrection of the language of the Bible. He was convinced, as were other Jews, that if they willed it and were energetic about it the Jews could effect their national resurgence as the Balkan peoples had recently done. This conviction involved a complete misapprehension of the difference in the two situations. Only a handful of Jews lived on the soil of Palestine, and these had not yet discovered the magic wand with which to work the land and make it productive. The warmth with which certain periodicals espoused the Palestine idea had little immediate result. Confidence was wanting, and the attitude of the Turkish officials was not calculated to strengthen it.

But now came the Russian catastrophe and made the search for a solution a burning question. There was an overpowering urge to return to the ancestral home and to agricultural pursuits. Oliphant hastened to Brody and convinced himself of this urge by inquiries among the emigrants. He pleaded with the responsible Jewish authorities to yield to the urge, but could find no organized will to cooperate. The Turkish government for its part also put obstacles in the way, and those who were waiting in Constantinople for permission to enter into Palestine fell into a deplorable plight. The enthusiastic throng of Russian students who banded together under the slogan BILU[17] (*Beth Ja'acob Lechu Ue-nelecha* — "House of Jacob, come, let us go".) fared not much better. Most of them came from the University of Kharkov, were completely Russianized, and had quite forgot their Jewish origin. The tragic events had stirred them deeply and had aroused their Jewish consciousness; but they could see only one possible meaning in their being Jews, and that was to journey to the land of their fathers and there to work the soil with their hands. The idea took fire and the number of their adherents grew to 525; all wished to abandon their studies, emigrate to Palestine, and there establish model colonies on cooperative principles and so offer a solution not only for the Jewish problem but for the social problem generally as well. An idealism of extraordinary proportions sprang into being. There were orthodox rabbis who saw the inception of the Messianic age in this conversion of radical students, and took every means of forwarding their design. Unfortunately no use was made of this eager willingness. Only a small number of the BILU group ever succeeded in reaching Palestine and those that did met with difficulties enough to discourage the firmest resolutions.

The movement seemed to travel in circles. While the friends of Palestine in Russia were endeavoring to win the *Alliance Israélite* for their plan, and with the *Alliance* the various Jewish relief organizations, the people in Paris declared they would wait for the steps taken in Russia, that is to say, for the example of emigrants of means whose settlement would demonstrate the good faith of the movement. Into the literary war on the subject there was injected unexpectedly a brochure which offered a keen analysis of the situation, and so gave a new direction to the whole problem. This work was entitled *Auto-Emancipation; Admonition to his Brethren by a Russian Jew*[18] (Berlin, September 1882). According to the thesis of the author the prerequisite to the choice of a country for immigration is a thorough clarification of the question of the position of the Jews in the world, and the creation of a national consciousness and a national existence. His view of the situation was completely pessimistic. It was his conviction that hatred of the Jews would endure as long as the Jewish people itself; that the Jews, though dead as a nation, continued its existence and so created a fear of a phantom. "Judaeophobia" is a congenital demonic disease peculiar to the human race; it is not to be overcome by any reasonable means, and no polemic is capable of dealing with it. Antagonism towards the Jews, he argued, is an intelligible phenomenon, but one misunderstood by the Jews themselves because they possess no consciousness of selfhood; they struggle only for their individual existence but neglect the primal genius of their natural, national force. "What we lack is not genius, but self-respect and the consciousness of human dignity."

The only means of liberation is the creation of a Jewish national state, of a people occupying its own land, the *auto-emancipation* of the Jews, their attainment of a position as a nation with standing equal to other nations, by the acquisition of their own national home. Where this land should be, the author left an open question. What was wanted was not a holy land but a land that was the Jews' own; it need only be sufficiently large and give promise of becoming a productive center.

It was a physician who had laid his finger on the Jewish pulse, Dr. Leon Pinsker of Odessa. It was startling that this man, who was known as a Russian patriot, as a cosmopolite hostile to any radicalism, should make any such gloomy diagnosis as this:

> Our fatherland is the other man's country; our unity — dispersion; our solidarity — the general hostility to us; our weapon — humility; our defense — flight; our individuality — adaptability; our future — tomorrow.

His summons constitutes a rejection of emancipation:

> ... a rich gift, a splendid alms willingly or unwillingly flung to the poor, humble beggars whom no one, however, cares to shelter, because a homeless, wandering beggar wins confidence or sympathy from none.... In the midst of the nations among whom the Jews reside, they form a distinctive element which cannot be assimilated, which cannot be readily digested by any nation.

He saw the Jewish fate persisting ever the same in all ages and all lands and inescapable unless some new and decisive direction were given to it. Pinsker's therapy convinced neither party; the one denied the existence of a separate Jewish nationality, the other refused to allow the existence of a nationality in an undefined location and could justify it only with its seat in Palestine.

From the echoes brought forth by his conclusions, Pinsker realized that the "national resoluteness" which he called for could be found, if at all, only among the

Hoveve Zion ("Lovers of Zion"), and so, without compromising his fundamental principles, he joined forces with them. In many communities of the Czar's realm there were formed associations under various but similar names, whose common purpose was *Hibat Zion*[19] ("Love of Zion"). Their aim was to promote the settlement of Palestine and assist settlers there by their united moral and material forces. There was much enthusiasm, many contributions, and plenty of opportunities for using the sums collected.

Settlements of families of some means were made: those from Russia settled in Rishon le-Zion, not far from Jaffa, others, from Rumania, in Rosh Pinnah (near Safed) and Zichron Ja'acob, halfway between Haifa and Jaffa. Petach Tikvah was settled again. But it soon became apparent that for a successful settlement more was required than enthusiasm and the readiness to sacrifice. The pioneers contributed not only the strength of their bodies but also spiritual élan. The redemption of the land they looked upon as a sacred duty. The draining of every swamp, the clearing of every dunam, the building of every house, the digging of every well was marked as a sacred day. But what price the utmost devotion when the soil, like the human material, was unfit for colonization, when the means available were inadequate for giving the enterprise its start and setting it into motion, when officials put all manner of obstacles in the way, when expert knowledge and intelligent management were wanting?

These men and women were not brought up to such heavy labor or such painful deprivation; but they were inspired by an unswerving determination not to yield, to conquer the soil of their ancestors by the toil of their hands. They were prepared to make every sacrifice to win a future for themselves and their people; they took upon themselves a martyrdom which was to lead not downward to destruction but upward to resurgence. They collapsed under the combined attack of starvation, trachoma, malaria, and other tropical diseases; the slight assistance which the *Hoveve Zion* were able to send them did not suffice for their needs. But their heroism left no room for doubt that the work would eventually be successful, that the creation of viable colonies and a farmer class in Palestine was no idle Utopia.

This was the impression of Charles Netter when he visited Mikveh Israel in 1882; it was symbolic that this Jewish philanthropist came to his eternal rest in the Holy Land shortly thereafter. He did not hesitate to press upon his friends in Paris, through one of the colonists, the urgency of saving from collapse an undertaking so promising for the future. The same anxiety hurried Samuel Mohilewer, the Radom rabbi, to Paris. Both representatives gained the ear of the Grand Rabbin, Zadoc Kahn, and by him were brought into touch with Edmond de Rothschild (1845–1934). Rothschild[20] had frequently expressed his conviction that the return of the Jews to Palestine was a vital need, and that the center for the development of their spiritual and moral civilization must there be created. In the colonization which had been begun he recognized a step towards the realization of his ideal, and so he determined to take the enterprise under his protection. He overhauled the existing colonies, taking care of their hygienic as well as financial and administrative needs, and laid plans for new colonies. He saw to a rational plan for the establishment of colonies, he provided that they be equipped with houses and barns, with livestock and tools, with synagogues and schools, and all the appurtenances of an orderly communal life. He tided the colonists over the early hardships until they could produce a regular annual crop, and, most important, he provided for the drainage of the settled areas and for the eradication of malaria. He was fully aware of the difficulties which threatened his undertaking. His sceptical friends smiled and mocked at him for building on sand. The Turkish officials put every obstacle they could think of in the way of settlement; the colonists rebelled against being the wards of the Rothschild management; but Rothschild bore all patiently, in the conviction that he was working for the future. Success, however dearly purchased, did come. Fifty years later, Rothschild, now considered the Grand Old Man of Palestine colonization, could look with complete satisfaction upon the achievement of the great work which he had had in mind from the beginning — Israel rejuvenated upon the land of Israel.

The *Hoveve Zion* did not diminish their efforts. A great impulse was given to their work by the one hundredth birthday of Moses Montefiore, the divinely blessed pioneer of modern Palestine work. They wished to establish new colonies in his name, to convoke an assembly of all like-minded people in his honor, and to found a Montefiore Society for the Promotion of Agriculture. They dispatched David Gordon, the editor of *Ha-Maggid*, who was faithful to their cause, with a fulsome address to Ramsgate. But Gordon met with a cool welcome. The old gentleman was too feeble to be receptive to new ideas, and his relatives and associates too firm to permit him to assume new responsibilities. The hope that the name Montefiore would serve as a magnet to attract some of the Montefiore millions proved vain.

Nevertheless, the conference did take place, November 6–11, 1884. The meeting place was Kattowitz,[21] where the three empires of Russia, Austria, and Germany met at that time, and where the local community provided a favorable environment for the enterprise. This was the first Palestine conference of modern times. Its thirty-six delegates came from all the great countries of Europe and represented all professions, ages and religious tendencies. Dr. Leo Pinsker took the chair, and though he had not surrendered his former plans and still regarded the humanitarian problem as central, he nevertheless enjoyed general confidence and was named presiding officer of a provisional executive committee to prepare for colonization in Palestine. On his journey home he visited Heinrich Graetz in Breslau and succeeded in obtaining the cooperation of that famous and widely read Jewish author, who had emphasized the national content of Jewish history. When, shortly thereafter, Graetz learned from newspaper reports that the goal of the movement was not only philanthropic but also political, he withdrew his approval. This touched upon a decisive critical point. For although the conference had specifically stated that the efforts to colonize Palestine and to return the Jews to agriculture in no way involved the patriotism of the Jews, the attitude of Turkey to the new movement could not be a matter of indifference. Far from looking upon the colonization scheme as an improvement of the country, the Turkish government[22] saw in it the political danger of a second Bulgaria, and forbade the immigration and settlement of Jews, especially in the southern part of the country. It was ready to admit Jews into all parts of the broad Ottoman Empire excepting only Palestine.

It cannot be said that the intentions of the *Hoveve Zion* were greatly favored by fortune. It seemed as if everything conspired against them. It was not only the soil of Palestine, which in those very years chanced to produce mediocre and poor harvests. It was not only the beneficiaries of the *Halukkah*, to whose interest it was to spread unfavorable reports on the colonization and its prospects. It was not only the numerous opponents in Russia, who derived from various camps and held out various reasons for their negative attitude. The *Hoveve Zion* were troubled by great difficulties in their own ranks. Despite many promises and ample publicity, their income lagged far behind their requirements. No large undertaking could therefore be planned or be carried out. There was no unity among the groups or within individual groups. This confusion crippled their activity and brought despair to the settlers who expected help from Europe. In 1887 they were faced with an absolute blank, but the helpers to whom they appealed were themselves helpless. It was little wonder that unrest prevailed among the colonists and that they spread a spirit of recalcitrance to the Rothschild colonies also, where there was no pressing want.

The orthodox, who had originally expected a new era in Judaism from the Palestinian work, wished to remove the liberals from the management of the *Hoveve Zion* and particularly from the colonies which were being supported. The attitude of the rabbis assumed scandalous proportions in 1888–89, which was the year of the Release (*Shemitta*). They themselves favored the opinion that work could proceed on the soil of Palestine; but they allowed themselves to be intimidated by the intrigues of the opponents of colonization in Jerusalem, and later declared work prohibited during the year of the Release. Material for conflict was not wanting in the colonies themselves, and this cleavage provided tinder for a quarrel. These disruptive phenomena[23] were very depressing to a man of Pinsker's pure intentions, and it required all his idealism to continue with the prosecution of the movement. One handicap was the failure of the Russian government to recognize the movement. Recognition was finally attained in 1889, when the Society for Supporting Jewish Agriculturists and Artisans in Syria and Palestine was authorized. Its central offices were in Odessa, and so for a long period it was styled "The Odessa Committee." Dr. Pinsker was made chairman, and he retained the office until his death at the end of 1891.

The force of the idea was so irresistible that it spread despite all internal difficulties. It found centers of support in Germany, Austria, even in the United States, and some of particular importance in England. In England there were men who were personally acquainted with the East and believed in its future. They had learned to know the Jewish pioneers in Palestine and had faith in their potentialities.[24] An English army officer, Major, later Colonel, Albert E. W. Goldsmid (1846–1904), was deeply interested by the work of the BILU when he came into contact with it in Palestine, and upon his return to England he set to work with all the force of his vigorous personality, not only in behalf of the colonization idea, but for arousing Jewish national consciousness. At his side stood Elim Henry d'Avigdor (1841–1895), who had participated in the construction of railroads in Syria, and later, in England, became active in behalf of colonization. He was the organizer of the first *Hoveve Zion* in England and advocated a carefully thought-out plan for organization and work. He arranged for the purchase of an area in Hauran, and it was as a result of his work that Samuel Montagu, M. P., delivered a petition of the English *Hoveve Zion* to the British Premier, Lord Rosebery, for transmission to the Sultan. The scope of the requests was modest. Permission was sought for a limited number of selected agricultural workers to settle in Transjordania, for facilities to make the work of colonization possible, and for freedom from taxation during the time of transition were requested. The petitioners were careful to emphasize the peaceful and non-political character of their enterprise. But the petition failed of its purpose. The government in Constantinople was very distrustful of plans of this nature, particularly when they derived from England.

Ahad Ha'am

Into this spate of ambitious designs there burst a pointed barb of criticism which declared that, without a unifying basic principle, the entire scheme was preposterous. *Lo zeh ha-derech*, "this is not the proper way," cried its author to the Lovers of Zion — not indeed because he opposed them but, on the contrary, because he wished to avoid dissipation of valuable forces. The author called himself Ahad Ha'am, "one of the people," but his treatise and those which followed aroused such interest that he shortly became *the* one, towering above others, the mouthpiece of his own generation and the educator and leader of following generations.

Asher Ginzberg[25] was his real name; he was born in August 1865 in Skwira, in the Ukraine, and later lived in Gopishitza, province of Kiev, where his father held a profitable leasehold. He was the only son of a prosperous and respected family and received a careful education as well as the usual training in the rabbinic tradition. His family belonged to the élite of Hasidism and so he was not permitted to learn Russian, for the very sight of the alien alphabet was supposed to pollute the eyes. When he was twelve years old his father presented him to the rabbi of Sadagora, Eastern Galicia, of whom he was a devoted follower; but the boy found the usages of the rabbi's court repulsive. He developed an antipathy for Hasidism and inclined to the literature of the *Haskalah*. He prosecuted his study of Talmud and rabbinic literature with great zeal, and at the time of his marriage, at the age of sixteen, he had achieved a wide reputation in rabbinic responsa, and his advice in formulating decisions was sought by men who were themselves authorities. But Ginzberg also read in the literature of Jewish philosophy and of modern rationalism, and found support in Pissarev and other contemporary idols of liberal Russian youth. He felt the urge to go abroad, to complete his education by pursuing systematic, scientific studies. He traveled by way of Brody where he saw the shocking misery of the refugees with his own eyes, and went to Vienna. There he remained only a few weeks, for he distrusted his own

THE LOVERS OF ZION: AHAD HA'AM

capacities. Later attempts to work at the universities of Berlin and Breslau failed similarly.

But these journeys did produce one decisive result, a determination to master as much of foreign languages and general knowledge as he was capable of. He was especially attracted by mathematics and philosophy, and in particular by the celebrated champions of positivism, such as John Stuart Mill and Herbert Spencer, who exercised a strong influence on the formation of his own philosophy. In 1884 he went to Odessa, and there for the first time he came into contact with an environment that was spiritually aroused. The *Hoveve Zion* quickly became aware of his potentialities and drew him into their counsels. After a short interruption he took up his permanent residence in Odessa. His parents settled there also, in consequence of the May Laws which made it impossible for them to continue their leasehold. Asher Ginzberg's towering gifts were soon recognized. He belonged to Pinsker's circle and when the Odessa Committee was organized in 1889 it was natural that a place should be made for him upon it.

On the basis of his discussions of the Palestine problem and his investigations into the causes of previous miscarriages and disappointments, Ginzberg came to the conviction[26] that a thought as new as that of a Jewish national ideal required a certain amount of spiritual preparation, "a strengthening of faith and a kindling of the will to attain the goal." The goal was national, not individual. So had the life of Israel itself begun; the Torah had as its aim the welfare of the whole, by the side of which the welfare of the individual was inconsequential. Later development had given too much emphasis to the individual, and had formed the Jew according to this pattern. To swing the pendulum back, a "revitalization of the heart" must be undertaken; men must be educated to a sense of common responsibility. Colonization must be regarded not as an economic or philanthropic, but as a national problem. To yield to present self-interest was perverse, and such tendencies must be vigorously combatted.

> The heart of the people — that is the foundation on which the land will be regenerated. And the people is broken into fragments. So let us return to the road on which we started when our idea first arose. Instead of adding yet more ruins, let us endeavor to give the idea itself strong roots and to strengthen and deepen its hold on the Jewish people, not by force, but by the spirit. Then we shall in time have the possibility of doing actual work.

Ginzberg's essay made a profound impression. It evoked much opposition among men of more practical interests, who were eager to create something tangible and expected that spirit would then follow of itself. The attacks, some of them acrimonious, constrained the author to defend his point of view, and so he became a highly regarded publicist, partly against his own will. In sum, the differences between him and the *Hoveve Zion* were comprised in this, that they concentrated on numbers, whereas he concentrated on values; they saw the problem as an economic one, he as a moral duty; they thought in terms of settlements, he in terms of education; they regarded the individual and his needs, he the nation and its resurgence; they worked for the immediate present, he for the future if not for eternity. These thoughts recur constantly in the keen polemic of contemporary publications; they are the basic principles of Ahad Ha-'am's philosophy.

There was one group of men which was in complete agreement with Ahad Ha'am and recognized in him the leader of a new spiritual and ethical attitude. This group combined into a kind of Order, called *B'ne Mosheh*;[27] they were knights of a Jewish national renaissance on ethical principles. The circle was small but of high worth; its members were saturated with their mission and resolved to devote all their moral force to its realization. Rigid requirements had to be met by those who wished to join. Members were obligated to work with unity, system, discipline, truth and discretion, so that they might serve the common cause by faithful and appropriate common efforts, consciously avoiding exaggeration of available resources and wishful thinking. Their duty was not discharged by a day-to-day program, but by an educational task which would occupy them for many generations. A solemn oath bound each member to keep faith and to observe discretion with reference to the work of the Order. A formal ceremonial governed the meetings, so that the participants should at all times be conscious of their high calling. What was in effect taking place was a recrudescence of the ancient prophetic concept of "the remnant of Israel," which should become a nucleus for a newer and better Israel. A chosen group of high-minded men was ready to put their abilities and their spirit at the service of the spiritual and moral rebuilding of their people. It was in the nature of such an association that it should be limited to a small élite, for the number of reflective and spiritually-minded people is never very large. And in this instance the number was bound to be smaller, for the ideal which was to receive shape was still in the formative stage.

Poor judgment was shown in publicizing the association with a view to enlarging its membership; this move marked the beginning of the end. With the affiliation of local groups and with an augmented membership, differences of opinion on formal matters multiplied. Much energy was dissipated in mutual recriminations, and more essential work suffered. It was the principle of Ahad Ha'am, the first leader of the cause and its spiritual head, to leave as much as possible to the moral responsibility of the individual members and to lay down as little as possible in lifeless regulations. But expansion led to the opposite tendency. An attempt to remove the central office to Jaffa was unfortunate in that it brought the association into the conflict waged by Jerusalem against the freer thinking elements in general and directed especially against radical teachers. All the poisoned weapons which had been used in similar religious conflicts in the past were refurbished. The *B'ne Mosheh*, whose desire had been to remain non-partisan and to unite men of varying religious views into a common national enterprise, now suffered an internal cleavage. Thenceforward no contributions came from the *B'ne Mosheh*, but only suggestions. It dragged its existence on until 1897, at which time the greater part of the membership joined the movement of political Zionism, then in the ascendant; and, indeed, Zionism was indebted to the *B'ne Mosheh* for many of its decisive leaders, already trained in nationalist work. Menachem Mendel Ussischkin (1863–1941), for example, continued as a faithful leader for over fifty years.

Ahad Ha'am himself, in the reports on the actual situation in Palestine which he published after two visits to the country, set himself at variance with his following. He found it inspiring to see Jews working their ancestral soil with their own hands, but was repelled by the spiritual attitude of the inhabitants of Palestine. Upon the establishment of the Odessa Committee a boom in real estate developed which went far beyond the worst excesses of land speculation in a growing industrial city in any capitalist country. Inasmuch as the Turkish government rigidly forbade immigration of Jews, the day of reckoning was inevitable and the boom collapsed. What Ahad Ha'am saw were schemes for profit-taking, built chiefly on sand, and men who were seeking lucrative investments, not men who would devote themselves to an ideal. The critic who was decried as a dreamer made very keen observations on the dislocations in the Palestinian economy, in particular on its one-sidedness and want of self-sufficiency, and on the legal rights of the settlers. He was not content with criticism, but made useful suggestions for improvement.

Among his suggestions was the warning against increasing the number of immigrants by surreptitious means contrary to the will of the government. Not quantity but quality should be the decisive factor, not the extension of the colonies but their improvement should be the objective. Regeneration of the land of the Jews could only be achieved by men who lived in freedom and honor, who would give up the habits of the *galut*, who were not afraid of hard work if they could attain spiritual satisfaction thereby. Whether as a result of Ahad Ha'am's criticism or of the force of circumstances, there actually did come a pause in the establishment of colonies, and the older ones had a chance to consolidate and grow. Despite all obstacles a farmer class was actually in the making. In 1898 the American consul at Beirut, Syria,[28] reported to the State Department that nine hundred and sixty Jewish families, some five thousand souls, resided in twenty-two colonies. Development had begun and in time the land would "generously respond to modern influences." Within the Jewish population the view prevailed that reclamation of the soil was a religious service. The attitude of the Arabic Bedouins made the country insecure, and the corruption of officials, high taxes, obstacles to immigration, all combined to retard development; yet in spite of all this the consul reported "the prospects of Palestine brighter than ever. European influence, the tide of modern ideas cannot long be debarred."

Modern ideas affected the spiritual development also. Jaffa, called the rival of Jerusalem by the orthodox and feared as such, developed a modern school system. The use of Hebrew as the vernacular progressed; it became the language both of daily life and of a contemporary culture. It took root in the colonies also, and the colonists employed it in their work as in their leisure. They created Hebrew songs. Naphtali Herz Imber (1856-1909), who spent some time in Palestine as secretary to Oliphant,[29] became the bard of the new Jewish Palestine; his *Hatikvah* became the Jewish national anthem. Nationalist education made great strides within Palestine and without. In Russia, Hebrew was cultivated as a living tongue. Not only did the new higher schools support it, but the Hebrew publications also contributed to this development.

Because of the deterioration of his personal fortune Ahad Ha'am was constrained to adopt a calling and became manager of the publishing house of *Ahiasaf*[30] in Warsaw. This house served the cause of the national renaissance and diffused a meritorious Hebrew literature. Here Ahad Ha'am published the first collection of his essays (*'Al Parashat Derachim*, 1895) and in the following year he thought the ground prepared for a Hebrew monthly. The *Hashiloah* which he founded became the literary forum of the new movement. Here problems of the Jewish present and future were discussed, here the Hebrew storytellers, poets and thinkers of the new generation found a platform from which to give expression to their thoughts and feelings. From the *Hashiloah* there emanated a new atmosphere, a new spirit, a new style.

Ahad Ha'am's strength lay in his work as publicist. It was never his lot to present his philosophy as a unified system; but his essays, always dealing with a simple, concrete problem, always fresh, always lively, always imbued with a lofty idealism, were extraordinarily influential. His brilliant fancy, his original approach, his striking applications to the vital questions of contemporary Judaism, won readers who did not necessarily subscribe to his theoretical premises.

In theory he took his stand with the positivist philosophy, in practice he wished to appear, like Nathan the Wise, exclusively the Jew (Graetz, V, 323), but in a sense quite other than Lessing's individualist. For him the Individual was quite subordinate to the People. The People was the real ego, the bearer of a creative spirit, the source of national creativity. The biologic law of the nation was alike point of departure and goal. The Jewish people, or better, the ancient Hebrew people, received its peculiar form at the hands of Moses and the prophets who succeeded him; its task was to propagate truth and justice in the world, without limitation and without compromise. Alone of the peoples of the earth the Jews had rejected the cult of power and had paid honor exclusively to moral and spiritual values. From time to time, as a result of unfavorable external influences, its efforts in this direction had grown weak and negligent, but it had at no time entirely forsaken them. In the present, which posed problems never hitherto encountered, Judaism was assailed by various evils. In the ghetto, which maintained the Jewish spirit, it was cramped by limitations of space and means; in the open fields of the emancipation, where it had attained access to the world, it suffered from inner want of freedom, from the mortification of all hope for the future. Recovery could be expected only from the reawakening of spiritual identity, that is to say, by the restoration of the national, ethical and spiritual ideal of prophecy to its central position in life and by the creation of a spiritual center for its preservation and cultivation in Palestine. The numbers in this center might be insignificant; if only it were strong spiritually it would effect a quickening of the heart.

When all the scattered limbs of the national body feel the beating of the national heart, restored to life in the home of its vitality, they too will once again draw near one to another and welcome the inrush of living blood that will flow from the heart.... The influence of the center will strengthen the national consciousness in the Diaspora, will wipe out the spiritual taint of *Galut* and will fill our spiritual life with a national content which will be true and natural, not like the artificial content with which we now fill up the void.

This biologic concept of nationality led Ahad Ha'am to a new consideration of contemporary Jewish problems. The question of the purpose of the continuance of the Jewish people despite all its suffering was without meaning. It continued to live because it must, not to fulfill an imaginary mission to others, but by the law of its own being to live in accordance with its prophetic task. The religious problem had lost its edge; religious unity was gone; the old faith was undermined by philosophy and science; but the national unity was not disturbed. Various forms of belief could be accommodated and find a unifying element in ethical progress. The attitude to reform is changed. The question is no longer whether forms are antiquated or disruptive; from the national biologic point of view they are the expression of a given epoch, and cannot be changed by propaganda or caprice but by transmuting the spirit out of which they arose. Assimilation loses its terrors if the danger of being dissipated among various alien peoples is removed by the creation of a single central focus, by whose spirit all the scattered members of the people are unified and fructified.

According to a *bon mot* current at the time, every man possessed two countries, that of his birth and France. Similarly, according to Ahad Ha'am, every Jew had two countries; that of his birth, which controlled his political, economic and spiritual relationships, and Palestine, which governed his soul. The possibility of a conflict between these two spheres seemed to him unthinkable. The Jewish question then became a question of national will, of national education. In this direction Ahad Ha'am's doctrine attained a significance impossible to exaggerate in the generations that followed, even though political ventures thrust the national concept onto a quite different track.

CHAPTER II

Theodor Herzl and Political Zionism

THE *Judenstaat* AND ITS RECEPTION

WHILE Ahad Ha'am was publishing his essays, Theodor Herzl was writing his book, *Der Judenstaat*. The effect of this book was epoch-making. It brought into being a new movement in Judaism, political Zionism, which, after certain vicissitudes, received recognition, at the end of the World War in 1917, as a factor in international politics. Theodor Herzl[1] was one of those extraordinary figures who make history; not many such are vouchsafed to any people. His life was short and passed uneventfully until he recognized his special mission; and then it became involved in a maelstrom of struggle in which he rapidly exhausted himself. His brilliant personality, which rose suddenly, meteor-like, and disappeared undimmed, became the subject of heroic legend to a faithful and devoted following.

Theodor Herzl was born May 2, 1860, in Budapest, the son of a respected merchant, and in 1878 he moved to Vienna with his parents. He had the schooling customary in Jewish bourgeois circles, studied law, and obtained the degree of *Doctor Juris* in 1884. For a time he considered aspiring to the position of judge; but having, as a Jew, slight prospects of appointment or advancement, he turned to journalism. His maiden effort, accounts of travels in Spain, met with considerable favor in Vienna. The *Neue Freie Presse*, at that time a daily of world-wide importance, made him its Paris correspondent, and, upon his return to Vienna in 1896, the director of its belletristic department. Although Herzl's Zionist activities occasioned many conflicts with the owners of his newspaper, they were eager to retain so respected a writer on their staff and so Herzl kept his position until his death. His strength lay in the miniature art of the feuilleton, in his keen perception, artistic elaboration and spirited exposition. With the years his art, excellent from the start, developed to perfection, and his standing was that of a first-class writer. As a dramatist and storyteller he attained success only with those works which he wrote in the service of his ideal.

This ideal was the solution of the Jewish question by means of the politically unified will of the Jewish people. The Jewish question burst upon Herzl suddenly; previously it had been to him "a matter of indifference, lying under the threshold of his consciousness." Antisemitism "thrust it forward forcibly." A decisive factor was his first-hand experience of the Dreyfus affair, the fact that it was possible to arouse such passion against the Jews in so enlightened a country as France. In his capacity as newspaperman Herzl was present at Dreyfus' degradation. He was grieved by the depressing attitude of the crowd and turned to the writer sitting next to him, Hermann Bahr, the author of the *Enquiry on the Jewish Question*, and asked whether the crowd had no human feelings. The reply came: "You forget, sir, that this crowd is elated over the degradation of a Jew."

And so the ferment began to work in him and to seek for an outlet. For months he walked about as in a fever, conscious of the throb of inspiration; he "wrote as he walked, as he stood, as he lay, in the street, at table, and at night when inspiration routed his slumbers." His thoughts coursed and thrilled through his soul; he feared he would go mad. A friend to whom he gave the manuscript to read burst into tears; not because he was moved, but because he thought the author was in fact mad. There followed some weeks of grave crisis and then Herzl regained his balance and persevered in his plans. His desire was to withhold his *Solution of the Jewish Question* from publication, but to discuss it privately with men who could be of weight in carrying the plan out. But everywhere he met with scepticism or with only lukewarm agreement, and so he determined to resort to publicity. In 1896 he published an article in the London *Jewish Chronicle*, and a few weeks later he followed with his brochure entitled *Der Judenstaat*.

Let us summarize Herzl's thought, as far as possible in his own words:[2]

The Jewish question still exists. It would be useless to deny it. It exists wherever Jews live in perceptible numbers. Where it does not exist, it is carried by Jews in the course of their migrations. We naturally move to those places where we are not persecuted, and there our presence produces persecution. This external pressure in our upper classes causes unpleasantness, in our middle classes continual and grave anxieties, in our lower classes absolute despair. Antisemitism increases day by day and hour by hour among the nations; indeed, it is bound to increase, because the causes of its growth continue to exist, and cannot be removed.

Oppression and persecution cannot exterminate us. No nation on earth has survived such struggles and sufferings as we have gone through. Jew-baiting has merely stripped off our weaklings; the strong among us were invariably true to their race when persecution broke out against them. Old prejudice against us still lies deep in the hearts of the masses. He who would have proofs of it need only listen to the people where they speak with frankness and simplicity; proverb and fairy-tale are both antisemitic.

The longer antisemitism lies in abeyance the more fiercely will it break out. The infiltration of immigrating Jews, attracted to a land by apparent security, and the ascent in the social scale of rising Jews, combine powerfully to bring about a revolution. The Jewish question is a national question, which can only be solved by making it a political world-question to be discussed and controlled by the civilized nations of the world in council.

We are a people — One People.

We are one people — our enemies have made us one in our despite. Distress binds us together, and, thus united, we suddenly discover our strength. Yes, we are strong enough to form a State, and a model

State. We possess all human and material resources necessary for the purpose.

The distinctive nationality of the Jews neither can, will, nor must be destroyed. It cannot be destroyed because external enemies consolidate it. It will not be destroyed: this it has shown during 2,000 years of appalling suffering. It must not be destroyed. Whole branches of Judaism may wither and fall, but the trunk remains. The emigration societies for wandering Jews are created not for, but against, persecuted Jews — are created to despatch these poor creatures just as fast and as far as possible. The attempts at colonization made even by really benevolent men, interesting attempts though they were, have so far been unsuccessful. These attempts were interesting, in that they represented on a small scale the practical forerunners of the idea of a Jewish State. They have, of course, done harm also. The transportation of antisemitism to new districts, which is the inevitable consequence of such artificial infiltration, seems to be the least of these evils. Far worse is the circumstance that unsatisfactory results tend to cast doubts on the efficacy of Jewish labor.

No human being is wealthy or powerful enough to transplant a nation from one habitation to another. An idea alone can compass that; and this idea of a State may have the requisite power to do so. Let the sovereignty be granted us over a portion of the globe large enough to satisfy the reasonable requirements of a nation; the rest we shall manage for ourselves.

Herzl depicted the exodus of the Jews in the brightest imaginable colors as constituting an advance for all social classes and as a benefit for the states who would be relieved of their Jews:

The outgoing current will be gradual and continuous, and its initial movement will put an end to antisemitism. The Jews will leave as honored friends, and if some of them return, they will receive the same favorable welcome and treatment at the hands of civilized nations as is accorded to all foreign visitors. Their exodus will have no resemblance to a flight, for it will be a well regulated expedition under control of public opinion. The movement will not only be inaugurated with absolute conformity to law, but it cannot be carried out without the friendly intervention of interested governments who would derive considerable benefits from it and will further it.

As countries to which the immigration might be directed Herzl thought of Palestine and Argentina. He mentioned the advantages of each, without deciding between them.

He promised a seven-hour working day and other new and far-reaching social experiments. Problems relating to choice of a country for immigration and to the immigration itself were to be carefully prepared by a "Society of Jews" which was to be founded, and the execution of the plans was to be carried out through a financial instrument to be called the "Jewish Company" or the "Jewish Chartered Company," which was to be incorporated under English law, with its seat in London. Both bodies were to proceed with care and precision and so win the fullest confidence. Membership was to be voluntary. Those who were not like-minded would abstain, but those who did join would have the authority and the legal capacity to deal with governments. The nations would find their own conditions improved by the project of the Jewish state, and would be sympathetic to the Jews who were making their old hope of a Promised Land an actuality.

> Here it is, fellow-Jews! Neither fable nor fraud! Every man may test its reality for himself, for every man will carry with him a portion of the Promised Land — one in his head, another in his arms, another in his acquired possessions.
>
> We shall give a home to our people — not by dragging them ruthlessly out of their sustaining soil, but rather by transplanting them carefully to a better ground. Though we are creating new political and economic relations, we shall preserve as sacred all that is dear to our people's heart.

It is futile to enter into the details of the organization of the Jewish state as Herzl envisaged it in its minutest ramifications in his journal, in his brochures, and in his fascinating novel *Altneuland* (1902). For despite his efforts *not* to compose a Utopia, it was a Utopia that he composed; in this way no actual state ever came into being. But Herzl did inject new ideas into the forum of public discussion, to wit, that the Jews are a nation, that all Jews in the world are subjected to a common and unavoidable fate, and that this is to be dealt with not by struggling against antisemitism and not by philanthropy, but by open negotiations in the councils of the nations and by establishment of a Jewish state with their consent.

How came this cosmopolite among the prophets? How came this admirer of the Paris salons to advocate an exodus out of Europe? His best friends shook their heads and thought he had lost his mental balance.[3] For how could measures which involved a sharpening and deepening of the evil be regarded as a solution? But Herzl thought that the moral need was the more actual because Jews of his generation had dispensed with the inward counterpoise which our stronger ancestors possessed. Men jested behind his back, some laughed in his face quite openly, but he never allowed himself to be disturbed by the frivolous remarks of people whose insight he had never had occasion to rate very highly, and he retained his calm in the presence of jests, whether malicious or good-natured. And since his conduct in other respects was not unreasonable he was gradually allowed to devote himself to his whim, which many regarded as an *idée fixe*.

But the Jewish nationalist university men of Vienna,[4] who had been organized by Nathan Birnbaum and R. S. Landau, thought otherwise. They agreed enthusiastically. The territorial difference was soon bridged. Herzl quickly grasped the significance of the historic bond with Palestine, and "Zionists" of all countries put themselves under his guidance. News of his initiative swept through the ghettos of Europe with whirlwind speed; hearts in flight turned to him; large masses of people put unbounded faith in his wisdom and were ready to follow him unquestioningly.[5] He had put into words the inarticulate feeling that was cherished in the hearts of countless individuals and groups. He had proclaimed a magnificent goal, had aroused intense hope. Objective hindrances neither he nor his devotees could see. For them the only question was the willingness of the Jewish people; political and technical difficulties they were sure could be mastered with ease if only a mass movement could be stirred among them.

The trend of Herzl's thought was not strange to the friends of Zionism. A generation earlier, in the bloom of the period of liberalism, Moses Hess had written in a prophetic vein that the Near East would be made accessible and that the last of the national questions would be solved by the settlement of Jews in Palestine. But no one took the "communistic rabbi" seriously when he proclaimed a Jewish national consciousness. Perez Smolenskin (see page 222, above) found a strong echo, but his militant nationalism lacked the political aspect, the plan of the Jewish state. Herzl's ideas were to a certain extent identical with those of Pinsker (see page 257, above). Herzl had learned of *Auto-Emancipation* only after his own brochure was in print, for things Jewish lay outside his field of interest. He had not even read *Daniel Deronda*, which should have interested him as a literary man. It was perhaps providential that Herzl had no Jewish affiliations, for now no party could regard him as a renegade and all could give him their trust, which he did receive in the fullest measure. His definition of a nation as a "historic group of men of a recognizable cohesion, held together by a common enemy," in itself highly disputable, did not correspond with the concept of nationalism which his potential followers held. But it was not a matter of scientific definition, it was a matter of faith. And the people reposed their faith in the man who could write: "the Jews wish to have a State, and they shall have one. We shall live at last as free men on our own soil, and die peacefully in our own home." He could count on a following if only he would organize it.

Surprising help came from an unexpected source. William H. Hechler,[6] the chaplain of the British legation at Vienna, was one of those English enthusiasts whose lives are saturated in biblical imagery and to whom the restoration of Israel and Zion as prophesied in Scripture is a vital concern. He was intoxicated with Herzl's proposals and declared them a turning point "to fulfill prophecy." Now this enthusiast had very distinguished connections, as for example, with the Grand Duke of Baden, and through him with his nephew, the Emperor William II. From the beginning Herzl had conceived the idea of laying his plan before the German Emperor. He expected that that impulsive monarch would appreciate his extravagant idea and would advocate it to the Turkish Sultan who was his friend. It was Hechler who transmitted the *Judenstaat* to both princes. He hurried to Karlsruhe and procured an audience with the Grand Duke for Herzl. April 23, 1896, was the memorable day on which Herzl had his first opportunity to lay his plan for a Jewish state before a reigning prince. The Grand Duke was a chivalrous proponent of liberalism, one of the last and most distinguished. He discussed the proposals fully, gave his approval, invited Herzl to keep him informed, and indicated he would advocate the plan to the German Emperor.

At the same time Herzl was introduced to Constantinople by von Newlinsky,[7] the editor of the *Correspondence de l'Est*, who possessed remarkable political acumen and was on terms of intimacy with ambassadors, ministers and princes. Of the results of this journey Herzl reported to the Grand Duke as follows:

His Majesty the Sultan took my proposal under consideration. He expressed himself as definitely opposed to granting Palestine to the Jews as an independent State, but even so he did not discourage me entirely. Indeed, he showed me many marks of regard, and it was indicated to me indirectly that the affair might possibly go forward if the satisfactory form could be found. From the Sultan's entourage the suggestion was thrown out that the Jews might be permitted to found a vassal state in Palestine. Immigration would be facilitated by a grant of autonomy, and an annual tribute would be paid to the Suzerain.

Feelers to the Vatican were less successful. The attitude of the papal nuncio in Vienna was negative; the nuncio in Constantinople was instructed to work against Herzl's proposals. An accidental encounter with Prince Ferdinand of Bulgaria indicated the latter's sympathy. He even declared himself ready to speak for Herzl's reception at the Czar's court, though he had little hope for success.

The Organization of the Zionist Movement

The advance on the diplomatic front seemed extraordinarily favorable. Most statesmen were familiar with the *Judenstaat* and interested in its ideas even before they were approached personally on the subject. Herzl's self-confidence and his conviction of quick success grew enormously. But the response expected of Jewish notables was wanting. Financiers, philanthropic associations, and communities withheld approval. • They could be carried away neither by the plan of a Turkish loan nor by a gigantic colonization scheme in Palestine. They lacked Herzl's vision and faith. The difficulties seemed to them insurmountable, and the dangers to the position of Jews in various countries a matter not to be overlooked. Herzl's ideology seemed to them a flight from the nineteenth century. And the resentment which Herzl displayed in his transactions with Jews[8] was not calculated to reconcile opposition. Discouraging also was the rejection of the proposals on the part of eminent religious leaders.[9] The Chief Rabbi at London, Dr. Hermann Adler, who knew Palestine at first hand and had given his blessing to a pilgrimage of the Maccabeans then in progress, rejected the new concept of a nationalistic Judaism, and so did Dr. Moritz Güdemann, the Chief Rabbi of Vienna, a scholar and a man of the world, the first man of standing whom Herzl took into his confidence.

But Herzl did not want for companions for his journey. One of the first of the faithful was Max Nordau,[10] a physician by training, a writer by profession, widely known and recognized as an incorruptible critic of the times. He was born in 1849, the son of Rabbi Gabriel Südfeld in Budapest, and after 1880 he lived in Paris. Like Herzl he remained alien to all things Jewish until he too, like Herzl, was thrust into conscious Jewishness by antisemitism. Nordau was among the first in whom Herzl found instantaneous understanding and agreement, as soon as he acquainted him with his ideas. Nordau called the *Judenstaat* a great achievement, a revelation. The man of science decried for his realistic rationalism became a devotee of this new revelation and, in the sequel, one of its most vigorous literary proponents. From Cologne came Max I. Bodenheimer, a lawyer, and David Wolffsohn,[11] a merchant. Both had long been very active in Jewish national work; both were capable, active and practical; both were ready to do whatever they could to promote the success of the movement, and in particular to establish a connection with the Zionists in Germany. In Vienna there were plenty of men who agreed with Herzl and admired him, but these undisciplined enthusiasts were always in disagreement among themselves and did more to disrupt the work than to promote it.

The establishment of an international movement which rested upon propaganda and a large volume of intensive correspondence required systematic organizational work. But the friends whom Herzl trusted were not available for routine work, and his life was harried in consequence.[12] Only in the Anglicist Leon Kellner did Herzl find a "dear friend whose visits were points of light in all my vexation." Kellner became editor of the party organ, the weekly *Die Welt* which appeared for the first time June 4, 1897, in order to advocate the "conciliatory solution of the Jewish question." Its outward makeup and its militant tone did not promote conciliation. At least in Jewish circles its reception was anything but friendly, and even Zionists did not yield it the confidence which the central organ of a party might expect.

The periodical championed the idea of a world congress of Zionists which Herzl had convoked for the end of August in Munich. A sharp conflict among those concerned broke out in public print. True friends, among others the *Hoveve Zion* in England, were definitely opposed to the Congress; but Herzl insisted and the invitations went out. The Jewish Community of Munich[13] was terrified and protested against the honor intended for it, and the Congress was transferred to Basle. The Central Conference of American Rabbis unanimously deplored "any attempt for the establishment of a Jewish state" and expected that the establishment of such a state would bring "not benefit but infinite harm." The heaviest cannon was discharged by the executive committee of the Rabbinical Association of Germany.[14]

"In order to dispel false representations of the doctrines of Judaism and the objects of those who profess Judaism," this association made the following declaration in the daily newspapers:

The efforts of so-called Zionists to establish a Jewish national State in Palestine are in contradiction to the Messianic promises of Judaism as preserved in Holy Writ and in later religious sources. Judaism requires its followers to serve the fatherland to which they belong with full devotion and to promote its national interests with all their hearts and all their might. With this duty the worthy efforts which aim at the colonization of Palestine by Jewish agriculturalists are not in conflict, for these efforts have nothing to do with the establishment of a national state. Religion and patriotism alike, therefore, lay upon us a duty to beg of all who have the interest of Judaism at heart to abstain from the aforementioned Zionist efforts and in particular from the Congress which has been called despite all admonition to the contrary.

"A perplexing document," wrote Herzl. It was highly impolitic to transpose the struggle to the arena of dogma. Not only did immediate refutation come from orthodox quarters,[15] but many other prominent rabbis gave their support to the contemporary Zionist movement. Rabbi Samuel Mohilever, the old friend of Zionism, based his position expressly on the traditional Messianic promises. The mutually contradictory declarations did nothing to clarify the issues, but resulted only in a sharp divagation between Herzl's supporters and the "protesting rabbis."

The Congress took place in Basle, August 29–31, and brought the movement success far greater than had been anticipated.[16] Two hundred and four delegates from most of the countries of Europe, and also Palestine, Algiers, and the United States, were present. Filled with hope, they represented diverse ages and callings, spoke diverse languages, professed the most disparate philosophies; and still they could find a common ground for understanding and cooperation. They felt themselves to be in fact a Jewish national assembly. Herzl insisted upon so shaping the externals of the Congress that the delegates could find in it solemnity and inspiration; he showed a fine perception of impressive effects. In the festively decorated hall, the banner showing the blue and white[17] and the Star of David was unfurled, and thereupon became the Jewish flag. The transactions took place in the full light of publicity like those of all parliaments, and were attentively followed by numerous representatives of newspapers the world over. Herzl presided with the dignity and distinction natural to him. His extraordinary personality was at least as effective as his ideal. In his opening address Herzl reported on the purpose of the convocation and the tasks of the assembly. Then Nordau enthralled the audience with an impressive analysis of Jewish need, the material need of the Eastern Jews and the moral need of the Western Jews. With the reports from individual countries, Galicia, Rumania and the like, there was unfolded a shocking picture of the poverty, the misery, and the affliction of the Jews. Of Russia, where more than one half of the world's Jews lived at the time, nothing was said, for obvious reasons. This consideration was entirely just and necessary; nevertheless the silence was eloquent in showing how much the "international discussion" proclaimed in the opening address was yet to seek.

The same constraint appeared in the formulation of the program of the new movement. There was no more talk of a Jewish state; there was no mention of the assurances of international law in the first draft. It was only after long debate that the formulation which became known as the Basle Program[18] was adopted. This Program has been retained to this day:

Zionism seeks to secure for the Jewish people a publicly recognized, legally secured home in Palestine.

For the attainment of its goal the Congress set itself the following tasks:

1. The programmatic encouragement of the settlement of Palestine with Jewish agricultural workers, laborers and artisans; 2. the unification and organization of all Jewry into local and general groups in accordance with the laws of their respective countries; 3. the strengthening of Jewish self-awareness and national consciousness; 4. the preparation of activity for the obtaining of the consent of the various governments, necessary for the fulfillment of the aim of Zionism.

The form of organization was provisional, but despite numerous later alterations it remained unchanged in these essentials. The Congress was declared the "chief organ of the Zionist movement." It was composed of delegates chosen by electors who had paid a membership fee of at least a *shekel* (at the time, an English shilling). The Congress named an Executive Committee with its seat at Vienna, where an Inner Executive Committee with Herzl as president carried on the business of the organization. The Congress closed in a mood of exaltation and with unending ovations for its founder.

Herzl[19] saw in the Congress the embodiment of his Society of Jews. "The movement," he noted, "has its place in history; in Basle I created the Jewish state" — and then he added, "even though with opportunistic modifications and with weak execution." The newspaper accounts of the Congress were favorable; critical opinions came almost exclusively from the Jewish camp. Among the visitors to the Congress, but not a delegate, was Ahad Ha'am, "a mourner at a wedding festivity," as he styled himself. He was deeply disillusioned to hear only of politics and diplomacy and nothing of inner regeneration. To be sure Herzl's opening address contained the sentence: "Zionism is the return of the Jews to Judaism even before their return to the Jewish Land," but this thought nowhere came to the surface during the transactions. The redemption of Israel was to be expected at the hands not of diplomats but of prophets. The hour was not yet come, and the Congress was but a premature demonstration.

How wonderfully the two leaders who strove for the regeneration of the Jewish people might have complemented each other! Ahad Ha'am, the thinker who reckoned with the positive factor of a healthy people's force and energy and who wished to develop its power by hard and continuous toil, and, on the other hand, Herzl, the poet whose vivid fantasy expected that an imaginary outside world would furnish help and that a spontaneous drive of the popular will would follow. ("If you would have it so, it is no dream," is the closing sentence in *Altneuland*.) To Ahad Ha'am the primary object was to make the people's soul normal, to Herzl to make its body normal; Ahad Ha'am stood for moral strength, Herzl for political education.

A political movement[20] could be combined with any sort of general outlook; it required only the affirmation of the past and the future of Judaism, but made no sort of dogmatic demands. It was particularly fascinating to the educated youth, who, to use George Eliot's language, "found an interest in the world beyond the small drama of personal desires." Youth gave the ideal enthusiastic apostles and recruiting sergeants who worked as a permeating yeast in the Jewish communities. The communities of the West, whose conquest Herzl had set as his goal, took on a new aspect. They sprang into life with meetings, elections, resolutions and protests. There was talk of Palestine, of the Jewish people, of the need for studying Hebrew — all subjects which had previously been under a ban. Opposition was cried down in lively polemics.

For questions of immediate needs the Zionists of the West took little thought; even the colonization of Palestine was regarded with indifference, for Herzl had rejected infiltration and would approve only of open settlement on the basis of a charter. Upon these unrealistic objectives, relegated to a remote future, all attention was focused. The problem of the feasibility of their execution and of the possibility of combining loyalty to one's homeland with the effort to attain a new nationality was easily disposed of. The seriousness of this latter problem was not yet understood.

A purely political, secular movement was a new thing in Judaism, and its dangers were recognized by those among Herzl's followers who were faithful to tradition in beliefs and practice. Under the leadership of Rabbi Reines of Lida they united in the Mizrahi[21] Federation, which set as its goal the recognition and fulfillment of Jewish religious law within the Zionist movement. It was no part of the Zionist program to oppose such demands; the Mizrahi had a very large following in the

East and became an influential body in the movement. Ahad Ha'am also had a following, among whom Rabbi Marcus Ehrenpreis and Martin Buber, then a young student, were particularly outspoken and energetic. They labored unwearyingly to give political Zionism a foundation in the cultivation of Jewish cultural[22] values. It was from this circle that the much debated concept of a "Jewish art" arose. In consequence of this concept, the work of younger Jewish writers, painters and musicians came to give clear expression of their ties to Judaism. It is significant, however, that artists of the first rank refused to be classified in this category.

But to Herzl all speculation on aspects other than the political continued to be remote. Perhaps he would have been more responsive if the bitter need of his people, whom he had stirred up, had not driven him to action. He believed it necessary to convene a Congress annually, in order to keep alive the fire which had been kindled. Again, at these annual Congresses it was necessary to exhibit deeds. He forced the establishment of a Jewish Colonial Bank[23] as an appanage of the Jewish Company called for in the *Judenstaat*. This was to serve as the national financial institution. Of the obstacles with which this project met we shall have to speak presently; the Congress (August 28–31, 1898) was not stirred by it.

The Congress was stirred when a sport club passing the building in which the Congress convened gave the delegates standing on the balcony an ovation, calling out "Hurrah for the Jews!" This cry was strange to Jewish ears, and many of those participating in the Congress saw in the episode "the beginning of kindlier times."

Herzl's Diplomatic Journeys

After the close of the Congress a communication came from the Sultan, thanking the Congress for the telegram of greeting which had been sent him. This was an indication that he was not antipathetic to the movement. But a much greater sensation was to follow. The Emperor of Germany had decided to go to Palestine[24] and was prepared to receive a deputation of the Congress, with Herzl at its head, in the Holy Land. On October 17, 1898, Herzl arrived in Constantinople, and there learned that the Kaiser had granted him an audience. In Constantinople he had lengthy, informal conferences with the Kaiser and his Secretary of State (later Chancellor) Bernhard von Bülow on Zionism and other political problems. Arrangements were also made for the reception of the Zionist deputation in Jerusalem.

In the Jewish colonies of Palestine Herzl received the triumphant reception of a conqueror. On October 28 he took up a position, together with a student choir of Mikveh Israel, on the road from Jaffa; the Emperor and the Empress and their suite passed and were greeted by the choir with the strains of the German national anthem, *Heil Dir im Siegerkranz*. The Kaiser recognized Herzl, greeted him, and spoke to him of the beauty of the countryside and its great future if the water supply could be made adequate. On November 2 the Zionist deputation was received in Jerusalem in solemn audience. Herzl delivered an address in which he petitioned the Kaiser to secure the Sultan's approval for a Jewish Chartered Company for Syria and Palestine under German protection. His majesty was in a gracious mood and spoke again of the need of irrigation and of the large sums required for such an undertaking, which Herzl's "countrymen" (*Landsleute:* so the Kaiser referred to the Jews in all these conversations) could easily get together.

From the propaganda point of view the audience was an unexampled success, but it produced no tangible results. *Il n'a dit ni oui ni non*, said Herzl to his companion, Dr. Schnirer, as he left the royal pavilion. The Grand Duke of Baden, it is true, was optimistic. It was through his good offices that entrée to the Emperor had been obtained, and he had always encouraged Herzl with touching kindliness and patience. He now reported that the impression on the Kaiser had been very favorable, and that the Kaiser was willing to intercede with the Sultan when requested. But there the matter remained; no binding declaration was ever made. Disillusionment affected Herzl deeply. Failure was due not to his own inadequacy, as his own self-tormenting accusations charged, but, as he later discovered from authentic sources, to the sharp disagreement of the Sultan when the Kaiser spoke in favor of Zionism.

Herzl now had to direct his efforts towards winning the Sultan[25] over. The difficulties of dealing with the Sultan were augmented by Turkey's serious internal problems; the European powers pulled first in one direction and then in another. At the court itself, moreover, conflicting influences were at work, and since most of the officials were susceptible to bribery, one could never be sure which attitude they might favor at any given moment, or what party was bringing to bear the heaviest battalions of bakshish. Herzl himself had nothing positive to offer. He perceived that the Sublime Porte was pressed for money, and he toyed with plans for a loan; but there was no financier to back these plans — only Herzl's faith that he could find one.

After many vain attempts and negotiations through more or less honorable agents, Herzl learned that Professor Armin Vambéry of Budapest (1832–1913) had obtained for him the interview for which he so ardently longed. Vambéry,[26] one of the most distinguished linguists of his time, was a great favorite of the Sultan's and had long been attempting to influence the Sultan in Herzl's favor. On May 17, 1901, Herzl was received at Yildiz Kiosk[27] and was able to present his proposal to free Turkey of its public debt. As compensation he desired only that the Sultan should promulgate some recognizable and impressive measure of friendship to the Jews. The Sultan assured him that the Jews had always enjoyed his sympathy and that they did so still. Herzl had further opportunities to consult with the Sultan's counsellors on plans for putting Turkish finances on a sound basis. He emphasized that the Jews required a protector and must have one who was competent to act. When Herzl mentioned the demand for a charter, the response was made that no handicap would be put in the way of scattered Jewish settlements, it being assumed that the settlers would take up Turkish citizenship *before* immigrating and so automatically subject themselves to all Turkish laws, including the requirement for military service. Herzl was determined not to agree to such terms, but postponed his objections to the more favorable moment when the negotiations should be on the point of consummation. For the time being he asked only that the Jewish Colonial Bank be granted a charter for organizing a *Compagnie Ottomane-Juive pour l'Asie Mineure, la Palestine et la Syrie*. Vambéry gave his approval to this proposal.

Herzl left Constantinople utterly depressed. The Sultan had indeed bestowed upon him the highest order it was his custom to give and had shown him other marks of honor, but Herzl was repelled by the Sultan's entourage and by their intrigues. He took it hard that the Russian members of his Executive Committee were sceptical about the mission as a whole and even regarded it as a mistake. Even worse was Herzl's inability to negotiate the loan, despite feverish activity. Neither in the western countries nor in Russia could Jewish financiers be won over to the project.

In February 1902, the Sultan invited Herzl to new conversations. The results of the conversations Herzl formulated in a letter to his trusted friends as follows:

The Sultan offered colonization, on land granted by the government, in Asia Minor and Mesopotamia with the exception of Palestine; he demanded the establishment of syndicates which should attend to all financial enterprises such as banking, loans, mining developments, and the like. I had to refuse because I could only accept terms on the basis of our program, since the larger executive committee had not empowered me to conclude agreements of a different kind. But later I was semi-officially informed that I might deposit contingent collateral in banks for the various concessions. If this is to be taken seriously, negotiations can be initiated anew and will proceed more smoothly.

But while Herzl was conducting negotiations with the Executive Committee and with financiers, the wind in Constantinople veered, and it was thought Jews were no longer needed.

Herzl suspected that resistance in Constantinople was due ultimately to the intervention of Russia. In general he was afraid that difficulties were being put in the way of his scheme by the court at St. Petersburg. In view of Russia's significance in any solution of the Jewish question, he had long desired to lay his project before the Czar. Despite many efforts he could never succeed in obtaining an audience. But after the horrors of Kishinev (see page 379, below) the Russian government was eager for an opportunity to justify itself before the world. Herzl was received in St. Petersburg[28] by the Adjutant General of the Czar and by the two powerful ministers, Witte and von Plehve. The two ministers were opposed to one another politically, but they were at one in their judgment of the Jewish question. Each acknowledged that the Jews lived in fearful poverty; each deplored the large part Jews were playing in revolutionary movements. Each welcomed a proposal that might lead to the emigration of several millions of Jews out of Russia — Plehve did not wish to lose all the Jews, for he did not wish too much intelligence and capital to be withdrawn from the country. Witte declared himself ready, upon Herzl's offer, to allow subscriptions to the National Bank to be taken up in Russia if an affiliate of the Bank were established in the Czar's realm. Plehve refused confirmation of the proposals for the systematic work of the Zionist Organization. But he did do something considerably more important. With the consent of the Czar he delivered an official communication to Herzl in which he declared, in the name of the Russian government, that that government was ready to support fully at the Sublime Porte the plans for the establishment of a Jewish commonwealth.

This was an unexpected success, and was bound to strengthen greatly Herzl's position in the forthcoming negotiations. He had in his possession a communication of similar import from the Grand Duke of Baden,[29] in which the approbation of the German Emperor was held out in prospect, and he had permission to use both communications in his further negotiations; and so he proceeded on his course filled with courage and high hopes. First he secured the pledge of the Austrian Foreign Minister, and on January 23, 1904, that of King Victor Emmanuel III of Italy. The King was already acquainted with the project, spoke of it with great warmth and immediately instructed his Foreign Minister to put his good offices at Constantinople at Herzl's disposal. Only Pope Pius X, who had received Herzl on the preceding day, took a flatly negative attitude. He as well as his Secretary of State expressed themselves sharply against any settlement of Jews in Palestine. Even with the provision of special protection for the sacred sites of Christianity and Islam they could not be won over. We cannot at this stage determine whether the old juristic dictum was involved, *Roma locuta, causa finita*, or whether the Papal Curia would have shown itself more yielding in the face of a unanimous expression of will on the part of the great powers. In the contemporary political constellation the word of the Curia would not necessarily have been conclusive.

The only government which did not wait for Herzl's

proposals but invited him upon its own initiative was Great Britain. In May 1902 he appeared before the Royal Alien Immigration Commission which was in session at the time. The Commission had invited him as an expert[30] in Jewish migration, and to a certain degree they recognized him as spokesman for all Jewry. Upon this occasion Herzl was brought into contact with the English Foreign Minister, Lord Lansdowne. The English government recognized the need of doing something decisive for the amelioration of Jewish distress. It consented to Herzl's proposal to release the Sinai peninsula[31] to the Jews for colonization. This was not Palestine, to be sure, but a territory bordering on Palestine and one that had historical significance in that it had in the past served as an approach to Palestine. The territory was under Egyptian administration, and London recommended the project warmly to the British governor and the government of the Khedive. A commission of experts traversed the country and found it entirely suitable for settlement, despite certain shortcomings. The report was favorable, and Herzl went to Cairo to conclude the negotiations in person. But in Cairo he found an attitude of constraint, even of open hostility. After long wavering it developed that the Egyptian government had raised decided objections on the grounds that the quantity of water required for irrigation should not be drawn from the Nile.

Zionist Congresses and Debates

While Herzl was still in London, before this rejection at Cairo, prosecuting the negotiations for financing the project, the Colonial Secretary, Joseph Chamberlain,[32] one of the Empire builders, suggested to him another territory which he had seen on his travels and which seemed to him eminently suitable for Jewish mass settlement. This was the high plateau of Uganda in British East Africa. Conversations indicated that the Colonial

Office was ready to grant territory in Uganda, to be selected by a Jewish commission, as "an autonomous Jewish settlement, with a Jewish administration, Jewish local government and a Jewish official as its head, under the suzerainty of Great Britain." This was an extremely enticing offer, and seemed to fall into the lap of the Jewish people as a palpable gift. From the first moment Herzl made it very clear that Uganda was not Palestine and that he could therefore not accept it without reservations. Nevertheless, in view of the increasingly precarious situation of increasingly large masses of Jewish population, he did not feel justified in rejecting so promising an offer. He wished to leave the decision to the Sixth Zionist Congress, which took place at Basle, August 23–28, 1903.

These Congresses[33] had become a regular feature of the Zionist Organization. Attendance had increased at each succeeding meeting, but their value as demonstrations had naturally not grown at the same pace. With the exception of the year 1902, the Congress had met annually, but voices had long been heard advocating a less frequent convocation, and in fact the Congress later met biennially. In 1900 it convened in London and made a sensation in English society, more striking in non-Jewish circles than in Jewish. All the other Congresses took place in the familiar locale of Basle, and almost all ran off in the same way. The delegates and spectators were filled with great enthusiasm and were extravagant in their applause. But the Congress performed nothing noteworthy. For several years it was occupied with matters of organization, and here the difficulties of the problem were multiplied because it was not the will of the Jewish people but the laws valid in various countries that determined the legality of their procedures. Individual temperaments left their stamp upon the transactions of the Congress. Max Nordau's impressive addresses were display pieces. Their finely wrought aphorisms frequently provided telling expressions for use as propaganda. He employed the term *Luftmensch*, for example, to characterize the complete insecurity of Jewish existence, and it was his striking eloquence which gave the outside world a picture of Jewish misery. The relentless criticism which he, and other speakers, directed against the form of existing Jewish congregations and organizations and their contributions frequently exceeded the measure of what was just; he himself could show no corresponding services to balance those he criticized. In the Congress and in the movement generally a millenary mood was prevalent; there was a conviction that the Jewish world as it had been known was doomed to collapse and that the entire Jewish problem would quickly be solved by the Zionist Organization. Among the masses of the people hopes for liberation in the immediate future were aroused.

But the oratory of the Congresses and the applause which greeted them did little to promote this liberation. Action did not follow upon enthusiasm; the keenest critics were not always the most willing workers. This was made especially clear in the establishment of the Jewish Colonial Trust.[34] Quite apart from the many difficult formalities which had to be dealt with, the will of the people, of which so much had been said, failed, and the necessary subscriptions were not made available. It was only in 1902 that the Bank could take up its work, and it never became the strong and helpful financial institution which its founders had expected. The fate of the Jewish National Fund[35] was happier. This Fund had been proposed as early as the first Congress by the Heidelberg mathematician, Hermann Schapira; the Fifth Congress called it into being. The object was to create a substantial fund the principal of which was to remain untouched; when a certain income was available, land was to be acquired in Palestine and Syria (in practice none was acquired in Syria). Such land was not to become private property, but must remain national possession. This Fund enjoyed great popularity from its inception and met the popular desire of applying every energy to increasing the holdings of land in Palestine. The attitude of the Zionists from Russia was decisive in this regard. In their meeting at Minsk in 1902, under the influence of Ahad Ha'am, they had taken a resolution to turn their full attention to problems of the present. They pressed forward, therefore, to action in the field of national culture and national education. At each Congress reports on the progress of Jewish culture and the Hebrew language were received with enthusiasm. But when it came to reaching positive decisions, the orthodox group protested and the radicals showed no eagerness in questions of Jewish education. It was only after strong pressure on the part of the younger Zionists that resolutions were passed at the Fifth Congress, though in general terms, which advocated Jewish cultural work.

Such was the situation when the Sixth Congress assembled at Basle, August 23, 1903.[36] Herzl reported on his grandiose diplomatic success for the information of the Congress, and laid the East African question before it for decision. He declared most emphatically "that the Jewish people could have no other final goal in mind than Palestine, that the views of the Congress on the land of their fathers were and must remain unalterable," whatever attitude the Congress might take towards the offer of the British government, which could be helpful toward "ameliorating and alleviating the lot of the Jewish people." Among the 600 delegates there was surely not one who thought otherwise. The question was whether, in view of the burning need, the "Night-Shelter" (as Nordau styled it in a happy phrase) should be considered at all, or whether it should be rejected from the start. It was the hardest decision which the Congress could be called upon to make. The question was one of conscience, for the decision would affect not only this one project but possibly also the fate of the entire movement. As might be expected, passions ran high; excited discussions[37] took place in the Executive Committee, in the hall of the Congress and in its lobbies. In none of the national groups was there unanimity of opinion; in each there were delegates who were fully cognizant of the gratitude due the British government, but who refused any refuge whatever for the Jewish people except Palestine.

The most numerous opposition was found in the ranks of the Russian delegation, who looked upon the very mention of the Uganda project as treason to the Zionist idea. Although they knew the measure of Jewish distress at first hand and had just received a gruesome lesson at Kishinev, they preferred to reject any alleviation of their lot if it detracted from the Zionist ideal. This attitude did not suit the requirements of practical politics, but it showed an unsurpassable idealism and an unconquerable faith in final success. The Executive Committee proposed to set up a commission of nine members which would serve in an advisory capacity to the smaller Executive Committee in despatching an expedition to the territory to be investigated; the decision on the settlement of East Africa was to be reserved for a congress which was to be convoked for that express purpose. The proposal received 298 aye's and 178 no's; about one hundred delegates, in addition to the large Executive Committee, abstained from voting. The proposal was adopted, and the results of the voting met with vigorous approval on the one hand and storms of indignation on the other. In the midst of this excitement seven Russian members of the Executive Committee declared that in the meeting of that body they had already voted against despatching the expedition. They left the meeting under protest and their adherents followed them. Wild scenes ensued, and hysterical wails as if the Temple at Jerusalem had been destroyed anew.

The Congress seemed to be split; but that was not the case. The opposition returned and demanded assurances that the composition and instruction of the expedition to East Africa would be left to the larger Executive Committee which had to be specifically summoned for this purpose, and that this Committee should be convoked for receiving the report of the expedition and also for making the decision with reference to calling a new congress for action upon the report. These conditions were accepted, but the cleavage was not entirely healed, for excitement and distrust had penetrated too deep.

Herzl's health was delicate at best, and it became worse as a result of the work and excitement of the Congress. Furthermore, the struggle within the party grieved him deeply. He reckoned with the possibility of a schism and was prepared, in order to save the organization, to lay down his position. "If it should come to a split," he wrote in the deeply tragic sketch of his *Letter to the Jewish People*, "my heart will remain with the Zionists and my reason with the Africans. This is the kind of conflict which I can only resolve by my own withdrawal." What hurt him most was the fact that he was represented by the Russians as a traitor to the movement. In October 1903 the Russian leaders met at Kharkov[38] and delivered an ultimatum. If Herzl would not obligate himself in writing to drop the Uganda project and never to propose similar schemes and if he would not bind himself to consent to practical work in Palestine, they would establish a Zionist organization of their own in Russia. They had already taken measures to obtain official approval for such an organization.

All this came at a time when Herzl was putting forth the greatest exertions to make Plehve's promised advocacy effective in Constantinople and to obtain the approval of the Sublime Porte, through the agency of the Russian ambassador, for a charter for the Sandjak of Acco in Galilee. Regardless of his ailing health he traveled and negotiated towards these ends without intermission. He succeeded once more in pacifying the Russians and postponing the final decision until the next Congress. But Herzl never survived to see the next Congress. On July 3, 1904, in the flower of his age, Herzl succumbed to his heart condition at Edlach, near Vienna. He had spent himself in the service of the Jewish people. The towering cedar was felled in its full glory.

Consequences of Herzl's Death

"The sharp cry of horror, the long wails of woe which were the thousand-fold reverberations of the report of his departure, give the measure of his significance to this people."[39] "At the age of thirty-five he was utterly unknown to the Jewish people; nine years later he was its pride and its hope. That he should have attained such a place in Jewish thought and Jewish feeling is one of the marvels of his marvellous life." In such moving words Nordau mourned for his friend and leader. He called Herzl a model and an educator who had set a broken people upright, had given it hope, and had shown it its path. For nineteen hundred years no Jew had spoken with the rulers of the earth regarding the Jewish fate as he had, not as suppliant but as a claimant who explained the Jewish question as a problem of world politics and demanded its solution by the means afforded by world politics. Like many great men, he failed to attain his goal; but the nobility of his dream and the purity of his intent assure him a place of honor in history.

The Zionist Organization had lost its leader, who was, in the literal sense of the word, irreplaceable.[40] The heroic phase of the movement passed away with him. The administration was no longer entrusted to a president but to a presidial body; this was one of those unwieldy machines which regularly fail to work, and function only at unsuitable junctures. David Wolffsohn of Cologne was elected president; he had been one of Herzl's most trusted friends and most selfless co-workers. With Herzl he had built up the Colonial Bank and had fought for it shoulder to shoulder with him. He had accompanied his master upon his journeys to the German Emperor and to the Sultan, and he had been initiated into all his dealings with statesmen and financiers, and also into his plans for the future. He was conscious of his own limitations, but he had two advantages over Herzl: first, his thoroughly Jewish upbringing and his connection with Zionist thought from his earliest consciousness; and second, his skill in handling men and dealing with them. He understood the art of disarming opponents and breaking down their opposition. He took the movement over at a time of threatening crisis and succeeded in preserving its unity.

The antagonisms were violent. In the death of the lion the Russians thought that their time had come. The principle of the publicly recognized, legally secured home in Palestine they declared a mirage; Zionism meant a new path to the old love of Zion. The conflict created by the East African question was quickly liquidated. The commission which had been sent to East Africa to investigate reported that the land was more suitable for grazing than for agriculture and offered no prospects for a large settlement. The Seventh Congress (Basle, 1905) accordingly rejected the Uganda project; at the same time it also banned any colonization activity outside Palestine and its adjacent countries. The Colonial Office in London was greatly relieved, for hardly had the news of the offer of permission for Jewish settlement spread abroad than protests from the East African protectorate began to reach the government in London.

The vote did have one unpleasant consequence for the Congress and did cause a cleavage in the ranks. Israel Zangwill was so incensed by the declared will of the majority that he forgot his usual sense of humor and with his adherents left the Congress amid great turmoil. He founded the Jewish Territorial Organization,[41] whose stated object was:

to procure a territory upon an autonomous basis for those Jews who cannot or will not remain in the lands in which they at present live. To achieve this end the organization proposes: to unite all Jews who are in agreement with this object, to enter into relations with governments and public and private institutions and to create financial institutions, labour bureaus, and other instruments that may be found necessary.

Faithful co-workers of Herzl, like Max Mandelstamm, the oculist of Kiev, joined the new group, and new friends were won among those who wished to help the Jewish people but could not accept the nationalist point of view. Among the latter was the influential journalist and historian, Lucien Wolf.

Zangwill explained that Zionism was not to be given up, but that other, attainable, partial solutions were not to be excluded. He fought Congress Zionism with all the bitterness so often characteristic of the falling out of brothers. His zealous activity won much sympathy for his ideas. He received and examined projects for settlements in the most diverse regions of Asia, Africa and America; but not a single proposal could be translated into reality. Only at one point did territorialism achieve a certain success, and that was in directing a certain section of the mass immigration away from New York. With the help of the *Hilfsverein der deutschen Juden* and the funds put at their disposal by Jacob H. Schiff of New York, it was possible to direct some ten thousand immigrants to Galveston, Texas, whence, thanks to the special efforts of Rabbi Henry Cohen of that city, they were distributed in various sections of the southern states.

The Zionist movement was not greatly affected by the schism. Wolffsohn was able to close the Seventh Congress with the assurance that the crisis had been weathered. In the conflict between "political" and "practical" Zionism a formula of compromise was reached: the diplomatic efforts were to be continued,[42] but at the same time the systematic development of Palestinian work was to be prosecuted. The scope for political action was very greatly reduced when, as a result of the revolution of 1908, the Young Turkish "Committee for Unity and Progress" took the wheel, deposed the Sultan and attempted to build a state which should be, indeed, constitutional, but at the same time strongly nationalist. To grant permission for an autonomous Jewish group was altogether contrary to their program. Those who wished to work for Palestine had to make use of existing possibilities and forego far-reaching plans.

Progress in Palestine

As a matter of fact, despite the position taken by the Zionist Congress against infiltration, the process did continue. By 1914 the Jewish population of Palestine had grown to 85,000 souls, and the productive portion of the population was constantly on the increase. Among others, several thousands of immigrants came from Yemen, where they had suffered under harsh oppression and horrible poverty; conditions there had been much worse even than in Russia. They were used to hot climate and to hard conditions of life, and so provided a valuable source for labor; they were also highly skilled in certain trades, as for example, filigree work.

The Jewish agricultural colonies were consolidated at about the turn of the century. In 1900 Baron Edmond

Rothschild turned over the colonies he had founded and subsidized to the management of the Jewish Colonization Association, which was concerned with the technical training of the colonists as well as their education for independent living. New colonies were started by them as well as by several other groups. Special energy was shown by M. M. Ussischkin, who had been a zealous member of the *Hoveve Zion* since his student days, in reclaiming and cultivating the soil. He was the leader of the group called *Zione Zion* who fought any Jewish colonization outside Palestine, and within the country would brook no delay on account of political theories.

The Eighth Congress met simultaneously with the International Peace Conference at the Hague, expecting the recognition of the Conference. It established a Palestine office in Jaffa, which was put in charge of Dr. Arthur Ruppin[43] (1876–1943) who for 35 years thereafter placed a wealth of ideas, of wisdom and energy in the service of the upbuilding of Palestine. In the Palestine Development Company it established a central office for purchasing land and formulating plans for colonization. It attempted also to solve the problem of settling Jewish agricultural workers. After the Russian revolution of 1905 especially, and as a consequence of the revolution, numerous socialistic elements emigrated to Palestine, and the question of the future of the workers was thrust into the foreground. The number of Jewish colonies increased to forty-three at the outbreak of the World War. The land began to grow green again and to bloom. Vineyards, orange and almond orchards, and olive groves flourished. The production and consumption of goods increased from year to year. Unfortunately the country continued insecure, and the governmental administration unpredictable; youth could see no proper future or assurance of permanence.

The cultural development of the country proceeded

apace. The new generation demanded education and training to suit the time.[44] Hebrew gained more and more ground as the vernacular of daily life and the language of instruction. In 1903 Eliezer ben Yehudah established the *Va'ad ha-Lashon*, a sort of language academy, which was to watch over the development of the living Hebrew language and its application to the requirements of the present. In his *Millon* ("Thesaurus"), planned on a generous scale, he attempted to arrange and record all the known resources of the Hebrew language, from the earliest time to the present. Public libraries sprang up; the Jewish National Library founded by Dr. Joseph Chasanowitz of Bialystok developed particularly rapidly.

Schooling was improved. In the establishment of popular education the small and poverty-stricken Jewish community of Palestine quickly took first place in the Near East. Jaffa received a Hebrew *Gymnasium* and named it after Herzl; it was providentially situated at the edge of the city, on ground later occupied by Tel Aviv, the first Jewish city, built in 1909. Benzion Mossinsohn (1878–1942), who joined the staff at the start, directed it for 30 years, during a time of its finest bloom. Since this high school took a radical position on religious questions, the Mizrahi located its intermediary school, *Tahkemoni*, alongside it. In connection with the Lämel School (see p. 249, above) the *Hilfsverein der deutschen Juden* of Berlin built up a school system which in the course of time included twenty educational institutions in all parts of the country, from kindergartens to teachers' seminaries, and employed Hebrew as the language of instruction. Unlike their attitude in earlier generations, the populace now went along willingly, and were grateful for the improvement in educational facilities. The Bezalel School, a professional institution established at Jerusalem, cultivated industrial arts, opened new branches of industry, and raised the level of taste. A *Technicum*, or technical school which was to supply the deficiency of mechanically trained workers and at the same time create new possibilities for employment, was projected by the *Hilfsverein* for Haifa. Plans for this institution, which was to have a character quite new to the Orient, were prepared by a special governing body, in which the Zionist Organization as well as such generous benefactors as Wissotzki in Moscow and Schiff in New York were represented.

The realities of Palestine and the constant mass emigration of Jews from Russia and Galicia strengthened those tendencies in Zionism which placed the needs of the day in the foreground to the neglect of ideological considerations. Against Wolffsohn, who was concerned to save as much as possible of Herzl's political legacy, there was directed the concentrated attack of all who were dissatisfied on personal or other grounds.[45] Herzl dead was used by those who had embittered his life as a weapon against Wolffsohn and Nordau. Nevertheless the opposition forces were not able to change the administration, for they could not unite upon a successor. It was only in 1911, when Wolffsohn's health made it impossible for him to remain in office, that he was given a successor in the person of Otto Warburg, professor at the University of Berlin. As botanist and researcher in tropical plants, Warburg showed a special interest in the settlement of Palestine. He not only headed the Palestine Commission of the Zionist Organization, but called into being various institutions to aid in developing the land. He was always accessible to new ideas and suggestions if they showed some possibility of vitalizing the work in Palestine, even if they did not promise immediate success. He dissociated himself at once from schemes for a charter, and declared that work in Palestine was itself an end and not the means to an end, and that it was unthinkable that such work should not be prosecuted with all available resources.

At the Eleventh Congress, which took place in Vienna in September 1913,[46] the last Congress before the World War, the victory of this tendency was uncontested; significantly, Nordau remained away from this Congress. The thought of Homeland was completely abandoned. On the political side, absolute resignation prevailed. The life of the Jews in the Diaspora was accepted as an unalterable fact, and every Zionist was called upon to make *Eretz Yisrael* part and parcel of his life, to feel himself closely bound to Palestine spiritually and economically, and to arrange his interests and order his life accordingly. It was not quite the point of view of Ahad Ha'am, who now came to be valued, but his influence is clearly discernible. Cultivation of Hebrew language and literature and the development of a Hebrew school system were strongly urged, and it was determined to build a Hebrew University in Jerusalem.

In this way opinion was prepared for the great coup which became known as the Palestinian language war.[47] Zionists and non-Zionists had for a long time worked together peacefully in the Directorate of the Technicum, and they were agreed that for the moment Hebrew was insufficiently developed for instruction in complicated technical matters and that a period of transition was necessary. But now the Zionist members unexpectedly presented an ultimatum on behalf of Hebrew as the exclusive language of instruction. A large proportion of the students and also of the teachers in the schools of the *Hilfsverein* in Palestine showed their loyalty to Hebrew by means of a strike. Strong passions were loosed. In all countries where Jews lived, the Zionist Organization fanned the flame. The conflict reached the United States, and the American members resigned from the Board of Directors. In a few months the World War broke out, and the struggle was suspended. But the episode demonstrated two things: first, the Palestinian *Yishub* had, for the first time, shown independence and had demonstrated that it would not allow itself to be governed by its "benefactors"; and secondly, the Zionist Organization suddenly realized the necessity of building up its own school system. The Organization as such was able to assume this task because it could now rely on the loyalty and generosity of its members and on the devotion and pedagogic ability of Palestine's teachers.

Curious are the ways of history. The development of Palestine was sharply curtailed by the World War, only to be confronted with undreamed of possibilities at the end of that War. After it had apparently been decently interred, the concept of a publicly recognized, legally guaranteed homeland for the Jewish people was revivified. Its resurrection introduced a new chapter in Jewish history.

CHAPTER III

The Jews in the British Empire: Effects of Immigration

THE IMMIGRANTS AS A PROBLEM

POLITICALLY and socially the Jews of England[1] had reached a high level about 1880. Some were elected to the highest municipal offices, others were sent to Parliament. Emancipation attained its climax when Queen Victoria named Nathaniel Meyer Rothschild a peer in 1885. Rothschild was the first Jew to enter the House of Lords; later he was followed by others. Shortly thereafter Henry de Worms, later Lord Pirbright, became Undersecretary of State for Colonies (1888-1892), and Matthew Nathan, who had distinguished himself as a soldier in Africa and India, began a brilliant career in the Colonial Defense Commission, as governor of various departments.

The leaders of English Jewry regarded it a high duty to intercede for their brethren who were being persecuted for conscience's sake; and Her Majesty's Government lent a willing ear to the representations and petitions of the Anglo-Jewish Association, and raised its voice against cruelty wherever it was feasible to do so. At that time all the world looked to the British Empire as the embodiment of power and freedom; and the Jews of London, whose philanthropies had attained a princely scale, were reckoned the most distinguished and the most secure Jewish community in the world, the shield and buckler of their brethren in every peril.

It was from London[2] that the first alarm concerning

the Russian pogroms of 1881 was issued; it was from London that the first collection of relief moneys was sent to enable the victims of persecution to immigrate to the United States. But it was inevitable that some portion of the refugees were stranded in England.[3] The number was not large considered absolutely — some three thousand annually; but in the course of years the accumulation was considerable. They arrived penniless and disheartened. The Poor Jews' Temporary Shelter gave them lodging, which they were supposed to use for a period of two weeks; but they remained only six days on the average, so eager were they to find employment and to gain their livelihood by the work of their hands. They worked under inhuman conditions, endless hours in unhygienic rooms for starvation wages. But they persisted and gained the reputation of being the most willing and industrious workers to be found. They could not expect charity, for the Jewish Board of Guardians gave support to no one who had been in the country less than six months; it wished to avoid the odium of attracting paupers to the country. In common with the Russo-Jewish Committee, the Board did assist many to continue on their travels to the United States. Those who remained in the country, mostly unskilled workers, the Board sought to fit into some occupation and to promote their chances for employment by educating them and teaching them trades. The process was necessarily lengthy and could not be carried out with equal success for all immigrants. New arrivals retarded progress by necessitating a fresh start. But in the meanwhile the earlier groups had largely surmounted the greater difficulties and were so stabilized that many ventured to complain of the working conditions they had formerly accepted.

Until 1881 the number of foreign-born inhabitants was relatively small in England. The compact mass which now crowded into a few streets and a few occupations in the East End of London or in Leeds seemed an alarming phenomenon. The average Englishman could not imagine that any government could contemplate the destruction rather than the protection of its own citizens, that people who called themselves Christians could so cruelly misuse their innocent fellow-citizens. He could easily be made to think that what was taking place was a malevolent invasion of a ragged proletariat which must lead to a decline of the living standard and the dignity of the English worker and of the standing and esteem of the English working classes. The era was one of prodigious technical revolution, brought on in part by the use of machinery and the export of cheap staples. Socially-minded politicians[4] took note of the abuses of home work and the sweat system, and their spokesmen attributed all of these dislocations to the immigration of the Jews; it was their low standard of living, they alleged, which depressed the English labor market. This propaganda drew its arguments from the arsenal of the enemies of the Jews and sugar-coated them with patriotic, social, and political phrases; it succeeded in having a special parliamentary commission[5] appointed to investigate conditions thoroughly. The detailed report of this commission threw light upon gaps in the existing laws for the protection of workers and upon abuses in their administration. But it established the fact that these evils existed independently of the immigration and that the latter was not considerable enough to arouse alarm.

The Jewish immigrants came off rather well as a result of this inquiry. Their moral qualifications were much higher than those of immigrants of other nationalities. They were described, indeed, as "generally dirty and uncleanly in their habits"— a consequence of their grim poverty and intolerable living conditions — but they were generally praised as "thrifty, industrious, peaceable, for the most part an inoffensive race, moral in their habits, respectable in their family life, fond of their children, and never drunken."

It is interesting to observe the consequences of this judgment. Out of the virtue of sobriety the charge was drawn that the Jews did not contribute to the excises on spirituous liquors, and this charge was then expanded: they did not participate in the burdens of the state but remained aloof. This was utter nonsense, for in contrast to other foreigners the Jews had burned their bridges behind them, were seeking a new home, were grateful when they found one and therefore ready to give it full loyalty. The charge was made that they kept themselves separate and did not enter upon mixed marriages — as if, with the exception of the few aristocrats who were interested in rich Jewish heiresses, the English were so eager to intermarry with Jews. It was not long before these same guardians of the temple expressed concern over the fact that the immigrants did not remain Jewish enough, that they gave up too many of the traditions which they had brought with them. It was also charged that they did not settle in the rural districts — this at a time of a general flight from the land, when genuine Britons were migrating daily from the countryside to the large industrial cities. Nothing was too ridiculous or too infamous to charge against these foreigners and against these alone. Only a few could realize the human problems involved, the mass flights, and the necessity of allowing for a period of transition and of giving the newcomers a chance.

The first attack collapsed, but the opposition gave itself no rest. Immigration did not stop, could not stop, for the conditions which occasioned it continued and were aggravated by new complications, such as famine in Russia and Galicia and new restrictions in Rumania. The Society for the Prevention of Immigration of Destitute Aliens threw aside its cloak of politeness and pointed directly to the overcrowding of the East End of London with pauper Russian Jews. The point was reached where the barbed statement could be made that the propagandizing group could easily stage a riot against the Jews after the continental pattern if they wished to do so.[6] But the English population could not be hoodwinked by mischief of this sort made in Germany. Nevertheless public opinion was not unaffected by the agitation and it was particularly welcomed in those circles which opposed the old policy of the Open Door. The address from the throne in 1896 announced the preparation of an alien law, but such a law was never presented.

During the Boer War the Jews, including the newest immigrants, performed their duties as citizens fully, but the agitation continued. Major, later Sir, W. Evans-Gordon[7] demanded in Parliament that rigorous measures be taken against immigration. All the familiar arguments were repeated, and, in addition, fear was expressed lest infectious diseases be brought into the country and lest criminals and other undesirable elements gain admittance. Evans-Gordon traveled in the regions where Jews lived in great misery and submitted a memorandum embodying his observations. He noted certain moral shortcomings in the Jews of Poland (including Galicia), but in the main he repeated the favorable impression which the earlier inquiry had reported. Nevertheless a Royal Alien Immigration Commission[8] was established for the purpose of investigating "the character and extent of the evils which are attributed to the unrestricted immigration of Aliens, especially in the Metropolis." The transactions of this commission took the form of a partisan tribunal against the immigration of Jews. The conclusion of the long investigation was the rejection of an absolute prohibition of immigration and the recommendation of supervision on the American model, looking especially towards the exclusion and return of "undesirable aliens." By general agreement the Jews constituted a very small percentage of those who could be designated "undesirable," but the expression was so elastic that it permitted of capricious administration.

The government was faced with a difficult task in carrying its Alien Bill.[9] Its leader, A. J. (Lord) Balfour, declared that he was himself free of hostility towards the Jews, and there is no reason to doubt him; his ministers attempted to alleviate the situation by designating a territory to be settled by Jews (see p. 295, above). But one cannot be certain of similar good-will among his following and among the officials who were charged with the execution of the law. Israel Zangwill warned openly "that England was catching the epidemic which rages everywhere against the Jews." On the other hand, public opinion, supported by church associations, gave clear evidence of sympathy for the Jews of the East End, whose numbers had been increased by victims of persecutions at Kishinev and other martyr sites. After much discussion the Alien Act became law on January 1, 1906, and, though limitations were not severe, the period of free immigration was past. The number of Eastern Jews who remained in England declined considerably; on the other hand, English shipping realized enormous profits from the transportation of Jews immigrating to America. The seed of hatred could produce fruits even in the United Kingdom, as the Jews of Limerick, Ireland, discovered. There, Father Creagh, a Redemptorist priest, spread such terror against them that for a time they were completely boycotted and were not even able to purchase food (1904).

Problems of Religion and Culture

The Jewish community had to bear the burden. It felt itself responsible for the immigrants and was faced with the problem of caring for them as human beings and as Jews. But the imposing exterior of the English

Jewish community hid its inner weakness. Its favorable situation had acted as a soporific. Whether the persecutions had served to stir them up or whether the coincidence was accidental, gratifying symptoms of a spiritual awakening appeared during the 80's.[10] The participants in this renascence were chiefly foreign-born or the sons of foreign-born. The group called "The Wanderers," of which mention has already been made, was led by Asher I. Myers, the publisher of the *Jewish Chronicle*, which was the most widely read and influential Jewish weekly of the time and which maintained a high standard of excellence. Among its other members were Israel Zangwill, the Jewish Dickens, who observed Jewish life critically and affectionately and depicted it with golden humor; Lucien Wolf, the historical conscience and diplomatic spokesman of English Jewry; Joseph Jacobs, a living fountain of scientific ideas and inspiration who, in addition to his scholarly researches, pointed the way to the study of the present and to the sociological investigation of Jewish conditions; Moses Gaster, a passionate leader, a polymath and a distinguished scholar in the field of folklore; Israel Abrahams, the first English-born scientific student of Judaism, who united a rare charm of personality with breadth of knowledge; and, last but not least, fiery Solomon Schechter, who preached the abolition of the idols of fashion and a return to Jewish learning and to a simple Jewish faith. Schechter's discovery of the Hebrew original of the Book of Sirach, and his unearthing the *Genizah* of the Ezra Synagogue in Cairo, brought luster to English scholarship, and its reflection illuminated the Jewish community. Schechter had come to England as tutor to young Claude G. Montefiore, the great-nephew of Sir Moses Montefiore. Montefiore was unique in his environment in that he dedicated his rich gifts to the study of Jewish religion and his energy to the deepening of Jewish religious consciousness.

Each of these men had a special message for the community and their combined influence was soon seen in a deepening of Jewish life. A tangible result was the Anglo-Jewish Historical Exhibition of 1887,[11] "in which were shown most of the antiquarian remains of the history of the Jews in England, together with a collection of objects of ecclesiastical art and miscellaneous Jewish antiquities." This exhibition had beneficial results. In England and in all the countries of Europe it awakened a sense for the preservation of Jewish historical documents and for the appreciation of artistic values in the formation of Jewish life. A series of significant lectures was dedicated to the exposition. Heinrich Graetz,[12] now a septuagenarian, came to London for the exposition. He admired it greatly and praised it as "a new and golden page in Jewish history." Graetz thought that English Jewry gave promise of making the greatest contributions to Judaism. "Establish your claims to leadership," he admonished the English Jews, "by founding a Jewish academy and preparing a Jewish encyclopedia!"

A year later Israel Abrahams and Claude G. Montefiore founded the *Jewish Quarterly Review* which became one of the representative scientific journals of its time. The *Review* was not only an inspiration to scholarship, but it also fructified the life of the present. In 1893 the Jewish Historical Society of England[13] was founded; it still continues active in investigating and presenting the history of the Jews of England and its colonies. These studies were popularized and circulated throughout the country; the associations which cultivated them were centralized in a Union of Jewish Literary Societies. In the same year the Union of Jewish Women was organized, a significant step for conservative England, where nothing was ever changed except under necessity and where the women had previously taken no special part in community life.

The problem which took precedence over all others was that of the new immigrants, who gradually attained the majority. The London ghetto remained overcrowded, the rise of its inhabitants very slow, and the possibility of clearing the slums slight. Existing Jewish schools were enlarged. The Jewish Free School[14] of London with its two thousand pupils became the largest Jewish parochial school in the world. In his autobiography, its best known alumnus, Samuel Gompers, the American labor leader, tells how much he owed to the education he received at that school. For those children who attended the general schools, supplementary instruction in Jewish religion was introduced. But this did not satisfy the majority of parents; they sent their children to the old-fashioned *Heder* in addition, and thereby aroused the objection, on the part of some, that a heavy burden was being laid upon the strength and health of the growing generation.[15] The synagogues and ritual institutions were also unsatisfactory to the newcomers, and in 1887 they combined into a Federation of Synagogues, which later called its own Chief Rabbi. But not all inhabitants of the ghetto shared the desire to retain permanently what Zangwill called "the picturesque primitiveness of the Orient." They were in no sense a stolid, conforming mass which clung stubbornly to old habits in a new environment.

Many were captivated by socialism, and England became the original home of the Jewish workers' movement.[16] This was never very strong; the following of the Jewish unions was small and impermanent. But this does not mean that there was no class-conscious proletariat; upon occasion ten thousand or more Jewish workers participated in a strike. The extreme radical group was strongly anti-religious in its attitude, and at times there were serious conflicts between the Jewish workers of the various camps. A perplexing problem was that of the youth. Some of them had undergone frightful experiences in their childhood, and the transition from the constraint of Russia to the freedom of England was not always accomplished without moral strain. The unavoidable conflict between the older generation, with its roots in the ghettos of Eastern Europe, and their children, who had grown up in England, often took on tragic forms. The Children of the Ghetto felt their way, step by step, but the Grandchildren of the Ghetto rushed ahead at the double quick. Zionism[17] served, in a measure, to alleviate the conflict by teaching appreciation of certain Jewish values. It had enthusiastic followers in the ghettos of London and Manchester long before it gained a footing among England's English Jews.

Ahad Ha'am relates that, upon his return from Palestine in 1900, he attempted to interest the Chief Rabbi, Dr. Hermann N. Adler,[18] in Palestinian matters. Adler would not receive him because he was preoccupied with matters concerning *shehitah*, and Ahad Ha'am complained that the most influential rabbi in all Judaism should be prevented from putting all of his energy to the service of the spiritual and moral interests of the Jewish people by a purely technical matter. The remark characterizes the weakness of an institution which was once regarded as a source of strength, but which proved to be handicapped by centrifugal tendencies. But if the Chief Rabbi regarded the protection of Jewish tradition as his principal task, he was bedeviled in its performance by divers groups, particularly in the eastern ghettos. These people could not understand that the prevalent social forms and habits in Great Britain were different from those in their own homeland, and their resistance was strengthened by rabbis and laymen with an appetite for power. The situation was anomalous: serious efforts were being made to ward off attacks, and yet there was vigorous opposition on the part of those for whom protection was primarily intended. These difficulties recurred upon divers occasions: in connection with the problem of *shehitah*, with that of Sunday closing laws, and in the regulation for divorce. On the one hand, the conditions of Jewish life had grown more complicated, and, on the other, the cosmopolitan tolerance of old England had passed away. The need for unity was the more pressing.

The Chief Rabbi had to wage a war on two fronts. He had to contend at once against intransigence and indifference. The religious life of the community stagnated. Without renouncing the synagogue, considerable numbers were completely indifferent towards it and its institutions. At this juncture Claude G. Montefiore, with the help of Israel Abrahams and Lily H. Montagu,[19] established the Liberal Jewish Union. The purpose of the Union was to attract those who were estranged from Judaism, by means of supplementary services, instruction, and discussions. They wished to avoid a schism, and so sought workers from the ranks of the United Synagogue, such as Simeon Singer. Singer was an excellent preacher, to whom nothing Jewish was alien; he had given support to Herzl. But within the community there was vigorous opposition to this new heresy, and an attempt was made to boycott the Union and its leaders. Yet this did not hinder the growth of the Union into a congregation, which was consolidated as the Liberal Jewish Synagogue and followed the ritual of the American Reform congregations. Its work affected other congregations, such as the West London Synagogue; after long quiescence this congregation also introduced new reforms. The problem of indifference was not solved however; nor was that of cooperation with Christian circles, upon which Montefiore laid great weight.

Whether or not the phenomenon was connected with the increase in Jewish population (in 1911 Jews comprised about .5% of the population), the attitude towards the Jews did not continue unbiased; continental tendencies had gained a footing in English life and in English politics. Individual English Jews did, indeed, attain high positions. Herbert (later Sir Herbert and Lord Herbert) Samuel[20] was named Chancellor of the Duchy of Lancaster and so became the first Jewish member of the English Cabinet (1909). He was followed by Rufus D. Isaacs (Lord Reading of Erleigh, 1913) who, after an unparalleled career in the law, became Lord Chief Justice (1912). But these distinctions must be balanced by a disturbing outbreak of Judeophobia. While the English press was protesting against anti-Jewish excesses in Russia, attacks were being made upon Jews in South Wales. English public opinion did not countenance such attacks, but had not the strength to keep racial and religious animosity out of political life.

The Jews in the Empire

Of the English colonies, Australia, in consequence of its great distance and rigorous immigration laws, received only a small access of Jewish population. The situation was different in South Africa,[21] where the gold and diamond mines began to be worked about 1880 and occasioned a great boom. Favorable economic conditions naturally attracted numerous immigrants. Barney Barnato of London and Alfred Beit of Hamburg were both diamond kings; they combined their interests with those of Cecil Rhodes to form the largest diamond concern in the world. But it was not these powerful businessmen, who aided the cause of British imperialism, that were decisive for the development of the Jewish community, but the increment from Eastern Europe. Though their numbers, in relation to the total immigration, were not great, they sufficed to give a foreign aspect to the few existing congregations, upon which the newcomers looked down with their usual contempt. The eastern group grew steadily, not only because of increasing pressure in Russia, but also because those who settled quickly fetched their friends and relatives. The Jewry of South Africa came to be comprised predominantly of immigrants from Lithuania, and that fact gave it a certain unity and strength.

The land was new and capacious. The white population grew by leaps and bounds, new settlements were made every week, and frequently the Jewish trader was the pioneer of a settlement. The older Jewish immigrants had spoken English, but the mother tongue of the new was Yiddish, and they continued to cultivate it. In 1906 it was recognized by the government as a current language. Yiddish made it easier to learn Afrikaan and to form connections with the Boer population. The Jewish traders provided isolated farmers with necessary articles, and the farmers were glad to welcome them. Villages grew into cities, and with the growth of population the Jewish community grew also. Jews entered various other callings including industry and agriculture. In the Boer Republic they possessed no political rights and, what affected them most keenly, they were accepted neither as pupils nor teachers in the state supported schools. In practice exceptions were not unusual, and relations between the peoples were favorable. Many Jews fought on the side of the Boers against the English; the majority were evacuated as foreigners and were forced to flee to Cape Town. Notwithstanding their sympathy for the Boers they welcomed the change when the entire region was united under a democratic government by the formation of the Union of South Africa.

The spirit of freedom was manifested by the admission of Jews to all offices of honor. The case of Hyman Liberman of Cape Town,[22] who, in his term as mayor, opened the City Hall and as president of the Jewish congregation opened the new synagogue (1905), is unique in the annals of Jewish communities. The community flourished under the supervision and labors of its rabbi, Alfred Philip Bender (1895-1937), who gave it a modern organization and, most important, promoted its educational work in various directions. He established a Jewish public school, an extremely important enterprise in view of the prevailing school conditions. He introduced impressive religious services for the young, and attracted them to the congregation. Charitable institutions of modern character were quickly established. Soon after Bender's assumption of the rabbinic post his prestige was increased when he was named professor of Hebrew at the University of Cape Town.

Numerically the Cape Town community was soon outstripped by that in Johannesburg.[23] Immediately after the foundation of the city, in 1877, its Jewish congregation was established and the first synagogue in Transvaal erected. The community experienced a sharp setback during the Boer War, but later its growth was very rapid and in 1914 it numbered almost 20,000 souls. From the very beginning it possessed leaders who had been brought up in the modern spirit. In 1898, J. H. Hertz, who was to go to London as Chief Rabbi in 1911, became rabbi at Johannesburg. In 1903, at Hertz's instigation, a Board of Deputies of the Transvaal and Natal was founded; later it was expanded to represent all the Jews of the entire Union. In the Russian Jewish congregation, J. L. Landau (1866-1942) became rabbi in 1903. Landau made a reputation as a Hebrew poet, and also taught at the university.

The Jews of South Africa were subjected to all the economic crises which the country experienced. On the whole their economic condition was favorable. They were active and alert, traveled to Europe frequently on business, and participated in world movements in Judaism. Zionism, for example, quickly found a fruitful field for its labors in South Africa.

Canada,[24] too, had a considerable share of immigration. The proximity of the United States, the extent and fertility of the country, and the sparsity of its population were inducements to immigration but prevented a firm and independent development. The reception of the first refugees was very cordial. All charitable work was on a voluntary basis, and the personal interest and warmth with which they were met encouraged the immigrants and made it easy for them to settle down, so that they could soon help others to settle. When immigration became particularly heavy, in 1888, the Young Men's Hebrew Benevolent Society of Montreal, which had always felt responsible for the immigrants, approached Baron de Hirsch and solicited the same interest on behalf of immigrants to Canada as he showed in those to the United States. The petition was promptly heeded; permanent assistance was promised and given. In 1891 the Baron de Hirsch Institute was opened. This provided shelter for newcomers and also secular education, with evening classes for adults. The Institute became more important as immigration grew after the turn of the century. Not content with this work, Baron de Hirsch and later the Jewish Colonization Association, which established a separate Canadian Committee, promoted the settlement of Jews as farmers. The government favored these efforts by putting land at their disposal gratis. As in almost all other countries these settlements began with a very difficult period of trial. Their success was retarded by unfavorable location and failure of crops. According to a census of 1920 there were 3,500 Jewish persons in Canada living by agriculture, and the annual value of their products was a million dollars.

These figures signify little in view of the greatly increased immigration which took place, especially in the bad decade between the pogrom of Kishinev and the World War. Whereas there were only something more than 16,000 Jews in Canada in 1901, in 1911 the number was 50,000, or 1.03% of the total population, and in 1921 it had grown to 126,196, or 1.44%. This enormous absolute increase was received into the cities, of which some, like Winnipeg and Vancouver, were founded during this period and grew at an astounding rate. The Jews wandered from east to west along the railroad, and many settled at the stations fixed by the railroad. Their small stores became central points for the agricultural regions round about. There farmers not only found their necessities, but frequently an interpreter for the various languages spoken in the country, someone to read and write their letters, and sympathetic understanding for their human problems. At these railroad stops villages came into existence, and also Jewish congregations. They are to be found strewn over the whole broad dominion. But the main body of the Jews settled in a few large cities. Montreal,[25] Toronto, and Winnipeg contain about three-fourths of the total Jewish population. The character of the congregations was determined by the character of the immigrants, who brought a conservative attitude into an essentially conservative country. It is significant that, as late as 1921, 87% of the Jewish population recorded their mother tongue as Yiddish. Proximity to the United States determined the character of charitable institutions, hospitals, orphanages and the like; all such establishments followed the pattern set in the United States. The relief organizations for the victims of pogroms and for work in Palestine found ready support in Canada. All the leading rabbis of the country come from the United States. The complexion of the congregations is predominantly conservative; only a few have accepted the reform point of view.

A problem peculiar to Canada is that of education in the Province of Quebec, where Catholics and Protestants have long had separate state school systems under denominational supervision. The large community of Montreal is in this Province, and the Jews found themselves in the anomalous position that only those who possessed real property, and so contributed to the support of the schools, could claim rights for their children, whereas the others could not. After a friendly understanding with the Protestants, the law was altered so that the Jews were incorporated with that group and enjoyed equal rights within it. But Jews are not eligible for election to the School Commission, although the number of Jewish pupils constitutes a very high proportion of the whole.

CHAPTER IV

The Jews in America and the Immigrants

Problems of Adjustment

NO region on earth was more deeply affected by immigration than America, and in particular the United States.[1] In the decade 1880-1890, the average immigration of all nationalities was more than a half million annually and in this vast number there was room for many Jews. The Jewish immigration differed from the rest in that the newcomers were regularly penniless and dependent upon the assistance of their coreligionists. In the summer of 1881, even before the first reports of the pogroms had reached America, some hundreds arrived unexpectedly, and soon there were thousands of refugees in the harbors of New York, Philadelphia and Baltimore. "The condition in which they arrived," writes an eyewitness,[2] "baffles description; terror was written all over the faces." They came with their few possessions hastily bundled together, came, unlike most of the earlier immigrants, together with their families. They aroused general and deep sympathy in the non-Jewish immigration officials as in the Jewish charitable establishments.

The Jews of the United States had never withheld their sympathy from their fellows who were made to suffer for conscience's sake; they had rendered effective help in Persia, in Morocco, and especially in Rumania. But now the misery was at their doorstep; and no one can say that they met their great moment with petty spirits. No one could foresee that it was an avalanche that had been set in motion and that the pressure in Russia would burden American Jewry for forty years; but the nature of the situation was grasped as by instinct, and assistance was so organized that it served as precept and example for later generations. The emergency awakened a feeling of solidarity among American Jews, and informed their relations to the Jews of the world. To be sure, human institutions are never perfect, and the objects of care are never fully at one with the ways of the organizations which provide care; but that there was a will to give adequate and constructive help could be denied by no one. The efforts on behalf of immigrants during the next decade constitute a glorious page in the annals of humanitarian benefactions. The Jews of the United States proved worthy of the freedom and the well being which had been vouchsafed them, and in responding to appeals for help they proved they deserved their blessings.

In the old world such emergencies had been met by the organized community. In the new world the community as a whole was not organized, but the sense of obligation was so strong that various groups combined to form a Russian Emigrants Relief Fund.[3] Very soon it was realized that the enormous need could not be met by money alone, that personal service was essential. The members of the Relief Committee toiled to the full limit of their energy. Those who were in position to give employment took on as many of the "greenhorns" as they could, so that they might learn techniques and become employable elsewhere. The problem of sheltering the first immigrants and providing them with the most pressing necessities was not solved before new immigrants crowded in; in a single week more arrived than had formerly come during the whole year.

In many places Hebrew Immigrants' Aid Societies were formed for receiving the newcomers, and in order to avoid division of energy they incorporated themselves with the organization of that name which operated in New York. In the West and the South great readiness was shown, especially on the part of the members of the Independent Order B'nai B'rith, to welcome the newcomers and introduce them to employers. But the preponderant number remained in the East and were concentrated in the city of New York.

Among the immigrants there were some idealists, particularly those with academic backgrounds, members of the league *Am Olam* ("Eternal People"),[4] who cherished a single purpose, that of settling in the country and cultivating its soil. It was made possible for these idealists to establish an agricultural colony in Louisiana; but they did not realize what great reservoirs of experience and money would be necessary to make such an enterprise successful. All were willing to work; most despised the easy calling of peddler. Those who understood trades found work without difficulty, at the risk of occasional unemployment. Those who had not learned a trade sought work as unskilled laborers until they became capable of seeking some better employment.

The preponderant majority of immigrants were tailors or other needle-workers; these found and accepted work under wretched sweatshop conditions (see p. 239, above). The clothing trade underwent enormous expansion; low wages and intense competition went together. Scarcely had the newcomers disembarked when they were eagerly seized upon, but their pressing need and their unfamiliarity with conditions were mercilessly exploited. As in England, they were forced to work endless hours under murderously unhygienic conditions for starvation wages.

Morris Rosenfeld (1862-1923), the great poet who had himself toiled in a sweatshop, describes his experiences in gripping verses:[5]

> Oh, here in the shop the machines roar so wildly,
> That oft, unaware that I am, or have been,
> I sink and am lost in the terrible tumult;
> And void is my soul ... I'm but a machine.
> I work and I work and I work, never ceasing;
> Create and create things from morning till e'en;
> For what? — And for whom? — Oh, I know not!
>   Oh, ask not!
> Whoever has heard of a conscious machine?
>
> No, here is no feeling, no thought and no reason;
> This life-crushing labor has ever supprest
> The noblest and finest, the truest and richest,
> The deepest, the highest, the humanly best.
> The seconds, the minutes, they pass out forever,
> They vanish, swift fleeting like straws in a gale.
> I drive the wheel madly as tho' to o'ertake them,
> Give chase without wisdom, or wit, or avail.
>
> At times, when I listen, I hear the clock, plainly;
> The reason of old — the old meaning — is gone.
> The maddening pendulum urges me forward
> To labor and labor and still labor on.
> The tick of the clock is the Boss in his anger!
> The face of the clock has the eyes of a foe;
> The clock — oh I shudder — dost hear how it drives me?
> It calls me "Machine" and it cries to me "Sew!"

Not everyone felt the bondage of the factory as oppressive as did the gifted poet, but there must have been many who felt themselves degraded to the level of mere machines.

After its first fury there was a pause in the storm of immigration during the winter months of 1882. Next spring emigration was organized in Europe, and it was agreed that the United States should be the principal receiving country. On the basis of the experiences which they had gathered and under the pressure of the crushing burden they had borne, responsible persons in New York expressed their misgivings at so optimistic a plan. They demanded that only such immigrants as were willing and able to work, trained artisans if possible, should be directed to America. Their admonition was futile. Agreements based on the American demands were disregarded in London;[6] the Mansion House Committee there treated the Americans as if they were not quite adult, and by their disdain and willfulness caused great injury to the work in hand. It was only after long and careful negotiation that friction was eliminated.

It was vitally necessary that the controversy be settled, because immigration continued in large volume and American capacity for philanthropic endeavor was put to a severe test. Aside from demands upon the physical energy of those willing to assist, there was need of mutual understanding between them and the immigrants, and the lack of such understanding caused dissatisfaction on either side and increased the difficulties of the task. Not only the language they spoke but the world in which the minds of the immigrants moved was alien to the natives. Most[7] had brought with them rosy dreams of the land of abundance and liberty, and the reality which they found confronted them with a new bondage. The transformation into a new existence made extraordinary demands upon spiritual resources. The immigrants came from Jewish villages and found themselves in non-Jewish metropolises, from patriarchal Russia and found themselves in industrial America, where they discovered that people whom they regarded as friends and neighbors made them feel the merciless power of capital. Along with nostalgia, many were heartbroken because of their material degradation. All the good-will in the world and all the readiness to help could not bridge over these irreconcilables.

In this difficult crisis Michael Heilprin (1823-1888) appeared as an angel of deliverance.[8] He was born in

Pietrkov in Russian Poland, migrated to Hungary as a youth, and there participated actively in the revolution of 1848. After its collapse he traveled to the United States by way of France and England. He was an uncommonly well informed man and became a valued contributor to Appleton's *New American Cyclopedia* and to various important journals. His knowledge of Hebrew subjects was sound and his two-volume work, *The Historical Poetry of the Ancient Hebrews* (1879-1880), was well received. He avoided association with Jews, was member neither of a congregation nor a charitable organization. But when the plight of the Russian Jews became known, he threw himself into relief work body and soul. He was the right man in the right spot. He brought to his task not only knowledge and energy, but also sympathy and understanding; he knew the mentality of the immigrants and could make it intelligible to the natives. He himself called his indefatigable work "a laborious stirring which almost amounts to martyrdom." There have been few social workers who have won such unqualified recognition on all hands as did this selfless and devoted helper. It was to the lavish expenditure of energy in this work that his friends attributed his rapid aging and his early death. "Those who had the advantage of knowing him more intimately and who got a glimpse of the untiring energy which he threw into his work on behalf of the unfortunate of our race, especially the Russian immigrants, will agree with me that his death is indeed a national loss."[9]

The author of this sympathetic characterization was another protecting angel, Jacob H. Schiff (1847-1920). Schiff[10] was born in the old community of Frankfort and came to New York, as a very young man, in 1865. Ten years later he became a partner in Kuhn, Loeb and Company, a banking firm which attained world-wide importance through Schiff's activities. He had a leading part in the development of American railroads; and in their long and painful history the railroads have had few promoters who brought so full a measure of clarity, vision and selflessness to their work. Schiff was a genius of beneficence. His kindliness was apparent in his countenance. The characteristic thing about his philanthropies was not that he gave generously of his great wealth, but that he devoted so much time and energy, of which commodities he possessed no greater share than other men. "He would attend to the most extraordinary things, and to all of them with the same degree of conscientiousness." President William H. Taft put it well when he characterized the man and his work: "He was an effective doer of good works; he was a supporter of everything making for human benefit; his intelligence in the uplift of mankind was as great as his generosity, which was never-ending." Schiff's interest in Jewish matters began early, and he was always distinguished by the reverential regard he showed to Jewish scholarship and Jewish scholars. During the forty years of his active career there was scarcely a worthy Jewish movement in the United States in which he was not to be found at the forefront. He was a recognized leader of American Jewry during the critical period in which that Jewry attained world importance.

When the overwhelming stream of immigrants made necessary the erection of temporary barracks to shelter them, it was Jacob Schiff who financed the undertaking. The plight of her fellow Jews turned the gifted poetess, Emma Lazarus (1849-1887), into an enthusiastic Jewess who recalled the Jews to a realization of their own dignity and worth. It was on her numerous visits[11] to the barracks which Schiff had built that she realized the need of giving their inmates work in order to guard them from the crippling consequences of idleness. In the columns of the *American Hebrew*, which quickly grew to be an outstanding Jewish periodical, she kindled the ardor of the larger community for the task of training the refugees, and more especially their children, in the technical arts and in trades. Due to her efforts the Hebrew Technical Institute was established in New York and similar schools were set up in Boston, Philadelphia and Chicago.

These schools were a farsighted provision for the future. For, although the number of immigrants declined in the period immediately following, immigration continued. Each new Russian ukase which straitened the living space of the Jews increased the number of those eager to migrate. The reports the newcomers sent to their old home pictured the new land and its prospects in enticing colors. Wretched poverty in Austria-Hungary, and particularly in Galicia, put great masses on the move; far fewer came out of the Rumanian inferno. Altogether approximately two hundred thousand Jews migrated from Eastern Europe to the United States in the years between 1881 and 1890,[12] that is to say, a number almost equal to those in the country in 1880.

It was no light task to make such great masses employable. But the situation was much more favorable than in England, for America was hungry for workers. The first newcomers were far from accumulating riches, but they did find a livelihood. None of them became a public charge. Those who were needy were helped by the United Jewish Charities, which came into being after the dissolution of the Emigrants Societies. The newcomers lived in overcrowded and unhealthy dwellings in the most wretched fashion; whenever they could do so they would actually deny themselves food in order to be able to bring their relatives from abroad. Nevertheless, as was shown by an inquiry, the state of their health was not bad; their children flourished and developed properly.

Michael Heilprin was an enthusiastic partisan of the back-to-the-land movement and was happy to find that many immigrants expressed a strong desire to devote themselves to agricultural pursuits. He made it his business to raise funds for this purpose. Settlements were attempted in several states, but unfortunately all of them miscarried.[13] One time it was the water that was at fault, another time it was a crop failure; once drought, again frost and hail spoiled flourishing crops that were almost ready to harvest. Always it was complete lack of experience and consequently ill-chosen ground which was to blame for the failure. The settlers worked with all their might and contented themselves with the barest minimum, but none of the settlements survived its difficulties longer than four years. Individual farmers could set their teeth and outface failure until their soil rendered a return, and indeed many did so. But for closed colonies the requisite experience and capital were never available. Most of the enthusiasts were forced to return to the city disillusioned. A few colonies in southern New Jersey, like Alliance, Carmel, Rosenhayn, maintained themselves because their proximity to large cities provided them a favorable market and because the Baron de Hirsch Fund stood behind them.

Heilprin's influence in the creation of this Fund was considerable. In Constantinople Maurice de Hirsch was in contact with Oscar S. Straus (1840-1926), the United States ambassador to Turkey.[14] Straus informed de Hirsch of the miserable condition of the immigrants in America. Prepared, as always, to give productive help, de Hirsch asked for a plan, and one was prepared by Michael Heilprin and met with de Hirsch's approval. He made the income, and later the principal sum, of ten million francs ($2,400,000) available, and left the disposition of these moneys to the judgment of an American committee. Upon this committee sat men most experienced in such affairs, among others Schiff, Straus and Judge Mayer Sulzberger. In addition to temporary help immediately upon landing, such as providing shelter, distributing immigrants in the interior of the country and the purchase of tools for artisans, measures were taken for providing permanent help by making the immigrants self-sustaining. There was much difference of opinion in matters of detail, but eventually unity was achieved. In 1890 the Fund began to operate, and the American administration was given broad powers.

While these negotiations were in progress, a crisis in American immigration policy arose. The country was now almost fully settled, the labor market stiffened, and demands for restriction of immigration began to be heard. There was a pronounced sentiment in favor of tightening the immigration laws or at least putting teeth into the laws already on the books. Jewish immigration was, indeed, only 2.5% of the whole, but it was nevertheless the principal object of attack. Jew-hatred controlled the situation and was the basis of an attempt to poison public opinion. The United States Commissioner of Immigration, Schultheiss, a member of the investigating commission despatched to Europe (see p. 230, above),[15] declared that in his opinion the reports of the "alleged" persecutions in Russia were exaggerations of English propaganda. He was himself under the influence of Muscovite propaganda. He discovered that the Jewish Pale of Settlement embraced the most fruitful provinces of the Czar's realm, but he forgot to add that the Jews were not permitted to live upon the land and were excluded from agriculture. He juggled with the concept of Russia as designating the interior provinces only, in order to create the impression that the Jews residing in annexed Poland were all aliens. Following the model of the Moscow press he painted these Jews in the darkest possible colors. According to his account, the English relief committee and the Baron de Hirsch Fund were only devices for releasing a horde of undesirable paupers against the welfare of the United States.

Public opinion was alarmed by such attacks as these, and that at a time when the frenzy let loose in Moscow (see p. 205, above) had thrown more than 150,000 Russian Jews upon the shores of the United States in a short space of time. The Jewish relief committee found themselves in a serious dilemma; they must avoid anything that might be interpreted as "assisted immigration," and at the same time they could not withhold their help from "enforced immigration," nor look idly on while the right of asylum was sacrificed to hatred and prejudice.

The government, too, was confronted by a grave choice. Upon the question of the right of asylum it was prepared to give free rein to its humanitarian impulses, but it could not shut its eyes to the danger which constantly increasing immigration brought in its wake. To the representations of Simon Wolf, who was the stout champion of the Jews in Washington, John W. Foster, the Secretary of State, replied:[16]

Unquestionably a great and sudden influx of expatriated and destitute aliens of any race would be a grave misfortune to any country, and American Hebrews act both patriotically and humanely when they advise Jewish refugees against coming hither, but at the same time endeavour to render self-supporting those who finally come. Obviously the support of great numbers of dependent persons is a tax upon the resources of the country, even though paid from funds, and, quite as plainly, industrial conditions here might be seriously disturbed by the sudden arrival and the enforced competition of a multitude of needy people. Hence it is important to the last degree that the volume of this expected refugee immigration be not excessive or threatening and that with entire certainty it be promptly and widely distributed so as to supply a real want in scattered communities and interfere as little as possible with existing and normal industrial conditions.

Immigrants' Progress

It was a stroke of good fortune that at this very time the Baron de Hirsch Fund began its work and energetically set about providing for immediate needs.[17] It helped distribute the Jews over the country; many found a healthier and more profitable environment. The number of Jewish communities grew by hundreds. Together with other agencies the Fund took up the task of remedying the wretched state of New York slums, which were a standing mockery of all hygienic principles. Philanthropy of itself was not sufficient. These efforts became effective only when those immediately concerned showed a vigorous interest in abolishing the slums. The Fund also attempted to introduce the newcomers to the language and habits of their new home and to provide vocational training so that they might more quickly become self-supporting.

The Educational Alliance,[18] into which the Technical School expanded, developed an extraordinarily intense and diversified program of educational activities. It began in the forenoon with speeded up courses for children, who could not be accepted in the public schools until they were able to use English. In the afternoon children who were released from school were taught manual arts, sports and music, and were provided with a more attractive atmosphere than could be found in their tenement houses. In the evenings adults came to learn English and to perfect themselves in their vocations. In this building there were combined "an American school, a social settlement, and an adult educational agency of a superior kind." There was a constant coming and going of some three thousand persons daily, and of an even greater number later; after ten years the stone steps of the building were so worn down that they had to be replaced. One cannot overestimate the contributions of this organization to the improvement of the situation of the immigrants and the support it gave to their spirits.

Finally, the Fund attempted to direct Jews to agriculture.[19] At Woodbine, N. J., a colony was established in which small industry was combined with small farming;

and eventually the first Jewish Farm School was instituted. Here too there were innumerable difficulties, but they were all overcome by the devoted zeal of the director, S. Sabsovich. The colony persisted, and organized the first Jewish communal administration not only in the United States but in the whole world.

By no means all of the immigrants of the 90's were penniless. Many had saved the remnants of their property and were able to establish themselves with their own means. Many were skilled artisans or professional men, and so able to find work. But the proportion of those who possessed nothing and had no trade, and who were therefore in need of immediate help, was large enough. There were immigrants also who received and assisted newly arrived fellow countrymen and made their first steps in the new country easier. The situation in general was alleviated by the fact that immigration declined from the high point it had so suddenly reached. Relative calm in Russia and labor shortages in the United States retarded the pressure if they did not entirely remove it.

Immigration changed the structure of American Jewry; the preponderant majority of the Jewish population now consisted of wage earners. Many attained independence, some even became great entrepreneurs, but the mass belonged to the proletariat.[20] There were as yet no laws in the States to protect labor, and employers used their power pitilessly in view of the plentiful supply of those who sought work. Every incoming ship exerted a depressing effect upon labor conditions. Fear of starvation and ignorance of conditions forced the newcomers to accept any offer, however poor. Workers already on the spot, mostly of German origin, were friendly towards their Jewish fellow workers, but were annoyed when the latter fell upon their rear in the struggle for wages. Among the immigrants there were, indeed, convinced socialists who joined their Russian or German comrades. But the masses were not to be won over until Abraham Cahan[21] (born 1860), a socialist schooled in the Russian secret societies, decreed that propaganda among the immigrants must employ their own language and their own frames of reference. And so Yiddish, the language of the proletarian masses, became the language of Jewish socialism; and so socialism became the cry of the Jewish masses. There were many varieties of Jewish socialism, from the most radical to the most moderate, but it was principally the trade union idea that gained ground among the masses.

The Jewish worker came to understand how seriously he injured both himself and the generality of workers when he insisted upon his individualism and, as an individual, sold his labor upon unfavorable terms. Gradually unions of the various trades were formed, and these fought at the side of other unions. In October 1888 they combined under the leadership of Bernard Weinstein and Henry Miller, with the cooperation of the great labor leader Samuel Gompers (1850-1924), into the United Hebrew Trades.[22] These unions grew steadily in strength and numbers and fought stoutly for the material improvement of living conditions of the Jewish laboring population and for their cultural uplift. The stubborn resistance of the employers which the workers had to face and the obstinately fought strikes which they waged make a familiar story whose details need not be recounted here. The Jewish labor movement is a highly significant factor in American life and it exerted a strong influence upon Jewish society. After Abraham Cahan founded the *Jewish Daily Forward*, in 1897, labor's widely read daily press[23] exercised a marked educational influence upon the Jewish masses.

In the 90's children of the new immigrants began to attend colleges and universities, and their intelligence and eagerness gave rise to the hope that their new country could expect great things of them. The services rendered to the United States in various fields by the immigrants of earlier generations and their children justified these expectations.[24] The architecture of Dankmar Adler of Chicago (1844-1900) won universal admiration; Mendes Cohen of Baltimore (1831-1925) solved the most difficult problems of railroad construction; Fanny Bloomfield Zeisler of Chicago (1863-1927) was a pianist who spread the fame of her American home over all Europe; David Belasco of San Francisco (1854-1931) was a theatrical director and dramatist who delighted the public far and wide; Benjamin Altman (1840-1913) was a far-seeing merchant and art collector whose treasures belong to the gems of the Metropolitan Museum of New York City. The contributions of Jews to public health and child aid are inestimable. Of the many meritorious names only the following can be mentioned: Adolphus S. Solomons of Washington, D. C. (1826-1910), whose most important service is the foundation of the American Association of the Red Cross; Felix Adler of Ithaca (1851-1933), the founder of the Ethical Culture Society, whose European studies suggested the idea of the kindergarten, an institution which he spread in this country; Nathan Straus of New York (1848-1931), who provided pasteurized milk for children of the poorest families and thereby saved the lives of millions of children in all parts of the world, and of whom a popular vote in New York testified that he had done more for the welfare of the city than any other individual; Emil Berliner of Washington (1851-1922) who, besides being a famous inventor, manifested a great interest in the prevention of tuberculosis; Lillian D. Wald of New York (1865-1940), who in her home in Henry Street founded the first visiting nurse service (1892) and the first city-school nursing system before there was anything of the kind anywhere else in the world; and lastly Adolph Heinrich Joseph Sutro of San Francisco (1830-1898), who made a large part of his property into a public park and left it with other valuable bequests to the city's welfare.

The number of Jews who distinguished themselves in municipal, state and federal offices is legion. Adolph Meyer (1842-1908) became Brigadier General in the Louisiana militia and from 1891 to his death represented his state as congressman. Julius Kahn of San Francisco (1861-1924) set a record. From 1889 to his death he was elected congressman, with short interruptions, and when he died his widow continued in his position for twelve years. Oscar S. Straus was ambassador to Turkey under three administrations. He was a member of the Permanent Court of Arbitration at The Hague and, as Secretary of Commerce and Labor (1906-1909), the first Jewish member of an American Cabinet.

The patriotism which the Jews showed in the arts of peace they carried over into the arts of war. In the Spanish American War[25] (1898) some 4,000 Jews served under the colors; in addition to officers and men of the regular army and navy, there were volunteers in the federal army and in the regiments recruited by the states. Among them were many of the most recent immigrants who had received military training in the armies of Austria-Hungary, Rumania and Russia. Many distinguished themselves in battle. Theodore Roosevelt liked to speak of his Jewish comrades in the Rough Riders which he organized. The highest rank was obtained by a naval officer, Adolph Marix (born in Germany in 1848), who had the difficult assignment of directing the investigation of the sinking of the Maine, which provided the final occasion for the outbreak of war. Marix was cited "for eminent and conspicuous conduct in battle." Later he reached the rank of admiral. The war resulted in the liberation of Cuba and the Philippine Islands from Spanish rule, and thereby made it possible for Jews to settle in these islands.

The few thousands of Jews who settled in Argentina[26] were insignificant compared with the millions who streamed into the United States. Whether or not Baron de Hirsch was well advised in acquiring land in the Argentine is difficult to decide; but it is certain that his idealistic hopes were not fulfilled. Not only were the people selected as colonists not always suitable for the project, the soil, too, was unsatisfactory and proved to be much too small for large-scale colonization, especially with an extensive type of agriculture. The administration did not understand the character of the settlers and had no feeling for their spiritual and religious requirements. The system of scattering settlements and separating by long distances groups which belonged to a single colony, thus making communication with one another and religious services difficult, resulted in much bad blood. The ample means of the Jewish Colonization Association made it possible for the colonists to survive a plague of locusts and a drought; and by the introduction of intensive cattle-breeding they were able to show a profit.

The slow development of the rural settlements promoted the growth of urban population in Argentina. Aside from the Russian immigrants, Jews also came from Morocco. In 1897 the first synagogue in the new South America was erected in Buenos Aires, and Jewish life became more active. At the same time a weekly paper for farmers, called *Der Yiddisher Fonograf*, came into being. Jews soon began to participate in the awakening political life of the country. Enrique Dickmann (born 1874), one of the first agricultural settlers, removed to the city and became a founder of the socialist party in Argentina.

Religious and Cultural Organization

It was not necessarily a consequence of the immigration, though surely not unrelated to it, that in the 80's North American Judaism became conscious of its religious and spiritual obligations. The peace between congregations of diverse tendencies which I. M. Wise had effected was not of long duration. A break came as early as 1883.[27] The leader of the positivist tendency was Leeser's successor, Sabato Morais (1823-1897), who had brought the Sephardic tradition of the ancient congregation of Livorno to Philadelphia. His stature was not heroic nor were his spiritual gifts extraordinary; but the warmth of his personality, the genuineness of his convictions and the purity of his intentions made him an effective teacher. "No one ever listened to him but he caught the fervor of his earnestness and enthusiasm." He advocated embracing contemporary culture but was firmly opposed to any conscious alteration in the forms of Jewish life and worship. His precept and example contributed much to the preservation of the conservative spirit in Philadelphia and informed a generation which gave enthusiastic leaders to American Judaism.

Morais found unexpected support in Alexander Kohut (1842-1894), who is best known as the author of the *Aruch Completum*. In 1885 Kohut became rabbi of the progressive congregation, *Ahavat Hesed* in New York, and with the full fervor of his rabbinic authority he preached against "unauthorized radical reform." Reform of this sort Kohut characterized not as reform but as surrender. His protest summoned another New York rabbi, Kaufmann Kohler (1843-1926), into the lists. Kohler was a distinguished scholar in the field of the history of religions and he allowed himself to be guided by his researches without regard for imponderables and for experience. He preached the uttermost extreme of reform. But no one could criticize reform's failings more sharply than he did:

> Its great shortcomings consist in its neglect of domestic devotion, in its constant appeal to reason instead of cultivating sentiment. Reform abolished the old regular services, the Hebrew daily prayers, but did not train our children to communicate with their God in fervent devotion at the beginning and close of each day. It did away with old formulas of praise and benediction, but failed to imbue every step or enjoyment of the Jew with religious life. It allowed the old fires of self-consecration, of sanctification of human life at its various solemn epochs, to cool down.

But Kohler also saw the decay of orthodoxy and was convinced that only a complete transformation of Jewish spirit and Jewish ceremonial could be constructive.

> Judaism must drop its orientalism, and become truly American in spirit and form.... It will not do to offer our prayers in a tongue which only few scholars nowadays understand. We cannot afford any longer to pray for a return to Jerusalem. It is a blasphemy and lie upon the lips of every American Jew. Neither ought we any longer to retain the Pentateuch lessons unrevised and unabridged, either in an annual or in a triennial cycle.

The controversy[28] was followed with tense interest by the congregations, whose members desired clearly expressed direction for their own attitudes. The answer was to be given by a conference of rabbis called to meet in Pittsburgh on November 16-18, 1885. The conference was presided over by I. M. Wise, but Kohler's spirit dominated it. Its "declaration of principles" is a peculiar document which can only be understood on the basis of contemporary intellectual currents. Nothing was said of faith or piety; the advantages of Judaism over other religions were indeed mentioned, but not clarified. It was not a *Confessio Judaica* but a homage to the latest European school of thought in science, in history of religion and particularly of the religious evolution of Israel. The laymen did not get much out of this platform; they did not learn what to believe and what to do, but only what not to believe and not to do. There was an emphatic denial of the validity of Mosaic legislation.

We accept as binding only its moral laws, and maintain only such ceremonies as elevate and sanctify our lives, but reject all such as are not adapted to the views and habits of modern civilization.... We hold that all such Mosaic and rabbinical laws as regulate diet, priestly purity and dress originated in ages and under the influences of ideas entirely foreign to our present mental and spiritual state. They fail to impress the modern Jew with a spirit of priestly holiness; their observance in our days is apt rather to obstruct than to further modern spiritual elevation.

Kohler called this "Pittsburgh Platform"[29] a declaration of independence, and like the greater declaration it was regarded as a summons to arms. Sabato Morais declared it intolerable that the only institution for training rabbis in the country should be entrusted to the direction of a man under whose presidency such resolutions could be adopted. With the cooperation of the Sephardic congregations he proceeded to establish the Jewish Theological Seminary of America which set as its goal

the preservation in America of the knowledge and practice of historical Judaism, as ordained in the Law of Moses and expounded by the Prophets and Sages of Israel in Biblical and Talmudical writings.

Morais himself undertook the direction of the Seminary and Alexander Kohut became its professor of Talmud. The Seminary began on a modest scale, but it survived and became a rallying point for the forces of conservatism.

I. M. Wise replied by founding the Central Conference of American Rabbis,[30] which was organized in Detroit, in July 1889, and determined to hold annual meetings at which attitudes would be taken "to all matters pertaining to Judaism, its literature and its welfare." In theory it was possible for all American rabbis to join the Conference, for it never accepted a platform like that which had been adopted at Pittsburgh; but experience showed that the organization stood firmly upon the ground of reform. The Conference attained a large membership with surprising rapidity; only nineteen rabbis had been present in Pittsburgh, but a hundred joined the Central Conference. Wise was repeatedly elected president, as long as he lived. The Conference regarded its most important task to be the creation of unified practice in worship and instruction in the numerous congregations, and the provision of the necessary agencies to this end.

From the beginning of his activity Wise had worked for a uniform prayer book for all reform congregations, and such a prayer book now became a reality. The *Union Prayer Book*[31] (1894-1895) did not follow Wise's own *Minhag America* but Einhorn's *Olat Tamid*, and departed markedly from tradition. It was immediately adopted in many congregations and fashioned the form of their worship. The introduction of this prayer book and its supplementary volume marked the completion of the process which Wise had begun with his concept of American Israel. American Israel was now cut off from the spirit of Universal Israel — and that at a time when American Israel's body was undergoing so radical a transformation. I. M. Wise looked coldly upon the "idiosyncrasies of late immigrants;" he did not realize that within these immigrants lay slumbering the constructive power of the next generation.

Independently of the religious differences, and in fact bridging them, the cultural needs came to the fore and received attention. One of the most energetic representatives of this aspect of Jewish life was Judge Mayer Sulzberger of Philadelphia (1843-1923), a distinguished jurist, a sensitive connoisseur of art and literature, and a man "of unswerving loyalty to his faith, convinced of the importance of founding educational establishments which fostered Judaism, a leader in every endeavor which tended

AMERICA AND THE IMMIGRANTS

to the mental, moral and physical betterment of his brethren." It was due to Sulzberger's energy that The Jewish Publication Society of America was founded[32] in Philadelphia in 1888, with the cooperation of Rabbi Joseph Krauskopf. Two previous attempts to form such an institution had miscarried, but the present Society survived and showed a rapid growth in strength and significance. The function of the Society was the dissemination of sound Jewish books in distinguished format. Since 1899 it has published *The American Jewish Year Book*. It has brought out such solid works as Heinrich Graetz's *History of the Jews* and Israel Zangwill's novels and sketches. The complete list of the Society's publications cannot be presented here, but one in particular must be mentioned. With the cooperation of scholars representing all religious tendencies the Society fulfilled a desideratum of long-standing by producing a new English translation of the Bible.

Four years later, on the four hundredth anniversary of the discovery of America (1892), largely upon the initiative of Cyrus Adler whose fruitful work we shall have occasion to deal with in the sequel, the American Jewish Historical Society[33] was established. The function of the Society was "the collection, preservation and publication of materials having reference to the settlement and history of the Jews on the American Continent." The first president of the Society was Oscar S. Straus. The Society extended its work to all parts of the continent, gave great encouragement to research, and contributed considerably to the collection and scientific investigation of historical sources. It was at the instance of the Society that the work of Meyer Kayserling (1829–1905), the rabbi of Budapest, was translated and published in English under the title *Christopher Columbus and the Participation of the Jews in the Spanish and Portuguese Discoveries*.

At the World's Columbian Exposition in Chicago (1893) a parliament of religions was called, and owing to the influence of Emil G. Hirsch, the powerful preacher of prophetic universalism, Judaism was given a dignified position in it.[34] For the first time in history it appeared as an equal among equals, and was enabled to set forth before the entire world its doctrines, its work and its goals. The impression upon the world as a whole was not as deep as had been expected, for 1893 offered too many intense sensations to permit the retention of so mild a one. But the consequences within Judaism were significant. A Parliament of Jewish Women[35] was meeting in Chicago at the time, and the enthusiasm incident to this meeting led to a resolution to make a permanent institution of it. The National Council of Jewish Women was established, for the purpose of teaching the importance of Jewish religious education, work among the youth, and social aid. At the same time the Jewish Chautauqua Society[36] was founded under the direction of Henry Berkowitz, upon the model of the American Chautauqua societies. The aim of this Society was "the dissemination of knowledge of the Jewish religion;" it directed itself primarily to those Jews who lived outside the great centers, widely dispersed and with no Jewish inspiration or teaching. Later it directed its activities to colleges.

Before very long Zionism[37] brought a new leaven into American Judaism. Herzl's *Judenstaat* (1897) evoked vigorous discussion; former members of the *Hoveve Zion* and new devotees were enthusiastic over Herzl's idea. I. M. Wise, who was, to all seeming, the most influential Jew in the United States, regarded the question as sufficiently important to lay before the Central Conference of American Rabbis at once. The grand old man was almost beside himself as he spoke of the revolutionary element that had forced its way into Jewish life; and he rejected it root and branch. The Conference unanimously resolved upon

> the total disapproval of any attempt for the establishment of a Jewish state. Such attempts show a misunderstanding of Israel's mission.... Such attempts do not benefit, but infinitely harm, our Jewish brethren where they are still persecuted by confirming the assertion of their enemies that the Jews are foreigners in the countries in which they are at home and of which they are everywhere the most loyal and patriotic citizens.

A later and more detailed discussion underscored this position; the stale sentiment to which G. Poznanski had given utterance in Charleston, S. C., in 1841, was repeated: "America is our Zion and Washington our Jerusalem."

Only three Americans participated in the first Congress at Basle. Richard Gottheil (1862-1932) attended as an observer, and upon his return he gathered those that were interested in the movement and, together with his young disciple, Stephen S. Wise, and Dr. Harry Friedenwald of Baltimore, he founded the Federation of American Zionists. The Federation brought out its own monthly organ, *The Maccabean*. It was difficult to create a movement in the heterogeneous and generally self-willed elements of American Judaism. Zionism broke through religious affiliations and gradually spread among various groups. It was not to be a decisive factor in American Judaism for a long while; on the other hand, it was not to be ignored.

The first organization to take a friendly stand on the new movement was the Union of Orthodox Jewish Congregations in the United States and Canada, whose platform declared that "the restoration of Zion is the legitimate aspiration of scattered Israel, in no way conflicting with our loyalty to the land in which we dwell or may dwell at any time." It was long before the orthodox congregations in the United States formed any kind of union. The great mass of immigrants, though they had given up large areas of traditional practice, must be considered as belonging to the orthodox group. Reckoned by numbers they constituted a power, but an ostrich-like individualism rendered any attempt at organization futile. Repeated attempts were made to name an orthodox chief rabbi, but each met with obstruction. Finally, through the efforts of Dr. H. Pereira Mendes,[38] the Sephardic rabbi, one of the co-founders of the Jewish Theological Seminary, a union was achieved. It was not an orthodox union of the Russian type, and its program was based on American conditions. It affirmed traditional Judaism unqualifiedly and, without naming reform, it consciously took a position in opposition to it.

It was, as a contemporary remarked, a half-hearted orthodoxy, and so wanted power. "Orthodoxy, reform, conservative," Judge Sulzberger, a keen observer, wrote at the turn of the century, "all have been found to be names, and it is no bad thing to be uncomprehended in or by any of them. He who has scholarship, talent and enthusiasm may be more appreciated for the first time in our history than he who leads a party."[39] The hunger for learning led to the creation of a monumental work of Jewish culture, *The Jewish Encyclopedia.*[40] An enterprise which had been planned for fifty years in old Europe and had never been realized was undertaken by the Jewish community in America with youthful venturesomeness. Isidore Singer (1859-1939) had knocked in vain at the doors of the rich and influential in Paris, Vienna and Berlin. It was in the United States that he found a forum for scholarship: Jews and non-Jews who undertook responsibility for the work and organized the enterprise; the (non-Jewish) publishers, who were experienced in projects of the same character; and at last the necessary material support for its execution, since the work could not be expected to be self-sustaining. It was the first time that American Judaism had taken the lead in a significant enterprise. It is noteworthy that the Americans were confident of their own ability to assemble and direct a whole army of specialists from many countries.

The Jewish Encyclopedia [its Preface states] endeavors to give, in systematized, comprehensive, and yet succinct form, a full and accurate account of the history and literature, the social and intellectual life, of the Jewish people — of their ethical and religious views, their customs, rites, and traditions in all ages and in all lands. It also offers detailed biographical information concerning representatives of the Jewish race who have achieved distinction in any of the walks of life. It will accordingly cast light upon the successive phases of Judaism, furnish precise information concerning the activities of the Jews in all branches of human endeavor, register their influence upon the manifold development of human intelligence, and describe their mutual relations to surrounding creeds and peoples.

It was no light task that the publishers set themselves. Aside from the thousand details of history, biography and bibliography which had to be assembled and sifted, there was need to present fundamental concepts systematically — and here the science of Judaism had been negligent. It was also necessary to consider Jewish life of the present in its anthropological and sociological aspects — and here scientific investigation was in its infancy. *The Jewish Encyclopedia* became not only a source of information, but it inspired specialists to complete studies or begin new ones. Many scholars who are now named with respect won their spurs in work upon the *Encyclopedia*. In the short space of six years (1901-06) the twelve large volumes were ready, handsomely got out and rich in illustrative material.

Every collective work has its weaknesses and every first attempt its difficulties. But considered by and large *The Jewish Encyclopedia* is an outstanding scholarly contribution of permanent value. The Jewish encyclopedias in Hebrew and Russian were entirely dependent upon it, and later independent attempts leaned heavily upon it. No one could be offended if, of those who were responsible for the work, the palm is given to Joseph

Jacobs, "the eager humanist and the enthusiastic Jew." He was versatile and original, had a clear insight into facts and problems, and united scholarship with literary art.

The scholarly work was followed by the scholarly man, embodied in the magnetic personality of Solomon Schechter.[41] Schechter lived in the academic atmosphere of Cambridge in England, far from the struggle of Jewish parties, and was not embarrassed in holding a truthful mirror up to each. He embraced no system of Judaism but Judaism in its entirety, what he liked to call "Catholic Israel." To him Judaism was what had seemed to be Judaism, by common consent in all places and at all times; and the surest means of preserving Judaism, he thought, was a knowledge of Judaism and of its rich legacy. He had the courage to declare war upon the idols of the hour, upon the higher criticism of Wellhausen and Kuenen; he had the courage to oppose faith in the intangible and the emotional to the absolute dominion of rationalism.

The Jewish Theological Seminary had been merely vegetating and was in need of regeneration if it was to be preserved. It wanted a dynamic and authoritative leader. Eyes had long been turned towards Schechter, but the institution had to be strengthened before the call could be extended him. It is significant that two members of reform congregations, Jacob H. Schiff, "*the* Yehudi of New York," and Louis Marshall, "the ideal man in every respect," along with Sulzberger, Adler and Solomon Solis-Cohen, were largely instrumental in bringing Schechter to America. In the spring of 1902 that scholar came to New York in the fullness of his strength and brought new vitality to American Judaism.

But before we speak further of these matters we must bring ourselves up-to-date by glancing at events in Eastern Europe which exerted a decisive influence upon Jewish work in America.

BOOK FOUR
THE WORLD UNREST

CHAPTER I

The Terror in Rumania and Russia

THE RUMANIAN POLICY OF DECEPTION

RUMANIA set the record in maltreating the Jews. Russia was more brutal, but Russia had the courage to confess its brutality. Rumania, on the other hand, practiced the "cold" pogrom and washed its hands in innocence. The Rumanian[1] Jewish policy was characterized, and is so today, by hypocrisy and deception. The Rumanians always boasted of their tolerance and their liberalism; and these protestations were calculated to furnish an alibi for intolerance and obscurantism. In Rumania the party which called itself liberal was the embodiment of Jew-hatred; the policy of the conservative party was not quite so narrow toward the Jews and took into consideration other aspects of Rumania's situation, though it too was not free of Jew-hatred. Under the ceaseless, inexorable and brutal incitement of the Anti-semitic League it could not be otherwise. Significant of the theory and practice of creating anti-Jewish sentiment was the custom of issuing solemn proclamations during the Easter season in which, in bombastic and unctuous style, the Jews were charged with responsibility for the crucifixion. To what end?. In order to introduce an appeal for boycotting Jewish business completely. So were the sanctities abused for base material interests.

The hocus-pocus which declared that the Jews were aliens in the country in which they and their fathers had been born, in which they had received their education and had rendered their military service (see p. 74), provided limitless possibilities for willful and capricious treatment. The European powers[2] were content with this sleight of words, for their interest was in questions of political power, not of justice; they failed to perceive that this deception was but a symptom of the depravity of the governing class. Provisions in the constitution to the contrary notwithstanding, the land was governed by a small clique of boyars which assured itself and its partisans a luxurious existence and wished to suppress all the working classes, the peasants no less than the Jews. There was incessant agitation against the Jews in the press.[3] A consistent principle was followed, in that civil, social and natural rights were regularly interpreted as political privileges, to the sole end that Jews be excluded from many vocations.

There were some few statesmen who eschewed this duplicity and demanded liberal legislation and justice, but the majority of politicians thought only of their own purses and of preserving a favorable atmosphere in Western Europe. They suffered from a persecution complex, as if a mere quarter of a million Jews could dominate the country, force their way into all vocations and oppress the Rumanians. To the suggested solution that the Rumanians be brought up to work and so be enabled to compete with the Jews, they turned a deaf ear. The natural consequence was that the Jews were tormented and ruined, and the Rumanian people in no wise helped. The country which was fertile and rich in minerals was constantly on the brink of bankruptcy.

The campaign of extermination against the Jews began as soon as the Rumanian politicians realized that the European powers could be toyed with. Under the pretext that the peasants were being seduced to drunkenness, everyone not enrolled as a voter (a euphemism for Jews) was forbidden to sell brandy in rural communities and in small towns and villages which were connected with rural communities.⁴ By an arbitrary interpretation of the regulation it was enforced much more rigorously than the letter of the law demanded. The Jews were made penniless. But their exclusion from the trade contributed nothing to the abolition of alcoholism; in the place of Jews, Rumanian citizens and officials or aliens of the Christian faith became tavern-keepers, and they promoted drunkenness under the protection and to the advantage of the great landed proprietors.

The next victims were the Jewish peddlers. In the cities every kind of peddling was forbidden and the term was extended to embrace every conceivable manner of selling. In the country permission to peddle was made to depend upon bureaucratic conditions which also amounted to a practical exclusion of the Jews. Again 20,000 became penniless and were added to the great army of starvation.

This was only the beginning. New laws were constantly being created which limited activity in almost all vocations and trades in which Jews were to be found in considerable number to Rumanians, native or naturalized. This legislation was harmful to Rumanian economy, particularly to the export of produce, but such a consideration did not concern the antisemitic lawgivers as long as they attained their immediate goal of working an economic injury to the Jews. In 1900 an American commissioner of immigration⁵ summarized the special legislation affecting the Jews as follows:

> A Jew may not secure, hold or work land in a rural district; he may not reside in a rural district; he may only reside in one of seventy-one towns designated as abiding-places for the Jews. He may not follow the occupation of an apothecary, a lawyer, stockbroker, a member of the Bourse or Stock Exchange, a peddler or regular dealer. These are only a few of the callings denied him. To be deprived of the right to own, rent or labor on a farm or garden in a peculiarly agricultural country must be recognized as a tremendous handicap in the race of life, but to follow that up with the closing of the greater part of the avenues of endeavor in urban centers greatly intensifies the hardships to which he is subjected. And, as though the foregoing category was

not considered sufficient, a still further impediment is found in the regulation which forbids employers of labor to employ Jews until they have first employed two Christians.

Two points merit special mention because they are significant for the "tolerant" and "liberal" spirit of Rumania. One concerns public health. Jewish physicians[6] (with the exception of those few who had been naturalized) were graciously allowed to practice in those localities in which a Rumanian scorned to settle. The moment a Rumanian physician appeared upon the scene the Jew must clear out, whether or not the people had been satisfied with his ministrations. An equally crude aspect of the problem appears in the fact that the number of Jewish patients admitted to hospitals, even public hospitals to the support of which Jewish taxation contributed, was limited. It happened in Bucharest in 1896 that a Jewish workman sought admission to a hospital; it was recognized that the case required emergency treatment, but the man was rejected and in a few moments he collapsed and died on the street. A newspaper which was not friendly to Jews protested against the absolute want of humanity and common decency, of which instances could be cited from all hospitals almost daily. But not a word of protest was heard from the Christian clergy, which was so influential in Rumania, nor from the humanitarian royal poetess, Carmen Sylva. The Jewish community was willing to take upon itself the expense and burden of maintaining its own hospitals, but the government forbade the erection or support of such hospitals; apparently the intention was to destroy the Jews.

The second point concerns schooling.[7] The Rumanians thought the Jews were too eager for education; in 1891, 39% of all pupils in the public schools were Jewish — and this despite the claim of the politicians that the Jews remained alien and were unwilling to assimilate themselves. It was determined that the Jews should be cured of this zeal for education. The first step was to introduce tuition charges for "aliens;" then it was provided that only as many Jews could be admitted as there were places available in the schools. Since the number of schools lagged far behind the needs, it was easy to refuse Jews admission. Later they were excluded from the higher schools and from the professional and agricultural schools. They were nominally admitted to commercial and handicraft schools, but conditions of admission were so difficult that they amounted to practical exclusion.

Now education was the one point on which the Jews were most sensitive and susceptible. Every effort and every sacrifice was made by communities and individual patrons, by the *Alliance Israélite Universelle* and later by the Jewish Colonization Association, to build up a Jewish school system. But the government interfered in the administration. It limited the Jewish schools to several elementary classes, narrowed instruction in Jewish religion to the minimum, and did not even hesitate to meddle in religious questions, as for example when it required the schools to give instruction upon the Sabbath or would not allow the pupils to cover their heads when receiving instruction in Hebrew. Such crudeness had never previously been shown by a civilized state.

The next attack was directed against Jewish artisans.[8] Their function was recognized as extremely necessary to the country's economy, but as they were Jews it was determined to starve them out. A law concerning artisans, proposed in 1902, provided that each artisan must secure special permission to continue in his trade and that this permission could be secured only by submitting an attestation of good conduct from the applicant's last place of residence; that is to say, permission depended upon the caprice of police officials. Foreigners who applied for examination as master workmen must adduce proof that similar privileges were granted to Rumanians in their own country. In public works Rumanians were to have the advantage, and tenders from foreigners were to be received only if Rumanians were given similar advantages in their own country. Both these regulations implied the complete exclusion of Jews, for they had no other country and would therefore never submit the required proof of reciprocal privileges.

The rigor of the laws was exacerbated by the arbitrariness of the police and the hostility of the judiciary, which regularly took a position unfavorable to the Jews and denied them the protection of the law. Officialdom in all grades was honeycombed with members of the Antisemitic League;[9] a number of ministers were leaders in the League, and the principles of the League became the law of the land. They stated openly that their goal was to torment the Jews so thoroughly that they would be ready to leave the country.

What was the attitude of the Jews towards all of these coercive measures? They fought for their rights, but if they had been bold enough to give utterance to their opinion they would have been expelled on the basis of the law against foreign revolutionaries. Among others who might be named as rebels were Moses Gaster (1856–1939) and Elias Schwarzfeld (1855–1915), who contributed far more to the knowledge of Rumanian language and literature than did thousands of "genuine" Rumanians. Correspondents of foreign newspapers who represented conditions accurately were expelled from the country. When England,[10] as one of the signatories of the Berlin Congress, made representations, Jews were punished in reprisal. To the populace the Jews were represented as personal devils; it was small wonder that in every period of need the citizen directed his dissatisfaction against the Jews. Each generation became familiar with the sound of crashing window panes, plundered shops, or beaten people, now in one place, now in another. Native Jews founded an association[11] comprised solely of former soldiers, and this association protested tirelessly against injustice; but the general attitude of the country was such that protests of this sort were wholly without effect, and finally the association was dissolved by the government.

The Jews loved the country, but realized at last that they had no choice but to emigrate, and it is ironical that increasing emigration frightened the officials in charge. One of the first groups of Palestinian pioneers (see p. 258, above) came from Rumania, and at the First Zionist Congress at Basle petitions were presented from 37,043 Rumanian Jews, from all of the seventy-one localities in which Jews were permitted to live, asking for immediate settlement in Palestine. These people were serious about the upbuilding of Palestine, and they were ready to put their proven skill and energy at its service. But the preponderant number of emigrants made for North America.[12] At first the number was not excessive; until 1890 it amounted to only 6,967 persons. It is significant that emigration began to increase in 1885 after the issuing of the law on peddling; it took a spurt after each new severity in the law, so that by 1900 it had almost doubled (12,789), and from that date to 1910 it almost quadrupled (47,301). The net result was that, in the course of thirty years, more than a fourth of all Rumanian Jews had removed to the United States. Many of them were workmen or farmers, and so were able to find subsistence in their new home. Baron de Hirsch remembered the Rumanian Jews from his Turkish period and took special thought of them in his benefactions.

About the turn of the century there occurred an event such as the world had never yet seen; the Rumanian Jews set themselves in motion in a march of despair. In 1899 Rumania and Bessarabia were visited by famine. Economic life was at a standstill, national credit was exhausted, and the government demanded impossibly high taxes. Opportunities for Jews, which were limited enough at best, were now so completely confined that people literally died of starvation and exposure. In their despair the Jews determined upon flight, with no plan and no goal in view.[13] They cast away their scanty possessions and set out. One group in Berlad started the cry, "We go afoot!" The notion caught hold, and in many places smaller and larger troops set themselves in motion. Trains of lamentable figures filled the roads; with bundles slung over their shoulders, starving and gasping, they dragged onward. Even those that were prosperous, even the rich, despaired of any solution of their grim situation save flight.

The Rumanian government sought to stem the tide by denying passports; but in vain, for the measure was overflowing. The Rumanian officials felt they were being exposed; Europe must not discover actual conditions in the country, for Rumania required a public loan and the first reports of the mass flight of the Jews and its causes had shaken the credit of the state. Rumania attempted to pacify Europe, to minimize the emigration, and even to extort a statement from the Jews that it was only the acute famine and not the chronic suppression that had driven them to flight. The government was forced to resign, and Peter Carp became presiding minister. But the Jews had no faith in his ministry, for several arch-antisemites that sat in it took vigilant care that he should not "liquidate Rumania in favor of the Jews." His attempts to alleviate some of the regulations were futile, and he was forced to resign after he had negotiated his loan.

Of the Jewish wanderers some thousands turned towards the East. They had heard of the dream of settling Cyprus and half hoped that they might be admitted into

Palestine. Many thought that the Turkish government would permit them to settle along the Anatolian railway. And in fact the Sublime Porte was receptive to the idea, but the locale and the work required people of a different character, and in the case of most the experiment was a failure. The enormous expenditure had been useless.

Those that turned to the West[14] met with unexpected difficulties at the Austrian and Hungarian borders. Many were actually thrust back into their homeland where entry was denied or penalized by heavy fines. The Jewish community of Budapest and the *Israelitische Allianz* of Vienna were faced with problems they had never before known. There was need both of organization and of funds. A conference held in Paris (June 1900) sought to organize the relief work, to alleviate famine in the country as far as possible, and to regulate the flow of migration so that undifferentiated hordes streaming in should not aggravate existing hostility against Jewish immigration. From England a number of unsuitable immigrants were relentlessly returned to Rumania, to serve as a warning against unselected immigration; and this caused much bad feeling.

In London, Lord Rothschild[15] informed the Foreign Office of the causes of the sudden increase of immigration from Rumania, and in Washington Jacob H. Schiff and Oscar S. Straus laid similar information before President Theodore Roosevelt. Negotiations looking towards a naturalization agreement with the United States, which had been begun, were interrupted by cunning King Carol,[16] "for the reason that it would complicate the already troublesome Jewish question in that country." These negotiations induced John Hay, the Secretary of State, to study the matter more deeply and to compose the Note whose thorough factual grounding and lofty moral tone have made it a famous document.[17] Never before had a statesman confronted the Rumanian government with their sins with such clarity and penetration. Here are some of the pertinent paragraphs:

The United States welcomes now, as it has welcomed from the foundation of its Government, the voluntary immigration of all aliens coming hither under conditions fitting them to become merged in the body politic of this land. Our laws provide the means for them to become incorporated indistinguishably in the mass of citizens, and prescribe their absolute equality with the native born, guaranteeing to them equal civil rights at home and equal protection abroad....

... [In Roumania] the ability of the Jew to earn even the scanty means of existence that suffice for a frugal race has been constricted by degrees, until every opportunity to win a livelihood is denied; and until the helpless poverty of the Jew has constrained an exodus of such proportions as to cause general concern.

The political disabilities of the Jews of Roumania, their exclusion from the public service and the learned professions, the limitation of their civil rights and the imposition upon them of exceptional taxes, involving, as they do, wrongs repugnant to the moral sense of liberal modern peoples, are not so directly in point for my present purpose as the public acts which attack the inherent right of man as a breadwinner in the ways of agriculture and trade. The Jews are prohibited from owning land, or even from cultivating it as common laborers. They are debarred from residing in the rural districts. Many branches of petty trade and manual production are closed to them in the overcrowded cities where they are forced to dwell and engage, against fearful odds, in the desperate struggle for existence. Even as ordinary artisans or hired laborers they may only find employment in the proportion of one "unprotected alien" to two Roumanians under any one employer. In short, by the cumulative effects of successive restrictions, the Jews of Roumania have become reduced to a state of wretched misery. Shut out from nearly every avenue of self support which is open to the poor of other lands, and ground down by poverty as the natural result of their discriminatory treatment, they are rendered incapable of lifting themselves from the enforced degradation they endure. Even were the fields of education, of civil employment and of commerce open to them as to "Roumanian citizens," their penury would prevent their rising by individual effort. Human beings so circumstanced have virtually no alternative but submissive suffering or flight to some land less unfavorable to them. Removal under such conditions is not and cannot be the healthy, intelligent emigration of a free and self-reliant being....

The United States offers asylum to the oppressed of all lands. But its sympathy with them in no wise impairs its just liberty and right to weigh the acts of the oppressor in the light of their effects upon this country and to judge accordingly.

Hay's Note was transmitted not only to the Rumanian government but also to all the signatory powers of the Berlin Congress. The latter[18] courteously acknowledged its receipt, but none declared itself ready to join the British government in intervening against the injustice which had been demonstrated. Upon the Rumanian government the Note had effect to the extent that it failed to enforce the most injurious provisions of the law regulating artisans. Meanwhile the acute economic crisis had passed, but Jewish emigration continued. The Jews could expect little good of the new ministry of Sturdza. The duplicity of this statesman[19] is illustrated by the statement he issued upon assuming office. He explained that a distinction must be drawn between the two groups of Jews in Rumania: the Spanish, who were superior, and those in Moldavia, who were not Jews at all but converted Mongols who had been under Austrian or Russian protection until 1828. When it came to military service, he was as content with the one as with the other; for naturalization he rejected the one as well as the other — unless foreignness was remedied by specious baptism. He complained that most Jews did not speak Rumanian and were not assimilated, but he barred them from the schools in which the youth might have learned Rumanian and come to love the language. He deplored emigration because it took the more competent elements out of the country, but he did nothing to make life tolerable for industrious people who felt a strong bond with their homeland.

On the contrary, every crisis in the country was blamed upon the Jews. The agrarian unrest in 1907[20] was represented by the government's press bureaus as a consequence of the hard treatment of the peasants at the hands of Jewish land lessors. But when the unrest rapidly developed into a general peasant revolt and threatened the great estates, the officials employed strong military force to suppress it promptly. In the situation of the Jews only one item was altered during this period. In the Court of Appeals the special Jews' oath[21] with its degrading medieval formula was abolished (1909), thanks to the persistence of the chief rabbi of Jassy, Dr. Niemirower (1871–1939). The court subsequently made repeated, but ineffectual, attempts to return to the old usage.

INTERNATIONAL POLITICAL CRISES AND THE JEWS

Crisis in the Balkans became acute and permanent with the annexation of Bosnia and Herzegovina by Austria (1908); and the sympathies of the not inconsiderable Jewish populations were engaged. In the newly created *Landtag* of the combined duchies the religious communions, including the Jews also, received the right of separate representation. But evil nationalist passions were let loose over the entire peninsula and battles between various groups were waged with grim cruelty. The Greek[22] population had long shown its hatred of the Jews upon every possible occasion, and now it distinguished itself by excesses against them. Into the hands of the Greeks there fell (1912), among other cities, Saloniki; the majority of the inhabitants were Jewish, and they dominated the economic life of the city. The remarkable strength of Saloniki's powerful and tireless Jewish dock workers was generally recognized. On the Sabbath the workday life of the town ceased. In the Turkish period this was accepted as natural, but when the Greeks came they attempted to outflank the Jews and drive them from their positions. They seized upon the approved technique of calling the patriotism of the Jews into question on the grounds that they were firm supporters of the party of Young Turks, which had originated in Saloniki, and could not change their convictions from day to day. Numerous Jews, laborers as well as merchants, emigrated. The Greek government made sincere efforts to secure peace, and succeeded insofar as it was possible to do so in the disturbed condition of the times. The Bulgarian and Serbian governments also sought to curb the excessive zeal of their countrymen, and granted their new Jewish fellow citizens the same complete equality that the old Jewish settlers enjoyed. The attitude of Rumania to any new Jewish citizens that might fall to its lot, especially such as had previously enjoyed equal rights, was a matter of concern.

Sir Edward Grey was shocked when he was informed of true conditions in Rumania[23] by the representations of the Anglo-Jewish Conjoint Committee. An opportunity for intervention came when Rumania took part in the Second Balkan War (1913) and received an access of territory. Again it was the government of the United States, at the suggestion of the American Jewish Committee, which introduced the question of securing explicit assurances of civil and religious rights for sections of the population which were to be transferred under the terms of the treaty. The Rumanian plenipotentiary declared that such provisions were to be assumed as a matter of course and were therefore unnecessary; but he added an express assurance that the suggestion proferred would be complied with and that all sections of the population of the newly won provinces would be granted full civil and religious equality. In consequence of earlier experiences with the government at Bucharest those concerned for Jewish interests were unwilling to be satisfied with mere declarations, but before decisive steps could be taken the World War broke out and the Rumanian government was spared being put to the test.

The annexation of Tripoli[24] created a new situation in Italy. In Tripoli the Jews lived in closed corporations according to their own law. The Italian government had no desire to change conditions and found itself in the situation of having to recognize such institutions as a chief rabbinate and Jewish courts of law, which it had never tolerated in the mother country. It is significant that the war passions of the nationalist groups called forth an antisemitic campaign in the press; aside from the clerical press such things had been unknown in Italy.

Across the Sereth in Bukovina[25] Jews and Rumanians lived together amicably. The small country owed its prosperity in large part to the work and energy of the Jews; for a time it was called the Eldorado of the Jews. Together with the administration and the German settlers the Jews were the strongest supporters of Germanism, and it is partly due to them that the small country with a preponderantly Rumanian and Ruthenian population became a stronghold of sound German culture. With the collapse of the liberal constitutional party in Austria, the Germans took up antisemitism and sought to spread hatred against the Jews. They succeeded in small places, where they preached an economic boycott against the Jews and reduced them to the beggar's staff. But the Jews retained their position in the economy and the culture of the cities; they supplied a large proportion of the doctors and an even larger proportion of the lawyers. Czernowitz, the capital, elected a Jewish mayor several times, and after 1897 sent Benno Straucher as its representative in the Austrian parliament (*Reichsrat*). Though no Zionist, Straucher was the first deputy who consciously followed a Jewish policy. Nathan Birnbaum's[26] doctrine, that Jews should strive for national and cultural autonomy in countries where they lived close together in large numbers, struck root in Bukovina. At a conference in Czernowitz (1908) it was resolved that Yiddish language and culture should be given equality with Hebrew. The government of Bukovina recognized the Jews as a national community with complete equality of rights.

This situation was very different from that in neighboring Galicia.[27] There the Poles prosecuted their campaign of extermination against the Jews, and despite the remedies offered by various physicians the misery of the Jewish population assumed ever gloomier proportions. In view of the poverty of the country and the declared or tacit boycott on the part of the Poles, the program of made work promoted by the Baron de Hirsch Fund, in conjunction with the Jewish Colonization Association and the local Relief Association for the Necessitous Jewish Population of Galicia, could have but little success. Between 1900 and 1910 no fewer than 152,811 persons emigrated to the United States alone,[28] but even this considerable emigration brought no relief because of the excess of the birth rate. The census of 1910 counted 871,906 Jews, or approximately 11% of the whole population. If they had acted as a united group the Jews could have made their numbers count in dealing with the Poles, for they possessed legal equality. But there was no union. The Hasidim who controlled the masses and the rich who strove for social recognition threw themselves into the arms of the Poles and justified the Poles' worst political and economic misdeeds. The nationalists, on the other hand, were split into bourgeoisie and socialists, and so weakened their own position. Galician elections,[29] over which the Poles claimed an absolute monopoly, always resulted in foul scandals and often in bloody battles. After general suffrage was introduced in 1907 the Jews of Eastern Galicia in combination with the Ruthenians elected three of their number to the Imperial Parliament. Together with Straucher these deputies formed a Jewish bloc in parliament and followed a Jewish policy insofar as their small number permitted. But they were not returned at the next election; among the Poles and the Social Democrats chauvinist tendencies were strengthened.

National-Democratic doctrine gained the upper hand among the Poles, and preached the complete exclusion[30] of Jews from economic life. The tavern law of 1910 reduced 11,000 families to penury at a single stroke and added 50,000 starvelings to the sum of wretchedness. If the Jews ventured to announce a policy of their own, they were branded as traitors by the Poles. They did not permit closed Jewish groups to arise, but they were equally hostile to assimilationist tendencies on the part of Jews. Even the Polish socialists, who were all nationalist, declared that a Jewish national consciousness on the part of workers constituted a menace to the class struggle.

The Jewish Socialist Labor Party (*Poale Zion*) issued a significant statement at the beginning of the World War (1915):

The awakening of the Jewish masses of Eastern Europe to national consciousness, a natural process called into being by historical necessity, has met with not the slightest degree of understanding among the entire Polish people with very few exceptions; they have not even shown the good-will to consider this profound transformation which has occurred wherever Jews live together in great number and to deal with it with requisite attention. With the rise of a Polish merchant bourgeoisie, which regarded the existence of a Jewish merchant class an irksome competition, an antisemitic movement appeared in wide circles of Polish society. This movement shrinks from no device for undermining and suppressing the Jews economically, nor, on the political side, does it hesitate to deprive the Jews of civil rights. Constantly increasing disturbances in the amicable relations of the two peoples have become apparent. In consequence of fatal and irresponsible activity on the part of large sections of the Polish citizen body, a cruel hatred of Jews has taken possession of a large proportion of the Polish population. This hatred knows no bounds and is constantly deepening the rift between the two peoples. The conflict has become exacerbated and is drawing to a crisis, yet the Polish press and publicity has not changed its practices in dealing with the Jewish question; there is the same indifference, the same ignoring of facts, the same misdirection. The rapidly developing Jewish press is mocked and scorned. Jewish literature, youthful and flourishing, which has won a name in Europe by the excellence of some of its representatives, and, in a word, the entire cultural upsurge of the Jewish masses during the past decade, have been completely ignored.

The problem of self-preservation was a more potent factor than Polish theory, and large masses joined the Jewish national movement[31] in all its various shadings. They cultivated Hebrew as the language of the educated and Yiddish as the language of the people. The literary center was in Russia — the active Jewish intelligentsia of Galicia lived in western countries for the most part — but the Socialist Party formed the bond of union.

Stirrings in Russian Jewry under the Last Czar

In Russia the illness and death of Alexander III gave the Jews a breathing spell. The capacities of his successor, Czar Nicholas II[32] were not equal to the responsible position which he had inherited. He was not every inch the king, but every inch the neurasthenic. Even in a period less pregnant with storm this spineless man, incapable of decision, helpless without support, would have failed. He was afflicted with a pronounced intellectual and moral weakness and had an irresistible inclination towards cunning, underhanded and scheming devices. He wavered constantly between unlimited absolutism and modern democratic forms of government. At the beginning of his reign he seemed not incapable of noble impulses, and he surprised the world by his peace manifesto of 1898; but his true nature was cruel and bloodthirsty; he wound up by being closely implicated with the Black Hundred and shielding their crimes.

His myopia amounting to blindness prevented him from recognizing the demands of the age. Russia had just passed through the transition to large industry; factories had been set up, mines were being exploited, and the network of railroads was being greatly expanded. All of this brought with it the rise of the class of industrial workers. The government was interested in the welfare of the workers in the old patriarchal fashion, but it could not prevent the growth of a proletarian class consciousness which was opposed to the prevailing order. The workers eschewed charity and demanded rights. The cumbersome structure of the state with its weaknesses becoming increasingly apparent, the corruption of the officials, and the ambiguous attitude of the Czar, all conspired to favor revolutionary activity, which increased perceptibly and embraced ever larger circles.

But the Czar looked upon every expression of dissatisfaction as the criminal work of the intelligentsia, which he and his equally scheming Czarina hated and would gladly have wiped off the face of the earth. He despised public opinion and would trust only his own intuitions which he regarded as divinely inspired; weak and mortal humanity he believed incapable of correct judgments. Nevertheless he was as unsteady as a reed and was completely under the control of his advisers, who were frequently as incompetent as they were conscienceless. Small wonder that the revolutionary movement gained in strength; in 1905 it extorted a constitution and finally, in 1917, it brought on the fall of the monarchy.

For the Jewish population the reign of Nicholas II had a profound and fateful significance. Let us glance first at the economic aspect.[33] Industrialization was not without its effects upon the Jews. A small upper class acquired considerable wealth and a strong position as manufacturers, entrepreneurs, bankers and wholesale merchants. But the great mass of Jewish handicraftsmen, who were at a disadvantage in any case because of insufficient training and inadequate tools, were now altogether cut off from competition. A thorough inquiry of the population and vocational distribution of Jews in Russia and Poland, made by the Jewish Colonization Association, demonstrated that the Jewish handicraftsman could not compete against large-scale machine production. Efforts to raise the standard were hampered on the one hand by legal restrictions and on the other by the nature and habits of the Jews. The Jew was disinclined to factory work; he disliked becoming a tool in a lifeless mechanism. Furthermore, Jewish workers, for a number of reasons, could find employment only in Jewish enterprises; these were situated chiefly in Poland and Lithuania, were limited to the production of a small number of articles, and by reason of their small size could offer only the most unfavorable working conditions. Following the example of the Polish workers the Jews combined in order to obtain higher wages and shorter hours. First they established collective strike funds, their organization being purely economic. Later these associations took on a political coloring and drove a wedge between the employers and employees of the ghetto. In 1897[34] various groups combined into a central organization which was called the General Jewish Workers' Union of Lithuania, Poland and Russia, or more briefly, the Bund.

The awakening of a Jewish proletarian class consciousness set the masses in motion and resulted in demands for freedom, at whatever price it might be obtained. Not only the freedom of the individual was sought but also the freedom of the community, not only civic but also national equality, not only religious but also and especially cultural autonomy. The primacy of religion yielded to secular demands. The instrument for reaching the masses was the Yiddish language, and Yiddish now made great gains in importance and in cultural value. Yiddish became the language of the popular broadside, of socialistic journalism, of popular education and entertainment. From being a political expedient it became a cultural force, from a convenience a national weapon. Economic improvement, civic freedom, national cultural rights: these were the demands that were presented in the Yiddish language.

A conflict arose on the question of national rights. In

1897, the year in which the Bund was formed, the Zionist movement was also organized. It, too, sought to influence the masses; it, too, was unconcerned about religious tradition; it, too, spoke out for national demands. But its interpretation of "national" was different. For the realization of its demands it looked outside Russia, and it stood aside from Russian political movements. This fact was observed by the public officials, who accordingly favored Zionism; and the Zionists themselves claimed that they sought to draw the masses, and particularly the youth, away from political radicalism. Between the Bund and Zionism an internecine war of brothers was waged. The opposition continued unreconciled when, later, socialist groups were formed among the Zionists and under the title *Poale Zion*, transferred the center of their interest to Palestine.

The Bund, on the other hand, had its own difficulties within the Social Democratic Party. The Polish Social Democrats roundly rejected the Jewish national program on the ground that it constituted treason to proletarian interests. Russian Social Democracy was organized only in 1898 and found the Bund already functioning; its views on this point were consequently less pronounced. The Bund demanded that the Russia of the future be composed of a federation of nationalities and that the Jews be regarded as one of these component nationalities. This view was sometimes accepted and sometimes rejected, and the relations of the Bund to the party varied accordingly. The representatives of the Jewish workers' groups received a hearing for their demands at the Socialist Internationale.

Socialism and Zionism[35] alike strove to become popular movements, to win the interest and arouse the enthusiasm of the masses. They stirred the people up, admonished them to take the shaping of their fate into their own hands, to make themselves independent of their former leaders whose interests were not those of the people. The awakening masses attained a new spiritual orientation and showed themselves susceptible to an extraordinarily lively cultural and literary activity. They were now approached with a realistic popular education along nationalist lines, not with an ivory-tower enlightenment. They were not asked to assimilate to suit someone else's desires, but to intensify their own values to suit their own desires.[36]

The leaders came from the people and remembered that they belonged to the people; they cultivated the things that were dear to the people, its usages, its beliefs, its hopes. Folkways upon which the educated classes had looked down, now were considered an important element in national life. The enlightened classes had long ridiculed Hasidism because of its extravagances; now, as the belief of the people, Hasidism rose in the scale of values. Judah Leib Perez (1851–1915), who had begun his career as a rationalist, dedicated his poetic gifts to celebrating the folk life of the Jews. His sympathetic sketches ushered in the fashion of glorifying Hasidism. Along with Perez, Mendele presided as the kindly genius of Yiddish literature. Shalom Aleichem (1859–1920) was gifted with keen observation and inexhaustible humor; he gave the people realistic representations of all their various folk types. Realism in literature enlarged its audience and interested numerous Yiddish readers in England and the United States. The Yiddish theater was aware of its new possibilities and rose far beyond the level of vaudeville.

Neither did the classic Hebrew authors scorn to write Yiddish. Since Ahad Ha'am the lines which Hebrew literature was to take had been sketched out; its aim was integration with contemporary world culture.[37] Critics like David Frischman and Reuben Brainin raised its level; Micha Joseph Berdyczewski ("Ben Gorion," 1865–1921) preached the transvaluation of all old values. The youthful Chaim Nachman Bialik delighted readers with his lyric genius. It was he that gave expression to the yearnings of his generation:

> We are the mighty!
> The last generation of slaves and the first generation of freemen!
> Alone our hand in its strength
> Tore from the pride of our shoulders the yoke of bondage.

Pogroms as Czarist Policy

For the Russian government it was axiomatic that the revolutionary movement must be overcome, and a commonplace that the Jews, whose youth had been thrown into the arms of the revolution by the increasing rigor of special legislation, were the ringleaders. The government sought to suppress the Bund, as it sought to suppress all opposition tendencies, and had long kept its spies within the movement. Sugar-plums and cat-o'nine-tails were as little effective as they had been with the Social Democrats. Revolutionary ferment embraced ever widening circles, intellectuals and nobility, workers and peasants, and not least foreign groups such as Poles, Finns and Armenians. Acts of terror were the order of the day. Only groups that lived off the government, bureaucrats, police, the military and the frightened owners of large estates, were concerned to preserve the corrupt and rotten system. To the Czar the danger and the threat to throne and altar were pictured in the darkest colors; the plotters wished to draw him into their intrigues.

In order to make the Czar more susceptible, a crime was perpetrated of a character then unknown; even those in the plot could not realize how far its ramifications were destined to spread. The fabrication which was later to be known as the *Protocols of the Elders of Zion*[38] was smuggled into the Czar's court. It contained an alleged scheme for a Jewish world conspiracy which had been planned and recorded in an imaginary assembly of Jewish leaders. It has been amply and conclusively demonstrated that these *Protocols* are a gross forgery from beginning to end, and that they were fabricated by Russian emigrés in France as early as 1895, before anyone dreamed of a Zionist congress. The whole wicked contrivance sprang from the brain of Russian reactionaries, and then suited to the taste of like-minded persons in other countries; so diabolic a scheme could never have sprung from the head of a Jew. The document was disregarded at the time, but it left its poisonous effect on the Russian court. Now the bitter hatred which had been the special preserve of the Grand Duke Sergius dominated the entire royal family. The Czar[39] used the word "Jew" (*zhyd*) as synonymous with "enemy;" he called all his opponents, especially the English and the Japanese, "Jews." The Jews alone were to blame for the misfortunes which their own guilt had brought upon them.

The Czar sought protection against the peril which he was made to believe endangered his life, and gave the Ministry of the Interior to Wencelas von Plehve. This protégé of Pobiedonostzev strove to prove worthy of his patron. He showed no mercy in suppressing everything that did not seem to him to be thoroughly Russian. At the same time this arch reactionary gave himself the airs of being a modern who appreciated liberal thought, and did not exclude liberals from his department. He was the embodiment of all that was diabolical in the old regime, and became that regime's grave-digger. His principal opponent in the administration was Sergei Witte, who believed that the very existence of the Russian empire was imperilled by Plehve's policy of suppression.

In the memory of the Jews, Plehve lives on as the hangman of Kishinev.[40] Positive proof of his guilt has not yet been discovered, but he can surely not be acquitted of complicity. His regime promoted the conviction on the part of officials, police, military, in the schools, and in the greater part of the populace, that the Jews stood outside the protection of the law, and that the government desired for them to be railed at and maltreated. The central government issued a veritable stream of accusations, open or secret, to the effect that Jews were injurious to the state and to individuals. Enormous quantities of blood-thirsty broadsides demanding that Jews be murdered, printed by a committee of the Holy Synod and approved by the censor, were put into circulation. Governors and other highly placed representatives of the government openly threatened that under certain conditions they would organize riots against the Jews — disorder produced by the guardians of order, a product of Russian bureaucracy's manufactory of terror!

It was in such an atmosphere that several smaller pogroms were instigated at the turn of the century and that the ground was prepared for the pogrom of Kishinev. Of the responsibility of the Russian government Leo Tolstoi[11] has written as follows:

The outrages at Kishinev are but the direct result of the propaganda of falsehood and violence which our Government conducts with such energy. The attitude of our Government towards these events is only one more proof of the brutal egoism which does not flinch from any measures, however cruel, when it is a question of suppressing a movement which is deemed dangerous, and of their complete indifference (similar to the indifference of the Turkish Government towards the Armenian atrocities) towards the most terrible outrages which do not affect Government interests.

In Kishinev[42] the ground had been prepared for years by atrocious publicity, subventioned by the government, particularly favored by official censorship and enjoying the collaboration of government officers in positions of responsibility. The Jews were railed at as exploiters and bloodsuckers, and violent measures against them were called for. The blood-myth played an important role in their repertory. Whenever a death occurred under mysterious circumstances the Jews were blamed; but when, as usually happened, the mystery was cleared up, readers heard nothing of the explanation. Easter was the open season for the blood accusation. The attacks of *Bessarabetz*, the local newspaper hostile to the Jews, created such an anti-Jewish sentiment that even high police officials could speak lightly in public of the forthcoming expulsion and slaughter of Jews. It was determined that Jewish socialists and revolutionaries should all be incarcerated within the Pale. The Greek bishop refused to utter a humane word of conciliation. The governor gave assurances that no attack need be feared. The Jewish community, whose fifty thousand souls constituted a third of the population, was lulled into security by this assurance, and contented itself with admonishing its people not to leave their homes on Easter.

Easter Sunday happened to be the last day of Passover. Until noon all was quiet. But it was the calm before a storm which had been carefully plotted and prepared. In the early afternoon half-grown youths attacked Jews; they spread over the principal streets with lightning speed and hurled stones into windows. The police looked on without interfering. This was the prologue and the demonstration that had been awaited. About three o'clock men dressed as workmen appeared in the streets and shouted, "Death to the Jews! Beat the Jews!" Simultaneously twenty-four small bands rushed into the streets inhabited by Jews. They broke windows and even shop doors, rushed into houses, destroyed furniture and household goods, stole money, ornaments and other valuable articles, and struck down any that offered resistance. Shops were destroyed or plundered and their contents divided on the spot. Students, officials and ladies of good social standing were eager to share the booty. The police and the military did not stir, except to receive their share of the plunder. An alleged ukase of the Czar permitted the plundering and guaranteed immunity. A large store of wine provided necessary refreshments and incited the fury of the plunderers to a pitch of beastliness.

Up to this point the rioters did not yet venture on murder. But about five o'clock fury had grown so intense that a Jew was pulled from a tram-car and done to death. The police remained inactive, and so murder continued until by evening ten Jewish dead were counted. The chief of police rode by the points of danger, and when he was asked whether murder was permitted he made no reply. Evening interrupted the orgy, but the night was used to prepare worse misdeeds. Strangers who had been called into the city for the occasion were provided with axes and clubs. A council of war decided on an attack upon the following day. The Jews prepared to defend themselves, but they had scarcely assembled to offer resistance when the police stepped in and dispersed or arrested them. The city was in the hands of the rioters.

> On Monday from three A. M. until eight P. M., mobs raged in the midst of the desolation and ruin which they had themselves heaped; they plundered, robbed, and destroyed Jewish property; they stole, pillaged, and spoiled; they hounded, assaulted, abused, and tortured Jewish persons. Representatives of all classes of the population participated in this frightful witches' Sabbath: soldiers and police, officials and priests, children and women, peasants, workers, tramps.

The governor did not stir, though he was asked for help. He explained that the military — five thousand men were at his disposal in the garrison — could not be employed without orders from the central government. Finally, at about five o'clock in the afternoon, the necessary telegram arrived from St. Petersburg. The soldiers took up positions, and without a single shot having to be fired, the streets were cleared in short order — a clear indication of the ease with which the whole misfortune might have been averted. The mob was still allowed to attack the Jews in their hiding-places in the suburbs without hindrance. Many women and girls were brutally raped; numerous murders were committed; there was untold destruction and devastation.

"No pen or tongue," said an eyewitness, "can add anything to the fiendishness of the mobs who swarm to the streets crying 'Kill the Jews! Burn their houses! Spare not at all!'" Bialik[43] visited the "city of slaughter" and fixed the horror of the destruction in a gripping poem. He calls upon a spider as the witness of the brutal horrors:

> She saw it all, and she's a living witness,
> The old gray spider spinning in the garret.
> She knows a lot of stories — bid her tell them!
> A story of a belly stuffed with feathers,
> Of nostrils and of nails, of heads and hammers,
> Of men who, after death, were hung head downward,
> Like these, along the rafter.
> A story of a suckling child asleep,
> A dead and cloven breast between its lips,
> And of another child they tore in two,
> And many, many more such fearful stories
> That beat about thy head and pierce thy brain,
> And stab the soul within thee, does she know.

The horrors of Kishinev revealed such bestiality as was not thought possible in the twentieth century in a society which called itself Christian.

The mob [wrote Maxim Gorki],[44] merely the hand which was guided by a corrupt conscience, driving it to murder and robbery, was led by men of cultured society. But cultivated society in Russia is really much worse than the people who are goaded by their sad life and blinded and enthralled by the artificial darkness created around them . . . . Cultivated society is not less guilty of the disgraceful and horrible deeds committed at Kishinev than the actual murderers and ravishers. Its members' guilt consists in the fact that, not merely did they not protect the victims, but that they rejoiced over the murders; it consists chiefly in committing themselves for long years to be corrupted by man-haters and persons who have long enjoyed the disgusting glory of being the lackeys of power and the glorifiers of lies.

In St. Petersburg, where no very tender feelings for the Jews were cherished, even the authorities were shocked by the lawlessness and by the complete apathy of the official guardians of law and order. The Czar himself complained of Russia's misfortune. The governor of Bessarabia and the police chief of Kishinev were discharged. Many of the attackers were arrested, but the principal ringleaders, whose violence and murder were matters of common knowledge, were left completely at large. Reports to foreign countries were withheld, but since the proximity of the Rumanian border made it impossible to prevent leakage, all the government's machinery was set in motion to deny the facts. First the existence of a serious emergency was denied altogether. Then an attempt was made to explain the uprising by putting the blame on the Jews. But the official efforts at explanation bore the marks of their disingenuousness upon their face; they sought to prove too much and convinced no one. So a story was officially circulated that the Jewish owner of a carousel[45] had struck a Christian woman in a quarrel and so had occasioned the disturbances; the truth was that the carousel belonged to a Christian German, and that neither quarrel nor disturbance had taken place there. Then it was claimed that the disturbances were the result of a spontaneous outbreak of indignant peasants against Jewish exploiters. But the malefactors were not peasants and the victims were mostly poor handicraftsmen and small shopkeepers who were very far from being exploiters. The attack had been long and carefully prepared, and the connivance of the officials, if not their active cooperation, had been assured.

An impartial investigation[46] might have established the ultimate responsibility for the excesses, but the investigators and the courts hesitated to follow up the clues. The representatives of the Jewish plaintiffs sought to throw light upon the background of the riots, and the lawyers for the defendants were also concerned to point out the culprits who were really responsible, in the interest of those who had accidentally been taken into custody.

They did succeed in unmasking the notorious speculator Pronin, who was the mainstay of the *Bessarabetz*; he appeared before the court as a witness to the guilt of the Jews, and left it as an exposed accomplice of the criminals. But the court could not be induced to examine Baron Levendal, the representative of the General Safety Organization, who had turned up in Kishinev several months before the pogrom on an unexplained mission and had then disappeared, equally mysteriously; common opinion and all available evidence pointed to the guilt of this man. Nor would the court examine other similar *provocateurs*. The defense attorneys were hampered in their work and gave up their briefs. The well-known Russian advocate, Karbatchev of St. Petersburg, likened events in Kishinev to an arena of the ancient Roman circus, where a delighted crowd was diverted by a horrible spectacle which began at a word of command and at a word of command suddenly ended.

The reaction of the outer world to these horrors is indescribable.[47] One must have lived through the expressions of indignation; they cannot be retailed at second hand. The German emperor, William II, informed the Czar that such inhumanity was unheard of; his royal kinsmen at the Danish and English courts are said to have made similar representations. Indignation was most intense in the United States.[48] President Theodore Roosevelt did not exaggerate when he said: "I have never in my experience in this country known of a more immediate or a deeper expression of sympathy for the victims and of horror over the appalling calamity that has occurred." All newspapers excoriated the Russian barbarity. In all important cities public meetings were held at which speakers representing all classes and all faiths gave passionate expression to their horror at the brutality and inhumanity of what had happened at Kishinev. Dr.

Jacob Gould Schurman, the president of Cornell University, uttered his indignation before a meeting in New York:

> O Christ! What crimes have been committed in Thy name against the race which gave Thee to the world! Thy gospel of peace and goodwill to man has brought the Jews at the hands of Thy unworthy followers too often only hatred, pillage and massacre. It was no accident that these Kishinev horrors fell at the Easter season. That blessed occasion was used only to accentuate religious differences, to foster outrageous misrepresentations regarding the religious rites of the Jews, and to intensify the spirit of bigotry, superstition and intolerance, which easily produce, not only hatred, but strife and murder. Thus religion, or rather the perversion of religion, undoubtedly played its part in bringing about the massacre at Kishinev.

Everywhere resolutions were adopted expressing the deep distress of American citizens at the detestable attacks upon peaceful people and the hope that such excesses would be impossible in the future. The Independent Order B'nai B'rith, under the leadership of its president, Leo N. Levi (1856–1904), prepared a petition[49] to the Czar in which American citizens appealed to the creator of the peace manifesto to "add new lustre to his reign and fame by leading a new movement that shall commit the whole world in opposition to religious persecution." In a few days this petition, which was presented in only a few states, bore the signatures of 12,544 American citizens of all classes. The Czar refused to accept the petition. Since the French as well as the English uttered not a word, out of fear of Russian military power, and since Herzl himself excused his negotiations with Plehve on the ground that politics could not be affected by sentimentality, the President of the United States could not well be expected to expose himself further. The State Department in Washington received the petition into its archives; its contents had been made public and so it had served its purpose.

American citizens without distinction of creed participated in relief work for the victims of the pogrom.[50]

Besides forty-nine dead there were more than ninety maimed or seriously injured and five hundred less seriously injured. About six hundred shops were plundered and seven hundred homes destroyed. The homeless and bereft were estimated at 10,000, and an even larger number were impoverished. In Kishinev itself those that had been spared by the persecutions, with slight exceptions the more prosperous members of the community, organized a relief committee, and their energetic efforts were supported by contributions from all of Russia. Russian writers and thinkers sent the relief committee expressions of their warm sympathy and of their aversion for the horrors that had taken place. Hearts and hands were opened in Western Europe. A conference of the various relief organizations took place in Berlin; it unified and systematized relief for the sufferers of Kishinev and took special thought for rehabilitating lives that had been crushed.

Panic seized the Jews of Russia when they were confronted with the possibility of such gruesomeness and realized that they might be delivered over to destruction utterly helpless under the very eyes of the officials. What had happened in Kishinev today might be tolerated or even instigated elsewhere tomorrow. The number of immigrants to the United States mounted rapidly, and there was considerable increase also in immigration to Palestine, Canada and South Africa. But the horror of Kishinev had another consequence in the establishment of self-defense[51] organizations. Hardly had peace been restored when people asked how it could happen that so numerous a Jewish population, including able-bodied men in their number, could allow themselves to be slaughtered without raising a hand in defense. Where, as Bialik scornfully asked, were the descendants of the Maccabees slumbering? Now they awakened. Throughout Russian

Jewry there was a call to arm and defend themselves, to meet the enemy with revolver in hand and to make him pay dearly for his attacks. The call was enthusiastically received by the Jewish youth, and in the Jewish centers large groups joined the defense organizations. Unfortunately the purpose of this organization was not always clearly understood; even after the pogrom epidemic of 1905 each tiny group stuck fast in its ideological web and would hear nothing of ideas on common defense. On the other hand, the movement was joined by some noble-minded Christian socialists. The defense organizations suffered from lack of funds and from double-dealing on the part of the police, so that they could not reach the requisite strength. Nevertheless their very existence and possibility of their being mobilized served as protection against pogroms that were threatening or beginning.

The ruins of Kishinev had not yet been cleared away when similar excesses occurred in Homel,[52] in the province of Mohilev, where some 60% of the population was Jewish. On August 29, 1903, a fight took place on the market place, and the peasants scattered out of fear of the Jews. One peasant was fatally stabbed. The police arrested only Jews. Decent citizens strove to restore calm, and also warned the Jews of a pogrom which had been planned for September 1. The police gave assurances that they could easily control any uprising, and soldiers were available. Nevertheless a troop of workers armed with stout clubs and iron rods swarmed into the city, and before the eyes of soldiers and police broke into the houses of the Jews and destroyed furniture and household goods. The Jewish self-defense succeeded in pressing the plunderers back, but the soldiers prevented them from pursuing their advantage and protected the pillagers, who were thus able to proceed with their work undisturbed. Later the police fired a few shots, the crowd dispersed, and the pogrom was ended.

But the Jews again had their dead, their wounded, and those whom the attack had driven mad. Four hundred families had suffered serious loss and injury; prosperous families were reduced to such beggary that they could not afford a hovel. Again a striking feature was the malicious joy with which the Christian population greeted the slaughter of the Jews. The attitude of the officials was no less remarkable. The governor hastened to the scene and in a callous and impertinent speech to the assembled Jews placed the entire blame upon them. The indictment for the trial which was to take place assumed a similar tone. Facts were turned topsy-turvy; the Jews were made solely to blame, and the presiding justice tolerated no questions which might serve to clarify the facts of the case. Again the muzzled representatives of the Jewish defendants were constrained to lay down their brief, and jurists all over Russia sent word approving their course. The court tacitly acknowledged the justice of the defendants' case by imposing light penalties for the extremely grave charges upon which the Jews were held. The real culprit was the bureaucracy, which had been playing politics. It was not put into the prisoner's box but it was condemned nevertheless.

The duplicity of such excesses as those in Kishinev and Homel was too much even for the lawlessness of the Russian reactionary forces. Some remedy had to be found. The Holy Synod addressed an admonition to the clergy asking them to instruct their people that hostility to the Jews was sinful. Plehve[53] resorted to the time-honored device of appointing a commission on the Jews, and like other such commissions it accomplished nothing. If any of the governors concerned ventured, as did Prince Sergei Urussov on the basis of his experience in Bessarabia, to mention faults in the existing laws concerning the Jews and in their administration, he called the ill-will of the all-powerful minister down upon his head. Plehve's man was

General Trepoff,[54] who declared "each measure good and acceptable that is directed against the Jews." Nevertheless the proposal was made to the commission that they grant the Jews fundamental equality with other citizens and proceed to discuss individual points where departure from this principle seemed imperative. The commission lasted only a short while. At the end of January 1904 the Japanese attacked the Russian fleet, and the Russo-Japanese War began.

Plehve demonstrated upon the five fingers of his hand that Russia, being so greatly superior in population, must indubitably conquer little Japan.[55] The same flippant mentality which had organized the pogroms, the same disregard for human life, imposed this adventure upon Russia. Like all tyrannical rulers of history, Plehve looked upon war as a means for diverting interest from mounting internal problems. "We need a little victorious war," he is reported to have said, "to stem the tide of revolution." And the Czar who had issued his peace manifesto a few years before, swelled with childish vanity when he received telegrams informing him of patriotic parades. He could not imagine that he was sitting upon a powder keg; he could not know what dangers he conjured up when he set it afire.

There was no popular enthusiasm for this war in the Far East, which was entered upon for the sake of the imperial ambitions and the financial interest of the royal family. The Jews[56] felt the effects at once, when two thousand of them who had received permission to settle in Port Arthur and along the Trans-Siberian railway were forthwith expelled. Characteristically enough, they were not even permitted to use the railway; the reason given was that the line was overloaded with troop transport, but there was no such traffic from east to west. In the bitterness of winter they had to cover more than a thousand miles on foot, and because of domiciliary limitations they could not even lodge at convenient stopping places. It can easily be understood why many Jews subject to military service sought to evade war duty by flight: there was another jump in emigration figures. Nevertheless tens of thousands of Jewish soldiers and a disproportionately large number of Jewish physicians took part in the campaigns. They had their full share of dead and of those distinguished for bravery.

At home the professional pogrom-mongers spread a new lie: the Jews were supporting their racial kindred, the Japanese, by every means in their power. All signs pointed to the preparation of new horrors for the Easter season, but excesses of this nature were highly inconvenient to the government at this juncture, and so strict orders were issued to the governors not to allow them. Accordingly there were no excesses, and that fact alone proves clearly that the will of the central government was the paramount factor in these orgiastic outbreaks. The situation of the government, indeed, became ever more precarious. Plehve's mathematical calculation proved mistaken; the Russian armies suffered defeat after defeat. Revolution and terror raised their heads in the country. Plehve and, a few months later, Grand Duke Sergei, together the heads and fountains of all evil, fell victim to bombing attacks. Absolutism was forced to make concessions. Some crumbs of the royal grace even fell to the lot of the Jews; some of the most oppressive provisions of the domiciliary laws were abrogated.

The Constitutional Movement and Czarist Reaction

These were the birth pangs of a new era which were throbbing through the body politic of the Russian people. Those that were forward-looking were more insistent in their demands, the reactionaries more brutal in their use of force. Among the mass of petitions[57] with which the government was flooded some came from the large Jewish communities. Voicing their complaints and their hopes they said,

that the cruel system of endless restrictions and disabilities undermines the very basis of their existence, that it is impossible to continue such a life.... that they are waiting for a radical repeal of all restrictive laws, so that, enjoying freedom and equality with all others, they may, shoulder to shoulder with the other citizens of this great country, work for its welfare and prosperity.

The League for the Attainment of Equal Rights for the Jewish People in Russia was established in April 1905 as an official mouthpiece for the Jews; the League, largely under the influence of S. M. Dubnow's fight for national autonomy, stated as its goal "the realization to their full extent of the civil, political, and national rights of the Jewish people in Russia." The League demanded proper representation of national minorities in every electoral district in the forthcoming parliament. It sought to sway public opinion in Russia so that specific mention of the rights of the Jews should be made in the resolutions which demanded equal rights for citizens.

These efforts imply a certain lack of faith in Russian popular sentiment, and the misgivings were justified by events. Witte himself, who was one of the few Russian politicians who could look facts in the eye, who realized that special legislation against the Jews was unjust and cruel, acknowledged that the Jews were justified in asking equal rights with the Russians, but declared that it was improper for the Jews to concern themselves with Russian politics and to appear as spokesmen for the Russian people. "It is not your business to teach us," he said. "Leave that to Russians by birth and civil status, and mind your own affairs!" Witte's argument was specious; no one could be entitled to demand rights for himself if he was not prepared to join others in the fight for their rights. Yet his defeatism won Witte the approval of many

Jews. Only a few who possessed political insight, such as Vinaver, an outstanding lawyer who was to become a deputy in the *Duma*, and Paul Nathan, the expert on Jewish needs, disagreed with him.

The reactionaries turned at once to a counterstroke against "revolutionaries and Jews." Reaction wished to make the one unpopular by associating it with the other; it wished to identify the Jews with the revolution and to represent the revolution as a Jewish conspiracy which could only bring harm to the Russian people. Reactionaries in the ranks of the nobility sought for help among the people and found it in the Black Hundreds.[58] Under the protection, and sometimes under the actual direction, of the police these bands committed all kinds of violence and in particular fell upon Jews and revolutionaries. In many places it was perfectly clear that incitement to brutality came from higher officials and police officers, and that their humble tools were only obeying orders blindly.

In Zhitomir[59] there was ceaseless agitation, until one day a carefully prepared attack was made upon the Jews and served as the signal for a regular battle. Peasants from the vicinity reinforced by a crew of outsiders beat Jewish persons and plundered Jewish property. Police and military stood by to protect the attackers and prevented the Jewish self-defense from making a stand. The results of the two-day battle (April 24–25, 1905) were: fifteen Jews and one Russian student who fought on their side killed, sixty seriously wounded, several suicides, and several cases of insanity. The governor did not lift a finger to restore order. When new danger threatened on the third day a number of Jews forced their way to the governor and threatened general slaughter if he did not restore quiet at once. This burst of despair impressed the governor, and he issued stern orders for the suppression of the unrest. These were effective, and showed how easily the excesses might have been nipped in the bud if the officials had shown any inclination to prevent them. In Bialystok the military itself provoked the Jews and then fired at them for hours mercilessly, not even allowing physicians to treat the injured (July 30, 1905). "Human cruelty has reached its climax," the protest of the local Jewry stated. "Men surpassed the bloodiest beasts in their fury. And these men were representatives of the administrative and military power."

The year 1905 marks an important turning point in the internal history of Russia, for it brought the end of absolutism.[60] The transformation, so meaningful to the world at large, was carried out by elemental force. It began with a bloody Sunday in St. Petersburg in January and ended in December with barricaded battles in the streets of Moscow. The participation of Jews was relatively slight; all peoples and classes in the broad realm of the Czar were stirred by the ferment. Count Witte had given a Jewish deputation the usual commonplace about the extraordinarily large number of Jewish revolutionaries, but in his memoirs he tells a different story of the tempest which tore the empire completely asunder and drove it to chaos. Of the situation in October 1905 he reports as follows:

The country was in a quandary, and when the revolution boiled up furiously from the depths, the authorities were completely paralyzed.... A general feeling of profound discontent with the existing order was the most apparent symptom of the corruption with which the social and political life of Russia was infested. It was this feeling that united all the classes of the population. They all joined in a demand for radical political reforms. The upper classes, the nobility were dissatisfied and impatient with the Government. Their dream was an aristocratic constitutional monarchy. The merchants and captains of industry, the rich, looked forward to a constitutional monarchy of the bourgeois type. The "intelligentsia," i. e., members of various liberal professions, hoped for a constitutional monarchy, which was eventually to result in a bourgeois republic modelled upon the pattern of the French state. The students, not only in the universities, but in the advanced high school grades, recognized no law — except the word of those who preached the most extreme revolutionary and anarchistic theories. Many of the officials in the various governmental bureaus were against the regime they served, for they were disgusted with the shameful system of corruption which had grown to such gigantic proportions during the reign of Nicholas II. The *Zemstvo* and municipal workers had long before declared that safety lay in the adoption of a constitution. As for the workmen, they were concerned about filling their stomachs with more food than had been their wont. They fell completely under the sway of the revolutionists and rendered assistance without stint wherever there was need of physical force.

The upshot of the confusion was the memorable manifesto of October 17 (30), in which the Czar set forth to his government his firm resolve "to grant the population the unshakable foundations of civic freedom on the basis of real personal inviolability, freedom of conscience, of speech, of assemblage, and of association." The Jews were not specifically mentioned[61] here, but the law creating an imperial *Duma*, to which the manifesto referred, made suffrage independent of race and religion. The grant of equality to the Jews could therefore be assumed, although some found it strange that, whereas Jews were eligible for election to the *Duma*, they were not allowed to reside where the *Duma* met.

But very soon the question of civic rights became secondary to that of mere existence. The October manifesto was promptly followed by a pogrom epidemic[62] of inhuman proportions. Plehve had said, "I will choke the revolution in the blood of the Jews," and now his words came near literal fulfillment. In hundreds of places political excitement ran to demonstrations and counter-demonstrations, and in almost every case these turned into a pogrom against the Jews. Between October 18 and 29, greater or smaller pogroms and attempted pogroms took place at 690, or, by a higher estimate, 725 localities in the provinces of Bessarabia, Kherson, Ekatrinoslav, Tchernigov, Kiev, Podolia, to a lesser degree in Tauria and Poltava and certain provinces outside the Pale of

Settlement. Nine hundred persons were killed, leaving 325 widows and 1,350 orphans (among them 166 full orphans), a number were crippled for life, and some seven or eight thousand were injured. In addition, thousands of houses, shops and synagogues were destroyed; the property damage was reckoned as being in excess of six million rubles. A frightful panic seized areas inhabited by Jews. More than 200,000 persons were directly injured or suffered indirect consequences of the excesses.

The world was so appalled by the unexpected reports from Russia that it noted only the political implications of the groups concerned and did not at once realize the gruesome meaning of these events. Gradually it was learned that the pogroms all followed one and the same pattern.[63] First there was a "red" demonstration, and then this would be countered by a "patriotic" demonstration.

> It was always the crowd following the portrait of his Majesty — a proceeding which had never taken place before — there was always a Jew shooting at it, there was always the same revolver shot with identical results, including the powerlessness of the authorities to repress the pogroms, which were nevertheless carried out by a small band of men. And the population gave their own version of these pogroms, which on the face of it certainly supplied a better explanation of the uniformity of these occurrences. According to their version, the crowd of patriotic demonstrators consisted of the dregs of the population, of hooligans recruited by the police and frequently paid; the shot, which mostly hurt no one, was fired by a police agent, and then the crowd, led by the police, commenced to sack and kill until given the signal to desist.

Behind this movement was the powerful police system, equipped for spy work and malicious provocation, and expert in organizing riots. They were furnished with money, and their bands of ruffians were taken from place to place on the railroads; immunity was assured them before they went into action. The populace never rose against the will of the officials. It was by the basest lies and most unprincipled agitation that they were roused to the necessary pitch, so that the pogrom could begin as soon as its directors had given the signal previously agreed upon. Minute accounts of these epidemics of murder and pillage are available, and there is no single instance where a pogrom broke out contrary to the will of the officials or where one could not have been ended in a moment at the will of the police and the military.

Odessa[64] furnishes a typical example of official irresponsibility and barbarity. The toll of three days rioting amounted to 302 Jewish dead, of whom fifty-five were members of the self-defense; seventeen Christian members of the self-defense; 5,000 wounded; 1,400 businesses ruined; 3,000 artisans reduced to beggary. The man responsible for this death and destruction was Colonel Neidhard, the chief magistrate in the city. He gloated over the reckoning he was paying out to Jews and revolutionaries, particularly those at the university. "Here is your Jewish freedom!" he called mockingly to the anguished Jews. His conduct was not that of a guardian of order but of an *agent provocateur* of the most evil kind; he incited to murder with cold-blooded cruelty. The massacre lasted for precisely three days, as had been arranged, then Neidhard gave the signal to discontinue, calling out to his hooligans, "Enough, brothers, go to your homes!" He was a worthy brother indeed to these cutthroats, and he had a fitting tool in the military commandant who was attached to him. "We all sympathize most heartily with this pogrom," the attaché said to his police officers. The thoroughgoing investigation established Neidhard's brutal inhumanity, and even though he was not sentenced he was condemned. The Christian citizens of Odessa turned with loathing from the scenes of cruelty; and it must be noted in general that in many places there were citizens who devoted themselves to the protection of the Jews without thought of self. Police officers also frequently ventured to follow their conscience rather than command to murder. On the other hand, the distressing phenomenon must be recorded that the "class conscious proletariat" frequently allowed itself to be drawn into participation in the attacks. Despite its revolutionary schooling it had not yet come to realize that Jews too had a claim on human rights. If this was the attitude of the progressive group, what was the outlook for the future? The answer of the Pale was a panicky flight. More than 500,000 Jews emigrated between 1903 and 1907, 90% of them to the United States.

A view of the pogroms as a whole indicated that a powerful organization[65] disposing of extraordinary resources was at work, and investigation showed that a lawless rump government was functioning at the seat of the court in St. Petersburg. The leader of the gangster organization was General Bogdanowicz, a corrupt extortioner who collected a militia of adventurers and drilled them to the watchwords "Death to the Jews, death to the students, death to the intellectuals!" as well as "For the Czar!" Long before the October Manifesto was issued the counter-revolution had been organized with the twofold purpose of letting a quantity of radical blood and then pointing to the disorders which they themselves engineered as a proof that such savages were not fit for a constitution. Broadsides without number were scattered through the land. They were crammed with foul lies, and they incited to violence against Jews and revolutionaries in the crudest language.

These summonses were printed by a police officer who had installed a secret printing press in the rooms of the Ministry of the Interior. When he was discovered, he remarked cynically: "We are in a position to start a pogrom, when and how we please, with ten or ten thousand men!" The broadsides were paid for out of the Czar's secret funds, and they bore the approval of General Trepoff. Trepoff held the local post of Court Commander, but in reality he was the most powerful person in the general police organization. As early as the beginning of October he had issued an order not to spare bullets. He had put his signature to an appeal to murder Witte, "the Jewish Minister." He was exposed, with the full consent of the assembled *Duma*, as a "quartermaster and police spy by education and pogrom-maker by conviction." Here was utter anarchy, under the pretense of maintaining order.

The Czar was wholly in the toils of anti-Jewish propaganda. If he had listened to Witte's accounts of his experiences in the United States he would have learned of the great appreciation Russian Jews had won for their constructive work there and he would have been informed too of their devotion to the Russian homeland. But he preferred his underground sources of information. In January 1906 his Foreign Minister, Count Lambsdorf,[66] submitted a memorandum bearing the intriguing title, *On the Anarchists*. He was sure that the Russian revolution was staged by foreign nations, but he attributed the principal guilt for its course and its direction to world Jewry which was united in the *Alliance Israélite Universelle* and allied with international Freemasonry. Accordingly, he suggested a triple alliance with the German Empire and the Vatican, "for the purpose of organizing a vigilant supervision, and then also for an active joint struggle against the common foe of the Christian and monarchical order of Europe." This poisonous brew, apparently drawn from the witches' cauldron of the *Protocols of the Elders of Zion* which had been newly printed by the imperial press in 1905, was annotated by the Czar with his own individual remarks: "Negotiations must be entered into *immediately*. I share entirely the opinions herein expressed." The whole thing was nothing else than an intrigue counting on the ignorance and prejudice of the Czar. It failed of success only because the same minister, opposing the country's foreign policy, was intriguing for a union with Germany and, consequently, soon lost his portfolio.

It is due to the existence of the imperial *Duma* that these reports, which throw so shocking a light upon Russian officialdom, could come into being and be published abroad. One can understand why the radicals feared that any thought of popular representation in the pogrom-infested atmosphere would become a farce and why they considered boycotting the election. The Jewish Bund shared this feeling and prevented primaries among other Jewish groups also. But to the surprise of all, the elections showed a strong liberal majority, in which the Constitutional Democrats (Cadets) had the leadership. Twelve Jewish deputies and a number of baptized Jews were elected. The Jewish members of the *Duma* had no common program, but they agreed to act together on all points which involved the equal rights of the Jews. This problem was barely touched, and the question of a constitution was not considered at all. But in a penetrating debate on the pogroms the *Duma*[67] threw a clear light upon the machinations of the central office of the murderous network and uncovered its secret ramifications. Stolypin, the Minister of the Interior, tried to hush matters up and gave assurances that there would be no recurrences under his administration.

But while the *Duma* was debating upon illegalities, reports arrived of a new pogrom in Bialystok. The disorder started with a shot during a religious procession, and followed each detail of the customary pattern. "There was pillage, devastation, a raid upon the Jews who were killed in the streets, in the houses, in the trains and at the railway station, even in the restaurants, before the eyes and with the approval of the officers and officials."

A commission of the *Duma* was despatched to the spot at once, and submitted the following report:

1. There was no race hatred, either religious or economic, between the Christian and the Jewish populations of the town of Bialystok.
2. Undisguised hatred of the Jews existed only among the police, who imparted it to the troops, on the ground that the Jews were participants in the Liberal movement.
3. The pogrom was prepared beforehand, and this was known for some time by the administration as well as by the population.
4. The immediate pretext of the pogrom was also premeditated and prepared by the authorities, and it cannot therefore be considered as an outbreak of national and religious fanaticism.
5. The action of the army and the civil authorities was in open violation of the existing laws.
6. The civil and military authorities not only remained inactive before the pogrom, but in many cases, in the persons of their agents, they themselves were guilty of murder, mutilation and pillage.
7. The official reports on the reasons, the pretexts, and the course of events are contrary to the truth.

The *Duma* was dissolved and the majority of its members assembled in Finland, where they issued the Viborg Manifesto, in which they urged the Russian people to supply its autocratic government with neither taxes nor conscripts. They showed great confidence in the population, though they possessed no tangible means for following up their words with deeds. The government prosecuted those who had participated in the assembly and withdrew their right to election. Thus it happened that none of the former Jewish deputies could be elected to the second imperial *Duma*, and that the Jews were represented by only four, quite unknown, members. The life of this *Duma* was also short. The Jewish question was brought up, against the will of the government, under the heading of freedom of conscience, but no decisive resolutions were adopted.

After the dissolution of this *Duma*, Stolypin, the presiding minister, consummated a coup by which he altered the electoral law to conform to the wishes of the nobility by making the franchise depend on landed property. As in many other countries, so in Russia, the first revolutionary impulses produced loud wails on the part of the propertied classes who trembled for their possessions and privileges and wished to exclude unpropertied classes from any share in legislation. In Russia reaction of this sort was supported by the Union of the Russian People. This Union[68] had made itself indispensable to the government in crushing the revolution, and Stolypin, who claimed credit for pacifying the country, made a pact with it.

And so this group "of dark-minded and ignorant people, which consisted of plain thieves and hooligans, led by unhanged villains, among whom there were some noblemen," gained a decisive influence upon the policies and the administration of the country. In these anarchists of the Right the emperor and empress saw their saviors, the possibility for the restoration of Russian autocracy. When Dr. Dubrovin, the leader of the Union, felicitated the Czar upon the coup, the Czar replied with circumspection that he would rely upon the group in future. He did support it with money, and on occasion conspicuously wore the insignia of this society of adventurers who served only their own interests and showed no hesitation in exploiting the basest instincts of the masses. The Czar was completely taken in by their patriotic phrases; a clearer-headed observer like Count Witte characterized them as "the embodiment of savage, nihilistic patriotism, feeding on lies, slander and deceit, the party of savage and cowardly despair, devoid of the manly and clear-eyed spirit of creativeness."

During the seven years preceding the World War this unscrupulous society made Russia the scene of endless disturbances; few ventured to oppose the mad course of events, and the Jews were the preferred victims. After looking into the Jewish regulations, Stolypin[69] came to the conclusion that the times demanded their thoroughgoing revision and undertook "to remove all restrictions which are the source of irritation and are manifestly obsolete." His memorandum on the existing Jewish regulations (December 1906) is an outspoken indictment of the system. The council of ministers approved a step-by-step abrogation of the restrictions. But as soon as the "True Russians" heard of the resolution they began to protest most vehemently. The sovereign emperor yielded to their desires forthwith and refused to sign the minute which was submitted to him. Instead of clarifying the mind of the Czar, the presiding minister shamelessly decided to falsify the resolution of the ministerial council and give it a meaning opposite to its original intention, so that the Czar could give it his approval.

Stolypin knew from what quarter the wind blew and returned to the policy of suppressing non-Russians and particularly of crushing the Jews. The third imperial *Duma*,[70] which met at the end of 1907, was dominated, not only by a plebeian tone and crude expression, but also by the dark spirit of the Black Hundred; and the government yielded at every point. Dubrovin was able to promise his gangsters the Czar's pardon if they should be found guilty, and for such thugs this was encouragement to unrestrained terror — every Jew must expect an attack at any time. In legislation and administration this "party of hatred," as the ambassador of Russia's ally, France, called it, always emphasized the anti-Jewish tone. It censured the suggested amelioration in the execution of the domiciliary law and effected new expulsions; it obtained particularly rigorous exclusion from resorts and watering places. In provisions for the inviolability of the person, it made express exceptions to the disadvantage of the Jews. The reactionary group hailed the proposal of the Octobrists to exclude Jews from the position of justice of the peace in a Christian state.

Above all, the *Duma* introduced new rigors into the

percentage norms for schools and universities. It not only made into law the old regulations which had been disregarded after the revolution, but it extended the law to apply to private institutions, though these were largely maintained by Jewish funds. The Jewish question was handled with greater cruelty than ever before. In this atmosphere of hatred it was a mockery to summon an assembly of rabbis to St. Petersburg and to expect that it would offer suggestions for dealing with the Jews. It is nothing short of miraculous that the deputy Nisselovitch was able to obtain 166 signatures for a proposal to abolish the Pale of Settlement. In this *Duma* there was not the slightest chance for the adoption of such a proposal. The Black Hundred regarded the demand as dangerous and brought out its most effective weapon for destroying all Jewry by staging an agitation concerning ritual murder.

In Kiev, in the middle of March 1911, a thirteen-year-old lad, named Andrei Justschinski, disappeared. All signs indicated that he had been done to death in the home of the mother of one of his companions, a nest of thieves, fences and murderers, because he knew too much about their crimes. The body was found near a brickyard belonging to a Jew, and so, at the instigation of the "True Russians," one of the watchmen of the brickyard, Menachem Mendel Beilis[71] by name, was accused of the murder. He actually had as much to do with the murder as the Dalai Lama or a lighthouse-keeper in Patagonia, and it is noteworthy that in the trials which followed Beilis himself was kept completely in the background. It was not against him that the charge was directed, but against the entire Jewish people, which was to be exposed in the person of this cipher. It was difficult to build up a charge out of thin air, and the Minister of Justice in person spent two years contriving unexampled subterfuges and illegalities before he could assemble the materials and opinions necessary to raise the charge that Beilis, "aided and abetted by persons unknown," had committed a ritual murder.

The case roused the revulsion of the entire civilized world. The Russian intelligentsia, and in particular the bar association in St. Petersburg, protested loudly against this barbaric justice; professors of Russian universities utterly refuted the conclusions of the "experts" engaged by the minister. Competent scholars from every part of Europe agreed with the professors, and representatives of culture everywhere protested against this perversion of every concept of law. At the time only published material was available, and no one realized the depths of baseness, deceit and forgery which the subsequent opening of the Russian archives have since revealed. The Minister of the Interior summarized public opinion quite correctly when he said that it was convinced "that there were no traces, no hints of such a crime, and that this whole case was arranged and staged by the Russian government with special secret purposes." The trial in Kiev took the form of a conflict between the powers of light and the powers of darkness, and the powers of darkness were defeated. A police report compares the fiasco in Kiev with the débacle of the Russian fleet at Tshusima. The prosecution did succeed in persuading the carefully chosen jurors that a case of ritual murder was involved, but they refused to be convinced that Beilis had committed it, and so he was discharged. One cannot but admire the simple peasants in the jury box for having had the courage, in the face of the irresistible pressure brought to bear upon them, to follow their natural feelings of justice, while the professional representatives of the law yielded to the terror of the "True Russians" in their disgraceful perversion of all notions of justice.

During these years the scourge of Jew-hatred spread over Poland[72] also. Although the Poles, like the Jews, were among the peoples hated and persecuted by the Russians, they nevertheless found it just to release their own hatred of the Jews. The occasion for fanning antisemitism, which was always latent, into a flame was provided by the flight of numerous Jews from Russia to Poland, where not all the barbarous domiciliary restrictions were in force. These "Litvaki" were the particular favorites of the Poles; upon them could be placed the blame for whatever annoyed the Poles, particularly the spreading radicalism and terror — as if Poland had not had an organized social democratic party before Russia. In 1905, when the Poles were concentrating their demonstrations around the Church, and the Jews around the Bund, Polish leaders regarded it as their duty to preach tolerance and to warn their followers by the example of "barbaric" Russia. But a few years later the wind turned, and complaints were made that the Jews were an element in Russification. The rising national Polish democrats seized upon the antisemitic platform and fought all Jews, native as well as foreign, with the weapon of economic boycott. When in 1912 the Jews of Warsaw ventured to reject an antisemitic candidate for the imperial *Duma* and to vote for a Polish socialist, economic war to destruction was declared against them, and it was with such a declaration that the Poles entered on the World War.

Life in the Pale

The passage through the vale of tears pressed hard on Jewish life but did not submerge it. Russian barbarism could not enslave the Jews nor rob them of their vitality. Through peril and distress these millions continued to assert themselves, some in praying, weeping and fasting, in humble faith in their God; others in sharp rebellion against Him; all firmly resolved not to yield lightly but to persist heroically. The masses were quickened by faith in the liberation of Russia, in socialism, in Zionism. The ghetto was not fallow. Ideologies sprouted like mushrooms in a meadow, and men attacked them or defended them and were so filled with them that they would lay down their lives for them. The old communities continued; new ones came into existence as far east as Irkutsk, Harbin, Vladivostok. The communities were supplemented by new organizations with political, social and cultural aims. The Russian constitution granted freedom of assembly, and the lively Jewish spirit made rich use of this liberty. Action and conflict was not limited to religious concerns, nor exhausted by the traditional modes. Secular activities, even disruptive movements, found admittance into the ghetto and engulfed it like a whirlpool, stirring every fiber and every passion.

Apart from a handful of millionaires in the capitals, who concerned themselves little about the Jewish future, three groups could be distinguished. The large mass of pietists, loyal to the advice of their rabbis, were convinced that they could master their fate by reciting psalms. Their prayers would be answered some day; "they must be heard, and they will be heard." "The Lord of the world lives for ever and can wait. Finally and ultimately justice always triumphs." The activists likewise burned with faith, but were convinced that they had to take their fate in their own hands:

> People sick and grey, not wholly dead, not wholly living,
> No savior from without can come
> To those that live — and are enslaved.
> Their own messiah they must be,
> And play the savior and the saved.

Such exhortations of poets like Frug echoed the feelings of the younger generation. The ideal of the bourgeois class was Zionism, a Hebrew Renaissance on the soil of the forefathers which they were ready to colonize — if necessary, at the cost of their lives. The increasing class of manual workers clung to the ideal of socialism. Their aim was to liberate the Russian and with it the Jewish people, and their dogma was that the revolution needed to overthrow the existing order was worth dying for.

The miserable status of his people was brought home to every Jew when he faced the problem of providing an education for his children. The wealthier class sent their children abroad to attend schools and universities. These students were bound to pick up all manner of western ideas and "isms" which they brought back home. Earnest efforts were made to establish within the country new schools which would admit Jewish students, but their fate was at the mercy of the bureaucracy. The Jewish Colonization Association helped by improving vocational training of every sort.

The educational efforts on modern lines did not diminish the energy for traditional training. The *Yeshibot* weathered all storms from without and within and educated prospective leaders. Woloszyn continued to be an inspiration; Rabbi Raphael Schapiro managed to maintain its activities despite the prohibition of the government. It found friendly rivals in Slobodka, organized by Rabbi I. Blaser as the main center of *Mussar*, where Rabbi Moses Mordecai Epstein (later of Hebron), attracted many students; in Telschi, where R. Joseph Loeb Bloch, and in Grodno, where R. Simon Skop enjoyed equal fame. A new phenomenon was the *Yeshibah* on Hasidic lines, founded by Rabbi Sholom Baer Schneerson in Liubawich. A modernized *Yeshibah* was opened in Lida by Rabbi Izhaq Reines, the *Mizrahi* leader; in Odessa Rabbi Chaim Tschernowitz, known by his nom de plume *Rav Tzair*, ventured to establish a *Yeshibah* on quite a new principle, the amalgamation of Jewish training with general academic education. St. Petersburg established an Institute for Higher Jewish Studies and published the *Yewreiskaya*

Enciclopedia. The Historical Ethnographic Society published a quarterly, *Yewreiskaya Starina,* edited by the famous historian Simon Dubnow. Cultural alertness helped to overcome the misery of the Pale. Odessa, not hampered by age-old traditions, was the center of all progressive ideas and movements in the sphere of Judaism. The names of Mendele, Lilienblum, Bialik indicate the standard supported by the intelligentsia among the leading businessmen. Ahad Ha'am's legacy, the *Hashiloah,* found a faithful trustee in Joseph Klausner; it remained the organ of the Hebrew Renaissance, the platform on which the young essayists, novelists, poets were introduced to the public. If Zalman Schneur's gentle verses express a pessimistic mood, Saul Tschernichowski shows a surprising admiration of Greek serenity and an optimistic assertion of life. In the north, Warsaw and Wilna were the spiritual centers which created the pattern of education and guided the outlook on life. Perez continued to enrapture by his symbolism. Young Sholem Asch, the first Yiddish writer to enter the world arena, projected the ghetto figures on the world scene with remarkable genius. The favorite of the ghetto was Sholom Rabinovitch, better known as Sholom Aleichem (1859–1916). He depicted the Jewish Pale realistically, in all its narrowness and wretchedness. But his fine sense of humor lifted the mind over the misery of daily life. His readers laughed with him, and the very fact that they had not forgotten to laugh gave them the courage to face life, and the strength to outlast their tormentors.[73]

CHAPTER II

The Jews of Western Europe Before the First World War

Economic and Social Progress

THE turn of the century was a period of booming industrial activity. Central and Eastern Europe experienced enormous economic expansion.[1] The capitalist system attained its full development. Distant countries and regions of the earth with rich and undeveloped natural resources were drawn into the economic process. Production and use increased in an unexpected degree, and the standard of living of all classes rose. Karl Marx's theories of the progressive impoverishment of the masses were given the lie by actual facts. Within socialism a moderate revisionist group arose under the leadership of Eduard Bernstein, and many Jewish socialists joined it. The economic advance affected all countries, though its pace was not everywhere the same. Its progress was most obvious in Germany. Here an increasing population, intelligent and energetic, turned, despite the resistance of the entrenched landed gentry, to industry, export and overseas trade, and enormously improved the general welfare of the country. In the growth of the cities, their activity and their wealth, the Jews had a considerable part, in most cases much larger than their relative numbers would indicate.

The effects of capitalism were by no means all salutary.[2] Concentration of capital gave far-reaching influence to one wing of the upper class. In Germany and Austria-Hungary the number of Jews who attained prominence in the management of great corporations and in the directorates of important industrial and transportation companies was quite high. But at the same time the number of small independent concerns declined, and it became increasingly difficult for Jews to obtain employment in large corporations. In a bank in which Jews occupied managerial positions, for example, a Jew who applied for a lesser or a quite small position would be turned down. The "middle class" movements, which were organized and encouraged as protection against the ravages of capitalism, showed, in almost all countries, an anti-Jewish tendency. The expansion of great department stores under Jewish initiative offered convenient and timely material for agitation. Despite antisemitic grumbling against them, Jewish businessmen felt quite secure in their economic position. They were as little disturbed by boycott slogans as they were by the constant saber rattling which threatened European peace long before 1914.

It is pleasant to note that along with energetic piling up of material possessions and light-hearted enjoyment of their revenues there went a vigorous idealism, a vibrating sense of responsibility. The Jewish communities experienced a period of impressive generosity; they expanded their work in amount and in variety. Here too the pace varied. Germany developed the most intense activity, but it was apparent everywhere that the period of stagnation was over. There was a growing realization of responsibility for Judaism and a growing readiness to maintain and strengthen it. The Jewish communities had energetic honorary executives and could dispose of considerable incomes. Aside from substantial current income, they received rich foundations. Noteworthy among such foundations was that endowed with five million marks by Baroness Julie von Cohn-Oppenheim,[3] the only daughter of the former court banker of Emperor William I, bequeathed to the *Israelitische Kultusgemeinde* of Dessau. Its purpose was to provide for the propagation of religious activities, charity, and education in the Jewish communities of the principality, as well as to create charitable institutions throughout the state for the common good. Such foundations were not unique, though they rarely provided such large sums and for such broad purposes. The most distinguished continental Jewish community of the period was indubitably that of Frankfort on the Main.[4] Its distinction did not rest on its size — in 1910 it numbered no more than 26,228 persons — but upon its intensely Jewish religious life and learning, the communal feeling of its members, and the rare combination of such outstanding leaders as Marcus Horovitz, its scholarly, versatile, and energetic rabbi; Julius Plotke and Julius Blau, the presidents of the community, both with a deep sense of responsibility for universal Israel; Charles L. Hallgarten, a genius of philanthropy; Hermann Baerwald and Salo Adler, far-seeing educators; and finally Bertha Pappenheim, who aroused Jewish womanhood and gave it leadership. This splendid example impelled other communities to realize their potentialities.

Of these not the least was the capital, Berlin.[5] In 1900 its number exceeded 100,000, and the community included numerous distinguished scholars, writers and artists, as well as leading merchants and industrialists. The community possessed an annual fixed income of several million marks derived from taxation, and collected a similar sum in voluntary contributions for charitable and educational purposes. Berlin was the accepted center for all organizations which were concerned with nation-wide needs. Under the leadership of Martin Philippson, the veteran *Deutsch-Israelitischer Gemeindebund*[6] extended its activities, particularly in the field of social service.

Because of geographical position and economic importance Berlin was also the focal center for all relief work in Eastern Europe. In the period of pogroms and of the Balkan crisis, Germany became the clearing house for emergency relief and permanent assistance. The *Hilfsverein der Deutschen Juden*[7] worked hand in hand with the Frankfort Russian Relief Committee. The *Hilfsverein* was founded in 1901 and directed by James Simon in association with Paul Nathan. Simon was a princely merchant, with a great reputation as a collector and patron of the fine arts. Nathan combined clear political thinking with selfless devotion to the cause of humanity. The development of the *Hilfsverein* matched the pace of contemporary enterprises in other fields, and expanded greatly at home and abroad. The promptness and precision of its intervention in case of catastrophe — from Kishinev on through the great wave of Russian pogroms and the various persecutions and expulsions of Jews before the World War — its efforts to make its assistance reach beyond immediate emergencies, and its skillful negotiations with the governments involved brought it universal respect. Very soon after its foundation it won a position of confidence and leadership in relief work. In 1904 it was entrusted with the establishment of a central office for work relating to Jewish emigration, and during the following decade it dealt with no fewer than 200,000 immigrants.

In addition, the *Hilfsverein* built up a school system in the Near East. In the Balkan countries and especially in Palestine it established educational institutions, from kindergarten to elementary and intermediate schools, to training schools for teachers. Its school work embraced fifty institutions and 7,000 pupils. It planned the *Technicum* at Haifa. The aim of these schools was to make the local Jewish populations productive. It promoted the renaissance of Hebrew in Palestine; in Turkey it recognized the need of knowledge of German by reason of the growth of German interests in that country, and here its work was encouraged by the German government.

In Paris the invasion of France's old monopoly on work in the Orient was regarded with displeasure, and the *Alliance Israélite Universelle* made its resentment felt. In order to take the wind out of the *Hilfsverein's* sails it established, with its old and faithful German adherents, a German advisory board of the *Alliance* (1906) under the direction of Ludwig Max Goldberger,[8] a cosmopolitan financier with great organizing ability. Its purpose was to expend moneys collected in Germany in such a way that their objectives should not conflict with the government's Near Eastern policy. Competition had the favorable effect of rousing somnolent energies within the *Alliance* and worked to the advantage of the common philanthropy.

Harmony between the *Hilfsverein* and the *Alliance* could not be achieved by even so conciliatory a personality as Berthold Timendorfer,[9] who had directed the German District of the Independent Order B'nai B'rith for nearly three decades. Timendorfer brought the Order to a high state of prosperity, caused it to cooperate substantially with all central organizations which engaged in social and educational Jewish work, and encouraged the Austrian District to increase its activity also. The antagonism between the *Hilfsverein* and the *Alliance* came to light upon every occasion when common action was called for. When, in view of the continuing emergency, the Jewish Colonization Association suggested a central organization of all relief organizations, the American Jewish Committee (see p. 434, below) refused to participate because it did not wish to be drawn into a quarrel involving two states.[10]

Defense Organizations and Philosophical Literature

Organization was the watchword of the hour. Where there were no legal restrictions, the number of Jewish organizations increased in all countries. In Germany, with its patchwork diversity of state regulations, what had been wanting for a long while was a single important organization which should embrace all the Jews of the empire, represent them before the world, and protect their rights. The stronger the economic position of the Jews became, and the higher they climbed on the social ladder, the more tormenting they found certain disabilities in public life. They were at a constant disadvantage, for example, in obtaining posts as judges and as teachers in higher schools and universities. Particularly galling, in view of the hierarchical social order of the time, was their exclusion from the officer caste in the active army and in the reserves. The Prussian Minister of Justice, whose function was the guardianship of law, declared with cynical frankness that the principle of the equality of all citizens before the law was not applicable to Jews. Martin Philippson[11] who, as rector of the University of Brussels, had been attacked because he was German and who had been passed over in Germany because he was a Jew, suggested the institution of "Jews' Days" as a protest. Following the model of the "Catholics' Days," Jewish doctrine was to be presented to the public, but attention was also to be drawn to the abuses under which the Jews suffered. The timorous opposed this procedure vehemently. After negotiations extending over several years, Philippson's idea was embodied in an organization embracing all the Jews of Germany, the *Verband der deutschen Juden*[12] ("Association of German Jews"), founded in 1904.

The *Verband* had no public legal standing, but it did possess, and this was more important, the confidence of almost all Jewish groups, and it could approach the national and state governments as authoritative spokesman for all Jewry. It advised governments and legislators when issues of importance to Jews were in question, as for example, the elementary school law, the Sunday observance law, or the question of visas for Russian passports. It prevented the prohibition of *shehitah*. It fought for equal rights not only of individual Jews, but of the Jewish religious community as a whole. The fact that a liberal policy again prevailed, amid the numerous compromises which contemporary German politics made necessary, and that the *Verband* could count on the support of the Catholic Center, which sought to secure legal guarantees for tolerance, had the effect that it was more successful than any earlier organization for representing the rights of the Jews. Every second year there was a public general meeting. These meetings were brilliant exhibitions of all that was outstanding within Judaism. Important aspects of Jewish doctrine were discussed, the political and social situation of the Jews was illuminated, and resolutions expressing the Association's demands were adopted for submission to the government. In the *Korrespondenzblatt* which it issued and its large publication on *Die Lehren des Judentums* ("The Doctrines of Judaism"), the Association developed a successful apologetic activity.

The fact that at least as much emphasis was laid upon religious and cultural work as upon political was an expression of the new religious attitude which, after the turn of the century, came to the fore in Germany and affected the Jews also. Nietzsche's war against naturalizing and brutalizing civilization had been effective. Henri Bergson[13] (1850–1941) had pointed the way to intuition, to the immediate and inward meaning of the puzzling manifestations of life. He had taught that life is to be understood not as an accumulation of experiences but as creative evolution. The new generation turned back to an idealistic concept of life; it sought for a unified explanation of existence.

Hermann Cohen[14] (1842–1918), the founder of the neo-Kantian school of philosophy, was not content with the subjective experience of faith but insisted that its objective bases be investigated. With the intensity of a seer he admonished men to a serious comprehension of the problem of religion. In his system of ethics he proclaimed monotheism as the ultimate basis of universal ethics. The prophetic idea of God constitutes the tie between nature and morality. It teaches that God, the Creator of nature, is likewise the original Source of morality and its warrant; the moral idea is not fancy but actuality, and its hope for the "world to come" and for the "days of the Messiah," as Jewish tradition designated the remote future, was not the mere mouthing of enthusiasts. The messianic idea, the complete expression of the Jewish idea of God, involves a faith in the actuality of morality. It presents an endless task: faith, which is of the nature of *Should* rather than *Is*, must increasingly acquire the character of *Is*.

In the prophetic idea of God, religion is released from the trammels of myth; the prophets are the creators of actual and fundamental notions of morality. To them the philosophical ethics owe their tendency to universality and their notion of universal history. At the height of scientific thinking, the basic ideas of the prophets turn from religion to systematic ethics. Religion is to be resolved in ethics; such transformation is not its completion but its fulfillment. Ethical monotheism is the end goal upon which the historical religions in all their variety must converge.

When Cohen approached the crowning work of his life,

the systematic presentation of Judaism, he realized that his philosophic formula had not made adequate room for the vital religious sense which was a potent factor in his own inward life. He therefore decided to give religion a new significance in his system of philosophy, to recognize its peculiar character if not its independence. Essentially this peculiarity rests upon the position of religion in relation to the needs of the individual. The God of ethics is the God of humanity, but the God of the individual is the God of religion. It is the individual who feels a tie to his fellow man, who extends a hand to his fellow man in sympathy (and social sympathy is an aspect of moral faith), not out of respect for the merit of his fellow man but out of love. The individual, moreover, is oppressed by a sense of sin and yearns for liberation from guilt and restoration to moral freedom. In his consciousness of guilt the "single" man becomes a religious individual; he seeks and finds God who grants him pardon. The relations between God and man are those of love in a twofold form: God's love for man, and man's love for God. To "love God with all your heart and with all your soul and with all your might" signifies that all the facets of human personality must enter in the love of God.

It was on the basis of such a faith that Cohen wrote his last work, *Religion der Vernunft aus den Quellen des Judentums* ("The Religion of Reason from the Sources of Judaism"). As the title suggests, the framework of the book retains Cohen's system of pure reason; but religion is brought into relationship with all aspects of civilization. Man's moral and religious ideas, the ethical and the religious aspects of the idea of God, constitute a unified whole. The structure is supported by a foundation of biblical and rabbinic sources which, being presented with acute penetration and devout faith, serve to dignify and exalt Judaism. Cohen's feeling of responsibility for the future of Judaism loomed ever larger in his consciousness.

He regarded a triumphal tour through the Jewish centers of Russia (1913) as the high point of his life. With his death (April 4, 1918), speculative Judaism lost a high-minded leader.

Under the influence of such idealism the new generation showed a warm interest in the spiritual resources of Judaism. It was concerned to establish some connection between research and present-day needs. At the end of 1902 the *Gesellschaft zur Förderung der Wissenschaft des Judentums*[15] ("Society for the Advancement of the Science of Judaism") was established, with its seat in Berlin and with the participation of scholars in the various countries of Europe and in the United States. The wide range of interest shown in the Society is indicated by the fact that Martin Philippson became its president and Rabbi Jacob Guttmann, a recognized authority on the history of medieval philosophy, its vice-president. In addition to numerous monographs which it issued or subsidized, the Society undertook the publication of the *Monatsschrift für Geschichte und Wissenschaft des Judentums*, and assured the continued existence of this old and respected periodical in good times and in bad. The *Monatsschrift* was a common forum for contributors of all countries and of varying convictions and proved that fruitful collaboration was possible on the common ground of science. The journal won an interested following beyond the limited circle of specialists; interest in Jewish research and its results was wider spread than ever. The Society set to work with optimistic energy and set itself goals that could hardly be attained by its available collaborators. Its monumental undertakings, such as the *Corpus Tannaiticum*, the *Germania Judaica*, and the *Grundriss einer Gesamtwissenschaft des Judentums*, have remained mere torsos. But the very fact that such works were planned is significant and creditable. And in the *Grundriss* three works which present Judaism in a systematic form have appeared:

Moritz Güdemann's *Apologetik des Judentums*, Kaufmann Kohler's *Theologie* and Hermann Cohen's *Religion der Vernunft*.

Contemporary interest brought new vitality and new methods to Jewish research. Respect for it in university circles grew to such an extent that sixty leading German theologians and philologians, among them scholars of international reputation, such as Theodor Nöldecke and Julius Wellhausen, petitioned the Ministry of Education to remove an old injustice by establishing a chair for Jewish scholarship at a university.[16] The outbreak of the World War prevented the further prosecution of this plan.

New Religious Currents

Reawakened idealism pervaded the religious field also. In France[17] religious life had long stagnated; but the separation of Church and State (1905) induced the Jews to form voluntary associations (*Associations Cultuelles*), on the old basis of the consistorial organization, and these undertook responsibility for the budget which had hitherto been borne by the state. In the rabbinic association, which was founded in 1907, there was some agitation for seasonable reforms, but these were rejected under the influence of Baron Edmond de Rothschild, who was traditionally-minded. Nevertheless a *Union Libérale Juive* was founded at this time; it reformed the prayer book and educational procedures and introduced Sunday services in addition to those on the Sabbath. When it sought admission to the consistory this congregation was forced to give up many of its reforms, but it continued to stimulate innovations. Prophets of the Jewish renaissance in France, such as Edmond Fleg and Aimé Pallière, the youth leader, found a basis for their work in the program of the *Union*.

Even the Jewry of Italy[18] stepped out of isolation and awakened to communal endeavors. Their political situation was very favorable. Despite their small numbers they produced a considerable body of scholars, jurists, administrators, officers, and statesmen. Graziadio Malvano was director of the Ministry of Foreign Affairs for decades and exerted a decisive influence on foreign policy. General Giuseppe Ottolenghi (1838-1904), an observant Jew, was Minister of War. Luigi Luzzatti, who enjoyed an international reputation as economist and social statesman, was several times Minister of Finance and in 1910 presiding minister. Shortly before, Ernesto Nathan was mayor of the capital, Rome. The Jews of Italy were brought into relations with those of Europe when Samuel Hirsch Margulies[19] was called to Florence as chief rabbi (1891-1921). Margulies reorganized the *Collegio Rabbinico Italiano* and restored the old scholarly tradition of Italian Judaism. He provided an impetus to Zionism in Italy, and heade the Pro-Falasha movement.

Joseph Halévi (1827-1917), the well-known Parisian Semitist, had been sent to Abyssinia by the *Alliance Israélite Universelle* in 1868 to study the Falashas.[20] He brought important personal impressions from his travels, but he lost his materials in consequence of the Franco-German War. The contact which had been made was not followed up. The Falashas had for centuries manfully resisted the attempt of Christian missionaries to convert them, and their courage was now strengthened by contact with Jews. The reports of missionaries that there was a community of Jews who believed in Christ was proven false. Halévi never gave up hope for renewed contact, and his pupil, Jacques Faitlovitch, undertook an expedition to the Falashas equipped by Baron Edmond de Rothschild (1904). His report of the loyalty and persistence of the Falashas in their faith was stirring and called for immediate attention to the problem. But the *Alliance* refused its help. It was Margulies who then aroused the interest of the Jews of Italy and Germany, and later those of the United States to undertake missionary work among the Falashas. Young Falashas were educated in Europe, became teachers in the model schools founded with the assistance of the Italian government in Addis Ababa (Abyssinia), and were enabled to send teachers educated there into the interior of the country.

In Germany the mood was that of religious war. The Free Association for the Interests of Orthodox Judaism,[21] founded by S. R. Hirsch, had led a quiet existence, modest and retiring, for twenty years. In 1905 it became a militant organization and sought to impress upon government officials as well as upon Jewish individuals the necessity for a complete separation of Jewish religious groups from one another; it described the groups as belonging to different denominations, on the analogy of Catholic and Protestant. Its model was Hungarian orthodoxy, which was recognized in 1908 as the Hungarian Autonomous Orthodox Confession and separated from the rest of Jewry. The Free Association consolidated the energies of the orthodox and helped those adhering to the traditional Jewish way of life; but it injured the whole body of Judaism by accentuating separatism and making it a political issue.

Those who were actually faithful to the letter of the Jewish law, and affirmed their obligations to it by deeds as well as by words, constituted a vanishing minority, even in Hungary, let alone Germany. The great majority was made up of those who had tacitly given up Jewish observances because of convenience; but they had not made their conduct into a principle, nor did they possess the strength to combine into an organization. Others were depressed in conscience by having to represent religious views and requirements which took no account of the numerous transformations in philosophy, natural science, and views on the Bible. They observed similar struggles in Protestant and Catholic modernism. In 1908 people so minded united, under the leadership of Rabbi Heinemann Vogelstein and Judge Bernhard Breslauer, into a Union for Liberal Judaism[22] (*Vereinigung für das liberale Judentum*). Their program was the promotion of religious life; they urged the deepening and the spiritualization of Judaism, the creation of a form of service which should appeal to the heart and the soul, and the removal of the contradictions between doctrine and practice. These were old demands, and large numbers of people believed them desirable; but there was wide diversity of opinion in matters of detail. In 1912 the Union of Liberal Rabbis in Germany, under the leadership of Cäsar Seligmann, proposed a new formulation of principles under the title "Principles of a Program for Liberal Judaism" (*Richtlinien zu einem Programm für das liberale Judentum*). They set forth the bases of their position fully. Retaining the eternal verities and the basic moral prescriptions of the Jewish religion, they advocated the extension and fresh creation of forms of faith and observance. In connection with their general principles they set up a series of individual requirements.

The program was moderate, for the Union was aware of its responsibility for Jewish life in the present and in the future. But hotheads at either extreme declared war upon their formulation. The radicals found the requirements too numerous and too positive; with a conciliatory gesture they acknowledged the good intentions of the authors, but they specifically rejected their theses. The orthodox, on the other hand, found the Principles too trivial and too negative. They stormed against their "destructive tendency." They declared that religious education carried on in the spirit of the Principles constituted a danger to Judaism, and they asserted that rabbis who subscribed to them were unworthy of occupying a rabbinic post. Declaration followed upon declaration, and there was profound unrest in the Jewish congregations of Germany. The agitation was ended only by the outbreak of the World War. The struggle had contributed nothing towards clarifying concepts and strengthening tradition.

The campaign against the Principles was waged under the auspices of the *Agudat Yisrael*,[23] the world organization of orthodox Judaism. The *Agudah* was founded in Kattowitz in May 1912, and was directed from Frankfort by Jacob Rosenheim. Its goal was the "solution of the contemporary common problems of Judaism in the spirit of the Torah." Its means were the combination and common action of orthodox groups in the East and West, large scale promotion of the study of the Torah and of Jewish education, measures of relief, and, finally, representation of the interests of observant Jews to the outer world and defense against attacks directed against the Torah and its adherents. Before the *Agudat Yisrael* had time to develop its organization the World War broke out. The war immediately affected the regions of Eastern Europe where orthodoxy prevailed, and faced the new movement with unexampled problems.

Into the internal Jewish struggle of the period the Zionists injected a new factor. They introduced a political note into the discussions, and, since internal problems were only loosely related to their ideology, they threw their weight to one side or the other out of tactical considerations. They were like the ferment of new wine, and their criticism was sharp. They themselves carried little responsibility, for their own ideal of upbuilding Palestine then seemed relegated to the remote future. The point of their attack was "assimilation," but they were themselves quite thoroughly assimilated; even the renaissance of Hebraism affected only a small stratum in western countries. In practical questions their program was never logical or consistent. In Galicia and Bukovina, for example, they issued such contradictory slogans for election campaigns that even their own adherents became confused; many an election was lost to the Jews because of the scattering of their ballots. They trifled with the nationality into which they were born without holding out the prospect of substituting another for it; they mocked at those who declared their loyalty to their homeland and their civic rights. In religious questions they were fundamentally opposed to the liberals, although it was common knowledge that their preponderant majority did not stand upon the ground of tradition. The briskly fanned blaze against the *Hilfsverein* (see p. 307) blew the bottom out of the barrel. Those attacked took refuge in publicity and issued a vigorous declaration against Zionism and Zionists in the daily press of Germany (February 1914). Feelings grew more intense, and though the World War put an end to the agitation, the relations between the parties continued strained.

The Deep-Rooted Prejudice

If the ultimate causes of conflict are sought,[24] they can be found in the contrast between individualism and group consciousness, between rationalism and emotionalism, between classicism and romanticism, between a feeling of security and the premonition of catastrophe. A solution of any of the vexing religious, political or social problems was not involved in it; the Zionists with all emphasis on differentiation and on solidarity with world Jewry, the Orthodox with full emphasis on Jewish tradition insisted on full political equality just as did those who were willing to yield on the forms of Jewish life. The non-Jewish world was but little troubled over these conflicts within Judaism. To them the Jew remained a Jew, regardless whether he belonged to the *Agudat Yisrael* or to extreme Reform or had even deserted Judaism. It was a peculiar situation. The Catholic Church, while favoring conversion of Jews in France, in Austria and Hungary, worked in

Germany for perfect toleration in religious matters, to be granted to Jews as well as to Christians. The intolerant were those who called themselves progressive, the Protestants and the Dissidents who saw no salvation except for those who followed their lead. The Synagogue and the Talmud were still the stumbling blocks they had been a hundred years before, although a large percentage of Jews had no connections with the one or the other.

Full citizenship notwithstanding, each group believed itself entitled to control over the Jews. The states no longer considered citizens, but nationals. Cultural idealism was being pressed to the wall by blood-centered realism. It was a truism in Paris as well as in Berlin, in Vienna as well as in Budapest, that Jews had an extraordinary share in all cultural pursuits, that in these fields much depended on their active or financial cooperation. And still they were considered as a foreign body. Their contributions were accepted; their fellowship was rejected. Not only the Folkists, who in a *Semi-Gotha* or *Semi-Kirschner* pilloried all members of the nobility who had some Jewish blood — and they were, indeed, not few — rejected all writers and artists of Jewish extraction who had dared to enrich the European world with their creations, but even the moderates and so-called liberals gave such evidence of narrowness as to demand a mental sacrifice of the Jew before considering him equal. Werner Sombart,[25] the famous economist who in a fascinating book had emphasized the paramount share of the Jews in promoting capitalism and rejected enforced assimilation, formulated his views as follows: "The European states grant to their Jewish citizens full equality of rights; but tact and intelligence will prevent the Jews from making full use of this equality." The similarity of Max Nordau's views does not affect the situation. Should Jewish research workers or judges neglect their abilities in order not to become worthy of promotion? Or should

Jews acquiesce when they realize that baptism opens all the roads which are barred to loyal Jews? It is hard to believe how many absurd ideas and suggestions were uttered at the time in regard to the future of the Jews.

This was how the problem presented itself in 1905 to the mind of the liberal, personally unprejudiced Christian students of Judaism. They would certainly have objected to any coercion of conscience, to any totalitarian demands of "modern education;" but in the case of the Jews such liberals felt no scruples in insisting upon coercive alienation of their traditional character. There were enough Jews in the so-called upper strata who did not require such beckonings to be repeated and who were all too glad to follow. The Jews would have had every reason to consolidate their forces in order to avoid self dismemberment. In Germany these principles were uttered with brutal frankness; in other countries the imminent dissolution of Judaism was counted upon, but it did not become a subject of public admonition.

Their own sociologic conditions provided the Jews with sufficient ground for misgivings; for, however brilliant the façade seemed, the structure within was brittle and offered no security for the future. The bases of communal life were visibly weakened in western countries. The number of marriages and births decreased; the number of mixed marriages increased. The figures were not everywhere equally catastrophic, but everywhere they were on the increase, in orthodox Amsterdam precisely as in liberal Berlin, in a Jewish center like Budapest not less than in the Scandinavian or Italian Diaspora. Concentration of Jews in great cities was a continuous process, and so was concentration in a handful of callings. The consequence of the decline in the birth rate was an unhealthy shift in the distribution of age groups; the center of gravity had not yet shifted to old age, but there was a tendency in that direction. Serious observers in all camps uttered

Cassandra cries and admonished men to change their callings and their places of residence. It was not only physical well-being that suffered, but also spiritual welfare. The continuous cessation of small Jewish congregations permanently destroyed centers of Jewish education and Jewish worship. Perhaps a Jewish sociologist in Berlin[26] was overly pessimistic when he predicted "the decline of the German Jews;" but certainly a cry of alarm was justified, and not only for Germany, but for all countries in which Judaism had been emancipated.

CHAPTER III

The Jews of America at the Beginning of the Twentieth Century

The Process of Americanization

EVENTS in Eastern Europe exerted very strong pressure upon the Jews of America. Mention has already been made of the immigration to Canada (see p. 323, above). In Argentina[1] the agricultural settlements in the Baron de Hirsch colonies advanced slowly but steadily, with the Jewish Colonization Association caring for the economic and cultural welfare of the settlers. But there was also a strong current of immigration to the cities. Buenos Aires developed rapidly as a city, and its Jewish community grew to considerable proportions, including both Ashkenazic and Sephardic elements. It was not easy to mould the disparate elements into a new organization, and much credit for doing so is due to Rabbi Samuel Halphon. Among his other accomplishments was the introduction of a rabbinic court of arbitration and regular instruction for the young. It speaks well for the moral standing of the community that as early as 1900 it undertook decisive steps against the participation of Jews in the white slave traffic. In Brazil, too, Sephardic as well as Ashkenazic Jews settled, especially in the large cities. Rio de Janeiro, São Paulo, and other industrial centers saw synagogues rise in their midst. The Jewish Colonization Association attempted agricultural settlements, but these were not successful, and the settlers migrated to the cities.

Immigration to the United States took on proportions that were unexampled, even after the heavy immigration of the preceding period. From 1899, when Jewish immigrants from all countries were counted together under the designation of Hebrews[2] — to the acute discomfort of native Jews — until 1914, approximately a million and a half Jews immigrated to the United States, and so doubled the total number of Jews in the country. For some years Jews constituted more than 10% of the total number of immigrants; the rise and fall of Jewish immigration charted a curve of the intensity of anti-Jewish agitation in Eastern Europe. There were, to be sure, experienced organizations and anxious relatives to take the part of the immigrants, yet despite the best will in the world it was a huge task to distribute and establish such overwhelming numbers of penniless individuals and families. Older men who could not be retrained were given pushcarts and allowed to peddle cheap wares. But the younger men, and they were in the majority, used their strength and sought employment at workbench and factory. It happened that American industry[3] was in a period of great expansion; it needed and welcomed new resources of labor. The economic curve turned upward and downward sharply, and at times demand for labor was slack, but those who could find employment were provided with a decent livelihood. Farming also proved attractive.

The distribution of immigrants through the country was governed by the labor market. Throughout the states hundreds of new communities were formed or greatly enlarged. But despite all the efforts of the Industrial Removing Committee and the temporary diversion of immigration through the harbor of Galveston, it was inevitable that the preponderant majority fell to the share of the industrial centers in the North and East, and that of these more than half settled in New York and its environs. New York contained the greatest number of Jews that had ever been concentrated at a single place, and Chicago and Philadelphia approached the figures of the most populous communities of Europe. The center of gravity of American Jewry was definitely fixed in the East. Chicago became the center for the Middle West. West and south of Chicago the communities were sparsely sown and, with a few exceptions, such as Kansas City, St. Louis, New Orleans, San Francisco, and later also Los Angeles, not large.

The crowding of huge masses of people in the metropolises created insurmountable problems of health and education.[4] The misery in which most of the newcomers were forced to live is indescribable. The ghetto grew more and more crowded and it became the refuge of questionable characters that shunned the light of day. As unwholesome as was the outer aspect of the narrow streets, the interiors of the overcrowded dwellings in the tumble-down and dilapidated tenement houses were equally bad. The atmosphere in which the numerous younger generation grew up was not a cheerful one, and yet many who have gone far in life think back on their youth in New York's Lower East Side with gratitude.

Life in the ghetto may have been joyless, but it was not hopeless. Its denizens had no sooner recovered from the stunning impact of new experiences in America — and many needed years for the process of recovery — than they devoted all their intellect and all their energy to overcoming the handicaps of the "East Side gutter." The land to which they had come seemed to them the promised land, the land of hope; in this land everyone saw limitless possibilities for developing his potentialities if only he would accommodate himself to its practices and demands.

Americanization proceeded at a pace which astonished all educators. The newcomers were not discouraged by the shady sides of American life and persisted resolutely upon their way. The Educational Alliance[5] was besieged as never before. Its director, David Blaustein, who himself came from Russia, possessed deep understanding of the character and the problems of the immigrants and of their requirements in an environment which was so alien to them. One aspect of Americanization was the rapid increase in physical robustness. Anthropologists[6] who took measurements in the ghettos of various states were astonished at the favorable and rapid growth, posture, and muscular power of the immigrant Jews under the influence of air and light and of access to games and other physical exercise. The ghetto passed the test of the World War with flying colors. "The boys from the East Side stood out for conspicuous bravery and utter disregard for self. ... There is no better soldier than the Jewish boy:" this is one[7] of many similar commendations from commanding officers.

The urge to education was innate in the Jew. It was the dream of the poor ghetto dwellers to see their daughters teachers, their sons doctors. Nor did the young people require goading. From the workbench or factory they made their way towards college, university, the professions, and official careers. There was still much room for pioneering and expanding in the United States. Jews had but a slight share in the ever increasing number of trust companies, but the golden age of private enterprise had not yet passed. Jews won prominence in banking and finance; many of them prospered in commerce. The clothing industry in its various ramifications was almost a Jewish monopoly. In the metal and in the hides and skins business they were outstanding in the United States as they were in Europe. Many distinguished themselves in journalism; the *New York Times* owed to Adolph S. Ochs (1858–1935) its phenomenal rise to world-wide leadership. Jews were to be found among the outstanding physicians and lawyers of the country. In the field of research, Edwin R. A. Seligman (1861-1939) became a leader in the social sciences and Albert A. Michelson (1852-1931) in the natural sciences. The latter was the first Jew and the first American scholar to be awarded a Nobel Prize.[8]

The high esteem which Jews enjoyed found expression in the speeches of prominent non-Jews at the celebration of the 250th anniversary of the settlement of Jews in New Amsterdam. Upon that occasion (November 16, 1905), President Theodore Roosevelt praised the loyalty and the contributions of his Jewish fellow citizens in the following terms:[9]

While the Jews of the United States... have remained loyal to their faith and their race traditions, they have become indissolubly incorporated in the great army of American citizenship, prepared to make all sacrifice for the country, either in war or peace, and striving for the perpetuation of good government and for the maintenance of the principles embodied in our Constitution. They are honorably distinguished by their industry, their obedience to law, and their devotion to the national welfare. They are engaged in generous rivalry with their fellow-citizens of other denominations in advancing the interests of our common country. This is true not only of the descendants of the early settlers and those of American birth, but of a great and constantly increasing proportion of those who have come to our shores within the last twenty-five years as refugees reduced to the direst straits of penury and misery.... In a few years, men and women hitherto utterly unaccustomed to any of the privileges of citizenship have moved mightily upward toward the standard of loyal, self-respecting American citizenship; of that citizenship which not merely insists upon its rights, but also eagerly recognizes its duty to do its full share in the material, social, and moral advancement of the nation.

Such generous recognition on the part of the first citizen of the country was very welcome to the old inhabitants, and much more so to the newcomers, who were not used to good-will on the part of rulers. Such recognition was a stimulus to greater devotion to their new home. They took their civic privileges seriously, and in many places became a factor to be reckoned with. There was, to be sure, no "Jewish vote," and Jewish opinion varied greatly in political and especially in economic matters; there was only one question on which Jews of all parties were equally sensitive, namely, upon that which touched upon Jewish honor and security.

Defending Jewish Honor and Rights

And indeed occasions for unified action on the part of the Jews were not wanting. It was not given to everyone to establish himself quickly, and all required a certain period of transition and acclimatization. Not all were successful in their work; not all could retain their spiritual balance in the rapid change of fortune; not all could remain unaffected by the evil usages of their environment; some became asocial, some were even pushed into a path of crime. Among the young there were not a few who required special care. The Jewish communities and charitable associations did all in their power to prevent such social tragedies. But young America saw the repetition of an abuse common in old Europe: statistics were juggled and figures were arbitrarily chosen to spread mistrust and hatred of the Jew.[10] Against such abuses Jews of all schools of thought made common cause.

But there was no nation-wide institution which was competent to speak for all the Jews in the country. They had individual representatives but no representation; to use an American expression, "they had no address." Events in Eastern Europe naturally reverberated in the United States. Horrors like those of Kishinev[11] or of the October pogroms aroused immediate sympathetic anguish. Quite naturally the immigrant body participated largely in the collections for the victims and in the protest against the persecutions. In public meetings Rabbi Judah L. Magnes aroused feelings for self-protection and self-liberation; by reason of his youthful idealism and his sincere and moving eloquence Magnes had great power over the masses. A particularly impressive protest was a cortège of 100,000 Jewish mourners through the streets of New York arranged (in 1905) by the labor leader, Joseph Barondess; this was the first Jewish protest march in the world, and it met with warm sympathy on the part of the Christian population. The great suffering forged closer bonds between the Jews of America and those of Europe. They perceived that it was their cause that was being fought out on the other side of the ocean and they were eager to provide front-line assistance and protection.

But such assistance was occasional in nature; for each new emergency the machinery had to be erected and set into motion anew. This involved a waste of time and energy. It was Jacob H. Schiff, ever ready to help, who urged his co-workers in Jewish tasks to create an organization[12] which should always and constantly concern itself with the interests of the Jews not only in the United States but also abroad, and which should be able to speak for the Jews with authority to the American public and its government. This was easier said than done, for centrifugal tendencies were very strong. It was not only that certain individuals saw their influence threatened; great organizations, such as the Independent Order B'nai B'rith and the Union of American Hebrew Congregations, which had hitherto habitually spoken for the entire community, rebelled at the new thought. It required the diplomatic skill and energy of Judge Mayer Sulzberger of Philadelphia to overcome the opposition and to bring all sections of the country and all classes of the population under the single roof of the American Jewish Committee.

Judge Sulzberger, who was distinguished by brilliant intellect and warm sensitivity, by Jewish scholarship and by his feeling of solidarity with his people, became the first president of the Committee. His right-hand man and later his successor was Louis Marshall, whose "character, knowledge, natural ability, high reputation" Sulzberger warmly praised. Marshall was an outstanding representative of the American bar, distinguished alike for the volume of his knowledge, the acuteness of his thought, and the clarity of his presentations. The third member of the group, and its third president, after Marshall's death in 1929, was Cyrus Adler. By education and inclination Adler was wholly bound up with Judaism, and he never refused to undertake new burdens in its service. His was a rare combination of enthusiasm and realism; his thoughts were for eternity, but gifted with wise statesmanship, he never lost sight of reality and of the demands of the moment.

The American Jewish Committee described its functions as follows (November 11, 1906):

To prevent the infraction of the civil and religious rights of Jews, in any part of the world; to render all lawful assistance and to take appropriate remedial action in the event of threatened or actual invasion or restriction of such rights, or of unfavorable discrimination with respect thereto; to secure for Jews equality of economic, social and educational opportunities; to alleviate the consequences of persecution and to afford relief from calamities affecting Jews, wherever they may occur.

The country was divided into twelve districts from coast to coast. Together these districts sent sixty representatives to the Committee, apportioned according to the size of their Jewish populations. A committee of nine members together with the officers formed the Executive Committee. The Committee realized that effective work required the broadest possible basis, and so sought its members from the various groups in American Jewry. But members were nominated rather than elected by public ballot, and the Committee was attacked on that account. The resentment of the Russians against the earlier German immigrants also contributed to the opposition.

There was no lack of business for the new organization, though there was no need for relief work at the moment. Even while time was being consumed in negotiations relating to the form of the Committee, proposals for limiting immigration were being agitated. The fact that the country had been thought of by the Pilgrim Fathers as a "shelter of the poor and persecuted" had long been forgotten by those who represented themselves as the successors of the Pilgrims. The "Immigration Resting Committee" made a great to-do and used strong language, which is habitual in the United States upon such occasions. Theses and statistics were presented of such a nature as to render the good faith of their proponents suspect. Representatives of the American Jewish Committee[13] studied these concoctions and demonstrated their falsity and the injury they worked to the country. Their reply was of great service not only to Jewish interests but to all who sought a refuge. The soundness and wholesomeness of their political campaign was also a meritorious contribution. The Committee succeeded in having victims of religious and political persecution exempted from the increased tax which had been imposed upon immigrants. Educational tests were voted from time to time, but these were vetoed by the presidents. The process of naturalization was made more difficult, and this could not be prevented.

A political question which had long concerned and annoyed public opinion in the United States involved the refusal of the Russian government to grant passport[14] visas to American citizens of the Jewish faith. The United States recognized no limitation of political rights on grounds of religion and treated all Russian subjects equally, without regard to their religious beliefs. It therefore requested reciprocity on the basis of the commercial treaty of 1832, but the representations of the American envoys continued unsuccessful. At the beginning of the nineteenth century the State Department was less forceful in its demands, because it sought the friendship of

Russia. But with the growing number of American citizens of Russian origin, relations with the realm of the Czar increased, and with them the needs of American citizens to travel freely in Russia. Proposals repeatedly came up in Congress to insist upon the dignity of American citizenship and to renounce the trade agreement. President Theodore Roosevelt wished to avoid a break, and when Count Witte was present in the United States the President made strong representations to him and handed him a personal note to the Czar in which he emphasized the urgency of the matter. One group of Russian ministers was inclined to yield, but the government as such would not agree to the request and irritated American public opinion by further provocations.

The Russian government refused to recognize naturalization of its subjects and claimed permanent jurisdiction over those who had become citizens of another country. Instead of protesting against this assumption, the American Secretary of State issued a circular in which he warned American Jews not to request passports for Russia, for these would only be granted if the visa of the Russian government could be counted upon. The American Jewish Committee entered an energetic protest against this untenable position, which surrendered the honor of American citizenship.

The situation was exacerbated by unscrupulous business practices on the part of the Russians. Their propaganda induced Jews to sail to Europe on Russian vessels, but entry to Russia was made impossible, for Russian envoys refused their visa. Important American personalities received invitations to visit Russia, the government being quite willing to make exceptions for such Jews. Jacob H. Schiff repeatedly refused to enter into commercial relationships with Russia and declined personal invitations so long as the Czar's government refused to grant the poorest Jew the same rights as it did him. He looked upon the problem as a matter of principle. The Russian government had declared that it was unable to grant foreign Jews privileges which it denied its own Jews. Schiff insisted that discrimination against foreign Jews be abolished, so that the Russian government could not deny to its own Jews what it granted to foreign Jews.

In the course of the years indignation over the affront to American citizenship and the disregard of United States passports grew very high. Before the presidential elections of 1908 both major parties adopted planks on the subject in their respective platforms, and the successful candidate, William Howard Taft, gave assurances of his disapproval of the Russian policy both before and after the election. But actually he did nothing, and the cases involved grew more numerous and more flagrant. The Jewish organizations turned to the President personally. In a lengthy conference with a Jewish delegation President Taft expressed much good-will, but showed no understanding of the nub of the problem. Louis Marshall pointed to the inexorable logic of international law, and the President countered by mentioning his consideration for individual firms and the danger of the loss of their Russian investments. The Jewish delegates left the White House in a state of despondency. Jacob H. Schiff was the first to find his voice, and he called out, "This means war." In a courageous letter[15] which he addressed to the President a few days later he repeated his determination to make a fight of it.

Since no help was to be expected of the government, the Jewish leaders decided "to appeal to the people of the United States." In nearly all cities mass meetings were held, denouncing Russia's course. Several states adopted resolutions requesting the government to act. The press was almost a unit in demanding the abrogation of the treaty. Resolutions for abrogating the treaty were introduced in the House of Representatives as well as in the Senate. The agitation began in the latter part of February and continued to the end of the year. On December 19 and 20, 1911, both Houses of Congress unanimously declared for the renunciation of the treaty. The President apparently welcomed the support of the people against the pressure of Big Business.[16] On December 31, 1912, the trade agreement with Russia, which had been in force for eighty years, was in fact abrogated, abrogation to take effect at the end of the following year. For the representatives of the Jews it was a great satisfaction that right had prevailed over might. Before negotiations for a new treaty could be got well under way the World War broke out, and with it fundamental changes in the Russian situation.

In addition to attending to such matters as these within the country, the American Jewish Committee extended its care to Jews abroad. In the numerous collections which were necessitated by various emergencies it worked in close cooperation with the Jewish organizations of Europe. It collaborated with them also in matters pertaining to the security of Jewish rights. It was United States Ambassador Henry White[17] who, at the Conference of Algeciras, "had a provision inserted in the treaty by which the security and equal rights of the Jews of Morocco, both those living in the ports and those living in the interior towns, are guaranteed by the signatory nations" (April 2, 1906). At the regulation of the Balkan situation in the Conference of Bucharest in 1913 (see p. 367, above), it was the representative of the United States who supported the inclusion of a clause to secure equal rights for the Jews.

Community, Religion and Culture

In addition to such problems as concerned the entire body of Jews in the United States or in the world, there were many of a local nature, involving only a single city or a single state, such as laws concerning Sunday observance, divorce, education. The Jews had no representative body to deal with such problems. New York's Jewry comprised more than a million souls, a greater number than the combined population of several states, and the needs arising out of the peculiar nature of its agglomeration were numerous, yet it possessed no communal representation, no institution to take responsibility for the whole body and act as its spokesman. There was no organization sanctioned by law. Among the old congregations there was more antagonism than cooperation. The new immigrants loved their *Landsmannschaften*, or societies of persons deriving from the same locality. There were as many *Landsmannschaften* in New York as there were cities and villages in Poland and Russia, but there was no union among them and each went its own way. There were thousands of associations of religious, philanthropic, cultural, and social character, but there was no single association to bind them together and to fashion the amorphous mass into a unified organism. Moreover, there were hundreds of thousands who visited neither synagogue nor *Landsmannschaft* but who had no desire to deny their Jewish identity. And even if the elders were confirmed in their ways, what was to be done to retain the youth for Judaism? Who was to take responsibility for this task?

In Europe, in an analogous situation, the community would step in. Judah L. Magnes had come to know the beneficial effects of communal organization as a student in Europe, and fought for the introduction of a communal organization in a form appropriate to the United States. He began by creating the *Kehillah* ("the Jewish Community"), a "central, authoritative, and representative body of the Jews in New York City." The aim of the *Kehillah*[18] was "to further the cause of Judaism, and to represent the Jews of this city with respect to all local matters of

Jewish interest." It was to abstain from interfering with the autonomy of individual congregations and associations and from participation in party politics. Its program was rich and varied, as befitted the number and variety of the greatest Jewry in the world.

In addition to religious and ritual questions, there were questions of education, of religious training, of Americanization; in addition to social care of underprivileged children or unemployable and handicapped Jews, there were differences between employers and employees and the institution of courts of arbitration to occupy the *Kehillah*. Public officials regarded the *Kehillah* as the spokesman for the Jews. It represented the Jewish view in questions of Sunday observance and civil marriage laws. It participated in the work of the American Jewish Committee as a body.

The idea was sound, and was imitated in several other cities. But the initial democratic alertness was not supplemented by the unity and the readiness to sacrifice which were essential for the preservation of the organization. To bring men to the point where they would surrender individualism and subordinate themselves to a communal organization was evidently a consummation impossible to achieve. There was no common ground which could contain orthodox, reformed, agnostics, socialists, and their various shadings. In Europe the very inertia of an ancient tradition could suffice to drag its existence on in a period when ideologies grew weak. But in the United States a new tradition had to be established, and it was expected to represent both religious and political interests. Centrifugal forces did not permit of such centralization. Magnes nursed his offspring until it attained the age of *Bar Mitzvah*, when it quietly died of anemia. An offspring of the *Kehillah* movement, in a measure, is the Federation movement, an attempt made to unite the various Jewish charities under one roof and to avoid waste of money and energy.

Another effect was the effort to improve Jewish education. An inquiry, initiated on behalf of the *Kehillah*, uncovered an appalling state of affairs. A large proportion of Jewish school children had no religious training at all, many attended old-fashioned *Hadarim* or *Talmud Torahs* whose teachers had no understanding whatsoever for healthy pedagogical methods and repelled the pupils instead of attracting them. Samson Benderly, a Palestinian, founded the Bureau of Jewish Education[19] which has functioned ever since and has made valuable contributions to the improvement of *Talmud Torahs* and of Hebrew teaching in general.

In its efforts to solve the problem of maintaining Judaism in the United States and securing its future, the *Kehillah* could look to the preliminary labors of Solomon Schechter. Schechter had taken up his work in New York at the end of 1902, and from his first appearance he made it clear[20] that he was resolved to turn the course of American Judaism and steer it in a new direction. It was his aim to make the Jewish Theological Seminary of America, to the presidency of which he had been called, a bulwark of positive Judaism, and he devoted his impressive spiritual and moral energies to the accomplishment of this task. He gave new meaning to the idea of progress. His watchword was "Catholic Israel," that is to say, all-embracing Judaism, without qualification. In its basic concept Judaism was to feel its indissoluble bond with Judaism of all ages and all countries; it could sustain difference of opinion in its midst, it did not require absolute conformity or exert the coercion of a system, but it presupposed continuity. Schechter rejected systems of theology and ethics; he taught these subjects by the examples of what had actually existed, in the words of the Jewish sources in all their breadth and fullness. It was from this precipitate of Jewish life that the Jew was to learn his religion, the inward and spiritual quality of Jewish doctrine, and the religious content of Jewish law. Drinking from the fountain of living water should make him immune against fashionable prejudices as fostered by rationalism and Bible criticism. It was spiritual Jewish autarchy, respect for authority, which Schechter postulated.

The impulsive emphasis of his teaching was a challenge to Reform Judaism. The ideas attacked by him were just that positivism and individualism on which Kaufmann Kohler[21] had based his theology. In 1903, after an interim following Isaac M. Wise's death (1900), Kohler had been appointed president of the Hebrew Union College, and conflicts between the two schools of thought were inevitable. Twenty years ago the aggressor, Kohler now was forced into the defensive. The Reform Synagogue had not kept pace with the changed structure and problems of American Jewry. It was built on spontaneity, but the response to the inner voice had not proved strong. People felt too comfortable in their material life to give hard thought to spiritual needs.

The new immigrants were attracted by the decorum of the reform synagogues but they did not feel at home there. They continued under the impress of their group experiences and clung to memories of them, even after they had shaken them off in their actual lives. They fashioned their private lives as seemed convenient to them, yet they wished to see their synagogue not English but Jewish. They did not ask for an historic or scientific evaluation of their institutions; they loved their folk usages, their folk melodies, and they loved the Hebrew language, regardless of whether they understood every word in the service or not.

The expansion of reform Judaism was checked by these new currents. The newcomers inclined not to rationalism but to emotion, not to occidentalism but to orientalism. The Zionists found moral support in Schechter's emphasis on the national aspects of Judaism; they took up the gauntlet thrown down by Reform and cast it in their opponents' face. Even within Reform's own ranks there was some opposition. In 1907 Stephen S. Wise founded the Free Synagogue in New York,[22] which followed the reform ritual, but relaxed its rigidity and admitted Zionist ideas. In general the Free Synagogue maintained the principle of full freedom for the discussion of all problems relating to Judaism from its pulpit. About the same time Judah L. Magnes reverted to a more conservative ritual. All this was not a turning point, but a ferment which excited understanding for folkways, for the traditional aspects of religious life. In course of time it became manifest even in reform circles that the issue was not how to pull down but how to sustain the fundamentals of Jewish self-preservation.

To Schechter growth seemed intolerably slow.[23] He was depressed because his work did not find the lasting response which he had expected, because the orthodox organizations in particular stood aside, demanding uncompromising conformity, and condemned even scholarly collaboration with men of other tendencies. Opposition delayed the consolidation of his ranks. Although the number of congregations which accepted his program and called his pupils as rabbis grew steadily, it was only in February 1913 that he could proceed to the establishment of the organization which was called the United Synagogue of America.[24] Its seat was New York, its direction was in the hands of a board, with Cyrus Adler at its head, and its spiritual leadership in the hands of the Rabbinical Assembly of America. The aims of the new conservative association were formulated as follows:

> To assert and establish loyalty to the Torah and its historical exposition; to further the observance of the Sabbath and the dietary laws; to preserve in the service the reference to Israel's past and the hopes for Israel's restoration; to maintain the traditional character of the liturgy, with Hebrew as the language of prayer; to foster religious life in the home, as expressed in traditional observances; to encourage the establishment of Jewish religious schools, in the curricula of which the study of the Hebrew language and literature shall be given a prominent place.

This was the maximal program, which the founders had in mind for some ideal future. They were far from insisting that all congregations which entered the United Synagogue must accept the program in its entirety. Its formulation was capable of interpretation, and so broad enough to contain various shadings. Like any party of the Center, the United Synagogue had its weaknesses and was attacked both from the Right and the Left; but its program suited the inclinations of large numbers of people, and it became a power in American Israel.

The bond which united Kohler and Schechter was their common enthusiasm for the scientific study of Judaism. Each strove with emulous rivalry for the development of the institution which had been entrusted to his care. They called gifted young scholars to their faculties and built extensive libraries with the professed intention of making America the cultural center of Judaism. A decade after his arrival Schechter could remark[25] that American Jewry had made more numerous and more valuable contributions to Jewish cultural life in that short span of time than it had in the entire previous 250 years of its existence. Scholarly resources were further enriched by the Dropsie College for Hebrew and Cognate Learning,[26] opened in 1909 under the presidency of Cyrus Adler. The

College is non-professional and non-sectarian and is open to all qualified students without limitation "on account of creed, color, or sex." In this broad and liberal foundation it affords wide opportunities for study. It has demonstrated the westward movement of Jewish study by taking over the publication of *The Jewish Quarterly Review*, which previously appeared in England.

The link between Schechter and Kohler was Jacob H. Schiff, who did not agree with all the utterances of either, but who cherished high regard for both as scholars. Schiff's thought always moved in the direction of strengthening Jewish life and of propagating Jewish cultural ideals in the widest possible measure.[27] It was he who financed the new Bible translation[28] and the Schiff Classics of the Jewish Publication Society. It was he who responded to the frequently emphasized need for training teachers by providing funds to enable both the Hebrew Union College in Cincinnati and the Jewish Theological Seminary in New York to establish teachers' institutes.[29] The problem of Jewish education had come to the fore and it was very timely to further the endeavors which were being made in this field.

The religious associations take in scarcely half of all the Jews in the United States, even including the considerable number of the orthodox who have not departed a single hair's-breadth from the habits of their home land and resist every attempt at organizational affiliation. Of the remaining half, one section desires its Jewish identity forgotten. The fashionable are engulfed in the Society for Ethical Culture and in Christian Science. A few have been lost to the Church through mixed marriages and through striving for "exclusive" social contacts.[30]

Jewish college students, whose numbers grew by leaps and bounds, presented a particularly serious problem. To the considerable surprise of their Christian teachers these representatives of the coming Jewish generation were far removed from all things Jewish. Their spiritual potentialities were high, but for their interest to be engaged emphasis would have to be placed on the cultural aspects of Jewish life and not on partisan formulae. Inspired by these considerations sixteen students of Harvard University organized a club to which they gave the symbolic name "The Menorah Society" (1906). The objective was to spread light on the cultural position of Judaism, present as well as past, and to stress Judaism as a formative element of a philosophy of life. The idea found support in colleges of the East and the Middle West. University instructors, who during their student years had cooperated with the Menorah, carried its light to their new academic activities and kindled it at new centers. In 1913 the students organized an Intercollegiate Menorah Association which envisaged far-reaching educational tasks and tried to influence the character of the American Jewish college graduate. As expression of their tendencies, the Menorah Society founded a magazine, *The Menorah Journal*, which since 1915 has been published by Henry Hurwitz, Chancellor of the Intercollegiate Menorah Association. The variety of *The Menorah Journal*'s contents and its high literary standards attracted numerous readers.

The preponderant majority of American Jews belong to the working class. Though Jewish in spirit, they were on the whole unwilling to affiliate themselves with congregations. The Jewish workers' movement, like American labor in general, preferred to hew close to the line of labor interests and eschew political or party slogans.[31] The needle workers, among whom Jews were most strongly represented numerically, fought many a hard strike and finally laid the ghost of the sweatshop. But working conditions were still intolerable and those most responsible were upstarts who, a score of years before, had sweated under the same system they now practiced. The operation of new expensive machinery made workers more and more dependent on the employers. The older labor leaders were not equal to the situation; new men recently arrived from revolutionary Russia fanned into flames the discontent of the workers. From 1907 on, a series of strikes took place, culminating in the "Great Revolt" of 1910. The women's wear industry of New York came first, and the men's clothing industry of Chicago followed. Myriads of workers walked out; the clothing industry was paralyzed. After weeks of arbitration — this was Louis D. Brandeis' first contact with a Jewish organization — the employers had to give in. But the fight continued within the unions, for the unskilled workers had the feeling that the union bureaucracy had betrayed them. Their uprising led to a secession; a new union was created, no longer exclusively, but still in large majority Jewish, the Amalgamated Clothing Workers of America. Under the leadership of Sidney Hillman (born in Lithuania, 1887) it became the best organized union in the country. It afforded its members the greatest advantages morally and economically.[32]

The Jewish socialists did bring with them two tendencies derived from Russian Marxism: one against organized religion, and the other for a world proletariat. They did not wish, however, to be swallowed up by a world proletariat, but to continue their distinct identity as a Jewish group. The means for assuring their continuance was Yiddish life and letters, which were zealously cultivated in secular schools, in the press, in literature, and in the theater.[33]

Yiddish culture developed an astonishing vitality, and, paradoxical as it may sound, it became a potent factor in Americanization. America was paramount not only in the forms of its expression but also in the stock of its ideas and in the range of its interests. It may seem even more paradoxical that this culture, which sprang up and was nurtured in the ghetto, became vital and robust when it wrenched away from the ghetto and stood upon its own feet in open opposition to synagogue and *Bet ha-Midrash*.

The Yiddish press took over the techniques of the great dailies, and like them attracted hundreds of thousands of regular readers. The more naive these readers were, the greater was the influence of their newspapers upon their outlook on politics and economics, on religion and education. These dailies also provided a link with the Jews of the world. Yiddish literature steadily emancipated itself from amateurs and sensation-mongers and attracted professional writers who had been trained in world literature and who translated classics of the Russian, English, German, and French languages into Yiddish, and so gave Yiddish a universal aspect. It attracted a writer like Sholem Asch, widely recognized despite his youth, to settle permanently in New York. It inspired talented novelists like Leon Kobrin and Zvi Libin, who, among other subjects, dealt realistically with the vicissitudes of the new immigrants. A poet of stature arose in "Yehoash" (Solomon Bloomgarden, 1871–1927), who drew his inspiration not only from the Jewish past and from life in Russia but also from the American environment. In addition to his original works, Bloomgarden inspired the masses by means of a fresh translation of the Bible. Yehoash did not live to see the publication of this great work in its completed form.

The Yiddish theater became extremely influential. Here one could sit with eyes and ears agape; one could be amused and could learn. The Yiddish theater started with melodramas on a provincial level, but from 1890 on it grew perceptibly in strength and content. Stars like Bertha Kalisch and the couple Jacob P. and Sarah Adler became factors in popular education. Adler sought to improve the repertory, and found in Jacob Gordin a reformer who not only refined the language of the Yiddish drama but, following famous models, strove to make a moral institution of the stage. Triumphant success was brought to the Yiddish theater by Kobrin's realistic and effective plays and especially by David Pinski's versatile talent. For the masses the theater became a place of devotion and reflection. Only the more populous ghettos, to be sure, could enjoy regular performances; the smaller ghettos swallowed reports of presentations and received vicarious exaltation, and occasionally saw a company on tour. The Yiddish group staged a remarkable drama of national life, entirely free of chauvinism.

BOOK FIVE
THE FIRST WORLD WAR AND ITS CONSEQUENCES

CHAPTER I

The World War

THE WAR AND THE JEWS OF EUROPE

ON August 1, 1914, the First World War broke out, bringing with it black catastrophe and shaking Europe and its civilization to their very foundations.[1] Ten million dead, fifty million maimed and crippled, the progress of a century destroyed, every moral standard erased, every animal instinct aroused — such were the consequences of the war. At the outbreak of the war, to be sure, the nations of Europe were filled with righteous enthusiasm and convinced that they must put forth every effort to assure the security of their homeland. But the enthusiasm vanished as the war dragged on, as it demanded the most exacting personal sacrifices of every individual, and so caused men to lose sight of any moral goal. For four and a half years murder and assault, robbery and deception were praised as deeds of glory, and men were imbued with a brutality and bestiality which has plagued them ever since. The complete failure of all governments, victor as well as vanquished, authoritarian as well as democratic, shattered men's faith in the wisdom of statesmanship and encouraged a tendency towards anarchy or towards flight from responsibility. The faults of statesmen and war leaders had to be atoned for by the people and are today being atoned for by their children.

The deluge did not strike all peoples with equal force; the Jews[2] were among those hardest hit. It was the Ninth of Ab when the conflict between the chief belligerents began, and like many another Ninth of Ab that day was the beginning of woe ineffable for the Jewish people. Though it possessed no territory of its own, it was exposed to invasion, like Belgium and Serbia. The scenes of battle in the east and southeast were the regions of the Russian Pale of Settlement, thickly populated with Jews, from the Baltic to the Black Sea, Galicia and Bukovina, Carpatho-Russia and Rumania, Turkey and Palestine. Approximately three quarters of all the Jews of the world were under the immediate scourge of the fury of war. As urban dwellers and as owners of stores they suffered by invasion in any case. But Jew-hatred rendered their situation worse and greatly increased the volume of destruction of Jewish lives and Jewish property, far beyond the martyrdom which war of itself demanded. Germans and Russians alike expected that the Jews of the border regions would assist their advances, or used the fact that they failed to do so as a pretext for attacking them and their possessions. In the first years of the war the border regions changed hands several times, and it was an easy thing, when one army was in occupation, to accuse the Jews of having welcomed and assisted the opposing army. The Poles in particular were pleased to make such charges against Jews. Occasionally their own priests undeceived them and helped truth prevail. Courts-martial were not fond of long investigations and generally pronounced quick and summary punishment against those accused. But when charges were examined, a different state of affairs came to light. At Brzezany in Poland, for example, documents of the German occupation were found which indicated that the Jews had refused to collaborate with the Germans, that a Jewish notable had been condemned to death in consequence, and that he had been released only as a result of the pleas of the populace and of the Christian clergy. In the case of the charge against the Jewish mayor of Mariampol it was demonstrated that the denunciation originated with a certain Mohammedan, who was in the service of the Germans as a spy.

In the course of the campaigns[3] not fewer than a million and a half Jews were under arms on both sides, and to this figure must be added the considerable number of men and women in the civil and labor services and those who gave voluntary assistance in nursing and welfare work. There was no question on the part of the Jews that they must offer the supreme sacrifice for their country's sake. Russian revolutionaries fought in the Czarist armies; German Zionists hurried from Palestine at the risk of their lives to join their colors; Jews from overseas undertook the hazardous journey to Europe in order to enter army service. The loyalty of all groups to their country proved to be deeply rooted. In the partisan politics of peace time, superpatriots had suspected the patriotism of their political opponents, but in the hour of danger the baselessness and the baseness of all such denunciations became manifest.

Jews showed the same heroism, the same zeal, as did their comrades of other faiths.[4] They shared in distinctions and in losses. In the French, Italian, British, and also in the Austro-Hungarian armies it was natural that some should be promoted to positions of command. The highest rank was attained by Sir John Monash (1865–1931), who rose to be Lieutenant General and Commander of the Australian Expeditionary Force. In the Russian and Rumanian armies also, those in immediate command saw to it that Jews should receive justice. They were not cut off from awards of merit, and there were some promotions. In Germany the ban on naming Jews as officers was broken immediately after the outbreak of war, and it became clear how ridiculous were the grounds for the ban offered by the War Office in parliament as late as 1914. It was decidedly not the fault of the Jewish officers that Germany lost the war.

The proclamation of domestic truce at the outbreak of the war in no wise abolished Jew-hatred. "The Ethiopian cannot change his skin," nor could the Russian Black Hundred, nor the antisemitic parties in Germany and Austria cease their agitation. The longer the war lasted, and the more its hardships came home to the individual, the more frequently were the Jews made scapegoats: from Leeds in England to the Black Sea, wherever Jews lived, the same phenomenon occurred. For everything that went wrong "the Jews" were blamed: the scarcity of food, the lack of consumers' goods, the outbreak of the war itself. The civil administration, the armchair colonels in their comfortable berths, engineered their own policies, and these were mostly hostile to the Jews.

In Russia[5] not a single one of the Jewish disabilities was abrogated. As if war had confronted the administration with no more important task, limitations on residence, in the professions, and on attendance at schools were vigilantly maintained, and generally to the extreme letter of the law; only in the rarest cases was a latitudinarian interpretation accepted in view of the exigencies of the war. The percentage norm was insisted upon even for children of front line fighters, for whose education the government was obligated, and parents were pitilessly turned away when they sought to visit seriously wounded sons in hospitals.

Mistrust of the Jews, on occasion given utterance by personages in high position, led to the evacuation of the Jews from the western provinces of Russia which were threatened by the German advance. To transport such masses of people over so great a distance would have been well nigh impossible even in normal times. In time of war there were naturally no means of transportation, not even the most primitive, and so the journey itself became a form of martyrdom. Countless individuals were forced to make the journey on foot, and especially cruel commanders so marshalled the Jews that they served as rifle parapets. When these refugees arrived in the interior of Russia, hairsplitting discussions began as to whether or not they might remain at their place of exile, whether or not they should be allowed to move about freely, whether they should be put to work and at what. If the evacuation had been a temporary emergency measure its difficulties could have been overcome; but as time dragged on the attitude of the bureaucracy brought catastrophe. To be sure, there were other attitudes in Russia. The merchants of the capitals showed understanding of the situation, and the organizations for war relief were responsive to it.

In Germany[6] certain groups of armchair patriots began, at the very beginning of the war, to gather material against Social Democrats, Catholics, and Jews; the fact that a man was a Protestant would guarantee his being a model patriot. Antisemitic deputies repeatedly voiced the slander that the Jews were not doing their full duty in their country's hour of need. Constant burrowing led to action on the part of the Prussian Minister of War, who held authority over three-fourths of the army. He ordered a census[7] to be taken on November 1, 1916, to determine the number of Jewish soldiers at the front, the number in reserves or in armies of occupation, the number working in army bureaus, and the number excused from service. This was a calculated insult to the Jewish soldiers, to those who had fallen or been wounded in action as well as those whose lives were in constant peril. With the customary strutting and puffing about the honor of an officer, the intention to insult was denied, but the execution of the measure betrayed its original hateful purpose. Even so the inquiry did not turn out to the discredit of the Jews. The Minister of War made the results public and turned to farfetched exculpations when he realized, in consequence of determined Jewish protests, how grotesque his measure had been. What was right in Germany was surely acceptable in Austria and Russia. There, too, demands were made for a census of the Jews, but the censuses were never carried out. A similar suspicion even reached Great Britain[8] and the United States, after it entered the war. Here the Jews were likewise forced to prove that they were doing their duty. Figures showed that their representation in the armed service was greater than their proportions in the population would indicate.

Two points in the gigantic struggle offered the extraordinary spectacle of Jews fighting as Jews in their own closed formations.[9] Such a thing had not happened for 1300 years; it was involved in the role which the Jewish settlements in Palestine had already played and were yet to play. When Turkey entered the war, Russian subjects of military age had to leave the country. Many fled to Egypt and put themselves at the disposal of the British government for military service in a Jewish unit. The leading spirit among them was Joseph Trumpeldor, who had lost his right arm in the Russo-Japanese War and had been promoted to the rank of captain, along with other honors, because of his bravery. Five hundred men were recruited; they were fitted out with 750 mules and as the Zion Mule Corps were dispatched to the assistance of the British army at Gallipoli. Hebrew was their language of conversation, commands were given in Hebrew, they carried the blue and white banner of Palestine, and they bore the Star of David as their emblem: it was as if ancient history were being resurrected. The assignment of the Corps was a thankless one. They were required to assist in a campaign which had been most inauspiciously begun. Their commandant, Lieutenant Colonel J. H. Patterson, was full of praise for his intelligent and brave troop, who shunned no danger and suffered considerable losses in consequence of their courageous action.

The same officer also commanded the second Jewish

troop to be organized during the World War. The troop was known as The Jewish Legion and later as The Judaeans;[10] it was employed in the closing act of the British campaign in Palestine. It was the Zionist writer, Vladimir Jabotinsky, as bold as he was gifted, who from the very beginning of the war fought for the idea that Jews must campaign for the conquest of Palestine in voluntary formations by the side of the Allies. He recruited volunteers for such a troop among the Russian Jews in England and America also. In 1917 his propaganda met the wishes of the British government and the British General Headquarters; at a critical moment in the war they wished to secure the sympathy of the Jews of the world and so encouraged the formation of unified Jewish regiments. But this design met with vigorous opposition. Not even all Zionists welcomed it, let alone the native English Jews. The latter sought to sabotage the entire undertaking and succeeded in having the distinct name and uniform of the troop dropped; actually they were designated the Royal Fusiliers. As a result of the dispute, the number of men assembled did not exceed 5,000, and they left for Palestine in February 1918. Among those offering their service was the sculptor Jacob Epstein, who, however, never reached the front. In Palestine they met with the hostility of the Egyptian Expeditionary Force. As we shall later see this Force took every means to discredit the whole idea.

Jewish casualties of the war in killed and wounded were numerous.[11] Exact accounting showed the names of more than 12,000 dead in Germany. Hungary also counted more than 10,000 Jewish dead. Russia had the largest number of Jewish soldiers, there being 350,000 at the beginning of the war. Exact statistics of casualties are not available, in consequence of the collapse of the Russian armies, but it can hardly be an exaggeration to set the number of Jewish dead of all armies at 120,000. The best known war casualty was Rabbi Abraham Bloch[12] of Lyons, France; Bloch handed a dying Catholic aviator a crucifix when no priest was near, and in the performance of this labor of love he was torn to pieces by a grenade. At the moment it appeared that such an act of heroic self-denial must produce peace among men. And in fact their common danger did make for cordial relationship among comrades-in-arms; but the experiences of the post-war period showed how quickly men forget their anxious moments and the comrades of their time of need.

The large number of dead and missing brought the unhappy situation of the '*Agunot*[13] to the fore in Jewish communal life. Thousands of young women were driven to despair because rabbinic tribunals refused to accept available proof of widowhood as sufficient and so made remarriage impossible according to Jewish law.

JEWS IN THE WAR ZONES

Palestine[14] was among the regions hardest hit, although Turkey did not enter the war at its beginning. The country was dependent upon import and export, and both were completely cut off. Food prices rose rapidly and sources of income dried up. The income of the numerous recipients of foreign aid also ceased; money could not come in from abroad, and drafts were not honored. In September 1914 the Turks declared the treaty provisions which granted foreign powers special privileges abrogated. Most Jews were placed in a precarious situation, inasmuch as they were not Turkish citizens. Many accepted Turkish citizenship, but about 18,000 were forced to leave the country. The Russians, particularly those of military age, fled to Egypt; about 13,000 refugees were counted there.

Kemal Pasha, the military governor of Palestine, in character an avatar of the Gestapo, assumed a particularly hateful attitude. As a Turkish chauvinist he feared the Zionist movement and let the Jewish colonists feel his displeasure. He would have liked to expel them all from the country and confiscate their lands. He rejected their applications for naturalization. As a result of the intervention of foreign powers — the United States Ambassador at Constantinople, Henry Morgenthau, in particular was able to avert the severest hardship — Kemal Pasha moderated his attitude for the moment; but with the growing danger to the country his fury grew. In the spring of 1917 he determined to remove all of the Jews out of Palestine to Syria; the movement was to begin by emptying the youthful city of Tel Aviv and by expelling the Jews from Jaffa. The Armenian atrocities which were disturbing the whole world at the time alarmed the Jews with the prospect of similar horrors. It was due to the intervention of the Queen of Holland and the King of Spain that the German and Austrian governments made representations at Constantinople as a result of which Kemal Pasha rescinded his order.

Galicia and Bukovina[15] with their numerous and impoverished Jewish population were the first to bear the brunt of Russian attack. The Russians drove in no fewer than six times, and each time they were beaten back by the Austrians. The devastation wrought by the armies fighting in these regions is indescribable. The Jewish population hastily threw together what possessions it could and fled to avoid the frightful rule of the Russians. The fate of those left behind, and particularly of others who were dragged off as hostages, proved the genuineness of the threat. The farther the Russians advanced the more numerous were the hordes of refugees who cluttered the roads. The Austrians hurriedly set up refugee camps; these left much to be desired from the hygienic point of view and showed shocking mortality rates, especially among the children. Hundreds of thousands were evacuated to Vienna and western Austria and to Hungary. As long as war enthusiasm lasted the population made the best of these war victims. But when food became scarce and starvation threatened they began to murmur at the unwanted consumers. Beginning with 1916 complaints about the billeting of the Jews and calls for their removal became louder and more malicious.

It was impossible for the refugees to return to their homes, for eastern Galicia and Bukovina remained in Russian hands until the middle of 1917; and central and western Galicia were so devastated by war that they could not receive their original inhabitants. The Jews were no longer welcome in their homeland, moreover, for in the meanwhile the government had fallen into the hands of the Poles. The Poles had again become the favorite children of the family of nations. Both sides in the war flattered them and held out prospects of independence. The Polish people proved unworthy of its great hour.[16] It used the power which had been given it for the purpose of oppressing other nationalities which resided in the country. It was especially unbridled in its Jew-hatred; it begrudged the Jews a share in food and raw materials as well as in education, and even refused to allow the cooperation of Jews in Red Cross work. It put into force during the war the plan for a boycott which it had proclaimed before the war. It disregarded the fact that much Jewish blood had been spilt before independence could be promised Poland.

The German and Austrian troops which were systematically advancing in Russian Poland and western Galicia counted upon the services which could be rendered the invading forces by so numerous and intellectually agile a population as were the Jews. The Jews were important in transportation and commerce, and thanks to their Yiddish speech communication with them was easy. The natural disinclination of the Jews for the Czarist regime was counted upon. At the beginning of his advance the German Major General Ludendorff[17] addressed a proclamation phrased in choice Yiddish, *An meine libe Jiden in Poilen*. He promised the Jews the protection of his army and complete freedom and equality for the future. The Austrian army did the same. But the Czar, too, was not niggardly with promises. At first the battle moved back and forth. In the Russian-Polish border regions the Jews suffered severely under the first onset. In addition to the destruction of entire localities there were pillaging and executions due to mistrust or denunciations. In the summer of 1915 the superiority of the Central Powers in this sector of the war became apparent; Poland, Lithuania, and parts of the Baltic provinces were occupied. Wherever they could the Russians evacuated the Jewish population, and those that were not driven into the interior of Russia they crowded into the interior of Poland, especially in Warsaw. The determined attack worked serious injury to the Jewish population, but the raging soldiery was soon supplanted by the army of occupation. Individual commanding officers, whose power went to their heads, played the part of dissolute pashas; but on the whole the forces of occupation strove to bring order into the country and to draw the populace to collaboration, not so much, to be sure, for the advantage of the populace as for the interests of German war economy.

However that may have been, a *modus vivendi* was developed between the Jews and the occupation authorities. At the very beginning of the war a Committee for the East[18] had been formed in Berlin; this Committee represented all Jewish groups, and made it its business to furnish the authorities of the occupied region with information regarding the peculiar circumstances of the Jews and to mediate between the authorities and the Jewish population. The Committee succeeded in creating an atmosphere of good-will. The occupation authorities had no desire to increase the suffering of the populace beyond the measure inevitable in a state of war, and the Jews were spared suffering in excess of their unavoidably hard lot.

The occupation authorities had a special Jewish department established in which all relevant questions were considered. Hermann Struck, a celebrated etcher, and Arnold Zweig,[19] a celebrated writer, both working at the "Upper Eastern Command" at Wilna, made sketches of "the Eastern Jewish countenance." They caught not only the externals but also all that was hidden behind the beards and the side-locks. Soldiers and officers came into closer relations with the populace and, in consequence of daily contacts, largely lost their prejudice against Eastern Jews. German Jewish soldiers were deeply impressed by the solidarity and the inward Jewish piety which they observed, and by the feeling of comradeship and hospitality with which they were met. The Jewish department took measures for the restoration of the Jewish community life and educational system. It created no small sensation when a *yeshibah* was opened in Lithuania under the patronage of a Prussian general.

Collaboration in Poland[20] was not as free of friction as was the case in the "Upper East" because there German policy sought to win the favor of the Poles, and for a long while found it difficult to determine a satisfactory delimitation with respect to the Austrian sphere of influence and an appropriate form for Polish independence. It is significant that, whereas the administration in Lithuania treated the Jews as a separate nationality, they refused them similar recognition in Poland. The *Referat für jüdische Angelegenheiten* ("Board for Jewish Affairs") which was set up by the Government General at Warsaw, directed by the German Reichstag deputy, Ludwig Haas, in cooperation with the representative of the *Agudat Yisrael*, Rabbi Pinchas Kohn, was in charge of the restoration of communal life and the regulation of religious and educational matters. In providing for the schools they had to fight not only the Poles, who were unwilling to tolerate schools using any but the Polish national language, but also the Jews themselves, who could not agree upon a single national language and split into Hebraists and Yiddishists. To the Poles, Yiddish was particularly unsympathetic because of its kinship to German. The Bund, moreover, took exception to the subventioning of schools at which religious instruction was given.

The German occupation authorities also regulated the Organization of Jewish Religious Associations in Poland. They granted the communities a legal basis and saw to their division into districts and the unification of the districts under a superior council. Needless to say, all parties were not equally pleased with the law, and in particular those who longed for national autonomy. But the law was basically so sound that it was taken over by the new Polish Republic after the conclusion of peace.

A desperate problem was that of feeding and clothing the multitude; this could not be solved from Germany because Germany itself was suffering as a result of the blockade. Poland was thoroughly impoverished; the harvest of 1915 was completely destroyed and that of 1916 largely destroyed. The produce was not sufficient to sustain the Polish population, and their leaders refused to share their scanty bread with the Jews. Starvation and epidemic threatened the country. At this juncture only the good-will of the occupying authorities and effective help from neutral countries abroad could save the situation. Eyes were turned to the United States in particular.

American Jewry's Sense of Responsibility

The stature of the United States as a world power became evident at the beginning of the war; both sides made great efforts to obtain its material assistance and moral support. For the public opinion of a democratic country, and especially for its Jewish masses,[21] the alliance of the Entente with the Czar was a great obstacle, and the propaganda of both parties laid their finger upon this sore point. It was natural that the Jews should follow events in the eastern theater of war with feverish tension. In America, where a detached and complete view of the entire situation was possible, the belief was prevalent from the very beginning of hostilities that Europe would be brought to the edge of the abyss by its self-mutilation, that it would be in need of a new political orientation, and that eventually the United States could exert a decisive influence.

Need was soon clamoring at the gates.[22] An urgent appeal came from Henry Morgenthau, the American Ambassador in Constantinople, on behalf of the Jews of Palestine, who were reduced to pressing want by the outbreak of the war. The American Jewish Committee in cooperation with the American Zionist Federation immediately despatched the sum requested, and the latter organization later followed with considerable additional assistance. The Zionists also called attention to the need for all-embracing relief work for the necessitous Jews in the European theater of war, and the SOS from Europe was heard very soon. Various Jewish organizations made collections for the needy, and each succeeded in interesting its own following. But the cries for help became more insistent, and, in order to make sure that the sums generously contributed should be distributed from a unified source and to the best possible effect, the various organizations active in relief work combined at the end of 1914 to form the American Joint Distribution Committee for the Relief of Jewish War Sufferers.[23] The Committee was non-partisan and international; not only all of the United States, but Canada, Cuba, and other countries entrusted their relief moneys to it. Its seat was in New York. Felix M. Warburg, who devoted himself wholeheartedly to this work, was its chairman, and he was assisted by a staff of co-workers. Originally conceived as a temporary war measure, "the Joint," or "the JDC," as it came to be called, became a permanent establishment as the result of the constantly recurrent emergencies in Jewish life. It did not cease operating after the end of the war, and its achievements are beyond praise and without parallel in the history of human helpfulness. About eighty countries have come into the orbit of its work. It has disbursed upward of 120 millions of dollars for relieving material and spiritual need, for aiding emigration, for reconstructing lives. Aside from this, the Committee was of assistance in transferring private aid at a time when ordinary bank communications had ceased.

The hope of the war victims in the free and prosperous Jewry of America was not deceived. The warm-hearted appeals which pictured the emergency as "unparalleled in history," as indeed it was, and the sufferers as "near to extinction," as indeed they were, were readily credited and contributions were subscribed of a size which had never before been thought possible. By the end of 1915 a million and a half dollars were collected, but incoming reports made it clear that this sum was entirely inadequate. For 1916 the goal was set at five millions, and nearly that sum was actually obtained. Mass meetings were held in all cities, and the generosity displayed bordered on the miraculous; money and jewels were eagerly contributed. On a single evening in New York almost a million dollars was collected; Chicago and Philadelphia together gave half a million.

The money was distributed purposefully. In Palestine[24] the chief need seemed to be a reduction in the price of food and the supply of as great quantities of food as possible. The military required such amounts that existing stocks were quickly exhausted. With the approval of the United States government the collier *Vulcan* was despatched to Palestine in 1915 with 900 tons of food, but the local government allowed the Jewish population to receive only 55% of the cargo. In February 1916 a new vessel laden with medicinal material sailed; it was highly welcome, for typhus and Asiatic cholera had begun to spread in the land.

Judah L. Magnes traveled to Europe in order to learn of conditions in the war regions at first hand. He could not obtain a visa for entering Russia. There the existing communities had formed a Central Relief Committee in St. Petersburg,[25] with which 150 local committees were affiliated. As early as the summer of 1915 that Committee dealt with 100,000 exiles, whose situation was aggravated by the fact that they were not allowed to work. By 1916 the number had grown to 350,000. People of means introduced self-taxation, and the Jewish Colonization Association supported them with aid received from America. The National Russian Relief Committee, too, was aware of the Jewish sufferers. The rich merchants of the large cities preserved the much admired Russian magnanimity.

In Lithuania and Poland things looked worse. More than a million and a half Jews were in the areas occupied by Germany and Austria, and a large fraction of them were completely dependent upon outside support. Local Jewish organizations cooperated with the *Hilfsverein der deutschen Juden* in Berlin and the Joint towards alleviating their misery. In consequence of the blockade against the Central Powers money alone did not suffice; there was need of food, clothing, and raw material for work. The Polish relief committee displayed an odious chauvinism and excluded Jews from its beneficiaries; it even shut them out from collaboration in the relief commissions. When the merchant guild of Moscow contributed a sum of money to relief in Poland, they found it necessary to stipulate the percentage to be made available to Jews, to the shame of the Poles.

The need was so pressing that Magnes[26] proposed a goal of not less than ten million dollars for the American relief drive of 1917. The amount seemed fantastic, but it was collected. Julius Rosenwald of Chicago, a businessman of great wealth, who took no joy in earning money if he could not spend it generously for the common good, promised a million on condition that the remaining nine million be raised. His example fired other wealthy men to assume 10% of their community's quota, and so the entire sum was obtained.

In 1917 the United States entered the war on the side of the Allies. The new cares and duties which fell to the Jews and to the Jewish Welfare Board[27] did not reduce the readiness of American Jews to give. Cooperation with the relief committees in Eastern Europe now became impossible. Thanks to the willingness of the Department of State in Washington and of the authorities of the German occupation, relief work could be continued through a Dutch committee. But no relief efforts could permanently prevent the outbreak of such epidemics as starvation typhus; in large cities like Warsaw and Wilna the toll of epidemic was shocking.

Revolution and Civil War in Russia

The year 1917 brought a number of events of great political importance which were momentous for the Jewish fate. At about the same time that America was entering the war, revolution in Russia[28] abolished the rule of the Czar and the regime of absolutism. It was an inexpressible relief to public opinion in America to find itself released of the onus of armed alliance with Czarism; Jews in particular had been uneasy in such an alliance. The importance of the Russian revolution in the history of the world cannot be overestimated. The new constitution abolished all laws which laid disabilities upon any citizens of the realm on the grounds of difference of religion or race. In order to avert any future abuse the decree enumerated in detail the issues involved: freedom of residence and freedom of movement, abrogation of all limitations on possessions and property, upon work and occupation, access to positions in the administration and the army, access to educational institutions of every grade; complete freedom of religion and the use of language other than Russian were also provided for. Overnight then, the Jews were granted full equality.[29] They appreciated the significance of the event and were duly grateful. They realized that their position within the state was now fundamentally changed, and they strained every effort to support the new government and bring the war to a victorious conclusion.

The revolution also had its seamy side. Its first concomitant was chaos[30] and the dissolution of the army. Bands of starving deserters spread over the country and pillaged, and Jewish property seemed particularly attractive. Soon counter-revolution raised its head. The Black Hundred fell upon the Jews with charges that they were Russia's misfortune and that they were to blame for the fall of the monarchy. What the real trouble was with Russia was pointed out by its ally, David Lloyd George, who, on the basis of his experiences during the war, called the Russian government "brutal, tyrannical, corrupt, rotten to the core;" and of the Czardom he said: "It fell because every fibre of its power, influence and authority had rotted through and through; it tumbled to pieces at the first shock of insurrection." But too many people were directly affected by the collapse to take it placidly, too many hungry men were ready to accept the Czar's shilling. German spies were at work, spreading anti-Jewish proclamations and promising the restoration of the Czar.

The German High Command did more. It gave free passage to the leaders of the extreme Left, the Bolshevists. The revolution of the Right combined with that of the Left. It was the program of Bolshevism to accept every aid and every ally that made difficulties for the existing government. So the Bolshevists chimed in with the chorus of those who were agitating against the Jews, and took active part in pogrom-like attacks. Beating Jews was no part of their program, but they agreed to such attacks as a strategic propaganda device. An unfortunate offensive of the Russian army against the Central Powers, and the support by the Kerensky government of a general who coveted dictatorship, contributed to strengthen Bolshevism. Throughout the summer of 1917 revolutionary battles and hostility to the Jews continued. The end came with the victory of the Bolshevists on November 7, 1917, and the establishment of the dictatorship of the proletariat.

A concomitant phenomenon of the Russian revolution was a turn towards the Allies on the part of the Poles. Hitherto they had wavered between Russia and Germany, but now they turned sharply from the Central Powers. The German proclamation of an independent Poland proved to be a complete fiasco. Only a wretched handful turned out for the army which Germany expected, but numbers of Polish legionnaires turned up in the armies of the Allies. This had an incidental effect on the Jews: Jewish workers were transported to the industrial regions in Upper Silesia and the Rhineland, where they were forced to supply heavy labor.

The Bolshevist government, under the leadership of

Lenin, proceeded to the expropriation of farmland and the nationalization of banks, mines and factories. By the summer of 1918 property to the value of a billion rubles was expropriated; it is needless to remark that the Jews, insofar as they were possessors of capital, suffered from these measures. Leon Trotzky (originally Leba Bronstein), the Foreign Minister, demanded on the radio that the warring powers declare an armistice and conclude a peace which should rest upon the self-determination of peoples. Only Germany accepted the armistice, and after lengthy complications it concluded the peace of Brest-Litovsk on March 3, 1918; among other concessions Russia recognized the independence of its western border states. The German army formed a rampart from Reval and Riga to Kiev and Odessa, and maintained peace and order. External war was thus ended for the Soviet Republic, but not internal war. The Bolshevists had by no means a majority of the people behind them, nor even of the workers. Their opponents continued the struggle; a social revolutionary, Dora Kaplan, even ventured upon an attempt on Lenin's life. His party defended itself by a reign of terror which knew no mercy and made Bolshevism a nightmare to the world powers.

Immediately after the fall of the Czar, the Ukraine[31] began to set up its own national state. It was prepared to grant national autonomy to its Jewish minority (5% of the total population) and created a People's Ministry for Jewish Affairs. Democratic elections for the national assembly were proposed, but could not be carried out because a wave of pogroms made the country unsafe. Bands of starving deserters like those in Russia ranged over the country to rob and pillage. When the Ukrainian Republic desired to sever its connection with Soviet Russia, the Jewish parties voted against the dismemberment of Russia. Matters came to the point of actual war with the Bolshevists, and the armed Ukrainians threw themselves upon the Jews in blind fury. The leaders of the army deplored this brand of heroism but could do nothing to prevent it, for they had no troops with which to suppress the insubordination.

Even after the Germans took over the protection of the country in the spring of 1918, Petlura, the Minister of War, gave free rein to the vengeful feelings of his soldiery, as he styled it, toward alleged Bolshevist tendencies. The Jews paid with many lives and large contributions to his war chest. On the other side, the Bolshevists accused the Jews of having fired upon the Red Army, and demonstrated their heroism by "conquering" villages in the border territory and filling them with corpses. When somewhat later the Hetman regime introduced a new constitution, the Jews were again between the hammer and the anvil, for the peasants accused them of having called the Germans in. The German occupation, however, did not allow serious excesses.

The Balfour Declaration

The other great surprise of 1917 came in the autumn in the form of the Balfour Declaration,[32] which expressed the good-will of the British government for a Jewish National Home in Palestine. How the ground was prepared for this significant declaration can be read in the *History of Zionism* by Nahum Sokolow, who was one of the godfathers of the Declaration. Chief merit for bringing it into being belongs to Dr. Chaim Weizmann, at the time Professor of Chemistry at the University of Manchester in England. In Turkey's entry into the war Weizmann's perspicacity saw the possibility for a change in the status of Palestine, the prospect of broad Jewish colonization on a basis of autonomy. At the Zionist Congresses he had led the opposition of those who would subordinate every political calculation to practical work in Palestine. That was well enough when there was no prospect for a political decision. But now the possibility of new negotiations had arisen, particularly in view of the Allies' proclaimed intentions concerning the restoration of small nations. Weizmann and his friends were able to spread his convictions among all the Jews of England. Those among them that had political influence were inclined to favor only a cultural autonomy. But Weizmann insisted upon national and political autonomy also, and won the agreement of the English press and of British statesmen to this view.

As a chemist Weizmann had made a discovery important for British defense; he had declined a proffered distinction for himself, but instead asked for a sympathetic reception of the idea which he represented. This brought him into touch with members of the war cabinet and won him their sympathy. As early as March 1916 the Foreign Office sounded the Russian[33] government on its attitude towards an "agreement relating to Palestine which would satisfy the aspirations of the Jews," having as its goal the "conversion of the Jewish elements in the East, the United States of America, and other places to the cause of the Allies." At the moment no progress was made, but in February 1917, when the situation in the Near East was nearer settlement, conversations were resumed at the home of Dr. Moses Gaster, and the matter was energetically prosecuted by a small group of Zionists.

Independently of these efforts, work in a similar direction was undertaken in the United States.[34] Zionists there had realized from the beginning that the war might offer an unprecedented opportunity for some permanent achievement for Israel in Palestine. Shemaryah Levin, a fascinating popular speaker and Zionist propagandist, was sojourning in New York at the outbreak of the war and was unable to return to Europe. He was a member of the Zionist Executive, the only member, indeed, in a neutral country and so able to correspond freely. In collaboration with American Zionists, who seized upon the opportunity to demonstrate their intentions and their effectiveness, Levin convoked a conference "of all American Zionists." The conference met on August 30, 1914, established a Provisional Executive Committee for General Zionist Affairs, and elected Louis D. Brandeis[35] its president.

Zionism thus acquired a leader of spiritual and moral stature such as it had not possessed since Theodor Herzl. As a jurist Brandeis enjoyed the highest esteem because of his passionate struggle for human rights as against the formality of the law, for the rights of the economically weak against the might of capital. As "the People's Attorney" he was honored and feared. He was a champion of the principle of social justice. He worked upon the structure of constitutionality and law so as to adapt it to the changed forms of society. President Wilson called him "a friend of all just men and a lover of the right" when, to the consternation of all representatives of Big Business, he nominated him as Associate Justice of the Supreme Court of the United States in 1916.

Brandeis had been quite remote from Jewish life, but he was gripped by the Zionist idea, and from 1912 he professed Zionism. Now he saw a possibility of actualizing the idea, and he felt in duty bound to work for its actualization. Taking the presidency meant for him devoting his full energy and enthusiasm to the task. Former leaders of the movement were astonished at the seriousness with which he took his responsibility, at the care he devoted to grasping all its details, at his systematic procedure. His first concern was to preserve as much as possible of what had been done in Palestine. He admonished the Zionists to concentrate all their strength on this one point, and in fact unexpectedly large subsidies reached Palestine.

In 1915 the functions of the Zionist Executive, which had hitherto had its seat in Berlin, were transferred to the

American Federation. This move gave the American Federation a position of leadership, and it retained its position after the business office of the Zionist Organization was established in neutral Copenhagen and after the London Zionists developed greater activity. Confidence in the movement was strengthened by the fact that a man like Brandeis was at its head. Under his administration there were no debates but only energetic work for the specific goal of procuring men and means for the upbuilding of Palestine. One of Brandeis' dicta was "Members, money, discipline, that is true preparedness."

Some of Brandeis' moves were pregnant with momentous consequence. As early as 1914 he explained Zionist goals to President Wilson and sought to engage the interest of the British and French ambassadors. The attitude of both envoys was positive; the British ambassador gave approval to very broad concessions. Brandeis insisted that Zionists live up to their responsibilities and so conduct themselves that the general public would repose confidence in them and give them opportunities to display their good faith in positions of responsibility. A new zeal animated the old party members, and visitors from Europe and especially from Palestine added fire to their energies. The Jewish press, and especially the Yiddish newspapers with their extensive influence, gave wide publicity to Zionism and the Jewish national ideas. President Wilson was kept informed of progress, and in the spring of 1916 he initialed a short memorandum expressing approval of Zionist aims.

Meanwhile further conversations in London led to the elaboration of a positive proposal on the part of the Zionists, which was approved by members of the British government who were consulted. The agreement of the French and Italian governments and the good-will of the Holy See were assured. The approval of the President of the United States was made explicit to the British mission led by Lord Balfour, the British Foreign Minister, which dealt with important matters of common interest.

It was not long before Dr. Weizmann was able to make a public declaration at a meeting of the English Zionist Federation:[36] "I am entitled to state in this assembly that His Majesty's Government is ready to support our plans." But immediately there appeared in the London *Times* a detailed protest of the Conjoint Foreign Committee of the Board of Deputies of the British Jews and the Anglo-Jewish Association against the upbuilding of Palestine on a political basis, against Jews being privileged over other groups of the population, and against the application of the principle of Jewish nationality to the Jews of other countries. Other personages, who later organized into a League of British Jews, joined in the protest.

The reaction of public opinion was not what these people had expected, but rather inclined to the Zionist point of view. The outspoken support of the Russian Zionists, who had grown very active after the revolution, and resolutions of hundreds of Jewish mass meetings in Great Britain "in favour of the reconstruction of Palestine as the National Home of the Jews" strengthened the position of the Zionist leaders. The whole summer was passed in conflict and wavering, whose effects were felt by the government and made formulation of its declaration difficult. But finally, and after constant consultation with President Wilson, a satisfactory formula was reached and transmitted to Lord Lionel Walter Rothschild, the president of the English Zionist Federation.[37] The document is sufficiently important to be reproduced verbatim:

> Foreign Office,
> November 2nd, 1917
>
> Dear Lord Rothschild,
>
> I have much pleasure in conveying to you, on behalf of His Majesty's Government, the following declaration of sympathy with Jewish

Zionist aspirations which has been submitted to, and approved by, the Cabinet.

"His Majesty's Government view with favour the establishment in Palestine of a national home for the Jewish people, and will use their best endeavours to facilitate the achievement of this object, it being clearly understood that nothing shall be done which may prejudice the civil and religious rights of existing non-Jewish communities in Palestine, or the rights and political status enjoyed by Jews in any other country."

I should be grateful if you would bring this declaration to the knowledge of the Zionist Federation.

Yours,
Arthur James Balfour

The Balfour Declaration was compared to the edict of King Cyrus of Persia which permitted the Jews in Babylonian exile to return to Palestine in 539 B. C. E. In all Jewish centers it was the occasion of infinite rejoicing, accompanied by overflowing gratitude to Great Britain. Some dated a new era from the Declaration (*ahare hazharat Balfour*). The Declaration was not the charter which Herzl had sought, but it was the basis for future construction. After Cyrus, too, the community had begun with a small settlement, which eventually expanded into the large state of the Hasmonaeans. The Balfour Declaration took no position on the disputed question of Jewish nationality, but it was addressed to all the Jews of the world and spoke of them as a unity. It strengthened enormously the prestige of the Zionist Organization to which it had been delivered.

The Central Powers could not fail to meet the challenge of the Declaration. They too had a burning interest in binding the confidence and the resources of the Jews to their cause. As allies of Turkey they could not, indeed, proclaim the dismemberment of that country, but the Berlin government repeatedly promised the Zionist leaders there that they would forward their plans in every way. At about the same time that the Balfour Declaration was issued, the Turkish Grand Vizier declared[38] that it was the purpose of the Imperial Ottoman government to favor the budding Jewish settlement of Palestine by granting free immigration and colonization, local self-administration, and the promotion of the development of autonomous cultural institutions. The German government welcomed this declaration and expressly subscribed to it. The Zionists were in the same happy situation as the Poles, having obtained assurance from both warring parties. Of President Wilson, who was steadily being advanced to a position as *arbiter mundi*, it was said that both P's, Poland and Palestine, lay equally close to his heart.

British and Jews in Palestine

But the British had disposed of the lion's skin before they had caught the lion. Palestine was still in the hands of the Turks. The British army, with the Arabs of Mecca fighting at their side, had indeed won a battle at Rafah on December 23, 1916, but that brought them only to the border of the Holy Land.[39] The Turks, with the assistance of the Germans, fortified Gaza, which was a naturally strong position, and the Palestinian Arabs helped them throw back the British attacks. General Allenby was placed in supreme command and given reinforcements, and by his mastery of the tactics of flanking movements and of the use of cavalry he succeeded in getting the upper hand. He first stormed Beer Sheba, on November 3, 1917, and so broke the back of the resistance. The Turks fled along the coast, with the English cavalry blocking their path. Gaza and all the surrounding fortresses fell into Allenby's hands. The way to the north was open, and Jaffa was the next objective. The Turks still attempted to offer resistance here and there, and many Jewish colonies suffered from gunfire, but the advance of the English was irresistible.

For obvious reasons General Allenby was unwilling

to shell Jerusalem. He surrounded the city on all sides, and on December 11, 1917 (Kislev 26, 5678), he marched into the Holy City at the head of his troops. Seventy years before Disraeli had dreamed, "The English will take the city, and they will keep it;" what was then a dream was now a fact. The victors were greeted by the Jewish population with uproarious jubilation. It happened that they were in the midst of the Hanukkah celebration, and in the entry of the British they saw a fresh divine miracle for their liberation. Jews everywhere believed the fulfillment of the Balfour Declaration was at hand. The entire Christian world regarded it as a great triumph that the Holy City was redeemed from the domination of the Crescent. In a proclamation, issued in Hebrew as well as other languages, the victor expressed his profound respect for the Holy City and gave assurances of his unqualified protection of all its sacred sites.

It was only in February 1918 that Jericho could be taken. The Turks continued to hold strong positions and the process of driving them from the highlands of Samaria was slow. A British attempt to hold Es-Salt in Transjordania and to block the road to Hedjaz was unsuccessful. Fighting ceased until autumn.

Meanwhile the Jewish battalion[40] arrived in Palestine. Since its arrival in Egypt it had been given to understand that it was not welcome there. The staff of the Egyptian Expeditionary Corps followed its own policies and sabotaged those of the central government at London. Many of its officers were confirmed in their opposition to the battalion by their dislike of all things Jewish. Their attitude slowed down recruiting, for which numerous Jews from Palestine and Egypt and from distant America were eager. It was clearly the intention of the general staff to disband the battalion. In the course of a few months it was shifted about in twelve different formations. General Allenby had promised that a Jewish brigade would be formed upon the arrival of new troops; his own staff prevented this step by a consciously mendacious report that no additional Jewish troops could be expected, whereas they had already actually landed in Egypt. Information that the War Office in London had bestowed the designation "The Judeans" upon the Legion was kept from them for a year. Colonel Patterson, as commandant of the Jewish Legion, suffered many a personal affront, but he would not sever his connection with the troop because he valued their military discipline and diligence as well as their bravery and fearlessness. The least that could be said of the attitude of the general staff, he wrote, is "that it was unworthy of the British tradition of fair play."

Since the Jewish Legion was after all not disbanded, they were subjected to all manner of hazing to make their lives miserable. During the hottest months of the summer they were posted in the valley of the Jordan, where the climate is murderous and where British soldiers were never sent for any length of time. Their position in the Jordan valley (Mellahah) was not only a sizzling inferno but it was under the constant fire of Turkish snipers. The Legion was forced to continue on the alert day and night. Finally, in the middle of September, the order came to march. In order to protect the flank of the great offensive to the north they were to hold the Turkish army of Transjordania in check. On September 20 they stormed the ford of the Jordan at Um-esh-Shert, not far from the place where Joshua had once crossed the Jordan in the opposite direction, and opened the road to Nimrin and Es-Salt. These places they then had to occupy and mop up. The British army report and expressions of opinion by the generals who participated in the campaign explicitly acknowledged the Legion's contribution to the victory. But Palestinian and Egyptian newspapers could print nothing of all this.

This campaign led to the occupation of Amman and took the entire Turkish army east of the Jordan out of the war, but it was only incidental to the chief blow which General Allenby directed against Nablus and which he decided by a memorable cavalry attack along the coast and through the Emek towards the east. He cleared Galilee of enemy troops, cut all their lines of communication, and pursued the Turks to Aleppo and Damascus. This was the first step towards ending the war. On November 11 the general armistice was signed.

Immediately after the conquest of the southern portion of Palestine the British government established an Occupation Enemy Territory Administration[41] with local military governors. It was their task, insofar as such things were possible during the progress of the war, to restore what had been destroyed, to raise the level of nourishment and hygiene of the sorely afflicted population, and to set the ordinary processes of trade and traffic into motion again. This would have been a difficult assignment even for a trained civil administration; it was practically impossible for army officers who had brought with them neither the training nor the love which the job required. The task became no easier and it was carried out with no greater joy, when, after the victory, the military administration was extended to cover the entire country.

In March 1918 the British government despatched to Palestine a Zionist Commission[42] which "should act as an advisory body to the British authorities in Palestine in all matters relating to Jews, or which may affect the establishment of a National Home for the Jewish people in accordance with the Declaration of His Majesty's Government." This commission (*Va'ad ha-Zirim*) was under the leadership of Dr. Weizmann and had upon it Jewish representatives from the Allied countries. It sought to remove the more dismal consequences of the war, to organize the Jewish group, to repatriate those who had been banished or had fled, to alleviate famine, and to create work in the cities and in the country. Their efforts on behalf of health were supported by the American Zionist Medical Unit which was equipped by the women's organization, Hadassah. The unit supplied linen, clothing and shoes, and, like the Red Cross, also provided for medical care and hygienic prophylaxis. Among other things it freed Jerusalem of the plague of mosquitoes.

A brilliant event was the laying of the cornerstone of the Hebrew University[43] on Mount Scopus, which towers over the Holy City and offers a magnificent view of the Mediterranean and of the mountains of Moab (July 24: Ab 15). This was a bold undertaking in a territory under enemy guns and in the midst of the pressing poverty of the country, but it was the clear expression of an intention "to create during the period of war something which is to serve as a symbol of a better future" and "to stimulate the Jewish people to reach further truth." All officials, British and Arabic alike, and representatives of all religions participated in the celebration. The occasion was profoundly significant as a proclamation of peace.

As fruitful as were the efforts of the Zionist commission it cannot be doubted that its mission was premature. Conditions were only just beginning to be regulated. Upon that stony ground every step had to be taken with care so that no one's toes should be trodden upon. Only with the greatest prudence and with the most careful consideration of the character of the people could innovations be attempted in this most conservative corner of the conservative Orient. Not even the Jewish communities looked upon it as an unmixed blessing when foreign visitors, however high their authority might be, wished to press changes upon them. As soon as the commission arrived in Egypt the Arabs gave indications of their mistrust, and Weizmann had to exert himself to dissipate their anxiety. Moreover the English occupation authorities, who were just learning to feel their way in an alien world, were shocked at finding a sort of parallel government set up beside them. Two worlds were in conflict. On the one side were the hot-blooded Zionists with their glowing hopes and their absorbing ambition to achieve and to advance, and on the other the British military, which were outspokenly hostile to the experiment or at best detached and impartial. This was the root of the misunderstanding which at times flared into bitter hatred between the Zionists and the English administration. "Everywhere was a sense of frustration, hope deferred, promises cheated of performance."

The victory of British arms did bring the day nearer upon which hope could be cherished for the establishment of a civil administration and the building of the National Home.

CHAPTER II

The End of the War: Pogroms and Treaties of Peace

The Heritage of War

ON November 11, 1918, bells rang out to proclaim the armistice, and nations heaved a great sigh of relief. Mass murder was halted. Even the vanquished did not despair, for they trusted in President Wilson's Fourteen Points, which promised a just peace and the prospect of a League of Nations which would establish the basis for benevolent and fair cooperation. If this had been a war to end all war, the peace was not too dearly purchased no matter what it cost. But the sequel proved otherwise. Lasting peace was further removed than ever. The European victors were much too self-centered to translate into deeds the noble principles for which they had proclaimed they were fighting.

The principle of a League of Nations was opposed by the principle of national chauvinism; narrow-minded autarchy came to the fore in matters ranging from law to economics. It is characteristic that the most vocal partisans of nationalism were veteran groups, legionnaires, free corps, or merely gangs of freebooters. Where great armies were being demobilized, weapons were not hard to come by. There was no lack of men who were accustomed to their use, and human life and property were not valued highly.

The third principle was that of world revolution, represented by Moscow, whither the capital of the Russian Empire had been removed. An apocalyptic mood was spread by the catastrophic desolation which the World War had wrought.[1] Youth physically exhausted and spiritually diseased returned from the fields of battle to see their hopes and their ideals shattered, and grasped at the phantom of a classless society in which nationalization of property would abolish all friction between individuals and between nations. The psychosis of defeat brought new politicians to the fore, mostly young men with noble aspirations but completely immature judgment, with fanciful plans for national well-being but with no sense for earthly reality. Conflict between extremes seemed inevitable. In particular the anarchic period between the armistice and the conclusion of the peace encouraged every sort of disorder and violence.

As at every new birth in the history of the world, the Jews felt the birth pangs keenly. They were the more painful in the degree that the changes were more incisive. To judge by former experiences, the Jews would have been made the whipping boy even if the conduct of each and every one of them had been exemplary. Even before the end of the war nationalistic and reactionary groups in Germany[2] urged that Jews be deprived of all rights or even that they be banished; and like-minded people in other countries kept abreast of these suggestions. The fact that individual Jews were active in the Russian revolution, some even taking leading parts in it, provided a welcome pretext. The revolution was interpreted as a piece of Jewish vengefulness and Bolshevism as the Jewish plan for world conspiracy and world destruction, in order to justify a crusade against the Jews, as we shall see presently — as if revolutions are made by individuals and not caused by circumstances, and as if the campaign of calumny against the Jews had not already been started before the war and before Bolshevism. Perhaps the very fact that Jews were looked upon as being outside the law led so many young Jews along the path of revolution.

In the conquered countries as in Russia, it was defeat[3] that unleashed revolution. When he allowed Lenin and his Bolshevist friends free passage through Germany, General Ludendorff's intention was to introduce the virus of confusion into Russia, and he expected that he would be able to keep Germany immune from infection. By the peace of Brest Litovsk the enemy was lodged in his own capital. The Russian ambassador in Berlin, Adolf Joffe, was an active agitator for world revolution.[4] In November 1918, workers' and soldiers' soviets after the Russian pattern were established, the navy refused obedience and the mutiny spread to the army. The Kaiser did not abdicate quickly enough, so that the ruling house was deposed and a republic proclaimed.[5] General Field Marshal Paul von Hindenburg performed a highly patriotic service when he led the German army back from the western theater of war, and carried out demobilization in an orderly manner without undue disturbance. The difficult task of rebuilding the Fatherland devolved upon unofficial popular leaders (*Volksbeauftragte*) — among whom were two Jews, Otto Landsberg of the majority socialists and Hugo Haase of the independent socialists — whose purpose it was to lead the revolution along the peaceful path of constitutional government. The elections for the national assembly showed a preponderant majority for the Left. Berlin was still suffering from revolutionary tremors, and counsel was taken on the new constitution in the quieter atmosphere of Weimar. The author of the first draft, Hugo Preuss, a minister of state, was a Jew; a fact which contributed little to the popularity of the Weimar Constitution in Rightist circles.

The radical elements shortly split with the socialists and formed a Communist Party. Their resistance forced the government to throw itself into the hands of the military, which was a fateful step for the future of the republic. Disturbances were suppressed by armed force, one of its victims being the socialist Rosa Luxemburg,[6] who was done to death by the soldiers in January 1919 as she was being carried to prison. In Berlin attacks upon the Jewish quarter were feared, and protection was provided by a self-defense formed by Jewish front-line veterans.[7]

In Munich there was greater disturbance than in Berlin. Munich had no great workers' proletariat, but long before the war it had had an inflammable cultural proletariat. There the socialist writer Kurt Eisner,[8] a radical opponent of war, had proclaimed the republic on November 7, 1918, and was named presiding minister. His Jewish birth was a constant provocation to attack. He came into the *Landtag* on February 21, 1919, in order to offer his resignation after a vote had gone against him, and was shot down by Count Arco Walley, who himself had Jewish blood in his veins. Disturbances continued in Munich, and in March a soviet republic was proclaimed there. At first its tendency was moderate. Gustav Landauer[9] wished to induce social revolution by the spread of popular education and by establishing a society based on intelligence and honor; he scrupulously avoided violence and cruelty. He spoke to the masses and to small groups of individuals "always ready to help, encourage, teach, console," and a foreign observer noted that nothing had ever moved him so much as the sheer goodness and humanity which emanated from this genuinely Jewish prophetic figure. But after a few days his principles were overridden by the communists, who employed violence and force, following their Russian model, taking hostages and murdering them. The army quickly gave the experiment its quietus. Gustav Landauer was beaten to death by the soldiers, the Russian communist Eugen Leviné-Niessen condemned and shot, the writer Erich Mühsam and the young poet Ernst Toller sentenced to long terms of imprisonment. The consequences of the disorder were that various reactionary elements combined forces and that Bavaria became the hotbed of popular partisan groups and of raging Jew-hatred. An immediate consequence was the expulsion of foreign Jews en masse.

In Hungary[10] the struggles were more intense and more fateful for the Jews. State and society collapsed completely, and everything necessary for restoring normal life was wanting: clothing, raw materials, tools, articles of ordinary daily use. The relentlessness of the victorious powers in maintaining the blockade increased tenseness, and the radical propaganda of soldiers back from the war found fruitful soil. A number of them had been trained as Bolshevist agitators in Russian prison camps, and now preached their new doctrine in their own home. Count Michael Karolyi gave radicalism free reign in his government. He hoped to obtain thereby more favorable peace terms from the victors, and to direct the revolution along constitutional lines. He failed on both accounts. The Bolshevist tendencies within the government were strengthened, and the Allied Powers increased their pressure by demanding the surrender of the border regions which Hungary's greedy neighbors coveted.

The consequent confusion and despair were used by Bela Kun as an occasion for proclaiming a soviet republic and putting himself at its head. As a captive of war Bela Kun had come into Lenin's company, was recognized by him as a tractable agitator, entrusted with the Bolshevization of the Hungarian captives, and finally released to continue his calling in his home country. He was by nature and in all respects a subaltern in character, but he knew the Bolshevist catechism backwards and forwards and he knew how to attract starving workers and soldiers with talk of the world revolution and the dictatorship of the proletariat. With the following he thus acquired, he expanded his sway over the whole country. Only in such an atmosphere of despair could a man with nothing but demagogy to recommend him attain such power. He did his job thoroughly and introduced the entire Moscow program of complete socialization and Bolshevization. He organized workers', soldiers' and peasants' soviets and their appropriate peoples' tribunals everywhere. He also took up the mandatory campaign against capitalists and counter-revolutionaries and was not sparing in terror. His people's courts were not chary of capital sentences, and frequently his hangmen did not wait for the sentences. Executions and murders of hostages were numbered by the hundred.

At only one point did Kun depart from the communist program. Towards the advancing foreign troops his policy was out and out national. He did not hesitate to tear the mask of hypocrisy from the faces of the victor nations and to expose the disparity between their deeds and their professed principles. He organized a red army and was able to repulse the Czechs, but after some initial successes he was forced to yield to the Rumanians. His following also turned against him, for he could provide neither bread nor work, and his movement lacked the militant proletarian class consciousness. After 130 days his rule collapsed, and on August 1, 1919, he fled to Vienna with most of the members of his government. One of the most evil of his adherents, Tíbor Szamuelly, fell into the hands of the troops and committed suicide. The Jewish community refused burial to this perverse bloodhound.

A few days later the Rumanians occupied Budapest. The Bolshevist regime was ended, but not the misery and the unrest of the people. In the meanwhile counter-revolutionary elements had gathered their strength and, in the autumn, Admiral Horthy and the counter-revolutionary army moved into Budapest. The new parliamentary elections showed a counter-revolutionary majority. The Awakening Magyars and the Help Hungary organized and swore fearful vengeance upon the Jews.[11] The number of Jews who had occupied leading positions in the revolutionary movement was so striking that no effort was required for anti-Jewish passions to be aroused. That the preponderant majority of the Jews belonged to the bourgeoisie and had therefore suffered severely under the soviet republic, and that in Budapest alone, for example, forty-four Jewish hostages had been murdered, could not avail to turn wrath aside. Nor did it avail that Wilhelm Vászony, the Minister of Justice, the first and only Jewish Minister of a constitutional Hungarian government, had given timely warning against the socialist propaganda. As is always the case at such times, no account was taken of the deserts of the Jews, but the evil deeds of individuals were charged to the entire body.

The White Terror raged unrestrained. The first to feel it were the 30,000 Galician refugees who had been evacuated to Hungary during the war and were now pitilessly thrust out with no notion of where they might go. The problem of the Galician refugees kept recurring in various countries during those hard months, but nowhere was the solution so heartless. The next to be dealt with were the native Jews. Again following a Bolshevist model, officers of the anti-Jewish league forced their way into Jewish homes in the dark of night, robbed the houses and dragged the people off; of many the corpses were found later, but most disappeared without a trace. The terror began in smaller places, and it was continued in Budapest. Three thousand Jews are said to have been done to death in this way. The crimes were so shocking that respected representatives of both Christian Churches protested publicly against the mass slaughter of innocent persons. The old Tisza party too was mindful of its liberal traditions, but its words were drowned out in the general disorder.

The chief of the government, who was concerned for

the restoration of order, discovered a fine-sounding phrase. The policy of Hungary, he said, must not be antisemitic, but Christian. This meant, for him, that the suppression of the Jews must be achieved by means of legislation. Students of the university and of the polytechnic school had sought to drive Jews from these educational institutions by the use of force. The teachers at the university did not approve of force, but they sought to attain the same end by peaceful means. Now legislation took cognizance of the question, and on September 27, 1920, decreed a *numerus clausus*[12] for higher institutions of learning. This was the beginning of a statistical attitude to establish the relative influence of Jews in various phases of public life and then attempt to suppress them. A frightful panic seized Hungarian Jewry. In Budapest alone not fewer than 6,915 Jews sought baptism in 1919–1920, and the number of mixed marriages increased greatly. With the gradual improvement of the situation in the country passions were allayed; but the era of tolerance was over, and henceforward racialists called the tune.[13]

Polish and Ukrainian Terror

Reverberations of the jubilant echoes had hardly ceased after the armistice in the autumn of 1918, when alarming reports from Poland reached Western Europe. In America, Ignace Paderewski had represented that the soul of the Polish people was as pure and harmonious as the strains of his own music, but from the Vistula and the Bug sour notes penetrated to the ears of the world. The Poles desecrated their hour of liberation by their attitude towards other nationalities. Like the other successor states they wished to carve the largest possible slices out of the German and Austro-Hungarian cake and to confront the peace conference with a *fait accompli*. If it was possible to do so they were determined to suppress and abolish everything that was not of the Polish nationality.

From eastern Galicia[14] they sought to expel the Ukrainians. When they stormed Lemberg on November 22, 1918, the officers promised their troops, after the good cossack manner, that as a reward they would receive permission to plunder the Jews for forty-eight hours. They set about the job systematically. The Jewish self-defense was disarmed, bars and bolts were removed from the Jewish quarter by squads of engineers with their equipment, houses and shops were broken into and fired upon indiscriminately, blocks of houses and synagogues were set afire, persons seeking to escape were driven back into the flames, and fire-fighting apparatus was forbidden to function. This was a genuine Russian pogrom; seventy-three were killed on the spot, and many died of their wounds later.

The protectors of Poland in Paris, London, and Washington had hardly recovered from this first shock when worse excesses were reported from the campaign against the Russians. In Pinsk the participants in an orderly and licensed business meeting of the Jewish Cooperative were attacked by soldiers and gendarmes, searched, robbed of their valuables, and denounced to the commandant as Jewish Bolshevists. Without further question and without reflection he had fifty of them shot forthwith. A number of women, who had also been arrested, were kept in jail, stripped and flogged, and taken through a gauntlet of Polish soldiers in that condition. The following morning the men who had been arrested but not sentenced were taken to the cemetery in which those that had been executed were buried; they were told to dig their own graves, and after this harrowing experience released.

Somewhat later, April 16–19, 1919, similar crimes occurred when Lida and Wilna were stormed by the Poles. In Lida "they plundered the town: more than thirty noncombatant Jews were killed. Others, quite innocent, were made responsible for the shots fired from their houses, and executed; and others, equally innocent, murdered. The same allocation of deaths must be made in Wilna, where the total number was more than twice as high. The plundering was accompanied by a great deal of violence and brutality."

Was there any point, the Poles and their adherents asked, in raising such a furore over the killing of three or four hundred Jews at a time when world-shaking transformations were taking place and millions of men in the flower of their youth had given their lives? The question overlooked the difference between soldiers on an active campaign and innocent victims of a bestial commanding power. Moreover these explosions were merely symptoms of the inflammable tinder which was being scattered broadcast in the country and in the army. Excesses against the Jews became a customary feature of daily life. Jews could not walk the streets without being attacked, beaten and robbed by soldiers; a favorite pastime was to cut Jews' beards off forcibly. Jews could not travel on the railroads without being pulled off, mauled, even killed. During the months between November 1918 and January 1919, soldiers regularly attacked and plundered Jews and set their houses afire. Peasants were on hand with their carts to fetch their share of the booty. Citizens took possession of the stores of Jewish merchants as if they were their guardians. Excesses are known to have occurred at 130 localities, from small villages in remote border regions to the capital Warsaw itself.

Most distressing of all, neither the military nor the civil authorities uttered one word of protest against such lawlessness.[15] For them Jews were outside the common limits of the law; anyone might deal as he liked with their lives and property. Although they had unhesitatingly given assurance of their loyalty to the new Polish state, they were represented to be enemies of the Polish people. Polish society had only hatred and contempt for them; there were exceptions, but they were neither numerous nor influential. It had been the traditional privilege of the Polish *Schlachta* to treat the Jews as a whipping boy. But now — and this was the advance of democracy — citizens, peasants, soldiers, and occasionally workers also claimed the same right.

Conditions were so intolerable that the United States and the British Parliament sent missions to Poland to study the situation on the spot. At that time (June 1919) the competent authorities found their tongue and expressed their dissatisfaction with the excesses. Even General Haller, whose officers and men had been permitted to commit the greatest outrages with immunity, now declared that the excesses were unworthy of the Polish army. But it was too late. The poison had penetrated too deep, and the atmosphere of good-will, which alone could guarantee health and stability to the new state still bleeding from its deep wounds, was nowhere to be found.

What good-will on the part of the government could achieve is shown by Czechoslovakia,[16] whose leading statesman, Professor Masaryk, not only taught ethics but practiced ethics, and made it clear that religious persecutions would not be tolerated. Returned soldiers and legionnaires were no more angelic in his country than in others; they, too, suffered from hunger and need and seized upon every opportunity to gain booty. In Czechoslovakia, too, excesses could not be prevented — in Holleschau, Moravia, there were even a number of dead — but the government left no doubt that it condemned attacks upon life and property and that it would impose just penalties upon the guilty. It also gave the Slovak Babbits, who wished to use their new freedom to drive the Jews from their former economic positions, clearly to understand that the new state recognized no differences on grounds of religion.

In Poland it was the elementary hatred of primitive self-assertion that was revealed, but in the Ukraine[17] it was the cannibalistic bloodthirstiness of subhuman barbarians. The departure of the German troops left utter chaos; for more than two years there was no consolidated government. In addition to regular armies, detached bands roamed over the country. Many places changed masters ten times, and each victory was crowned with a foray of vengeance against the Jews. Greedy and bloodthirsty officers drove their dehumanized followers to the complete extermination of the Jews. The instincts of the *Haidamaks* were revived; there was slaughter such as neither Russian nor Jewish history had previously recorded; only the unspeakable Armenian atrocities offer a parallel.

With the fall of the German power the *Hetman* whom they supported also fell. A national Ukrainian government was formed, called the Directorium. The Bolshevists were willing for the Ukraine to remain independent provided it continued in the Union of the Soviet Socialist Republics. They sought to conquer the country with their Red Army, and the Directorium opposed them with its national army, called variously the Active Army of the Ukrainian Democratic Republic or the Ukrainian Republican Army, under the *Ataman*, S. V. Petlura. Many *Atamans* and their cossacks served under Petlura, others led their own troops. Petlura was unsuccessful, and was forced to withdraw towards the west in defeat. But the Czarist General Denikin, with the support of the Allies, assembled a volunteer army and occupied the Ukraine during the second half of 1919, when the Bolshevists drove him out. Aside from the regular fighting, bands of peasants with primitive weapons contributed to the disorder. Each of the parties attacked the Jews; the one side, because they were allegedly Bolshevist; the other, because they were anti-Bolshevist; all sides, because they were unarmed and easy to plunder. It was as if Hell had spewed forth all its fire and from all sides the flames were hurled upon the Jews.

> The recent epidemic of pogroms [says the report presented by the Committee of the Russian Red Cross of Kiev] is distinguished from those that preceded, first by its long duration, and then by its refined cruelty, the merciless thoroughness and naked bloodthirstiness with which the crimes were carried out.

All of the principal leaders disclaimed responsibility for the incredible bestiality. Petlura gave assurances that he, like the Directorium, condemned the pogroms, and Jewish partisans of the Ukrainian Peoples' Republic vouched for his innocence. But his followers have no fewer than 493 pogroms upon their conscience. Under Petlura's command was the Battalion of Death which perpetrated blood baths at the very beginning of hostilities at Ovrush, Zhitomir, and Berdichev. To his army belonged the young wastrel Simosenko, who directed the bloody battle of Proskurov, the cruelest of the campaign, with the savage Zaporog cossacks and the *haidamaks*. Simosenko made his lawless bands swear that they would not plunder but only kill, and they kept their plighted faith. In a few hours 1,600 Jews were killed in cold blood; so was a priest who appeared in his full vestments, crucifix in hand, and adjured the mob to refrain from murder. When a telegraphic order arrived from the front to put an end to the slaughter, Simosenko flippantly remarked, "All right, it will do for today," and whistled the signal which stopped the butchery in an instant. That cruelty of this sort was ingrained in the character of the Zaporog cossacks was shown by events in neighboring Felshtin, where, on the following day, blood flowed in streams and 500 dead were counted as well as 120 wounded. Of

Petlura's following also was the abominable Grigoriev, who had originally commanded a Soviet army and now distinguished himself by egregious violence.

Petlura belonged to a democratic government, which possessed a Minister for Jewish Affairs; it sharply disapproved of all these excesses, and demanded strict punishment of the guilty.[18] He promised all that was asked and issued appropriate proclamations. But nothing further happened; the evil deeds were not investigated nor the evildoers punished. It was no secret that the commander-in-chief looked with a kindly eye upon many of the excesses, and passed them off with the remark, "Let the boys have some fun." Under his eye, too, there went on an incendiary newspaper campaign whose battle cry was "Kill the Jews; save the Ukraine!" When Petlura's army moved into Kiev for a single day, August 31, 1919, his cossacks found nothing more important to do than cruelly torture and kill thirty young Jews who had been assigned by the municipality to protect the Jewish quarter. It was only when his army was driven off to Polish territory and the Poles demanded that their guests respect the local usages, and when the Ukrainian missions sought to win the support of Western European statesmen that pogroms and excesses were forbidden. Since the seriousness of the order was unmistakable, the excesses did in fact stop. On May 26, 1926, Petlura was shot down in Paris by Shalom Schwartzbard, a watchmaker originally from the Ukraine. A French jury acquitted him of the deed when the facts of the pogroms were set before them.

The Denikin movement proved to be a bitter disillusionment for the Jews. They had welcomed it at first because they had expected that it would restore a strong and orderly Russian empire. But they very soon discovered that the controlling spirit of the movement was that of the Czarist army and the Black Hundred. It began with insults and abuse of Jewish volunteers and delegates, and ended with pogroms. Not fewer than 213 pogroms were perpetrated by Denikin's army, and all were marked by unusual cruelty. The pillagers belonged to the officer class, and they stole with the refined instinct of gentlefolk for articles of value. Denikin himself expressed a devastating judgment of his following when he called them "a villainous crowd, debased morally to the lowest depths." "They were," he said, "not volunteers for the sake of a principle, but a crew made ripe for pogroms in consequence of the bestial instincts aroused by war and revolution." This "crew" has more than 5,000 dead upon its conscience; 600 in Fastov alone, and 300 in Krivoye Osero; and the numbers of violated women and girls reached enormous proportions. But Denikin could never summon courage to forbid pogroms in clear and explicit terms; his subordinates understood his position, and Mai-Maievski issued orders that localities where pogroms were impending be made ready for emergency. Denikin feared that a protest might provoke "an unnecessary turmoil" and eventually a charge that he had sold out to the Jews; yet he was not afraid to burden his conscience with so many crimes. That pogroms were not a natural necessity was proven by Generals Wrangel and Kolchak who suppressed them in the White armies which they commanded.

The Bolshevist Red Army was also responsible for more than a hundred pogroms, but with them plunder rather than murder was the main objective. Similarly, the principal motive of the peasant bands was robbery, but their want of discipline and primitive brutality spared neither the lives of men nor the honor of women. The tragic balance sheet[19] of this year of fury no one can read without a deep shudder.

Hundreds of thousands of Jews have been robbed of their last shirt; hundreds of thousands have been maltreated, wounded, humiliated; tens of thousands have been massacred. Thousands of Jewish women became the victims of bestial instincts of savage hordes. Hundreds of thousands of Jewish women are haunted daily by the one idea that to-morrow they will no longer be able to hold their heads erect. The panic which seized on the Jewish population of these regions is without precedent in all history.... The Jewish masses in the Ukraine are on the verge of madness, and many have actually lost their reason.

These unfortunate beings, having lost all that makes life worth living, their nearest, their homes, everything they had, all means of existence, mutilated physically and broken morally, how can they solve the problem of their existence? Where are they to find a shelter? How to save the children from dying of starvation and cold, and all the accompanying miseries?

To these desperate questions of the report of the Red Cross, the people in the United States sought to provide a positive answer, insofar as it was possible to do so in the face of such overwhelming woe. This was no matter for political protests, for where there was no responsible government the best will of the administration in Washington could attain no results. The greatest pressure the United States could exert was through its large-scale relief work. It proved it could produce not words alone but deeds also for the welfare and healing of suffering humanity. Under the direction of Herbert C. Hoover, later President (1929-1933), the American Relief Administration[20] was organized and its work of deliverance in the affected regions was greeted as a miracle from heaven. The Joint Distribution Committee was able to fit its work into that of this organization and so overcome the enormous difficulties of communication and financial exchange which confronted operations in Central, Eastern, and Southern Europe.

In the first five years after the war $47,000,000 were collected by the Joint Distribution Committee for relief purposes, and in addition large sums were remitted to individuals by private drafts. The representatives of the Joint Distribution Committee, who traveled about the regions of Europe smitten by famine and pestilence, worked with self-sacrificing devotion. Two of them, both in the flower of their years, Israel Friedlaender, a distinguished scholar (born 1876), and Bernard Cantor (born 1892), were attacked and murdered by bandits in southern Russia in the summer of 1920.

In addition to the distribution of food, clothing and medicaments, attention was given to the disinfection of persons and houses from dirt and bacilli, to the restoration of water supply and bathing arrangements, to the establishment of clinics, and to the provision of physicians, dentists and nurses. Special attention was devoted to saving the children who had been so badly abused. Under the leadership of the Independent Order B'nai B'rith adoption of orphans (sixty per cent were full orphans) was arranged for, and support and education in the new or the old world was assured them. In Poland and the Ukraine itself help was given by organizations like the OSE[21] (*Obtschestwo Sdravoochraneniya Evreyev*—"Society for the Protection of the Health of the Jews"). For years this organization had worked in the field of child protection and child care; it had experienced and trained personnel, and devoted itself to careful popular instruction in hygienic requirements.

A pressing problem was offered by the hundreds of thousands of refugees who had escaped from the pogrom regions or had fled from Russia and the Baltic provinces before the Bolshevists. Numbers of them wandered about the highways not knowing where they could find rest. Their problem was made more difficult by the fact that it was impossible for most of them to obtain the documents necessary for emigration. In Eastern Europe registers of birth and death were not always carefully kept, and even in normal times it was difficult to procure adequate documents in those regions. But now so many official buildings and records had been destroyed during the war and the confusion following upon it, that transcripts were not obtainable, and inhabitants who might have given oral information were so scattered that they could not be counted upon. The United States, the traditional haven of refuge, was not yet barred. Jewish immigration, which had declined greatly during the last year of the war and amounted only to 14,292 in 1920, reached the high figure of 119,036 in 1921; but there was already a strong anti-alien sentiment. Canada, Argentina, and South Africa, each took a certain percentage of refugees annually, but the number was far from sufficient to meet the pressing need. Large resources of money and a separate organization seemed essential to overcome the crucial problem. The Jewish World Relief Conference was organized in Carlsbad, Bohemia, in August 1920. Its purpose was to do work like that of the Joint Distribution Committee in Central, Eastern, and Southeastern Europe, and it succeeded in a limited degree. In 1921, together with the Hebrew Immigrant Aid Society and other associations working in a similar direction, it founded the organization called EMIGDIREKT, the United Committee for Jewish Emigration. The Joint Distribution Committee and the Jewish Colonization Association, which had held back at first, now took part in the new enterprise, and the combined forces brought a pause in the catastrophe. Among their other tasks they had to create transit facilities through the many new states.

Minority Rights

The Peace Conference continued its consultations in Paris for six months, until the basis for the new treaties was reached. They were called after the Treaty of Versailles which Germany was forced to sign (June 28, 1919), for that treaty contains the basic principles which controlled the treaties with the smaller states which followed. After a mere twenty years that treaty already belonged to ancient history, nor can one say of it *de mortuis nil nisi bene*.[22] It brought to the world not peace but unrest,

POGROMS AND TREATIES OF PEACE

for it was built not only upon hatred and vengeance, but, what was much worse, upon untruth and unrighteousness. The "principles of justice, liberty, and tolerance" were only emblems for outward show; they were not the principles which informed the peace.

It was inevitable that in the expected formation and expansion of states the Jewish question should come under discussion.[23] The number of Jews in the areas under consideration was large; their situation had always been precarious, and the war had proved it to be completely untenable. Whatever the Jews did, however they expressed or conducted themselves, it was always interpreted to their disadvantage. And what would it be now when the newly formed states, in the heady intoxication of freedom, would cast aside all restraints upon their nationalism and themselves take up the policy of suppressing foreign nationalities under which they had themselves so long groaned? The Czechs declared the Jews were Germans; the Slovaks, Rumanians; the Croats declared they were Magyars; the Poles declared they were Russians and Germans; and so it went. But the overwhelming majority of Jews in those countries maintaining complete loyalty to the state, wished nothing more than to remain Jews, constituting a separate group in religion, language, dress and usages. There was another problem. In a city like Vienna there lived 200,000 Jews from all parts of the Austro-Hungarian monarchy, because of the right of free movement which the constitution guaranteed all citizens. But now that the empire was broken up and ten different nationalities created, would the city in which the Jews had become rooted continue to recognize them as citizens and tolerate their continuing active? One needs only to cite a small segment of reality to recognize the problematical character of the situation. The problem could only be dealt with by international agreement.

Other sections of the population, to be sure, were confronted with the same difficulty and could not transfer their loyalty overnight. But of them consideration was taken, and time was allowed. Furthermore, each of them had a "big brother" who could stand behind it and make his power felt. But the Jews had no "big brother;" in every country they were a minority. Everyone made demands of them, and their right to exist was seldom recognized.

Eastern Europe, the region which embraced the most numerous Jewish settlements, was now being put on a new basis of national rights, and the fitting moment had come to state the rights of the Jews, not only as individuals but as a group. Success in the Palestine question had aroused a chimerical hope in the leading minds in Zionism that the Jews would be recognized as one of the small nations and admitted upon an equal footing with them into the counsels of the Peace Conference. On October 25, 1918, Zionist Headquarters issued the Copenhagen Manifesto[24] in which it stated Zionist demands upon the Peace Conference. Aside from the establishment of a National Home in Palestine and full equality for Jews of all countries, two points which no one disputed, the Manifesto also demanded "national autonomy, cultural, social and political rights for the Jewish population of countries largely settled by Jews, as well as of all other countries whose Jewish population demands it, and admission into the League of Free Nations."

The effect of the Manifesto was that everywhere in Eastern Europe "Jewish National Councils" were formed and demanded the recognition of the Jews as a national minority. The delegates they sent to Paris organized themselves into a *Comité des Délégations Juives auprès de la Conférence de la Paix*.[25] Their aspirations were resolutely opposed by the *Alliance Israélite Universelle*, and the Jewry of France for which it spoke. The *Alliance* and French Jewry would hear absolutely nothing of national rights, and advocated only the recognition of Jews as a religious community. The French were joined by the English delegates, who, however, asked that the minorities be granted "the autonomous management of their religious, educational, charitable, and other cultural institutions."[26]

The extremes were to a certain extent reconciled in the position of the *Agudat Yisrael* and the American delegation. In the United States proposals for establishing an American Jewish Congress,[27] which should discuss Jewish demands in the future reconstitution of Europe, were heard at the very beginning of the war. Friends and foes of the Congress idea agreed that it should be called at the end of hostilities when steps towards a peace conference were in prospect. The respectable number of 335,000 ballots were voted for delegates, and the Congress met in Philadelphia on December 15, 1918. Judge Julian W. Mack, Brandeis' successor as president of the Zionist Federation, became its president, and Louis Marshall, president of the American Jewish Committee, one of its vice-presidents. Stephen S. Wise, whose dynamic personality was coming to the fore in the leadership of Jewish affairs, exerted a great influence upon the Congress. The conclusions of the Congress, which were given expression in resolutions designated as a Bill of Rights, are summarized in the petition which was submitted to the United States delegates to the Peace Conference. They were asked

to use their high and kindly office to the end that it shall be made a condition precedent to the grant of autonomy, independence or freedom to any nation or land, that all the inhabitants thereof shall have equal civil, political, religious and national rights without distinction of race or faith and that such rights shall be guaranteed to them and their descendants in perpetuity.

To the leaders of the American Jewish delegation goes the credit for avoiding the spectacle of an open collision between opposing Jewish demands and for finding a common platform upon which the various delegations could unite.[28] Of recognition as a national minority, as they soon discovered, there could be no question. Not even President Wilson could be won for such a view, to say nothing of the representatives of any of the nations affected. The minorities of whom it was expected that cognizance would be taken belonged in the main to the conquered nations, and no victor nation was inclined to grant such concessions to them. The Jews differed from all minorities in that they made no territorial claims and so offered no problem of irredentists. Still it seemed highly inadvisable to the statesmen to grant the Jews the invidious distinction of forming a state within a state and thus perpetuating the hatred against them.

But it was evident to all that the minorities could not be left to the caprice of the new governments after all that had happened. The Jewish delegates worked hard in the interest of all minorities. It is due to their insistence on the recognition of full equality that the new states were forced to undertake an obligation[29]

> to embody in a treaty with the principal Allied and Associated Powers such provisions as may be deemed necessary by the said powers to protect the interests of inhabitants of that State who differ from the majority of the population in race, language or religion. [The detailed provisions of the treaties] affecting persons belonging to racial, religious, or linguistic minorities shall be recognized as fundamental laws; they constitute obligations of international concern and shall be placed under the guarantee of the League of Nations.

These basic provisions were accepted in the treaties with Poland, Austria, Hungary, Czechoslovakia, the Serb-Croat-Slovene State (Yugoslavia), Bulgaria, Rumania, and Greece. States which had been formed without the blessing of the Peace Conference, such as Lithuania, Latvia, Estonia, and Finland, could only be admitted as members of the League of Nations if they solemnly pledged themselves to respect the rights of minorities.

In addition to the general provisions, individual treaties had particular provisions, made necessary by special conditions in the countries concerned. Thus in the treaty with Greece[30] the Jewish Sabbath was officially recognized as the day of rest for the Jews of Saloniki:

> In towns and districts where there is resident a considerable proportion of Greek nationals of the Jewish religion, the Jews should not be disturbed in the observance of their Sabbath.

In the treaty with Rumania[31] a clause provided that

> All persons born in Rumanian territory who are not born nationals of another State shall *ipso facto* become Rumanian nationals.

And on express provision was subjoined:

> Rumania undertakes to recognize as Rumanian nationals *ipso facto* and without the requirement of any formality Jews inhabiting any Rumanian territory, who do not possess another nationality.

The Rumanian statesmen objected to this provision vigorously, on the grounds that they had intended of their own accord to grant extensive rights, but when the Allies remained firm the Rumanians did not refuse their signature.

The fullest assurances were employed in the case of Poland[32] where it was expected that some 3,000,000 Jews, more than 10% of the population, would be affected. The first provision was against the limitation of the use of languages other than Polish:

> No restriction shall be imposed on the free use by any Polish national of any language in private intercourse, in commerce, in religion, in the press or in publications of any kind, or at public meetings. Notwithstanding any establishment by the Polish Government of an official language, adequate facilities shall be given to Polish nationals of non-Polish speech for the use of their language, either orally or in writing, before the courts.

The assurance of civic rights was broadened by the provision that minorities

> shall have an equal right to establish, manage and control at their own expense charitable, religious and social institutions, schools and other

educational establishments, with the right to use their own language and to exercise their religion freely therein.

Furthermore the government was obligated to assure the minorities instruction in their own language and

where there is a considerable proportion of Polish nationals belonging to racial, religious or linguistic minorities, these minorities shall be assured an equitable share in the enjoyment and application of the sums which may be provided out of public funds under the State, municipal or other budget, for educational, religious or charitable purposes.

And so that there could be no doubt that the provisions mentioned were to apply to the Jews also, an express statement was added:

Educational Committees appointed locally by the Jewish communities of Poland will, subject to the general control of the State, provide for the distribution of the proportional share of public funds allocated to Jewish schools . . . and for the organization and management of these schools. The provisions . . . concerning the use of language in schools shall apply to these schools.

Finally it was provided — naturally with the exception of military service — that Jews could not be forced to violate their Sabbath or be made to suffer any injury whatever by reason of their observance of the Sabbath. Permission to work on Sunday instead of on the Sabbath was refused.

The treaty between the Allies and Poland firmly anchored the principle of equality of all minorities and of the Jews, as individuals and as a group. It assured the provisions growing out of this principle against circumvention or wilful alteration. It refused, indeed, to recognize national minorities as political entities and to allow them proportional representation as such; it avoided anything which might be interpreted as a relaxation of the structure of the state. Yet anyone concerned with substance rather than slogans could only acknowledge that all conceivable guarantees for their own cultural and religious existence, the concrete goal of all Jewish national programs, were here secured. Nahum Sokolow agreed with the American leaders that the treaties were a huge success, for they "at last absolved the Jews of Eastern Europe from the serious disabilities from which they have so long suffered and will forever end the grave abuse of the past. They will enable the Jews as well as all other minorities to live their own lives and to develop their own culture."[33]

For the Poles the bitter pill was sweetened by a personal communication from Georges Clemenceau which urged the analogy of previous treaties and the needs of the immediate situation.[34] Nevertheless the Poles continued their obstructionist tactics and only at the last moment decided to put their signatures to the treaty which was set before them. But the conditions which had been imposed upon them seemed so frightening that none of the remaining states would accept the religious and cultural provisions. In a personal conversation courtesies were exchanged between Paderewski and the Jewish delegates, and it appeared "that a better era was now dawning."[35] But it was only the laws and not the people that were changed, and so this hope was not fulfilled.

CHAPTER III

The Jews of Europe in the Post-War Era

Antisemitism and Reconstruction

OVER Europe of the post-war era there hovered not the spirit of Woodrow Wilson but the shadow of Adolf Hitler. After 1917 the war aim of all forward-looking men had been: neither victors nor vanquished. The peace negotiations knew only victors; reality only vanquished.[1] The stretches of desolated countryside, the numerous mass burials, the many monuments to the Unknown Soldier, constituted a flaming indictment against the crime of war. The outlook of the generation that had lived through these horrors was profoundly shaken; all feeling of confidence and of security had perished. Disillusion was so complete that energy for reconstruction could hardly be summoned. Reconstruction was made difficult because the men who made the Peace of Versailles had mortally injured the heart of Europe without realizing that the injury must affect the entire organism. And independent of all negotiations the Russian colossus had gone its own way, had set itself upon a new social and economic platform, had separated itself from the family of nations. The attitude of the nations towards Russia was equivocal; they abhorred the Russian revolution, but were eager for Russian markets. They repelled Russian statesmen, but enticed Russian commercial representations.

War and Bolshevism, then, were the two factors which produced unrest in the world. But because the world lacked the faculty of self-examination it required a scapegoat, and following primordial habit it found one in the Jews. And so it came about that the post-war era, which proclaimed that the world was to be rebuilt with justice and good-will, saw also the sudden resurgence of the Jewish question and the rise of hatred in forms which had not been heard of since the days of the Spanish Inquisition. Nerves which had been strained by war and starvation were receptive to any hallucination.

Seeking for an alibi, the eminent strategist, General Erich Ludendorff,[2] who was completely lacking in a sense of political reality and of truth, discovered the explanation that Germany's defeat had been brought about by a stab in the back. The unhappy people who had been quite unexpectedly hurled from their proud hopes of victory to the abyss of defeat —"we have been lied to and duped," exclaimed the leader of the Prussian Junkers — clung to this myth and planned vengeance upon the enemies that had been pointed out to it: the radicals and the Jews. Circles dispossessed by the revolution contributed to the cost, the propaganda machine of the war period which was still intact was set into motion, and the remotest villages were stirred up by agitators. There was a hail of broadsides with forged talmudic citations calculated to demonstrate the faithlessness and the treachery of the Jews. Even where hatred of Germany persisted, there was eagerness to consume this product of German manufacture and to use it in rousing passions against the Jews.[3]

The anti-Jewish canards gained credit in view of the depressing news of destruction and cruelty which came out of Soviet Russia. It was a commonplace that Bolshevism was nothing but a Jewish conspiracy,[4] and the Jewish names of Bolshevist leaders were made to serve as irrefutable proof. This is not the place to examine the causes and methods of so complicated a phenomenon as

Bolshevism, nor is it our task to exculpate the adherence of certain Jews to the movement. No one considered that men like Trotzky (Bronstein), Radek (Sobelsohn), Zinoviev (Radomislowsky), Kamenev (Rosenfeld), regarded themselves not as Jews but as representatives of the international proletariat, nor that their influence was eclipsed by that of Lenin and Kalinin, of Stalin and Bucharin. Here the Jew was trapped, the Jew as revolutionary, the Jew as conspirator, the Jew as Antichrist!

Russian monarchists who journeyed through the world stirring up hatred, took care that these charges should be substantiated by "authentic" documents in black and white. They carried in their bags copies of the *Protocols of the Elders of Zion*.[5] These they offered to Jews for large sums and, when the Jews could not be cozened, they sold them to their enemies. This criminal conflation, of whose origin we have already spoken (p. 377), purported to contain a plan for a Jewish conspiracy to destroy and dominate the world, and Bolshevism was alleged to be nothing else than the phase of the plan which aimed at world revolution. Immediately after the armistice translations of this Russian fabrication appeared in France and England, in Germany and Poland; and although lie was written upon its face and its falsity was immediately demonstrated by Christian scholars and journalists,[6] it was widely read and believed. Even in so mad a period no huge reading public could be expected for such insanity, and so it was popularized[7] and expounded in periodical articles and confirmed by pseudo-scholarly historical excursuses on the misdeeds of Jews and Freemasons. In many countries the Freemasons would not even accept Jews as members, but by a method practiced by some Catholic writers they were indiscriminately drawn into the whirlpool as followers and accomplices of the Jews.

Sergei Nilus, the remarkable devotee who published the *Protocols* several times and each time with a different account of their origin, apologized for not being able to demonstrate their genuineness and provenance completely: "We must not search for direct evidence." Search is indeed otiose, for the model of the *Protocols* from which all their wisdom was borrowed was discovered in 1921. It was the *Dialogue aux enfers entre Machiavel et Montesquieu ou la Politique de Machiavel au XIXme siècle*, which had appeared anonymously in Brussels in 1864. The author, Maurice Joly, a non-Jew, criticized the policies of Napoleon III. The book was later turned into Russian by agents of the Russian secret police working in Paris, in order to be used in making charges against the Jews before the Czar. These facts were proven beyond doubt, yet the *Protocols* found an ever increasing public; there was no European language into which they were not translated, no country in which they were not exploited. Even in the United States, as we shall see, they played a fatal role; they were exported to Japan and China, and the Arabs in Egypt and Palestine were provided with them. What was at work was not an Internationale of Jews but an Internationale against Jews, not a conspiracy of Jews but a conspiracy against them. The *Protocols* became the basic text of Nazism; it was according to the formula of the *Protocols* that Nazism set about subjugating the world.

But first they poisoned men's minds against Jews everywhere. In every country there existed or came into being groups who welcomed political retrogression and hailed this means for deceiving the people. The same Jews who had lately fought shoulder to shoulder with their countrymen were now branded as traitors and conspirators. Not only was this true in Germany, which had been humbled and needed a whipping-boy, but also in the western democracies which had annihilated their rival. A century earlier a principal argument for recognizing the Jews in France[8] was "their blood has mingled with ours;" but now a narrow nationalism worked for the separation of the Jews. A century earlier the spokesman of public opinion in England was Thomas Babington Macaulay, who marshalled powerful arguments for regarding the Jews as British citizens. The spokesman for contemporary English opinion was Hilaire Belloc,[9] who never wearied of emphasizing the danger in the Jews and their foreignness and who advocated their separation from the state. His book, *The Jews* (1922), is crafty and deceptive, "wise as serpents, harmless as doves." There is one truth in this untruthful book, the observation that the age of liberalism, of tolerance, and of the recognition of the rights of man was past.

In their place racial doctrines[10] occupied the foreground. Not only the color of the skin but the contours of the skull, the shape of the nose, pigmentation of the hair and eyes, determined the capacities of peoples for cultural and moral excellence. Observations of natural science were forged into a political weapon. Count Gobineau had proclaimed the revelation and Houston Stuart Chamberlain was his prophet. Each people, the Germans foremost among them, so ordered its imaginary scheme that it occupied the highest rung on the stepladder of race: it, that is, and its current allies. When Germany hated Poland, the Slavs were inferior beings; when it sought their alliance, then not Germans only but all Aryans constituted the noble race; and when the Japanese came to support the crimes of the Axis, they were promoted to the rank of yellow Aryans. Germany showed the greatest zeal in transforming this pseudo-science into a religion. One of its dogmas was the inferiority of the Jewish race, and innumerable pens were set into motion to spread this doctrine among the nations. Racial teaching spread like an epidemic. The stand of serious anthropological science was a matter of indifference; it was cried down by the clamor of political hirelings.

One of the few fields in which men of varying origin and philosophy could still work together was the youth movement.[11] Along with the growth of the youth movement generally, the Jewish youth movement increased in extent and energy after the war in all the continental countries of Europe; Great Britain did not participate fully in the Jewish youth movement, though it was the home of the Scout movement. The movement showed great inclusiveness; all tendencies from the most radical to the most conservative were represented in it. But certain aspects of the movement, corresponding to the general characteristics of youth, were universal. Among these was the cultivation of sport, which now became a considerable factor in Jewish life. Among these also was a rebellion against traditional ways of living, against the concentration of Jews in cities and in a limited number of callings. Youth demanded a bond with nature and a preference for all kinds of handwork, which implied a far-reaching change in occupation. With inconsiderable exceptions, therefore, the youth movement was interested in the upbuilding of Palestine. This was true not only of the world-wide organization of *He-Ḥalutz* which made work in Palestine its goal, but also of the *Union Universelle de la Jeunesse Juive* directed by Aimée Pallière in Paris, and of the majority of the Jewish youth organizations in Germany.

The supposed solidarity and power of the Jews was at the furthest remove from the actual situation. They were in a state of frightful wretchedness, and there was a deplorable lack of a feeling of cohesion. The number of war profiteers among them appeared disproportionately large, for Jews were preponderantly engaged in commerce, and the newly-rich made themselves especially conspicuous. They were not alone of their kind. In his *Between Two Worlds*, Upton Sinclair has shown the sort of drones that swarmed over every corner of Europe where gain or pleasure was to be pursued. The fortunes of the Jews were not stable[12] and could not survive a crisis. For the greater part they disappeared as quickly as they were won. Older fortunes too suffered enormous devaluation; one need only think of the liquidation of all private property in Russia.

The great masses who were desperately poor before the war now had to drain the cup of suffering to the dregs. The last remnants of their furnishings and clothing were gone. In their search for bread many wandered footloose in strange countries and met the cold reception of strangers. To appreciate the situation one need only read such reports as those of the officials of the Joint Distribution Committee on the lamentable plight of Jewish refugees from the East in Paris.[13] They were hungry and cold, and were brusquely turned away by the native Jews because the latter feared that the presence of these foreign and tattered figures would occasion an increase of Jew-hatred.

The situation in Germany was worse. There the census of 1920 had shown an increase in the number of Jews[14] from the amputated territory of the Reich, because many Jews from Alsace-Lorraine and practically all of the Jews from the provinces ceded to Poland had migrated to Germany. Because of the geographical situation of Germany it was inevitable that many refugees from the eastern countries settled there, some prosperous and so welcome, others needy and so regarded as an added burden to the prevalent poverty. The antisemitic propaganda played this up, and was echoed by the Association of National German Jews,[15] which, "while frankly acknowledging their descent, felt themselves so indissolubly fused with German character and German culture that they could not feel and think otherwise than as Germans." The Association rejected "any historical or cultural community with the millions of Jews who, despite their dispersion over the globe, had retained a common religious and national consciousness." The Association declared that the question of the eastern Jews and their immigration was not a Jewish but a German problem. It demanded of the Zionists that they emigrate or consider themselves foreigners.

The membership of the Association was not large, but their social position made their influence great. It could not exert much influence upon the German government, whose tendency was democratic; but it promoted the agitation of the circles of the Right and worked much harm by its provocative stand. It was the most alarming but not the only example of the anti-Jewish obstructionism of wealthy Jews.

The voice of reaction, which had fallen to a whisper because of the collapse of the Reich, quickly rose to new strength. Discharged officers and retired officials swelled the numbers of the discontented, and deposed princes and big industry footed the bills for agitation. The Jews served as a centripetal object of propaganda. The Weimar Republic[16] with its democratic constitution was called the Jews' Republic; the black, red and gold flag, which had been selected to represent Germany and Austria, the Jews' banner; and the government, regardless of whether Jews sat in it or not, the Jews' government.

To make difficulties for this government, to promote its collapse, to supplant the "Jewish" spirit with the Teutonic, was looked upon as a national duty. Adolf Hitler's small but constantly growing National German Workers' Party (Nazi) was a typical expression of this mood. The antisemitism of the post-war period had a national rather than religious direction; its primary emphasis was on racial differences. It did not ask whether a Jew was useful, whether his work was helpful or not; it demanded his complete exclusion from state and society. Its methods were the methods of rowdyism then current.

Walter Rathenau, first as Minister of Reconstruction and then as Foreign Minister, had made the first successful attempts to reach a rapprochement with the former enemies of Germany; popular songs were made to incite hatred of Rathenau, until he was foully shot down by cowardly assassins (June 24, 1922). The system as well as the man was the object of the attack. The state funeral which was granted him, perhaps the only such ever granted a Jew, served at the same time as a demonstration for strengthening the republic.

How completely confidence in its stability was shaken was shown by the events which followed immediately. The governing classes in France, whose mouthpiece was Raymond Poincaré, proceeded in a vindictive and arrogant mood to the utter ruin of Germany. The occupation of various German cities, particularly in the Ruhr region, followed the plummet-like and bottomless fall of German currency. It was the expression of the unspeakable confusion and depression that Adolf Hitler, with the assistance of Erich Ludendorff, could venture upon his burlesque beer-hall *Putsch* (November 9, 1923) which, to be sure, laid the popular specter for several years. It was inevitable that the catastrophe brought to the German monetary system by the inflation[17] was entered upon the debit account of the Jews. It was a fact that a small number of Jews, particularly from the eastern ghetto, foresaw the situation and estimated the value of the German mark more accurately than did the leading statesmen and financiers. But it is also a fact that the great mass of Jewish merchants and industrialists did not possess this foresight and lost all their possessions. The middle classes and the not inconsiderable number of widows and others who lived upon fixed incomes, all, in fact, who had their property invested in sound securities, were completely impoverished. The Jewish congregations not only lost their funds but were now called upon to extend their benefactions to classes that had formerly themselves lavishly given to charitable causes and never expected to be supported by them. The Independent Order B'nai B'rith, whose membership was composed principally of well-to-do merchants and professional men, had always stoutly maintained the principle, "Nothing for ourselves, everything for others;" now, so insistent were the demands for help, it realized that charity must begin at home.

Spiritual Reconstruction

As by a miracle Germany recovered economically, and even experienced some years of prosperity. In a highly capitalized and cartellized economy the Jewish merchant and industrialist never again attained the position he had held before the war, but, insofar as he was not excluded from the normal economic processes, he began to prosper again and even accumulate fortunes. He showed a praiseworthy willingness to sacrifice and put considerable sums at the disposal of Jewish congregations and their federations of charities.[18] The communities were able to carry the increased burden of the poor; in addition to their old tasks they could devote greater care to the health of underprivileged children, and could undertake more intensive work for youth and adult education.

The Jews organized state associations (*Landesverbände*)[19] which kept up a constant activity, especially in maintaining the religious life in small communities which without such assistance would be doomed to extinction. They were active in promoting religious and cultural enterprises generally, cared for the maintenance of institutions for training rabbis and teachers, and promoted work in Jewish scholarship. So, for example, they assisted in the establishment of the *Akademie für die Wissenschaft des Judentums* (founded in 1919).[20] They cooperated with the national association of front line veterans in the settlement of retired soldiers upon farms, an undertaking which quickly proved successful. They were the official representatives of the Jewish community in governmental matters; the prevailing democratic administration was inclined to recognize the Jewish religion as on a par with the Christian denominations in every respect. The Weimar Constitution made it possible for a number of state associations to organize into an autonomous corporation and to enjoy the advantage of a legally recognized body. It was the fault of the representatives of the Prussian communities that such a corporation was not formed; they could not summon the energy, as the South German associations could, to ignore petty party differences and to unite on fundamental principles.

Unity was the pressing need of the hour, for Judaism was surrounded by foes upon all sides. The frontal attack of the opponents of the Weimar Republic was directed primarily against them. Even if the splendor of Hitler's star had proved transitory, there were enough racialists and other anti-democratic forces at work to destroy the Jews. Every crime of any individual Jew was inflated to the proportions of a great scandal and served as potent propaganda material. Excesses against Jews and desecrations of synagogues and cemeteries were frequent occurrences, although officials and courts of justice were strict in meting out punishment. Despite increasing popular hatred, the number of mixed marriages increased from year to year. In another direction communism worked for the disintegration of Judaism and attempted to convince the young in particular that their future could be secure only on the side of Moscow.

Nevertheless, this heavily battered Central European Jewry did not succumb; on the contrary, it again won the spiritual hegemony in Judaism. Berlin, Vienna and Prague were the clearing houses for Jewish cultural currency. Germany and Austria led in Jewish publications, quantitatively and qualitatively.

The disintegrating forces — not forgetting certain extravagances in art and literature — were compensated for by centripetal currents. The post-war generation was distinguished by self-respect and earnest concern about the Jewish future. The upbuilding of Palestine combined Zionists and non-Zionists in an enterprise of practical idealism which stirred the imagination. *Noblesse oblige* constrained Jews who had obtained high positions in public life not to withdraw from Jewish leadership. If Nobel Prize winners like Albert Einstein in Berlin, Richard Willstätter in Munich and a luminary like Sigmund Freud in Vienna professed their Jewish affiliation, if a writer of Jakob Wassermann's rank struggled along his way as German and Jew and wholeheartedly affirmed each, their example could not fail to impress the cultured classes and especially the young generation.

The latter found spiritual guides of stature. Franz Rosenzweig (1886–1929), prematurely cut off by a sickness contracted during the war and becoming a legendary personality, exercised an enormous influence. In his principal work, *Stern der Erlösung* ("Star of Redemption"), he placed revelation at the center of his religious system and insisted upon the revitalization of old-fashioned Jewish learning. He found a numerous following.

He became the leading pioneer of a new Jewish type who fused into a new unity the practical devotion to Jewish ritual characteristic of the Orthodox, the freedom and incisive thinking characteristic of the Liberals, and the inner bond with the people and the land of Israel characteristic of the Zionists.[21]

Together with Martin Buber (born 1878)[22] he undertook a new translation of Scriptures. Their goal was twofold: to render the Jewish concept of the biblical word faithfully, and to present it in a German form which should correspond to the highest demands of language and of style. Their version was enthusiastically received by Jewish youth of all wings, but no less gratefully welcomed by educated Christians. Buber dedicated his best energies to influencing Jewish youth and to training them to an inwardly conceived and seriously realized Jewish life centered around the new Palestine. Like him, Leo Baeck (born 1873)[23] by his thoughts and his personality exercised great influence upon wide circles, Jewish and non-Jewish alike. The number of important posts of honor which were bestowed upon him is an indication of the extraordinary confidence reposed in him. Since Moses Mendelssohn no representative of the Jewish view of life had attained so broad and so cordial a recognition. In Prague the circle formed around Hugo Bergmann, Max Brod and Siegfried Weltsch worked zealously for the clarification of the spiritual and religious problems of Judaism.[24]

In France the Jews of Alsace-Lorraine felt at home on their return and needed no adjustment. From about 1924 the immigration of Jews from Eastern Europe increased; they brought with them new organizations and new problems. Paris became headquarters of world-wide Jewish organizations like the *Comité des Délégations Juives*, the ORT, the OSE which joined the *Alliance*, the Jewish Colonization Association and the HICEM. Paris once more was the heart of the world; yet the Jewish pulse beat slowly notwithstanding the stirring poetry of André Spire and the expressive paintings of Marc Chagall. Religious personalities like the former Catholic, Aimée Pallière, and the assimilated Jew, Edmond Fleg, told of their innermost religious experiences, but the inspiration of their writings was felt more deeply outside than inside France.[25]

In England the first "Pastoral Tour" of the Jewish communities of the British Overseas Dominions (1920) helped to bind together the Jewish communities of the Empire and to stimulate their religious activities. Chief Rabbi J. H. Hertz, who made the tour, was always on the alert to spread knowledge about Judaism and to prevent any offense to Jewish religion. A religious genius was vouchsafed on the community in Claude G. Montefiore (1858-1938), but a thinker of his unbending liberalism was not the type to attract a large following in that conservative country. He was too noble a soul to antagonize other men's convictions; persuasion was his weapon, not polemic. The World Union for Progressive Judaism, which was founded under his aegis in 1926, did not attain its proper place within the Jewish hierarchy; it lacked the militant zeal of other similar organizations.

The saddest victim of the peace treaties was German Austria and its capital Vienna.[26] It was as if an organism had had its ribs amputated and had then been condemned to continue a vegetative existence. Yet no possibility for continuing existence was provided. Sooner or later the state was doomed to collapse of exhaustion. It staggered under the enormous burden of an army and an administrative organization suitable for a great power, with provision for communication, commerce and finance based upon a huge hinterland that no longer existed. More than 90% of the Jewish population of approximately 200,000 souls lived in the capital and were more sharply affected than the Christians by the constriction of the country's vital arteries. The abysmal fall of the imperial city condemned this community to death by starvation.

The savior of the community's spirit was its chief rabbi, Hirsch Perez Chajes[27] (1876-1927), who had been brought to Vienna shortly before the collapse. Chajes was a scholar enormously erudite in Jewish and general learning and naturally inclined to scientific research. But he recognized it as his duty to steer the craft of his community through the raging storm. The bookworm became an organizer and social servant on a grand scale. "Day and night he labored, not only for the poor, that they might live, but for the well-to-do, that they might be spared political intrigue and persecution." Youth had the principal place in his affections. In cooperation with Anitta Müller (later Mrs. Cohen), a woman of singular energy and deftness in social work, he provided that thousands of starved children should enjoy long holidays abroad where they could have better nourishment and grow robust. He organized a Jewish school system and by the foundation of his *Paedagogium*, which was imbued with his spirit and guided by his enthusiasm, he made Vienna the focal point for training Hebrew teachers for Eastern Europe and Palestine.

The equality of rights guaranteed by the constitution was faithfully observed in Austria.[28] The Social Democrats possessed a stable majority in Vienna. Among their leaders was Hugo Breitner, whose model housing projects called forth universal admiration. The Christian-Socialists strove for a Christian class state, but in view of Austria's dependence upon the League of Nations they could not oppose the constitution. After 1927 social peace in Austria was undermined; a mighty decision seemed probable and imminent. The situation was rendered more critical by chronic economic crises which became acute after 1931. Various great financial scandals, in which adventurous speculators of Jewish descent were involved, turned public opinion sharply against the Jews. But the constitution was transformed only in 1934, when Hitler was already knocking at the gates. In the internal struggles of the *Israelitische Kultusgemeinde* the Zionists attained a majority in 1927. They directed the community in accordance with their principles, and when the new constitution demanded national differentiation, the Zionists made the process easier.

The Struggle for Survival in the Succession States

The Eastern succession and the Baltic states had one thing in common: contrary to the obligations upon which they had entered, both oppressed their minorities.[29] They assumed the bearing of nations united in race, although even in 1930–1931, after much had been done to "improve" statistics, Czechoslovakia still showed 33%, Poland 31%, Rumania 28%, and Latvia 26% of "foreign" populations. They regarded citizens of a different race or religion, not as national comrades who were to cooperate in the upbuilding of the new state, but as enemies, to be eliminated as far as possible. To be sure, the peace negotiations had assured all citizens of equality, and these assurances were ratified by the constitutions. But a man cannot quiet his hunger with the right of voting or of free assembly, and the leaders of the new states were cleverer than the great statesmen of Versailles in that they realized that national economy afforded them the amplest opportunities for oppressing their minorities.[30] It was particularly easy, in the case of a minority with an occupational distribution as one-sided as that of the Jews, to use economic repression to deprive them of the oxygen which they required for life.

The economic aspects of the peace treaties were the worst. The disparate sections carved out of a large entity could only survive if they could live peacefully with one another and cooperate in the upbuilding of their countries, which were naturally poor and now completely impoverished as a result of the war. But events proved such cooperation impossible. The hostile brothers thought it necessary to confront each other armed to the teeth, and burdened their peoples with heavy expenditures for well-equipped but unproductive armies. In addition they set up customs barriers against one another; each wished to establish a national economy, and, since the hinterland requisite to such an economy was wanting, such an economy could only be achieved by means of state subventions, which put another unnecessary burden upon the people. In all of these states national economy meant exclusion of minorities, and, except in Czechoslovakia, exclusion of Jews. Jews could count neither on state subventions nor on credit at the state banks, and they could not obtain contracts from the state or its subdivisions. The spread and increase of state capitalism barred the Jews from considerable areas of commerce, industry and finance.

Many had gained their livelihood in retail trade, and these were now pushed to the wall by the newly established cooperatives which were encouraged by the state. The cooperatives were an intelligible and legitimate economic development, which would have had a greater justification if they had worked out to the equal advantage of all citizens, including the Jews. Many citizens found employment as officials or workers for the state and the communes, but only in the rarest instances were Jews so employed. Occasionally an individual Jew would be called to some high post, but they were not employed in the rank and file. Where there were any, as in Galicia where they had continued from the Austrian period, they were doomed to extinction. Forming at least 10% of the total population, the Jews of Poland in 1923, which was in some ways the honeymoon of the new Polish republic, had a 2.23% representation in the civil administration. During the next decade this representation was reduced to 1%. In a city like Warsaw, one-third of whose population was Jewish, there were in 1928 altogether two Jews among 4,300 employees of the municipal tramway system, and the situation in other cities in Eastern Europe was no better.

Similar methods were employed against other minorities, but not with the same rigor. The consequences were not so intolerable for them, for a considerable proportion were peasants, who were not loved, to be sure, but who were essential. The Jews were strongly urged to change their occupations, though no way by which this could be done was pointed out to them. No land was put at their disposal. On the contrary, in Galicia and Rumania,[31] where some Jews possessed considerable landed property, this was expropriated and distributed to native peasants. The easiest way to satisfy the land hunger of the peasants was to use land which belonged to the minorities. All sorts of handicaps were put in the way of Jews who sought to follow trades. It was difficult for them to obtain certification as master workmen, so that they could not then train Jewish apprentices, who were in turn not received by non-Jewish masters.

This "peaceful" repression was exacerbated by boycott.[32] The intensity of the boycott was not always the same; it depended on the passions of the current political campaign and on the current economic situation. But the boycott was an ever-present weapon which might at any moment be drawn from the scabbard and put to use. The World War had shown how effective propaganda can be. In this way the economic life of the Jews was systematically undermined; a "cold pogrom" was carried out, and it achieved its end of making the Jews poor and wretched.

That the Jews did not succumb to a man was due to the modesty of their requirements. They were used to getting along with less than the minimum and had developed a certain immunity to hunger. It was of course inevitable that the health of some, and more especially of their children, should be undermined by chronic undernourishment and by constant excitement and that serious complications should follow.[33] They sought means for self-help, and they obtained the help of the great Jewish relief organizations, principally that of the Joint Distribution Committee.[34] It provided assistance in restoring ruined dwellings and buildings. Together with the Jewish Colonization Association it sought to restore, promote, and create anew credit cooperatives and loan funds which had been numerous before the war. It cooperated with the ORT in restoring and maintaining trade and technical schools. It sought to provide rational training for handicraftsmen and to furnish them with modern tools. This was only a palliative against the deadly attacks of the power of the state, but at any rate of some help.

Another palliative was emigration.[35] Probably half or more of the five million East European Jews would certainly have gone to Palestine, but with the limited resources of Palestine only a few could reach that haven. In 1924 the United States barred its doors and assigned very small quotas to the successor states carved out of Russia and Austria. Most of the immigration was taken up by Canada, Argentina and other South American republics, and by South Africa.

Despite their pressing poverty the East European Jews built up an imposing school system. The peace treaties had granted autonomy in education, and the Jews devoted all their energies to it. They created elementary and intermediate schools which provided for 225,000 pupils; they created their own textbooks, their own methods, and their own system of teacher training. Despite the scantiness of their means and the newness of their undertaking, their modern methods won the approval of all students of pedagogy. This is all the more remarkable, for they had only their own resources to fall back on; so far from helping, the governments only hindered them. Even the *Agudat Yisrael* found it advisable to provide modern secular education, for girls at least, if not for boys, and at the same time to train them in the skills necessary for housekeeping. It is to be noticed that attendance at *yeshibot*[36] also greatly increased at this time, but the *yeshibot* had undergone a certain transformation by introducing instruction in handicrafts and agriculture, and had thereby renewed the ancient ideal of *Torah im Derekh Eretz*.

Recognition of the Jewish school system on the part of the government was made more difficult by the fact that it presented no unity, but was divided into two fragments with different national languages. There was a warm contest as to whether Hebrew or Yiddish should prevail, and no one could suggest a means of reconciliation. Internal Jewish life as a whole was dominated by party strife. Despite their common need, orthodox and Zionists, the "folk" party and the socialists, were in constant conflict. In any election there were dozens of competing ballots, and as a result of this scattering, Jewish representation in state and communal bodies was not as large as Jewish population figures would justify, and the house of Jewish self-government was divided against itself.

If we glance at developments in the several countries, we notice that Finland and little Estonia[37] were the only exceptions. The latter, with its 4,000 Jews, about .35% of the population, and its patriarchal conditions, was the only country of Eastern Europe to grant the Jews complete autonomy and to observe the grant faithfully throughout its short history, or until 1940. Estonia also established a chair for Jewish studies at its national university of Tartu (Dorpat).

In neighboring Latvia[38] the law of 1921 made the grant of national civil rights dependent upon proof of residence over a period of twenty years. As in all these countries, proof was difficult to obtain. A proposal to amend the law was rejected on the grounds that it would only aid

Russian officials and Jewish merchants or handicraftsmen, and that the cities ought to grow smaller rather than larger. No increase in the Jewish population needed to be feared. Jewish population decreased rapidly as the result of the dangers incident to war and Bolshevism, and even when refugees returned and figures rose from 80,000 in 1920 to 96,000 in 1925 (not quite 5% of the entire population), the percentage of Jews lagged behind that of the general population. This was true even of the capital, Riga, where 40% of all the Jews of the republic lived.

In the main Latvia was a peasant state, and the division of large estates and land reforms were probably carried out more consistently there than elsewhere. Its long coastline, indeed, invited export trade, and despite state capitalism it could not altogether dispense with Jewish middlemen, but there was a tendency to restrict them. Latvia was the first of the new states to regulate the rights of minorities by law and to grant them complete cultural autonomy. State and communes assumed the necessary expense for maintaining the requisite schools, cared for the training of Jewish teachers, and supported Jewish cultural institutions. Until the introduction of dictatorship in 1934 these provisions were faithfully observed. Jewish cultural life flourished; in addition to the schools recognized by the state there were a number of private schools, and in 1931 a *yeshibah* was established at Dünaburg. The percentage of Jewish students at the national university declined rapidly, partly because the Letts, who had previously been indifferent, began to attend the university in droves, and partly because the professions offered little prospect to Jews. Despite its favorable laws, the state named not one Jewish judge and only very few Jews to other state posts.

In Lithuania[39] the Jews comprised half of all the minorities; their number was 153,000, or 7.5% of the total population. They were unqualifiedly in favor of Lithuanian independence, and the champions of independence made broad promises to the Jews. Consolidation was delayed by the attack of the Bolshevists and the seizure of Wilna. The constitution of 1922 did not, indeed, realize all that had been hoped for, but it did guarantee, in addition to civic and political equality, a considerable degree of Jewish national autonomy. The Jewish communities were combined under a national council, and this council with a minister of state for Jewish interests had the right to tax and a voice in common Jewish affairs, particularly in the matter of Jewish schools. These schools were under the Ministry of Education; their maintenance was a charge upon the state and the communes. In matters of administration, local minority groups which constituted 20% of the population were entitled to use their own language, so that the Jews could employ Yiddish in almost all the cities in which they lived. To promote Jewish cooperatives, Jewish peoples' banks were established, and these were affiliated with a central bank.

But the high promise of these provisions was short-lived. The very first *Sejm* refused to fix the Jewish ministry in the constitution, and in 1924 the Christian-Democratic regime abolished it. Subventions for the schools were systematically diminished. In 1925 existing Jewish communal organizations were dissolved; a new law limited them so narrowly that the Jewish population abandoned further work on the recognized communities and formed voluntary associations (*Adat Yisrael* and *Ezra*) for religious and social functions.

The direction of the economic policy is indicated by the stated principle, "Our cities must become Lithuanian." There was no intention to drive out or kill the 32.2% of Jews who formed the population of these cities; the purpose, in pursuance of the policy of agrarian reform, was to eliminate the Jewish merchant class. Rigorous observance of Sunday was ordained by law in order to injure the Jews, who were mostly orthodox and kept the Sabbath. Examinations for artisans were made more difficult. Jews were slowly but surely crowded out of the professions of medicine and law. It need hardly be added that there were almost none in the service of the state and of the communes, nor that, despite their material troubles, they maintained an intensive religious and spiritual life with study groups, *yeshibot*, theaters and a Yiddish press.

Poland[40] possessed the largest Jewish population in Europe, absolutely and in relation to the population generally. It was several years before the land-hungry state was consolidated. After the repulse of the Bolshevists, the annexation of Wilna and East Galicia and the award of Eastern Upper Silesia, it counted approximately 3,000,000 Jews. Every third citizen of the state was a non-Pole, and every third non-Pole was a Jew. In the cities, where almost all the Jews lived, every third inhabitant was a Jew. Poland had Jewish communities of a size unknown elsewhere in Europe. Warsaw, for example, had more than 300,000 Jews, Lodz (1931) 194,000, Lemberg about 100,000, Wilna 55,000, Lublin 44,000, and so on.

Here was a large and, as experience proved, useful group; properly distributed and directed they could have rendered valuable service to the state, but the governmental policy saw in them only a disruptive element which it sought to destroy. The economic policy of Poland as a whole was unbalanced, because it was directed by nationalist rather than economic considerations. The evil was aggravated by the elimination of so industrious an element as the Jewish, with the result of increasing the impoverishment and degradation of a numerous section of the population. Strabismic preoccupation with a single symptom made diagnosis difficult and therapy impossible. Pressure upon the Jews was as little effective in saving the Polish republic from constriction in the devaluation which resulted from German inflation as it was in protecting her from the general depression and unemployment later. But every crisis of this sort only served to renew the alarm against the economic power of the Jews, who were actually powerless, and as a battle cry for issuing new restrictions. It was a vicious circle: Polish economy suffered, and the Jews were again bled. Unemployment affected them much more seriously than the non-Jews, for the various forms of state care were barred to them. The result, according to the calculations of an authoritative statistician, was that in 1934 20% of the Jews of Poland were well situated, 25% were in many respects independent, 25% could maintain themselves with help from the outside, and the remaining 30% were hopelessly lost. The increase in the number of paupers seeking aid of the Jewish communities corresponds with this calculation, and observations for 1935 indicate further deterioration.

Actual equality of the Jews was obstinately opposed by almost all Polish parties and by the Catholic Church. The National Democrats were uncompromising in the detestable propaganda in which they preached the anti-Jewish boycott. Despite the measures for the equality of minorities which were prudentially ordered at Versailles and embodied, perforce, in the Polish constitution, a whole series of czaristic ordinances on foreign peoples remained in force. Parliament and government always found new pretexts to postpone their abolition. It was only in 1931, a full decade after the constitution came into force, that they were all abrogated. Power alone could impress Polish politicians, and when the Jews by reason of their unity and their electoral understanding with other minorities were represented by thirty-five deputies and twelve senators in the *Sejm* of 1922, the government could not ignore them — and especially when a currency reform and a permanent seat in the council of the League of Nations were being envisaged. The National Democratic ministry of Grabski, which had formerly pecked away at the Jews, now made all manner of promises; but before they could be actualized, the coup of Marshal Pilsudski (May 1926) destroyed the ministry's power.

The new government repudiated all antisemitic excesses. It was in constant danger of attack by the National Democrats, and it needed the support of the Jewish minority, which, however, never again reached its former strength in the *Sejm*. The elections of 1928 yielded only thirteen deputies and six senators for the Jewish group, and from 1930 the Pilsudski party had a safe majority.[41] But the economic depression gave the National Democrats new strength. They sent out their young hotspurs of the student organizations to undertake a general attack against the Jews.

Their school policy is only a special aspect of the Polish Jewish policy. The Treaty of Versailles was unequivocal in establishing the right of the Jews to their own schools and to subventions for these schools out of public funds. But in actuality these schools[42] were harassed at every step. Just as the Russians had formerly suppressed the Polish schools, so now the Poles attempted to make it impossible for the schools of the minorities to function. A proposal of the socialists to grant the schools autonomy was snowed under. Even those Polish public schools which were attended by Jewish children exclusively and gave no instruction on the Sabbath were liquidated after 1930. The children were forced to attend Catholic schools; these would not employ Jewish teachers, who lost their livelihood in consequence. In the higher schools in Galicia there were still Jewish teachers from the Austrian period; the Polish republic appointed scarcely a handful. By creating their own school system the Jewish population relieved the general community of a heavy burden; the subventions were ridiculously small, far less than the Jews were entitled to on the basis of their numbers and their taxation, and each year they were diminished. The city of Warsaw, for example, granted the sum of 60,000 zlotys for Jewish schools in 1927; the following year the sum was reduced to 17,000 zlotys, and in 1934 the subsidy was cancelled altogether. In 1935 the Polish Ministry of Religion and Public Enlightenment granted a subsidy of 183,000 zlotys out of its budget of approximately 300,000,000 zlotys.

To be sure, the universities were included in this budget, and, according to law, Jews had the full right of admission. But from the beginning the National Democrats worked for the introduction of a *numerus clausus*.[43] This was contrary to the constitution, but the students took matters into their own hands. The medical students admitted Jews to courses in anatomy only if they could supply a proportionate number of Jewish cadavers for purposes of dissection. This new contrivance of a percentage norm spread over Polish and other East European universities. Their purpose was achieved. The number of Jewish medical students decreased by 45% in the decade between 1923 and 1933, and the number of Jewish dental students by 70%; there was a corresponding rise in the number of Christian students.

In the other faculties the number of Jews was larger, but no greater than their proportion in the population of the cities, and it was constantly on the decrease. What was the sense of attending a university when they knew that insurmountable obstacles would be put in the way of their advancement? They could obtain no appointment or employment in public service. When asked for the grounds of this exclusion, a high official replied cynically that he could not answer, for the state was not concerned with the religious beliefs of its officials. Indeed it had no need to be concerned, for its choice was uniform.

The intention was to keep the Jews out of the universities altogether, and the winter semester of 1931 was ushered in with physical attacks upon Jewish students. In Warsaw and Wilna the disturbances were carried into the Jewish quarter; people were injured and property damaged. The Jewish students boldly took to defense; there were injured on both sides, and in Wilna there was one dead among the Polish students. An attempt to accuse two Jewish students of premeditated murder, and so to build up a sensational case against all Jewry, collapsed. The government disapproved of public agitation of this character, and so furnished its protection; indeed an ancient privilege of the universities prevented the police from trespassing on their premises. The National Democratic press did not deny its share and approved of the excesses. It declared it would not rest until the *numerus clausus* was introduced, and the party immediately put forth a proposal to that effect. The proposal was rejected by the government and a parliamentary majority, and was disapproved of by most university professors. A new contrivance of introducing so-called ghetto-benches for Jewish students was reduced to an absurdity by distinguished Polish scholars. But the tension was not relieved; the aim of destroying the Jews intellectually and culturally persisted.

Despite their pressing poverty and despite the handicaps imposed by the government, the Jews of Poland maintained an extraordinarily vital cultural life.[44] Two important associations cared for modern educational institutions: *Tarbut* for those using Hebrew, and the Central Jewish School Society (*Zisho*) for those using Yiddish. Each system maintained hundreds of elementary and higher schools, evening courses for adults, the requisite teachers' training schools, and libraries. The *Agudat Yisrael* strove to improve the *Hadarim* and to provide suitable education for girls; furthermore it maintained numerous *yeshibot*. There were also higher Jewish schools where Polish was the language of instruction; these were called Braude Schools, after their founder the rabbi of Lodz. It was Braude also who brought about the establishment of a Jewish Scientific Institute in Warsaw; the Institute had a section devoted to social sciences as well as one devoted to Judaic studies. The Yiddishists established the Jewish Scientific Institute in Wilna (*YIVO*) which engaged chiefly in historical, sociological and folkloristic research, and used its world-wide connections to collect an extensive library and a body of archives. Poland remained the center of talmudic scholarship. Eliahu Klatzkin of Lublin (died 1932 in Tel Aviv), Israel Meir Kahan of Radin (1833–1933), and Chaim Oser Gorodsenski (died 1940) were everywhere esteemed as outstanding authorities. Samuel A. Poznanski of Warsaw (1864–1921) and his successor, Moses Schorr (1875–1941), made important contributions to scientific Jewish and Oriental studies.

The Jewish press[45] enjoyed a very wide public. Yiddish publications had the largest circulation; next, but by a great interval, Polish; while the circulation of Hebrew publications was relatively small. Numerous Jewish writers were at work. Jacob Kahan achieved a great reputation as a naturalistic poet. In Abraham Stybel, Hebrew literature found a Maecenas who devoted millions to assure its progress along modern cultural lines. The Yiddish theater was a cultural factor of special importance. There were theaters in all large centers, and with the coming of the cinema in smaller centers also. Qualitatively as well as quantitatively both institutions matured rapidly. Their repertory was enriched by classics of western literature; staging and acting followed the best available models. In 1916 a group of enthusiastic amateurs formed a troupe in Wilna[46] which later undertook tours extending as far as America and achieved great success as the Yiddish Art Theater.

Communal politics were lively and partisanship keen. Questions of tactics as well as of ideology were fought over with emotional intensity. The pulverization of the party system, which dissipated the worth of the Polish parliament, affected Jewish life also. When the state was established, 74% of all the Jews declared their allegiance to the Jewish nationality, and the deputies in the first *Sejm* were chiefly nationalists and Zionists. But the masses[47] turned away from them, and after the introduction of democratic communal elections (1927) the *Agudat Yisrael* made startling advances and attained a majority in the large communities. Orthodoxy had a grip on the masses; the strongest influence was exercised by Hasidic rabbis. Much genuine piety existed among the petty bourgeoisie; those who lived far from the noisy agitation of the cities continued to pray and to meditate, to weep and to hope as their fathers and forefathers had done. But not even that most conservative group could escape history, and the wing of the Hasidim connected with the *Agudat Yisrael* and led by the Gerer Rebbe (R. Aryeh Löb b. Abraham Mordecai Alter) entered the political arena and threw the gauntlet to Zionists and Bundists. Surprisingly enough, it was the youth that showed the stanchest inclination towards orthodoxy and were most militant in its behalf. To be sure, a great part of this same youth later, under economic and political pressure, turned to the extreme of communism.[48] Party lines were not clear cut, and since no principles were at stake petty intrigues abounded. The Zionists were not concerned exclusively with Palestine but also with the welfare and the normalization of Jewish life in Poland. Its *Mizrahi* wing laid emphasis on the strict observance of Jewish ritual. The Bundists did not care for religion and were sometimes outspokenly anti-religious, but they fought for the improvement in the situation of the working classes and for the benefit of the Jewish proletariat; if they were not interested in Jewish political aspirations, they felt solidarity with working Palestine. The *Agudat Yisrael* also did not brush aside the upbuilding of Palestine. The *Agudists* were, of course, dissatisfied with the religious, or areligious, attitude of official Zionism, but *Yishub Eretz Yisrael* ("Resettlement of Palestine") stood forth as a biblical command and found the warmest support among leading *Agudist* rabbis. Poland supplied the largest contingent of immigrants to Palestine (125,154, or 46.6% of the total), and it was in Poland that youth organizations such as *He-Ḥalutz* and *Ha-Poʿel ha-Tzaʿir* (see p. 595), which prepared for agricultural and artisan work in Palestine, had their central offices. The hope of some day being able to live and work in *Eretz Yisrael* was the strongest spiritual support of Polish Jewish youth and upheld its morale.

The Balkan States

Poland's ally, Rumania,[49] had an old and tried formula for Jew-baiting. The number of its Jews had been tripled by its accessions of territory in Transylvania, Bukovina, and Bessarabia; estimates of the total vary between 800,000 and 900,000. In the peace treaty Rumania had automatically undertaken to give civil rights to its newly acquired Jews as well as those in old Rumania. But the constitution of 1923 made civil rights, for the other minorities as well as for Jews, depend on ability to produce certain documents. These were not always easy to obtain, and in consequence 20,000 heads of families, or 10% of all the Jews, were denied citizens' rights. Others depended entirely upon the good-will of local authorities, who possessed more power than the central government at Bucharest and were not only "unintelligent, annoying, and violent, but also a field of bribery."

Rumania had grown great overnight, and its administration offered manifold difficulties. The government was completely centralized and nationalist. All minorities were oppressed, but the Jews were an especial target because they could not count on protective measures sponsored by a kindred power. When their difficulties were mentioned[50] in Geneva, London, or Washington, the Rumanian representatives made a complete denial and pictured their government as wholly innocent. Discrimination in the first instance was of an economic character. State capitalism directed profits into the hands of a small and exclusive clique; taxation intentionally favored certain categories; employment in the service of the state and the communes was reserved for Rumanians; merchants and handicraftsmen were hampered by limitations — and all these items contributed to the impoverishment of the Jewish population. Certain favored individuals were able to interest the ruling clique in their undertakings, but the great mass sank to an ever lower standard of living.

The school and church policy of the state was a tragedy from its very inception. It constricted the educational system of the minorities at least as cruelly as had the most odious Hungarian laws of the period before the war. Jewish public schools were not tolerated, for the Jews — so it was asserted — had no language of their own and were required to have their children taught in the Rumanian language. Among the 80,000 Jews in Kishinev, the 45,000 in Czernowitz, the 18,000 in Grosswardein, practically none spoke Rumanian, and it was torture for little children to have to be taught in that language. Moreover the schools took no consideration of the religious requirements of Jewish children. In the higher schools there was a tacit *numerus clausus* for Jews, and the whole atmosphere made the attendance of Jewish children intolerable. If the Jews brought these facts to notice, they were told to establish private schools, but grave obstacles were put in the way of establishing and maintaining such schools. Jewish communal organization was subjected to regulations against which they protested and whose injustice liberal-minded people in Rumania acknowledged. The Jewish cult did receive a subvention, the state so far acknowledging its responsibility; but the amount was half a leu per person, whereas the Orthodox Church received more than forty lei per person.

All of this was within the framework of the law. The government pretended not to be antisemitic, but it tolerated the most shameless agitation against the Jews. The National Christian Defense League, the swastika party headed by A. C. Cuza, professor of economics at Jassy, was the driving power behind the agitation. Its program demanded not only the exclusion of Jews from all civic rights, from all civic posts and all schools without distinction, not only a 100% boycott in buying, selling, and employment, but also the proscription of all Jews in Greater Rumania. The party's organ, *Awakening Christianity*, went further and explicitly demanded that all Jews be murdered. And in the face of this agitation, the head of the state Church, the patriarch of the Greek Orthodox communion, dared to complain that the Jews were exploiters and creators of unrest.

Cuza's bodyguard, the National Rumanian Christian Students' Union, undertook the work of "cleansing" the universities.[51] After 1922 there were repeated scandalous instances of Jewish students, male and female, being attacked and beaten in the rooms of the universities. Needless to say, such brutality did result in a decrease in the enrollment of Jewish students. This path of glory took its rise in Jassy, and continued in other universities.

The universities were repeatedly closed, and the majority of professors, and with them the educated classes, protested against this rowdyism. His colleagues suggested that Cuza retire from his post, as being unworthy of an academic teaching position. But nothing availed; the disturbances were aggravated and spread from the universities to the Jewish quarters. The police director of Jassy, who had given evidence in a hearing against the rioters, was shot down by a leader of the band as he left the court house. The court acquitted the murderer as a national hero. A student from Czernowitz, who traveled alone to Bucharest for the purpose and fatally wounded a Jewish student in the court house, was similarly acquitted. In connection with a student congress at Jassy at the end of 1926 there were wild excesses against the Jews in various places, and these were repeated in an aggravated form a year later after a meeting at Grosswardein. The excesses were so outrageous that the government granted damages to injured individuals and communities and in 1928 dissolved the student organization. When, in 1926, Chief Rabbi Zirelsohn[52] of Kishinev discussed these events in the senate and that body refused to record his speech in its proceedings, the worthy rabbi laid his post down in protest.

> A hideous campaign of intimidation and brutality was being carried on against the Jewish citizens of the State, its motive being a mixture of arrogant intolerance and ignorant hatred.

So a commission of Christian clergymen from the United States summarized the impressions it had gained upon a journey undertaken in 1927 to investigate the shocking reports of the treatment of minorities. They affirmed that the terror had decreased in consequence of an agreement of the Liberal Party with the Jewish voters before the parliamentary elections. And in fact the situation was somewhat pacified. The government made concessions in the school question and saw that a number of

Jews were employed by the communes. The Association of Rumanian Jews[53] worked in the new Rumania, as it had done in the old, for closer adjustment to the environment. It laid special stress upon spreading the knowledge of the national language; prayer book and Bible were translated and educational periodicals published. Even the Jewish national group took no exception to this degree of assimilation, though it continued to stress Hebrew and Yiddish.

The interval of mutual understanding was ephemeral. When the world-wide economic crisis made itself felt, the wave of antisemitism rose again and the movement became more vigorous and rougher. Of the access of strength which Nazism brought it we shall have to speak in the sequel.

Of the remaining Balkan states, Jugoslavia[54] carried equalization out faithfully, as its predecessor Serbia had done. The Jewish community, Sephardic and Ashkenazic, comprised 68,000 persons, or 5% of the total population. They combined into an association which reconciled differences resulting from the past and united for common efforts. Zionism found a broad following in the country and the Hebrew language was zealously cultivated. The greater number of Jews spoke Serbo-Croatian, and all Jewish periodicals appeared in that language. In Bulgaria,[55] which had 48,000 (.8%) Jews, the animosity of the population made the grant of equality difficult. The uniform Jewish group, practically exclusively native-Sephardic of long standing, created a very respectable school system. In Greece[56] the great problem was Saloniki, where the living space of the Jews was constantly narrowed, with the result that emigration was considerable. It is interesting to note that the King of Spain recognized the Sephardic Jews of the Near East as Spanish citizens, invited them to return to Spain, and granted them a six-year option for doing so. Not many took advantage of the invitation; most were attracted to the East, to *Eretz Yisrael.*

The development in the Turkish[57] republic is significant. For centuries the empire had freely granted autonomy to its minorities, but the new nationalist tendency demanded the unification of the state. The tendency was first expressed in an ordinance which required that after 1927 Turkish be used as the language of instruction in the schools, and that schools could be directed only by Turkish subjects. The *Alliance Israélite Universelle* was able to retain its old schools only with great effort and at the sacrifice of many of its former rights. The Jewish communities took over most of the existing schools. Furthermore, in connection with the new order in the state and the abolition of the Caliphate, the Jews were subjected to pressure and in 1926 the minority rights agreed upon in the Treaty of Lausanne were renounced. This spelled the end of the centuries-old office of *Haham Bashi* ("chief rabbi") and of the unified organization of the Jewish communities. At the same time the position of the Jews in economic life suffered. Preference was given to Turks, Jewish interests shrank visibly, and the only solution in sight was increased emigration.

The Jews in Italy and Liberal Europe

By the annexation of Trieste, Fiume, and Merano, Italy[58] acquired an access of 12,000 Jews, no inconsiderable number in view of its own small Jewish population. Most of these new Jews had been brought up as Italians. The new Fascist regime did not alter the political position of the Jews. There were already sowers of disorder in the party, but in 1923, on the occasion of an official reception, Benito Mussolini, the head of the government, declared his decided opposition to antisemitic policies to Angelo Sacerdoti, the *Rabbino Maggiore* of Rome. Jews participated in the Italian Fascist movement and produced an incredibly large number of high officials in view of their small proportions in the general population. Among them were several ministers, as for example Lodovico Mortara, son of the scholarly rabbi of Mantua, who had previously sat as judge in the highest court. There were numerous Jews among the officers of the army and navy, and not a few among the university teachers and the distinguished representatives of Italian science.

When the concordat with the Vatican gave the Catholic Church important concessions in respect of the educational system, consideration was expressly taken of the requirements of the Jewish schools also. A law governing organizations (October 30, 1930) gave the Jewish communities a unified construction and associated them into a union so that they might be affiliated with the Fascist system of administration. The law abolished the voluntary basis of membership in the community which had previously been the rule, and made membership mandatory; it also provided model regulations on the competence of communities and rabbis. The *Collegio Rabbinico Italiano* was removed to Rome, under the direction of Professor Umberto Cassuto of the University of Rome, and a teachers' seminary was established in the island of Rhodes, where teachers were trained for service in Sephardic communities generally. It was intended that the Jewish community be incorporated into the state and cooperate in the spread of the idea of the Roman imperium.

When Hitler came into power the Jews were able to count upon Mussolini's intervention on their behalf. Italy also received a large number of Jewish refugees from Germany, made it possible for Jewish students to continue their studies, for Jewish physicians to take up their practice, and for *Halutzim* to prepare for work in Palestine. Zionist activities were not hampered, nor was cooperation in preparations for a World Jewish Congress. A change of policy came with Mussolini's adventure in Ethiopia (1935).

The Republic of Czechoslovakia[59] was the only new state whose government was absolutely free of antisemitism and would not even countenance the boisterousness of students. Regardless of their language it allowed the Jews to acknowledge Jewish nationality. Of the 350,000 Jews, 53.5% had themselves recorded as of the Jewish nationality in the census of 1921; the minority recorded themselves as being of the Czech, German, Magyar, or Ruthenian nationality. Jewry presented the same patchwork appearance as did the state as a whole. In Bohemia and Silesia the religious attitude was largely dejudaized, in Moravia it was conservative, in Slovakia orthodox, in Carpatho-Russia fanatic, mostly Hasidic after the manner of Eastern Galicia. It was impossible to attain unity among these strongly differentiated groups; a dozen communal organizations were in competition. In consequence of the peculiar electoral regulations and the factionalism among the Jews, the Jewish party was able to send two deputies to parliament only once, in 1929.

The Jewish national council in Prague established several Jewish schools. In Munkascz, against the vigorous opposition of the Hasidic rabbi, it set up a high school with Hebrew as the language of instruction; this school even received a subvention from the state. The Jewish population there and in Eastern Slovakia was much denser than that in the western provinces, had a much greater proportion of peasants, and was poverty-stricken. The Joint Distribution Committee and the Jewish Colonization Association sought to help at various times by setting up cooperatives. In Bohemia and Moravia, which were relatively prosperous, the communities made considerable contributions to help their needy sister communities. There the Jews lived more in accord with western civilization; in the eastern regions the *yeshibot* dominated Jewish spiritual life. Czechoslovakia remained a retreat of freedom and an asylum for those persecuted by Hitler and the Nazis.

The states which had remained neutral, like Switzerland, Holland, and the Scandinavian countries, showed admirable hospitality to refugees during the war, and after the war openhanded generosity to sufferers, particularly to suffering children.[60] They supported the upbuilding of Palestine generously. Their participation in the Jewish spiritual life of the larger countries became more active, and they made efforts to promote Jewish culture in their own lands. This was true not only of Holland with its ancient humanitarian traditions, but also of Denmark and Sweden. In the former, David Simonsen and in the latter Marcus Ehrenpreis, both veterans with European training, bore the spiritual scepter among the Jews.

Jewish Life in Soviet Russia

The Union of Soviet Socialist Republics[61] put itself completely outside the European family of nations. What actually went on in Russia, Bolshevism concealed behind an impenetrable curtain. The reports of occasional travelers showed exalted enthusiasm or abysmal dismay. Both extremes were justified; along with brilliant successes there were shocking failures; along with satisfaction and happiness despair and disillusion. Whether the economic experiment was successful and a new and perfect society created still cannot be determined with certainty. But that the past was destroyed and that the populace had to endure hunger and deprivation is quite certain, particularly in the early years of the Soviet regime when war and famine complicated the tasks of an inexperienced administration. In this catastrophic period the Joint Distribution

Committee, acting as agent of the American Relief Administration which was directed by Herbert C. Hoover, rendered essential service in saving Jewish individuals and institutions. It not only fed adults and children and cared for the improvement of health conditions, but by its reconstruction work it sought to restore people's capacity to work and to earn their livelihood.

On the condition of the Jews in Soviet Russia also contradictory reports reached the outer world, and either extreme reflected a measure of the truth. According to the constitution, Jews, men and women alike, enjoyed full equality, and actual practice followed the provisions of the law. But after the long and evil Russian tradition antisemitic sentiment could not disappear overnight, even among the intelligentsia and the officials. But those in authority refused to countenance it; they insisted that the Jews were a part of the Russian population and punished any manifestation of Jew-hatred severely. Many Jews whose philosophy was at variance with that of the Soviets were reconciled to the system by this attitude.

But other circles could not endure it that in place of the Czarist tyranny another tyranny had stepped in whose despotism they found more galling. Formerly it was only their bodies that were in bondage, now their souls too were enslaved. The practice of religion was nowhere forbidden in the Soviet Union, but neither was interference with religious practice. At times the leaders of the atheist movement intensified their activities and at other times they relaxed them. If one spoke to the appropriate people's commissars one received assurances of the most complete tolerance. But if one inquired of conditions under the competent Jewish commissars[62] (*Evsektia*) a different story came to light. "They are driving God out," the rabbi of Berdichev declared. "The Communist Jews have enthroned themselves and are reviling God. In the old days we had no strength in the

Town Hall, but God ruled among us and we were content and felt strong." The representatives of the Joint Distribution Committee were also reproached: "The people are being fed and made content, and thus you have strengthened the hands of a government that persecutes Judaism and rabbis. So, what has been gained? Is it not better to hunger than that Judaism should suffer?"

Some Jewish Bolshevists in high position thought it necessary to close synagogues and to penalize or banish rabbis in order not to become liable to the suspicion that their conduct towards the Jewish religion was less uncompromising than towards the Christian. But the greater number of commissars had cherished a resentment against religion from their school days and a hatred of its organized forms. They raged against the Jewish congregations, against their rabbis and their teachers. In any dictatorial system it is easy to contrive slanders and accusations which justify any desired punishment, and such accusations were now made. Any expression and any action might be interpreted as counter-revolutionary and contrary to law.

Among the intolerable regulations was the prohibition against imparting organized instruction in religion. Any father was free to teach his child as much religion as he wished, but no teacher or cleric might do so. Many preferred to undergo punishment rather than to neglect a self-imposed duty. "They give the children life, but what manner of life is it that is not Jewish?" Such a question reflected the despair of the man in the street. Included among the subjects in which instruction was forbidden was Hebrew, according to some because it was taught as a holy language and was therefore out of place in a communist state, according to others because it was the language of the counter-revolutionary bourgeoisie and the Zionists — and Zionists were interdicted as accessories of British imperialism. Many Jews could not conceive of Judaism without Hebrew, and taught it secretly; the language of the Bible was condemned to a sort of Marrano existence.

But the prohibition did not extend to academic institutions such as the Jewish Scientific Institute of Leningrad. There Hebrew was recognized as an object of scholarly study. Hebrew reached its artistic bloom, moreover, in the theatrical company called *Habimah*.[63] The company was formed in 1916 by Nahum Zemach among war refugees in Moscow. It enjoyed the patronage of such outstanding theatrical personages as Stanislavsky and Vachtangoff, and its work was governed by the principles of the Moscow Art Theater. It rejected the star system and the traditional stylized acting, and strove for naturalness and complete teamwork on the part of the entire company in the spirit of the plays which were presented. Their production of An-ski's *Dybuk* in Bialik's classic translation aroused unusual attention even in Moscow, which was used to theatrical productions of high merit. *Habimah* was placed under the Art Division of the Commissariat of Education and received a state subvention. Tours in Western Europe and North America made the company famous. But its natural locale was *Eretz Yisrael*, and there it has played since 1928 and has justified its reputation of being the first art theater in the Orient.

The privileged language of the Jews was Yiddish,[64] the idiom of the proletariat. Since the Jews possessed no territory, they could show their national identity within the Soviet Republics only by means of a common language. The preservation and cultivation of Yiddish was effected by folk-schools and also by other cultural institutions such as press and radio, theater and cinema. Universities like those at Kiev and Minsk established departments for the scientific investigation of Yiddish language and literature. It is needless to remark that these investigations were based on a Marxist interpretation of

EUROPE IN THE POST-WAR ERA 551

history. Even a communist orthography for Yiddish was sanctioned. But despite official patronage Yiddish lost ground; it could not flourish when its roots in Hebrew and in the Jewish religion had withered. The tendency of its development was in the direction of assimilation to Russian. Only 18% of all Jewish children attended Yiddish schools; the remainder went to Russian or Ukrainian schools. There was a decline in the Yiddish press also.

Economic problems, the burning question of subsistence, were the most difficult to master. The chief trouble lay in the bad occupational distribution of the Jews. There were very few peasants and factory workers, callings which were favored as being productive. There were many state and party officials, but these were not numerous enough to affect the balance. For merchants, agents, wagoners, and even for small handicraftsmen of the old sort, there was no place in the Bolshevist economy. The New Economic Policy (NEP) did provide a comfortable livelihood for some Jews, but these were not of the best class or such as would reflect credit on the community. The great majority of Jews were therefore what was called "declassed." The implications of the term are very difficult for anyone living outside the Bolshevist community to appreciate. Declassed persons formed the lowest class of Russian citizens; theirs was not only a moral degradation but a very tangible economic disability. They were required to pay higher taxes and higher rates for water, light, and other public conveniences. They did not have an equal claim on rations of food and clothing. They had to pay higher rents. Their children could be accommodated in the schools only after others had been provided for. They could be received into hospitals only if the space was not required for the higher categories: soldiers, workers, and peasants.

Allowing some 2,000,000 people to remain in the declassed condition created a most unhealthy situation, and the government saw a solution in settling Jews upon the land. As the Czar had done a century earlier, the People's Commissars now put land[65] in the Ukraine and the Crimea at the disposal of settlers and required only that the settlers bear the cost of establishing and equipping themselves. The government formed a Jewish commission, called KOMZET; under the direction of a non-Jewish People's Commissar, Smidovich, it prosecuted the task of settling the Jews upon the land with benevolent zeal. A private organization of Jews, called OZET, worked hand in hand with KOMZET. The response among the Jewish population exceeded all expectations. Assistance was provided for the settlers with a generous readiness to sacrifice. But Russian Jewry was too poor to make up a sufficient sum, and the Joint Distribution Committee came to their assistance. It also assisted ORT which had settled some thousands of Jewish families in the region of Odessa and White Russia in 1923, among them two thousand *Halutzim* who were preparing for immigration to *Eretz Yisrael*.

In order to strengthen the necessary work of upbuilding, the Joint Distribution Committee created a Russian representation in 1924, in the form of the American Jewish Joint Agricultural Corporation[66] (Agro-Joint). The management was undertaken by Dr. Joseph A. Rosen, a political refugee of the Czarist period who had returned to Russia as a social worker with the American Relief Administration. Rosen was an expert in the field of agriculture and thoroughly familiar with Russian conditions. He set to work with a carefully thought out plan to settle the largest possible number of people at the least possible cost and to make them independent. He had the satisfaction of seeing his work prosper. Not only did the old colonists of the Ukraine, who had been driven or frightened away by the confusion during the war, return to cultivate their land, but numerous new settlements were called into life, one after another. The cry "Back to the land" was eagerly taken up, and in a short while 50,000 persons were settled and earned their living as farmers, agricultural workers, or rural handicraftsmen. They were old city-dwellers, lost youth, men and women of all ages, and they all found satisfaction in work and happiness in country life; none wished to return to the city.

The work was strange and tiring, especially for the women, and life was hard, but they dwelt upon their own acres and could look to the future with hope. The Jews could care for their inner life and their religious interests better in the quiet of the country than in the noisy city. Relations with neighboring peasants, especially in the Crimea, were friendly; the Jewish settlers rose in the esteem of the peasants when they saw them working the soil with their own hands, like the peasants themselves.

For its part the government[67] advocated a dense settlement of Jews in the Crimea, so dense that they held out the prospect of a Jewish "state" with complete self-administration. The ground was ready, but in order to settle it there was need of large means. These could only come from the United States; and the Russian government promised to supplement such funds out of its own budget. But in the United States the word "state" was misconstrued — the autonomy which the several national soviet republics enjoyed was quite limited — and the necessary support was refused. Only a small portion of the land available was settled, and a favorable opportunity was missed. James N. Rosenberg of New York, however, who had traveled through the colonies and preached the saga of the soil in the United States, was able to collect eight million dollars in individual subscriptions, five million of which came from Julius Rosenwald, and to found the American Society for Jewish Farmers' Settlement in Russia. The Society purposed to use its means to promote the work of the Agro-Joint. The government promised its proportional share of the expenditure. "The scope of the work included not only farm settlement, but industrialization, training and other activities for the Jews dwelling in the cities, small towns, and villages."

The work of settlement so far succeeded that eventually 250,000 persons lived and did productive work on the land. Forty-two trade and farm schools, conducted in cooperation with the Jewish Colonization Association and ORT, trained several thousand young people so that they could take up work in the state factories. These organizations also promoted the system of cooperatives, in which tens of thousands of Jews contributed work which was recognized by the official organs. They claimed that "In less than a decade and a half, the work of the Agro-Joint helped to transform Russian Jewry from a down-trodden, almost helpless ghetto population into self-reliant and productive workers of the field and factory." Reality, of course, never quite measured up to expectations, for the economic crisis in America made the collection of funds exceedingly difficult. If the problem of the declassed was not completely eliminated, it was greatly reduced.

The project of turning the Sea of Azov into a Jewish lake could not be carried out, but KOMZET did not surrender its plan for an autonomous Jewish soviet republic, and started on new attempts in the Far East, in Biro-Bidjan[68] in the Amur territory. Sanguine hopes were centered in this settlement; optimists spoke of a capacity of a million inhabitants. The land was made available for "contiguous Jewish settlements," the region was recognized as a Jewish national district, and, if the extent of the settlement should justify such a designation, the prospect of its being made into an autonomous Jewish state was held out (1927).

There was a great rush of settlers to the new territory, and organizations like ICOR and AmBidjan in the United States devoted themselves to promoting the new project. But the project was a failure. The district was not suitable for agriculture and the settlers were not able to cope with the enormous difficulties involved. Of the twenty thousand who went to Biro-Bidjan only about half were still there in 1934.

Nevertheless, on May 20, 1934, Biro-Bidjan was raised to the status of a Jewish Autonomous Region, in order to give the Jews "the possibility of developing their own culture, nationalist in form, socialist in content." But all the well-meaning intentions of the government could not avail to attain this end. Exact figures for the development of the settlement are not available. Those that have been published are contradictory, and the highest are far lower than had been expected. Internal difficulties have also become apparent; as usual, they have been and are being represented as the work of opponents of the Soviet Republics. It is certain that a large percentage of the settlers were disillusioned and left Biro-Bidjan. The number of Jewish farmers appears to be less than the number of city-dwellers who work in industries and communications.

Yiddish is the official language of the district; public notices appear in that language. Yiddish schools, press, radio, theater, and cinema are all represented. But progress here is also very slow, for the population as a whole prefers Russian. Biro-Bidjan was a beautiful thought, but for the present it is no more than that.

The question of sustenance was relieved by the introduction of the five-year plan (1929), for hundreds of thousands of Jews now found employment in factories.[69] For the young who had grown up under the soviet regime the problem had become very simple. They lived as did all in their environment, and in consequence of common education and common work they were easily assimilated. Their connection with Judaism grew lax, and was further weakened by increasing intermarriage. How much of Russian Judaism which was so strong under persecution will survive under equality, particularly when negation of religion is no longer a pillar of government, is an enigma which the future will solve.

The Re-Discovered Marranos

The discovery that communities of Marranos[70] had survived in northern Portugal was one of the surprises of this period. A mining engineer from Lodz, named Samuel Schwarz, happened to find himself in that region, when he was warned against a small shopkeeper on the grounds that the shopkeeper was a Jew. This aroused Schwarz's curiosity and he struck up an acquaintance with the man designated. This was difficult to do in the prevalent atmosphere of suspicion, but Schwarz persisted. The younger generation had little to tell him, but when, after much effort, he had gained the confidence of their elders they informed him that in the north and east of Portugal, in the provinces of Minho (Braga), Tras-os-Montes (Bragança), and Baira Baixa (Belmonte, Castelo Branco), all remote from communications and civilization, thousands of simple families had with heroic courage kept their loyalty to the faith of their ancestors over a period of four centuries. Outwardly they lived as Catholics, and they observed their Jewish rites in secret. They could not imagine that Jewish prayers, Jewish festivals, Jewish usages could be practiced otherwise than in the form which had been handed down to them and which had grown dear to their hearts. After the separation of Church and State in 1910 it was no longer necessary for them to hide their faith, but secrecy seemed sacred to them and they held fast to it. Since that time, indeed, the youth had grown estranged from the old traditions, and mixed marriages impinged upon their closed circle. The older generation disapproved of such transgression strongly.

Independently of these remarkable events, a young officer in Oporto, Arturo Carlos de Barros Basto, by observing the peculiar habits of his father, awoke one day to the realization that he was a Marrano. He was so moved by a visit to the synagogue in Lisbon that the last doubts of his religious roots disappeared. He began to study the doctrines of the Jewish religion and learned Hebrew; but as long as his Catholic mother was alive he hesitated to take the decisive step of open conversion. In the World War he fought with the English in Flanders and distinguished himself for bravery in the face of the enemy.

Upon his return home de Barros Basto went to Tangiers, studied Judaism and entered into the Covenant of Abraham, acknowledged himself publicly as a Jew, and in token thereof took the Hebrew name Abraham Israel ben Rosh. He married a Jewess of Lisbon and required her to study Hebrew along with him. This enthusiastic champion of the faith recognized that his mission was to explain to his brothers of the faith, whose language he spoke and whose mentality he understood, that there was a living Judaism practiced by millions of people and to persuade them to follow in his footsteps. He transformed a number of Marrano conventicles into Jewish congregations. He made prayers and poems of the Sephardic ritual accessible in Portuguese translations. He founded a monthly which he called *Ha-Lapid* ("The Flame"), to bring light and warmth, doctrine and hope, to the Marranos. In order to assure the future of the movement he established at Oporto a *yeshibah* for teachers and precentors, and called it *Rosh Pina*.

When these things became known abroad all Jewry was astounded at the saga of the power of Jewish faith. The Sephardic congregations of London and Amsterdam regarded themselves honor bound to support de Barros Basto in his devoted work, to provide means for maintaining his institutions in the exceedingly poor communities, and, above all, to fulfill his fondest wish by erecting a synagogue as a monument in Oporto. By its name, *Mekor Hayyim* ("Fountain of Life"), and by the style of its architecture, it was to be a symbol proclaiming a new era. Oporto's last synagogue had been destroyed in 1497. When the new synagogue was dedicated in 1938, sowers of discord had already attempted to interfere with the work, and the difficult years which followed have not carried it far. Quieter times will be needed to strengthen the enterprise of revitalizing Judaism in Portugal.

The native community in Lisbon,[71] which had been reconstructed after the earthquake of 1740 and had been strengthened by accessions chiefly from Gibraltar and Morocco, also sought and found connections with world Jewry. Their leading representative, Moses Bensabbat Amzalak, a distinguished professor of economics, is at the same time a spiritual leader. He sought to renew the ancient cultural tradition and even planned to publish a scientific Jewish periodical in Portuguese. Joaquin Bensaude made serious studies of Portuguese navigation and its significance in the age of discovery; he demonstrated the importance of the preparatory work of Jewish astronomers. Political confusion in Europe confronted the Lisbon community with the exceedingly trying task of caring for refugees, and the community has responded in a spirit of cheerful sacrifice.

CHAPTER IV

The Jews in the United States (1919-1933)

Racism in America

PRESIDENT Wilson won the war but lost the peace. Not only did the European statesmen at the Paris Peace Conference rob his fourteen points of all their ethical content, but the Senate of the United States did not ratify the Treaty of Versailles and refused to enter the League of Nations. But the Jews could not follow this policy of isolation with reference to their brethren in Europe. The personal bonds which attached the great body of American Jews to their old homes and their family connections there were too close. Moreover the Jews in the war-torn regions looked across the ocean for material and political help. America had attained hegemony among the nations, and its Jews among their fellow Jews. They felt the principle of *noblesse oblige* deeply, and they gave their best attention to the problem of reconstruction in Central and Eastern Europe as well as in *Eretz Yisrael*.

At this decisive period American Israel was fortunate in possessing leaders of stature, endowed with wisdom and vision, men whose words as well as deeds exercised profound influence over their people. Towering above his peers was Louis Marshall,[1] whose authority was so widely diffused and widely recognized that Israel Zangwill, who was sojourning in New York shortly after the end of the war, coined the *bon mot*, "American Jewry is under

Marshall law." Benjamin N. Cardozo, himself a jurist of high distinction and a magnificent personality, wrote of him:

One feels that he has somehow been transformed into a great civic institution, coordinating the energies and activities of many men, so that with all his intensely human traits he has acquired, in his own life, a new and, as it were, a corporate personality. He is a great lawyer; a great champion of ordered liberty; a great leader of his people; a great lover of mankind. In this teeming center of Jewish life the calls upon his experience, his courage and his extraordinary abilities are equaled only by his readiness to meet them with never-failing cheer and sacrifice.

American Jewry was in need of strong leadership for it was soon exposed to an unexpected storm, to what Christian Americans called a "new and dangerous spirit, one that is wholly at variance with our traditions and ideals and subversive of our system of government."[2] The isolationists wished to guard the people against being swallowed up by European intrigues, but they tolerated the importation of the most evil outgrowths of European hatreds. War enthusiasm was followed by a period of sobering which developed into an intense dislike of foreigners. The Nordic principle was discovered, and the United States was declared the preserve of Nordic peoples. The arrogant Ku Klux Klan,[3] which had been slumbering for some decades, awakened to new life and extended its original program of suppressing the Negro to include Catholics, Jews, and all foreigners, who were all to be eliminated from political and economic life. This narrow-minded secret organization with its ridiculous mummery could have done no considerable damage if it had not been helped by the *Protocols of the Elders of Zion*, which provided effective material for agitation.

Capital and Society trembled, as they did in England, before the specter of Bolshevism. Anti-Bolshevist emissaries[4] used the social and financial resources of these groups to corrupt public opinion under the cover of anonymity and to sow hatred and prejudice among the citizens of the United States. Not only were the *Protocols* newly printed,[5] but a series of popular exploitations of their contents was spread broadcast. They purported to prove[6] a pretended conspiracy of Jews and Freemasons to overturn the economic system of the world by inciting warfare and revolution. This fable was given credence in the educated society of enlightened America, just as the Middle Ages gave credence to stories of witchcraft. They were accepted as true, though the publishers of the stories could not themselves suppress their doubts of their authenticity.

Henry Ford[7] was the most successful industrialist in the world, and believed that he was also the cleverest man in the world. He felt called upon to solve social problems, and put the columns of the *Dearborn Independent*, a weekly founded by the Ford Motor Company and distributed gratis in hundreds of thousand of copies, at the disposal of an unrestricted campaign against the Jews. In a moment of discouragement he had fallen into the hands of a number of journalists of the German racial school, and they abused his gullibility and wealth to set before the American public the dreariest fabrications of antisemitic fraud concerning the alleged international Jewish conspiracy. In order to strengthen the effect, the weekly articles were from time to time assembled into pamphlets under the title *The International Jew*.

The Jews suffered severely from this carefully thought out and concentrated attack, which ran absolutely counter to every American tradition. Such mass slander could not be ignored, and the large Jewish organizations felt it their duty to take a stand. A common declaration, signed by the representatives of the entire body of American Jewry, by the synagogue associations of the various shades and their respective rabbinic organizations, by the American Jewish Committee, the Zionist Organization of America, the Provisional Congress Committee, and the Independent Order B'nai B'rith, was issued on December 1, 1920, under the title *An Address to Their Fellow-Citizens by American Jewish Organizations*.[8] External proof that the *Protocols* were a base forgery was not yet available, but a detailed analysis demonstrated the falsity of the document on internal grounds and the utter impossibility of Jews being responsible for its contents. Similarly the baselessness of the assumption of the identity of Judaism and Bolshevism was shown, and the true purpose of the publication revealed. The Jews were not alone in protesting. A few days later representatives of thirty denominations and 150,000 churches were assembled in Boston at a convention of the Federal Council of the Churches of Christ in America and adopted a resolution

deploring all such cruel and unwarranted attacks upon our Jewish brethren, and in a spirit of good-will extending to them an expression of confidence, earnestly admonishing our people to express disapproval of all actions which are conducive to intolerance or tend to the destruction of our national unity through arousing racial division in our body politic.

On Christmas eve the American Committee on the Rights of Religious Minorities issued a similar protest condemning every effort to arouse passion against minorities. In the middle of January 1921 there followed a protest of 119 distinguished American Christians from every walk of life under the leadership of ex-Presidents Wilson and Taft and of William Cardinal O'Connell "against this vicious propaganda."

We call upon our fellow-citizens of Gentile birth and Christian faith, [they said] to unite their efforts to ours to the end that it may be crushed. In particular, we call upon all those who are moulders of public opinion to strike at this un-American and un-Christian agitation.

John Spargo, the writer, who had been responsible for this declaration, supplemented it by a brochure entitled *The Jew and American Ideals*. Jewish organizations, and in particular the Anti-Defamation League of the Independent Order B'nai B'rith, circulated literature in defense.[9] The American Jewish Congress, which had been planned for only a single meeting and had already been declared dissolved by its president, decided to remain a permanently active body. The permanent organization was founded in May 1922 in order

> to further and promote Jewish rights, to safeguard and defend such rights wherever and whenever they are either threatened or violated; generally to deal with all matters relating to and affecting specific Jewish interests.

Nathan Straus, the universally admired philanthropist, was the first president of the new organization, and in 1925 he was succeeded by Stephen S. Wise, who in one capacity or another has remained the spiritual leader of the Congress. Most of the tasks the new organization undertook were identical with those of the American Jewish Committee, and in times of great need they have worked together.

In the meanwhile the Constantinople correspondent of the London *Times*, Philip Graves, discovered the original model of the *Protocols*. Herman Bernstein, the writer (1876–1935), later American Minister to Albania, discovered the copies of the *Protocols* in Russian, which had been dedicated to the Czar, and in his *History of a Lie* he gave a detailed exposé of the crude motives and methods of the forger. In any other concern such compelling evidence would have made the further use and propagation of such base frauds impossible. But since it was a question of Jews, the discredited rubbish continued to circulate as current coin. Out of the stores of the *Dearborn Independent*, *The Ford International Weekly*, stench bombs continued to be hurled and to vitiate the atmosphere, and the marksmen had no reason to complain of want of success. The press, which was conscious of its responsibility, refused to publicize the matter, but there were representatives of public opinion such as judges, educators, statisticians, and a number of members of Congress who were only too eager to swallow these charges.

A dreary symptom of the devastating effect of racial prejudices was offered by the president of Harvard University, who could find no other remedy for a situation that troubled him than the establishment of a *numerus clausus* for Jews.[10] The Overseers of the University were sufficiently liberal-minded to reject the proposal directly. But that such a suggestion could have been made in a democratic country by the head of one of the oldest and most distinguished seats of higher learning was alarming enough. Other academic institutions employed the *numerus clausus* tacitly, its existence being an open secret. Many hospitals did not accept Jews as internes; in others the Christian internes made things so disagreeable for their Jewish colleagues that it amounted to a practical boycott.

At a time when Jews were being subjected to a constant, screaming barrage, their hands were strengthened when President Coolidge,[11] a thorough New Englander by descent and convictions, repeatedly and unequivocally expressed himself against racial hatred and in favor of the American tradition of tolerance which had undergone trial by fire during the World War.

The Jews [he declared in one of his speeches] have always come to us eager to adapt themselves to our institutions, to thrive under the influence of liberty, to take their full part as citizens in building and sustaining the nation, and to bear their part in its defense, in order to make a contribution to the national life fully worthy of the traditions they had inherited.[12]

But the hope that these exalted pronouncements of the President of the United States would drown out the outpourings of fanatical bigots was frustrated. Ford's buccaneers of the press continued unchanged their work of slandering Jews individually and collectively. It was the nemesis of the German spirit; it was as if the hydra of Ludendorff, whose head appeared to have been struck off, had sprouted a thousand new heads upon the soil of the United States and was devastating the body politic with its poison. For over six years the monster raged on, and it appeared that it would never be subdued. It was Aaron Sapiro, a young Chicago lawyer, who found a vital spot. Sapiro was attorney for a number of cooperative agricultural produce organizations. The slanderers on *The Dearborn Independent* accused him of running these organizations exclusively for his own profit, and Sapiro entered suit against Henry Ford.[13] Efforts were made to delay the action, but all pretexts were finally exhausted and the case came to trial in 1927 in Detroit, where all of the machinations of *The Dearborn Independent* were laid bare. Henry Ford suddenly came to realize the abysmal depths into which he had been drawn, and as a man of determination he seized the occasion for freeing himself.

After reaching an agreement with Louis Marshall, Ford made public a statement in which he acknowledged his error.

To my great regret [it read] I have learned that Jews generally, and particularly those of this country, not only resent these publications as promoting anti-Semitism, but regard me as their enemy. Trusted friends ... have assured me in all sincerity that in their opinion the character of the charges and insinuations made against the Jews, both individually and collectively, contained in many of the articles which have been circulated periodically in *The Dearborn Independent* and have been reprinted in the pamphlets mentioned, justifies the righteous indignation entertained by Jews everywhere toward me because of the mental anguish occasioned by the unprovoked reflections made upon them....

... I deem it my duty as an honorable man to make amends for the wrong done to the Jews as fellow-men and brothers, by asking their forgiveness for the harm that I have unintentionally committed, by retracting so far as lies within my power the offensive charges laid at their door by these publications, and by giving them the unqualified assurance that henceforth they may look to me for friendship and good will.... Finally, let me add that this statement is made of my own initiative and wholly in the interest of right and justice and in accordance with what I regard as my solemn duty as a man and as a citizen.

Marshall's reply is evidence for his wisdom, dignity, and magnanimity:

The statement which you had sent me gives us assurance of your retraction of the offensive charges, of your proposed change of policies in the conduct of *The Dearborn Independent*, of your future friendship and good will, of your desire to make amends, and what is to be expected from any man of honor, you couple these assurances with a request for pardon. So far as my influence can further that end, it will be exerted, simply because there flows in my veins the blood of ancestors who were inured to suffering and nevertheless remained steadfast in their trust in God. Referring to the teachings of the Sermon on the Mount, Israel Zangwill once said that we Jews are after all the only Christians. He might have added that it is because essentially the spirit of forgiveness is a Jewish trait.

Ford kept his word faithfully and forbade the reprinting of any of his previous publications against the Jews. But the damage had been done, the virus had been scattered, and it was used in quantities not only by Theodor Fritsch, the hero of antisemitic falsification in Leipzig, but also by the Klansmen in the United States. And, as if there were not enough points of irritation, the "Britons" of England felt obliged to dump their own wisdom regarding the *Protocols* upon the American market.

Immediate and irreparable harm was done in the field of immigration by the promoters of the Nordic doctrine. Out of fear that the expected impoverishment of Europe would direct an incalculable horde of immigrants to this country at the very moment of demobilization and widespread unemployment, a temporary bar and subsequent limitation of immigration were suggested.[14] President Wilson vetoed the bill, but in 1921 his successor signed a quota law to limit post-war immigration to 3% of the various nationalities according to the census of 1910. The law was a painful shock to thousands who had laid down their last penny to obtain permission to immigrate to the United States, of whom many were already en route. Cases of special hardship were alleviated by intervention, and many unfortunates were saved from deportation.

The law was to continue in effect for a single year; it was several times extended, but was slated to end on June 30, 1924. In the meantime an atmosphere of racial hostility had pervaded the atmosphere. Nordic and Protestant elements were to have a monopoly in the United States, and most of the Catholic peoples from the east and south of Europe were to be excluded. Accordingly the census of 1890, reflecting the period before the great immigration from Italy and the East, was made basic, and the quotas were reduced to 2%. Furthermore, beginning with July 1927 total immigration was to be limited to 150,000.

The exclusion of certain classes of immigrants and the limitation of the total number over long periods of time alarmed large groups of people, and among them numbers of Jews. For now those Jews who were forced to emigrate and had set their last hope upon flight to the United States found the gates barred. A consequence of the new quotas was that Jewish immigration from 1925 to 1930 was reduced to a fifth of what it had been in the preceding period. Furthermore, there were many cases of extreme hardship when earlier immigrants wished to bring their families over to join them. Jewish organizations felt their responsibility, and on June 22, 1924, the representatives of forty-five of them formed an Emergency Committee on Jewish Refugees.[15] The purpose of the Committee was

> to alleviate the plight of the stranded refugees, to repatriate those who wish to return to the countries of their origin, to investigate immigra-

tion conditions in other countries, and to help the settlement of refugees where opportunities are to be found.

The Committee was able to achieve a good part of its purpose, in cooperation with similar organizations in Europe.

The crisis in their own position did not diminish the concern of American organizations over questions of Jewish rights in the countries of Europe. New York became the clearing house for complaints regarding repressive measures against Jews and, in particular, regarding violations of minority rights.[16] The offices concerned were on the *qui vive*, with missions to Europe and the reception of delegates from Europe. It was from New York that negotiations with the envoys of the countries concerned, particularly Poland and Rumania, were undertaken. It was from New York that correspondence with the League of Nations was entered into, that personal representation was eventually maintained at Geneva, and that the implementing of the peace treaty was insisted upon. Since the various countries were concerned with American credit and with a favorable public opinion in America, this constant vigilance exercised at least a restraining influence upon the governments at fault. From the United States steps could be taken to oppose certain kinds of agitation which had become fashionable in the post-war period and which threatened to injure Jewish interests. It was possible to prevent impending calendar reform[17] which would have made Sabbath observance extremely difficult. No efforts availed to prevent the prohibition of *shehitah* in free Norway,[18] but a full explanation of the institution forestalled similar agitation in the United States.

After the war the United States was the richest country on earth, and all the world turned to the United States with their financial problems. Delegates of Jewish organizations and institutions in Europe were constantly on hand for the purpose of collecting funds. In most countries money values were such that great help could be given with a relatively small contribution in dollars. The Jewish population of the United States enjoyed a certain prosperity. At a time when billions changed hands the merchants naturally profited, and Jewish workers profited by high wages. The clothing industry, in which Jews were largely represented as tailors, manufacturers and merchants, experienced a boom which brought them large profits. This was the period in which the Jewish share in this industry was at its highest. In the large cities the real estate business was extraordinarily lucrative. There were speculators who lost their money as quickly as they made it. But by and large prosperity prevailed and men were ready to share it with those who were in need. Among the millions of immigrants of recent decades there were many who had needy friends and relatives in Europe and were anxious to save them from starvation. There were many who thought of the communities and the communal institutions of their old homes and wished to help maintain them. The amount that individuals remitted to Europe during the decade cannot be determined statistically, but it certainly approached the hundred million mark.[19] We do know of the great relief drives which were constantly in progress. The Joint Distribution Committee had been established as a temporary organization for the duration of the war; it continued as a permanent institution and between 1921 and 1930 it was able to disburse as much as forty million dollars. From prevention of famine and epidemics it proceeded to reconstruction. When David A. Brown declared, on the basis of his personal impressions in Eastern Europe, that he was willing to lead a campaign to collect fourteen millions of dollars, his design seemed chimerical. But the willingness to give was there, and he succeeded in this and in later drives. We have already indicated the magnificent benefits these collections made possible (see p. 467, above).

ZIONISM AND THE JEWISH AGENCY

The upbuilding of Palestine was among the undertakings which found warm support in the United States — aside from a few intransigent dissidents.[20] Zionism has its special American history. Post-war Zionism was associated with the name of Justice Brandeis; it was he that inspired the Pittsburgh program of 1918,[21] which urged the upbuilding of the land as a model community on the basis of the fullest social justice —"a combination of Amos and Isaiah," wrote Henrietta Szold. Immediately after the end of the war he visited Palestine in order to know it at first hand. Like all visitors he was fascinated by the beauty of the country; but he was also shocked by the inroads made by chronic malaria. He suggested that the abolition of malaria be undertaken as a preliminary to reconstruction, and he urged that to achieve this end large sums be devoted to afforestation and irrigation. The best experts were to prepare the economic bases for mass settlement. Zionist administration and propaganda should devote all their efforts to the single goal of actual constructive work.

Brandeis was thinking of the rapid settlement of the United States as an example. It is to be doubted that the experience of the United States could be repeated in an inhabited area like Palestine, where the difficulties were the result of outside forces and not due to shortcomings on the part of the Jews. Nevertheless everyone was eagerly awaiting the initiative of this farseeing and enthusiastic guide. But instead, at the first Zionist Conference after the Balfour Declaration, which took place in London in 1920, a break between Brandeis and the directorate of the Zionist Organization developed. It is not clear at this date whether the break was really avoidable, and to what extent it was caused by human, all too human, factors. Brandeis could not be at ease with the Zionist routine and bureaucracy and was visibly annoyed by it. Chaim Weizmann, who had not yet been formally named leader of the organization but was commonly recognized as such, formulated the opposition in popular terms as a conflict of "Pinsk versus Washington." The formulation was correct, for what was involved was a meeting, or lack of it, between diverse mentalities and temperaments. Mass psychology won, and, as is always the case, the prophet went unheeded. Brandeis and his friends were read out of the administration of the Zionist Organization. They withdrew to promote reconstruction work in Palestine by economic processes, and obtained the cooperation of the Joint Distribution Committee and the Jewish Colonization Association to that end.

The government of the United States concurred in the formulation of the Palestine Mandate (see p. 599, below). A resolution of both Houses of Congress approved of the principles of the Mandate (1922), and this was supplemented by a "Convention between the United Kingdom and the United States of America respecting the Rights of the Governments of the Two Countries and their respective Nationals in Palestine," dated December 1924.[22] This convention assured American citizens of the security of eventual investments of capital in Palestine and encouraged them to make such investments. Instead of the gigantic construction fund which Brandeis had visualized, there were annual collections for the *Keren Hayesod* ("Palestine Foundation Fund"). The appearance of Dr. Chaim Weizmann in the company of the magic figure of Albert Einstein gave the Fund an aspect of solemnity and exaltation and assured its success.

The objective of the collections was not only the material upbuilding of Palestine, but its spiritual upbuilding also, in the form of the Hebrew University in Jerusalem.[23] For this end men of various convictions extended helping hands. Sol Rosenbloom of Pittsburgh, a Brandeis Zionist, set up a large fund along with non-Zionists like Felix M. Warburg and Philip Wattenberg. J. L. Magnes not only put his influence at the service of this idealistic enterprise, but removed to Jerusalem with his family in order to prepare for the establishment of the future University. As early as 1921 the American Jewish Physicians' Committee was formed for the purpose of establishing and maintaining a medical center in connection with the University, and Hadassah stretched out a helpful hand.

Work for the University constituted a bridge to the non-Zionists, whose cooperation was indispensable if the success of the annual collections and the "cooperation of all Jews" envisaged by the mandate were to be assured. Louis Marshall[24] regarded it his ineluctable duty to promote, at whatever sacrifice, the possibility of upbuilding Palestine which had been offered to the Jews, and took the chairmanship of a Non-Partisan Conference of American Jews to Consider Palestinian Problems. After years of taking counsel this Conference won the cooperation of ever larger groups and increasingly found itself on common ground with the Zionists. Both parties combined to despatch a "Joint Commission to make a thorough survey and investigation of conditions in Palestine, including an expert study of the resources and of the agricultural, industrial, commercial and other economic possibilities of Palestine and neighboring territory, and to acquire a complete conspectus of Jewish activities and achievements in the Holy Land" (1927). Besides Felix M. Warburg and Lee K. Frankel of New York, Sir Alfred Mond (later Lord Melchett) of London and Oskar Wassermann of Berlin served on this Commission. They were accompanied by a number of experts. A carefully worked out memorandum drew their attention to the various problems which were to be considered. The report of the Commission proved to be favorable, and the non-Zionists declared their readiness to cooperate in an enlarged Jewish Agency. After certain difficulties in the Zionist camp had been overcome (see p. 602, below), a meeting of the Agency took place in Zurich in August 1929. Louis Marshall put all the weight of his authority behind the Agency, and considered plans for making its work effective by gathering funds for it. This was Marshall's last act on behalf of Judaism; several weeks later he died. Even his persuasive eloquence could not have produced the gigantic sum hoped for during the economic crisis which followed in the United States. It was difficult for his successor, Felix M. Warburg, to fulfill even part of what had been expected. The new constellation had the merit of establishing unity among the Zionists themselves and between them and other groups and of avoiding dissipation of strength in internal quarrels.

Cultural and Religious Progress

The disruption of communications during the World War had shown the folly of a large community remaining permanently dependent on overseas countries for cultural requirements. Until 1914, for example, the United States imported all its Hebrew prayer books and Bibles from Europe, and then it suddenly found itself cut off from its sources of supply. An incidental result of the war, of no great cultural or economic significance externally considered but extremely important nevertheless, was that the Jews of America now established Hebrew presses. Of these the most significant for its aesthetic merits and for completeness, was the Hebrew Press[25] of the Jewish Publication Society of America, located in Philadelphia. This Press has since assured itself of a place among historic Hebrew printing establishments, and, in consequence of the increasing concentration of Jewish spiritual energies in America, its significance in Jewish cultural life as a whole has grown.

Far-seeing men realized that spiritual interests required serious attention and energetic action. New York, which had more Jews than all of Europe with the exception of Poland and Soviet Russia, was enriched by two institutions for higher Jewish learning.[26] In 1922 Stephen S. Wise created the Jewish Institute of Religion as a "school of training for the Jewish ministry, research and community service." Wise stamped the institution with the impress of his own spirit. In accordance with the principles of the Free Synagogue, the Institute was not bound to any single specific interpretation of Judaism but made a place for all whose representatives were morally and intellectually worthy. In view of the attitude of the founder it is needless to say that strong emphasis was put upon contemporary problems of Jewish life, on national thinking, and on the upbuilding of Palestine.

Especially noteworthy is the stride towards recognizing modern scholarship, Jewish and general, taken by orthodox groups. The Rabbi Isaac Elchanan Yeshiva, bearing the name of the famous rabbi of Kovno as its symbol, had been in existence since 1896. Under the leadership of Bernard Revel (1885-1940) it was transformed into a Theological Seminary in which Jewish subjects other than Talmud and codes were also taught. In 1928 the charter was broadened, so that the Yeshiva added to its departments a regular American college, offering courses usual in the college curriculum in the humanities and the natural sciences, with its own High School for preparatory work. This was the first attempt to provide universal education and to face the demands of modern science in an orthodox Jewish atmosphere. If one remembers the remark made by Rabbi Solomon Tiktin of Breslau about 1840 in reference to Abraham

Geiger, that anyone who had attended a university was *ipso facto* disqualified to be a rabbi, and if one remembers that as late as 1870 Esriel Hildesheimer was attacked by his orthodox friends because he would not limit rabbinic training to the realm of the *halakah*, one can realize the magnitude of the transformation in time and environment. In 1922 the western center of orthodoxy established a Hebrew Theological College at Chicago with similar aims, but this institution has not as yet attained the organization and influence of its sister institution in New York.

The older Jewish scholarly institutions flourished.[27] In 1922 the Hebrew Union College for the first time called one of its own graduates to the presidency, in the person of Julian Morgenstern. The College undertook the publication of an annual volume of studies, which not only included the work of its staff and alumni but also offered hospitality to scholars not connected with the institution. The Jewish Theological Seminary started a learned series entitled *Ginze Schechter*, commemorating the name of Solomon Schechter and connecting it with the Genizah which he discovered. Both institutions competed in acquiring the most valuable collections of Jewish books and manuscripts in Europe in order to make them available for use on this side of the Atlantic. For the Hebrew Union College, A. S. Oko acquired the valuable collection of Jewish art and cult objects in the possession of Sally Kirschstein of Berlin and laid the ground for a Jewish Museum. In 1931, the Jewish Theological Seminary opened a Museum of Jewish Ceremonial Objects in its new building, under the direction of Alexander Marx; this Museum performs a unique function in the educational center of New York.

Two great universities received foundations for Jewish chairs. At Harvard, the Nathan Littauer Chair for Jewish Literature and Philosophy was endowed in 1925, and at

Columbia the Miller Foundation for Jewish History, Literature and Institutions in 1929. Yale became the seat of one of the Alexander Kohut Memorial Foundations and acquired a large scientific Jewish library.

Jewish scholarship in the United States had attained an important position, and Jewish scholars showed their awareness of their responsibility when in 1920 the foremost among them, under the leadership of Louis Ginzberg, organized themselves into the American Academy for Jewish Research. A few years later the Academy began the publication of its series of *Proceedings*, which offered a forum for further scholarly development.

But the religious situation continued unsatisfactory.[28] The old parties and programs had grown rigid, and, whatever their separate designations might be, all alike failed to attract new blood. In all of them Mordecai M. Kaplan saw weaknesses which made them impractical as vehicles for contemporary philosophical outlooks. He sought to substitute vitality for petrifaction, to make of the synagogue a vehicle for an outlook which should embrace and vitalize all of life. To the old view of Judaism as a faith he opposed a new view of Judaism as a civilization. The power of old-fashioned Judaism had rested in the idea of redemption, but that stage had now been left behind; the new Judaism must make its goal the development of a peculiarly Jewish life, a peculiarly Jewish creativeness, an "urge to Jewish survival by an inspiring and irresistible motive supplied with a definite method of self-expression." Such an ideology must do violence neither to Judaism nor to Americanism; it must, indeed, subserve both, for both have the right and duty to make their claims upon life. Jewish tradition must not overshadow American feeling towards life, nor Americanism crowd out Judaism; both must enter upon a cultural symbiosis.

According to an ancient Jewish dictum, the Holy One, blessed be He, the Torah, and Israel are one. Israel must form the basis; it must retain its identity within American life and preserve itself as a distinct group. It can do so if it strengthens and develops its institutions, if it elaborates its hereditary culture and the manifold expressions of its folk-spirit, if it cultivates the Hebrew language and its literary manifestations, if, in the spirit of Ahad Ha'am, it recognizes and promotes *Eretz Yisrael* as a cultural center. Judaism is the product of the life of the group, determined by the experiences of the group. Religion has always been an effective cultural factor, and as such its preservation is a matter of the highest importance, though certain details of its doctrines must be reconciled with philosophy and natural science. The importance of the Torah as revelation must be made relevant to contemporary life; it must suffuse life with inwardness; it must be conjoined with the aesthetic and the cultural. Judaism must not be relegated to an antiquarian nook in life, but must impregnate and pervade the whole fabric of life.

Kaplan's Reconstruction Movement has struck roots which transcend existing religious party lines; whether it is destined to bear fruit the future must show. The United States is not a favorable soil for movements. The American may be stirred momentarily by a drive or by the bizarre staging of a convention, but persistent effort on behalf of a movement is not his concern. Thus it comes about that even organizations with enormous followings are able to actualize so little of their philosophic principles in the lives of their membership. Why should a man disturb his comfort with reflections, when such matters can be left to the administrative machine of his organization?

Men who reflect make up a vanishing minority. Such a minority is comprised in the Menorah Association,[29] which remains true to its tradition of devoting attention to all cultural expressions of Jewish life. They remain outside of party affiliation, not because they are above it, but because they do not recognize the limitations of party; they see in the various concepts of Judaism the functions of a living organism which has various aspects and outgrowths but which is capable of discarding diseased members and preserving the sound.

For a considerable proportion of the intellectuals religion merges into social action.

The fundamental problem of our day [writes Waldo Frank][30] is how we are to transform the great traditional religious energies of Western Civilization into a modern social action adequate to recreate the world chaos in which we live and in which all that we revere is endangered. The basis of democracy is in our religious heritage; yet, as we know, the democracies have lost this in anything that we might call a working form. And the revolutionary isms have gone so far and tragically off the track as to turn entirely against religion, even against the spirit of religion. No wonder they fail! And must continue to fail.

The heart of the problem was and is the horde of philistines whose god is the dollar and whose cultural interests are limited by sports and parlor games. Among the children and grandchildren of immigrants from Eastern Europe the same phenomena occurred as were to be observed in the 60's of the preceding century among the German immigrants. But the earlier immigrants had been attracted by the reform congregations and had not leaped at one bound from absolute constraint to absolute liberty. The bridge from Pinsk to Washington is built slowly, and rung by rung. Many who regard themselves as enlightened are quite remote from enlightenment; they are merely at the stage at which Judaism seems to them not fashionable. They no longer speak the language of their parents, but they cannot yet understand the language of their children. In large cities the evil is lessened by the dynamic of the masses and by the work of community centers[31] and similar institutions, but in smaller communities the effects of isolation are devastating. In Europe the small communities were the mainstay of conservation, a reservoir to maintain the level reduced by the leveling forces of the large cities; but in the United States the process of leveling down begins in the small cities, where each individual synagogue officer is a sovereign power and is vigilant to see that Judaism does not display too much activity. To a large extent it is the Christian churches that expect certain cooperation from the rabbi; the Jews in his community would scarcely urge him to greater activity. They are largely without understanding of the significance of religion and historical consciousness.

Educational efforts made headway after 1910: teachers were trained, methods and textbooks improved, and the living Hebrew language greatly increased its influence. Many communities became conscious of their responsibilities and established educational bureaus and supervisors. But dissatisfaction was not eliminated; above all, the understanding support of the parents was lacking, and, where the interest of the parents is at a minimum, none at all can be expected from the children.

In more recent years attention has been paid to the urgent task of adult education. An Academy for Adult Education has come into existence; the Hadassah organization has been very active in this as in other respects; much has also been accomplished in orthodox circles. The young people presented still another educational problem.

Young men who were employed could be reached, in larger localities, through Jewish Centers or "Y's;" those who attended college were left quite to themselves. Their connection with Judaism, unless they were interested in the Zionist *Avukah* or the orthodox student societies, grew constantly weaker. It is significant that it was a non-Jewish professor, Edward Chauncey Baldwin of the University of Illinois, who called attention to the sad state of affairs. He pointed out that Jewish students displayed complete ignorance of anything pertaining to the Bible, and declared that positive measures to end so shameful a condition were more important than refuting antisemitism. The suggestion was accepted, and Jewish students again organized themselves for Jewish activities as they had once done through the Menorah Society. The pioneer in this work was Benjamin M. Frankel, a theological student, who, before his early death, was able to interest the Independent Order B'nai B'rith in the enterprise. The Order undertook financial responsibility for the work; it was called the Hillel Foundation,[32] after a hero of Jewish history. The organizations which, alarmed by the indifference of Jewish youth, had formed a Council of American Jewish Students Affairs, could find no more effective solution for the problem than that afforded by the Hillel Foundation, and as the Foundation spread from college to college the work of the Council became superfluous.

The name of Hillel is now part of the American university tradition, and on more than three score campuses, in association with the names of Wesley and Newman, it helps to integrate the spiritual values of the historic religions with the life of the university.

The program of the Foundation varies according to the size of the student body and the opportunities for influencing it. In addition to ordinary courses and discussion groups, open forums provide opportunities for exchange of views with non-Jews and for work in interfaith relations. In some universities, as at Illinois, Hillel work in religious education is accredited as a regular college course; in others the leader of the Hillel Foundation is a member of the college staff. In this way a focus is created from which Jewish students are stimulated to concern themselves with Judaism at a formative period of their lives and to prepare themselves for future leadership, to say nothing of the spiritual advantages that accrue to the individual by participating in voluntary common worship and the common celebration of Jewish festivals. Whether the future representatives of the greatest Jewish center in the world will be conscious of their responsibility and be true to it depends in large measure upon the extension and intensification of such work as this.

The labor group was a well organized class which led its own life and carried through its own educational program. Within the group itself a variety of reasons were offered for work in the field of Jewish education. Some emphasized the aim of restoring harmony between parents and children; others that of initiating their youth in Jewish values and of creating for them a friendly environment; still others desired "that the spirit of liberty shall permeate Jewish education." The Workmen's Circle, the *Po'ale Zion* and the Folkists organized their respective elementary schools and high schools in keeping with their specific ideologies. Even as the Labor group was making sacrifices by sending large sums of money for relief among the Jews of Eastern Europe, so they were lavish in their spending for the maintenance of educational systems which had their origin in Eastern Europe. There was, to be sure, one important difference between these schools and their European progenitors: the American schools, though employing the Yiddish language for instruction, followed a program whose aims and tendencies were in the direction of thorough Americanization.

Americanization and guidance towards the acquisition of higher culture were no longer problems but accomplished facts. This is shown by Yiddish literature itself.[33] The backgrounds of this literature were completely transformed. The new and numerous generation of Yiddish writers was altogether under the influence of the American experience. Their outlook was dominated by the countryside, the human types, and the habits of thought of their new home. They translated the classics of American poetry, such as Poe, Longfellow, Whitman, into Yiddish in order to acclimatize their audience, disregarding the difference of language, in the American scene. On the other hand, excellent translators, such as Isaac Goldberg, introduced the American public to outstanding Yiddish authors.

Yiddish press and Yiddish literature enjoyed their great period. Their readers were reasonably prosperous and willing to pay for cultural sustenance. The Yiddish theater also profited. New theatrical enterprises shot up like mushrooms, and their repertory was enlarged by translations from other literatures and by new creations in Yiddish. The Yiddish Art Theater presented the art of the Moscow theater to New York audiences. Leivick's *Golem* trilogy, with its brooding thought and its yearning for redemption, aroused such interest by its subject matter and the manner of its presentation that it was produced on Broadway in an English version, to say nothing of translations into other languages. The new art of the film was quickly exploited by the Yiddish stage. Indeed the 20's marked the high point of Yiddish culture in the United States. Cessation of immigration from the East and the economic depression caused the depletion of the Yiddish theater and the decline of the Yiddish press. In other American countries, such as Argentina, Brazil and Mexico, Yiddish remained the predominant culture among the Jews.

If the representatives of Yiddish were now under the influence of American culture, the "assimilated" Jews were most certainly so. The time had come when Jews appeared in the American literary arena in numbers and won for themselves a passing vogue or a more enduring fame.[34] They were not only forward-looking publishers and translators from Latin American, German, and Scandinavian literatures; they were themselves substantive authors. Even before the World War the younger generation of writers had fought against colonialism, provincialism, and sentimentality. The war had taken millions of men, whose view had never reached beyond the steeple of their village church, into a strange continent and had widened their horizons. Not only England, but France, Belgium, and Russia also were making efforts to spread knowledge of their culture and their spirit in the United States. In the drive for a maturer outlook, Jewish writers and critics took an active part. They were not constrained by old ties; they were naturally cosmopolitan in outlook; and because most of them had made their place in the world by their own efforts, they had a clearer view of the hardships and the problems of life. They had a rooted aversion to the tedious, and inclined to the sensational; all rebelled against philistinism.

The Jews also had their part in the revival of the theater and the opera. When the Theater Guild in New York undertook to cultivate artistic drama without regard to box-office success, there were Jews among the financial patrons of the enterprise and for a long while its direction was in Jewish hands. The 20's were the great period of the films.[35] Eminent artists were attracted to their production; staging and decor became enormously impressive, and the tone-film was invented. The name Hollywood acquired a special meaning in world civilization. The great share which Jewish entrepreneurs, Jewish writers and composers,[36] Jewish directors and Jewish stars have had in raising this institution from a simple pastime for simple people into a solid factor in our culture is commonly recognized.

In the plastic arts headquarters of the rebellion were located at 291 Fifth Avenue, where from the beginning of the century Alfred Stieglitz,[37] a master of artistic photography, ventured to present exhibitions of the masterpieces of the Paris impressionists. His salon was the haven of youthful talents, whom he assisted materially and supported spiritually until they could make their own way. Stieglitz was the godfather of modern art in the United States. In architecture the problem was to combine the requirements of the modern business building with aesthetic demands. Louis J. Horowitz, who came from Poland as a young man, found artistic solutions for a number of important structures.

Shining lights of American culture were world-famous scholars, such as Franz Boas (1858–1942), one of the pioneers of anthropological research; Simon Flexner, one of the leading bacteriologists, for decades Director of Laboratories of the Rockefeller Institute for Medical Research; his brother Abraham, distinguished in the field of scientific education and deserving of particular merit in the improvement of medical education.

Business, Philanthropy, and Effects of Economic Depression

The slightness of Jewish participation in the colossal development of finance, commerce, and industry is striking. In these fields, which were elsewhere regarded as the special domains of the Jew, the Jews of the United States never reached the front ranks. In the heavy industries only the Guggenheims[38] need be mentioned. Meyer Guggenheim (1828–1905) became one of the leaders in the extracting and smelting of copper and lead; he also mined silver, gold and other metals. His sons carried on his work and made themselves famous by magnificent philanthropies. Daniel Guggenheim contributed millions to the promotion of aeronautics, apart from his general benefactions. In memory of his son John, Simon Guggenheim established a fund which provides gifted scholars and artists, without distinction of sex, race, or religion, with a period of freedom for developing their special talents.

Prominent Jewish merchants, mostly self-made men, distinguished themselves by their social outlook, and the annals of their home cities record their works. Out of the great number of names which might be cited a few may be taken at random.[39] Like many others, Edward A. Filene (1860–1937) of Boston was president of a department store, but his interests ranged far beyond his business. Following European models he introduced Credit Union Associations into the United States, which made small loans to their members at low rates of interest. Many states encouraged these unions by law, and while Filene was still alive they combined into a larger association. Filene brought about the establishment of the American Chamber of Commerce and the International Chamber of Commerce. He worked for international peace, and established the Twentieth Century Fund, which carries on important social and economic studies.

At Portland, Oregon, on the west coast, Ben Selling (1852–1931) was a modest and unassuming man, with poetic sympathy and the mind of a dreamer. In him the ideal of social righteousness found concrete embodiment. He was not able to complete his high school course because his father needed his help in his business, but his generosity made it possible for many children of his state to receive a satisfactory education. The president of the University of Oregon eulogized "his high-minded and intelligent conception of public service;" he found him "profound in wisdom, keen in his understanding and farsighted in his vision — combining in a rare degree the technical understanding of the trained mind, the human compassion of a great soul, and the desire to serve of a great altruist."

Finally mention must be made of Julius Rosenwald (1853–1932), the princely merchant of Chicago. From modest beginnings he rose to be head of the greatest mail-order house, perhaps the greatest retail organization in the world, but he remained simple and modest. He denied that his success was due to any special mercantile gifts, but he could not deny that he was a genius in philanthropy, or, for he hated the word, in correcting social injustices. He felt particular sympathy for those who were oppressed by society. His benefactions for relief and reconstruction among the Jews have already been mentioned in passing. The Negroes honored him as their greatest benefactor next to Abraham Lincoln, because he worked for their spiritual emancipation and social uplift. When he was convinced of the merits of a cause he gave in generous measure, but he made his gifts contingent upon the gifts of others to the same cause, and thus he multiplied his benefaction. Together with his like-minded wife he established a fund of many millions, but he provided that the capital sum of this fund be exhausted within a given space of time. His principle of avoiding funds created in perpetuity with provisions to remain binding in an unforeseeable future was a new departure in philanthropy, and the example was followed by others; it made incalculable sums available for the national needs of the moment. President Herbert C. Hoover, the director of the most extensive humanitarian undertaking of all times, wrote of Rosenwald: "He diverted his wealth into those channels which inspiration and study convinced him were for the best service of his fellow-men. Where there were no channels, he surveyed and dug them, recognizing no barriers of creed and race."

In October 1929 the world economic crisis laid hold of the United States. There had been depressions and unemployment from time to time in the past, but the depression of 1929 transcended all previous experience.[40] It was a landslide that carried everything with it. Overnight masses of people were impoverished, not only those who had speculated with their property, but those who had habitually invested it on sound and conservative principles. The depression halted the tendency to new undertakings. Capital disappeared and unemployment spread unchecked.

The depression weighed heavily upon Jewish life. Impoverishment had a twofold effect. Individuals who had previously contributed freely to charitable institutions now found it impossible to do so; and many who had previously been donors were now constrained to apply for assistance. The number of those applying for relief rose, on the average of all the states, by 50%; in an ordinarily prosperous community like Baltimore it rose by 77%. A special hardship became apparent: Jews and Jewesses applying for employment were refused because of their religion. It was always known that they were at a disadvantage, but as long as plenty of positions were available, no special attention had been paid to the situation. Synagogues, Jewish hospitals and orphanages, which had erected elaborate buildings during prosperity, frequently by assuming heavy mortgages, now found that they could neither maintain them nor even retain them. Emergency measures had to be taken; budgets were reduced, mergers arranged. Synagogues and Talmud Torahs had to be closed, rabbis discharged. For eighty years congregations had constantly expanded and retrenchment had been unknown.

Immigration ceased, and with it the burdens it had occasioned. But it required the utmost exertions to fulfill the obligations undertaken towards the Jews of other lands, and in particular of Palestine. Depression smoothed the road for communism and attuned men's ears to propaganda from Moscow. Numbers of workers in opposition to the unions enrolled in the radical camp and found adherents among the youth and the intelligentsia. Danger to the community was accentuated by the fact that this movement did not campaign with its visor up. The experience of the depression ended a carefree period in the United States — limitless possibilities had reached their limit — and made it necessary to construct an economy on planned lines.

A new government introduced a New Deal, and encountered the opposition of Big Business; according to the time-honored practice, the sluices of antisemitism were opened and dissatisfaction was directed against the Jews. Agitation was facilitated by the fact that a number of Jews had influence in the cabinet; and the wide spread of unemployment made larger numbers susceptible to this propaganda. The United States became a breeding-ground for fascist groups, which appeared under various odd names and whose programs exhibited a parti-colored kaleidoscope; the one point upon which all agreed was in creating incitement against the Jews. They could not affect official policies, but they could poison large areas of public opinion, and they could disturb the long cherished conviction of the adherents of democracy that "it could not happen here." Vigilance was the watchword.

CHAPTER V

The Jewish National Home in Palestine

Foundations of British Policy

THE history of the Balfour Declaration parallels the history of the Jewish emancipation. The step was taken; it called forth approval and opposition; its effects were curtailed by administrative contrivances and governmental interpretations; and yet it succeeded in great measure in advancing a noble end. When His Majesty's Government empowered A. J. Balfour to issue a declaration upon the future of Palestine,[1] it behaved like a feather-headed son who disposes of his father's legacy without bothering to inform himself of its extent. Aside from the fact that the country was still in the hands of the Turks, it had already been pledged upon several previous mortgages. Sir Henry McMahon[2] had made broad territorial promises to the Sheriff of Mecca; according to McMahon's understanding Palestine was not included, but the Arabs have never acknowledged such an interpretation. Moreover, Sir Mark Sykes, one of the warmest advocates of Jewish claims, had reached an understanding with George Picot, the representative of the Quai d'Orsay, looking to the partition of Syria and Palestine between France and England. The right hand knew not what the left was doing. The French Foreign Minister, Pichon, assured Nahum Sokolow of his wholehearted approval of the Balfour Declaration in a flowery letter. But when the Palestine question came up for discussion at the Peace Conference, the French representative doubted that the disposition of Palestine was in the jurisdiction of the Allies; he brought forward the Sykes-Picot understanding and the ancient historical claims of France. When France claimed authority, Italy, which was in the dark on previous secret understandings, could not, as a Catholic power, hold its peace. It knew it had the support of the Papal Curia, which had similarly approved of Zionist claims in the beginning and had subsequently taken a more ambiguous attitude.

This period of transition and uncertainty laid the ground for later difficulties. Emir Feisal,[3] the spokesman for the Arabs at the Peace Conference, approved the Balfour Declaration and declared that he was satisfied with the prospect of Arabs and Jews living side by side peacefully in Palestine. But the Palestinian Arabs were infected by the ferment which was active in Egypt and Syria at the time. And the OETA (see p. 482, above), instead of striving for reconciliation, confirmed the Arabs in their resistance. It gave them to understand that no final decision had yet been taken.

There were whispers that the military administration was opposed to a Jewish Palestine and hostile to Zionism and that it hoped to frustrate the policy of the government in London. In the spring of 1920 matters came to the point of an armed uprising in Syria. During the fighting, Bedouins attacked the most northerly of the Palestinian colonies, Tel Hai.[4] Joseph Trumpeldor, who had hastened to Palestine as a *halutz* immediately after the armistice, defended the colony heroically against superior force. He and five of his comrades, among them two girls, paid for their courage with their lives (February 29, 1920).

In March anti-Zionist demonstrations were organized at many places in Palestine, and were tolerated by the military administration. Higher officers heard speeches inciting to violence and did nothing. The military officials were warned but took no precautionary measures.⁵ On the critical day of *Nebi Musa* (April 4) they did nothing to prevent armed Arabs from swarming into the ancient city of Jerusalem, plundering Jewish businesses and attacking the inhabitants. The Arab police showed partiality to the insurgents. The military administration proved so incompetent that excesses took place on the two following days also and even increased in intensity. Five Jews and four Arabs were killed, 211 Jews and twenty-one Arabs wounded.

> Who could ever have conceived [writes an eyewitness, a non-Jewish senior British officer] that it should be possible, in the Holy City of Jerusalem, that for three days Jews, old and young, women and children, could be slaughtered, that rape should be perpetrated, synagogues burnt, scrolls of the Law defiled, and property plundered right and left, under the banner of England!

The only energy the British command showed was in keeping the Jewish Self-Defense at a distance and arresting twenty of their members, their leader, Vladimir Jabotinsky, at their head. It was an act of revenge against Jabotinsky, who had previously been thrown out of the army by what Colonel Patterson calls "strange and un-English devices," that he was now sentenced "on a ridiculous charge"— so again Colonel Patterson — to fifteen years of penal servitude. Upon the intervention of London the sentence was remitted. The military had wrecked their own administration, and were removed three months later. They had done little honor to the name of England, but they had succeeded in sabotaging the Balfour Declaration, which never achieved the result intended for it.

Gradually the situation was clarified. Palestine was declared a mandated territory⁶ under the sovereignty of the League of Nations; and, since the United States had refused its cooperation, Great Britain was generally acclaimed as the mandatory power, for there was general confidence in British fair play. Even before the treaty of peace with Turkey was signed, conditions of the Mandate were regulated by the Supreme Council at San Remo (April 25, 1920). Great Britain received a Mandate over Western Palestine, with the biblical boundaries of Dan to Beersheba, and was instructed to carry out the provisions of the Balfour Declaration; it was given a separate mandate over Transjordania.

The preamble of the Mandate agreement[7] repeats the Balfour Declaration and emphasizes, moreover, that "recognition has been given to the historical connection of the Jewish people with Palestine and to the grounds for reconstituting their national home in that country." The mandatory power was required to procure conditions in the country which would secure "the establishment of the Jewish National Home." A Jewish Agency was to be recognized as a Public Body. It was to be consulted and to cooperate with the administration of Palestine, particularly on questions concerning the establishment of the Jewish National Home and the interests of the Jewish population, but also concerning the development of the country generally. At first the Zionist Organization was to function as the Jewish Agency, but subsequently, with the consent of the British government, it was to "secure the cooperation of all Jews who are willing to assist in the establishment of the Jewish National Home."

Without confining the rights and the position of other sections of the population, the administration of Palestine was to make it possible for Jews to immigrate and to form closed settlements in the country, including the public domain and waste land so far as available. A citizenship law made it possible for Jews who settled in the country permanently to acquire Palestinian citizenship. A satisfactory legal and judicial system was to be introduced and the economy of the country, particularly agriculture, was to be promoted. The administration was empowered to authorize the Agency "to construct or operate upon fair and equitable terms, any public works, services and utilities, and to develop the national resources of the country." The Palestine administration was obligated

fully to guarantee respect for the personal status of the various peoples and communities and for their religious interests. In particular, the control and administration of *Wakfs* (Moslem pious foundations) shall be exercised in accord with religious law and the disposition of the founders. . . . . Complete freedom of conscience and free exercise of all forms of worship, subject only to the maintenance of public order and morals, are ensured to all. No discrimination of any kind shall be made between the inhabitants of Palestine on the ground of race, religion or language. No person shall be excluded from Palestine on the sole ground of his religious belief.

The mandatory power undertakes the full protection of the holy sites of all religions and is accountable to the League of Nations for their adequate protection. English, Arabic, and Hebrew are to be the official languages of Palestine. The festival days of the various religious communities are to be recognized as legal holidays for their communities.

On July 1, 1920, the British government put the country under civil administration. Sir Herbert Samuel[8] of London was installed as High Commissioner, the title being intended to conform to the character of a Mandate. Samuel was no Zionist, but he was a loyal Jew, and he had contributed greatly to mutual understanding between the Zionists and the British government. From 1905 to 1917, with short interruptions, he had been a member of the British Cabinet; subsequently he served in other important posts, as for example, as special commissioner for Belgium; and in all the positions which he held he won the highest confidence. Distinguished for conscientiousness, expert knowledge, and administrative skill, he was the ideal man for the difficult position. "His appointment was a stroke of genius on the part of Mr. Lloyd George, entirely justified by the results:" this was the opinion of one who was able to observe the man and his work at first hand. He was a man of natural dignity; the Jews reposed their confidence in him, and he sought to win the confidence of the Arabs and Christians also.

The British government[9] was faced with an enormous task. It had to reorganize a country which had been neglected and desolate for centuries, to show consideration for Turkish law and administration, and make the transition to modern usages. It had to care for public security, law, orderly administration, and just taxation, to attend to health conditions and water supply, to improve education, to construct roads, and much else. It had to improve economic conditions, and particularly to promote agriculture and handicrafts. And lastly it had to secure peace between the various religious communities.

All of these things the government undertook to do; and to secure the cooperation of the population it convoked an Advisory Committee upon which representatives of the Arabs, Christians, and Jews sat with the officials of the government. The British administration became a potent factor in civilizing the country. It would have been hailed as a blessing from heaven if there had been no Jewish problem; however, without the revenue from the Jews it could not have accomplished a fraction of what it actually did accomplish. The Zionist Commission pressed for free immigration at the earliest possible moment, first for those whom the Turks had forced to leave the country during the war, and then for the thousands of young people who were ready to devote their energy and intelligence to the service of the country. These young Jews from Eastern Europe had caused some resentment. They had not the manners taught on the playing fields of Eton and Rugby, but rather the nonchalance characteristic of the contemporary youth movements. They had been released from the pressure to which they had been subjected and had come to the national home which had been promised them. There they felt at home, and they were eager to redeem the country by their labor.

Most of them were under the influence of Aaron David Gordon (1856–1922), the philosopher of labor from Deganyah. Gordon[10] was a Jewish Tolstoi; he preached the gospel of work. Work, he taught, binds man not only to nature but to the entire universe, and in particular to his own country. Only by means of its own work could a people strike root in its own country. A nation can be rejuvenated only by the rejuvenation of its people. Ethical principles alone should be the basis of relations between people and nations. Gordon had no use for political programs, and was as opposed to political Marxism as he was enthusiastic for life in a community. His ideas dominated the *He-Ḥalutz* pioneer movement. There were some radical Marxists among the Palestinian immigrants, as there were among the self-conscious youth of all countries at the time. There were even some Bolshevists who made their way into the country for propaganda reasons, although Bolshevism was fundamentally opposed to Zionism.

Absolutely considered, the immigration[11] figures were not alarming; but they were quite large when compared to the previous Jewish population, and they seemed even larger, since all immigrants had to disembark at the single port of Jaffa. Permission to immigrate could be obtained only by those who possessed means for self-support or who could show that the Zionist Commission guaranteed them remunerative employment for a full year. There was plenty of new and essential work. Jewish capitalists invested in new industries, the Jewish construction firm *Solel Boneh* contracted for building roads and urban dwellings, Jewish land associations like *Keren Kayemeth* and PICA bought land which they drained and reclaimed for cultivation. The young workers toiled with a good will, although conditions were far harder than they could have expected. Not all found what they had been seeking in Palestine, and many emigrated again. It was not a simple matter to coordinate the various tendencies among the immigrants.

On May 1, 1921, the workers of Jaffa staged a parade and a number of communists tried to break it up. The confusion was used by the Arabs, Moslems and Christians alike, in fraternal unity, as an occasion for a murderous attack upon the Jews.[12] Forty-seven Jews were killed, among them the writer and labor leader Joseph Hayyim Brenner, and 146 wounded; the efforts of the Jewish self-defense and the intervention of armed force accounted for forty-eight Arab dead and seventy-three wounded. Attempts to attack neighboring colonies were forestalled. An investigation was started by the government at once, and established the existence of deep hatred for the Jews on the part of the Arabs. The Arabs had gradually grown used to the Jewish settlers of the period before the war, but they could not bear the swagger of the new immigrants and their contempt for the backward Arabs. Their dislike was intensified by a fear, which had been purposely and ingeniously exaggerated, that the Jews would soon be swarming into the country in countless numbers and would crowd the Arabs off their soil. Outside forces had been responsible for generating this fear, but it created great excitement at the moment and produced a united front against the Balfour Declaration. Immigration temporarily was stopped entirely, and when it was resumed the number of immigrants was smaller than it had been the preceding year.

Sir Herbert Samuel realized that it was impossible to govern a country against the predispositions of 80% of its inhabitants: the census of 1922 had shown 589,000

THE JEWISH NATIONAL HOME

Moslems, 83,000 Jews, and 71,000 Christians. Samuel regarded it as his first task to reconcile the Arabs to the Mandate government. He created a Supreme Moslem Council,[13] which had authority over the not inconsiderable religious foundations and over appointing and deposing judges of the Mohammedan religious tribunals. As head of this Council, a highly influential post carrying a government salary, Haj Amin Effendi el Husseini, a rabid Arab nationalist, was appointed in 1922.

Haj Amin's responsibility for the disturbances of 1920 had been clearly demonstrated, and he had been sentenced to ten years' imprisonment at hard labor. But he was soon pardoned and released. He had fled to Transjordania, and had returned upon being elected to the high post of Mufti of Jerusalem. When he was named President of the Supreme Moslem Council in addition, he became the most powerful man in the country and far the most powerful in the entire Arab world. Responsibility for two high positions did not calm his passions; he remained an irreconcilable and unscrupulous opponent of the Balfour Declaration and of English policies. The British administration had literally nurtured an adder in its bosom.

Shortly after the events in Jaffa an Arab delegation appeared in London and demanded that the Balfour Declaration and the plan for the Mandate government be given up and that the Arabs be granted their independence. The reply of the government constituted a statement of British policy in Palestine. In it the Secretary of State for Colonies, Mr. Winston Churchill,[14] laid at rest the fear of any intention to establish a Jewish state.

When it is asked [the decisive passage of the statement reads] what is meant by the development of the Jewish National Home in Palestine, it may be answered that it is not the imposition of a Jewish nationality upon the inhabitants of Palestine as a whole, but the further development of the existing Jewish community, with the assistance of Jews in other parts of the world, in order that it may become a center in which the Jewish people as a whole may take, on ground of religion and race, an interest and a pride. But in order that this community should have the best prospect of free development and provide a full opportunity for the Jewish people to display its capacities, it is essential that it should know that it is in Palestine as of right and not on sufferance. That is the reason why it is necessary that the existence of a Jewish National Home in Palestine should be internationally guaranteed, and that it should be formally recognized to rest upon ancient historic connection.

This prudently weighed statement was intended to allay the alarm of the Arabs and the disillusion of the Jews and to induce cooperation between the groups. The Zionists agreed with Churchill's interpretation, although they found that it whittled down the promises which had been made to them. But the Arab politicians remained intransigent. They continued to operate with the bogey of a Zionist condominium, and firmly refused to negotiate with the Palestine administration on creating instruments for self-administration until the British government should basically alter its policy.

Sir Herbert did not give up hope of reconciliation. He trusted to time and to the developments which the advantages of English administration must make apparent. The Mufti and his clique[15] styled themselves the "people of Palestine;" but the great mass of the population consisted of poor peasants or fellahin, who possessed tiny plots of land from which their primitive methods extracted diminutive crops which the impassability of the roads made it impossible for them to dispose of advantageously. Moreover, they were heavily indebted to the rich Arabs, or effendis, and under the insecurity of the Turkish administration they received the short end of every deal. The advantages which the new administration had brought were very real to them. They profited not only by the greater security, just taxes, orderliness in legal procedures and in land laws, not only by the improved roads, but also and primarily by the installations for education and public health. They bore practically no share of the expense, whereas a disproportionately large share came from the imposts and excises paid by Jews. Arabs also enjoyed the advantages of purely Jewish institutions, like the excellent health services provided by Hadassah and, later, the Nathan and Lina Straus Health Center. And lastly, Jewish purchases of real estate, rural and urban, brought the Arabs enormous sums, the large landlords directly, and the peasants indirectly. These advantages became increasingly evident daily; they would surely open the eyes of anyone not willfully blind.

Meanwhile, on June 24, 1922, the Mandate[16] was issued by the League of Nations. It was to go into effect on September 29, 1923, but its provisions were altered. The character of the Mandate over Palestine was different from that of other Mandates. In addition to the usual obligations of mandatory powers as set down in the constitution of the League of Nations, it made special provision for "establishment in Palestine of a National Home for the Jewish people." It therefore guaranteed Jews, and in particular the Jewish Agency which was their representative, certain privileges in the country. The Agency was not a Palestinian but a world-wide body, and so recognition of it was unusual in the ordinary framework of international usage. The British government which introduced this policy and the fifty-two member nations of the League which approved it were fully conscious of the problems involved, but were confident that the experiment would meet with good-will and that difficulties would be solved as they were encountered. Unrestricted Jewish immigration was not permitted, but, as in the mercantile age, permission to immigrate was made dependent upon bringing in a certain amount of capital or occupational ability, the latter with reference to the "absorptive economic capacity of the country." The Arab population was so preponderant and its rate of increase so great that there could be no threat of its being outnumbered at any humanly foreseeable time if eight or ten thousand Jews, which was the number anticipated, should be allowed to immigrate annually.

The demands of the Mandate were foreign to the training and outlook of the average administrative official, and the greater number of English officials met them with passive resistance, which on occasion might assume active form. Recognizing Jews as an equal or even privileged part of the population was a notion beyond the ken of the familiar routine of the Colonial Office and its servants. It may be that ardent insistence on the part of the Jews disturbed the placid existence of many an official; most of them found cooperation as provided in the Mandate distasteful. They knew their Bible well enough, but they were not aware of the historical continuity of the Jews who stood before them with the characters in the Bible.

With no Jewish problem the task of the administration would have been idyllic. The Arabs would have rested on their laurels, as those of Transjordania actually did. It was the Jews who were the leaven and who were always in motion. Indeed, the principal reason for admitting them into the country was that they should, in cooperation with the mandatory power, introduce modern cultural and economic conditions into the country after its lethargic sleep of centuries. The Jews knew what the country had produced in the remote past and saw the enormous possibilities offered by its present if it were managed with understanding and with love. They were willing to contribute their strength and their very lives, and wished for nothing more than to build up a country with which, as the Mandate recognized, they were historically bound. But when they mentioned any such desires, they were regarded as disturbers of the peace. The British governments of the post-war period were mostly weak and shied away from making any decisive stand. Before any step was taken towards fulfilling the terms of the Mandate, the anxious question of possible effects upon the Arabs was first canvassed.

It is indeed noteworthy that no British government rejected the Mandate. The Balfour Declaration had come into being as the result of an extraordinary and peculiar historical situation and a certain sentimentality; and it could hardly be expected that the same mood would prevail in Downing Street permanently. Attitudes were determined by points of view: pro-Jewish or anti-Jewish, pro-Arab or anti-Arab. The Arabs charged that the Jews influenced press and Parliament in England, and indeed the Jews did have more connections with the West; but the Arabs had no reason to complain that their cause was not emphatically set forth. They quickly mastered the devices of European propaganda, including the arts of exaggeration and deception. The court of last instance was the League of Nations. The Permanent Mandates Commission of the League took its task seriously; they were vigilant in seeing that the Mandate was fulfilled and that neither party violated it. The annual reports of the Palestinian government were carefully scrutinized, and complaints and petitions of both the Jews and the Arabs were examined. Criticism was unsparing, though its form continued highly respectful as long as possible.

Foundations of Jewish Policy

The Mandate gave the Zionist Organization international recognition. The Zionist Organization was the Jewish Agency,[17] and even though it had been instructed to seek the cooperation of all Jewish groups, it nevertheless held the initiative. As the Jewish Agency the Zionist Organization was responsible to the mandatory power and to the League of Nations. It could not, as it had previously done, lay its chief emphasis on propaganda, nor could it make itself dependent upon a congress where much of the talk was directed outside the chamber walls and decisions were taken with a view to group interests. In 1920 the annual conference elected Chaim Weizmann to the Zionist Executive, and from 1921 on the Congress elected him president of the Zionist Organization, and therefore of the Agency also. Weizmann's[18] position was never easy. He was attacked by the Zionists because he demanded too little, by the British administration because he demanded too much. With statesmanlike circumspection he avoided bringing matters to a head and so causing a break with the mandatory power. He also disclaimed thoughtless utterances which might have irritated Arab sensibilities. At one moment he was attacked by one faction, and again by another; always the opposition invoked the name of Theodor Herzl. And on each occasion Weizmann was able to overcome the opposition. Only with Vladimir Jabotinsky did matters reach an open break. Jabotinsky had grown up under an imperialistic philosophy; he demanded a more vigorous stand against Great Britain and urged the formation of a Jewish legion to give support to Jewish claims. There were absolutely no resources of power to give substance to such a program, and its announcement could only supply water to turn the mills of Arab propaganda. Weizmann, on the other hand, realized how much had been achieved despite the passive resistance of British officialdom, and wished to use the only weapon available to the Jewish people, the demonstration of the value of Jewish nationalism by means of actual achievement.

Among the tasks of the Jewish Agency was that of procuring funds for colonization. It was not proposed to let the national home fall into the lap of the Jews as a gift. Upbuilding the homeland was set as a task for all

Jews, and it was expected that they would finance the project by their common efforts. Colonization costs money anywhere; it costs a great deal when it is not undertaken for profit and in a land not blessed with raw materials. The Zionist Organization as such was unable to produce the necessary means. The method of raising them was one of the points at issue between the Organization and Justice Brandeis. His plan had been to take up a large capital subscription and to approach the problem of colonization from the economic point of view. But the annual Zionist Conference held at London in 1920 determined upon the establishment of the *Keren Hayesod*,[19] or *Eretz Yisrael* Foundation Fund. This was to be a neutral institution, to afford Jews of various opinions an opportunity to cooperate in building the new Jewish Palestine. Zionists were obligated by the Congress to tax themselves to the extent of a tithe, and non-Zionists were to be won over to contribute like amounts voluntarily.

The Fund was to bear the costs of immigration, preparation for colonization, education, religion, and sanitation. It was placed under a directorate half of whose members were chosen by the Zionist Congress and the other half by non-Zionist contributors; in its composition this directorate foreshadowed the Jewish Agency as subsequently expanded. In most countries cooperation with opposition groups was without friction; the concrete task presented by Palestine was important enough to dwarf minor differences of opinion. The income of the *Keren Hayesod* became the spinal column of the Palestine budget. Continuous collections had the advantage of constantly directing interest to Palestine; the same end was served by the Pro-Palestine Committees, to which both Christians and Jews belonged, which were established in various countries. But they had the disadvantage of necessitating constant advertisement. Palestine was in a display window uninterruptedly and always under the necessity of showing new attractions, which a developing economy cannot well be expected to do. The new interest in the resurgent country attracted tourist traffic to its rich and varied scenery. Many who came to know the country chose it to live in and invested their capital there. The constant flow of capital from abroad resulted in an active credit balance and unexpectedly high bank deposits, despite the adverse balance of trade.

The British administration was regulated by an Order-in-Council (August 10, 1922).[20] Sir Herbert Samuel's efforts were directed to the peaceful development of all of Palestine, from which all sections of the population would derive benefit. His work was successful, and the country made great forward strides.[21] It had wanted only a loving hand to bring it to flower. It was as if the soil had been touched with a magic staff and freed from an ancient curse. Prophetic promises were being fulfilled, swampy and barren sands were turned into gardens, the poor and backward land was made to thrive and progress. The farmer did his work and enjoyed its produce, and his living conditions improved perceptibly. Western Palestine became an oasis of prosperity in the Near East.[22] For fifteen years the government recorded an excess of income over expenditures. It was able to undertake many financial transactions, such as the purchase of the railways and the liquidation of its share of the Ottoman national debt, without having to burden the inhabitants of the country with special taxation. It was also an oasis of peace, when all the countries round about were experiencing uprisings. Most of the British troops could be sent home.

In fulfillment of the Mandate the High Commissioner planned the gradual introduction of instruments for self-administration. He announced elections to a Legislative Council,[23] in which it was intended that the Arabs should

THE JEWISH NATIONAL HOME

have a strong representation. But the Arabs refused to participate, on the grounds that they could claim a safe majority; they intended, by this means, to make the Mandate nugatory. The Moslem-Christian Union sabotaged the election. The government had suffered a defeat, but it pocketed the affront and made further attempts to win the dissidents over. These now felt so sure of themselves that they undertook to submit a *Report on the State of Palestine during the Four Years of the Civil Administration* to the Permanent Mandates Commission (1924). They protested against the Mandate; they declared it a "gross error to expect understanding." At the same time the Peasants' Party of Palestine, which represented the fellahin, entered a statement. It contested the right of the Arab Executive to set itself up as the representative of the Arab people of Palestine, on the grounds that they were interested only in their own welfare and did not enjoy public confidence. They also disputed the accuracy of the "facts" adduced by the Union and signified their desire to cooperate with the government.

The simple peasant learned to know his Jewish neighbor better and knew that he was at least as easy to live and work with as the effendis. He saw, too, that even Jewish trees did not spring up out of thin air, that the fear of immigration had been greatly exaggerated, since the flow was regulated to the capacity of the country. When harvests were poor and there was nothing to export or when foreign markets could not take Palestinian exports, there was unemployment and the immigration quota was reduced; there was even a considerable emigration.[24]

On the whole the economy was secure against financial crisis, because there was no question of profits. The great number of the Jewish immigrants were moved by enthusiasm. They had come to the country for the sake of an idea, and in the service of this idea their work took wings. It was no slight transformation to which they had to accommodate themselves. There was the climate, whose heat and drought they had not anticipated, and the new kind of work, whose difficulty they had not foreseen. But they never shirked.

From the ground up they had to create the very elements on which agriculture depends. They cleared the land, terraced the hillsides to make soil, constructed a water-system in an arid and hitherto unwatered land, built barns, houses, a school, and took the land under cultivation.

This description refers to Kiryat Anavim,[25] in the rocky hillside near Jerusalem; it applies more or less to all the colonies which came into being at that time. The greatest need was for water and woodland. Wells were dug, and tree nurseries set out. The great achievement of the early years was the reclamation of the Emek Jezreel. The deadly swamps were drained, malaria abolished, and the soil prepared for cultivation. The cost was sweat and blood, and sometimes life itself, but the price was paid. These pioneers were not like colonists in other countries, who go to seek a better place to work; theirs was an ideal to which devoted service must be rendered, the ideal of *Yishub Eretz Yisrael*.

It was not capital but labor which gave the upbuilding its character. The strongest group, numerically as well as morally, was the Federation of Labor (*Histadrut ha-'Ovedim*).[26] Labor became the predominant factor in the upbuilding of *Eretz Yisrael* as well as in the Zionist Organization. Along with the national and religious motives, most immigrants cherished the ideal of constructing a socially just society. They brought with them all the demands of the labor movements in highly developed capitalist countries without stopping to ask if such demands were applicable to a country in the process of colonization. A rigid social theory, lack of experience and organizing ability, were at first responsible for some failures; but time and training gradually brought the remedy.

The aim of the organization was to create a collective society freed from the curse of capital, where neither employers nor employees were known, but everyone did his share of the work. Many settled in collective communes (*K'vutzot*) whose members had no private earnings from their produce but were provided by a common purse for their necessary expenditures. The settlers reduced their desires for the material pleasures of life to a minimum, "they lived to bear and to forbear." They sturdily endured the hardships of their experiment and trustfully worked for the final success. Radical theories of this character impeded the upbuilding, accentuated the differences between groups of diverse origins and tendencies,[27] and created friction with the older colonists, who had meanwhile, in large part, become settled bourgeoisie.

But neither deprivation nor downright need nor conflict could affect the happiness of the settlers. With the proud security of the Shunamite of the Bible they could say, "I dwell among my own people," and that satisfaction made hardships and discomfort negligible. Life "by right and not on sufferance" was a blessed experience which gave the Jews of *Eretz Yisrael* a totally new aspect.[28] They were upstanding and forthright, healthy and happy. They developed a genuine folk life, with games and sports, with folk songs and folk dances. Without despising intellectual interests, many thought there had been too much of brooding and discussion. Despite its poverty the new *Yishub* quickly acquired theater and opera, and it is significant that, from the first, performances were made accessible to the working groups. It was inevitable that the upbringing and culture of the new immigrants should be influenced by the East European countries of their birth, but they sought to transform the legacy which they had brought into Jewish values. On principle they spoke, read, and sang only in Hebrew; with the relentless fanaticism which prevailed in the nationalist states of Europe they stubbornly demanded Hebrew of Jews and non-Jews alike. And they had their way. The new *Yishub* was completely Hebraized, and in this the youth of the older settlements joined with the new. The greatest stress was laid upon education, and in education the emphasis was upon love of the country and its language. In the last days of his life Eliezer ben Jehudah must have been rejoiced to see the approaching fulfillment of the dream of his youth.

Religious life too received new impulses of vitality. The Sabbath became the universal day of rest for all Jews, whatever their attitude to the prescriptions of the *Shulhan 'Aruk* might be; and this was an asset which had never been enjoyed in the Diaspora. Towards Friday evening all work ceased, and until the following sunset the atmosphere in the Jewish settlements was pervaded by a solemn and festive air. Passover, as the festival of liberation, was given special significance, and at *Shabu'ot* the bringing of first fruits was resumed. The occasion was profoundly impressive when the High Commissioner appeared in person at Rishon le-Zion and solemnly pronounced the scriptural benediction for the first fruits (Deuteronomy 26.5 ff.). *Hamisha 'Asar bi-Shebat* became the arbor day on which trees were planted, and pupils were brought out of their schools to set their young trees in the ground. On a folk festival like *Purim* joy reigned supreme.

The festivals gave the year its rhythm, and insofar as they were connected with the land they were celebrated even by those who would have no part in religious observance and, like their radical comrades in London or New York, made no scruple of mocking religion. There was much strife between the orthodox and the socialists, and coercion could not bring peace. Buckets of crocodile tears were shed over exuberant youth. Jews who had put themselves beyond all Jewish law could not endure that similar neglect could take place in *Eretz Yisrael*. Catholics[29] complained that a cinema had been brought to Jerusalem and that there was dancing in the Holy City (it was forbidden, as a matter of fact, in the Old City), as if any capital in the world, Rome included, could keep these elements of modern civilization out. Arabs complained that the Jews had introduced their western notions regarding the relations between men and women, as if their daughters would not have been very happy to dance with English officers and officials. The chief plaint of the Arab leaders was that they could not compete with Zionist agriculture, as if they were not equally free to use modern tools, to employ modern methods, to multiply their income from dairy and poultry products by introducing blooded stock. If they had used the money which they spent for congresses, junkets, and agitation on improving the internal conditions of the country, they would have done it a much greater service.

Such were the *Yishub's* pedagogues. Perhaps their criticism was salutary for curbing the high spirits of aspiring youth. But the *Yishub* also had leaders of stature.[30] A. J. Kook (1866–1935), the chief rabbi of the Ashkenazim, was a talmudic authority and devoted to the development of the *Yeshibah Merkazit 'Olamit* ("The Central Universal Yeshibah") which he founded. He possessed the rare gift of being able to grow along with the growth of his field of service. He regarded the possibility of actualizing the ancient Jewish dream as so miraculous a dispensation that he welcomed anyone who would cooperate towards its achievement. Himself a man of deep, mystic faith and scrupulous observance, he yet rejected no one who thought and lived differently than he did. He wished to embrace all, righteous and unrighteous alike, and he trusted to the power of love, as had Hillel of old, to bring men nearer to the Torah. The poet Chaim Nachman Bialik was the most popular personality of the *Yishub*, and at once became its conscience. He loved young people and loved to be with them, and he gave them guidance and direction. It was he that created the institution of *'Oneg Shabbat*, an effort to employ the means of today in order to bring to the people of today the inner exaltation and happiness appropriate to the day of rest. He made serious studies of the past of Palestine, seeking elements that might be useful in its present. He studied medieval Hebrew poetry in order to spread the knowledge of the classics. He composed only rarely, but he frequently appeared in public as a speaker, and his natural, unpretentious style was always effective. Ahad Ha'am also settled in Palestine, but he came as a broken and suffering man. There was much in the country that was not to his taste, but he rejoiced to be present at the burgeoning of a spiritual center in *Eretz Yisrael*. He was pleased that many Hebrew writers had settled here and gratified to be surrounded by members of his old circle at Odessa.

Among the educators David Yellin (1864–1941) was outstanding. Yellin was born in Jerusalem and had spoken Hebrew and Arabic fluently from his youth. He was therefore uniquely fitted to act as intermediary between the two peoples, and his relationships within Judaism fitted him to perform a similar function as between Sephardim and Ashkenazim. Yellin was one of the Jewish members of the government's Advisory Committee, for years he was president of the *Va'ad Le'umi*, and everywhere his conciliatory attitude and his resourcefulness were effective. He assumed a grave responsibility as one of the originators of the Hebrew school system, and as director of the Hebrew Teachers' Seminary his influence upon education was paramount. Menachem M. Ussischkin was a man of great strength of will. He came to Palestine with the Zionist Commission and immediately took a leading position. He had been a leader of the *Hoveve Zion* in his youth, and his aim was to acquire as much land as possible for the *Keren Kayemet* and gradually to bring it under cultivation. He was unyielding in his demands for nationalization and Hebraization and he intimidated the officials in the government offices by his emphatic insistence on the full implementation of the Mandate.

Pinchas Rutenberg (1879–1941) was of a different type. The substance of his existence was not politics but work. He was an engineer, and his aim was to supply Palestine with electric current. He had the brilliant idea of harnessing the fall at the confluence of the Yarmuk with the Jordan to a power station. As early as 1921 he had secured the necessary concessions by agreement, and for carrying his project out he founded the Palestine Electric Company, which became instrumental in the further development of the country. His first power plant was opened at Tel Aviv, and others followed at Haifa and Tiberias.

Tel Aviv[31] had sprung up on the sand dunes of the Mediterranean with American speed. In 1920 its inhabitants numbered 2,500; four years later there were ten times as many. It possessed no municipal rights as yet, but in Meier Dizengoff (1861–1936) it had a leader of unusual energy. Dizengoff had cooperated in the foundation of Tel Aviv as a suburban development in 1909, and it was his pride to see it expand into an independent metropolis and a center of trade and industry. Other foresighted men worked for modern, planned, garden cities in Jerusalem, Haifa, and Tiberias.

The bloom of *Eretz Yisrael* was not without its influence

upon the Diaspora.[32] For more than a century the Jews of the West had been made somewhat uncomfortable by the mere mention of its name. But now interest in it grew, and not as a museum of a remote antiquity but as the herald of a new present and future. The land was open to safe and convenient travel, and its scenery and people could be studied. It provided poets and thinkers, painters and sketchers, with rich inspiration for their future work. The deepest impression was made by the renaissance of Hebrew which became a complete instrument of communication for all the needs of daily life and showed a capacity for development which no one had credited it with. The youthful energy of the educational system and the vitality of the literature in so small a country were striking, and the folk elements in Palestinian song and dance charmed and attracted many admirers. A notable aspect was the interest in cultivating Jewish music. The Society for Jewish Music in St. Petersburg had begun the movement; it was transplanted to *Eretz Yisrael* and influenced Jewish composers the world over.

The high point in this period of pioneering was the dedication of the Hebrew University[33] in Jerusalem on April 1, 1925. The Holy City was filled to overflowing with visitors. The Zionist Organization had invited the world's cultural élite to be its guests. There were only the modest beginnings of a university at the time: a Judaistic, a biochemical, and an electrobiological institute; but the very notion of establishing a university in the Holy City fascinated governments and universities the world over, and they designated their representatives to be present at the opening. Such a galaxy of cultural dignitaries and scientific standard-bearers were assembled on Mount Scopus as could rarely be seen even at the centennial celebrations of the world's oldest and most distinguished universities. Leopold Pilichowski's monumental painting attempts to fix for posterity the overpowering impression of the illustrious gathering. Bialik summarized the significance of these events in the apposite remark that here the Jewish people were laying the foundations for the heavenly Jerusalem. Weizmann stated that the University had indeed been founded by Jews and would use Hebrew as the language of instruction, but that it was open to all without distinction and that it proposed to establish a universal fellowship. Lord Balfour's oration placed the opening of the University in the grand historical perspective of Jewish spiritual enterprise, and he expressed the wish that peaceful collaboration in the land of the prophets might serve to bridge over distinctions of religion and race.

Balfour was greeted everywhere as a prince of peace. Only the Moslem-Christian Committee used the occasion of his presence for a political demonstration. It instigated a general strike of the Arab population, and assembled for prayer "for deliverance from Zionist aggression supported by British arms." It designated the Balfour Declaration as "the ultimate ruin of the Moslem-Christian population throughout Palestine," and protested "against the great calamity that has befallen us and our country." These grotesque untruths would have been merely amusing if they had not involved serious danger to the distinguished guest. His desire to see the fabled city of Damascus might have cost him his life if the French police had not maintained constant vigilance and advised him to leave the country betimes.

The festivities were over and workaday life returned to its routine. But even workaday existence was very exciting in Palestine in 1925. A hundred immigrants arrived daily, 33,800 in the course of the year.[34] Most came from Poland, being forced to emigrate by the economic crisis and tax regulations which were hostile to commerce. These immigrants were different from their predecessors. They were predominantly of the middle class and possessed a certain amount of capital. They did not wish to settle upon the land but to engage in commerce and industry. Building activity in the cities rose feverishly. Tel Aviv experienced a boom. Real estate values reached a dizzy height. The population doubled, and dwellings were provided for them at a lightning rate of speed. This unhealthy overexpansion quickly collapsed. The year 1926 began with a sharp depression in business and trades, and in 1927 the difficulties were accentuated by drought and a devastating earthquake. More than 7,000 Jews left the country in 1926 in panic; but there were 13,000 newcomers, and in 1927 emigration exceeded immigration by 2,300. Despite this relief the number of unemployed grew by several thousand, and bankruptcies were numerous.

Instead of the prosperity which Sir Herbert Samuel had depicted in his final report, his successor, Field Marshal Lord Plumer,[35] found a disturbing depression. At first the Jews were restrained in their attitude to Lord Plumer, but they found in him understanding and sympathy for the critical situation which had arisen. He arranged work projects on the part of the government which gave employment to Jews. The Jewish Agency also did all that it could to avert catastrophe.

Individuals were hard hit by the crisis, but the country as a whole showed great powers of resistance. Agriculture continued successful, and vital industries established before the boom held their own. It was in the years of the depression that the Joint Palestine Survey Commission (see p. 572, above) traveled through the country, and their impressions of its future were such that they advocated the expansion of the Jewish Agency. These economic leaders looked with great misgivings upon the possibilities of a city like Tel Aviv which had neither natural resources nor a hinterland, but they realized that it possessed imponderable and incalculable assets when they observed the tireless zeal of its inhabitants in developing new possibilities for trade and commerce. And in fact the faith and energy of the Jewish population opened many fields which seemed inaccessible or unprofitable by the sober calculation of the scientific economists.

Gradually the depths of the depression were traversed, unemployment decreased, emigration and immigration attained a balance, and gigantic undertakings like the coffer-dam of the Rutenberg works or the harbor installations at Haifa quickened men's hopes. Complete calm prevailed in the countryside, which was consolidating its progress. Lord Plumer felt justified in reducing the number of troops and police to the minimum. Internal Jewish conditions were regulated by the formation of the *K'nesset Yisrael*.[36] This regulation did not fundamentally alter existing conditions. It sanctioned the supreme rabbinic council which the government had established in 1921 and had clothed with functions similar to those of the Supreme Moslem Council; Sephardim and Ashkenazim each received a chief rabbi and three assessors. The *Va'ad Le'umi* was recognized as the supreme secular body, exactly as it was constituted by the Zionist Commission. It became the parliamentary representation of the Jews — and it manifested the weakness of modern parliaments, including disruptive quarrels among "fractions." It had the authority to levy taxes for the requirements of religion, education, the care of the poor, the sick, the orphaned, and for administrative purposes. Any place with a population of at least thirty adult Jews or Jewesses constituted a community whose delegates (*nibḥarim*) elected to the *Va'ad*. Within the communities complete freedom of conscience was assured. Dissidents were free to have their names stricken from the communal lists. Only one *K'nesset Yisrael* was recognized, and no schisms were permitted. This policy annoyed the *Agudat Yisrael* greatly. They wished to introduce the Hungarian system of separatism, and when they could not succeed in doing so they did in fact have their adherents withdraw from the communities.

The Jewish population began to see new grounds for hope; they were confident that a new stream of energy would issue from the expanded Jewish Agency. After a hard struggle, Weizmann succeeded in gaining the approval of the Zionist Executive Committee for the agreement which he had concluded with the non-Zionists. Ratification by the Zionist Congress, which was called to meet at the end of July in Zurich, was considered certain. The first meeting of the expanded Jewish Agency, at which policies were shaped, took place at Zurich,[37] August 11-14, 1929. The wisest heads in contemporary Judaism participated in the meetings and hailed the union between Zionists and non-Zionists. It was generally expected that a new era for *Eretz Yisrael* and for the Jewish people would be ushered in by their collaboration. But the ink was scarcely dry on the constitution which they formulated when alarming reports arrived from *Eretz Yisrael*.

Conflict and Investigations

The subject of strife was the Wailing Wall (*Kotel Ma'arabi*), which was the only sacred Jewish site in Jerusalem.[38] From time immemorial Jews had gathered there to pray and to wail. Suddenly a rumor spread with the speed of wildfire to the effect that Zionists intended "to take possession of the Mosque of Al-Aksa gradually." The sin the Jews had committed was this. Once for the long service on Yom Kippur they had brought camp stools along for the use of the elderly and the feeble. Officially this was forbidden, but the Turks had winked at the practice and the English administration did not believe it necessary to alter the status quo. In 1928 the worshipers had the unhappy thought of erecting a paper curtain to separate the men from the women. On Rosh Hashanah there was no disturbance, but before Yom Kippur the Arabs, to whose own ideas the separation must have been congenial, pressed the English police to forbid the procedure. Since the curtain was not removed, the police appeared in the midst of the service (September 24th) and removed it by force. The worshipers were stirred to a high pitch of excitement; and Jews the world over were profoundly alarmed when they heard that the mandatory power had so tactlessly disturbed divine worship at the most sacred site in Judaism on its most solemn sacred day.

Formal right was on the side of the Moslems. The Wailing Wall and the street which was its approach were the uncontested property of the *Waqfs*, or sacred foundations. The Jews could claim the right of use and wont, but they had no written documents to substantiate their claim. Moral and human right was indubitably on the side of the Jews. They had only this one holy site and wished to do nothing more than call to mind their sacred traditions, to weep, and to pray. If the Supreme Moslem Council had possessed even the slightest understanding for religious needs they would have grasped the situation and have found some *modus vivendi*. But the Mufti could only see a unique opportunity to whip up religious passions of all the Mohammedan peoples of the world for a sort of holy war.

The Wailing Wall became a battle cry and undermined peace in Palestine as it did the prestige of the British government. In order to represent the situation as perilous, the Mufti founded a Society for the Protection of the Buraq. But his administration did even more.

Upon the extension of the Wall they erected a new cult structure, and the English who regarded the portable paper curtain as a disturbance of the status quo saw no objection in this structural change, nor in the fact that a passage to the Temple area was made. In the new structure a muezzin was installed, who called loudly to evening prayer at the time the Jews held their service. On Sabbath mornings the dervishes who were stationed there raised a frightful hubbub which disturbed the Jewish worshipers. Furthermore, the inhabitants of the neighborhood used the passageway to drive their cattle or dump their waste during the period of worship. It was an intolerable situation, created by no religious necessity but by malice.

The government had no notion of what was happening. In June 1929 the High Commissioner, Sir John Chancellor,[39] declared to the Permanent Mandates Commission that he had grounds to assume that relations between the two peoples were improving, and proceeded to spend his summer holiday in Europe. It was in those very weeks that the Moslems continued their building operations and the Jews founded a *Liga L'ma'an ha-Kotel* to protect their rights in the Wall. The situation grew so critical that the Zionist Executive in London impressed upon the Colonial Office that there was danger of an explosion, but in Jerusalem no precautionary measures were taken. The chief of the government omitted to do everything he should have done and did all that he should have omitted. Against the advice of the Zionist Executive he permitted 300 youths to demonstrate on Tish'a b'Ab (August 15th); the parade went off without disturbance, but not quite in accordance with the wish of the officials. On the following day, which was a Friday, 2,000 Moslems, some brought from a distance, swarmed out of the Mosque, after services, through the new gateway and attacked the caretakers; they destroyed and burned prayer books and other religious utensils which they found. The police were helpless in the face of the raging mob. The government did nothing, not even when a Jewish boy was stabbed in the back by Arabs. They tolerated the incitement in the Arab press which used excerpts from the *Protocols* and made outspoken threats against the lives of the Jews. They refused to issue a pacifying statement to point out the baselessness of the charge that the Jews had intentions upon the Mosque of Omar and had even damaged it. The only point at which they acceded to the Jews was in arranging personal conferences with outstanding Arabs. These took place on August 22nd; in consequence of the opposition of a single Arab no agreement could be reached, and the conversations were adjourned.

On the 23rd the storm which had been predicted by the newspaper *Falastin* broke. Disregarding every warning, the chief of the government took no defensive measures. Arabs armed with knives and clubs rushed out of the Mosque and were urged on to the Jewish quarter by the ringleaders. It was two hours before the police received permission to use their weapons — the Jewish police had been publicly and conspicuously disarmed — and so the mob had ample time to loot and murder. In the Old City at Jerusalem mobile troops were brought in and quickly subdued the malefactors. But in suburbs like Moza and Kalandia they raged on; at Talpiot they had prepared such a quantity of munitions that they could continue the fight behind their barricades for twenty-four hours before British auxiliaries could drive them out. In Hebron, the city of Abraham, a murderous attack had surprised the entirely defenseless Jews on Friday. On the Sabbath day they were attacked anew, and savagely slaughtered without consideration for age or sex. "Over sixty Jews were killed, including women and children, and more than fifty injured. Much Jewish property was destroyed, synagogues were desecrated, and a Jewish hospital looted. Only the courage of the one British police officer in the town prevented the outbreak from developing into a general massacre."

Nablus was the headquarters for attacks upon Jewish agricultural settlements; these generally defended themselves bravely. In Tel Aviv and Haifa there were dead and wounded also, and the government did what it could to hamper the self-defense of the Jews. When troops arrived from Egypt and Malta, the Arabs drew back. In Safed where, in consequence of an accident, the military were two hours late in arriving, the mob was able to burn the ancient Jewish quarter with its humble alleys down to the ground and to plunder the Jews; here they left fourteen dead. The results of this week of murder (August 23–29) were that the Arabs had killed 133 Jews and wounded 339, while they themselves lost 114 dead and 232 wounded by the action of the military.

It was by no means "the Arab people" that had risen against the Jews. On the contrary, there were plain indications of Arab sympathy. Workers and peasants assured Jews of neighboring settlements that nothing would happen to them; sheiks of individual villages offered their children as hostages for the security of the Jews, and kept their word faithfully. Arab officials and police officers protected endangered Jews at their own peril. Even in bloody Hebron and Safed there were a number of Arab families who gave their Jewish acquaintances protection. Investigation showed that it was the lie concerning the alleged attack upon the Mosque of Omar that had infuriated so many Arabs.

The High Commissioner[40] returned to his post in great haste and in a sharply worded proclamation dated September 1st he condemned the disturbances as

atrocious acts committed by bodies of ruthless and bloodthirsty evildoers, of savage murders perpetrated upon the defenseless members of the Jewish population regardless of age and sex, accompanied as at Hebron by acts of unspeakable savagery, of the burning of farms and houses in town and country, and of looting and destruction of property.

He ordered a searching investigation and held out the prospect of payment of damages to innocent victims. The religious heads of Palestinian Jewry united to issue a defiant protest in which they established the complete failure of the government and sought protection for the Jewish population. The Mufti washed his hands in innocence and laid the entire blame at the doors of the Jews. He organized an Arab boycott against Jewish goods, and then went to London to work on the government and public opinion. In London the leaders of the expanded Jewish Agency had the painful duty of devoting their first public announcement to the sad events in Palestine. They emphasized that the Jewish people would not be distracted by deeds of violence from their firm resolve to rebuild the Jewish National Home, and they received the assurances of the British government that it would abide by the Balfour Declaration.

To pacify public opinion an investigating commission was despatched to the scene from London. It consisted of one member of Parliament from each of the three major parties and was headed by Sir Walter Shaw, a superior judge. Their report appeared in May 1930 and it was a fateful document. The commission found no reason other than racial animosity responsible for the outbreaks, and they found the attitude of the English officials irreproachable. The report[41] could do no other than state the notorious excesses of the Arabs, but it sought to minimize their criminal responsibility. It then proceeded to discuss the ultimate political causes of the unrest and found the root of the trouble in the presence of the Jews, their immigration, and their economic activity. The report was a running attack on the Balfour

Declaration; it did not recommend that it be rescinded but it urged a new "clear statement of policy" in regard to its intention and in regard to the position of the Zionist Organization in the administration. It recommended a revision of the regulations on immigration and consultation with non-Jewish authorities upon desirable limits. It declared that the land was thickly settled and requested a scientific investigation of the areas capable of cultivation and the prospects of introducing improved methods.

The Arabs were elated over the report, particularly over the immediate cessation of immigration. The British government identified itself with the Shaw report, although one of the three members of the commission dissociated himself from it, giving his grounds for dissent, although the Jewish Agency charged that it was inadequate and contradictory, and although the Permanent Mandates Commission rejected it entirely. The Mandates Commission devoted a special sitting to the report, and, although the Colonial Office was represented by a skillful and eloquent advocate, it refused to accept the report and condemned the mandatory administration as a whole. The British government defended itself against this criticism, but a plenary session of the League of Nations adopted the conclusions of its own commission.

In accordance with the Shaw recommendations, Sir John Hope Simpson,[42] an expert on soils, undertook an investigation of the soil of Palestine and came to the depressing conclusion that the arable area was only half as large as had been previously supposed, and that it could not even assure the Arab agricultural population the minimum requirements for existence.

Until further development of Jewish lands and of irrigation had taken place and the Arabs had adopted better methods of cultivation, there is no room for a single additional settler if the standard of life of the Fellaheen is to remain at its present level. On State lands, similarly, there was no room, pending development, for Jewish settlers.

THE JEWISH NATIONAL HOME

For the sake of fulfilling the Mandate he recommended an active policy of agricultural development, having as its object close settlement on the land and intensive cultivation by both Arabs and Jews.

He expressed the hope that, in the course of time, space for settling 20,000 additional families might be found in this way.

Sir John found serious and widespread unemployment among Arab industrial workers also, and therefore considered the immigration of Jewish workers similarly inadmissible. But since the country urgently required new capital and Jews would not invest capital unless they were able to employ Jewish workers, he conceded that a certain limited number of Jewish workers should be admitted in order to create a "derived demand" for Arab workers. Sir John's pessimistic report invited the criticism of other experts; he did not exclude the possibility of different conclusions, and ten years later he himself recommended larger settlements of Jews. But his report was presented, and the government of Ramsay MacDonald, the most helpless of all the feeble British postwar governments, accepted it. It even omitted the two clauses concerning eventual possibilities of Jewish immigration. In a White Paper the government acknowledged the Mandate, although it was now completely without substance, and proposed the creation of a Legislative Council (October 1930).

Dr. Weizmann[43] declared that the announcement of the government, which was accompanied by grave aspersions upon Jewish efforts, constituted a complete reversal of its position. In protest he laid down his office as president of the Jewish Agency, and Felix M. Warburg and Lord Melchett also resigned. Public opinion in Great Britain and in the House of Commons was not on the side of the government. The government sought a rapprochement with the Agency, and the upshot was a letter addressed to Dr. Weizmann by the Prime Minister (February 13, 1931). The letter was in the form of an interpretation of the White Paper for the purpose of allaying "mistrust and misapprehension;" in reality its tone was friendlier than that of the White Paper in every point which did not directly touch on Arab sensibilities. The Jews contented themselves with this gesture, and the Arabs saw in the "Black Letter" a new rejection of their claims to self-administration. This was at a time when the neighboring Arab states were making gigantic strides in the direction of attaining autonomy. In 1932 a party of independence, *Istiqlal*,[44] was formed among them, in which the youth was largely represented. The inexorable goal of this party was complete autonomy. At first it sought contacts with the Jews, but later it was very outspoken in its opposition to Jewish rights.

In the meanwhile the international commission for adjudicating the matter of the Wailing Wall[45] had pronounced its decisions (May 31st). Neither of the parties was enthusiastic about the results, but the report did state clearly what was permitted and what was prohibited. Despite conflicts elsewhere the area about the Wall remained calm in the period following.

Progress in an Era of Conflict

The political tension had been relieved, and quiet prevailed even if there was no peace. The people of Palestine, Arabs and Jews alike, went about their affairs; there were difficulties enough, but on the whole their affairs prospered. Immigration[46] of Jews continued; a moderate number were admitted legally; a number at least as great came in illegally. Eventually the government recognized 6,000 of these "self-smugglers" as immigrants. Over the constant illegal immigration of Arabs, from Transjordania, from Hauran, and from Syria, it spread the cloak of Christian love. And despite all the calculations of the experts the people did not go hungry. On the contrary, "the economic position of the Arabs as a whole continued to improve. Wages rose, markets for country-produce expanded, more roads and bridges and schools were built." The Arabs made landless by the settlement of the Jews turned out to be a myth; the number of cases which stood up under examination proved to be negligible. The opening of the harbor at Haifa and of the pipe-line from the oil fields of Mosul and all their related industrial undertakings, the completion of the Rutenberg power station, and the beginning of work on the potash works at the Dead Sea ushered in an industrial future for Palestine such as could be found nowhere else in the Near East. The Imperial Airways included Palestine in their network, and it became an important station for communication with India. In agriculture the intensive development of citrus fruits along the coast provided ample opportunities for work and for profit. Palestine became an oasis in the world-wide economic crisis.

Sir Arthur Wauchope,[47] High Commissioner after the autumn of 1931, saw his duty in the fulfillment of the requirements which the League of Nations had emphasized, namely in the promotion of the Jewish National Home and in cooperation between Jews and Arabs. The latter aim he sought to achieve by forming joint committees which were to be consulted by the government on special questions. For a while this substantive work went off successfully, but suddenly the Arabs refused to collaborate. On the Jewish side the chauvinist Revisionists became active and caused frequent alarms, collisions with other Jews, with Arabs, and with the police. But these minor disturbances were insignificant in the face of the indubitable gains. In Jewish immigration Sir Arthur saw a factor for growth, not for complications.

Whether this first active intervention of a High Commissioner in the terms of the Mandate might have gradually led to pacification and collaboration it is difficult to say, for peaceful development was too suddenly interrupted by external forces. On January 30, 1933, Adolf Hitler came into power, and it became clear that tens of thousands of German Jews must unconditionally leave Germany. The Zionist movement saw its great hour; it had created a haven of refuge for an emergency which no one could have foreseen. The *Yishub* of Palestine strove emulously with the Jewries of other countries to help, to create openings for settlements, and in particular to assure the children a future in which they could develop their powers and make free use of them. Henrietta Szold crowned a long life rich in blessings by organizing this Youth '*Aliyah*. To old Zionists it seemed the obvious solution: if they were not tolerated in their homeland, their natural place was in the Jewish National Home. And many non-Zionists looked upon Palestine as a satisfactory solution of their immigration problem. German officials favored emigration to Palestine by making a transfer of property to that country possible.

Everything conspired to raise the number of immigrants[48] to undreamed of heights. Intelligence — to say nothing of a number of world-famous physicians, scholars and artists—education, and practical experience had never before streamed into the country in such quantity. Aside from human resources in education and training, this '*Aliyah* brought much capital and many industrial products. A new chapter in Palestinian upbuilding began. Agricultural enterprises were augmented and industrial activity intensified. The spurt in new undertakings seemed to the Jewish Agency to justify a request for a considerable immigration of workers. Although the government curtailed these requisitions and estimated the economic capacity of the country at a lower figure, from 1933 to 1935 no fewer than 130,000 Jews immigrated from Germany and other countries which were feeling Nazi pressure. This boom had no bad economic effects on the country; on the contrary all signs pointed to a promising upsurge. The difficulties of incorporating so numerous and varied an element, in large part sceptical of the ideals of the older community, into the grooves laid down by previous cultural development, constituted an internal problem for the Jews and has not yet been satisfactorily solved.

The Arabs[49] protested at the very first increase in immigration; they became more restless as the figure rose and began to endanger their unquestioned majority, and as the Jews, in consequence of the pressure abroad which had grown intolerable, demanded a more rapid development of the Jewish National Home. Arab agitation became more vocal, their boycotts more heated, and they struck at the hands which were repeatedly extended to them from Jewish quarters. The Arabs disregarded internal conflicts and directed a general attack against the principle of the Mandate. They demanded that the Jews be prevented from immigrating and from acquiring land and that a democratic form of government be instituted. The High Commissioner rejected all demands that were not in consonance with the Mandate, but held out the prospect of meeting the national demands in the form of a Legislative Council if the communal self-administration introduced in 1934 proved practicable. Despite constant disturbances of the peace he remained true to his principles, and at the end of 1934 he informed both peoples of his plan to institute a Legislative Council to represent all groups of the population. The competence of this Council was to extend over questions of finance and internal administration, but not over questions of policy. The Arabs were not satisfied with the proposal but were willing to negotiate. But this time the Jews rejected the project on principle. The Jewish Agency set all its machinery into motion to make its protest an expression of Jews the world over. The opposition of the Agency drove the Arabs to espouse the project, and they threatened to take their fate into their own hands if their demands for autonomy were not satisfied. Palestine fell into a state of constant alarm. Collisions, assaults, and political murders were the order of the day.

While these matters were still under dispute, another external event occurred to hasten developments. Italian imperialism attacked Abyssinia and demanded that the Mediterranean become *Mare Nostrum*. Benito Mussolini,[50] the anti-communist hero, borrowed a page from the Bolshevists and roused the Arabs to the folly of allowing themselves to become victims of British imperialism. In his internal policy he also followed the example of the Bolshevists, by punishing as treason adherence of Italian Jews to Zionism; only a few years earlier he had encouraged Italian Zionism. From Bari, where the crusaders had embarked for the Holy Land during the Middle Ages, his radio carried warlike words in Arabic to Palestine, to incite the Arabs against Great Britain. All the world recognized the danger; only the Colonial Office noticed nothing amiss; and it was a long while before they awoke to the realization that there was nothing to prevent the British government from broadcasting in Arabic. But it had grown too late. The Arabs had made the new slogans their own.

In the spring of 1936 the organization which the Arabs had prepared according to totalitarian methods was ready,[51] and they only awaited a suitable moment to strike. On April 21, 1936, their headquarters called for a general strike, and the call was universally heeded. All Arabs refused to work or pay taxes, and put themselves on a footing of non-cooperation with England. In a short while, high Arab officials in the administration and the judiciary declared their solidarity with their racial brethren. Moreover the neighboring Arab countries signified their complete approval and solidarity.

Open rebellion against the Mandate broke out. The Arabs did not stop at passive resistance but ambushed police and military, attacked railroads and highways, and cut telephone lines. Individual Jews were murdered, entire Jewish colonies attacked. Attempts of the High Commissioner to reach an understanding without shedding blood were flatly rejected by the Arab Higher Committee, as the insurgents styled themselves; their attitude was completely uncompromising. Troops were summoned and the strike leaders were arrested and sent to concentration camps, but none of these measures brought peace. Under the leadership of a Syrian chieftain warlike bands were formed. They infested the hill country and carried on a regular guerrilla warfare which the English were not able to put down despite their superior equipment and technique. Finally reinforcements were brought in and martial law declared, and after some five months the military mastered the disturbances. The strike had worked the gravest economic injury to the Arab population, and large numbers were quite ready to yield. But it was October 12th before a pacifying message arrived from the neighboring Arab kings and the Arab Higher Committee called off the strike and the terrorization of the orderly processes of life.

The casualty lists amounted to 80 dead and 308 wounded on the part of the Jews. "As to material loss, the Jewish Agency reports the destruction of 80,000 citrus trees, 62,000 other fruit-trees, 64,000 forest trees, and 16,500 dunams of crops." The Arab losses were estimated at 1,000 dead in battle or by acts of terror, and a correspondingly higher number of wounded. The extent of material losses, direct and indirect, and the deficit in government revenue cannot be calculated. An irreparable loss for the Arabs was the fact that the Jews, in order not to expose themselves to constant danger at Jaffa, withdrew from the harbor there and constructed a new one at Tel Aviv. Originally regarded as an emergency installation, it became a permanent fixture.

Naturally the Jews were depressed by these events, but there was no panic. The work of construction continued uninterrupted, and only a negligible fraction of the 400,000 Jews of Palestine emigrated in disillusionment. While the Arabs were projecting destruction, the Hebrew University enlarged its scope, and the Palestine Philharmonic Orchestra, founded by the world-famous violinist, Bronislaw Hubermann, prepared for its first performances. No less a maestro than Arturo Toscanini directed its first concert, which took place at Tel Aviv on December 26, 1936. This was an important cultural event, and all the population with the exception of the Arabs shared in it. And on the following evening, a thing which could happen only in Palestine, the concert was repeated for the unemployed who were unable to pay admission.

This event must have been a remarkable experience for the Royal Commission which was then working in Palestine under the presidency of Earl William Robert Peel, sometime Secretary of State for India. For eight long weeks the Commission had labored to get a clear picture of the situation and of the causes of unrest by means of inspections and hearings; the Arab Higher Committee had boycotted the Commission at first and appeared only as it was in the act of adjourning. The Commission elaborated a thorough and instructive report which was presented in the House of Commons in July, 1937. Its conclusions[52] were defeatist. The Mandate had proven impossible to implement, and the only path to a permanent peace was to be sought in partitioning the country. The Commission recommended the establishment of an independent Arab state which was to be united with Transjordania, an independent Jewish state, and a third neutral state under the Mandate to be associated with the other two by reciprocal agreements. It sketched the proposed boundaries, the possibilities of exchanges of territory and populations, and touched on many related problems. Sales of land to Jews in the territory of the proposed Arab state were to be forbidden entirely, and in the other states they were to be made only under certain precautionary regulations. Immigration to the future Jewish area was to be limited to 50,000 persons for a five-year period. The Jewish state was to present the Arab state the sum of two million pounds sterling to enable it to start operations.

If the Shaw report was a misfortune, the Peel report was a catastrophe. "The statement by the Royal Commission and the British Government that the Mandate was unworkable actually made the Mandate unworkable." But since the final solution was postponed to a distant future — and we may say here, was never put into force — the effect of the report was to undermine the authority of the Mandatory government at once and to provide new fields of support for the revolt in Palestine. The Peel report met with criticism on all hands[53] and caused great confusion. Commons declared the plan hasty, and referred it to the League of Nations for further suggestions. The League ordered that a technical commission be despatched to make precise proposals for drawing the boundaries.

Of those immediately concerned, the Arabs rejected the report, although it went very far in the direction of meeting their complaints, on the ground that it did not put a complete stop to immigration. On the Jewish side,[54] Weizmann and one section of the Palestinians were inclined to negotiate for improvements in the plan. But at the twentieth Zionist Congress (1937) Ussischkin led the opposition, as he had once done when the Uganda project was under consideration. The predominant majority of American Zionists agreed with his position. Weizmann finally succeeded in procuring a majority resolution to empower him for further negotiations on the basis of the Peel report. But during the next few days the Jewish Agency held its meeting, and its non-Zionist members unanimously pronounced against the plan. Matters almost came to a schism, and only after difficult negotiations was a compromise reached which did not completely negate the resolutions of the Zionist Congress.

The Arab Revolt against England

In Palestine[55] the Arab revolt had not completely subsided. Even while the Royal Commission was present there were constant excesses, minor and major. Especially in Galilee attacks upon Jews were a daily occurrence. But in Jerusalem also there were bomb explosions, and it was not known whether they were caused by Arab provocateurs or by a Jewish self-defense. Excesses continued uninterrupted during the entire summer of 1937 and exacted a toll of numerous victims among the population. There were casualties also among the English soldiers and police officials. Shots were fired into the residence of the High Commissioner. The military establishment was reinforced, but still proved inadequate to deal with the revolutionaries. Finally on October 1, 1937, the government delivered a decisive blow. It arrested the members of the Arab Higher Committee, dissolved the committee and its subsidiaries, and deposed the Grand Mufti from his post as president of the Supreme Moslem Council. The Mufti sought asylum in the Mosque of Omar, which was then surrounded by British troops. How he succeeded in getting to Beirut is a puzzle. The British paid dearly for their want of vigilance. From Beirut and later from Bagdad and Teheran he directed the revolt against the British Empire; and eventually he landed where he belonged, in the train of Adolf Hitler, where he functioned as Hitler's mouthpiece to the Arab peoples.

Measures had been taken too late. The poison had now been sown so far and wide that it was not enough to stop its sources. The adherents of the Mufti formed local commissions and a sort of provisional government which organized a regular civil war and continually caused loss of life. The terrorists had grown so wild that neither heavy penalties nor military defeats restrained them. They were as violent against their own people, such as the National Defense Party who disapproved of self-mutilation caused by boycotts and disorders, as they were against the Jews.

It was no enviable post that Sir Harold Alfred McMichael entered upon in the spring of 1938. All fury to the contrary notwithstanding, he refused, as his predecessors had done, to bar Jewish immigration. To be sure the Jewish Agency and the government were not in agreement on the schedule for immigration, and it is plain that there was a legitimate difference of opinion on the economic capacity of a country which was in turmoil and whose future was uncertain. The point of greatest conflict was the issue of illegal immigration. The government could not tolerate such immigration, and the Jewish Agency could not prevent it in view of the frightful need of the Jews in Europe.

For the Arab guerrilla leaders the struggle had resolved itself into a question of force. They wished to abolish the British regime, and they took their vengeance where the danger was least, upon the Jews. Five hundred is probably not too high a figure for the toll of Jewish dead as a result of the terror of 1938 and 1939, and the number of wounded was perhaps twice as large. Public security was at a low state, a murderous attack might be expected at any moment. A Jewish self-defense (*Haganah*) was formed, and it sought to prevent violence with heroic vigilance. It is not to be wondered that youthful hotheads wished to answer terror with terror. The *Va'ad Le'umi* and the Zionist Executive adjured them "not to stain the purity of the Jewish people's struggle for freedom." In the autumn of 1938 the High Commissioner was forced to declare martial law and to hand the command over to the troops which had newly been brought in.

In November 1938, His Majesty's Government published the report of the technical commission.[56] The report was so discouraging that it dropped the partition plan completely and returned to the proposal for a round table conference between Jews and Arabs.[57] This conference was called for February 1939 in London. But relations were now so strained that direct discussion between Jewish and Arab leaders was out of the question. Neither of the delegations nor the government had any constructive plan to offer. What the government finally suggested was an independent and unpartitioned Palestine in which the Jews were to be a permanent minority by limiting immigration and the acquisition of land in perpetuity. The negotiations were broken off with no results achieved and confusion worse confounded. To what extent the attitude of the government was influenced by the "Cliveden Set," which exerted so unwholesome an influence upon British policy at the time, has not yet been determined. Parliament and public opinion were not behind the government. Needless to say, the Jewish Agency protested vigorously against this projected travesty of the Mandate.

But the Colonial Office acted with precipitation, and yielded to rebellion and force. Before it could obtain the approval of the League of Nations, it began to enforce the restrictions on immigration and on the purchase of land.[58] The Jewish population of Palestine protested in dignified demonstrations, but used no force; it did not wish to spoil the justice of its cause with injustice.[59] The Permanent Mandates Commission declared, with a small majority, that these measures were not in consonance with the Mandate. The plenary session of the League adjourned its vote until the autumn, but on September 1, 1939, the new World War broke out.

To a country like Palestine which depended upon export and import and the flow of capital, the war brought hard times. When Mussolini followed Hitler (May 1940), the Mediterranean and the Suez Canal were *de facto* closed to commercial traffic. The air forces of the Axis made Haifa a frequent target and exacted a large toll of dead in defenseless Tel Aviv. Despite enormous increases in domestic production, food and all consumers' goods were scarce and dear. A beneficial result was peace between Arabs and Jews; common need brought neighbors together.

For Great Britain, Palestine became a mustering ground of great importance, since Egypt turned a cold shoulder. Upon the outbreak of war the Jews of Palestine did not hesitate to pledge their full cooperation to the allied cause.[60] They drew a sharp line of demarcation between Great Britain's struggle for existence and the mistakes of transitory ministries. The Arabs hesitated to declare their solidarity, and officials in London became more anxious to appease them. Even the cabinet of Winston Churchill lacked the courage for an unequivocal stand. It rejected, on threadbare grounds, the offer of a Palestinian Jewish legion under British command. What the oracle of the Atlantic Charter holds in store for the Near East is still an enigma. The half million Jews of Palestine have proved to be a reliable and constructive element.

CHAPTER VI

Hitler's Total War Against the Jews

Hitler's Policy

JANUARY 30, 1933, was a black day in the history of humanity. Upon that day Adolf Hitler[1] was named Chancellor of the German Republic, and so placed in position to spread over Europe and over the whole world the evil which he had brought upon the German people. Today every child knows that the name of Hitler denotes the incarnation of perjury, the enslavement of all peoples (including the German), and cold-blooded mass murder. Hitler conceived it his mission to persecute Jews with a persistent and relentless hatred: "by warding off the Jews I am fighting for the Lord's work." Since he was guided not by principles but by expediency, he was able upon occasion to moderate his tactics, if not his Jewish policy, when diplomatic or economic considerations made it advisable to do so. Von Hindenburg, the aged president; von Neurath, the Foreign Minister; and Dr. Schacht, the president of the Reichsbank and later Minister of Economics, could occasionally win some concessions. But then came Hitler's evil spirits, such as the demonic Dr. Joseph Goebbels, his Minister of Propaganda; the sadist Julius Streicher, his pornographer; and the enemy of mankind, Heinrich Himmler, his executioner. All of these men served to fan the flame of his hatred.[2] The baseness and the villainy, the lying and deception which were concentrated upon the Jews beggar description. Never was so intense and persistent a drumfire directed towards the destruction of a mighty army as these strategists found it necessary to use in order to make it impossible for 550,000 Jews to exist in the midst of 65,000,000 Germans. "Even 'Aryan' children were stirred to spy upon Jews and Christian non-Aryans and to attack them, and to incite their own parents to extirpate the Jews altogether."[3] From this specimen the world might have learned whither the destructive spirit of the Nazis was leading, but they were gullible and were persuaded that this treatment of the Jews was solely a matter of internal German policy. It was fatal to the world at large (and to the Jews) that the world relied upon the promises of the Reich Chancellor and Reich Leader, of which he kept not one, and did not rather refer to the conclusions of his *Mein Kampf*, in which the true nature of the revolutionary Hitler was expressed.

How a demagogue could succeed in creating, out of an insignificant band of brooding fanatics, a movement capable of bearing dominion in forcing dictatorship and a totalitarian state upon a great and intelligent people, in forming a competent ministry out of a group of desperadoes, in creating an irresistible instrument of war in the sight of all the world and overrunning all of Europe with it, is a story which has been frequently told but never yet adequately explained. In our context the story is of secondary importance, for Hitler's Jew-complex is older than his grand strategy. It rests upon intensification of Schönerer's Teutonic Nationalism combined with H. Stuart Chamberlain's Aryan theories and enriched by Arthur Rosenberg with the wisdom of the *Protocols of the Elders of Zion*. Jew-baiting was a handy program[4] for enthralling the masses and raising them ever and again to a pitch of revolutionary excitement without incurring the resistance of influential classes. Jew-baiting could win easy victories and offer a prospect of material advantages. Every local boss could celebrate triumphs in this campaign. Hitler's special corps, his storm troops and his élite guard were systematically drilled to hate and to bait Jews. They were men of violence who translated such insults as "Perish the Jews!" into deeds. Their masterly contribution to German culture was the desecration of Jewish cemeteries; sacrilege to the dead was made at the same time a threat to the living.

When they seized power this band of adventurers became the ruling class.[5] Germany ceased to be a nation based on law; it became the stamping ground of rogues and gangsters. Quite aside from the abolition of all constitutional rights by an administrative decree, Hitler's will alone was paramount in law: "In might alone lies right!" His puppet jurists-in-ordinary declared that right is what an Aryan considers right or what is advantageous to the German people, that is to say, to the Nazi party. Goering, the chief of the Prussian police, declared: "I am not here to dispense justice, but to destroy and to crush." The veterans of the party laid aside all restraint and terrorized the people. Business houses, especially those whose owners were Jews, were surrounded by pickets who threatened anyone who wished to enter them. They avenged themselves upon political opponents after the manner of bandits of old.

The victims were dragged out of their houses, beaten, driven half-clothed through the streets, hung with insulting placards, and sometimes even exhibited on the stage of variety theatres for the amusement of the audience. In Nuremberg a number of arrested Jews were herded into a meadow and forced to tear up grass with their teeth. A number of political expropriations were carried out; the objects varied from watches to factories.

In the concentration camps there was greater cruelty; tens of thousands were tormented to death or driven to suicide. To the world at large the names of Dachau, Oranienburg, and Buchenwald connote martyr-sites. Over their entrance there might have been blazoned the inscription of Dante's *Inferno*, "Abandon hope, all who enter here!" But unscrupulous and brutal as was the conduct of the Nazis, they wished to appear as men of honor in the sight of the world. Within Germany they suppressed reports of the prevalent anarchy; Hitler himself was forced to issue a warning against criminal actions on the part of individuals. Press and radio were "coordinated." But the press of the world was filled with reports of events in Germany.[6] Hitler and Goebbels called the reports atrocity tales; to the man in the street this label became a full guarantee for the reliability of the reports. The party was exposed before the world, and its response was wild fury against the Jews. Jews living in Germany were to do penance for attacks in the world outside Germany. A general boycott of all Jewish enterprises was proclaimed, to last until withdrawn by the party. In addition thousands of public meetings were to adopt anti-Jewish resolutions.

The mere announcement of this boycott produced such a panic in non-Jewish industrialist circles that they and their representatives in the cabinet pleaded with Hitler to abandon it. They could not persuade the tyrant to cancel the boycott completely but they did get it limited to a single day, Saturday, April 1, 1933. Several days before, Nazi rowdies here and there had driven Jewish lawyers and judges from the courts and Jewish physicians from hospitals. On April 1, pickets were posted in front of all stores, factories and shops belonging to Jews, in front of offices of physicians, lawyers, engineers, chemists, photographers, and the like, in order to prevent anyone from entering. The demonstration was carried out with a flawless revolutionary technique. The material injury to the Jews was less than that to German economy and to the reputation of the German government.

The boycott revealed the completeness and efficiency of the Nazi espionage. They possessed complete lists of all Jews or Christians married to Jews and of their financial interests, and they spared no one their generous attention, neither those who had been seriously disabled by the war nor widows of war casualties. As a consequence of the boycott the conviction was spread that it was permissible and even desirable to destroy the economic activity of the Jews, and subsequent measures were based upon this principle. Newspapers, publishing houses, department stores, wholesale houses and industries were subject to constant attack until they were eventually forced to surrender. Of Hitler's ostentatious economic program not a single item was carried out. Department stores, exchanges and banks were not liquidated, nor was industry nationalized; the only achievement was that Jewish participation in such enterprises was completely eliminated.

In order to reassure aroused public opinion abroad Hitler cabled the following despatch to the United States:[7]

German Jews will be treated like other nationals in accordance with their attitude to the national government.

But a few days later he issued his first special legislation regarding the Jews. From the Reichstag he had extorted the power to issue laws even when they ran counter to the constitution. His Law for the Restoration of the Regular Civil Service, dated April 4, 1933, was intended to eliminate officials who had no professional training but who had been named for party reasons. A rider provided: "Civil Servants of non-Aryan origin must retire; as regards the honorary officials, they must be dismissed." Non-Aryan was construed to mean, in the first instance, descent from Jewish parents or grandparents, even if only one of them professed the Jewish religion. Thus the principle of race was recognized in legislation; no baptismal water could cleanse the stain of a Jewish grandmother.

Upon the insistence of President von Hindenburg an exception was made in favor of those who were already employed as officers of the civil service on the first of August 1914, or who, during the Great War, fought at the front for Germany or her allies, or who lost their fathers or sons in action. This concession resulted in a painful surprise for the Nazis. Despite available information to the contrary, they had denied that Jews had contributed their full share of front-line fighting and of sacrifice in the war. Now it was officially established that the number of front-line fighters and of casualties was very considerable.

The provisions of the civil service law were soon extended to embrace provincial governments and communes, federal services such as the postal system, telegraph, telephone and railways, university professors, lawyers and notaries, honorary officials such as arbitrators and jurors, physicians at hospitals, sick funds and health insurance, directors and supervisors of banks and other corporations; nor was it long before Aryans who were married to non-Aryans were included in these provisions. It became a point of honor with all professional organizations to put the Aryan clauses into effect. Many communes declared contracts with Jewish purveyors and physicians void. In private business enterprises the managements were dragooned into discharging Jewish employees. The whole thing amounted to a pogrom on a broad front to eliminate Jewish competition.

Conflicting tendencies were constantly at work.[8] On the one side were reckless party men who prosecuted their cold pogrom and sought to annihilate the Jews by systematically depriving them of air and sustenance. On the other side, conservative forces in the Foreign Office and the Ministry of Economics sought to protect German exports by restraining the zeal of the party men. The victors were regularly "the militant gangster groups," as United States Ambassador William E. Dodd styled them. The administration, first the local functionaries and then the federal officers, always yielded to their "spontaneous manifestations," carefully organized by the party. The result was a constant diminution in the "living space" of the Jews and their systematic exclusion from all callings. Whether a Jew was an employee or worked on his own account, some means was found to eliminate him. At first it was announced that private enterprises would be spared, but in consequence of the bureaucratic organization into cartels and estates and especially of their being subjected to the totalitarian Four Year Plan (1936), a period was put to their continuance. Factories were deprived of raw material, merchants of customers, traders of their place in the market, bankers of credit; all were constrained to yield to force.

In the professions[9] all attempts to convince the Christian population of the infamy of the Jews proved ineffective, and so a direct course was taken and licenses were revoked. From the beginning of 1937 no Jew could own or hold employment in a pharmacy. After October 1, 1938, no Jew could practice medicine or dentistry, except for the few who were permitted to practice among Jews. On December 1, 1938, the same regulation was applied to lawyers, again those few who could serve as legal consultants for Jewish clients being excepted. It was now no longer a matter of suppressing political influence, no longer a matter of race, but simply cold-blooded strangulation of Jewish existence.

The economic was followed by a cultural pogrom. On April 26, 1933, there appeared the Law against the Alienization of German High Schools, Colleges, and Universities.[10] A *numerus clausus* was fixed for non-Aryans. Their numbers were not to exceed 1.5% in any single institution; in the period of transition 5% were to be allowed. Children of foreigners, of front-line veterans, and also of mixed marriages were not to be counted in calculating percentages. Jewish children were tolerated in elementary schools, but they were given no protection against insult and injury resulting from the poisoned doctrine of race and folk. The government recommended that Jewish primary schools be established, but they allotted no funds for such a purpose although they continued to receive Jewish taxes. They refused permission for higher schools for Jews; the Jews were to be denied higher education.

The universities, too, introduced the *numerus clausus*; the Jewish students who were tolerated received yellow certificates, as a memorial of the ancient Jew's badge. Admission to any sort of examination for civil service was not to be thought of. Candidates for degrees in law or education were forced to discontinue their studies. Medical students who had passed their final examinations were given their diplomas only if they could prove that they were to be employed abroad. Intolerance waxed; the time came when Jews were not admitted to examinations at all. Students assumed the right to drive unpopular professors from the universities. Their representatives proclaimed a campaign of enlightenment "to overcome Jewish intellectualism and the phenomena of liberal degeneration associated therewith. . . . The un-German spirit shall be extirpated from the libraries." All "un-German" books were ordered publicly burned[11] on May 10, 1933. Whole wagon-loads of such books in the fields of the arts and sciences were brought together, and in order that a satyr-play should not be wanting to round out the drama, the Bible was not forgotten. The torches of the new inquisitors cast an illuminating light upon the culture of this "Germanic" spirit.

These bumptious upstarts decreed that Jews might publish their literary productions only in Hebrew, and that any works which they might issue in German must be labeled as a translation. With abject servility the association of German publishers agreed and stated that they would no longer publish the works of Jews. The same spirit spread like an epidemic to other associations which had to do with cultural matters, embracing journalists, actors, musicians, and many others. Finally the Chamber of Cultural Affairs came to the support of the party. It forbade all who were not members of the Chamber to appear before the public in any of the fields over which the Chamber had surveillance, and it declared that Jews were unworthy of such an honor. Racialism celebrated its orgies; it is difficult to remain unmoved by the spectacle.

The Response to Nazism

How did the real representatives of the German spirit comport themselves? It is by no means certain, though not impossible, that a mass levy of the spokesmen of the churches, the bar, the sciences and the arts would have given events a different turn. But it is a peculiar feature of Hitler's career that decisive opposition was never at hand at crucial moments. There can be little doubt that even among those who desired that the Jews be excluded from public life on grounds of competition or envy or prejudice there were many who disapproved of the methods employed, which completely disregarded all principles of law. But there were very few indeed who summoned courage to express their opinions.[12] Those who did gather their courage were either put into immediate personal jeopardy or driven to flight.[13] The official propaganda machine published data concerning the mass immigration of Jews and concerning the positions which Jews had extorted for themselves in Germany, and their releases made the average German citizen shiver. It was not difficult to refute the falsified figures by official statistics; but who had access to such publications, and who would take the time to check the accuracy of the solemn declarations of a Reich ministry? Consciences were gradually dulled, and the existing state of affairs was accepted. "The *Führer* so ordained, and he must have had sound reasons." Such an attitude was characteristic of the cultured Germans of the period.

But foreign observers saw the situation much more clearly. Michael Williams,[14] the publisher of the Catholic weekly *Commonweal* in New York, directed the following appeal to the League of Nations after a visit to Germany:

Between 200,000 and 300,000 Jews have been deprived of any hope of the future.... The situation of the Jews in Germany is deplorable beyond words.... Unless the present rulers of the great German people are cast aside by the civilized Germans they now oppress, Jews and Catholic Christians will be subjected to scandalous persecution. Plans for world dominance of the Nazi system are a menace to the institutions of free men of Europe and America. What you will decide to do is your concern. Either harden your hearts and let the worst crime of our age proceed in the deliberate extinction of nearly 1,000,000 men, women, and children, or come quickly and strongly to the rescue!

Germany was at the time still a member of the League of Nations. The Nazi regime which was otherwise flawless in its efficiency had overlooked the fact that there was one territory in which the German Empire was not unqualifiedly sovereign. In the agreement with the Poles regarding Upper Silesia (May 15, 1922) Germany had obligated itself to guarantee all inhabitants, without distinction of birth, nationality, language, race and religion, complete protection of the law and complete legal equality, and had engaged to introduce no legislative or administrative provisions which would result in a differentiation among the inhabitants. A petition[15] requesting the revocation of German racial laws in Upper Silesia, the restoration of the *status quo ante*, and reimbursement for damages was submitted to the Council of the League. The German representative in the League was too clever to plead for a lost cause. His acquiescence, however, did not prevent a discussion of the question in the Council of the League, and in the rarefied diplomatic atmosphere which prevailed in that august assemblage an opinion was expressed:

A minimum of rights must be guaranteed to every human being, whatever his race, religion, or mother tongue. That minimum must be independent of the effects of changes in public life which it was impossible to foresee.

The petition was granted, and Hitler suffered a diplomatic defeat. His laws concerning the Jews were rescinded in Upper Silesia, and at least 2% of the Jews of Germany obtained a breathing space. When the treaty with Poland expired (July 1937), the Nazis repaired their neglect of four years in four weeks of Satanic lust for vengeance and pillage.

Though governments imposed restraints upon themselves, their citizens and parliaments protested[16] vigorously and condemned Hitler's procedures as crimes against humanity and against the principles of modern life. In democratic countries parties of the Left organized boycotts against German goods and services. In the United States the campaign was led by the Anti-Nazi League to Champion Human Rights, and the American Jewish Congress seconded their efforts vigorously. Other groups, Jewish and non-Jewish, who contemned Hitler in equal measure, opposed the boycott because they feared his vindictiveness against the Jews living in Germany. Looking backward from the vantage point of the present, it is to be regretted that the weapon of boycott was not more consistently employed. Only violence could subdue a man of Hitler's violence, and an air-tight boycott would have been a fatal blow to the Nazi regime. Yielding did not spare the Jews of Germany a single drop in their cup of sorrow. At the time things seemed different. Even Ambassador Dodd, to whom the Nazi philosophy was most repugnant, urged his Jewish friends, when he visited New York in the spring of 1934, to relax the boycott, at least experimentally.

The mass of German Jews was forced to bow to Hitler's rod. At his first attack many who were imperiled because of political activity in the past, many who had been thrown out of their employment, many who perceived what the future threatened, fled abroad. Some parents sent their children abroad to obtain an education in a free atmosphere, in many cases never to see them again. The number of Jewish refugees in those early months is estimated at 60,000.[17] Palestine received half of these; European countries, including fascist Italy — at that time Mussolini called Hitler's racial doctrines barbarism — hospitably opened their doors to the other half. With unemployment generally prevalent it was not easy to procure licenses for foreigners to work; and no country had use for the numerous merchants, lawyers, writers and artists. Here and there physicians were admitted to practice. Generous provision was made for scientifically accredited scholars. Only few of the refugees were provided with money; a small number of them were able to transfer part of their possessions abroad by illegal means, which, incidentally, the most convinced Nazis also employed.

Many refugees were assisted by eager relatives. But the preponderant majority were confronted with starvation and sunk to abysmal depression; despair drove many back to Germany. As at every catastrophe, Jewish responsibility faced the emergency with spontaneous generosity. Relief committees[18] were formed at once in various countries. The Central British Fund for German Jewry became the clearing house for all of Europe. In New York the Joint Distribution Committee resumed its traditional role and organized a new drive. The proceeds served to support the refugees, to retrain them, to settle them in Palestine. A share was allocated to the maintenance of Jewish life within Germany.

Life in the Land of the Nazis

The immediate victims of Hitler's barbarism were struck as by a cataclysm of nature. Despite all that had gone before, they were sure that they were living in a state ruled by law. Feudal states like Russia and Rumania had stubbornly opposed equality for the Jews, but that a civilized nation could be so retrograde as to abolish all constitutional security seemed chimerical even to pessimists. To their consternation they learned that the barbaric impulses emanated from the leadership of Germany, that the revolution derived not from below but from above.[19] No official functionary would receive reports on anti-Jewish excesses, let alone take action against them. One could only be prepared for the worst eventualities. Only the Foreign Office could be stirred to action, in order to improve public opinion abroad; these officials urged Jewish bureaus to issue pacifying reports.

The misfortune of the Jews of Germany was accentuated by the fact that at the moment of danger they were without authoritative representation; as a result of unhappy party strife they were incapable of unified action. One man, vigorous in soul and spirit, highly regarded by Jews and Christians, stepped into the breach and sought to save what could be saved. Leo Baeck,[20] rabbi of the Berlin Jewish Community, staked his life in galling negotiations in order to forestall further misfortune and to assure the possibility of a continuing Jewish communal life.

Gradually the comatose paralysis wore off, and Jewish will to survive was aroused. The Jewish press[21] called for courageous endurance; the Zionist *Jüdische Rundschau* of Berlin in particular uttered brave words. For the

Jewish press a new epoch of expanded activity and responsibility began. It found its way into circles which had previously had no use for a paper devoted exclusively to Jewish interests; now these people were repelled by the Nazi spirit which infected the daily papers and were receptive to increased emphasis upon Jewish values. The conditions under which the Jewish papers worked were extremely difficult. They could not ignore the activity of the Nazis, and on the other hand their criticism had to show the utmost restraint. There was no prepublication censorship, but from time to time papers were banned without reasons assigned, and always for several months, which was ruinous economically. But the Jewish press persisted intrepidly for more than five years, until it was completely outlawed, and aided considerably in strengthening the morale of the Jewish population.

The Jewish population exhibited admirable vitality and remarkable devotion in the struggle for existence which had been forced upon them. The first attempt to deal with the situation was the establishment of a Central Committee for Relief and Reconstruction. Its purpose was to provide advice and financial assistance to merchants, artisans, landlords, in a word, all whose existence was threatened by the Nazis. The foreign relief committees, and in particular the Berlin office of the Joint Distribution Committee, cooperated actively.

A further task was the care of the youth, which had been thrust out of the schools by law or cruelty. To allow them to grow up as illiterates would have suited the fondest hopes of the Nazis, but it would also have gone counter to every Jewish tradition. For years there had been a warm contest between those who advocated Jewish secular schools and those who opposed them. Now the decision had come from without; there could be no question of any but exclusively Jewish schools. The task then was to establish schools where none existed and to inform existing schools with a living Jewish spirit and to fashion their curriculum so that pupils should be prepared for the life which was before them and eventually for emigration. Many who had been discharged from the public schools were available as teachers. The old teachers' seminary in Würzburg and another newly founded in Berlin, both enjoying the approval of the Ministry of Education, provided for a continued supply of teachers. Energetic measures were taken to shift objectives from liberal to manual arts and to supplement the training of those who were released from regular schooling. A Central Institute for Adult Education, under the leadership of Martin Buber, with headquarters in Frankfort on the Main, provided for the Jewish cultural and spiritual education of teachers and youth leaders. There was a widespread mood of inwardness and reflection and an eager desire to close up the great gaps in knowledge of Judaism.

But these efforts at reconstruction lacked a foundation, an appropriate representation of all Jews with authority to speak to the Jews and for them. The communal representatives chosen on old party lines had fallen short of the need. The younger elements desired a new body, not weighted with the party lines of the old, and with due regard for various groups they formed a National Committee of German Jews (*Reichsvertretung der deutschen Juden*). This body was able to count upon the confidence of wide circles and undertake the task of reconstruction with fresh energy. Leo Baeck, whose leadership could not be contested, was called to head a board of ten. Associated with him was Otto Hirsch of Stuttgart, an experienced administrator who possessed marked spiritual qualities along with a sense of the practical. He as well as his faithful collaborator, Julius Seligsohn of Berlin, were later tortured to death in concentration camps and became martyrs to the Jewish cause.

It was a hopeless struggle which the National Committee had to wage, under tragic conditions. The Committee's members were never admitted to factual discussions with competent authorities; attempts to inform members of the federal government on the actual situation were all fruitless. They could only accept decisions and pass them on. Nor did they find all requisite support within Jewry. Legal representation of the Jews was in the hands of the communities. These now felt that their right of primogeniture was being impugned, and their resentment was the cause of many hindrances. The full cooperation of the bureaus in charge of emigration and retraining was valuable, but here too the executive had constantly to be on the alert to preserve the balance between Zionists and anti-Zionists; even in the presence of the common enemy there were die-hards who disturbed cordial relations. Only the prudence and self-denial of the leaders made it possible to steer the bark of the National Committee safely through the stormy waves. Whatever degree of Jewish self-administration could be organized under such overwhelming external pressure they attempted and succeeded in organizing.

Independently of the National Committee but in personal contact with it, a Cultural Union of German Jews (*Kulturbund deutscher Juden*) was formed in Berlin, with branches throughout the Reich. Its program was twofold. It made it possible for the Jewish population, which was excluded from public institutions for entertainment and instruction, to attend plays and operas, concerts and lectures; and it gave employment to hundreds of persons who had been made penniless by the application of the racial laws. The substantial contributions of the Cultural Union met with enthusiastic approval among Jews. Dr. Goebbels, who flaunted Nazi magnanimity to the world, boasted that the Nazis had made it possible for the Jews to pursue their own cultural life. In reality he put every possible limitation upon the Cultural Union. Only Jews or Christians married to Jews could be members or visitors. Needless to say, the active personnel must be wholly comprised of Jews. At first the repertory was free, insofar as considerations of space and finance permitted; then it was discovered that Jews could not interpret German poetry and German music according to their true meaning, and the Jews were therefore not allowed to present such works. There were other dodges also; the institution was banned for weeks without previous warning, so that the undertaking suffered seriously. A newly established book-publishing enterprise had to work under similar hardships, and after being tolerated for a while it also was eventually suppressed.

All of these institutions to promote reconstruction could only have been created with the toleration of the government, and the fact that they were permitted shows that the government wished to make life for Jews in Germany possible. The revolutionary force seemed to wane; the government was occupied in elaborating the dictatorship and the totalitarian state and in the campaign against the churches; for a while the Jews were left alone. They were subjected to certain pin-pricks, as for example, the prohibition of ritual slaughter throughout the Reich — not, as the Nazis cynically admitted, in the interest of dumb animals, but in order to torment the Jews. It was enacted that citizenship could be withdrawn from "undesirables" (a euphemism for foreign Jews) who had become citizens during the Weimar Republic. If the "undesirables" were German citizens living abroad, like Albert Einstein, for example, their citizenship was withdrawn and their property confiscated. But there was a pause in regulations directed against the Jews, and it might seem as if now that the Jews had been beaten out of the household with blows and buffets some *modus vivendi* with the outcasts could be worked out.

But the parallel government, the Nazi party, saw to it that there should be no respite. Despite the bloody struggle within its own body, it never lost sight of its goal of racial separation. Discrimination continued, and in small places occasionally reached the stage of public disturbances.[22] Many places declared that Jews were not wanted, bakers refused to sell them bread, grocers other necessities of life. In Nuremberg they were first forbidden to use public swimming pools and excluded from hotels and restaurants. There the first "hostels for Jews," where only Jews could be accommodated and served, were established. In order to make shopping easier for the man in the street, business places were marked with a sign reading "German" or "Aryan." Emphatic warnings against consulting Jewish physicians and lawyers had to be repeated time and again; apparently they were not as effective as had been desired. The Jews did not allow themselves to be worked up into a panic; there was even a certain hopefulness when, upon the introduction of universal military duty (March 1935), the army[23] insisted that Jews physically fit should not be excluded from service.

Such a danger Goebbels and Streicher were bound to prevent at any cost. The packs were unleashed in the summer of 1935; in the capital the "folk-soul" began to seethe; in the provinces the temperature was even higher, and raids upon Jews became the order of the day. Poor Hitler, already annoyed by the persistent and not ineffective boycott against German goods and the insult to the swastika flag in the harbor of New York, was deluged with complaints of the presumptuous conduct of individual Jews. This alien people, he was informed, had taken it upon itself to control public opinion in Germany; recently it had organized a protest against a film shown in a Berlin moving picture theater. Thus spake *Reichsführer* Adolf Hitler in a solemn address to the German Reichstag which he hastily drummed up in connection with the Party Day at Nuremberg, as if he himself had been present in the dark theater and had observed the protesting Jews.

Trivial as was its justification, the legislation which followed, the detestable "Nuremberg Laws"[24] of September 15, 1935, were the great legislative revelation of the Third Reich which had been brooded over for several years. The first of these laws made the right of citizenship in the Reich a privilege of people of German or related blood and of ability to serve the German nation and Reich faithfully. Thus Jews were definitely robbed of their citizenship. Next the swastika was made the flag of the Reich and Jews were forbidden to display any but the "Jewish blue-white colors." The capstone was the Law for the Protection of German Blood and Honor. This law forbade marriage and all sexual intercourse between Jews and women of German or related blood, and imposed heavy penalties for transgression. It provided further that female domestic help of German or related blood, younger than forty-five years of age, must not be employed in households which contained a male Jew over sixteen years of age. These laws applied also to cross-breeds. Hair-splitting casuistry regulated the status of quarter, half, and three-quarter Jews according to the number of their Jewish grandparents. "The deputies cheered and yelled their approval," reported the correspondent of the United Press.

Hitler assuaged his bad conscience by explaining that these laws made it possible for the Jews to lead their own lives as they could in no other country. There were even stoneblind Zionists who saw the triumph of their principles in this complete separation of Jews. In reality the Nuremberg Laws were not statesmanship but malice. The status of Jews was regulated only negatively. They lost their citizenship. This meant that those functionaries who were still in office, besides 763 notaries — all veterans in the service or of front-line duty in the World War — were immediately discharged. The law was executed far and wide, with the thoroughness of which only Germans are capable. It had another consequence in that all Jewish organizations whose names included the words "German Jews" now had to adopt other names.

But what was it that had been regulated? What were the Jews? According to the law, *Staatsangehörige*, "belonging to the state," but according to its interpretation, guests. As guests their situation was anomalous, in that they had no home; in numbers they were a minority, but they received no minority rights and could be treated simply as aliens. As far back as civilization reaches the rights of a guest have been sacred; protection of his life, his honor, and his property was assured to the guest. But to the Jews of Germany these things were denied. Streicher, who celebrated his triumph at Nuremberg, declared, "The fight has just begun;" and it was this slogan which determined the direction matters were to take.

The rubric of "race defilement," which was the peculiar province of Streicher's fiendish sexual depravity, provided limitless matter for his weekly, *Der Stürmer*. The most intimate and delicate of human relationships were dragged out to public view with the greatest imaginable coarseness and vulgarity. The law was a convenient tool for blackmail.[25] In the courts which were set up, the flimsiest denunciation of an Aryan woman or her relatives was given more credit than the documented statement of a Jew. Denunciations of race defilement became a favorite weapon against Jewish merchants and industrialists. As soon as the prosecution stepped in and arrested a man who had been calumniated, the party intervened to put his business into Aryan hands even before a judicial decision could be reached. Indeed, the whole turmoil was aimed at the one end of forcing Jews from their livelihoods. The mouthings about blood and honor were only a front for brutal robbery of Jewish enterprises and Jewish property. Excuses for forcing Jews out of a given calling were never wanting. It was contrived with system and precision, and with little ado. For the occasion of the Olympic games of 1936 an effort was made to camouflage the situation in order to avoid anything that might produce an unfavorable impression abroad.

The Nuremberg Laws constituted so inexorable an attack that even those groups which had previously regarded it their duty to persevere in Germany now perceived that salvation could be achieved only by emigration. Various plans for systematic emigration were suggested and discussed with the government, but the government would grant certain indulgences only to petty capitalists. The great Jewish relief committee in London, which now called itself the World Council for German Jewry,[26] produced a plan for the orderly emigration of 100,000 Jews out of Germany; the cost was calculated at $15,000,000, which was to be raised in Great Britain and the United States. The money was to be had; what was wanting was a country to which the migration could be directed. Aside from Palestine and Shanghai in the Far East, there was no place on earth which would admit a sizable immigration. Countries like Argentina and Brazil, which were still in process of development, were opposed to group immigration. The numbers which the smaller South American states could receive were insignificant.

In the United States Jews hesitated to exploit possibilities for immigration; between 1933 and 1936 only 17,600 Jews immigrated to the United States from all countries. Children, it is true, were received with open-hearted hospitality. Experience had shown that the anxiety which preceded any large scale immigration had proved baseless; but this was now forgotten. The difficulties[27] attendant upon the immigration of so many merchants and professional men seemed forbidding, but the quality of the human material available was underestimated. Later, when immigration increased (1937: 11,352; 1938: 19,736), it appeared that these people shunned no kind of work. The spiritual strength of the women in particular had been underestimated. In times of prosperity, to be sure, they had loved a life of luxury; but in times of need their resistance was heroic, and their willingness to toil and endure proved them worthy of the glorious models of Jewish womanhood.

The Intensification of Nazism

The grand scheme for emigration collapsed. The Nazis sought new tricks.[28] They wished to be rid of the Jews, but not before they had properly plundered them. "Drive out the Jews with one suit and a handbag and throw them on the charity of the democratic world," was Dr. Goebbel's diabolic advice. After 1936 the Gestapo became the paramount power. The Gestapo[29] signified permanent terror, bestial brutality, a more deadly and efficient Ogpu, as its organizer, Heinrich Himmler, boasted. In its treatment of the Jews the Gestapo recognized no legal considerations whatever. It assumed complete and irresponsible dominion over Jews, like that of a slave owner over his chattels; the lives and property of Jews were alike at their disposal.

The hand of the Gestapo lay heavy not only upon individuals but also upon organizations. After 1937 Jewish organizations were subjected to constant abuse.[30] Pretexts were not lacking. On April 20 leading members of the Independent Order B'nai B'rith throughout Germany were arrested simultaneously, subjected to a rigorous examination, and released after their passports had been seized. The individual lodges and the grand lodge were banned; their capital, buildings and inventories were confiscated.

The next blow was directed against the Jewish congregations. On March 31, 1938, they lost their privileges as public, legal corporations, and could continue only as private associations. Membership and the payment of dues were thus left wholly to the discretion of the individual, and at the same time tax exemptions, which Jewish congregations, in common with Christian churches, had previously enjoyed, were now revoked. It must be said, to their credit, that members were loyal to their congregations and continued to pay their dues voluntarily; as a result of the emigration of the wealthy, of the increased demands for charity, and of the taxes which were now imposed upon them, the burden was heavy indeed.

Previous horrors were only a prelude to the events of 1938. The subjugation of Austria (March 12, 1938) brought a coarse and bestial gang to the surface, "the scum of the earth," to use Hitler's own favorite expression. Never had barbarian conquerors abused a captured city worse than these allegedly longed-for liberators.[31]

The Austrian National Socialists broke loose and avenged themselves with truly bestial cruelty upon their opponents. Large numbers of the leading men of old Austria were literally mown down. But those who suffered most were the Austrian Jews. For weeks the Jewish inhabitants of Vienna — apart from those who had been immediately killed and arrested — were beaten and robbed; their homes were plundered and their businesses confiscated. They were caught in the streets and compelled to wash the Austrian Storm Troopers' motorcars, to clean out the lavatories in the barracks, to scrape the political slogans of the former regime from the roads and pavements. Neither children nor old women were spared. Many died in the concentration camps at Dachau and Buchenwald; many took their own lives.

What was done in the name of the law, after the exuberance of the first occupation, was no better. Jewish associations and organizations, including congregations, throughout the country were immediately dissolved; Jews were not allowed to participate in the plebiscite on the *Anschluss* with Germany. Jewish and part-Jewish judges were discharged. In the course of a few weeks all the laws and regulations for excluding Jews from every sphere of life, which had been contrived in Germany in the space of five years, were applied to the Jews of Austria. The laws governing crossbreeds, who were more numerous in Austria than in the Reich, were made stricter. Tens of thousands of employees and wage-earners were made penniless in a short while.

At intervals of a few weeks raids were made against the Jews; upon each occasion a number of victims were taken to the concentration camps, and few ever returned. By the beginning of April the number of those arrested, of whom the Jews constituted the largest contingent, was estimated at 34,000; suicides were numbered by the hundreds. The Nazis did not allow the true state of affairs to be known in the outer world. Inconvenient newspaper correspondents were expelled; threats were made to the Czechoslovakian government in the event that details should be published in the newspapers of Prague.

In Hitler's own country, Austria, degradation and pauperization of the Jews was not enough. In his first speech at Vienna, Marshal Goering proclaimed that the city must be cleansed of Jews in the course of a few years. "The Jew must know we do not care to live with him. He must go." The Jews who had overnight become the plaything of the mob, who had been deprived of all police protection, who were even dragged from the synagogues in order to scrub the streets (a thing that had never happened in Germany), the Jews who had been crowded out of their livelihoods and their property, would have been willing enough to heed this demand if anyone had shown them where they could go. All borders were barred, for neighboring countries protected themselves against an influx of impoverished refugees. Peaceful liquidation of property was made impossible. Storm troopers searched homes, besieged shops, and, as in a state of war, "requisitioned," that is to say, robbed. Larger enterprises were handed over to commissioners for liquidation. Here was a crew that even the Augean stables of the Nazis could not endure; at least a dozen were sent to Dachau to be educated.

Before it was possible to make any sort of preparations for orderly emigration, individual localities such as Linz and Graz began to eject the Jews forcibly. Burgenland took the prize. There the old-established Jewish population was vilely beaten and driven out of its homes by the storm troopers. It also established a record by thrusting Jews out into a no-man's land. With insufficient clothing and food they were loaded on a dilapidated boat which then lay at anchor in the Danube. Neither Hungary nor Czechoslovakia would permit them to disembark in their domain; the majority returned to their certain misery in despair.

The annexation of Austria, which had taught Hitler that Europe would accept any violation of law calmly, was also a turning point in his Jewish policy. Henceforth he was bent upon relentless liquidation. First Goering laid hands upon Jewish property.[32] By a decree of April 26, 1938, all Jews, three-quarter Jews, and half-Jews, as well as Christian spouses of Jews, who possessed property of a value in excess of 5,000 reichsmark were required to declare their possessions at home and abroad, including valuables, to the proper authorities. "The commissar for the Four Year Plan may take measures which are necessary to secure the use of the property in accordance with the interests of German economy." This was a clear indication that the declaration would be used as a basis for confiscation of property. Bolshevism was on the march, though its application was limited to Jews.

Next in order were personal torments. Jews were treated like criminals. Their passports were revoked and others issued only for imminent emigration, in which case they were marked with a "J" to describe the bearer. Instead of a passport, every Jew had to carry an identification card with his photograph and fingerprints, like enemy aliens in time of war; even infants in cradles were under this obligation. If Jews had given names which did not seem sufficiently Jewish to the Nazis, they had to take the middle name of "Israel" or "Sarah." There was no such thing as personal security. One morning, by decree of the Gestapo, a certain number of Jews throughout the Reich were arrested. They were alleged to be asocial elements, but in reality they were decent people who for some small irregularity had been fined by a police magistrate in years past or whose automobile license plates were found to be insufficiently polished.

Previously consideration had been shown for Jewish religious practices, but now this too changed. When the *Führer* and Reich Chancellor was surveying perspectives in the city of Munich and the local synagogue seemed to interfere with his view he gave summary orders to pull it down. The building had to be vacated within forty-eight hours. This was the conduct of a man who charged the Bolshevists with desecrating and destroying houses of worship. What was right with Hitler could not be wrong with Streicher. He did not rest until the synagogue in Nuremberg was also razed. As in medieval times, the destruction was celebrated as a folk festival. The *Stürmer* demanded the destruction of all synagogues — an ominous presage of things to come.

Annihilation or emigration were the only alternatives. But what country would receive penniless immigrants? The League of Nations was incapable of mastering the problem of the 35,000 refugees in Europe. Their snail's pace could not match Hitler's seven-league boots. In this emergency the government of the United States stepped in[33] and directed an appeal to twenty-nine nations for a cooperative effort to facilitate the immigration of political refugees from Austria and Germany. President Roosevelt expressed a cordial hope that this enterprise would benefit a large number of victims of persecution, insofar as immigration laws of various countries permitted. But United States consuls were of a different opinion, and did all they could to make immigration difficult. They posted themselves like cherubim with flaming swords before the Garden of Eden, to keep the way of the tree of life.

A conference in which thirty-two nations were represented took place July 6–15 at Evian in France, and Jews were filled with sanguine hopes. This relief conference revealed the complete helplessness of the great powers of Europe. Their representatives could make handsome speeches, but could not rise to any constructive measure. Hitler's and Mussolini's observers gloated over their fecklessness. Only the smaller republics of Latin America showed any inclination towards real cooperation, but they were chiefly interested in immigrants who were experienced farmers. The only tangible result of the meeting was a wordy resolution proposing the establishment of a permanent refugee body. The adherence of the United States to this idea remained the only anchor of hope for those who were being persecuted and exiled.

In Central Europe events moved rapidly. The weakness which England and France showed at Munich made possible the dismemberment of Czechoslovakia, the expulsion of new masses of Jews from the Sudeten lands[34] and from Slovakia, and the creation of new no-man's lands. Troubles multiplied. The Polish government gave notice that it would not allow the return to Poland of Polish subjects who had lived abroad several successive years without showing their loyalty to Poland. This caused the German officials to undertake a summary expulsion of all Polish subjects from Greater Germany.[35] Following their traditional methods, the Gestapo routed some 12,000, according to moderate estimates, out of their beds, mostly men, rarely women, gave them scanty supplies which they had themselves to pay for, and loaded them on wretched trains which took them to the Polish border. In Zbaszyn (Neu Benschen) there were collected no fewer than 4,000 persons who were not permitted to enter Poland or return to Germany. The Polish government was apparently frightened by its own temerity and declared that the German interpretation of their proclamation was based upon a misunderstanding. Diplomatic negotiations made it possible for a portion of those who had been exiled to return to Germany, but their means of livelihood had meanwhile been destroyed. Others were released through the help of the relief committees in Warsaw, a number received certificates for Palestine, many had to spend a hard winter in completely inadequate barracks.

Pogroms and the Last Flight

There was a grim postlude to this Polish horror. A seventeen-year-old emigrant in Paris, Herschel Grynszpan[36] by name, received word that his parents had been carried off from Hanover, and he took a desperate resolve. Armed with a revolver he went to the German embassy and shot down Ernst vom Rath, an attaché who was completely innocent. This assassination came very conveniently for the Nazis; they now had the pretext they needed to let loose their bestiality. With wonted Nazi precision everything was got ready for an attack on a grand scale; only a signal needed to be given to let loose the storm.

The entire Jewish population of Germany was subjected to a reign of terror. The pogroms started simultaneously all over Germany. No attempt was made by the police to restrain the savagery of the mob.

Almost every synagogue in the country was burnt to the ground. Scarcely a Jewish shop escaped being wrecked. Looting occurred on a great scale. Parts of the fashionable district of Berlin were reduced to a shambles. Jews of all ages, of both sexes, were beaten in the streets and in their homes. Numbers were lynched. The caretaker of a synagogue is believed to have been burnt, with his family, to death.

This is one of the many firsthand summary reports on the pogrom of November 9, 1938. It might be supplemented by a thousand details of barbarous bestiality.

The news of the last few days from Germany [said President Roosevelt[37]] has deeply shocked public opinion in the United States. I, myself, could scarcely believe that such things could occur in a twentieth century civilization.

This feeling of revulsion and indignation was general throughout the world, and widespread even within Germany.

What did the Reich government do in the face of such anarchy? Dr. Goebbels made many speeches and wrote many articles to represent the inhuman excesses as spontaneous outbursts of national anger. But the artful liar involved himself in such contradictions as to betray the guilty parties. The government machine had not operated as flawlessly as usual. The "folk instinct" had been carefully plotted and skillfully directed, but in many places it was prematurely unleashed.[38] Gradually documents turned up which clearly proved the full guilt of high officials. If any doubt remained concerning responsibility for the Reichstag fire of 1933, that doubt was now dissipated. The methods that had been employed in that fire were the same as were used to commit arson in more than six hundred synagogues simultaneously.

Deep grief for Herr vom Rath did not prevent other ministers from affixing their signature to all the decrees and the cleverly contrived regulations[39] which set the seal upon the crimes of November. On November 11 all arms and ammunition still in the possession of Jews were confiscated without reimbursement. On November

12 a mulct of a billion mark was imposed upon Jewish subjects of the state as a penalty for their "hostile attitude towards the German nation and the Reich." On the same day Jewish owners were ordered to make immediate repairs of the damage that had been done to their stores and shops during the disorders. The Jews themselves had to bear the cost of clearing up the debris and making restorations; payments due on account of insurance policies against damages were confiscated by the government. On that same day there was issued a regulation with the significant title, "Decree for the Elimination of the Jews from German Economic Life." It provided that after January 1, 1939, Jews must engage in no form of independent trade and that Jewish employees must be discharged at once with six weeks' notice. Finally police everywhere were empowered to forbid Jews to enter certain precincts or to appear in public at certain hours. All places of entertainment were barred to Jews. They were further forbidden to drive automobiles; all licenses had to be surrendered before January 1, 1939.

Even school children had to do penance for Grynszpan's crime. As many Jewish pupils as still attended "German schools" or continuation schools were instantly dismissed; they could attend only Jewish schools, and in small places that was not an easy thing to do. All Jewish congregations, organizations and associations were suspended. Scientific institutions and schools were closed and their libraries, or as many of them as had escaped the great fire, were confiscated; only the *Lehranstalt für die Wissenschaft des Judentums* in Berlin was spared. The Jewish press was banned, and Jewish bookdealers and publishers forbidden to operate; the latter were subsequently embodied in the Cultural Union. These various administrative and cultural institutions could hardly have functioned in any case, for their leaders were mostly under arrest. As in the preceding summer a fixed contingent of arrests was prescribed for the whole Reich. Rabbis, teachers, heads of congregations and societies, and other prominent persons, were arrested, if they were not absent on journeys or had not sought refuge outside their own homes, and carried off to concentration camps by the thousands. We shall never know the number of those who succumbed to maltreatment. Only those who engaged to leave Germany at once were released.

Soon it was discovered that things had been carried too far. The vandalism which had been countenanced was an obstacle to the execution of Goering's Four Year Plan. The collection of so enormous an assessment without the cooperation of those affected caused a sharp decline in the general money market. For purely selfish reasons, then, the cooperation of the Jews was secured; after a short time permission was given for "so-called Jewish communities which do relief work and train persons leaving for Palestine" to resume their activities. In time public worship was allowed, where suitable accommodations were available; one can imagine the dread with which worshipers entered these synagogues. At the end of November the National Committee of Jews in Germany was again allowed to function. This was not the old representative body, but an enforced concentration of all Jewish work. Congregations and other institutions could only exist as sections or business offices of the National Committee. The Committee had to provide for all Jewish needs, in the first instance for schooling and emigration.

Those who had lived through the terror of recent weeks needed no added stimulus to emigrate.[40] A frightful panic seized Jewish households; there was no family which did not have some cause for mourning. Each ringing of the doorbell brought terror, for the Gestapo might be on one of its missions of violence. Objects as well as persons attracted the eye of the banditti. Furnishings stolen from Jewish homes were offered for sale in such abundance that they ceased to have any value. Real estate and business enterprises had to be liquidated, and whatever prices were set by the Labor Front had to be accepted without demurring. In many places food was not sold to Jews and the organs of the National Committee had to take measures to prevent starvation. At this juncture Goebbels announced 1,500 mass meetings to consider the question of the Jews. Did he really believe that the public was not yet adequately informed, or did he merely have to keep his noisy propaganda machine in motion?

A mass flight of Jews set in, and somehow they found places which would receive them. What reason supposedly had prevented the individual governments from doing in the summer, sympathy prompted them to do in the autumn.[41] Countries bordering upon Germany were inundated with penniless refugees. Holland, Belgium, France and Switzerland set up special barracks for transients and camps for children. Christian contributions added to the considerable sums collected for relief by Jews, and even governments made appropriations. Great Britain displayed its traditional hospitality. It offered temporary shelter to 20,000 adults and 5,000 children who intended to continue their travels overseas, on condition that their maintenance was assured. Many families took refugees into their homes. Under the aegis of Lord Baldwin, the former Prime Minister, a fund of more than £250,000 was collected — to say nothing of Jewish generosity. President Roosevelt protected 15,000 visitors in the United States against the danger of immediate return to the Nazi inferno by extending their permits for six months. For the first time the United States consuls found their immigration quotas filled. The relief committees in the United States made strenuous efforts to provide assistance and to arrange for resettlement and occupational readjustment.

The director of the permanent bureau of emigration[42] entered into negotiations with the German government on the possibility of organizing systematic emigration. The decisive issue was permission for the Jews to transfer their property, which had in any case been greatly reduced, and here the Germans were unyielding. The flight turned into a panic-stricken rout, which was exploited, as might be expected, by extortioners.[43] Travel agencies and consular employees sold Jews inadequate or invalid documents, which did not permit them to land when they had reached their destination. The case of the S. S. St. Louis is notorious. This boat arrived at Havana on May 27, 1939, with 900 passengers, but despite pleas to the Cuban president they were not permitted to disembark. Palestine saw similar tragedies; upon the obstinacy of the British administration rests the responsibility for hundreds of human lives.

Nazism for Export

Leading Nazis declared that National Socialism was not intended for export, but with their customary duplicity they made unceasing efforts to infect every country and every continent with their virus.[44] Every means, lawful or otherwise, was used to disseminate their oral and written propaganda. The chief aim of their agents was to spread discontent and to use the Jewish question as dynamite; Hitler calculated on antisemitism as a weapon for world conquest. This burrowing technique was enormously successful. Every country spawned broods of somber gentlemen who fancied themselves as future Hitlers in miniature and injected Nazi slogans into the politics of their own countries. In England[45] the Union of British Fascists raged furiously against the Jews.

The United States realized a boom in proponents of fascism, avowed or disguised; without exception they beat the antisemitic drum and so got them a following. In Latin America, the German element, which was strong numerically and economically, did everything in their power to force the Jews out of business life. European states like Norway, Holland, and Belgium had their Quislings, and France its Fifth Columnists, who cloaked their underground work with the pretext of combatting the domination of the Jews.

If such things could happen in countries where the government and the preponderant majority of the people were strongly opposed to fascism, what could be expected of those which were under Hitler's influence? After 1933, Danzig[46] assimilated its legislation and its administrative practice to that of the Third Reich. Memel accepted all the Nazi laws, after Hitler's occupation, and was emptied of its Jews. The price which Hitler paid for Mussolini[47] has not yet been established. The first symptom of the Duce's vassalage was his racial legislation. As long as Mussolini set the tone for the Axis he ridiculed antisemitism and racism. But after 1937 he allowed the fascist press to indulge in wild outbursts against the "Jewish race." After a visit by German racial experts the Italian Ministry of Culture found a group of bogus scientists who prepared a "scientific" opinion in which they set forth the concept of a peculiar Italian race, denied the Jews any part in that race, and declared that the alteration of the purely European character of the Italians by the admixture of a non-European race was intolerable. These hallucinations were the precursors of a tragic body of legislation.

By a decree of September 5, 1938, Jews were excluded from educational and cultural institutions of every grade, from elementary schools to universities to academies of sciences or of arts. Jews could be neither students nor teachers nor directors; nor could textbooks written by Jews be used. Jews were permitted to maintain their own schools. On November 17, 1938, a comprehensive racial law was issued. It was modeled after the Nuremberg Laws; it was more rigorous than those laws in that it added numerous economic disabilities, and more lenient in that it made exceptions in favor of casualties of the last four Italian wars and of the struggle for fascism. Native Jews were immediately enrolled in a special listing as "Italian citizens of Jewish race." Foreigners who had been naturalized after January 1, 1919, now lost their citizenship. Those of them that had settled in Italy, Libya, or the Aegean Islands after that date were now expelled. According to Mussolini's definition, anyone with two Jewish parents is a Jew, whether or not they adhered to the Jewish religion. Here the Church saw grounds for objection. It rejected the racial point of view in general, but was directly concerned when baptism was disregarded. Italian racial legislation contributed to the strain in Italy's relations with the Vatican. The Pope showed conspicuous favor to certain Jews of high scholarly standing who had been ejected from their posts.

The basic racial principles were supplemented by drastic regulations covering details; the ridiculous requirement that Jews bear Jewish middle names was included. Mussolini's racial legislation was rendered the more disgraceful because it affected a group among which he had found many trusted collaborators. Not all Italian Jews were fascists, any more than all Italian Christians were fascists; but there were many Jews who had devoted all their intelligence and bravery to the victory of fascism and to its conquest of an empire. The number of high-ranking officers who were forced to resign and the number who responded by suicide is significant. All the Jews of Italy and its colonies were ruined; all who were able to do so emigrated.

In Hungary,[48] another of Hitler's vassals, strong fascist organizations urged anti-Jewish legislation. The government met them half way. Its "Law for the More Efficient Protection of the Social and Economic Balance" (1938) provided that the number of Jewish employees in industrial, banking and commercial enterprises, and of Jewish physicians, lawyers and engineers should not exceed 20% of the whole number. Wherever the number was larger it had to be reduced to the stipulated maximum within a given period of time. The number of breadwinners who were thrown out of their vocations by this law was officially computed to amount to 16,000 within the space of five years; including dependents, 75,000 persons must have been affected. Those discharged in the very first year by far exceeded the expected number. Like other countries, Hungary formulated its own definition of Jew. Anyone who had not embraced Christianity before August 1, 1919, was a Jew; those baptized after that date received an indulgence if their parents had been born in Hungary before 1879. The protest of the Union of Hungarian Jews was of no avail; the law was adopted and enforced. Was it the effect of hysteria that 5,000 rushed to baptism, or was it an accurate calculation of privileges to be acquired under some future legislation?

Before a year had elapsed a second anti-Jewish law was passed (May 5, 1939), a "Law to Restrict Jewish Participation in Public and Economic Life." In its casuistical definition of the term Jew it did in fact show consideration for the new converts. The new law reduced considerably the quotas assigned in the year before and limited the exemptions in favor of front-line veterans of the World War. Jews had to leave all governmental positions at once, and to be discharged from important positions in the press, theater and cinema before the end of 1939. Jewish real estate, urban or rural, might be confiscated.

This was not an economic law, but a law of pure hatred. It met with vigorous opposition, especially in the Upper House, whose presiding officer resigned his post.

The law brought no blessings to Hungary. Baron Imrédy, who had drawn it up as prime minister, discovered that he was himself descended of a Jewess, and retired. Count Paul Teleki, who carried it through parliament, ended by committing suicide because of his despair at the enslavement of his country by the Nazis. The law hit the Jews hard, for it robbed a quarter of a million persons of their livelihood. The law was also applied to the 150,000 Jews who returned from Slovakia (Upper Hungary) and Sub-Carpathia. Theirs was a sad homecoming and it multiplied the misery of those who were already impoverished for racial reasons.

There was no economic depression in Rumania,[49] but a fascist spirit and fascist propaganda prevailed. The economic influence of the Nazis was paramount and eliminated the Jews from commerce and industry, and thus reduced a third of them to ruin. At the end of 1937, King Carol summoned an outspokenly Nazi cabinet under Goga-Cuza. This government retained power for only forty-five days, but it used its time for a cold pogrom. An examination of citizenship papers was ordered. The result was that by the end of 1939 more than a third of the Jewish population was robbed of its civil rights; considering the Rumanian methods of procedure one wonders that the number was not greater. Many physicians, pharmacists and lawyers were deprived of their practice; 12,000 families were forced out of trade in alcoholic beverages and production for the state monopolies and rendered penniless. Jewish factory workers were discharged, either as aliens or as persons of alien blood. Following the pattern of the Nuremberg Laws, Jews were forbidden to employ non-Jewish domestics less than forty years of age. Complaints of the American

Jewish Congress to the League of Nations hastened the fall of this cabinet. A period of internal confusion followed. One fascist group fought another, and the unstable king did not know whether he was coming or going. The only thing that was permanent was the anti-Jewish policy.

Poland[50] was hostile to Germany but admired its Jewish legislation. The ruling party of "colonels" knew only one remedy for the country's economic difficulties — the suppression or even the expulsion of the Jews. The Camp of National Unification (*Ozon*), established in 1937, included in its program the Polonization of commerce and industry and mass emigration of Jews. Openly anti-Jewish laws which would violate the Minorities Treaty were avoided; but general regulations were so contrived that they would eliminate Jews from fields in which they were numerous, as for example trade in meat and baked goods. Pogroms were also tolerated upon occasion.

After the dismemberment of Czechoslovakia[51] the Nazis incited various groups of the population against one another, in order to be able to appear as deliverers in the event of disturbances. In its misfortune the Czechoslovakian people reacted by a spurt of anti-Jewish feeling; some politicians thought that a campaign against the Jews would bring deliverance. Autonomous Slovakia proceeded to act; measures were taken for disenfranchising the Jews. On March 14, 1939, Slovakia declared its independence, and on the next day Hitler incorporated Bohemia and Moravia as a protectorate of the German Reich. Now the scandalous events which had taken place in Austria the year before were repeated. The Nuremberg Laws and all their economic provisions were introduced, communities and synagogues were attacked, homes and places of business plundered. Obstacles were put in the way of emigration until Jewish property was secured. Czech fascists poured oil onto the flames, but the masses of the people soon realized that it was their mortal enemy who was inciting them against the Jews. Emigration was accelerated by every available means. Several thousands of Jews were reported to have embraced Christianity, not because they had suddenly come to see the light, but because a specious baptism in some countries facilitated the acquisition of an immigration visa. The Slovaks demonstrated the level of their culture by special brutalities. They adopted the Hungarian racial laws and in addition forbade Jews to reside in the arable districts; this was the first step towards total expulsion.

Epilogue*

HITLER'S broken promises to the Czechs revealed his lust to dominate the world and to oppress its peoples. That meant war. Beginning with September 1, 1939, the war monster which he had painstakingly constructed has been spewing forth destruction. Hitler and his aides viewed the war as a means totally to annihilate the Jewish people. The blitz in Poland took a heavy toll among Jews and brought more than two millions of them under the Nazi heel. The Jews of Germany and the Protectorate had to suffer under the scourge of war infinitely more than the other inhabitants of the Reich. They were, moreover, deprived of their rights and their rations, and after a while were ordered to wear the yellow badge with the Star of David. Those bodily able were drafted for forced labor. All others had to envisage evacuation when it pleased the Gestapo to expel them from their lodgings and to strip them of their possessions. The 700,000 Jews of the occupied countries of Holland, Luxemburg, Belgium, France, Norway and the Balkans fared no better. The Nazis disregarded all conventions of international law and all rules of humanity. They invaded Europe as "the master race" and proved their mastery in looting and murdering. Needless to say, they extended their anti-Jewish laws to the occupied

---

*Professor Elbogen was reluctant to have his book appear without some cognizance being taken of events which transpired between the completion of its original text in 1942 and its actual printing. With characteristic consideration he forebore to trouble his translator and composed his Epilogue in English. As his last utterance it is printed substantially as it left his hands [Ed.].

countries. But their intention thus to make outcasts of the Jews failed; except for a few quislings, the populations manifested their sympathy for the Jews. Even among his satellites — except the Rumanians — Hitler did not find that limitless cruelty and savagery which he ordered.

The spectacular successes in the first Russian campaign (1941) added about 2,000,000 Jews to the victims of the bloodthirsty monster. Meanwhile his bestial administration had elaborated a system of cannibalism which has no parallel in history. *The Black Book of Poland*, based on authentic German documents, tells the grim story of a deliberate attempt to exterminate the Polish nation, of the most bestial excesses, "persecutions, murders, mass slaughter, torture of prisoners, brutal treatment and rape of women." For the Jews the Nazis had even worse in store. The first steps were: wholesale expulsions from their domiciles, concentration of all Polish and the evacuated German, Czech and Dutch Jews in a few ghettos where they were doomed to a slow but certain death through starvation and epidemic diseases. Up to the summer of 1942 about 3,000,000 Poles and 700,000 Jews were calculated victims of this unheard-of savagery.

But the 18th of July 1942 inaugurated a new chapter— the wholesale slaughter of Polish Jewry with no regard for sex and age. Heinrich Himmler, Hitler's Hangman No. 1, coldbloodedly outlined a program to reduce the number of Jews in Poland by one half in 1942 as a start to complete liquidation. Means of modern technique, like gassing and electrocution, were applied for mass murder; large digging-machines were installed near the places of execution to dig mass graves. The shocking newspaper reports of the end of 1942 about these horrible crimes were not sensational atrocity propaganda, but the saddest reality of which the State Department in Washington and the Foreign Office in London have taken cognizance. One shudders when reading about these bestialities; one hesitates to believe that so-called human beings are capable of such brutal devising and executing! The whole story will not be known until after the end of the war. As a matter of fact, the Jewish population of Poland — except those who are forced into slave labor for the German war machine — has disappeared; of the Warsaw Ghetto, which according to conservative estimates housed no less than 400,000 people at one time, a few hundreds may be left, perhaps continuing to wage their heroic struggle against extermination. The reaction of the whole civilized world was unanimous: the liquidation of the Czech village of Lidice and of the Jews in Poland will remain an eternal stigma on Nazi rule and on German racial wickedness.

Hitler's doom is beyond doubt. The Allied Nations have solemnly pledged their resolution that those responsible for these crimes shall not escape retribution. But where is the guarantee that such bestialities will never and nowhere be perpetrated again? Will the ghosts of the immolated Jews harass the conscience of the Christian nations and bar for all future any such barbarity? Every corner in Nazi-ruled Europe has witnessed acts of violence; every corner cries to Heaven for justice, exclaiming, like Job, "O earth, cover not my blood!"

Never would Hitler [wrote Sholem Asch in connection with the Polish mass murders] have dared to select one people for annihilation had not the road been prepared for him by all kinds and degrees of anti-Semites. A person's constitutional rights are secured only when his social standing in a community is secure. If a people is singled out for hatred, as a group, if the fact of just belonging to this group is considered enough to count as a crime, that people loses, in the eyes of its persecutors, the dignity and mysticism of a human being. Then justice is warped and animal instincts are brought forth. All who have prepared this ground of hatred towards the Jews and other races are exactly as responsible for the bestial slaughter in Poland as Hitler and his clique. Hitler only gathers the fruit of their well-planted seed.

The diagnosis is clear. The disease started with the hallucination of German racial superiority over the Jews and ended with the global war to win world domination for the master races in Berlin and in Tokyo. Equally clear must be the remedy: a united effort of the Allied Nations to disinfect public opinion from all the poisonous germs which the Nazi lying-machinery has spread. The dignity of human life must be restored, freedom from fear established for all human beings. The test of democracy is that its privileges be granted not to the strong alone but equally to the weak groups of the earth. There will be no lasting peace if the bogies are not dispelled, prejudices and wicked propaganda eliminated, if it will not be generally recognized that lie remains lie, slander remains slander, offense remains offense even when practiced against Jews. The experiment has been too costly for mankind to gamble with it.

* * * *

It is too early for post-war planning as far as the Jews of Europe are concerned. How many of them will survive the pandemonium? In what physical and mental conditions will they be found? Their need will be food and clothing, lodging and nursing. And when the first reaction to the changed conditions is over, how many of them, especially of the tortured younger people, will find the equilibrium to return to normal work? How many of those surviving will be able and ready to return to their former homes which they remember as scenes of terror? Will they have the strength to reorganize their communal life, rebuild their synagogues and schools, even to restore their cemeteries?

The Allied Nations will be confronted with a Jewish question of tremendous gravity. It will not be the well-known problem of curbing and boycotting Jews, but on the contrary of restoring their human dignity and their working capacity. Victory will not be won by crushing the enemy's armies, but by eradicating his ideology and by creating an atmosphere of good-will to make all peoples enjoy the four freedoms which President Roosevelt proclaimed. The task is not an easy one and not to be solved within a short time. Such an ordeal as all of Europe has passed through cannot be remedied in a year or even a decade — it demands the patient indulgence and the benevolent help of the entire world.

There will be ready cooperation from the invaded countries with firm democratic traditions. It may be that large groups even in Germany and Italy will be glad to be freed of the racialism of their totalitarian tyrants. But what about the sly French aristocracy, and the brutal Polish colonels, who evidently have not yet learned the lesson of their disastrous pre-war policies, and who, as members of the victorious Allied Nations, will make every possible effort to continue their intrigues? And what about the treacherous Slovaks and Croats, the greedy Magyars, the murderous Rumanians? At least two million Jews will have to live among these nations who, faced with numerous internal difficulties, will follow the old pattern of ascribing them to their Jewish neighbors. Does the past of these peoples offer any guarantee that they will maintain a democratic order in the future? Will the Christian Churches of these countries preach to their adherents tolerance and Christian love? Will the United Nations police them until they can be educated to honesty and freedom? The Minority Rights of the Treaties of 1919 proved a delusion partly because they were accepted under protest. Those who undertook to abide by them used them to emphasize the predominance of a majority group and not the equality of political, religious, social and economic rights for all groups. The execution of these treaties, moreover, was watched by an inadequate League of Nations, the leading members of which were more interested in power politics than in peaceful collaboration. Jews will not be the only group to need restoration, but they will be the neediest of all because they suffered most and were too little connected with national agriculture and industry which will provide bread to the other groups. Soviet Russia will continue to be the exception, incorporating the Jews in the national-economic process, but endangering their religious identity.

When Jews knock at the gates of the United Nations, what answer will they receive? Will they be admitted to the vast empty regions and unfilled quotas? Will their suffering be considered and a haven of refuge opened to them? If certain countries accord priority to agricultural settlers, cannot Jews be trained for agriculture? Has the experience in Southern Russia and in Argentina not proved that as farmers they are not inferior to their neighbors?

And what of Palestine? Did they not by their sweat and labor make the country thriving? And all this despite the lack of sympathy — to put it mildly — of the British Colonial Office and the violence of the Arabs? The Churchill White Paper of 1922 proclaimed that the Jews were in Palestine as of right and not by sufferance. Shall twenty years of intensive cultivation, followed by an heroic war effort, result in a forfeiture of this right? Shall the new White Paper, issued by a helpless Colonial Secretary and lacking the approval of the League of Nations, stand and bar, after 1944, any further Jewish immigration and land purchase?

No neutral observer can assert that the Jewish immigration deprived the Palestinian Arabs of their soil. On the contrary, Jewish colonization helped to reclaim swamps and develop Arab agriculture; the Arab population was not diminished but increased; their whole standard of life was improved. The rebirth of Palestine is one of the glorious events of our time and the noblest achievement of the Jewish people since the time of its dispersion. Is it conceivable that in the coming democratic order Jews will be punished for this contribution to world civilization? The more deeply Christian and Moslem peoples feel attached to the Holy Land, the more readily they ought to appreciate what Jews have done for its rebuilding!

As for the Jews, the renaissance of Zion is a noble task which challenges their pride and their sense of solidarity. Palestine is no longer an issue today, as it was a hundred years ago when used by malice to rebuke the Jewish claim on emancipation. Today the Jewish National Home in Palestine is a fact, legalized by all the nations of the world, developed and open for further development by a united Jewish effort. Anti-Zionism belongs to a past stage of history; and so does the original Zionist ideology. The Zionists of the British Commonwealth and the United States of America reject any thought of a double allegiance with no less emphasis than the anti-Zionists. Most of the shouting and fighting in Jewish circles results from confused ideas about fundamental religious, political and social conceptions. That some good-will and a little sense for realities can create a united front is shown by the common pro-Palestinian platform of the American Jewish Conference. Palestine is the only country in the world where Jews qua Jews can meet a normal life and accomplish normal achievements. The gradual emergence of a self-respecting Jewish type and a new Jewish culture will have a beneficent reaction on the Diaspora.

The Jewish *Yishub* in Palestine is far from being safely settled; no colony in the world ever reached perfection within twenty-five years. The country has numerous unsolved problems; the rapid growth of the last decade was neither organic nor healthful; nor was the artificial prosperity created by the present war. On the other hand, Palestine is the only country where Jews are responsible for their economic mistakes and have to bear their brunt. It is not likely that the fiction of Mandated Territories will be renewed after this war. Great Britain will have to revise her Near East policy and grant a new status to the Jewish settlers in Palestine. Whether they will demand a State or a Commonwealth is for them to decide, and a fair-minded Council of Nations may rule whether they are less entitled to it than Lebanon or other small groups which have some special claim.

The dominion of wickedness will be broken, but we shall still be far from the Millennium. Strenuous and unstinted efforts will be needed to heal the wounds the world bleeds from. Though trained in martyrdom, the Jewish people never before has experienced such a cataclysm as has our generation. But we go on! We trust in the unswerving help of our God and the God of our fathers! Through all the moral and spiritual crises of the last hundred years we have not given up our identity. We have saved our faith, saved our morale, saved our mental faculties. Battered from all sides, we were capable of giving to the world some of the greatest luminaries of the period. We don't despair! As long as Israel believes, Israel will not perish! We trust in God, and we go on!

NOTES

Most of the facts related in this volume were first published or discussed in the contemporary periodical press. The number of such periodicals, general and Jewish, ephemeral and lasting, is so enormous that bibliography will be reduced to indispensable references.

Since the beginning of our century several Jewish encyclopedias have been published in various languages. They cover the entire field; on some subjects they even did pioneer work. Of these *The Jewish Encyclopedia* (= *JE*), 12 vols., 1901 ff.; *Encyclopedia Judaica* (= *EJ*), 10 vols., A–L, 1928 ff.; *Jüdisches Lexikon* (= *Jü Le*), 5 vols., 1927 ff.; *Universal Jewish Encyclopedia* (= *UJE*), 10 vols., 1939 ff., are quoted regularly — not so much because of their content as for their rich references which save the trouble of repeating what was printed elsewhere and has no immediate bearing on our context.

Of scientific expositions of our period, the following were used constantly: Martin Philippson, *Neueste Geschichte des jüdischen Volkes*, 3 vols., 2d ed., 1922, 1930, 1911 (= Philippson); Simon M. Dubnow, *Weltgeschichte des jüdischen Volkes*, vols. IX, X, 1929 (= Dubnow, *Weltgeschichte*); id., *History of the Jews in Russia and Poland*, translated from the Russian by Israel Friedländer, vols. II, III, 1918, 1920 (= Dubnow, *Russia*); Salo W. Baron, *A Social and Religious History of the Jews*, vols. II, III, 1937 (= Baron). The attentive reader will realize differences in the presentation even when direct polemics are avoided.

Of popular books the following may be mentioned: Max Raisin, *A History of the Jews in Modern Times* (up to 1917), 2d ed., 1923; Abram Leon Sachar, *A History of the Jews*, pp. 284–392, 2d ed., 1940.

The full titles of the books quoted in the notes will be found in the Bibliography.

The following are abbreviations used in the notes, in addition to those listed above:

ADB — Allgemeine deutsche Biographie
AJYB — American Jewish Year Book
AZdJ — Allgemeine Zeitung des Judentums
CCAR, YB — Central Conference of American Rabbis, Yearbook
CJR — Contemporary Jewish Record
JCS — Jewish Communities Series
JHSE — Jewish Historical Society of England
JSS — Jewish Social Studies
MGWJ — Monatsschrift für Geschichte und Wissenschaft des Judentums
MJ — Menorah Journal
MPMC — Minutes of the Permanent Mandates Commission
PAJHS — Proceedings of the American Jewish Historical Society
RRC — Report of the Royal Commission

BOOK ONE

THE ERA OF LIBERALISM

CHAPTER I

EMANCIPATION IN CENTRAL AND
WESTERN EUROPE

[1] On the meaning of the revolution of the year 1848 for the democratic idea, see V. Valentin, *Geschichte der deutschen Revolution von 1848-49*, 1930-1. The numerous petitions of the years 1847 and 1848 appeared in various daily newspapers and were reprinted by the *Allgemeine Zeitung des Judentums*.

[2] A member of the Stuttgart rump parliament was Dr. Johann Jacoby of Königsberg (1805-1877), one of the most colorful personalities and toughest political leaders of the period; cf. *UJE*, VI, 24 f. Riesser was elected vice president, Oct. 2, 1848, and resigned about the end of November 1848. His speech for the equality of the Jews (Aug. 29, 1848) is printed in his *Gesammelte Schriften*, IV, 410 ff. On Riesser, see *ADB*, XXVIII, 586 ff.; Graetz, V, 598 ff.; Fritz Friedländer, *Das Leben Gabriel Riessers*, 1926.

[3] On Ludwig Bamberger, cf., besides his *Memoirs* (2 vols., 1899), *ADB*, XLVI, 193 ff.

[4] For the various wordings of the Prussian Constitution, see Ismar Freund, *Die Emanzipation der Juden in Preussen*, II, 520 ff. The interesting opinions of the universities and their faculties concerning the equality of the Jews are printed in M. Kalisch, *Die Judenfrage*, 1860, pp. 84-244.

[5] Zunz's appeal is reprinted in his *Gesammelte Schriften*, I, 301 f.

[6] In the year 1847 Prussia granted freedom of religion to dissenters, without mentioning Jews. The law on behalf of the Jews, *Über die Verhältnisse der Juden*, presented to the *Vereinigter Landtag*, was preceded by a Memorandum of the government. Both these documents are printed in the Minutes of the *Vereinigter Landtag* and reprinted s. t. *Vollständige Verhandlungen des Ersten Vereinigten Preussischen Landtags über die Emanzipationsfrage der Juden*, Berlin, 1847. The law was reproduced in Freund, II, 504 ff. The ignorance about Jewish things manifested in the parliamentary discussions is hinted at in Zunz's application for the creation of a chair on Jewish history in a Prussian university: cf. *MGWJ*, LX, 1916, pp. 334 ff.; ibid., LI,

1907, pp. 654 ff.; I. Elbogen, *Ein Jahrhundert Wissenschaft des Judentums*, p. 22.

[7] Fr. J. Stahl, *Der Christliche Staat*, pp. 19, 34. Born 1802, in Munich, as Julius Jolson, he became a convert to Protestantism in 1819 and changed his name to Stahl. He was appointed full professor of Public Law in Berlin in 1840 and became one of the leading scholars in his field. He was the founder of the legitimist Christian Conservative Party in Prussia and Germany which later became the Junker Party, the bulwark of reaction and anti-Jewish sentiment. On Stahl, see G. Masur, *Friedrich Julius Stahl, Geschichte seines Lebens*, I, 1930.

[8] On Württemberg, see A. Tänzer, *Die Geschichte der Juden in Württemberg*, 1937, pp. 92–95.

[9] On Baden, cf. B. Rosenthal, *Heimatsgeschichte der Badischen Juden*, 1927, pp. 285–314, and the very instructive Appendix IV, pp. 479–503, where the motivation for the law of 1862 is printed in extenso. On the previous struggle, see Selma Stern-Täubler, "Die Emanzipation der Juden in Baden," in *Gedenkbuch zum 125jährigen Bestehen des Oberrats der Israeliten Badens*, 1934, pp. 89–103. Moritz Elstätter (1827–1905), a lawyer in Durlach, was appointed Minister of Finance in 1866 and held this office for 25 years. 1871–1893 he represented Baden in the *Bundesrat*; see *UJE*, IV, 93.

[10] A painstaking study of the Bavarian disabilities was made by J. Gotthelf, *Die Rechtsverhältnisse der Juden in Bayern auf Grundlage der neuesten Bayrischen Gesetze*, 1853. On the struggle for emancipation, see the comprehensive studies of A. Eckstein, *Der Kampf der Juden um ihre Emanzipation in Bayern*, 1905, and *Die jüdischen Parlamentarier in Bayern*, 1902; J. Heimberger, *Die Staatskirchenrechtliche Stellung der Israeliten in Bayern*, 2d ed., 1912.

[11] On the Wagener amendment, cf. Ludwig Philippson, *Der Kampf der Preussischen Juden für die Sache der Gewissensfreiheit*, 1856; see M. Kayserling, *Ludwig Philippson*, 1898, p. 216 ff. On the reaction in Prussia, cf. "Die bürgerliche Gleichstellung der Juden in Preussen," in *Verhandlungen des Hauses der Abgeordneten*, 1860; furthermore, "Über den Judeneid," 1861, "Über die Judenfrage," 1862.

[12] All members of the Frankfort National Parliament spoke of the deep impression Riesser's speech for the election of the King of Prussia as German Emperor (March 1849) had made; cf. *Das Frankfurter Parlament in Briefen und Tagebüchern*, ed. by Ludwig Bergsträsser, 1929. Moritz Lazarus published a pamphlet, *Über die sittliche Berechtigung Preussens in Deutschland*, in 1850. Ferdinand Lassalle wrote in favor of the unity of Germany in his *Ulrich v. Hutten*.

[13] On Lassalle, see *ADB*, XVII, 740–780, where his biography is written by Hermann Oncken; Gustav Mayer, *Bismarck und Lassalle, ihr Briefwechsel und ihre Gespräche*, 1928; Otto Jöhlinger, *Bismarck und die Juden*, 1921, p. 50 ff.; S. Baron, *Die politische Theorie Ferdinand Lassalles*, and "Ferdinand Lassalle and the Jews" in *Hatekufah*, XXIII, 347 ff.

[14] On Lasker (1829–84), see *ADB*, XIX, 746 ff.; *EJ*, X, 665; *UJE*, VI, 538 f. On the occasion of Lasker's sudden death in New York City, January 5, 1884, the House of Representatives of the U. S. passed a resolution of sympathy to the German Reichstag which, however, Bismarck refused to accept. The House resented it as an offense to the American people, and the *Reichskanzler* tried to settle the incident by the declaration that he considered the wording of the resolution as a condemnation of his political course. The repeated discussions in the House gave occasion to eulogize Lasker's high idealism and great statesmanship. See *Congressional Record*, 48th Congress, first session, 1884, pp. 2074–79. The political writings of Lasker were published by Wilhelm Cahn: *Aus Eduard Laskers Nachlass*, 1902.

[15] On Bamberger's parliamentary activities, see Jöhlinger, l. c., p. 60 ff.

[16] On the status of the Jews in the new provinces, cf. Leopold Auerbach, *Das Judentum und seine Bekenner in Preussen*, 1890, pp. 264, 333–351; I. Freund, *Die Rechtsstellung der Juden im preussischen Volksschulrecht*, 1908.

[17] The law of full equality is found in *Stenographische Berichte des Norddeutschen Reichstags*; see also Freund, *Emanzipation*, II, 522. That very day the first Jew was appointed judge in Prussia.

[18] In presentiment of what would come, Ludwig Philippson published in 1871 a *Gedenkbuch an den deutsch-französischen Krieg 1870–71 für die deutschen Israeliten*, where he listed, as far as his material reached, the names of Jewish combatants and of those decorated.

[19] Extremely rich and interesting material is to be found in Sigmund Mayer, *Die Wiener Juden 1700–1900*, 2d ed., 1918, and in the same author's *Erinnerungen eines Kaufmanns*, 1917; cf. also M. Grunwald, *Vienna* (Jewish Communities Series), 1934, and Hans Tietze, *Die Juden Wiens*, 1933.

[20] Adolf Fischhof (1816–1893), one of the greatest figures in Austria's political life, found his biographer in H. Charmatz, 1910.

[21] On Goldmark (1818–1885), see the work of his daughter, Josephine Clara, *Pilgrims of 48: One Man's Part in the Austrian Revolution and a Family Migration to America*, 1930. Goldmark's children won prominence in American public life (cf. *UJE*, V, 26).

[22] On L. A. Frankl (1810–1894), cf. *UJE*, IV, 411 f., and his correspondence, edited by his son. On his poem, *Die Universität*, cf. Tietze, p. 189; Grunwald, p. 282, speaks even of a circulation of 500,000 copies and so does *UJE*.

[23] I. N. Mannheimer's (1793–1865) funeral oration is quoted in Grunwald, p. 273; his sermon ibid., p. 274. Cf. M. Rosenmann, *Isak Noë Mannheimer*, Vienna, 1922.

[24] Jews in the National Parliament, ibid., 265 ff. On B. Meisels (1798–1870), see *UJE*, VII, 447; Ginsburg in *Ha-'Awar*, II, 129 ff. On Hermann Jellinek's assassination, Grunwald, p. 286 ff.; Tietze, p. 191 f.

[25] The remark on the Constitution is that of Josef Unger, later a convert to Catholicism and Minister of Justice in Austria. Sigmund Mayer, who had lived in Vienna since 1847, described his feelings in his *Erinnerungen*, p. 326.

[26] Among the 711 journalistic publications listed by Jos. A. Helfert, *Die Wiener Journalistik*, 1877, no more than about twenty were published by Jews; but public opinion reacted vehemently; cf. Tietze, p. 199.

[27] The title of Jacques' pamphlet, which won an extraordinary circulation, is *Denkschrift über die Stellung der Juden*; the translation is that in Grunwald, p. 399.

[28] The articles of the Constitution of 1867 are quoted by Grunwald, p. 406 f. On the struggle about equality of rights in Galicia, see F. Friedmann, *Die galizischen Juden im Kampf um ihre Gleichberechtigung*, 1929 (= *MGWJ*, LXXII, 379 ff., 452 ff.); *UJE*, IV, 495 ff.

[29] Cf. I. Einhorn, *Zur Judenfrage in Ungarn*, 1847, and *Die ungarische Revolution und die Juden*, 1851; J. Bergl, *Geschichte der ungarischen Juden*, 1879; *JE*, VI, 499 ff.; *UJE*, V, 492 ff. The quotation is from G. Fülepp, cited by Einhorn, *Judenfrage*, p. 35.

[30] On the pogrom in Pressburg (Poszony), see Mayer, *Erinnerungen*, p. 139; *UJE*, ibid.

[31] I. Einhorn, *Die Juden und die Revolution in Ungarn*, p. 100 ff.

[32] On the Jewish Congress, see Leopold Löw, *Die jüdischen Wirren in Ungarn von Leon da Modena Redivivus*, I. *Vor dem Kongresse*, 1868; *Der jüdische Kongress in Ungarn, historisch beleuchtet*, 1871. The view of the rightists, in Israel Hildesheimer's *Zum Congresse*, 1868, and *Ausführlicher Rechenschafts-Bericht der ... Mitglieder des ungarischen israelitischen Congresses*, 1869.

[33] The *Landes-Rabbinerschule* (*Országos Rabbiképzö Intézet*) used to issue its publications in Hungarian and in German; see J. Bánóczi, *Die Geschichte des ersten Jahrzehnts der Landes-Rabbinerschule*, 1888.

[34] On the collective Jewish participation in the Italian *Risorgimento*, see *MJ*, XXVII, 1939, p. 260 ff.; XXVIII, 1940, p. 182 ff.; and the monographs in the monthly *Israel*, VIII–X, listed in Baron, *History*, III, p. 148. See also *EJ*, VIII, 701 ff.; *UJE*, V, 631 f.; A. Berliner, *Geschichte der Juden in Rom*, IIb, p. 160 ff.; Vogelstein and Rieger, II, 375 ff.; Vogelstein, *Rome*, 1941, p. 338 ff.

[35] On the Mortara case very much was written at the time: cf. *JE*, IX, 35 f.; *UJE*, VII, 656 f.; J. Meisl in *MGWJ*, 1933, p. 321. The dates differ in the various presentations; the text follows Raffaele de Cesare, *Roma e lo Stato del Papa*, Engl. transl. *The Last Days of Papal Rome*, 1909, p. 176 ff. Mortara always remained attached to his family but refused to discuss a return to his ancestral faith. He died, 1940, at Liège, Belgium, after having reached a high position in the Catholic hierarchy.

[36] On Giuseppe Finzi and other Jewish heroes, see *MJ*, 1940, 185 ff. On the volunteers who joined Garibaldi, ibid., 190 f. Among the poets

who inspired the soldiers of the *Risorgimento* was Davide Levi of Chieri (1816–1898): cf. *JE*, VIII, 25. Statistics of Jewish participation in the various wars for the liberation of Italy in *MJ*, ibid., 197, note 21.

[37] Cf. Sol M. Stroock, "Switzerland and American Jews," in *PAJHS*, XI, 7–52; Adler, ibid., 25–39; J. Brisac, *Ce que les Israélites de la Suisse doivent à la France*, 1916; Lucien Wolf, *Notes*, 1919, pp. 65 ff., 73 ff.; A. Nordmann, *Geschichte der Juden in Basel (1397–1875)*, 1913; id., "Die Juden im Kanton Basel Land," *Baseler Jahrbuch*, 1914, p. 180 ff.; and the literature listed in Dubnow, IX, § 52, p. 518.

[38] The ground is fully covered in S. Posener, *Adolphe Crémieux (1796–1880)*, 2 vols., 1933–34, abridged by the author and published in an English translation by E. Golob, 1940; on the effects of the revolution of 1848, see p. 144 ff.

[39] On the *Alliance*, ibid., 182 ff. See, further, Leven, I, 63 ff.; the articles in *JE*, I, 413 ff.; and *UJE*, I, 188 ff.; Dubnow, IX, 457 ff. A sharp criticism of the activities of the *Alliance* is found at the end of Philippson, I. The *Alliance* published monthly bulletins from 1861 to 1913.

[40] On the Jews of Algiers, see Posener, l. c., p. 198 ff., and J. Cohen, *Les Israélites d'Algérie et le decret Crémieux*, 1900. The illegal abrogation of the *Decret Crémieux* by General Giraud at the beginning of 1943 provoked prolonged and violent press polemics. A presentation of the matter in its historical aspects was given by Hannah Arendt, in *CJR*, VI, 115 ff. [The *Decret* was restored in October 1943.]

[41] On Spain, Secretary of State Blaine mentioned in 1881 "an offer of protection and assurance of right of domicile to Israelites of every race." Cf. Adler, *Correspondence*, p. 117; *PAJHS*, XXXVI, 35.

[42] On Belgium, see S. Ullmann, *Histoire des Juifs en Belgique jusqu'au 19e siècle*; on Holland, *UJE*, V, 436 f.; on Godefroi (1814–82), ibid., V, 8.

[43] On Denmark, ibid., III, 535 f. On Sweden, H. Valentin, *De svenska judarnas historia*, 1920; *CJR*, III, 156 ff. On Norway, ibid., 403; *UJE*, VIII, 242.

[44] On Great Britain, see L. Wolf, "The Queen's Jewry 1837–1897," in *The Jewish Year Book for 5658*, 1897, reprinted in his *Essays in Jewish History*, ed. by Cecil Roth, 1934, p. 309 ff.; A. M. Hyamson, *A History of the Jews in England*, chapters XXXIII, XXXIV, and end of XXXV; id., *David Salomons*, 1939; Cecil Roth, *A History of the Jews in England*, 1941.

[45] Wolf, l. c., p. 339 ff.

[46] The story is told by Jules Huret, *En Allemagne*, vol. III, "Berlin," chapter XX. No less narrow was the attitude of the *Evangelische Oberkirchenbehörde* in Berlin who, as late as 1871, in a circular letter to the Protestant ministers and in a public announcement, declared the conversion of Protestants to Judaism as "a symptom of mental depravity to be mourned by the whole community." A protest of the Executives of the Jewish Community in Berlin found the support of

quite a number of Christian notables of the capital. Abraham Geiger sharply attacked this medieval intolerance in an Appendix to his *Das Judentum und seine Geschichte*, III, pp. 161–190.

CHAPTER II

THE JEWS IN EASTERN EUROPE AND THE NEAR EAST

[1] For the different aspects of the East and the West, see I. Cohen, pp. 3, 7 ff., 17 f.

[2] Graetz's notes about the Jews in Russia stop with the year 1804. He failed to recognize in their afflicted position the thread of history. Historical studies in this field began only about the end of Graetz's life, and today we have a very extensive literature at hand. Apart from the pioneer studies in *JE*, X, 524 ff. and *Yevreiskaya Entziklopedia*, XIII, 616 ff., may be mentioned Dubnow, *Russia*, II; id., *Weltgeschichte*, IX — both with rich bibliographical notes; J. Hessen, *Istorya yevreyskavo naroda v Rossii*, II, 1927 (History of the Jewish People in Russia, dealing with Alexander III and Nicholas II). A certain value as source material, although tinged with personal impressions, may be granted to M. Lilienthal's "My Travels in Russia," in D. Philipson, *Max Lilienthal*, 1915, pp. 159–363; J. Lipschitz, *Zichron Yaakob*, 1925 ff. (the author was the leader of the orthodox party); P. Wengeroff, *Memoiren einer Grossmutter*, I, II, 1908 (describes the life of the Jewish upper class); I. Sosis, *Di geshichte fun di yidishe gezelshaftliche stremungen in Rusland in XIX yorhundert*, 1929; H. Frederick, *The New Exodus*, 1892.

[3] On Nicholas I, see A. Kornilov, *Modern Russian History*, 1924, I, 232 ff. None of the historians who wrote on the emperor mentioned the Jewish question. One of the courtiers who flattered the emperor and suggested the decidedly reactionary course was Count Uvaroff, on whose ambiguities see ibid., 280, and Solowjew, quoted by Th. Schiemann, *Geschichte Russlands unter Nikolaus I*, vol. II, 225, 1904. Of the thousands of Russian laws and statutes concerning the Jews which were enacted between 1649 and 1881, one half was signed by Nicholas I. Besides, he unearthed old anti-Jewish regulations and applied them in the most rigorous fashion. A collection of the laws concerning Jews was made by V. O. Lewanda, *Polny Khronologicheski Sbornik Zakonav*, 1874.

[4] On the "Conscription" = *Rekrutchina*, apart from the literature listed in Dubnow, cf. G. I. Bogrov's *Memoirs*; Mendele, *Winschfingerl*; Lipschitz, I, 107 ff.; Saul Ginsberg, *Historische Verk*, vols. II and III.

[5] See E. Tcherikower, "The Jewish Masses, the Maskilim and the Government," in *Zion*, IV (1939), 2, p. 150 f.; cf. D. Philipson, *Lilienthal*.

[6] The preparation of the statute of 1835 is described in Dubnow, *Russia*, II, 37 ff.; *Weltgeschichte*, IX, 199 ff.

[7] On the Kahal, see *UJE*, VI, 114, and the literature listed there.

[8] *Diaries of Sir Moses and Lady Montefiore*, I, 330 ff. Sir Moses's "Memoir" to Count Kisseleff, ibid., 363 ff. On the Jewish agricultural colonies in South Russia, see *UJE*, III, 290.

[9] On the Enlightenment Movement among Jews, see Raisin, *Haskalah*, p. 191 ff.; on I. B. Levinson, ibid., 204 ff.; on Lilienthal, ibid., 171 ff. and D. Philipson's biography. The deep impression which Lilienthal made on the Jewish youth is emphasized by Wengeroff, I, 126–141.

[10] Montefiore's Memorandum to Count Uvaroff, *Diaries*, I, 372 ff.

[11] On the total failure of the governmental schools, see Lipschitz, I, 172 ff.; Raisin, *Haskalah*, p. 202 f., rightly points out that, notwithstanding their faults, the rabbinical schools produced men like Gurland, Harkavy, Mandelkern, and Steinberg who won fame in Jewish letters.

[12] On the *Rasriaden*-law, see Dubnow, *Russia*, II, 141 ff.; *Weltgeschichte*, IX, 215 ff.

[13] On the Jewish garb, see *JE*, IV, 302; Dubnow, op. cit.; Wengeroff, I, 194 ff.; the bibliography in *UJE*, III, 381. The rules of 1853 for Poland in *YIVO*, historical section, I, 731 ff.

[14] On the enforced conscription Dubnow listed a rich literature. Recently several reports of former cantonists were published in *Reshumot*. Ossip Rabinovich's *Shtrafnoi* (1859) gave such a vivid picture of the Jewish sufferings at that period that it was translated into various languages. See also A. Levin, *Kantonisten* (Yiddish), 1934, and E. Tcherikower in *YIVO*, l. c.

[15] On Alexander II, see Kornilow, l. c., II, 3 ff.; Frederick, pp. 86–106, who surveyed the fact from a sober realistic viewpoint. The effect of the emperor's favorable attitude is evident from the opinions of the higher officials, as listed in A. Scholz, *Die Juden in Russland*, 1900, passim, and from the pro-Jewish utterances of the best known Russian writers in the press as well as in magazines and novels; cf. Sosis, p. 80 ff.

[16] See Dubnow, *Russia*, 157 ff.; *Weltgeschichte*, IX, 406 ff.

[17] The local and cultural shifting among the Russian Jews is noted in Montefiore's *Diaries*, II, 251 f.; Wengeroff, II, 168 ff.; likewise by U. S. Minister Foster, in his report of Dec. 31, 1880 (Adler, l. c., p. 84 ff.)

[18] A history of the Society was written by one of its promoters, L. Rosenthal, *Toledot hebrat marbe Haskalah be-Yisrael*, 2 vols., 1885–90, and recently supplemented by E. Tcherikower, 1913. It is significant that Mandelstamm's translation of the Torah into Russian, completed as early as 1844, was not printed nor allowed to be imported into Russia before the year 1862. The poet J. L. Gordon suggested the publication of a Russian translation of the Bible, mainly for the use of school teachers, and together with J. Gerstein published a translation of the

Torah (1875) which was very successful. He likewise edited and prefaced the *Compendium of Jewish Ethics* (3 vols., 1874 ff.) in the Russian translation of J. L. Lewanda. The Hebrew original, compiled by I. Schereschewski and Jacob Reifmann, was never published; cf. Klausner, IV, p. 420.

[19] The growing impoverishment of the masses — partly in consequence of the liberation of the serfs — is reflected in Mendele's satires; cf. Lipschitz, l. c.; Lestschinsky in Buber's *Der Jude*, I, 164; and Scholz, p. 24.

[20] Leven, I, 272 ff.

[21] Brafmann's *Kniga Kahala* ("Book of the Kahal"), first appeared in 1869, was reprinted several times and translated into various languages. It is significant that the Nazi geographer, S. Passarge, published a German translation with numerous notes in 2 vols., 1928. J. Levitats pointed out, in *Zion*, III, 1938, p. 170 ff., that the material published by Brafmann was authentic, but the conclusions drawn in his Introduction were biased.

[22] On the participation of some Jewish youth in the early revolutionary movement, cf. K. Sabsovich, *Adventures in Idealism*, 1922; Anatole Leroy-Beaulieu, *The Empire of the Tsars*, 1902–3, I, 197. Ambassador Foster at the end of his report, mentioned in note 17, emphasized that the Jews denied having an extraordinary share in the revolutionary movement.

[23] On the pogrom in Odessa, see Dubnow, *Russia*, 191; *Weltgeschichte*, 419. Leven, I, 272 ff., points out why the *Alliance Israélite* advocated a mass emigration to the United States. The Board of Delegates of American Israelites, however, insisted on a rigid selection, primarily of Jews fit for agriculture; cf. Kohler, in *PAJHS*, XXIX, 101 f.

During the 1870s complaints about the treatment of American Jewish citizens increased. Secretary of State James G. Blaine had a hard time studying and analyzing the Russian laws concerning foreign Jews. Cf. *Exec. Doc. no. 192, 1st session, 47th Congress*, 1881–82, vol. 22, p. 63 ff. His memorandum is preceded by a "Sketch of the Laws of Russia Relative to Foreign Israelites," written 1881, p. 58 ff. The same volume contains a "Memorandum on the Legal Position of the Hebrews in Russia," written 1872, which deals mostly with individuals expelled. Furthermore, on p. 21 ff. an "Abstract of a Report of Mr. V. Grigorieff, member of a Commission for the Improvement of the Life of the Hebrews, on the question of their place of residence," written 1875. Gregorieff arrives at the conclusion that the present status of the Jews involved dangers and that they have to be educated. The Secretary of State further reports conversations, at the end of 1880, with Russian Ministers, which did not sound very favorable.

[24] On the Jews in Poland, see Dubnow, *Russia*, 177 ff.; *Weltgeschichte*, 244, 412 ff., 516; Gelber, *Die Juden und der polnische Aufstand*, 1923, and the critical analysis of this book by J. Shatzky in *YIVO*, l. c., I, 423 ff.; J. Meisl, *Polen*, III, 316 ff., and the extended bibliography,

ibid., 417 f. Amusing episodes of Muraviev's life in Wilna are told by Wengeroff, II, 148 ff.

[25] For a thorough presentation of the conditions in the Balkans, see I. Loeb, *Situation*, 1877. For the decisions of the Congress of Berlin (1878) concerning Bulgaria, see L. Wolf, *Notes*, p. 25 ff.; on Serbia, ibid., p. 27 ff.

[26] The protracted sufferings of the Rumanian Jews provoked an extensive literature, listed in Dubnow, *Weltgeschichte*, IX, § 53, p. 518. Many details are to be found in the diaries entitled *Aus dem Leben König Karls von Rumänien*, 4 vols., 1894–1900.

[27] On the Conference of Paris (1856, 1858), see L. Wolf, *Notes*, pp. 18–23; Montefiore, *Diaries*, II, 19 f., 195 ff., 361 ff. The Conference did not expressly mention Jews because the powers were convinced that the term *toutes les classes de la population* included Jews. They did not reckon with the intrigues of Rumanian politicians. A withering criticism of the Rumanian formula was made by the famous Swiss jurist I. C. Bluntschli, *Der Staat Rumänien und die Rechtsverhältnisse der Juden in Rumänien*, 1879.

[28] On Crémieux's visit to Bucharest, see Posener, II, 150; Loeb, p. 147 ff.

[29] Sir Francis Goldsmid intervened several times in the House of Commons; see Leven, I, 93 ff., who also mentions the frequent appeals of the *Alliance Israélite* to the French government.

[30] The Board of Delegates watched the situation as early as 1867; Adler, l. c., p. 48; Kohler, l. c., note 23. Peixotto (*UJE*, VIII, 422 f.; *PAJHS*, XXIV, 2 ff.) constantly reported on the situation. On President Grant's message, see S. Wolf, *Presidents*, p. 74 f. On the Brussels Congress, see Leven, I, 183 f.; Kohler, l. c.; and *PAJHS*, XXIV, 25 ff.; on the two conferences in Paris, 1876, 1878, ibid., 29 ff.

[31] The United States envoy to Vienna, John A. Kasson, drew the attention of the Department of State to the Jewish question, June 5, 1878: Adler, l. c., p. 48 f. On the Jewish preparations for the Congress, see Leven, I, 212 ff.; *EJ*, IV, 274 ff.; and *Moses Gaster Anniversary Volume*, p. 545 ff.

[32] For extracts from the Protocols of the Berlin Congress, see L. Wolf, *Notes*, pp. 29–33. The details of the struggle with the Rumanian Parliament are reflected in Prince Carol's correspondence with his father, *Aus dem Leben*, III, IV. For the revised article VII of the Rumanian Constitution, see L. Wolf, *Notes*, 34 f.; the protest of the great powers, ibid., p. 35. Mr. Kasson informed the Department of State that, while Serbia was complying with the sanctions of the Treaty, Rumania was making difficulties: Adler, l. c., pp. 50–54. Leven, I, 279 ff., presents the events in the light of the Franco-German antagonism.

[33] On Jews in Morocco, see *JE*, IX, 24 f.; *UJE*, VII, 652; Montefiore, *Diaries*, I, 320 ff.; II, 114 ff., 145 ff.; Leven, I, 155 ff., 237 ff.; Edmondo de Amicis, *Marocco*, p. 268 ff., Engl. transl., *Morocco: its People*

and Places, p. 248. The poet H. W. Longfellow, while traveling in Europe, met a Jew from Morocco whom he presented as "The Spanish Jew" among the guests in his *Tales of a Wayside Inn*, 1863. On the intervention of the United States Government in the years 1863–65, see Adler, l. c., 39 ff. The Consul in Tangier left no doubt that the representations from London and Paris, "instead of mitigating, have certainly aggravated the condition of the Jews." The intervention of the year 1878, ibid., p. 41. The Board of Delegates, in 1881, designated Levi A. Cohen as its accredited agent in Tangier who might forward to the United States Consul authentic reports on wrongs done to the Jews, ibid., 43 f.

[34] The Madrid Conference was preceded by petty disputes about the right of protection of the agents and interpreters, Leven, I, pp. 240–260; for the resolutions on their privileges, see L. Wolf, *Notes*, 91 f. For the resolutions concerning religious liberty, see ibid., 92 f.

[35] That conditions had not improved and that the sultan was afraid to interfere in earnest, is clear from personal observation made by the U. S. Minister to Spain, Lucius Fairchild (report of April 20, 1881); Adler, l. c., 45 ff.

[36] On Persia, see Benjamin, II, 143 ff.; Montefiore, *Diaries*, II, 167 f. 237 ff., 256; Leven, I, 165 ff., 261 ff.; G. N. Curzon, *Persia and the Persian Question*, 1892, II, 510. The appearance of the delegate Nissim b. Shelomoh, who came to Canada in October 1848, attracted the attention of the newspapers of that time.

CHAPTER III

INNER DEVELOPMENT (1850–1880)

[1] Although I. M. Jost, in his *Neueste Geschichte* and his *Kulturgeschichte*, had dealt with the social aspects of contemporary history, studies of this kind were neglected among Jews up to the end of the century, when Joseph Jacobs resumed them. In 1922, J. Lestschinsky published his *Dos Idishe Folk in Zifern*. The rich material of the article "Statistik" in *Jü Le*, V, 630–698, offers in the main data from the period beginning 1871. For Hungary we have a comparative study by A. Benisch, "L'Extension et la répartition de l'élement israélite sur le territoire actuel de la Hongrie (1830–1930)" in *Magyar Statisztiki Szemle*, XII, 916 ff.; for Germany some hints in "Die Juden im deutschen Reich 1816–1933" in *Wirtschaft und Statistik*, XV, 147 ff. For a thorough research in the respective conditions in Prussia, see H. Silbergleit, *Die Bevölkerungs- und Berufsverhältnisse der Juden im deutschen Reich*, I, 1930. For extensive statistical data for that community see A. Kober's *Cologne* (JCS), p. 328 ff.

[2] For a beginning of research in this subject, see *JE*, IV, 191 f.

"The economic situation of the Jewish people in the various countries, as well as their contributions to economic life, have not yet been sufficiently investigated, although rich source material is readily available." So wrote S. W. Baron, in 1936, in his *History*, III, 155, and we have not made much progress since. Extremely instructive are the details given in S. Mayer, *Wien*, p. 402 ff. For Poland, see Ph. Friedmann, "Wirtschaftliche Umschichtungsprozesse und Industrialisierung in der polnischen Judenschaft 1800–1870," in *Kohut Memorial Volume*, 1935, pp. 178 ff.; for Germany, see *EJ*, VI, 980 ff. and Kurt Zielenziger, *Die Juden im deutschen Wirtschaftsleben*, p. 23 f. Most of the literature listed by Baron, ibid., deals with conditions of more recent decades.

[3] On Jews as financiers, see *EJ*, V, 1057 ff.

[4] On Jewish artisans we have some authentic material up to 1850, but from then to the end of the century the figures are but scanty. In Eastern Europe the artisans formed up to 25–30% of the Jewish population and up to 70–80% of all artisans. In Germany the figures were much larger in the former Polish provinces of Posen and Upper Silesia than in the rest of the country. In Western Germany, from the marshes of the North Sea to the Alps, Jews were numerous in cattle-breeding and cattle-dealing, as butchers and meat packers; in 1853, in Cologne 50% of the Jewish handworkers were butchers; Kober, l.c., p. 331.

[5] On Jews in agriculture, see *EJ*, X, 631 f. In Russia, besides the colonies initiated by the Government (p. 50), there were many Jews who farmed big estates and worked on them successfully. Between 1861 and 1880 the area owned by Jews grew ninefold. In Galicia, 1874, about 19% of the big farmers were Jews, but there were small Jewish farmers, too. Baron de Hirsch was impressed by the fact that many Jews in Rumania were excellent peasants, and that in Hungary they worked so successfully in agriculture that frequently the Catholic Church entrusted them with the farming of their estates.

[6] The names mentioned are a few from among many men prominent in their professions; cf. C. Roth, *The Jewish Contribution to Civilization*, 1938. Each of those mentioned has an article in *UJE*.

[7] Even S. W. Baron yielded to the exaggerated statement, "The press was soon largely dominated by Jews" (*History*, II, 284). The control of a few daily papers in *some* capitals does not mean domination of the press. Besides, none of the owners of the papers mentioned by him had any Jewish interests. Interesting as usual is S. Mayer's analysis of the press in Vienna after 1848: *Wien*, p. 313 ff., and for a somewhat later period, ibid., p. 391 ff. It is noteworthy that with all their dislike of Jewish journalists the statesmen did not scruple to use the services of gifted Jewish writers; ibid., 324.

[8] The rise in the incomes of the Jews is evident from the Jewish share in the communal budgets and from the budgets of their own communities. That Jews all over Europe were among the most generous citizens was recognized even in Russia; cf. Scholz, pp. 193, 236.

[9] The long list of honorary Jewish executives in the local and provincial administrations ought to be collected.

[10] The number of mixed marriages in capitals like Budapest, Vienna, Berlin, Paris, especially in the upper classes, was not insignificant.

[11] Cosmopolitanism is reflected in the works of almost all prominent Jewish writers of the period, whether Berthold Auerbach or Kompert, M. A. Goldschmidt or Ossip Rabbinowicz.

[12] On the changed status of the Jewish communities see M. Wiener, *Jüdische Religion im Zeitalter der Emanzipation*, 1933. For the changes in the legal status, see in the article "Jewish Community," in *UJE*, VI, 99–126.

[13] Philipson's verdict, in his *History*, I, 2d ed., p. 346; cf. Zangwill, *Grandchildren of the Ghetto*.

[14] S. Mayer, l. c., pp. 462, 515 ff.

[15] Steinheim's work appeared in 4 volumes between 1835 and 1865. It made no impression at that time, and only much later was it rediscovered and appreciated. M. Joel's *Kritisch-Religiöse Zeitfragen*, 1878, a polemical writing against Schopenhauer, D. F. Strauss and Eduard v. Hartmann, also made no impression.

[16] The manner of thinking of a secularized Jew is reflected by Mr. Pashof in George Eliot's *Daniel Deronda*.

[17] That the religious situation was most disappointing was a commonplace. All responsible Jewish bodies looked for more or less moderate reforms, but had not the efficiency to put them into effect. The *Consistoire Central* of Paris issued an invitation in 1867 to a Universal Jewish Synod; why the suggestion failed is not known. In 1868 a rabbinical conference took place in Cassel, Germany. The discussions centered around the liturgy; no definite action was taken on any other subject. Frankel and his pupils were absent; they held a meeting a fortnight later in Breslau. Religious problems were hardly touched. Much was expected from joint meetings of rabbis and laymen; but the Synods of Leipzig (1869) and Augsburg (1871) had no practical results. They, too, were boycotted by the Breslau Seminary. Heinemann Vogelstein, then rabbi at Pilsen, Bohemia, was the only pupil of Frankel who dared attend the Augsburg Synod. Besides the indolence of the congregations, the disunion of the leaders also was a serious handicap; cf. M. Philippson, I, 349 ff. Many details are given in D. Philipson, *Reform Movement*, chap. XI, and its interesting notes. A by-product of the Leipzig Synod was the foundation of the *Deutsch Israelitischer Gemeindebund*; see M. Philippson, I, 362; *EJ*, IV, 966 ff.

[18] On Geiger's work in Berlin, where he died, Oct. 24, 1874, see his *Nachgelassene Schriften*, V, 274 ff., 322 ff.; *Leben u. Lebenswerk*, p. 204 ff.

[19] How the observance of the Sabbath gradually fell into desuetude is described by S. Mayer, l. c., p. 298 f.; sarcastically in Zangwill's ghetto comedy, *The Sabbath Question in Sudminster*.

[20] In the strengthening of orthodoxy the inner migration had its share; for Vienna, see Mayer, pp. 370, 463. On S. R. Hirsch and I. Hildesheimer a rich literature is listed in I. Markon's articles in *EJ*, VIII, 95, 25 f. On the Rabbinical Seminary, see Wohlgemuth's monthly, *Jeschurun*, 1920, 218 ff.

[21] I. H. Weiss, in his *Memoirs* (*Zichronot*, 1895), reports on the flourishing state of the *yeshibot* in Moravia up to at least 1840, and they were such in Hungary. On the last *yeshibot* in Germany, see K. Kohler's "Personal Reminiscences" in his *Studies, Addresses and Papers*, p. 469 ff. On the decay of rabbinical studies in Galicia, see J. S. Bloch, *Lebenserinnerungen*, I, 3 ff. On the *École Rabbinique*, see J. Bauer, *L'École Rabbinique de France (1830–1930)*, 1931. On the origin of the modern rabbinical schools, see I. Elbogen, *Ein Jahrhundert Wissenschaft des Judentums*, pp. 24–37.

[22] On the Bible translations, see *UJE*, II, 339 ff.; on the prayer books, *UJE*, VIII, 621.

[23] On Philippson's Institute, see M. Kayserling, *Ludwig Philippson*, p. 252. Philippson had a special aptitude for satisfying popular needs, and most of his scientific and literary efforts were devoted to such publications. However, very little of his work survived his age.

[24] On Graetz as historian, see the Memoir at the beginning of the American edition of his *History* and *AJYB*, XLIII (1941), p. 489 ff.

[25] On Zunz's difficulties, see M. Lazarus, *Lebenserinnerungen*, 1906, p. 493 ff.

[26] On the writers mentioned and their work, see the respective articles in *UJE*. A vindication of Judaism in the form of a novel are W. Herzberg's *Jüdische Familienpapiere*, 1876. They found wide circulation and were translated into various languages; see ibid., V, 336.

[27] Of the excitement with which every weekly issue of the *Allgemeine Zeitung des Judentums* was awaited an era of mass publication cannot have any idea. In 1937, its successor, the *CV Zeitung* in Berlin, published a special number to commemorate the centenary of this first successful Jewish weekly.

[28] On Annuals, Calendars, *Jahrbücher*, etc., see the article "Periodicals" in *JE*, IX; "Periodicals and Press" in *UJE*, VIII, 437 ff.

[29] The aim of the following sketch is to give an idea of the spiritual evolution among Jews in Russia as a sociological phenomenon — not as a history of literature such as is given in Raisin's *Haskalah*, Klausner's *History of Modern Hebrew Literature*, Dubnow's *Russia*, II, and in many other books, like S. Spiegel, *Hebrew Reborn*, 1930, p. 167 ff. The social aspect is depicted in books like those of Morgulis, Wengeroff, Shomer Zunser, Sosis.

[30] For R. Itzhaq, see D. Philipson, *Lilienthal*, p. 342; for Israel Lipkin, cf. L. Ginzberg, *Students, Scholars and Saints*, 1928, pp. 145–194.

[31] Guenzburg (Raisin, 213 ff.; Dubnow, *Russia*, II, 133 f.) was under the spell of the Russian intellectuals' predilection for history; the next

two generations were under the influence of the realistic Russian literature.

[32] The conflict is thoroughly, but in a somewhat primitive form, described in Mendele's *Aboth u-Banim*.

[33] The change was so evident that even Turgeniev put in the mouth of a Lithuanian Jew words of despair about the next generation: "They believe in nothing."

[34] The triumph of the obscurantists is reflected in Lipschitz, I.

[35] On the Enlightenment in Yiddish-speaking circles, cf. *UJE*, VII, 128. It is to be kept in mind that some of the best Yiddish authors, like Gottlober or Mendele, were at the same time well known as Hebrew writers.

Chapter IV

THE JEWS IN THE NEW WORLD

[1] Besides the articles in *JE* and *UJE*, see: I. Markens, *The Hebrews in America*, 1888; Madison C. Peters, *The Jews in America*, 1905; P. Wiernik, *History of the Jews in America*, 1912; P. Masserman and M. Baker, *The Jews Come to America*, 1932; G. Cohen, *The Jews in the Making of America*, 1924; Lee J. Levinger, *A History of the Jews in the United States*, 1930 (popular).

[2] The distribution of Jews in the United States and their organizations are described in the "*Jewish Calendar*, compiled and published by the two Sephardic rabbis J. J. Lyons of N. Y. C. and A. de Sola of Montreal, Que.," in 1854. A little later, Benjamin II (Israel Joseph) toured the States from coast to coast and published his *Drei Jahre in Amerika 1859–62* (cf. *UJE*, II, 178). For scattered Jewries before 1848, see Anita Liburra Lebenson, *Jewish Pioneers in America*, 1931.

[3] In 1858, the Board of Delegates of American Israelites answered a questionnaire laid before it by the Federal Government on behalf of the Swiss Confederation and estimated the number of Jews resident in the U. S. A. as about 400,000 (!!), among them about 200,000 native born (Adler, l. c., p. 34) — an obviously highly exaggerated figure. Markens arrived at this figure in 1888 after a new huge wave of immigration had come in. A "Statistical Report of Hebr. Congregations of U. S. to Board of Delegates (1860–1)" in *PAJHS*, XXIX (1925), pp. 129–135, is incomplete.

[4] The aforementioned source says that Jews are to be found "in all and every honorable and respected profession." The conditions within the communities are vividly pictured by I. M. Wise in his *Reminiscences*. The book *In Memoriam Jesse Seligman* contains an autobiographical speech of this outstanding banker (1827–94) with very interesting details about himself and his brothers as well as their early business adventures. An unusual career was that of Adam Gimbel who in 1842 opened a store in Vincennes, Ind., and at the end of his

life controlled Gimbel Brothers' department stores in New York City and Philadelphia, Pa.

[5] The struggle against clericalism is manifest in D. Philipson, *Lilienthal*, pp. 101 ff., 474 ff.

[6] Strangely enough the Board of Delegates was so entirely forgotten that *The Jewish Encyclopedia* had not even an article about it, and the article in *UJE*, II, 427, does not amount to much. In *PAJHS*, XXIX (1925), pp. 75–135, Max J. Kohler discussed the activities of the Board on the basis of the scanty materials preserved. A recent study by Rabbi Allen Tarshish has not yet been published.

[7] "Jews and the American Anti-Slavery Movement" is discussed by M. J. Kohler, ibid., V, 137 ff. "Documents Relative to the American...Slavery Agitation" are re-published in *Moses Mielziner 1828–1903*, a biography by Ella McKenna Friend Mielziner, 1931, pp. 212–250.

[8] To the rich literature on J. P. Benjamin in *UJE*, II, 184, is to be added Rollin Osterweis, *Judah P. Benjamin, Statesman of the Lost Cause*, 1933; and Robert Douthat Meade, *Judah P. Benjamin: Confederate Statesman*, 1943.

[9] On the Jewish share in the Civil War, see S. Wolf, *The American Jew as Patriot, Soldier and Citizen*, 1895; S. W. McCall, *Patriotism of the American Jew*, 1924. The author analyzes the extant information about the participation of Jews in the Civil War and, p. 121, he quotes from an article by Mark Twain: "His [the Jew's] record for capacity, for fidelity and for gallant soldiership in the field is as good as anyone's." Cf. also *The Jewish Legion of Valor*, 1934. That Moses Ezekiel volunteered is mentioned by R. Kohut, *My Portion*, p. 286. Cf. *The History of the Jews of Richmond 1769 to 1917*, by Herb. T. Ezekiel and Gaston Lichtenstein, p. 118.

[10] The protests of the Board of Delegates (Kohler, l. c., XXIX) against the generals led to nothing. General Grant's explanation is found in S. Wolf, *Presidents*, p. 71.

[11] One of the most sensational incidents was the case of James Seligman, a banker who enjoyed the highest esteem of the President of the United States because of his efforts to secure the foreign credit of the Federal Government, but who was refused admission by Judge Hilton to his Saratoga Springs, Grand Union Hotel. On the other hand Solomon Heydenfeldt was elected Chief Justice of California as early as 1852.

[12] To the rich literature on "Abraham Lincoln and the Jews," in *UJE*, VII, 65, is to be added S. Schechter's "Abraham Lincoln: Memorial Address," 1909 (*Seminary Addresses*, etc., 1915, pp. 145–168).

[13] Judah Touro through his philanthropy became an almost legendary figure and the hero of some novels. Recently M. A. Gutstein, of Newport, R. I., published a monograph, *Aaron Lopez and Judah Touro*, 1939, and C. Adelman a bicentenary address: *Life and Time of Judah Touro*, 1936.

[14] Judge M. S. Isaacs in his letter to Gen. B. F. Butler, in the spring of 1864, emphasized the remarkable benevolence of the Jews as a class: "No Israelite is thrown upon public charity, although Israelites bear their share of public burdens, in the support of these communal institutions." He points out that in New York City they have a hospital ("The Story of Mt. Sinai Hospital" was published in the *Journal of the Mt. Sinai Hospital*, 1942) and an Orphans' Home, and a vast number of benevolent societies. "In other cities, Philadelphia, Cincinnati, New Orleans and Baltimore, similar benevolent institutions are liberally sustained, and wherever there are ten Jewish families, there is a benevolent society for resident or transient poor." (*PAJHS*, XXIX, 124). Even ten years earlier Lyons' *Calendar* mentioned numerous benevolent societies.

[15] On Rebecca Gratz and her family, see *UJE*, V, 86 ff.

[16] The history of the IOBB was first written by its great leader Julius Bien (1826–1909) and published in the *Menorah Monthly*, 1886–1889; see also *UJE*, II, 422.

[17] The activities and the difficulties of the early Ashkenazic congregations are referred to in I. M. Wise, *Reminiscences*; in Israel Goldstein, *A Century of Judaism in America*, 1930; in Edw. Davis, *The History of Rodeph Shalom Congregation*, 1926.

[18] A biography of I. Leeser by Miss Emily Solis-Cohen is in course of preparation; on the other two rabbis see Goldstein, l. c.

[19] I. M. Wise's *Reminiscences*, which unfortunately go no farther than the year 1857, were published in English translation by D. Philipson, 1900. An extended biography, *Isaac Mayer Wise, The Founder of American Judaism*, was written by his grandson, Max B. May, in 1916; for a tentative bibliography by A. S. Oko, see *HUC Monthly*, 1917.

[20] For the Union and its Constitution, see *JE*, XII, 344 f.

[21] D. Philipson, *Life*, pp. 1–24, where his previous writings on the subject are mentioned. Personal reminiscences of what Wise meant to the College and its students are related in M. Raisin, *Leaves from a Rabbi's Notebook*, p. 220 ff.

[22] On the struggle for Reform, see the biographers of Wise and Leeser. Cf. Philipson, *Reform Movement*, p. 339 ff. The arguments professed in these polemics are a repetition of the previous discussions in Germany. On the early Reform congregations, see ibid., pp. 334 ff.

[23] Einhorn's sermons, *Ausgewählte Predigten und Reden* (Einhorn was convinced that Jewish religious ideas and emotions could not find correct expression except in the German language), were published by K. Kohler, in 1880, whose centenary paper on Einhorn is printed in CCAR, *YB*, 1909, pp. 215 ff. — both augmented by E. G. Hirsch's Memorial Oration, reprinted in *David Einhorn, Memorial Volume*, 1911.

[24] Excepting the article on the "Selection of Israel," the principles adopted by the Philadelphia Conference were all negative. The number of those in attendance never exceeded fifteen, and there was

no unanimity. Cf. *Protokolle der Rabbiner Conferenz, abgehalten zu Philadelphia*, 1870. A. Geiger wrote an enthusiastic article about this meeting while it was still being planned in his *Jüdische Zeitung*, 1869, VIII, 1 ff.

[25] The ugly conditions within the Orthodox group are depicted in Weinberg, *Ha-Yehudim we-ha-Yahadut be-America*.

[26] See the article "West Indies" in *JE*, XII, 508 ff. The *Jewish Chronicle*, 1875, p. 687, reports that since 1845–46 a Jewish cemetery has been permitted in Venezuela, 1844 one in Santa Martha, Colombia, that in 1874 a burial ground was acquired in Peru and that in the same year the township of Barranquilla organized a Jewish section on the communal cemetery.

[27] On Jews in Canada, see M. Wolf in *AJYB*, 5686–1925, pp. 154 ff.; B. G. Sack, "History of the Jews in Canada," 1926 (in A. D. Hart, *The Jew in Canada. A complete record of Canadian Jewry from the days of the French régime to the present time*); L. Rosenberg, *Canada's Jews*, 1939; *UJE*, II, 652 f.

[28] See L. Herrman, *A History of the Jews in South Africa*, I, 1930; he also produced a new edition of Nathaniel Isaacs' *Travels*, etc., 1936–37. Cf. S. A. Rochlin in *Transactions JHSE*, XIII (1932–35), pp. 247 ff.; and *UJE*, V, 599 f.; J. H. Hertz, *The Jew in South Africa*, 1905.

[29] On Jews in Australia, see *UJE*, I, 619 ff.; *CJR*, II, 6, p. 27 ff. An *Oistralish Yidisher Almanach* (Australian Jewish Almanac) has been published in Melbourne since 1937.

[30] It is remarkable that the small Australian Jewish community in its early times produced such outstanding thinkers as Joseph Jacobs and Samuel Alexander, both born in Sydney.

BOOK TWO

THE INTERNATIONAL OF HATE

Chapter I

ANTISEMITISM AS A POLITICAL MOVEMENT

[1] Seventy years ago the word "antisemitism" was hardly known; today it is to be found in all dictionaries and analyzed in all reference books. Today it is a global scourge of mankind, symptomatic of the Nazi "New Order." The historian must be on his guard not to confuse the present brutal system of megalomaniac racialism with the beginnings of the antisemitic movement. It may be true that the embryo already betrays the traits of the adult, but this is evident only to retrospective reasoning. No doubt the germs of racial hatred were inherent in the movement from its start, but they were not primary

motives. Antisemitism is a very complicated phenomenon and has several roots: religious, economic, social, psychic as well as racial.

The aim of the present chapter is to show how the more or less conscious popular aversion to Jews was being exploited for a political organization, and we must bear in mind that conditions in 1873 were not what they were in 1933. Jew-baiting was not yet as fashionable as it became later under the misnomer of antisemitism. Moritz Steinschneider claimed priority rights on this name, which he had used in a letter opposing Ernest Renan's views on the character of the Semites. How this private correspondence could become known to Wilhelm Marr, who first used the term in public, remains a puzzle.

As frequently happens in political life, the beginnings of the antisemitic propaganda were not taken seriously; they seemed confusing and they mixed up too many different aspects of the situation. No comprehensive presentation of the beginnings of the movement and no exact bibliography of the numerous publications of that period exist. Rich information can be drawn from Erich Lehnhardt, *Die antisemitische Bewegung in Deutschland, besonders in Berlin*, 1890, p. 43 ff.; and M. Liebermann v. Sonnenberg, *Beiträge zur Geschichte der antisemitischen Bewegung*, 1880–85 (both anti-Jewish); and Johannes Menzinger, *Friede in der Judenfrage*, 1896, p. 179 ff.; for the first decade, see Jos. Jacobs, *The Jewish Question, 1875–84*, 1885. The first thorough sociological study of antisemitism was presented by Anatole Leroy-Beaulieu in his *Israel chez les Nations*, 1894 (English translation by Fr. Hellmann, *Israel among the Nations*, 1896). He was followed by Bernard Lazare, *L'Antisémitism*, 1894 (Engl. transl. 1903) who considered antisemitism under the aspect of socialism, and Count Heinrich Coudenhove-Kalergi, *Antisemitism Throughout the Ages*, an attempt to explain antisemitism as an expression of old religious fanaticism. Among Jews assimilationists looked on antisemitism as a symptom of a national disease provoked by transitory reasons and doomed to pass after conditions changed; while Zionists considered it as the constant shadow which follows the Jewish people as long as and wherever it moves. Modern Jewish investigations, like Constantin Brunner's *Der Judenhass und die Juden*, 1919; F. Bernstein's *Der Antisemitismus als Gruppenerscheinung: Versuch einer Soziologie des Judenhasses*, 1926, consider antisemitism as group pride and group defense. Arnold Zweig, *Caliban, oder Politik und Leidenschaft*, 1927, combined this thesis with the psychoanalytical theory and calls antisemitism a "difference affect." Quite recently Hugo Valentin in his *Anti-Semitism*, 1936, offered a historical and critical examination considering all aspects of this social phenomenon.

After the present generation's experience, many details of the early fight against Jews and Judaism have lost their significance and need not be enumerated here in full; they can be studied in the histories of Philippson, Dubnow, M. Raisin, who have extended accounts of the movement, while S. W. Baron gives an analysis of it.

² Richard Wagner's pamphlet, originally anonymous, published in 1869 under his name, provoked a number of sharp rebukes; it was published in English translation by Edwin Evans, 1910. Though Wagner later did not refuse Jewish cooperation, his slander became the textbook of racial antisemitism. If the rumors that the second husband of his mother, the Jewish actor Ludwig Geyer, was Richard Wagner's real father are true, his attitude represents a guilt-complex. Occasionally antisemites attacked him as a Jew and pointed to his Jewish face. His rabid Jew-baiting did not save Richard Wagner from the most slanderous abuses in a certain part of the antisemitic press.

³ Valentin, p. 16, quotes a striking story of the Swedish writer, Carl G. Laurin: " 'Here,' say the little peasant lads, 'the boys are good, but there' — pointing indignantly to the next village, a few stones'-throws away — 'there they are wicked.' " And the author adds: "I heard this when I was a child, and since then I have always thought how unsympathetic is the untutored mind towards what is strange. A great deal of culture and of the objectivity it begets is required before we can grasp that a foreign national character may be sympathetic."

⁴ On the nationalism of the period, see *Encyclopedia for the Social Sciences*, VI, 246 f.

⁵ The fact that some Jews in Germany joined the chorus of the slanderers of the Catholic Church offered to the Catholic press the excuse for vehement attacks against all Jews; cf. Leroy-Beaulieu, p. 47. The press of the orthodox Protestants, like the *Kreuzzeitung*, was only too willing to join arms with any foe of the Jews. Sebastian Brunner in Vienna, Abbé J. Leman (convert) and others attacked the Jews in the name of Catholicism.

⁶ The terrible fraud of the *Gründerjahre* was first exposed by Eduard Lasker in a speech before the Prussian Diet of February 1873. Jews used to emphasize this fact in order to prove that the boom was not a Jewish affair; non-Jews replied that Lasker had attacked the aristocratic swindlers who were his political opponents, and had spared the Jews. Wilhelm Marr (himself a descendant of Jews) who, as early as 1862, had written against Jews, now published his book, *The Victory of Judaism over Germanism*, which in 6 years went through 12 editions! Otto Glagau (not Glogau as is frequently misprinted), *Der Börsen und der Gründungsschwindel*, 1878, enjoyed a sensational success. For statistics about the real share of Jews in that blunder, see *AZdJ*, 1875, p. 661.

⁷ On the political constellation, see Jöhlinger, *Bismarck und die Juden*.

⁸ Stöcker published memoirs, *Dreizehn Jahre Hofprediger und Politiker*, which had a wide circulation. His emphasis was at first on the social and religious question; but very soon he realized that it was advantageous to shift the emphasis against liberals and Jews.

⁹ On the genesis of the *Antisemitenliga* and the later antisemitic

groups, see K. Wawrzinek, *Die Entstehung der deutschen Antisemitenparteien (1873–90)*, 1927 (*Historische Studien*, 168).

[10] Occasional remarks of scholars about Semitism and Aryanism had almost no effect on public opinion. Only later, when the political propaganda was in full swing, did books like E. Dühring's *Die Judenfrage als Rassen- Sitten- und Culturfrage*, 1881, or A. Wahrmund's *Das Gesetz des Nomadentums und die heutige Judenherrschaft*, 1887, obtain a market.

[11] The methods of antisemitic propaganda and terrorism were almost alike in all countries and have changed in violence only, not in substance. Theodor Fritsch in Leipzig, an antisemitic champion for fifty years (his *Handbuch der Judenfrage* first appeared in 1887), was a leader in these methods.

[12] The characterization quoted is that of the socialist leader August Bebel. Bismarck's views on the political incapacity of the antisemites are listed in Jöhlinger's book.

[13] Shortcomings of the Jews are pointed out in Philippson, II, 10; later on — even with a certain pride — it was emphasized that as human beings Jews were entitled to have their black sheep and their Shylocks just as any other group. Jewish self-accusations, attaining their heights in *Jüdischer Selbsthass*, are not wanting; the main exponent of them was Otto Weininger.

[14] Antisemites were exposed in the *Antisemitenspiegel*, *Antisemitenhammer* and similar publications. Their most pitiless critics were antisemites themselves who belonged to a different party or group. Hirsch Hildesheimer's *Jüdische Presse* and J. S. Bloch's *Österreichische Wochenschrift* contain abundant material of this kind, and Brunner, p. 80 ff., has a stirring collection of the filthiest insults of antisemites against antisemites.

[15] Cf. Bloch's *My Reminiscences*, I, especially p. 272 ff., on Ernest Schneider. On Stöcker, see H. L. Strack, *Herr Adolf Stöcker; christliche Liebe und Wahrhaftigkeit*, 1885, and Carl Witte, *Mein Conflikt mit Herrn Hof- und Domprediger Stöcker*, 1889, and Jöhlinger, *Bismarck*. On Guérin's penalties, see St. Arnoulin, *M. Ed. Drumont et les Jésuites*, 1902.

[16] A report on the Congress of Dresden according to the *Neue Freie Presse* of Vienna, in *Jüdische Presse*, 1882, pp. 429 ff.; for the resolutions, see *AZdJ*, 1882, pp. 652 ff.

[17] Since all figures have no more than relative value, even exact statistics are worthless without a proper framework. In the case of the Jews the figures were mostly misinterpreted, if not falsified. Even Treitschke used wrong statements about the immigration of Eastern Jews into Prussia; cf. Salomon Neumann, *Die Fabel von der jüdischen Masseneinwanderung*, 1880, and *Nachschrift*, 1881. Drumont preposterously asserted that, of the 250 billions of national property in France, the Jews owned no less than 80!! On the predominance of Jews in the press, see above, p. 91. The "criminality"

of Jews was first elucidated in Paul Nathan's *Die Kriminalität der Juden in Deutschland*, 1896, and Rudolf Wassermann, *Beruf, Konfession und Verbrechen*, 1907.

[18] In refutation of the generalizations see Leroy-Beaulieu, p. 75 ff.; Menzinger, p. 78 ff.

[19] Leroy-Beaulieu dedicated the bulk of his book to the Jew-myth. The result of his research is what had before been expressed in Russia: "The qualities of the Jews are their own; their shortcomings what we made of them."

[20] Many examples exist throughout the whole literature of antisemitism. The forgeries about the *Alliance Israélite* were exposed in the very first issue of the *Antisemitenspiegel*, 1890. A canard of recent times which concerns the United States is an alleged speech and letter against the Jews by Benjamin Franklin. That this is a 100% forgery was proved by the most reliable experts. Cf. their exposé in *CJR*, I, 2, pp. 45–54.

[21] Rohling's *Der Talmudjude* was circulated as early as 1871. From 1876 on new editions and translations followed one another. Rohling's ignorance and dishonesty were exposed in Franz Delitzsch's *Rohling's Talmudjude*, not to speak of the refutations of some rabbis (Philippson, II, 16). The situation thus produced is described in Bloch's *My Reminiscences*, I, 63 ff. The product of Rohling's trial against the latter were Fr. Kopp, *Zur Judenfrage: Nach den Akten des Prozesses Rohling-Bloch*, 1886; *Acten und Gutachten in dem Prozesse Rohling ca. Bloch*, I, 1890. Worthy protégés of Rohling were Aaron Briman (Dr. Justus), a convert of the meanest type, and his "pupil" Dr. Ecker. The fullest presentation of the talmudic material is J. S. Bloch, *Israel und die Völker*, 1923 (English translation 1927) and Michael Guttmann, *Das Judentum und seine Umwelt*, 1927. See also *UJE*, III, 1 ff. s.v. Canards.

[22] Against Rohling's accusation of ritual murder, cf. Franz Delitzsch, *Schachmatt den Blutlügnern Rohling und Justus*.

[23] The fullest presentation of the matter is H. L. Strack, *The Jew and Human Sacrifice (Human Blood and Jewish Ritual); an Historical and Sociological Inquiry* (English translation from the 8th German edition), 1909.

[24] The case of Tisza-Eszlár was a sensation for the whole civilized world, and the press of Central and Western Europe was full of reports about the trial. A comprehensive presentation of the investigation and the trial is given by Paul Nathan, *Der Prozess von Tisca-Eszlár: Ein antisemitisches Kulturbild*, 1892. A significant story about the level of the prevalent moral insanity was told in *Neues Wiener Tageblatt*, 1883: Count Pongrad visited the synagogue of Tisza-Eszlár and asked where the golden calf was located which (allegedly) had to be sprinkled every seventh year with the blood of a Christian virgin and was not allowed to be missing in any synagogue (*AZdJ*, 1883, p. 558).

[25] The quotations are from A. Nussbaum, *Der Polnaer Ritualmordprozess: Eine Kriminalpsychologische Untersuchung auf aktenmässiger Grundlage*, 1905, and its foreword by the famous criminologist Franz v. Liszt.

CHAPTER II

ANTISEMITISM IN WESTERN EUROPE

[1] That Bismarck's attitude towards antisemitism was entirely negative was clearly proved in Jöhlinger's book; but the government-controlled press did not abstain from emphasizing the share of Jews in the parliamentary opposition. Bismarck was, indeed, the target of the most uncouth slanders; Jöhlinger, pp. 111–132. The Prussian Minister of the Interior, Herr v. Puttkammer, and the Chief of Police of Berlin were thorough reactionaries and favored the antisemitic excesses; ibid., pp. 45 ff. It was against this lawlessness that Kaiser William I issued his order that the authorities must oppose the antisemitic movement with full energy and by all legal means (August 1881). Among the information which the emperor had received was a complaint of the banker Gerson v. Bleichröder about Stöcker's agitation (June 1880); Jöhlinger, pp. 141 ff.

[2] The numerous details about the excesses, which made a tremendous impression on contemporaries, can be read in Philippson, II, 20–26; Dubnow, X, 24–60.

[3] On the trial of Neustettin, see L. Auerbach, p. 57; and Sello, "Der Neustettiner Synagogen Brand Prozess" in *Das Tribunal*, I, 1885, p. 5 ff.

[4] The appeal of the Christian notables, in Philippson, II, 19, and Auerbach, p. 70.

[5] Treitschke's *Ein Wort über unser Judentum* and his reply to his numerous critics first appeared in his *Preussische Jahrbücher*, vols. 44, 45, and later as a separate pamphlet. Outstanding among the answers to him is Theodor Mommsen's *Auch ein Wort über unser Judentum*.

[6] The antisemitic attitude of the state administrations, in Philippson, II, 34 f.

[7] About the sincerity of these converts the Protestant missionary, de le Roi, is said to have expressed himself: "Never has a Jew become baptized through conviction."

[8] The changed attitude of the university students is significant. Up to that time not even the "aristocratic" fraternities had excluded Jews. Ludwig Bamberger and Berthold Auerbach, e. g., had the most cordial relations with the members of their fraternities.

[9] Paul de Lagarde combined with a warm interest for ancient Hebrew and Aramaic literature a deep contempt of contemporary Jews; cf. Anna de Lagarde, *Paul de Lagarde's Erinnerungen aus seinem Leben*, 1894; *UJE*, VI, 510.

[10] The failure of the courts to proceed in cases of collective injuries, of insults against the Jewish religion, etc., was pointed out in Maximilian Pamrod (= Max Apt), *Antisemitismus und Strafrechtspflege*, 1894.

[11] To the *Fall Stöcker* and the various attempts to remove this priest from his post, Jöhlinger dedicated the longest chapters of his book, 133–181, 194–199.

[12] On Stöcker's attempt to capture Prince William and Bismarck's counteroffensive, see ibid., 140, 171 f. William II's open disavowal of Stöcker's antisemitism, in Philippson, II, 37.

[13] *Verein zur Abwehr*, see *Jü Le*, V, 1173 f.

[14] On Xanten, see Paul Nathan, *Xanten-Cleve: Betrachtungen zum Prozess Buschhof*, 1892; *Der Xantener Knabenmord: vollständiger stenographischer Bericht*, 1893. On Konitz reports: *Privatdruck der gesamten Verhandlugen 25.X.–16.XI. 1900*.

[15] The German conquest of world markets was made easier through the fact that most Jewish businessmen in Europe as well as overseas spoke or understood German or Yiddish.

[16] Protestant pastors of the liberal wing did not stress the belief in the deity of Jesus and thus made conversion easy. It was a specious self-betrayal when well-to-do Jews, whose real motive was to remove the social and political ostracism from themselves or their children, excused their apostasy as an ascent to a loftier culture!

[17] The tragedy of the political allegiance of the Jews in Austria is clearly pointed out in J. S. Bloch, *My Reminiscences*, I, 152 ff., and similarly in Grunwald, *Vienna*, 426 ff. On the whole trend of the policy of nationalities, see R. Charmatz, *Österreichs innere Geschichte von 1847–1895*, 1907. The original program of the *Deutschnationale Partei* was drafted by Heinrich Friedjung, and one of those who cooperated with him was Victor Adler; this program was not antisemitic, but Georg v. Schönerer (at least since 1885) gave it an uncompromising racial character; much of it was later adopted by the Nazis.

[18] Details on the antisemitic movement in Austria, in Philippson, II, 69 ff.; Dubnow, X, 74 ff.

[19] On the Jewish share in the cultural life of Vienna, see Grunwald, *Tietze*, and S. Mayer, *Wien*, 362 ff., 458 ff.; Mayer, in his plastic way offers interesting details. In his *Erinnerungen*, 248 ff., 281 ff., he clearly depicts the Philistine atmosphere in the lower middle class.

[20] The turbulent scenes in the Vienna Parliament are well known; they are described in Bloch's *My Reminiscences*. Vol. II of the work is entirely dedicated to the shabby tricks of Pastor Deckert, a champion of the Christian Social Party.

[21] Lueger is portrayed realistically by S. Mayer (*Erinnerungen*, 256 ff., 294 ff.), who had known him intimately from the beginning of his political career. Some lines read as if they were a portrait of Hitler, the warm admirer of Lueger. See also Bloch, l. c., I, 227 ff.

[22] The trend of the economic policy in Austria is characterized by Charmatz, l. c.

[23] According to the statistics of 1894 the Army counted about 8% commissioned officers who professed Judaism; some of them, like Ritter von Eiss and von Schweitzer, attained the highest ranks though they were practicing Jews.

[24] Among the university professors of worldwide fame were Th. Gompertz, K. S. Grünhut and the physicians M. Benedikt, I. Neumann, W. Winternitz; cf. Grunwald, *Vienna*, 518 ff., 529.

[25] The situation in the Sudetenland, in H. Gold, *Die Judengemeinden in Mähren*; O. Thon, *Die Juden in Österreich*.

[26] On the Hilsner trial see the article "Polna" in *JE*, X, 116, written under the fresh impression of the events. See also T. G. Masaryk, *Notwendigkeit einer Revision des Polnaer Prozesses*, and the book of A. Nussbaum, 1906.

[27] As early as 1881–82, when the ritual murder slander was not yet fashionable, the Poles arranged the Ritter affair in Lutez; Ritter and his wife were first condemned to the death penalty in Rzeszow and, after appeals, twice again in Cracow, but were later absolved by a unanimous vote of the Supreme Court in Vienna, 1886: cf. L. Auerbach, pp. 64–69; Dubnow, X, 101. Enforced baptism of girls and their kidnapping to monasteries were frequent; the courts declared that before the walls of a monastery their jurisdiction ended. Cf. Bloch, I, 203 ff.

[28] Little was known about the conditions of the Jews in Galicia through general publications. It was Bloch's *Österreichische Wochenschrift* that constantly drew attention to their misery. A little later, S. R. Landau toured the country and reported on their incredible poverty in his *Unter jüdischen Proletariern*, 1898. Very instructive is the report given by Dr. Salz at the First Zionist Congress, 1897; *Bericht*, pp. 22 ff.

[29] On this election, see Bloch, *Erinnerungen*, I, 77 ff. Cf. pp. 211 ff., 343 ff.

[30] On the *Israelitische Allianz*, see *UJE*, I, 192, and the Annual Reports from 1873 to 1931.

[31] The details about the Baron de Hirsch Foundation were continually reported in the *Österreichische Wochenschrift*; the original by-laws, in *Die Neuzeit*, 1891, no. 2, p. 13; the English translation, in *JE*, VI, 415.

[32] For descriptions of the incredible misery about the end of the century, see the missionary's, R. Bieling, *Die Juden vornehmlich: Ein geschichtlicher Überblick über die Arbeit der Gesellschaft zur Beförderung des Christentums unter den Juden*, 1902, and Bertha Pappenheim's reports on her travels through Galicia.

[33] For the emigration to the United States, see S. Joseph, *Jewish Immigration to the United States, 1881–1910*, 1914.

[34] On the pogroms, see *Österreichische Wochenschrift*, 1898, no. 5, p. 82.

[35] On Istóczy's agitation and the pogroms, see the continuous reports in the Vienna Jewish weeklies: Philippson, II, 76 f.; Dubnow, X, 101.

[36] For the impressively large number of Hungarian Jews of worldwide reputation, see *UJE*, V, 498 ff. Sandór Roth, *Juden im ungarischen Kulturleben seit der 2. Hälfte des 19. Jahrhunderts*, 1934, after a general survey of the contributions of the Jews to Hungary's economy and culture, deals with the famous Jewish poets Jószef Kisz and Sandór Bródy and the convert Lajos Dóczi.

[37] The law of 1895 contains the paragraph: "The Jewish religion is hereby declared to be a legally recognized religion." The resistance of the Upper House was broken in 1896.

[38] Leroy-Beaulieu and N. Leven emphasized that antisemitism was a German importation, that France had no need of this German product and that its clericals never pardoned the Revolution and made common cause with the monarchists. The clericals tried very early to present the Revolution of 1789 as the work of Jews and Freemasons, and even a socialist like Fourier joined the chorus.

[39] On the anti-Republican movement in France, see Leven, I, 490 ff.; Philippson, II, 96 ff.; Dubnow, X, 227 ff.; Valentin, 68 ff. In a very instructive article, "From the Dreyfus Affair to France Today" (*JSS*, IV, 195–240), Hannah Arendt outlines the group-constellations within the Third Republic and the strange attitude of the House of Rothschild; cf. pp. 205 ff., 213 f.

[40] On Drumont's evolution, see G. Audiffrent, *A. M. Drumont*, 1889; I. Schapira, *Der Antisemitismus in der französischen Literatur*; *Edouard Drumont und seine Quellen*, 1927. The reply to Drumont's book, *La France n'est pas juive*, did not have a large circulation.

[41] The Antisemitic League was transferred to Algiers in 1898.

[42] One of the exquisite morsels which fell into the mouth of the *Libre Parole* was a list of the parliamentarians bribed by the Panama Canal Society which Jacques Reinach had forwarded to Drumont in order to expose his rival, Cornelius Herz. "The *Libre Parole* was transformed over night from a small and politically insignificant sheet into one of the most influential papers in the country" (Arendt, p. 204).

[43] The full story of the Dreyfus case is given in the voluminous book of the poet Wilhelm Herzog, *Der Kampf einer Republik: Die Affaire Dreyfus*, 1933: pp. 349–968 offer a "Chronicle of the Facts;" pp. 969–975 an extended bibliography of the most important publications. Definite proof of the innocence of Alfred Dreyfus was given in the publication *Militärattaché v. Schwartzkoppen: Die Wahrheit über Dreyfus: Aus dem Nachlass herausgegeben von Bernhard Schwertfeger*, 1930. Even this documentary evidence was declared spurious by Charles Maurras, *Au signe de Flore — souvenir de vie politique*, 1931, pp. 51–119, and Appendix. After Alfred Dreyfus' death (1935), his son published *The Dreyfus Case, by the Man Alfred Dreyfus and his son Pierre*, translated and edited by Don C. McKay, 1937. More recent literature in *UJE*, III, 509, and in Hannah Arendt's article.

[44] For an accurate statement of the Dreyfus case up to the time of its publication, see *JE*, IV, at the end, and Leven, I, 494–544.

[45] The first one to shed light on the tricks and intrigues of the trial was Bernard Lazare, then an unknown writer, in his pamphlet, *Une erreur judiciaire: La vérité sur l'affaire Dreyfus*, 1896. About the same time Senator Scheurer-Kestner informed several cabinet ministers of his impression that Dreyfus was innocent. Since he was of the Protestant faith, the Protestants were henceforth included in the attacks against the Jews. A little later Georges Clémenceau started his agitation for the revision of the Dreyfus trial. Émile Zola's *L'Affaire Dreyfus: Lettre a M. Félix Faure, Président de la République* was first published by Clémenceau in his daily, *L'Aurore*, on Jan. 13, 1898, under the headline "J'Accuse" which won worldwide fame.

[46] For the pogroms, see Herzog's book, pp. 603 f., 688, 718; and Leven, I, 518 ff., 523.

[47] Philippson, II, 105 ff., reported on the events in Algeria as an eyewitness.

[48] On the power behind the Paris mob, see Zola, in Herzog, p. 729 f. The attitude of the Paris population at the time of the trial against Zola is described in the *Diaries of Reichskanzler Prince Hohenlohe* who had his information from the converted Jewish journalist, Arthur Meyer of the *Gaulois*, one of the ill-famed antisemites of Paris. The quotation is in Herzog, p. 718.

[49] The discussion in the Chamber took place July 7; ibid., p. 720; six days later Esterházy was arrested. On July 18, the prosecutor examined Henri (ibid., 733 ff.) who confessed Esterházy's guilt and, when questioned by M. Cavaignac (August 30), confessed his share in the forgeries and committed suicide the same evening (pp. 755–57). Charles Maurras suggested the erection of a monument to the officer who had committed his forgeries "out of heroic patriotism"! A public subscription followed. The list of the subscribers was later published by P. Guillard, under the title *Le Monument Henri*, 1899.

[50] The year 1898 saw the first issue of *L'Antijuif*, the organ of the Antisemitic League of France. A little later the *Ligue pour les Droits des Hommes* was founded.

[51] On Guérin, see Arendt, p. 223; Leven, I, 538 f.

[52] For the procedure at Rennes, see *Conseil de guerre de Rennes. Le procès Dreyfus. Compte rendu sténographique*, 3 vols., 1900. Cf. Herzog, 862–891. The pardon of Alfred Dreyfus (September 19), ibid., p. 926.

[53] The proceedings of the trial of the Nationalists before the Senate as Extraordinary State Court are published in 4 vols.

[54] Herzog, p. 960. The last forgery in the Dreyfus case was discovered in 1902; the verdict of the Court of Rennes was annulled by a special court formed of all the departments of the Court de Cassation. The government avoided resorting again to a Military Court, and the anti-Dreyfusards never recognized the legitimacy of the acquittal.

[55] The legislation on the Clerical Orders was begun by the Cabinet Combes and continued by Clemenceau.

[56] Berthold Auerbach's *Briefe an seinen Vetter Jacob Auerbach* (1884), insofar as they were written during the last years of his life, strikingly illustrate the extraordinary social position of some Jews and the shock felt by them after the outbreak of this unexpected hostility.

[57] The figures on Jews baptized in that period are taken from the official statistics; cf. *JE*, IV, 252; *AZdJ*, 1894, p. 218.

[58] Lazarus read his paper Dec. 2, 1879. A year later he headed the *Jüdisches Komitee* and delivered his addresses, *Unser Standpunkt*. All these publications were reprinted in his *Treu und Frei*, 1887.

[59] The replies to Treitschke are listed in Dubnow, X, 27–31; Meisl, *Heinrich Graetz*, p. 126, note 57.

[60] The declarations of the rabbis were published in the daily and the Jewish weekly press. The "moral principles" were circulated through the *Deutsch-Israelitischer Gemeindebund*. For the views of the Budapest Rabbinical Seminary see M. Bloch, *Die Ethik in der Halacha*, 1886. D. Hoffmann's book appeared in enlarged form in 1895. A modernized and abridged edition of it was published by Arthur Liebermann in 1921. Noteworthy among the publications of Christian scholars in this respect is H. L. Strack's *Die Juden: Dürfen sie 'Verbrecher von Religionswegen' genannt werden?*, 1893. The *Einleitung in den Talmud*, by the same author, was originally written in order to prove that the Talmud was anything but a secret book.

[61] For details about the *Shehita*-problem, see Philippson, II, 123–128; Jeremiah J. Berman, *Shehita*, 1941, pp. 236 ff.; Drumont's confession in *Libre Parole* of July 21, 1894.

[62] Julius Fenchel, one of the "unknown soldiers" in the fight for Judaism was a man with neither wealth nor social standing but full of energy and enthusiasm. The beginnings of the IOBB in Germany are described in L. Maretzki, *Geschichte des Ordens Bne Briss in Deutschland, 1882-1907*. It is significant for the attitude of cultured Jews of that time that for decades no convention met without a discussion of the problem whether members represented a Jewish organization or an organization of Jewish individuals. Maretzki, a physician by profession, who was elected President of the German Grand Lodge in 1888, when the enlarged membership seemed to require a leader of academic standing, was a man of the purest idealism, a true disciple of Arnold Toynbee. He had to quit his office in 1898 because he had allowed his son to take the courses in Protestant religion given in the High School he attended. Maretzki offered the strange excuse that he wanted the boy to become acquainted with all religions and later to choose for himself! Of such queer ideas was the generation of the 1848'ers possessed! Maretzki was a true democrat and continued to work for his ethical and social ideals within the IOBB as an ordinary member. To his successor, Berthold Timendorfer (1898-1924), Jewish religion was a primary concern; and he was followed by a rabbi, Dr. Leo Baeck (1924-1937). This line indicates the process of renaissance among the Jews in Germany as well as in Central and Eastern Europe.

Fenchel, by the way, was the first to insist that the administrations of the Jewish communities in Germany be democratized.

⁶³ In Vienna Adolf Jellinek had urged energetic steps on the part of the Jews as early as 1882. Isidore Singer, who later became the editor of *The Jewish Encyclopedia*, urged the foundation of a really Jewish daily press (*Presse und Judentum*). On the "Union," see *EJ*, IX, 386 f., where the publications of that body are listed, and J. S. Bloch, *My Reminiscences*, I, 188 ff.

⁶⁴ On the Jewish Students' Organizations see *Jü Le*, III, 606–608. The fact that Jewish students appeared in public as Jews and were ready to fight duels for the honor of Judaism — no matter how we today appraise the brutal custom of dueling — made a deep impression, even on Christian students. It was reserved to Schönerer's nationalists in Vienna to declare that Jews had no honor and were not entitled to "satisfaction."

⁶⁵ As early as 1883 students of the Berlin University had founded the *Akademischer Verein für Jüdische Geschichte und Literatur*; according to its statutes this organization was interdenominational, but the number of Christian members throughout the 50 years of its existence was negligible. The organization was closely connected with the *Lehranstalt für die Wissenschaft des Judentums* in Berlin.

⁶⁶ On Zadoc Kahn and Isidore Loeb, see the issue of *Revue des Etudes Juives* dedicated to their memory, October 1938.

⁶⁷ On the "Wanderers" see N. Bentwich, *Solomon Schechter*, 59 ff.; on the Anglo-Jewish Exhibition, see *JE*, I, s. v.

⁶⁸ On Karpeles and his work, see *UJE*, VI, 325. Of the *Jahrbuch*, 32 vols. were published until 1938.

⁶⁹ This is not the place fully to portray the achievements of Jewish research or, as it is often called, Jewish science. More about it may be found in the writer's *Ein Jahrhundert Wissenschaft des Judentums*, 1922.

⁷⁰ The *Komitee*, like the *Literaturverein*, united men of all wings of Judaism. Its leading spirit was Paul Nathan who published several valuable apologetic works.

⁷¹ The *Zentralverein* (*UJE*, III, 93) was heralded by an anonymous pamphlet, *Schutzjuden oder Staatsbürger*, written by Raphael Löwenfeld, the translator of Tolstoi's works and the founder of the first people's theater in Germany. The leaders of the *Zentralverein* were Maximilian Horwitz (1893–1917) and Eugen Fuchs (1917–23). The latter's *Um Deutschtum und Judentum*, 1919, contains a series of lectures and articles which offer a full insight into the struggle and the ideology of the *Centralverein*. A history of it was written by Paul Rieger, *Ein Vierteljahrhundert im Kampf um das Recht und die Zukunft der deutschen Juden*, 1918.

⁷² Schechter's "Epistles to the Jews" were published in the *Jewish Chronicle*, 1900–1901 (Bentwich, l. c., p. 358, n. 14) and republished

in *Studies in Judaism*, First Series, Phila., 1915; for the reaction to these Epistles, see Bentwich, p. 108.

[73] Lazarus' *Ethik* was translated into English by Henrietta Szold, *Ethics of Judaism*, 2 vols., 1901. The book was highly praised by the orthodox scholar Jos. Wohlgemuth. Its philosophical approach was harshly attacked by Hermann Cohen (*Jüdische Schriften*, III, 1 ff.), but found a milder judge in Julius Guttmann, *Die Philosophie des Judentums*, p. 343 ff. The second volume, consisting mainly of notes left by the author, was issued in 1911 and has not been translated.

Chapter III

THE JEWS OF RUSSIA UNDER ALEXANDER III

[1] The historians of Russia begin to pay attention to the fate of the Jews after the first pogroms had taken place; cf. Kornilov, II, 265, 284; G. Vernadsky, *A History of Russia*, 1930, p. 169; Sir B. Pares, *A History of Russia*, 1937, p. 412 f. Harold Frederic, *The New Exodus: A Study of Israel in Russia*, 1892, told the story reproduced in the present chapter after having lived in Russia for some time. S. Dubnow also was an eyewitness, cf. his sources quoted in *Russia*, III, 194 ff.; *Weltgeschichte*, X, §§ 12–20, p. 556 f. Leven, I, 421 ff., gives an extended narrative of the events as observed in the circles of the *Alliance Israélite Universelle*, but strikingly remarks that the intervention of the *Alliance*, so effective in former decades, was of no avail this time. Philippson, III, is of little value.

[2] The ideology of Pan-Slavism is characterized by Aksakof's slogan *Para Domoi* = "It is time to go home," namely to distant Russia from the trends prevalent in Central and Western Europe.

[3] While the anti-Jewish press raged against Jewish competition in economic life, the Christian merchants of Moscow, as late as 1880, emphasized the valuable qualities of the Jews of their city, and protested against the importation of antisemitism then rampant in Germany; Frederic, pp. 91, 117. A protest of 1882, in Scholz, 246 ff.

[4] The pogrom-agitation in southern Russia started long before the murder of Alexander II and was stopped through his intervention; Frederic, p. 116. The same type of agent provocateur was to be observed later, after the assassination, about Easter time. The problem of the complicity of the Russian Government has been discussed on the basis of later events, but no evidence exists to prove the direct responsibility of actual members of the Government. On the other hand, there cannot be any doubt that the pogroms had been carefully prepared and organized. All indications point to complicity of the so-called "Sacred League," a group of terrorists from the Right. They asserted their readiness to protect the life of the emperor, although some of them, holding high offices at the time of Alexander II, had

been fully informed of the dangers menacing the life of the emperor and had done nothing to prevent them. One of their leaders, von Drenteln, the Governor General of Kiev, was considered the chief culprit by informed and responsible contemporaries. This is clear from the memoirs of Gen. Novicki, chief of the gendarmerie of Kiev (quoted by E. Tcherikower in *YIVO Historische Schriften*, II, 453) as well as from the reports of the Austrian Consul General at Kiev (quoted by Gelber, op. cit., 477 ff.)

The Russian censorship was on the alert not to allow the truth about the pogroms to get out of the country. The correspondents of the world press were not able to inform their journals. Like the diplomatic representatives of foreign countries, they were concentrated in the capital and far away from the centers of the atrocities. The first detailed information about the massacres was brought to the attention of the world through Joseph Jacobs' articles in the London *Times* of January 11 and 13, 1882. These articles alarmed public opinion of Great Britain and won the widest circulation in the American press and, through a German translation, on the continent of Europe. They were supplemented by a statement on "Russian atrocities" issued by the Russo-Jewish Committee of London. The map and the list of the pogroms were inserted in the *Congressional Record* of the U. S., XLVII, first session, as an appendix (pp. 651–58) to a speech delivered July 31, 1882, by the Hon. S. S. Cox, Representative from New York. The information on which Jacobs' articles were based was smuggled out of Russia through the office of Rabbi I. E. Spector of Kovno (cf. Jacob Lipschitz, *Zichron Ja'acob*, III, 1930).

About the time of the publication of these articles, Lucien Wolf toured the district of horrors and reported in the columns of the *Jewish World*. His collected articles appeared in a German translation, *Die russischen Verfolgungen: 15 Briefe aus Süd-Russland*, 1882. On Joseph Jacobs' eminent services on behalf of the persecuted Russian Jews, see *JE*, VII, 45. Among the diplomats accredited to St. Petersburg, the Austrian envoy, von Kalnoky, later Foreign Secretary of the Empire, sent very extended reports to his government and enclosed the information forwarded to him by the consuls, especially by Consul Zingria of Kiev. Since Austria was so close to Russia and the next refuge of the emigrants, the government had a lively interest in the matter. The reports were recently published by Gelber, op. cit., p. 466 ff.

[5] The report of U. S. Minister John W. Foster, of May 24, 1881, in *Executive Documents* no. 407, p. 53 ff. An extended bibliography concerning the pogroms, in Tcherikower's article, l. c., p. 463 ff.

[6] The analysis of the events follows Leroy-Beaulieu, *The Empire of the Tsars*, III, 551 ff.; the quotation on p. 179, ibid., III, 553.

[7] The Russian press quoted in *Die Judenpogrome in Russland*, herausgeg. im Auftrage des Zionistischen Hilfsfonds in London, 1910,

pp. 20 ff. The main contributor, A. Linden, was none other than Leon Motzkin.

[8] Ibid., p. 23 f.

[9] On Ignatiev's reputation, see Frederic, p. 114; on his greediness, ibid., pp. 70, 124 f. It is due to him that the responsibility for the riots was put on the Jews, and Count Witte later wrote that the pogroms meant to him a political game. His intrigues are analyzed in Dubnow, *Russia*, II, 259 ff., and in the report of the Russo-Jewish Committee as well as in Leven, I, 424–443.

[10] The Jewish delegation before the Czar, in Dubnow, II, 261; *Judenpogrome*, p. 28.

[11] Denunciations of the pogroms by bishops and other members of the clergy, in Scholz, p. 77 ff.; by governors, in *Judenpogrome*, p. 25 ff.

[12] A report of the Public Meeting at the Mansion House of February 1, 1882, was printed under the title *Outrages upon the Jews in Russia*. An appendix contained lists of 42 towns where similar protest meetings were held. The booklet was translated into French and German.

[13] Count Witte's *Memoirs*, translated by A. Yarmolinsky, p. 376.

[14] Pobiedonostzev was known as a very mean character (not "of unimpeachable honor:" Pares, p. 393): Frederic, p. 148 ff.; Leroy-Beaulieu, III, 178, 514; John S. Curtiss, *Church and State in Russia*, 1900, p. 42 f. Dubnow, II, 245, transmits the popular joke that people changed his name, which means "Victory-bearer," to Byedonostzev = "Misfortune-bearer." Kornilov, II, 275, calls him "the evil genius of Russia."

[15] Ignatiev, according to the facts reported by Frederic, was one of the shrewdest rascals imaginable. For his cunning approach to the Jewish question, see Dubnow, II, 259–273.

[16] The position of the Jewish representatives as described by an eyewitness, ibid., p. 274. Another remark on this assembly, in Tcherikower, op. cit., p. 465.

[17] The program of the *Novoye Vremya*, in Dubnow, p. 278.

[18] The May Laws were analyzed by Frederic, p. 128; Leroy-Beaulieu, l. c., p. 557 ff.; Dubnow, II, 309–312.

[19] For the application and extension of the May Laws, see the books just mentioned. "An Abridged Summary of Laws, special and restrictive, relating to the Jews in Russia, brought down to the Year 1890" appeared as appendix to *The Persecution of the Jews in Russia*, 1890. A French translation of it is in *Les Juifs de Russie, receuil d'articles et d'études sur leur situation légale, sociale et économique*, 1891. See also *52nd Congress of the U. S. A., first session, Ex. Doc. 235*, pp. 37 ff. A devastating exposition of the educational restrictions, in Frederic, pp. 154–162.

[20] Korolenko, in Scholz, p. 160 ff.; Schtschedrin, in *Judenpogrome*, p. 75. The protest of the intelligentsia, in Dubnow, II, 387.

[21] "High Commission for the Revision of the Current Laws concerning the Jews," presided over by Count Pahlen, former Minister of

Justice, see Dubnow, II, 336 ff. One of the members was Demidoff, Principe di San Donato, who as Mayor of Kiev had had ample opportunity to get acquainted with Jews and warmly advocated the repeal of all legal restrictions in his *Evreiskii vopros v Rossii*, 1883 (in French translation, *La Question Juive en Russie*, 1884; reprinted in *Les Juifs de Russie*). An extract of the "General Memoir" of this Commission, in Dubnow, II, 363 ff.

[22] The news about the prospective extension of the May Laws all over the Empire and of new savage laws against all Jews was published in the London *Times* in July 1890, and alarmed world public opinion. To be sure, the Russian government denied that any such measure had ever been discussed. The United States Minister to St. Petersburg reported to Washington that neither he nor the American Consuls had noted any unrest (Adler, *Correspondence*, p. 98 f.) but the secret decrees existed and were shown to Jews by one of the governors. Frederic, pp. 172–175, contains very definite information about the real situation.

[23] The report of the Guildhall Meeting (Dec. 10, 1890) and its resolutions were printed as an Appendix to *The Persecution of the Jews in Russia* and in French translation in *Les Juifs de Russie*. Pobiedonostzev, in a letter to Alexander III, foamed with rage on the events in London (see his *L'autocratie russe*, 1927, p. 601 f.)

[24] On the causes of the expulsion from Moscow and the events connected with it, we have a vivid description in Frederic, pp. 182–228; cf. *Ex. Doc.*, l. c., pp. 33–66; Dubnow, II, 400–411. The shameful story of the Russian loan transacted with the Rothschilds of Paris, in Frederic, p. 185.

[25] Cardinal Manning in his letter to the Guildhall Meeting, p. 77.

[26] Witte in his *Memoirs*, p. 381.

[27] Rabbi Spector's biography, *Toledoth Yitzhak* by Jacob Lipschitz, his private secretary, 1897.

[28] On Horace Günzburg, see Sliosberg, *EJ*, VII, 728; *UJE*, V, 131 ff. Ibid., on his son David, the eminent Jewish scholar.

[29] On Smolenskin, see R. Brainin, *Smolenskin we-Toledotav*, 1901; *UJE*, IX, and the special issue of the monthly, *Bitzaron*, VII, no. 6, of Adar 5703 = March 1943.

[30] See the articles in *UJE*.

Chapter IV

THE EXODUS: BARON MAURICE DE HIRSCH

[1] The mood of the Jews in the pogrom districts is described by S. L. Schwabacher, *Denkschrift über Entstehung und Character der in den südlichen Provinzen Russlands vorgefallenen Unruhen*, 1882; J. Rülf, *Drei Tage in Jüdisch-Russland: Ein Cultur-und Sittenbild*, 1882; *Die Judenpogrome*, p. 72.

² On the first arrivals in New York, see Philip Cowen, *Memories of an American Jew*, p. 93; *Hebrew Immigrants' Aid Society of New York: Reports of the President and Treasurer for 1882*; ibid., "Report of Moritz Ellinger," 1882.

³ President Benjamin Harrison, quoted by S. Wolf, *Presidents*, p. 156.

⁴ The growing number of immigrants in Galicia is reflected in the despatches of the Austrian Foreign Office, quoted by Gelber, l. c., p. 492 ff. On the chaos in Brody, see Schafir (pseudonym for Moritz Friedländer), *Fünf Wochen in Brody unter den jüdisch-russischen Emigranten, 1882*; C. Goldenstein, *Brody und die russisch-jüdische Emigration, nach eigener Beobachtung*, 1882; Abraham Cahan, *Bleter fun mein Leben*, II, 25 ff.; Leven, II, 417–423.

⁵ The proceedings of the Mansion House Meeting, in Dubnow, II, 290. The appeal of Victor Hugo on behalf of the French Relief Committee appeared May 31st, 1882. A similar appeal was published by Christian notables in Berlin. The Jewish Community of Berlin accepted a number of orphans and opened a new Orphan Asylum.

⁶ On the meeting in Berlin see the report of Moritz Ellinger, quoted above. On the *Deutsches Central-Komitee* and its branches, see Frederic, p. 293 f., "Report of the Commissioners of Immigration" (*Ex. Doc.* no. 235), I, 16 f., 22 ff., 26. The *Komitee* published a monthly report beginning May 1882. Statistics on the emigration of Russian Jews through German ports, ibid., II, 107 f.

⁷ The Conference of Russian Jewish delegates in St. Petersburg, in *Judenpogrome*, I, 79 ff.; Dubnow, II, 304 ff.

⁸ On the beginnings of the colonization in Argentina, see Leven, II, 474 f.; *50 Años de Colonizacion Judia en la Argentina*, 1939, p. 85 ff.

⁹ The scale of immigration is to be seen in S. Joseph, *Jewish Immigration to the United States*, 1914.

¹⁰ On the delegation to President Harrison, see Oscar S. Straus, *Under Four Administrations*, p. 106; S. Wolf, l. c., p. 160 ff. The result of this démarche was the Commission of Mr. J. C. Weber and Dr. Kempster whose report is quoted several times in this chapter. Cf. Leven, II, 431 f.

¹¹ The President's Message of September 9, 1891, in Wolf, l. c., p. 156 f.

¹² Although the Jewish papers of his time were full of his benefactions, Maurice de Hirsch has not yet found a biographer. The best written on him and on his wife, Clara de Hirsch, are O. S. Straus' article in *JE*, VI, 414 ff., and that of Mrs. Straus, ibid., 409 f. Cf. also N. Sokolow, *History of Zionism*, I, 248–262. Hirsch's article, "My Views on Philanthropy," appeared in the *North American Review*, no. 416, July 1891, and was reprinted in S. Joseph, *History of the Baron de Hirsch Fund*, pp. 275–77. His appeal to his coreligionists in Russia is reprinted in Sokolow, I, 254 f., and in Weber and Kempster, I, 18.

¹² His emissary to the Russian Government was Arnold White

(infra, p. 725) who published his conclusions in *The Modern Jew*, 1899, pp. 9–64, 294 ff.; cf. Dubnow, *Russia*, II, 414 ff.

[14] On the ICA, see the article in *JE*, VII, 178 ff., and on the transactions in Russia, Dubnow, II, 419 ff. The ICA detested publicity and did not print more than dry reports about the meetings of the trustees. However, all its transactions had to be presented to the Board of Trade in London and the latter's archives were used by the critics of the ICA.

[15] A filthy, typically antisemitic slander came from the American Commissioner Schultheiss; see the often quoted *Report of the American Commissioners*, p. 303.

[16] On the difficulties in Argentina, see *50 Años*, p. 147 ff.; White, l. c., p. 129 ff.

[17] Cf. L. Chasanowitsch, *Die Krise der jüdischen Kolonisation in Argentinien und der moralische Bankrott der ICA Administration*, 1910; and S. I. Hurwitz, "Crisis in Agriculture and the Jewish ICA Colonies," in *YIVO Bleter*, V (1927), 295 ff.

[18] White, p. 183, according to reports of the London Board of Trade.

[19] On the struggle of the first immigrants in New York see Cahan, II, and Gregorji Weinstein, *The Ardent Eighties*, 1929.

[20] On the beginnings of the Jewish Labor Movement, see Tcherikower, in *YIVO Studies in History*, II, 469–594.

[21] On the influx of Jews to England and America see Joseph, *Jewish Immigration*, p. 74 ff.

BOOK THREE

THE JEWISH RENAISSANCE

Chapter I

THE LOVERS OF ZION: AHAD HA'AM

[1] On Palestine a hundred years ago, see Edw. Robinson, *Biblical Researches in Palestine*, II, 81; III, 320. Very valuable source material is to be found in A. M. Hyamson, *The British Consulate in Jerusalem in relation to Jews of Palestine*, 1838–1914 (The Jew. Hist. Society of England), 2 vols., 1939–41.

[2] The *Halukkah* has been severely criticized from the Jewish side (*UJE*, V, 188), but even Robinson, who was not biased by Jewish prejudices, emphasized that it was "administered without much regard to honesty and served chiefly as a means of increasing their own influence and control over the conduct and consciences of their poorer brethren;" II, 87.

[3] Ibid., and Hyamson, passim (see Index, p. 591), on missionary activities. The first Anglican Bishop of Jerusalem was M. S. Alexander,

born a Jew, see *UJE*, I, 975. His contemporary, Warder Cresson, U. S. Consul in Jerusalem, became a convert to Judaism and one of the early advocates of Jewish colonization in Palestine: ibid., III, 410.

[4] *Diaries of Sir Moses Montefiore*, I, 167–196; II, 35 f., 44, 63 ff., 109 f., 171 ff., 261 ff., 272 ff.; see also Lucien Wolf, *Sir Moses Montefiore: A Centennial Biography*, 1885, pp. 260, 276; and P. Goodman, *Moses Montefiore*, passim. Sir Moses was in Palestine 1827, 1830, 1854, 1857, 1860 and after the death of Lady Montefiore (1862) in 1866 and 1875.

[5] About the criticism of Montefiore's work in Palestine, see the comprehensive study of Josef Meisl, *History of the Sir Moses Montefiore Testimonial Fund* (Hebrew), 1939.

[6] On the Hirsch family, see B. H. Auerbach, *Geschichte der Juden in Halberstadt*, p. 144 ff.

[7] L. A. Frankl described his trip and his efforts in his 2 vols., *Nach Jerusalem*, 1858; his work is a valuable source-book and an attractive narrative and was therefore translated into several languages.

[8] On Albert Cohn, see I. Loeb, *Biographie d'Albert Cohn*, 1878.

[9] On Kalischer, see N. Sokolow, *History of Zionism*, I, 202; II, 262 f.; *UJE*, VI, 295 f. The foundation and development of *Mikveh Israel*, in Leven, II, 297–319.

[10] On Graetz's trip to Palestine and his report see J. Meisl, *Heinrich Graetz*, 1917, p. 101 ff., and the Appendices, pp. 142–175.

[11] On J. M. Pines see Sokolow, I, 286; II, 290. On him and Frumkin, see the memoirs of Ephraim Cohn-Reiss, "Mi-zikronot ish yerushalaim," in *Reshumot*, VI.

[12] On the first colonies and their difficulties, see Hannah Trager, *Pioneers in Palestine (Stories of Petach Tikvah)*, 1924. Leven, II, 498 ff. Recently the outstanding colonies published memorial volumes on the occasion of their fiftieth anniversary.

[13] On George Eliot, see *UJE*, IV, 78. *Daniel Deronda* was translated into Hebrew by D. Frischmann, 1893.

[14] On Oliphant, see *Episodes of a Life of Adventure*, by Laurence Oliphant, 1887; *Memoir of the Life of Laurence Oliphant and of Alice Oliphant his Wife*, by Margaret Oliphant, 2 vols., 1891; II, 169 ff.; his *Eastern Project*; *Colonization in Palestine*. He also published a book, *Haifa, or Life in Palestine*. See Sokolow, I, 207 ff.

[15] On J. Brill, whose main interest in Palestine was stirred by the desire to fulfill all commandments relative to the Land of Israel, see Sokolow, I, 286; II, 286. On S. Mohilewer, ibid., II, 289 f.

[16] On Ben Yehuda, ibid., I, 287; II, 284, 384, and the biography at the introduction to the tenth volume of his *Millon*; *UJE*, II, 159.

[17] The Manifesto of the BILU in Sokolow, II, 332 f. The adventures of the first emigrants in *Reshumot*, VI, 280 ff.

[18] On Pinsker, see Sokolow, I, 217 f., 224 ff.; J. Klausner, *Sefer Pinsker*, 1921. An attempt to give a psychological explanation of Pinsker's personality was made by N. Touroff in *Bitzaron*, 1942

p. 678 ff. The first English translation of *Auto-Emancipation*, by Albert A. L. Finkelstein, was published in 1891.

[19] Of the immense literature on the "Lovers of Zion" the following may be mentioned: Sokolow, II, 281 ff., E. Deinard, *Dibre ha-yomim le-Zion*, 1904; S. L. Citron, *Toledot Hibbat Zion*, I; A. Druyanow, *Ketabim le-toledot hibbat Zion ve-yishub Eretz Israel*; B. Dinaburg, *Hibbat Zion*; Eppel, *Mi-tok reshit ha-tehiyyah*, 1937.

[20] S. D. Druck, *Baron Edmond Rothschild: The Story of a Practical Idealism*, 1928; id., *L'œuvre du Baron Edm. Rothschild*, 1936; A. Hermoni, *Ha-Baron Edmond Rothschild, abi ha-yishub*, 1935.

[21] On the Kattowitz Conference see Sokolow, I, 216; II, 418 f. The form of organization of the Lovers of Zion in Eppel, op. cit.

[22] The attitude of the Turkish government, in Adler, *Correspondence*, pp. 7, 10–25; Oscar S. Straus, op. cit., p. 80 ff.; the British consular reports from 1882 on discuss the question of protecting former Russian subjects resident in Palestine, and the measures against expelling foreign Jews from the Holy Land; see Hyamson, p. 412 ff.

[23] On the difficult situation of the colonies and the impotence of the Odessa Committee to help them, see Citron; Ahad Ha'am's criticism, Dubnow, II, 421 f. On the "Rothschild colonies," see the remarks of the British Consul in 1907, in Hyamson, p. 570.

[24] On Goldsmid and d'Avigdor, see Sokolow, I, 233 f., 239 f.; on Samuel Montagu's petition, I, 231, 239; II, 279 ff.

[25] Asher Ginzberg, better known as Ahad Ha'am, left autobiographical notes which were published in *Reshumot*, V, 88 ff.; VI, 101 ff. His critical essays are collected in 4 vols., *Al parashat derakim*, first published in 1895, latest edition 1921; some of them were translated into English in L. Simon's 2 vols., *Selected Essays*, 1912, and *Ten Essays on Zionism and Judaism*, 1922. His correspondence was published in 6 vols., *Iggerot Ahad Ha'am*, 1923–25. Cf., besides, the literature listed in *UJE*, I, 136; see Rav Tzair in *Bitzaron*, I.

[26] The famous essay, *Lo zeh ha-derek*, first appeared in *Hamelitz*, 1889.

[27] On the *B'ne Mosheh*, see the monograph of S. Tschernowitz, *Bene Mosheh u-Tekufatam*, 1914.

[28] The British Consular Reports since 1895, in Sokolow, II, 396 ff.; the American Consular Report in *Commercial Relations*, I, was quoted in Arnold White, *The Modern Jew*, p. 277, note. In 1898 Dr. Aaron Friedenwald of Baltimore, Md., visited the country, and in his letters to his family as well as in addresses delivered after his return told of the amazing symptoms of birth manifesting themselves in the cultivation of the soil and in the field of education, especially in the resurrection of the Hebrew language. Cf. Harry Friedenwald, *Life, Letters and Addresses of Harry Friedenwald*, 1906.

[29] On Imber's personality and eccentricities, see Rebekah Kohut, *As I Know Them*, pp. 190–200; Lipsky, p. 29 f. George A. Kohut was in

possession of the original manuscript of the *Ha-Tikvah* and presented it to the Library of Yale University.

[30] On *Ahiasaf*, see *UJE*, I, 71. Among other works the company published the *Hashiloah* from 1898–1921; vols. I–V were edited by Ahad Ha'am; vols. 6 ff. by Joseph Klausner.

Chapter II

THEODOR HERZL AND POLITICAL ZIONISM

[1] A source of incomparable value on Theodor Herzl and his work are his *Tagebücher*, 3 vols., 1922–23, and his *Gesammelte Zionistische Schriften*, 5 vols., 1934–35. The representative biography is that of Alex Bein, 1934, in an English translation of Maurice Samuel, 1940. In the bibliography of the latter book, pp. 523–530, not only Herzl's writings but publications contributing to the understanding of his work are listed.

[2] The quotations are from *The Jewish State*, English translation of S. d'Avigdor, with a preface by Jacob de Haas, 1904.

[3] The impression the *Judenstaat* made on his friends is recorded in *Tagebücher*, I, 345 ff.

[4] The Vienna students, ibid., pp. 343, 350 ff. S. R. Landau, ibid., pp. 346, 351 ff.

[5] The enthusiastic response of the Jewish masses, in Bein, p. 184 ff.

[6] On Hechler, see *Tagebücher*, III, Index p. 627; Bein, p. 191.

[7] On Newlinsky, see *Tagebücher*, ibid., p. 641; Bein, p. 192 ff.

[8] The *Tagebücher* and the different drafts of Memoranda and Addresses to the "Family" show that Herzl had a Rothschild-complex. It is not impossible that he would have come to an agreement with Maurice de Hirsch, but unfortunately the Baron died before he could see him again.

[9] Güdemann's pamphlet, *Nationaljudentum*, was the more disappointing for Herzl as he had fully informed the rabbi of his intentions and had even been encouraged by him. His answer, in Bein, p. 220; ibid. is mentioned also the polemic against Chief Rabbi Dr. Hermann Adler of London; but the quotation is misleading, because the words quoted were used by Herzl as a sarcastic allusion to Dr. Adler's background.

[10] On Max Nordau, see *UJE*, VIII, 233 ff. His *Zionistische Schriften* were published in 1909 and again in 1923; they include his famous speeches at the Zionist Congresses. After his death his widow published her memoirs of him, *Erinnerungen*, 1928. See also Anna D. and Maxa Nordau, *Max Nordau: a Biography*, N. Y., 1943.

[11] David Wolffsohn's *Autobiography* was published in Sokolow, II, 388; his biography was written by Emil Bernhard Cohn, 1939, and in this book are to be found many details about Bodenheimer. Of

course, both these most loyal collaborators are frequently mentioned in Herzl's *Tagebücher*; see the Index.

[12] On the collaborators in Vienna, see Bein, p. 210; *Tagebücher*, I, 624 ff.

[13] The correspondence with the Munich Jewish Community was published by Werner J. Cahnmann in *Historia Judaica*, III, 23 ff. The resolution of the CCAR in its *Yearbook*, IX, 12.

[14] The declaration of the Rabbinical Association of Germany appeared in the general as well as in the Jewish press. Herzl's reply is in his *Zionistische Schriften*.

[15] An orthodox view on the problem in H. Salomonsohn (=H. Brody), *Widerspricht der Zionismus unserer Religion?*, 1898, and in the letter of R. Samuel Mohilever to the I Zionist Congress.

[16] The transactions of the Congress were reported in *Zionistenkongress in Basel, Offizielles Protokoll*, 1898.

[17] The colors were those of the biblical fringes: Num. 15.38.

[18] Cf. the Basle Program as translated in J. de Haas' introduction to *The Jewish State*.

[19] Herzl wrote his remarks on the Congress in *Tagebücher*, I, 592 ff., 608 ff. Ahad Ha'am's impressions, in *Al parashat derakim*, II. On the echo of the Congress, see Bein, pp. 245 ff., 257 ff.

[20] Ad. Böhm, *Die Zionistische Bewegung*, I, 200 ff.

[21] The orthodox members of the Organization were early in touch with one another, but were not organized as Mizrahi before the year 1902 and more closely in 1904; cf. ibid., p. 206; *UJE*, VII, 599.

[22] On cultural Zionism, see Böhm, p. 203 ff. A biased polemic, in E. Deinard, *Koheleth America*, I, 55 ff.

[23] The Jewish Colonial Trust and the II Congress, in Bein, p. 268 ff.

[24] The Palestinian journey of the German Emperor, in *Tagebücher*, II; Bein, pp. 276-309. Prince Bülow in his *Memoirs* hardly mentions Herzl's reception, and this fact, too, makes it evident how far the Emperor and his advisers were from an understanding of the Jewish question.

[25] O. S. Straus, *Under Four Administrations*, p. 157, tells of his meetings with Herzl about the beginning of 1900 and his advice that it would be the best for him to go to Constantinople and there to discuss the plan of a Chartered Company.

[26] On Vambéry's career, see *Enc. Brit.*, XXII, s. v.

[27] On the trip to Constantinople and the transactions with the Turkish government, see *Tagebücher*, II, III; Bein, p. 342 ff.; A. Galanté, *Abdul Hamid II et le sionisme*, 1933.

[28] On the journey to Russia see *Tagebücher*, III, 431 ff., 459 ff.; Bein, 447 ff. Herzl's correspondence with Baron and Lady Bertha v. Suttner, in Tulo Nussenblatt, *Ein Volk unterwegs zum Frieden*, 1933.

[29] The letter to the Grand Duke, in *Tagebücher*, III, 493 f.; the audience with v. Goluchowski, ibid., 578 ff.; the audiences in Rome, ibid., III, 542-561.

[30] *Report of the Alien Immigration Commission*, 1903. The original text of Herzl's opinion was printed in *Zionistische Schriften*, I, 452 ff. The previous conversation with Lord Rothschild, in *Tagebücher*, III, 216 ff.

[31] On his stay in London and the El Arish project Herzl reported extensively in *Tagebücher*, III, 221 ff. Cf. Bein, p. 417 ff.

[32] On Uganda, see *Enc. Brit.*, XXII, 662 ff.; on Joseph Chamberlain, ibid., V, 202 ff. On the project offered for Jewish colonization, *Tagebücher*, III, 412 ff.; Bein, 435 f., 440 ff.

[33] Cf. *Stenographische Protokolle der Verhandlungen des 2. Zionistenkongresses*, 1898, etc. On the progress of Zionism and its institutions, see Sokolow, I, 262 ff.; II, 347 ff.; Ad. Böhm, *Die zionistische Bewegung*, I, 211 ff.

[34] On the Jewish Colonial Trust, ibid., p. 211; Sokolow, II, 341 ff. Zionist writers often attacked the Jewish financiers in Western Europe for their lack of support of this enterprise, but the millionaires of the East were no more ready to subscribe to the shares. Financial experts showed not much confidence in the scheme: cf. White's quotation from *Financial News*, in *The Modern Jew*, p. 218.

[35] On the Jewish National Fund, see Böhm, I, p. 226; on the Conference in Minsk, ibid., pp. 200, 296, 517; Bein, p. 405.

[36] *Stenographische Protokolle der Verhandlungen des 6. Zionistenkongresses*, p. 147 ff.; the vote, p. 236.

[37] Herzl's *Tagebücher* give some information about the discussions behind the stage. On his personal mood, ibid., III, 492 ff.; cf. Bein, p. 453 ff.

[38] The Kharkov "revolt," in *Tagebücher*, ibid., 522. The opposition was led by M. M. Ussischkin who had been on a tour through Palestine and thus prevented from attending the 6th Congress: cf. Böhm, I, 262 ff.; Bein, p. 478.

[39] On Herzl's personality, see Nordau's eulogy at the VII Congress: Böhm, I, 281 ff.; Bein's Epilogue.

[40] The confusion created by the loss of the leader is evident in Böhm, I, 291 ff., and in Emil Bernhard Cohn, *David Wolffsohn*. The resolutions, in *Stenographische Protokolle des Ausserordentlichen Kongresses* (July 28, 1905), p. 132, and Böhm, I, 318.

[41] On the JTO, see *JE*, XII, 685 ff., and the pamphlets published by the organization. On the Galveston Movement, see Adler, *Jacob H. Schiff*, II, 95 ff. A monograph on it is being prepared by Mr. Leo Shpall.

[42] Wolffsohn was in Constantinople in the autumn of 1907. The British Consul in Jerusalem reported, in November 1907, persistent rumors that the Sultan was inclined "to make liberal concessions to Jews:" cf. Hyamson, p. 569.

[43] On Ruppin's establishment in Jaffa, see Böhm, I, 415 ff. Of Ruppin's writings may be mentioned: *Soziologie der Juden*, 1930; *The Jews in the Modern World*, 1935; *Jewish Fate and Future*, 1940.

On the *Zione Zion*, Böhm, p. 309 ff.; on the Yemenites, ibid., 424 ff. The state of the Jewish colonies in 1914, ibid., 710-713.

[44] On the National Library, see G. Weil, "The Library's Fiftieth Anniversary," in *Kirjath Sefer*, XIX, 73 ff. The cultural development, in Böhm, I, 463 ff.; the schools of the *Hilfsverein*, in the annual reports of this organization. *Sefer Tel Aviv*, ed. A. Druyanov (in commemoration of the city's 25th anniversary), I, 1936.

[45] On the revolt against Wolffsohn, see Böhm, I, 485 ff., and E. B. Cohn, passim.

[46] On the Vienna Congress, see Cohn, passim, and Böhm, I, 608 ff.

[47] The official Zionist historiography based on the publication of the Zionist Organization, *Im Kampfe um die hebräische Sprache*, presented by Böhm, I, 412 ff., and others, asserts that the *Hilfsverein* made the attempt to suppress the Hebrew language. Dubnow (X, 488) even states that "it is a manifest fact that Paul Nathan acted according to instructions of the German Foreign Office, and that as representative of the *Hilfsverein* he found support in German diplomacy in Turkey." All this is absurd because it is well known that the *Hilfsverein* was first in organizing Palestinian schools with Hebrew as the language of instruction, that furthermore the members of the Board of the Technicum, who took part in the discussion in Berlin, had come to an agreement about the period of transition and that the conflict came as a surprise to all of them. This question of expediency was fanned into a conflict through the strike suddenly provoked in Palestine and the outrageous attitude of the Palestinian population towards Paul Nathan, cf. the latter's *Palästina und palästinensischer Zionismus*, which was printed for private circulation. The elements behind the storm are not yet clear. Neither the correspondence of Ahad Ha'am nor the remarks of Ephraim Cohn Reiss in his *Memoirs* shed sufficient light on the motives.

CHAPTER III

THE JEWS IN THE BRITISH EMPIRE: EFFECTS OF IMMIGRATION

[1] The 2d ed. of Hyamson's *A History of the Jews in England* contains a new chapter on more recent times but is very poor as far as realities are concerned and does not mention the complications resulting from the immigration. Cecil Roth, in his *History*, 1941, touches upon the immigration lightly, p. 266 f., and refers to L. Wolf's "The Queen's Jews" (*Essays*, p. 355 ff.), and to his own article on the Jews under George V, in *The Jewish Year Book* (England), 1937, p. 356 ff. On the leaders mentioned, see the articles in *UJE*.

[2] Among the first appeals to British public opinion on behalf of the Russian Jews was an article of Dr. Hermann Adler in *The XIX Century*, December 1881, p. 826 ff.

[3] On the first immigrants, see the *Reports* of the Jews' Temporary Shelter, the Jewish Board of Guardians, the Russo-Jewish Committee; G. F. Abbott, *Israel in Europe*, p. 443 ff.

[4] During the Eighties the problem of Labor attracted widespread attention: cf. Charles Booth, *Labour and Life of the People*; ibid., I, 564 ff., deals with "The Jewish Community." In the preceding chapters the living conditions of tailors (sweat-shops), tobacco workers, etc., are discussed in connection with recent immigration.

[5] In 1888 two reports were published: a) that of the Select Committee of the House of Commons on Immigration and Emigration of Foreigners; b) that of the Committee of the House of Lords on the Sweat System. The investigations brought to light inveterate, unheard-of grievances in many trades. Arnold White, a student of social conditions, at one time M. P., attributed all the evils to the recent Jewish immigration. He was a Jew-baiter of the Stöcker type and couched his haughtiness and bigotry in social arguments. His hatred of the Jewish immigrants to England is in contradiction with his respect for those Jews whom he had met in Russia while dealing with the Czar's government on behalf of Baron M. de Hirsch. His collected essays, *The Modern Jew*, 1899, betray his Judaeophobia; he was the chief trouble-maker during the whole period of Parliamentary inquiries.

[6] In a London meeting of July 25, 1891, after many hidden allusions to it, the labor leader Ben Tillet (d. 1943) urged special legislation for restricting the immigration of destitute aliens in order to prevent pauper Russian Jews from further degrading the East End of London: cf. the *Report of Weber and Kempster*, p. 305. How deep-rooted the prejudice was even among men of good-will is shown by the controversy between C. Russell and H. S. Lewis in *The Jew in London*, 1901. This book made an attempt at statistics of the London Jewish population, p. 150 ff., which is repeated in *JE*, VIII, 173 f.

[7] Major Evans-Gordon's book, *The Alien Immigration*, appeared in 1904.

[8] The *Report of the Alien Immigration Commission*, printed in 3 folio volumes and recounting 175 hearings of men and women from all walks of life (including Theodor Herzl, supra, p. 294), revealed nasty social conditions which had nothing to do with the Jewish immigration.

[9] Cf. Abbott, pp. 460–480.

[10] On the "Intellectual Progress," see *JE*, VIII, 170. On the "Wanderers," see A. A. Neuman, *Cyrus Adler*, p. 42 f.; N. Bentwich, *Solomon Schechter*, p. 59 ff. Cf. also Lucy Cohen, *Some Recollections of C. G. Montefiore*, 1939.

[11] The Anglo-Jewish Historical Exhibition (*JE*, I, 602 f.) published a *Catalogue* and a volume of *Papers read at the Anglo-Jewish Historical Exhibition*, 1887, which contain a Report of the Executive Committee.

[12] Graetz's paper, "Historical Parallels in Jewish History," ibid., pp. 1–19. His essay, recently reprinted in *CJR*, VI, 105 ff., first appeared in *The Jewish Quarterly Review*, I (1889).

[13] The Jewish Historical Society of England (*JE*, VII, 182) is still functioning. Its publications embrace volumes of *Transactions* and a series of standard works on Anglo-Jewish history. Its library, presented by F. D. Mocatta in 1905, subsequently became the richest repository of Anglo-Judaica, but was completely destroyed in an air raid on September 9, 1940 (*UJE*, VI, 131).

[14] On the Free School, see *JE*, VIII, 177; S. Gompers, *Seventy Years of Life and Labor*, 1925, I, 6 f. The "burden" of the *Heder* was pointed out by a circular letter of Lord N. Rothschild, addressed to the parents: cf. White, l. c., p. 150 ff.

[15] Glimpses of the social and religious conditions among the Jews in England are to be found in I. Zangwill's novels.

[16] On Aaron Samuel Libermann, who organized the first Jewish labor unit in London, see *UJE*, VII, 34.

[17] On Zionism in England, see Bein, pp. 344 ff., 347.

[18] On Hermann N. Adler, see *UJE*, I, 93 f. On the religious communities, *JE*, VIII, 174.

[19] Lily H. Montagu, *Samuel Montagu, First Baron of Swaythling*, pp. 22–28, affords an insight into the religious struggles; ibid., 33 f., mention that Sir Samuel hoped for incorporation of the Federation in the United Synagogue.

[20] On Herbert Samuel, see infra, pp. 596 f. On Rufus Isaacs, "The First Marquis of Reading," *UJE*, IX, 90–2.

[21] Hermann's book on the Jews in South Africa goes up to the year 1895. Cf. also *The South African Jewish Yearbook* and J. H. Hertz, *The Jews in South Africa*, 1905. Among the pioneers of the diamond industry was Harry Mosenthal: see *UJE*, VII, 660.

[22] On Cape Town, ibid., III, 23 f.

[23] On Johannesburg, ibid., VI, 166 ff.

[24] On Canada, besides the literature listed above, p. 701, see A. Rhinewine, *Looking Back a Century on the Centennial of Jewish Political Equality in Canada*, 1932.

[25] On conditions in Quebec, see "Montreal" in *UJE*, VII, 636.

Chapter IV

THE JEWS IN AMERICA AND THE IMMIGRANTS

[1] Besides the literature listed above, p. 698, Philip Cowen, *Memories of an American Jew*, 1932, is a very valuable source.

[2] On the first immigrants after the pogroms of 1881, ibid., p. 94 ff.

[3] See the printed report of the Hebrew Immigrant Aid Society which, at the end of the year 1881, replaced the Russian Immigrant's Relief Fund, for the year 1882. On the relief work in Philadelphia, see D. Sulzberger, "The Beginnings of Russo-Jewish Immigration to Philadelphia" in *PAJHS*, XIX, 125 ff.; H. S. Morais, *The Jews in Philadel-*

phia, 1894, pp. 206–235. On the Jewish quarter of New York City, see A. Cahan, *Bleter*, II, 72 ff.

[4] On "Am Olam," see *EJ*, I, 591. A. Cahan met members of the league in Brody and was astonished that they were not socialists (*Bleter*, II, 36). On the Louisiana Agricultural Colonies, see *Bericht über Catahoula Parish, La., Sicily Islands*, 1882; and *UJE*, III, 294.

[5] Translation of Rose P. Stokes and Helena Frank, 1914, p. 7 ff. On Morris Rosenfeld, see *UJE*, IX, 213.

[6] Disputes with the London Committee, in Cowen, p. 106 f. — the first but not the last instance of disunion among relief agencies which did much harm to the relief work.

[7] The disillusionment of the immigrants, in Weinstein, p. 23 f.; H. S. Goldstein, *Forty Years of Struggle for a Principle* (a biography of Harry Fischel), 1928, p. 10 ff.; A. Cahan, *Bleter*, II, 72 ff.

[8] G. Pollak, *Michael Heilprin and his Sons*, 1912. His is the unique case of a social worker who was held in highest esteem by all who came in touch with him. The diplomat Oscar S. Straus, the financier Jacob H. Schiff praise him no less than the socialist A. Cahan (*Bleter*, II, 96, 131 ff.); see Cowen, pp. 95 ff.

[9] The quotation is from Cowen, p. 98.

[10] On Schiff, see the address delivered by Louis Marshall (Dec. 19, 1920), published by Emanu-El Congregation of the City of New York; Cyrus Adler, *Jacob H. Schiff, his Life and Letters*, 2 vols., 1928. The words of President Taft, ibid., II, 362.

[11] On Emma Lazarus' cooperation, see Cowen, pp. 95, 103, 332 ff.

[12] The number of immigrants according to Samuel Joseph, *Jewish Immigration to the United States*, 1914, p. 114.

[13] Cowen, p. 98 f.

[14] Oscar S. Straus, *Under Four Administrations*, p. 95 f.; S. Joseph, *History of the Baron de Hirsch Fund*, 1935, pp. 10 ff.

[15] Usually only the first section of the *Report* is quoted, and it was this which was translated into French and German. The arguments quoted here were presented by Commissioner Schultheiss, ibid., 303 ff. Even the U. S. Minister to St. Petersburg, C. E. Smith, became a victim of false information; the newspaper, *Free Russia*, tried to spread the truth; see Adler, *Schiff*, II, 115 f.

[16] See *Official Correspondence relating to Immigration of Russian Exiles*, 1891, quoted in S. Wolf, *Presidents*, p. 156 ff. Cf. S. Joseph, *Immigration*, p. 199.

[17] The objects of the Baron de Hirsch Fund, in Joseph, *History*, p. 22; its work, ibid., p. 23 ff.

[18] On the Educational Alliance, ibid., pp. 253 ff.

[19] On Woodbine, ibid., pp. 48–115 (see also K. Sabsovich, *Adventures in Idealism*); on the South Jersey colonies, ibid., pp. 131 ff.; on the Jewish Agricultural Society, ibid., p. 116 ff., and L. G. Robinson in *AJYB*, XIV, 21–115.

[20] A. Cahan, *Bleter fun main leben*, II, p. 93.

[21] Bernard Weinstein, *Di idishe yunions fun America; Bleter; Geshichte un erinerungen*, 1929.

[22] *"Gewerkschaften: Sammel-buch zu fufzig jor leben fun di fareinigte idishe gewerkshaften*, issued by the United Hebrew Trades on the occasion of its 50th Anniversary as the Central Body of a Trade Union in Greater New York, ed. by H. Lang and Morris C. Feinstone, 1938. *Geshichte fun der yidisher |arbeter-bavegung in di Fareynikte Shtatn* (History of the Jewish Labor Movement in the United States), ed. for YIVO by E. Tcherikower, I, 1943; vol. II is in course of print.

[23] Cf. M. Soltes, "The Yiddish Press — an Americanizing Agency," *AJYB*, XXVI, 165–372.

[24] On all the personalities mentioned in the following pages, see the respective articles in *UJE*. Some found their special biographers, e. g., A. S. Solomons in *JE*, XI, 459; Nathan Straus, *AJYB*, XXXIII, 135 ff.; cf. Lina Gutherz Straus, *Disease in Milk*: *The Remedy Pasteurization*: *The Life Work of N. Straus*, 2d ed., 1917; Felix Adler, in *The Ethical Movement in America*, 1926; Sutro, in *JE*, XI, 604 f.; Rebekah Kohut, *My Portion*, p. 42 f.; Lillian D. Wald left a kind of autobiography in her *The House on Henry Street*; cf. C. Adler, *Schiff*, I, passim; Julius Kahn in *AJYB*, XXVII, 238 ff.; Oscar S. Straus, ibid., XXIX, 145 ff., and his *Under Four Administrations*.

[25] A preliminary list, ibid., II, 525 ff.; McCall, p. 125.

[26] On Argentina, see *50 Años de Colonizacion Judia en la Argentina*, 1939, and the articles "Argentina" in *UJE*, I; "Buenos Aires," ibid., II, s. v.; Leven, II, 473–497.

[27] On the crisis of the Union, see May, *I. M. Wise*, p. 306 ff. On Morais, *The Jewish Theological Seminary of America: Semi-Cent. Volume*, 1939, pp. 4 ff., 37 ff., 46 ff.

[28] On the ensuing religious controversy, ibid., 36 ff., and the present writer's article, "Alexander Kohut," in *AJYB*, XLIV, 76 ff., and the references, p. 80; D. Philipson, *My Life as Jew and American*, p. 50 ff.; H. Levy, *Reform Judaism in America*, 1933, pp. 51 ff.

[29] The Pittsburgh Platform, in D. Philipson, *Reform Movement*, 355 ff.

[30] The beginnings of the CCAR, ibid., and *Life*, p. 69 ff. The *Yearbook* has been published since 1890. An instructive summary of the activities of the CCAR in *UJE*, III, 88 ff.

[31] On the genesis of the *Union Prayer Book* and the repeated revisions of it, ibid., 90, and the works of Philipson.

[32] Judge M. Sulzberger, see *AJYB*, XXVI, 373 ff. On former attempts to organize a Publication Society, see *JE*, I, 519; *UJE*, VI, 138; "The 25th Anniversary of the JPS," in *AJYB*, XV, 19 ff. (was reprinted as a separate book). Krauskopf's part, in *AJYB*, XV (1913–14), 62 ff. Annual reports, ibid., I–XLV. Cf. Cyrus Adler, *Days*, passim; A. A. Neuman, *Adler*, p. 73 ff.

[33] American Jewish Historical Society, see Adler, ibid., 266 f.; Neuman, l. c., pp. 50 ff., 57 f. Cf. the *Publications* of the Society and *UJE*, I, 251.

[34] Cf. *Judaism at the World Parliament of Religions*, 1894; CCAR, *YB*, IV, 39 ff.; Philipson, *Life*, p. 89 f. On E. G. Hirsch, see Levy, ibid., 63 ff.

[35] On the Congress of Jewish Women, see *JE*, IV, 227; *UJE*, VIII, 116 ff.

[36] Ibid., VI, 94 f.

[37] The beginnings of Zionism in America, see Philipson, *Reform Movement*, 360 f. See, however, M. S. Raisin, *Dappim mi-pinkaso shel rabbi*, p. 208; Louis Lipsky, *Thirty Years of American Zionism*, 1927, p. 9 ff.

[38] On H. Pereira Mendes, see *AJYB*, XL, 41 ff.; *UJE*, VII, 479 f.

[39] Words of Judge Sulzberger in a letter to S. Schechter in N. Bentwich, *Schechter*, p. 169.

[40] On *The Jewish Encyclopedia*, see Preface to vol. I, especially pp. vi, vii.

[41] On Schechter, see Bentwich, l. c.; A. S. Oko, *Solomon Schechter: A Bibliography*, 1938. On the reorganization of the Jewish Theological Seminary, see the *Semi-Cent. Volume*, passim; Adler, *Days*, p. 243 ff.; Neuman, *Adler*, p. 85 ff.

BOOK FOUR

THE WORLD UNREST

Chapter I

THE TERROR IN RUMANIA AND RUSSIA

[1] The standard book on the Rumanian atrocities is Edouard Sincerus (Elias Schwarzfeld), *Les Juifs en Roumanie depuis le traité de Berlin jusqu'à ces jours*, 1901; an abstract of it is "The Situation of the Jews in Roumania since the Treaty of Berlin," *AJYB*, III, 63 ff. Bernard Lazare, *Les Juifs en Roumanie*, 1902, emphasizes the encroachments of the feudal caste upon the rights of peasants as well as Jews. The Rumanian propaganda tried to prove that the Jews were recent immigrants. Their own statements, however, traced Jewish communities back as early as 1843, so that at the end of the century, after at least two generations of Jews had served in the Rumanian army, they could no longer be called recent immigrants. Another argument of their propaganda was that living conditions in Moldavia (containing a large Jewish population) were much inferior to those of Wallachia (with a relatively small Jewish population), and the presence or absence of Jews was denounced as the only reason for the difference in these economic and social conditions, while the prepotent acts of the boyars against the population of Moldavia were entirely overlooked.

[2] On the reaction of the great powers, see Joseph Meisl, *Die Durchführung des Artikels 44 des Berliner Vertrags in Rumänien und die europäische Diplomatie*, 1925.

[3] On the attitude of the Rumanian press, see *Österreichische Wochenschrift*, 1900, no. 40, p. 714.

[4] On the law on the liquor traffic, see Sincerus, p. 19 ff.; that on peddling, ibid., p. 13 ff.

[5] U. S. Immigration Commissioner Robert Watchorn, quoted in *American Hebrew*, LVII, 1900, Oct. 19, pp. 647 f., 680 ff. He summarized his experience in the statement that immigrant Rumanian Jews "will be desirable accessions." Ibid., 645 ff., 679 f. D. Blaustein (infra, p. 430) summarized his views in his *Memoirs*, arranged by Miriam Blaustein, 1913, pp. 68 ff., 72 ff.

[6] On the curb on Jewish physicians and patients, see Sincerus, p. 100; *AJYB*, III, 71 ff.

[7] On the educational policy, see Sincerus, 119 ff.; Lazare, 48 ff. On the assistance granted by the *Alliance* and the ICA, see Leven, II, 386 ff.; ibid., 391, a list of existing Jewish schools.

[8] The artisans bill, promulgated March 16, 1902, in *AJYB*, IV, 199; cf. Lazare, p. 63 ff. When, in July 1902, a Congress "Pro Armenia" met at Brussels, an anonymous pamphlet, *Die Judenfrage in Rumänien: Eine Actensammlung*, was forwarded to Mme. Bertha von Suttner, the famous pacifist. The author, L. Ysaye, pointed out that the situation of Rumanian Jews was even more miserable than that of the Armenians. A number of authentic documents and a history of Rumanian Jews by Saniel Marcus corroborated that statement.

[9] The constitution of the *Alianta Antisemitica Universala* of 1895, ibid., and in Lazare, p. 80 ff. *Österreichische Wochenschrift*, 1900, no. 18, p. 329 f., proved that the *Alianta* had its headquarters in the Ministry of Cult and Instruction and maintained permanent connection with all antisemitic federations of foreign countries. The members were put under oath to preserve absolute secrecy about all projects and actions as well as the names of the members of the *Alianta*. Its outspoken aim was to make the life of the Jews miserable and to compel them to leave the country.

[10] The protest of Lord Salisbury (1885) and the reprisals against the Jews, in Lazare, p. 67.

[11] The *Association générale des Juifs indigènes*, founded in 1889 under the leadership of Adolf Stern, was dissolved in 1893. Its crime consisted in having depicted the situation of the Jews in a Memorandum addressed to the King, the Cabinet and the Parliament; cf. Lazare, p. 83 f.

[12] The immigration to U. S. A., in S. Joseph, p. 105 ff.

[13] The Jewish weeklies of the period, especially those of Vienna, are full of details about the terrible situation in Rumania and the desperate flight of the Jews. These reports were accompanied by a number of monographs about the Jewish situation in that country. "The

flight from the Modern Egypt" became a topic of the New York daily press too. Extracts from these discussions, in the *American Hebrew*, LXII, 1900, Oct. 5, p. 592 ff. See also Cowen, *Memories*, p. 254 ff.

[14] See Leven, II, 438, whose statements are based on authentic reports. Ibid., 441 f., on the Conference of Paris.

[15] Lord Rothschild's intervention, in L. Wolf, *Notes*, p. 36 f.; that of Jacob Schiff and other American Jewish leaders, in *PAJHS*, XXIV, 81 ff.; 108 ff.

[16] King Carol's attitude is referred to in Adler, *Correspondence*, p. 61.

[17] The famous Note of Secretary of State John Hay appeared in *Foreign Relations of the U. S.* (*1902*), p. 910 ff. and was frequently reprinted.

[18] The fate of the Note, in L. Wolf, *Notes*, p. 37 f.; *Foreign Relations* (*1903*), p. 702 ff.; 1904, p. 706.

[19] The duplicity of Prime Minister Sturdza is evident from Adler, *Correspondence*, p. 70.

[20] On the agrarian crisis of 1907, see *Encycl. Brit.*, s. v. "Roumania;" Leven, II, 443. H. Kraus, *Reminiscenses*, 115 ff. The immigration to U. S. A., in Joseph, l. c., p. 76. For the Memorandum of the Joint Foreign Committee of British Jews to the Secretary of State for Foreign Affairs, in November 1908, see *PAJHS*, XXIV, 137 ff., Kraus, l. c., 198 ff.

[21] The abolition of the oath *more Judaico*, *UJE*, VIII, 218, s. v. "Niemirower."

[22] On Greece, see *UJE*, V, 92.

[23] On Rumania, L. Wolf, *Notes*, pp. 45–54 and *PAJHS*, XXIV, 83 ff.

[24] On Italy and Tripoli, *AJYB*, XVI, 253.

[25] On Bukovina, see Dubnow, X, 422 f.; *UJE*, II, 574.

[26] On Birnbaum, ibid., 369 f.

[27] On Galicia, see Leven, II, 368–373; Dubnow, X, 418 ff. and the literature listed p. 561; cf. especially M. Rosenfeld, *Die polnische Judenfrage*, 1918. Cf. Bertha Pappenheim's writings on her travels in Galicia, in *UJE*, VIII, 386.

[28] Immigration to U. S. A., in Joseph, p. 111.

[29] The elections and the Jewish Club, see Dubnow, X, 419 ff.

[30] The economic boycott, ibid., 424 f.; Rosenfeld, p. 92 ff.

[31] Dubnow, X, 506–514.

[32] On the character of Nicholas II there is but one opinion among historians of Russia. Intimate glimpses at his personality are to be found in Count Sergei Witte's *Memoirs*, English translation by Avram Yarmolinsky, 1922. Cf. Vernadsky, p. 167 f.; Pares, p. 403 f.

[33] About the end of XIXth century solid statistical investigations of the reality of Jewish life in Russia were started. The *Comité Provisoire en vue de la formation d'une société pour le travail agricole et professionel parmi les juifs* of 1887 gathered valuable though not complete material. The most comprehensive studies were made by Ivan S. Bloch (1836–1901) who won world-wide fame as one of the outstanding exponents

of pacifism. After extended studies he published, *Le bienêtre matériel et moral des populations résidant dans la zone juive et en dehors de cette zone: Données et enquêtes sur la question juive*, 5 vols., 1901. Unfortunately all but 25 copies of this monumental work were destroyed by a fire, but one of Bloch's associates, A. P. Subbotine, published an extract of it, *La Question Juive*, 1903, in Russian. The ICA made independent investigations and published them under the title, *Recueil des Matériaux sur la situation économique des Israélites en Russie*, 2 vols., 1906, and drew interesting conclusions from the results.

[34] On the beginnings of the Socialist Movement among Jews in Russia and Poland see the literature listed in Baron, III, 161, and *UJE*, II, 589, above all A. Tartakower, *Toledot tenuat ha-obedim ha-yehudim*, 3 vols., 1929-1931.

[35] Recently Simcha Lew published (in Yiddish) *Perakim idishe geshichte* (Chapters in Jewish History: Social and National Movement among the Jews of Poland and Russia during the years 1897-1914). So far only the first part covering the years 1897-1903 was published, 1941. Part of his material, mostly coming from archives in Russian Poland, sheds light on the antagonism between Zionists and Socialists. E. Tcherikower et al., *Di jidishe sotsialistishe Bavegung bis tsum Grindung fun Bund*, vols. I-III.

[36] For the national trend of Jewish literature, see Dubnow, *Russia*, III, 58 ff.; *History*, X, § 39; J. Klausner, *Yotzrim u-bonim*, 3 vols., 1927 ff.; M. Kleinmann, *Demujot we-komot*, n. d.; F. Lachower, *Toledot ha-sifrut ha-ibrit ha-hadasha*, vol. IV.

[37] The attitude of candy and whip operated by the Russian police towards the Labor Movement was also adopted in respect to the Jewish Labor Movement: cf. A. N. Buchbinder's books on the subject in Russian and Yiddish and Lew, p. 44.

[38] The genesis of the *Protocols* was disclosed in Herman Bernstein, *The Truth about 'The Protocols of Zion'*, 1935, and John S. Curtiss, *An Appraisal of the Protocols of Zion*, 1942. They were fabricated outside Russia between 1896 and 1900 by General Rachkovsky, the Russian police chief in Paris (Bernstein, p. 37 ff.; Curtiss, pp. 70, 76, 80). According to one view, quoted by Curtiss, p. 77, the *Protocols* had been forged still earlier. They came into the hands of the strange saint Sergei Nilus, who was convinced that he could redeem the world by intrigues. In order to impress the Czarina he published in 1901 a pamphlet, *The Great in the Little — the Coming of Anti-Christ and the Rule of Satan on Earth* (in Russian).

[39] On the Czar's prejudice, see a letter to his mother, quoted in *Secret Letters of the Last Tsar*, ed. by Edw. J. Bing, 1938, p. 15; his use of the term *Zhydie*, in Witte, p. 189.

[40] Count Witte, who was Plehve's archenemy, called him the organizer of the pogrom of Kishinev (*Memoirs*, 262, 380), but there is no evidence of his immediate guilt. The "strictly confidential order" to the Governor of Bessarabia of March 25 (April 6) about a forth-

coming pogrom, published in *The Times* of London, England, was denied by Plehve, but later supported by *The Times*. His responsibility lies in having tolerated the press campaign against the Jews, especially the outrageous propaganda of Krushevan's *Bessarabetz*, in having despatched to Kishinev Baron v. Levendal who by unanimous consent was considered the pogrom-monger, and in not having mobilized the local garrison which, as later became manifest, was able to quell the uprising in a very short time.

[41] Leo Tolstoi in W. C. Stiles, *Out of Kishinev*, p. 274 f.; Dubnow, *Russia*, III, 76.

[42] Details about the massacre of Kishinev, in *Die Judenpogrome in Russland*, II, 6–24. The whole atmosphere and the failures of the authorities are analyzed in *Memoirs of a Russian Governor: Serge Dimitrovich Urussov*, transl. by Herman Rosenthal, 1908, pp. 79 ff., 47 ff. Cf. also Michael Davitt, *Within the Pale*, 1903, pp. 91 ff.

[43] *Be-'ir ha-haregah*, transl. by Maurice Samuel, p. 69.

[44] Gorki, in *Out of Kishinev*, p. 276 ff.

[45] Cf. ibid., p. 198.

[46] One of the first eyewitnesses to report to Europe was Siegmund Bergel, *Kischinev und die Lage der Juden in Russland*, 1903.

[47] On the trial, see *JE*, VII, 513 f.; Urussov, p. 74 ff.; *Judenpogrome*, II, 24–37.

[48] On the attitude of the population of the U. S. A., in Cyrus Adler, *The Voice of America on Kishineff*, (the author called it "a little volume ... very dull, which had a good effect;" cf. A. A. Neuman, *Adler*, p. 90).

[49] Ibid., pp. 468–481.

[50] The number of victims and the amount of damage is cited according to *Out of Kishinev*, p. 23 f.; *Judenpogrome*, I, 108 f., 178.

[51] Ibid., I, 383 ff.; Dubnow, *Russia*, III, 80, 90. Zangwill's raillery at the numerous factions within the organization, in his *Ghetto Comedies*.

[52] On the pogrom of Homel, see *Judenpogrome*, II, 37 ff.; Dubnow, l. c., III, 87 ff.; 101 ff.

[53] On Plehve's attitude toward Herzl, see the latter's *Tagebücher*, III, 460 ff.; supra, p. 292. On the commission to discuss the situation of the Jews, see Urussov, pp. 142 ff., 171 ff. To counteract Plehve's efforts, Krushevan published in his paper, *Znamia*, the first Russian translation of the *Protocols of the Elders of Zion* (Curtiss, p. 20 f.; *UJE*, IV, 52), but at the moment the publication had no effect.

[54] On Trepoff, see Witte, *Memoirs*, p. 327 ff.

[55] On Plehve's conception of the meaning of the Russo-Japanese War, ibid., p. 250; Urussov, p. 177.

[56] On Jews in this war, see *Reshumot*, II, 159; Dubnow, l. c., III, 94 ff. For the curb on further pogroms, see Dubnow, l. c., 98; Urussov, l. c.

[57] The Jewish petitions, in Dubnow, p. 108 ff.; Witte, p. 381 f.

[58] Ibid., p. 38 ff.

[59] On Zhitomir, see *Judenpogrome*, II, 44 ff.; on Bialystok, ibid., 61 ff.; Dubnow, l. c., 115 ff.

[60] On the Russian Revolution of 1905, see Witte, p. 253 ff. (the quotation is from p. 266 f.); Kornylov, p. 276 ff., 298 ff.; Vernadsky, p. 177 ff.

[61] The discussions whether Jews shall be admitted to the *Duma*, in Dubnow, III, 122.

[62] The pogroms of the counter-revolution, in *Sources for the History of the Russian Counter-Revolution*, I, 1908; *Judenpogrome*, II, 81–536.

[63] Dubnow, III, 124 ff. The quotation is from Sémènoff, *The Russian Government and the Massacres*, 1908, p. 152 ff.

[64] On Odessa, see *Judenpogrome*, I, 199; II, 130.

[65] The disclosure of the pogrom organization within the administration was made by Prince Urussov in his memorable speech in the first *Duma*; see Sémènoff, p. 156. The facts were supported by Witte in his *Memoirs*, pp. 191, 327, 331, 273.

[66] The memorandum of Count Lambsdorf, in L. Wolf, *Notes*, p. 57 ff. It is no mere chance that the year 1905 saw a revised and enlarged edition of S. Nilus, *The Great in the Little*, which for the first time included the *Protocols* under the special title, *Anti-Christ as a Near Political Possibility (the Protocols of the Sessions of the Zionist Sages. 1902–03)*. Cf. facsimile of the two title pages in the Appendix to Bernstein, *Truth*, and *UJE*, IV, 51. According to one of his versions of the origin of the *Protocols* — in the different editions he has several and some are contradictory — the manuscript had been delivered to him in 1901! See also Curtiss, p. 22. It is significant that the book was printed in Tsarskoe Selo, the winter residence of the Czar, in the printing office of the government. The copy presented to His Majesty is now in the possession of the Library of Congress in Washington, D.C. In 1906 George V. Butmi published a book, *Enemies of the Human Race*, and added "Protocols taken out of the secret depository of the main Office of Zion. Extracts from ancient and modern Protocols of the Sages of Zion of the Universal Organization of Free Masons"!! Butmi, who has his own story about the origin of his manuscript (Curtiss, p. 16 ff.), emphasized that his sages had nothing to do with the Zionist Organization. The book is called "third edition," but no previous edition is known; cf. Curtiss, p. 107; *UJE*, IV, 54.

[67] Extracts from the printed Minutes of the first *Duma* in Sémènoff, l. c. The report on the pogrom of Bialystok, 1906, ibid., pp. 216–223.

[68] The Black Hundreds, in Witte, p. 342; Kornylov, p. 312 ff.; Vernadsky, p. 179 ff.

[69] Stolypin's attempt to mitigate the anti-Jewish legislation, in Witte, p. 383 f.; Dubnow, l. c., p. 141; Leven, I, 470.

[70] The third *Duma*, in Dubnow, l. c., p. 153 ff.; Kornylov, p. 329.

[71] The Beilis Case (*UJE*, II, 139 ff.), intended as the climax of

the administration's anti-Jewish campaign, obtained world-wide notoriety. A stenographic report (in Russian), 2 vols., 1913, reproduced the proceedings of the court. On the machinations in preparing the trial we are informed by one of Beilis' counsel, Arnold D. Margolin, in his *The Jews of Eastern Europe*, 1926, pp. 155-247, and by one who had access to the Russian archives, A. B. Tager, *The Decay of Czarism: The Beiliss Trial*, 1935.

[72] On Jews in Poland, see Beatrice C. Baskerville, *The Polish Jew*, 1906; Dubnow, III, 166 ff.; Witte, p. 262, observed that, as a consequence of the anti-Jewish riots in Russia, a great many Jewish artisans and workmen emigrated to Poland and that they infected that country with the revolutionary spirit. That this is not quite true is evident from the fact that the Polish Socialist Party existed long before this immigration of Jews. Roman Dmowski, leader of the National Democrats, in a conversation with Louis Marshall (in 1918), confessed very bluntly the reasons why he had propagated the anti-Jewish boycott since 1908, cf. *Memorials submitted to President Wilson concerning the Status of the Jews of Eastern Europe . . . by American Jewish Congress*, 1919, p. 17 ff.

[73] A plastic picture of the energetic Jewish life in Russia and Poland shortly before the World War was given by Scholem Asch in his *The Three Cities*. The first quotation is from this book; the verses of Frug are given as translated by Maurice Samuel in E. Fleg, *Anthology*, p. 338. The cultural efforts, in Dubnow, *Russia*, III, and in the article "Yeshiva" of *UJE*, X.

CHAPTER II

THE JEWS OF WESTERN EUROPE BEFORE THE FIRST WORLD WAR

[1] On the economic situation, see W. Sombart, *Der moderne Kapitalismus*; Baron, II, 273; III, 99. Some figures about the Jews' share in taxation, in W. Sombart, *Die Juden und das Wirtschaftsleben*, p. 218 ff. Cf. Philippson, II, 255 ff. and *UJE*, IV, 558 ff. with numerous details.

[2] J. Segall, *Die beruflichen und sozialen Verhältnisse der Juden in Deutschland*, 1912.

[3] *Baronin Cohn Oppenheim Stiftung*, see *Jü Le*, I, 736.

[4] The volume *Frankfort* of the Jewish Communities Series unfortunately contains nothing about the communal achievements around 1900. Some hints are to be found in the articles of the encyclopedias on the persons mentioned; on Bertha Pappenheim, see also Rebekah Kohut, *My Portion*, pp. 272-283.

[5] The Jewish Community of Berlin published regular reports on its administration, but these contain dry figures and nothing about the life of the community. From 1911 on it published the monthly *Jüdisches Gemeindeblatt*, which about 20 years later was transformed into a

weekly. Some of the outstanding businessmen like Wilhelm Hertz, Ludwig Max Goldberger, Aron Hirsch, Berthold Israel, Oskar Tietz; famous physicians like Hermann Senator, Adolf Baginsky, Leopold Landau; lawyers like Hermann Staub, Eugen Fuchs, Hermann Veit Simon; scientists like Adolf Pinner; philologists like Ludwig Geiger, belonged at one time or the other to the administration of the community.

[6] Cf. the very informative *Mitteilungen des Deutsch-Israelitischen Gemeindebunds* and *EJ*, V, 966 ff.

[7] The *Hilfsverein* (*UJE*, V, 360) published annual reports. It is significant that in N. Leven's *Cinquante ans d'histoire* the name of the *Hilfsverein* is not mentioned even where its work could not be passed over. On Paul Nathan (*UJE*, VIII, 110), see Ernst Feder, *Paul Nathan: Ein Lebensbild*, 1928.

[8] See *UJE*, V, 17 f.

[9] On Timendorfer, see *Jü Le*, V, 951.

[10] The resolution of the American Jewish Committee, in *AJYB*, XI, 246 f.

[11] See *UJE*, VIII, 487 f.

[12] On the genesis of the *Verband der deutschen Juden*, see Philippson (who was one of the initiators), II, 64 f.; on its activities, see the biennial reports and its other publications, *Jü Le*, V, 1166. Of *Die Lehren des Judentums*, the first volume was published in English translation by A. H. Koller, under the title *Foundations of Jewish Ethics*, 1929.

[13] For the rich literature on Bergson, see *UJE*, II, 201 ff. and in the eulogies at his death.

[14] On Hermann Cohen, ibid., III, 244 f., and recently H. Slonimsky in *Historia Judaica*, IV, 81 ff.; D. Gawronsky in *Bitzaron*, II, 18 ff.; III, 30 ff. Cf. Jacob B. Agus, *Modern Philosophies of Judaism*, N. Y., 1941, pp. 57–128.

[15] On the *Gesellschaft*, see the annual reports published separately and later on in the *Monatsschrift*. Cf. the present writer's article in *MGWJ*, LXXII, 1928, p. 1 ff.

[16] The application of German university professors in connection with the foundation of the University of Frankfort in *Christliche Welt*, 1914.

[17] On France, see Philippson, II, 180; *UJE*, IV, 379, 381.

[18] On Italy, see ibid., V, 632.

[19] Margulies, ibid., VII, 356.

[20] Falashas, ibid., I, 271; IV, 234.

[21] On the *Freie Vereinigung*, see *Jü Le*, II, 785; *EJ*, VI, 1159; Philippson, II, 175 ff.

[22] On *Liberales Judentum*, see D. Philipson, *Reform Movement*, p. 393 ff.; C. Seligmann, *Geschichte der Reformbewegung von Mendelssohn bis zur Gegenwart*, 1929; *Jü Le*, V, 1175 ff. On the *Richtlinien*, ibid., IV, 1452 f.

[23] *Agudat Yisrael*, see *UJE*, I, 128.

[24] They are presented in the controversy between Martin Buber and Hermann Cohen in the later's *Jüdische Schriften*, II. The tension went so far that at the beginning of the World War a German propagandist sent to New York City, who happened to be a Zionist, made efforts to alarm American Jewry against the *Hilfsverein* and its relief work: see Bogen, *Born a Jew*, p. 89 f.

[25] To obtain a clear insight into the situation, cf. the polemic of Hermann Cohen against Professors Noeldeke and Schmoller, in his *Jüdische Schriften*, vol. II; Werner Sombart, *Die Zukunft der Juden*, 1912, and the inquiry, *Judentaufen*, 1911. Cf. also Cohen's polemic against Martin Buber, ibid., and the latter's replies quoted in the notes.

[26] F. A. Theilhaber, *Der Untergang der deutschen Juden*, 1911; 2d ed., 1921.

Chapter III

THE JEWS OF AMERICA AT THE BEGINNING OF THE TWENTIETH CENTURY

[1] On Argentina, see Leven, II, 485–497 (on the basis of ICA reports); *50 Años de Colonizacion Judia en la Argentina*, 1939; *UJE*, I, 470 f.; II, 580 ff.; III, 300 ff. On Brazil, ibid., II, 513, III, 302.

[2] On the new numbering of Jewish immigration, see *Immigration Commissioners' Reports*, XLI, pp. 178 f., 265–293; S. Wolf, *Presidents*, pp. 238–264. On the actual immigration, Masserman and Baker, p. 296 f.

[3] On the boom of American industry, see L. M. Goldberger, *Das Land der unbegrenzten Möglichkeiten*, 1901.

[4] On the mentality of the newcomers, see, e. g., P. Cowen, *Memories*, p. 289 ff.; Rebekah Kohut, *As I Know Them*, 1928, pp. 1–49; *An Eastside Epic: The Life and Work of Meyer London*, by Harry Rogoff, 1930. A painful, realistic description of New York's ghetto is Michael Gold's *Jews without Money*, 1930, but much more cheerful are the memories of Eddie Cantor, *My Life Is in Your Hands*, 1928; Judge Jonah J. Goldstein in *New York Times*, May 5, 1941.

[5] D. Blaustein (*UJE*, II, 390) in *Memorial Volume*, ed. by Miriam Blaustein, 1913.

[6] Cf. Franz Boas, *Changes in Bodily Form of Descendants of Immigrants*, 1911.

[7] The quotation is from *AJYB*, XXI, 149.

[8] Cf. G. Cohen, *The Jews in the Making of America*, 1925.

[9] The quotation is from "The 250th Anniversary of the Settlement of Jews in the U. S." in *PAJHS*, XIV (also separately), p. 19. The list of Jewish members of Congress, of Governors, etc., in each volume of *AJYB*.

[10] On juvenile delinquency, ibid. On the charges by Commissioner Bingham, see Ernst K. Coulter in *Outlook and Independent*, Aug. 12, 1931.

[11] The reaction on the Kishinev massacres, in L. Lipsky, *Selected Works*, I: "Thirty Years of American Zionism," 1927, p. 34 ff.; Oscar S. Straus, *Under Four Administrations*, p. 170 ff.; Cyrus Adler, supra, p. 733. — Negotiations with Count Witte in his *I Have Considered the Days*, p. 163; A. Kraus, *Reminiscences*, p. 157 ff.; C. Adler, *Schiff*, 128 ff.

[12] The beginnings of the American Jewish Committee, by no means an easy birth, in Cyrus Adler, *Days*, p. 246; A. A. Neuman, *Adler*, p. 94 f.; the Constitution in *AJYB*, X (1908–9), 238 ff. From that volume on the *AJYB* published the annual reports of the Committee.

[13] The Memoranda of Mayer Sulzberger and Louis Marshall on the question of immigration are remarkable legal studies of far-reaching scientific and moral value beyond the Jewish question.

[14] On the question of the Russian passports see the comprehensive article in *AJYB*, XIII, 19 ff.; XIV, 196 ff. (The difficulties with the Russian government had started as early as 1881, see Adler, *Correspondence*, p. 86 ff.) See also id., *Days*, p. 293; S. Wolf, *Presidents*, pp. 258 ff., 298–319; A. Kraus, *Reminiscences*, p. 190 ff.; L. Wolf, *Notes*, p. 75 ff.

[15] Jacob H. Schiff's letter to President Taft, in C. Adler, *Schiff*, II, 147 ff.

[16] The IOBB awarded President Taft a golden medal: see Kraus, l. c., p. 193 ff.; Wolf, *Presidents*, p. 321 ff.

[17] U. S. Ambassador Henry White's initiative at the Algeciras Conference, in L. Wolf, *Notes*, 98 f. The previous intervention of Jacob H. Schiff, in Adler, *Schiff*, II, 156 ff.

[18] On the *Kehillah*, cf. *The Jewish Communal Register of N. Y. C., 1917–18*, p. 59 ff. which contains the Constitution; p. 45 ff., a brief history of the *Kehillah* written by Harry Sackler.

[19] S. Benderly (*UJE*, II, 164) contributed an article on "Educational Agencies," pp. 347–466. On the Bureau of Jewish Education, see *UJE*, III, 639.

[20] See Schechter's *Seminary Addresses and Other Papers*, 1915.

[21] K. Kohler's *Studies, Addresses and Personal Papers*, ed. by H. G. Enelow, 1931.

[22] Cf. the Free Synagogue's *Bulletins*, published since 1907; on S. S. Wise, see *UJE*, VIII, 193.

[23] Schechter's dissatisfaction, in Bentwich, p. 191 ff.

[24] The organization of the United Synagogue, ibid., p. 209; A. A. Neuman, l. c., 164 ff. Schechter died Nov. 20, 1915. Remarkable among the tributes to his personality, because coming from a religious opponent, is that of D. Philipson, l. c., 258 ff.

[25] The quotation is from N. Bentwich, *Schechter*, p. 209 f.

[26] On the beginnings of Dropsie College, see C. Adler, *Days*, pp. 273–282; A. A. Neuman, *Adler*, pp. 102–115.

[27] Schiff's sponsorship of Jewish letters, in Adler, *Schiff*, II, 62 ff.

[28] On the difficulties connected with organizing the translation of the Bible, see Adler, l. c., 287 ff., A. A. Neuman, l. c., 152 ff. and D. Philipson, *Life*, 195 ff.; *AJYB*, XLII, 693 ff.

[29] Adler, *Schiff*, l. c., ibid.

[30] On centrifugal trends among American Jews, see O. I. Janowsky, ed., *The American Jew*, N. Y., 1942, especially the chapters "Historical Background" and "Jewish Education." Cf. M. M. Kaplan, *Judaism as a Civilization*, N. Y., 1934, pp. 19–46.

[31] On the labor movement, see H. Burgin, *Di Geshichte fun der yidisher arbeter-bavegung in Amerika*, 1915; the biography of Meyer London, and the book by E. Tcherikower quoted above.

[32] Cf. Joel Seidman, *The Needle Trades*, 1942, and the literature listed in *UJE*, VIII, 144; on Hillman, ibid., V, 368 f.

[33] Yiddish as a cultural factor, *UJE*, VIII, 188; VII, 129; *AJYB*, XXVI, 165 ff.

BOOK FIVE

THE FIRST WORLD WAR AND ITS CONSEQUENCES

Chapter I

THE WORLD WAR

[1] Nobody can describe the horrors of the World War more powerfully than David Lloyd George did at the beginning of his *War Memoirs*. The horrors were, of course, far surpassed by those of the Second World War; this war, however, is but the sequel of the first one. The catastrophic impression on the minds of the younger generation was evident throughout the post-war literary production and found its climax in the barbaric pronunciamentos of all types of Fascism.

[2] How Jews were affected by the war is to be seen in the brief historic sketch of A. G. Duker, in *CJR*, II, 5, p. 6 ff. See also J. Kreppel, *Die Juden der Gegenwart*, and the current reports in *AJYB*, XVII–XXI.

[3] The figures of Jewish participation in the war effort are based on estimates: cf. *Jü Le*, V, 1379 ff.; Duker, l. c., p. 8 f. In the trial of S. Schwartzbard (p. 498), H. Sliosberg stated on the witness stand that more than 500,000 Jews served in the Russian army and that 70,000 were killed: cf. H. Torrès, *Le procès des Pogromes*, 1928, p. 208.

[4] Long but incomplete lists of decorations and promotions were published in *AJYB*. For a list of outstanding Jewish generals, also incomplete, see J. Kliersfeld, *Sare Zaba mi-Yisrael* ("Jewish Officers"), 1941.

[5] In Russia, while the officers who were in touch with Jewish soldiers recognized their heroism and proposed many of them for decoration, the Grand Dukes and the leading generals indulged in the old prejudices against Jews. Outstanding in this respect was General Yanushkevich, Chief of the General Staff, who declared all measures practiced against Jews "too mild" (Florinsky, *The End of the Russian Empire*, 1931, p. 71). When bridges were blasted he had but one explanation, namely, that the Jews were responsible (Lloyd George, *War Memoirs*, I, 448). No wonder that a strategist haunted by this bogey suffered defeat after defeat; his private letters reveal that as early as 1915 he had scruples about his personal insufficiency (Florinsky, p. 211). The antisemitic and anti-British sentiments were shared by the Petrograd police, too (ibid., p. 149 f.). The Council of Ministers repeatedly protested against the absurd accusations and the brutal deportations of the Jewish population and declared this policy one of the causes of the complete military defeat of Russia (p. 213 f.). See also Duker, p. 10 f. The enforcement of the anti-Jewish laws, in *AJYB*, passim; as late as the winter of 1916–17 discussions about the Jews' right of settlement took place.

[6] The statement in the text is based on personal information. The growing antisemitism of the home warriors in the armchairs is a fact attested by all observers.

[7] On the *Judenzählung*, see *Jü Le*, II, 460 f., and the monthly, *Im deutschen Reich*, 1916–17; Duker, p. 20 f.

[8] Ibid., p. 22, on discrimination in England; and *AJYB*, XXI, 148 ff., on "American Jews in the World War;" ibid., 31 ff., on the Jews of France in the Great War; 98 ff., on British Jewry.

[9] J. H. Patterson (*UJE*, VIII, 414 f.), *With the Zionists before Gallipoli*, 1916.

[10] Id., *With the Judaeans in the Palestine Campaign*, 1922; W. Jabotinsky, *The Saga of the Jewish Legion*; *UJE*, VI, 133 f.; ibid., VI, 2 ff., on Jabotinsky and the literature listed there. Cf. *AJYB*, XXI, 120 ff.

[11] Duker, p. 9, estimates the number of Jews killed at 170,825, i e., approximately 2% of the total killed. Of details we know Sliosberg's estimate of 70,000 killed in the Russian army. Hungary's war victims included 10,000 Jews (cf. L. Venetianer, *Magyar szidoság története*, 1922). 12,000 Jews killed in the German army are listed in the *Krieger Gedenkbuch*, published by the *Reichsbund jüdischer Frontsoldaten*; see J. R. Marcus, *The Rise and Destiny of the German Jews*, 1934, p. 80.

[12] On Rabbi Bloch, see *UJE*, II, 395.

[13] The huge number of dead and missing married men of early age created the serious problem of the "Agunah:" see *UJE*, I, 132, and L. M. Epstein, *The Solution of the Agunah Problem* (Hebrew), 1940.

[14] The destinies of Palestine during the War, in "Ambassador [Henry] Morgenthau's Story," 1918, in the reports of the American Jewish Committee, in *AJYB*, XVII ff.; Duker, p. 18 f.; A. S. Yahuda, in *The Jewish Forum*, March 1941.

[15] Galicia and Bukovina, in Duker, p. 13 f.

[16] The behavior of the Poles was so shocking that the two Grand Old Men of Europe who sponsored the idea of a free independent Poland, Georg Brandes of Copenhagen and Luigi Luzzatti of Rome, felt compelled publicly to protest against their misuse of liberty. The American Jewish Committee on the basis of authentic material prepared a booklet, *The Jews in the Eastern War Zone*, and presented the first copy of it, with a petition to intercede, to Pope Benedict XV: cf. *CJR*, IV, 127 ff.

[17] Ludendorff's Manifesto was reprinted in *Reshumot*, VI, 459 ff.; a propaganda periodical, *Kol Mevaser*, is mentioned by Duker, p. 15.

[18] The *Komitee für den Osten* (*Jü Le*, I, 1433 f.; *EJ*, V, 636 f.) published its own monthly, *Neue jüdische Monatshefte* (1916-20), for the discussion of the "Jewish Question." Among the contributors were Hermann Cohen, Franz Oppenheimer, Eugen Fuchs. In 1916 Martin Buber started his monthly, *Der Jude*, as a representative organ for the discussion of the Jewish question from the national point of view.

[19] Intermediaries of high efficiency were the Jewish Chaplains of the German Army; some of them published their experiences. Hermann Struck and Arnold Zweig, *Das Ostjüdische Antlitz*, appeared in 1920. Gronemann's *Hawdoloh und Zapfenstreich*, 1927; cf. Arnold Zweig's anti-militaristic novel *Der Streit um den Sergeanten Grischa*, 1927, (in English translation, *The Case of Sergeant Grischa*).

[20] On the misery caused by the complete evacuation of Poland, see Pares, *History*, p. 459, and Duker, p. 15 f. On Haas, see *Jü Le*, II, 1309; Kohn, ibid., III, 755.

[21] On the attitude of American Jews at the beginning of the war, see Lipsky, l. c., p. 43.

[22] On the relief work in the United States, see Duker, p. 25 f.

[23] In *UJE*, VI, 170 ff.; Joseph C. Hyman offers a summary in his *Twenty-Five Years of American Aid to Jews Overseas: A Record of the JDC*, 1939. Cf. Boris D. Bogen, *Born a Jew*, 1930.

[24] On the work for Palestine, see *AJYB*, ibid., 219 f.; Lipsky, p. 47 ff.

[25] H. Sliosberg (supra p. 739) stated that round 26,000,000 rubles for relief were distributed by him among 223,000 people.

[26] On relief in Lithuania and Poland, see Duker, p. 23 f. "Magnes outdid himself;" this was the impression telegraphed by J. H. Schiff to Julius Rosenwald in gratification over the response: cf. Adler, *Schiff*, II, 282.

[27] On the origin of the Jewish Welfare Board (*UJE*, VI, 147), see Adler, *Days*, p. 301 ff.; Neuman, *Adler*, pp. 147 ff., 183 f.

[28] On the conditions which led to the Russian revolution of 1917, see among others, D. Lloyd George, *War Memoirs*, II, 659; III, 1608. Sir Bernard Pares, a lifelong student of Russia who lived there during the war, wrote a monograph about the fall of the Russian dynasty. In his *History*, p. 471, he summarized his opinion in the words: "The

dynasty fell of its own insufficiency, and the immediate occasion of its fall was the rule of the Empress and Rasputin."

[29] The laws on personal freedom in the new Russian Constitution, in *AJYB*, XIX, p. 306; Duker, p. 17 f.

[30] The chaos in Russia and the rise of Bolshevism, in Pares, p. 472 ff.; Vernadsky, p. 238 ff.; *The Bolshevik Revolution 1917–1918: Documents and Materials*, by James Bunyan and H. H. Fisher, 1934; William Henry Chamberlain, *The Russian Revolution 1917–1921*, I, 1935.

[31] On the conditions in the Ukraine, see Abraham Heller, *Die Lage der Juden in Russland von der Märzrevolution 1917 bis zur Gegenwart*, 1935. Only a few copies of this book are in circulation; the bulk of the edition was confiscated by the Gestapo.

[32] A. J. Balfour met Weizmann as early as 1906, and the Zionist idea as explained by the latter appealed to him. When Weizmann called on him almost ten years later and offered concrete suggestions, he met with "long-standing sympathy." Weizmann had been introduced to D. Lloyd George, too, but the thinking of this statesman then centered around ammunition and he remembered Weizmann only after the chemist had proved useful to the British war effort (*Peace Reminiscences*, II, 584 ff.). His invention was incidental, but it offered Weizmann the opportunity to stay in London and to share in the discussions with the circles around Sir Herbert Samuel and Sir Mark Sykes. Furthermore, he did his work under the auspices of the Admiralty of which Balfour was the First Lord at the time, to be appointed Chief Secretary of the Foreign Office in 1916. Mrs. Blanche E. C. Dugdale (*Arthur James Balfour*, I, 433; II, 213–34) emphasizes that the Balfour Declaration was neither a recompense for Weizmann's services nor a speculation on the favor of the Jewish socialist masses or the capitalists, that indeed both of these groups opposed this policy. Weizmann who, in *UJE*, II, 45 f., gave his own very brief tale, pointed out that the British War Cabinet had also to cope with the opposition of the military circles.

[33] The inquiry in Petrograd, in L. Stein, *Zionism*, 1925, p. 138 ff.; 2d ed., p. 111 ff.

[34] On the events in U. S. A., see Lipsky, l. c., p. 44 ff.

[35] On Justice Brandeis, see *UJE*, II, 495 ff.; the evaluation of his Jewish activities, in Jacob de Haas, *Louis Dembitz Brandeis*, 1929.

[36] The quotation is in Sokolow, II, 56; see ibid., p. 58 ff., on the objection of British Jews.

[37] A facsimile of the Balfour Declaration, in *UJE*, II, 47.

[38] The declaration of the Central Powers, in *Neue Jüdische Monatshefte*, January 1918, II, 147; ibid., 435 ff. is a statement in favor of the Jews in Lithuania.

[39] On Lord Allenby's campaign, cf. *AJYB*, XXI, 134 ff.

[40] The curb on the Jewish Legion, in Patterson, *Judaeans*, p. 40 ff.

[41] The work of the OETA, in *RRC*, p. 153 ff. It was obvious that the military administration's lack of experience would cause many

difficulties (Sir Ronald Storrs, *Annotations*, p. 423 f.). The real meaning of the Balfour Declaration allegedly was not known to them, and resentment ran high when the Zionist Commission arrived and made the intention of the Government manifest.

[42] On this Commission, see Sokolow, II, 140 ff. That an understanding with British authorities was possible is shown by the address of Major Ormsby Gore (later Lord Hankey), ibid., p. 143 ff. Things were different with the OETA. One may rely on Sir Ronald's statement that he wanted to be absolutely fair, but his excessive apology betrays a bad conscience. His arguments are taken mostly from the later discussions of the Palestinian problem, and not from conditions prevalent in 1918. He overemphasizes what the Arabs lost when they became detached from the Ottoman Empire. Is this not the natural lot of every *Irredenta*? Did the Polish nobility, e. g., not give up by far more conspicuous positions at the courts of Vienna and Berlin? And is it really true that the Arabs were so happy under the Turkish rule? Sir Ronald mentions that their language was forbidden (p. 423), that the income of the *Waqf* had partly to be delivered to Constantinople (p. 436)! It was one of the tasks of the OETA to explain the new situation to the Arabs, and it is tragic that just the contrary was done. Most of the commanding generals were absolutely against the policy of the London Government. One may be sure that later on the British officials had plenty of difficulties with Zionist leaders of Russian extraction, but Sir Ronald projects his later experiences to the period of the Zionist Commission. Its strong man, M. D. Eder, was born and brought up in England. M. M. Ussischkin did not enter the country before the summer of 1919.

[43] The laying of the cornerstone of the Hebrew University, in Sokolow, II, 145.

Chapter II

THE END OF THE WAR: POGROMS AND TREATIES OF PEACE

[1] The universal exhaustion after the World War was such that the latter was compared to an earthquake. "The hectic reaction of the younger generation," in Vera Brittain, *Testament of Youth*.

[2] The resolutions of the German Nationalists, in *AJYB*, XIX, 244.

[3] Detailed official reports about the German request for an armistice, which Ludendorff had proposed in the summer of 1918, in Ralph Haswell Lutz, *Fall of the German Empire, 1914–1918*, 1932, II, 455 ff.; Arthur Rosenberg, *The Birth of the German Republic*, transl. by Ian F. D. Morrow, 1931, p. 233 ff. Rosenberg was a member of the Reichstag's Committee of Inquiry into the causes of German collapse in the World War and reporter for the *Dolchstoss-Frage* ("Stab in the Back").

How far from the truth Ludendorff's and his fellow Nationalists' abuses of the Jews were is proved by the fact that two prominent Jews vehemently opposed the unconditional surrender suggested by General Headquarters. Walter Rathenau published in *Vossische Zeitung*, October 7, 1918, his appeal to a *levée en masse* (Lutz, II, 464 ff.), and Max M. Warburg implored the Chancellor of the Reich to desist from dealings with the enemies and to continue the fight to the finish: (*Memoirs of Prince Max v. Baden*, English transl. II, 1357).

[4] Louis Fischer, *Men and Politics*, 1941, p. 26 ff., reports Ambassador Joffe's confession about his subversive activities.

[5] On the revolution in Germany, see Arthur Rosenberg, *History of the German Revolution*; Ernst Haase, *Hugo Haase, sein Leben und Wirken*, 1929. On Otto Landsberg, see *UJE*, VI, 529 f.; Hugo Preuss, ibid., VIII, 633.

[6] Rosa Luxemburg, ibid., VII, 243.

[7] The anti-Jewish agitation, in H. Valentin, *Anti-Semitism*, p. 108 ff. When the Versailles Treaty was being discussed in the summer of 1919, the two Jewish Reichsministers, Landsberger and Preuss, resigned from the government because they refused to sign it.

[8] On Kurt Eisner, ibid., 110 f.; *UJE*, IV, 41.

[9] On Gustav Landauer (*UJE*, VI, 526), cf. *Gustav Landauer: Ein Lebensgang in Briefen*, ed. by Martin Buber, 1929; Julius Bab, *Gustav Landauer*. The quotation is from Valentin, l. c., p. 239.

[10] On the Hungarian Soviet Republic, see *UJE*, V, 496 ff.; VI, 487; v. Kaas and v. Lazarovics, *Der Bolschewismus in Ungarn*, 1930; Huszar, *Die Proletarier-Diktatur in Ungarn*. All the discussions of this experiment have an anti-Jewish bias which is also evident in the novel of the brothers Tharaud, *Quand Israel était Roi*.

[11] On the anti-Jewish terror, see *AJYB*, XXII, XXIII. Bogen, l. c., pp. 259–64.

[12] The specific *numerus clausus* in *UJE*, VIII, 251.

[13] In the year 1926 the Union of Hungarian Jews compiled *The Jewish Minority Rights in Hungary: Report . . . . . presented to the Board of Deputies of British Jews*.

[14] Alarming news from East Galicia came first through the daily press and was later followed by similar reports from Congress Poland. Then Israel Cohen of London toured the country and published *A Report on the Pogroms in Poland*, 1919. Similar reports were printed in the U. S. A. through the American Jewish Congress. These publications deeply impressed public opinion in Great Britain and the U. S. A. As a result of the alarms the House of Commons in London appointed a committee of investigation consisting of Sir Stuart Samuel and Captain P. Wright. Their *Report on the Mission to Poland* was presented to the Parliament. Both of them, as well as the British diplomat Sir Horace Rumbold, made every effort to exculpate the Poles,

but it was impossible to conceal the horror of the facts. President Wilson was shocked when Louis Marshall and Cyrus Adler brought the terrible news to his knowledge (Adler, *Days*, p. 313 f.). Paderewski's request to establish the truth of the rumors resulted in despatching to Poland a mission of investigation; cf. "Mission of the U. S. to Poland .... Report by the Hon. Henry Morgenthau on the work of the Mission," *66th Congress, 2d. Session, docum. 177*. Morgenthau's secretary, Arthur L. Goodhart, published a book, *Poland and the Minority Races*, 1920.

[15] Most instructive is the information given by Boris Bogen, *Born a Jew*, about his experiences as relief worker in Poland. On Morgenthau's difficult position between Jews and Poles see ibid., p. 202 ff. A volume, *Gevat (Ha-Kevutzah al Shem Kedoshei Pinsk): Mekorot ve-Korot*, was dedicated to the martyrs of Pinsk, Ein Harod, 1937.

[16] On the attempts to organize pogroms in Slovakia, see Kreppel, p. 243. On Masaryk, *UJE*, VII, 393 f.; Oscar Donath, *Masaryk und das Judentum*, 1920.

[17] Of the plentiful source-material on the pogroms in the Ukraine may be mentioned: E. Tcherikower, *In der Tekufe fun Revoluzie*, I, 1924; *The Pogroms in the Ukraine under the Ukrainian Government 1917–1920: Historical Survey with documents and photos*, 1927, published by the *Comité des Délégations Juives* in French and English; E. D. Rosenthal, *Megillat ha-tebah*, recording all the communities affected by the pogroms; A. Heller, op. cit.; William Henry Chamberlain, *The Russian Revolution, 1917–1921*, 1935, II, pp. 223–31. A memorial volume, *Felshtyn-Zamlbuch tzum Ondenk fun di Felshtyner Kdoishim*, was published in N. Y., 1937.

[18] An attempt to whitewash the Ukrainian government, in Margulin, p. 126 ff.

[19] An estimate of the pogrom casualties was made by N. Gergel, in *YIVO Shriften far Ekonomik un Statistik*, I, 1928, p. 106 ff., at 34,719 killed and at least the same number wounded and crippled. However, Chamberlain, l. c., 240, mentions S. Gusev-Orenburgsky, *Book about Jewish Pogroms in Ukrainia in 1919*, who estimates the number of victims at 100,000, among them 35,000 deaths; while E. Haifetz, *Material Gathered by the All-Ukrainian Committee for the Relief of Victims of Pogroms*, p. 176, has an estimate of 70,000 killed by Ukrainians, 50,000 killed by Denikin. In any case, the number of victims was horrible and by far exceeded those of the October pogroms, 1905.

[20] The ARA published a voluminous report on its activities. The Jewish share in the work, in J. C. Hyman, *Aid*, p. 27 ff.; Bogen, *Born a Jew*, p. 279 ff. On I. Friedlaender, see *UJE*, IV, 450 f.; on B. Cantor ibid., III, 18.

[21] On OSE, see *UJE*, VIII, 332. On *Jüdische Welthilfskonferenz* and *Emigdirekt*, ibid., IV, 99 f.; HICEM, ibid., V, 356 f.; HIAS, ibid., VII, 555; W. Kaplun Kogan, *Jüdische Wanderbewegung vor und nach dem Weltkrieg*, 1930.

[22] That the peace treaties were not what was expected is evident from D. Lloyd George, *Peace Memoirs* — not to speak of other publications about the same subject.

[23] On the newly created Jewish problem, see L. Chasanowitch and L. Motzkin, *Die Judenfrage der Gegenwart*, 1919.

[24] Cf. *Bericht über das Kopenhagener Bureau der Zionistischen Organisation*, 1920; A. Böhm, *Die Zionistische Bewegung*, I, 689 f.

[25] See the article of Bernard G. Richards, who was one of the pioneer workers of the American Jewish Congress, in *UJE*, III, 312 f. The *Comité des Délégations* published a series of *Bulletins* on Jewish affairs, nos. 1–26.

[26] The view of the *Alliance Israélite Universelle* was published in *La Question juive, devant la Conférence de la Paix*, 1919, and in *Paix et Droit*; that of the Joint Foreign Committee, in *The Peace Conference: Report of the Delegation of the Jews of the British Empire on the Treaties of Versailles . . . . . and the Annexed Minority Treaties*, 1920. A vivid picture of the internal strife is given by Adler, *Days*, p. 309 ff.; Neuman, *Adler*, p. 176 ff.

[27] On the long and sometimes confusing discussions about the convocation of the American Jewish Congress, see B. G. Richard's report in *Jewish Communal Register*, 1918, p. 1384 ff. Cyrus Adler remained up to the end of his life an outspoken antagonist of the Congress idea: cf. *Days*, p. 306 f.; Neuman, l. c., p. 138 ff.

[28] The hard task of the American delegation to reduce the utopian demands of the East European delegates to a reasonable political basis presentable to the Peace Conference and the no less difficult transactions with the various committees and experts of the Conference are reflected in the diaries of Judge Julian W. Mack and Dr. Cyrus Adler. Louis Marshall, "The World Court and the Protection of Racial and Religious Minorities" in the Appendix to Luigi Luzzatti, *God in Freedom*, 1930, pp. 735–794, presents an elucidating summary of the problem and its solution. The standard work on the question is Oscar I. Janowsky, *The Jews and Minority Rights*, 1933; cf. Kurt Stillschweig, *Die Juden Osteuropas in den Minderheitsverträgen*, Berlin, 1936. Cf. also *UJE*, VII, 573 ff.

[29] The quotation is from *AJYB*, XXII, 101 ff.

[30] The treaty with Greece, in Janowsky, p. 373.

[31] Rumania, p. 409 (*AJYB*, ibid., 127).

[32] Poland, ibid., 105; Janowsky, p. 373.

[33] The quotation is from ibid., p. 373.

[34] The letter of G. Clemenceau to Paderewski, *AJYB*, l. c.

[35] For the satisfaction among the delegates, see Adler, *Days*, p. 324 f.; Neuman, l. c., p. 185 f.

Chapter III

THE JEWS OF EUROPE IN THE POST-WAR ERA

[1] "The Big Four were making a desert and calling it peace," wrote Vera Brittain, *Testament of Youth*, p. 470.

[2] Ludendorff's reports to the competent authorities of the Reich as collected in Lutz, l. c., do not yet know of the "Stab in the Back." This excuse is a post-war interpretation and was elaborated in Ludendorff's *Kriegsführung und Politik*, 1922. What Jews had to suffer on account of this lie is hinted at by Valentin, p. 226 ff., and M. Lowenthal, *The Jews of Germany*, 1936, p. 331 ff. A further step was to make Jews responsible even for the outbreak of the war.

[3] The bulk of the material used by the Nazi propaganda came to the fore during this period. Lowenthal, l. c., has a long list of this kind of publications. Alfred Rosenberg won his laurels thereby, and Adolf Hitler devoured the stuff. Significant is the widespread circulation of Arthur Dinter's pornographic books.

[4] Dietrich Eckart, the wizard to whom Hitler dedicated his *Mein Kampf*, led with his book, *Der Bolschewismus von Moses bis Lenin*, 1919. On the real share of Jews in Bolshevist leadership, see Bulaschof (=Benjamin W. Segel), *Bolschewismus und Judentum*, 3d ed., 1923; cf. the article "Communism," in *UJE*, III, 317 ff., and the thorough discussion in Baron, *History*, III, 162 f.; Valentin, p. 255 ff.

[5] The salesmen of the *Protocols* were White Russian reactionary émigrés. Copies of this concoction were circulated among delegates to the Peace Conference. "A year later translations of the *Protocols* began to appear throughout the world with the prolificacy of poisoned fungi" (Bernstein, *Truth*, p. 45).

[6] The first to disclose the plagiarism of Joly's book was Philip P. Graves, Constantinople correspondent of the London *Times*, in his paper, August 16–18, 1921. (The assertion that Joly was a Jew has no foundation; he was of pure Catholic extraction.) Later another source which inspired the *Protocols* was discovered in Sir John Retcliffe's (pseudonym for Hermann Goedsche) novel, *Biarritz*, 1868, where one chapter is entitled "The Jewish Cemetery in Prague and the Council of the Representatives of the Twelve Tribes of Israel," itself influenced by Joly. A thorough exposure of the forgery followed in Benjamin W. Segel, *The Protocols of the Elders of Zion. The Greatest Lie in History*, authorized English translation from the German [ed. 1923] by S. Czaczkes-Charles. "With Ten Letters of endorsement from eminent German Non-Jewish Scholars," 1934. Much more material was used for the same purpose by Herman Bernstein, *The Truth about 'The Protocols of Zion'*, 1935. In the meantime, in a trial before a court in Berne, Switzerland, a number of prominent Russians presented authentic proof that the *Protocols* had been fabricated by the Russian Secret Police in Paris. On the basis of all the known

material, John S. Curtiss wrote *An Appraisal of the Protocols of Zion*, 1942. The same writer gave a summary of his analysis in an article in *UJE*, IV, 46–52. Ibid., 52–60, Theodor H. Gaster offered a survey on the exploitation of the *Protocols* showing that even earnest statesmen used this brazen invention when it seemed to serve their antiBolshevist policy. See also the discussion in Valentin, pp. 165–183; Baron, II, 294 f.

[7] Popular evaluations of the *Protocols* are to be found in most of the introductions preceding the translations. So in "*The Cause of World Unrest*. With an introduction by [H. A. Gwynne] the editor of *The Morning Post*," 1920.

[8] About the situation in France, see J. Bonsirven "Chronique du judaisme français: Y-a-t-il en France un réveil de l'antisémitisme?" in *Études, publiées par des pères de la Compagnie de Jésus*," CCXXII, 1935, 97 ff., 226 ff.

[9] H. Belloc, like many Jew-baiters, pretends to be friendly to the Jews and to have Jewish friends, but his statements and his statistics are one endless chain of bigotry. Great Britain after the World War introduced national discriminations which were intended against Germans but mostly affected Jews of German birth.

[10] To what grotesque nonsense the race theory leads is demonstrated in Valentin, pp. 135–164; in the article "Aryanism," *UJE*, I, 517, with many references, p. 529. See also Francis Hogben, "Biology and Modern Race Dogmas," in *CJR*, IV, 3 ff.; Fritz Kahn, *Die Juden als Rasse und Kulturvolk*, 1922; F. Hertz, *Race and Civilization* (from the German), 1928; Baron, II, 298 ff.; III, 159.

[11] On the Youth Movement, see *UJE*, X, 612 ff.; on Sports, ibid., VII, 264, s. v. Maccabi; Halutzim, V, 188; Israel Cohen, p. 92 f.

[12] Richard Lewinsohn (Morus), *Jüdische Weltfinanz?*, indicated in the title of his book that he did not believe in the legend that the Jews controlled world finance, and in the course of his book he refuted it. See also Valentin, p. 210 ff.

[13] On the misery among immigrants in Paris, see Bogen, l. c., p. 256 ff.

[14] "Invasion of Eastern Jews" was a part of the nationalistic propaganda. The highest estimates of Jewish immigrants to Germany from Eastern Europe are put at 80,000, but this immigration extended over a long period, and of the recent immigrants many left during the inflation period.

[15] *Verband der Nationaldeutschen Juden*, see *Jü Le*, V, 1167; Baron, II, 423.

[16] "Jews and the Weimar Republic," in Valentin, 195 ff. Harry Count Kessler, *Walter Rathenau, sein Leben und sein Werk*," 1928; Gottlieb, *Walter Rathenau Bibliographie*, 1929; Julius Bab, in *MJ*, Autumn 1942, p. 254 ff.

[17] On the inflation in Germany, see G. Stolper, *German Economy 1870–1940*, 1940, p. 155 ff. That the classes which became the profiteers

of the inflation were heavy industry and agrarians, two groups to which very few Jews belonged, is agreed upon by all economists; cf. Hugh Quigley and R. T. Clark, *Republican Germany*, 1928, p. 197 ff. The proletarianization of the German-Jewish middle class is proved in Kurt Zielenziger, *Juden in der deutschen Wirtschaft*, 1930, p. 275. Isr. Cohen, p. 186, mentions the growth in the number of suicides.

[18] The National Federation of all Jewish Charities, Welfare Funds, etc., organized in 1917, was after the war recognized by the Reich as a central charitable body on the same footing as similar institutions of the Christian Churches or the Red Cross. The Federation published regular bulletins, *Zedakah, Zeitschrift für jüdische Wohlfahrtspflege und Statistik*, and *Führer durch die jüdische Gemeindeverwaltung und Wohlfahrtspflege*: see the article "Zentralwohlfahrtsstelle," in *Jü Le*, V, 1562 ff.

[19] On the territorial Federations of Jewish communities, see *UJE*, VI, 107.

[20] On the Academy for Jewish Research, see *EJ*, II, 1.

[21] The characterization of Rosenzweig is given by Ernst Simon, in *Jü Le*, IV, 1501 f. Most fascinating are his letters, *Briefe*, ed. by Ed. Rosenzweig, 1935. On N. A. Nobel (1871–1922), by whom Rosenzweig and other youths of his age were deeply impressed, see *UJE*, VIII, 230.

[22] On Buber, ibid., II, 569 f., and Hans Kohn, *Martin Buber*, 1930. After Rosenzweig's death Buber continued the publication of the Bible translation, and the work was almost complete when the Schocken Publishing House (like all Jewish publishers in Germany) was discontinued by order of the Nazis in 1938. Simultaneously the Jewish Community of Berlin prepared a German translation of the Bible; it was published in 4 volumes by H. Torczyner, 1934 ff.

[23] Leo Baeck's (*UJE*, II, 26 f.) systematic work, *The Essence of Judaism*, appeared in English translation in 1936. His collected essays were published under the title, *Wege im Judentum*, 1933, and *Aus Drei Jahrtausenden*, 1938.

[24] On the Prague circle of Max Brod, etc., see *UJE*, II, 537. Beer Hofmann, ibid., 136 f.

[25] Ibid., IV, 382.

[26] On the plight of Austria and its capital, see, e. g., Kurt Schuschnigg, *My Austria*, 1938, p. 83 ff.

[27] On Chajes, see M. Rosenfeld, *Oberrabbiner Hirsch Perez Chajes: Sein Leben und Werk*, 1933. The quotation is from Rebekah Kohut, *My Portion*, p. 292. Anitta Müller, in *UJE*, VIII, 34.

[28] Ibid., p. 629.

[29] See Lloyd George, *Peace Memoirs*, p. 1393, on the "flagrant, direct and gross violations of the Minority safeguards." The rich literature on the Minority Rights, in J. Robinson, *Das Minoritätenproblem und seine Literatur*, 1928.

[30] Oscar I. Janowsky, *People at Bay: the Jewish Problem in East-Central Europe*, 1938. A survey of "Occupations" exercised by Jews, in *UJE*, VIII, 265–279.

[31] That Rumania discriminated against the Jewish landowners in carrying out the land-reform is mentioned by Lloyd George, l. c., p. 1400.

[32] Anti-Jewish boycott, see *UJE*, II, 487 f.

[33] On the nervous shock caused to Jews by their many sufferings, F. Schneerson, *Di katastrofale zeiten un di wachsendike doires*, in Yiddish and German.

[34] On JDC, see Hyman, *Twenty-five Years*, p. 34 ff. On ORT, see *UJE*, VIII, 329 ff.

[35] On migration, see *UJE*, VII, 550 f.; Israel Cohen, pp. 200 ff., 204. On education, see the special issue, "Erziehung," of Buber's *Der Jude*, 1926; and *UJE*, III, 636.

[36] On *Yeshibot*, see M. Wischnitzer, "Traditional Judaism and Manual Labour," in *ORT Economic Revue*, II, nos. 4–5, p. 12 ff.

[37] On Finland, see *UJE*, IV, 308; Estonia, ibid., 171.

[38] On Latvia, ibid., VI, 549 f.; Janowsky, p. 81 ff.

[39] On Lithuania, see *UJE*, VII, 135 ff.; VI, 114 f.; Janowsky, p. 80 ff.

[40] On Poland, see *UJE*, VIII, 573 ff.; Janowsky, pp. 50 ff., 90 ff.; A. G. Duker, *The Situation of the Jews in Poland* (Conference on Jewish Relations), 1936; Simon Segal, *The New Poland and the Jews*, 1938.

[41] The intervention of the American Jewish Committee, in *AJYB*, XXVIII, 490 ff.

[42] On the educational policy, see Janowsky, l. c., and the publication *Wilno*, a book dedicated to the city of Wilna, ed. by Ephim M. Yeshurin, publ. by Wilner Branch 367, Workmen's Circle, in New York City, 1935, p. 296 ff. Wilna is described as the "cradle of the secular Jewish school."

[43] On the *Numerus Clausus*, see *UJE*, VIII, 252; L. Motzkin, *La Campaigne antisémite en Pologne* (*Cahiers du Comité des Délégations juives*, nos. 1–4), 1932.

[44] On *Tarbut*, see *UJE*, VIII, 576; *Wilno*, l. c., p. 307. The Jewish schools participated in the International Exhibitions at Locarno, 1927 and in Nice, 1932, ibid.

[45] On the press, see *UJE*, VIII, 442, 446.

[46] On the Wilna "Theatertruppe," see *Wilno*, p. 572 ff.

[47] Cf. *EJ*, I, 1060.

[48] On Jewish communists, see *UJE*, VI, 110 ff.; and Valentin, p. 241.

[49] On Rumania, see Janowsky, pp. 68–79; *Roumania: Ten Years After* (by the American Committee on the Rights of Religious Minorities), 1929; S. W. Baron, *The Jews in Roumania*, 1930; Zsombor de Szasz, *The Minorities in Roumanian Transylvania*, 1927, p. 334 ff.

[50] A joint statement of the American Jewish Committee and the American Jewish Congress, in *AJYB*, XXIX, 419 ff.; correspondence with the Rumanian Minister to Washington, ibid., XXX, 299 ff.;

[51] On Rumanian antisemitism and the university riots, see *UJE*, I, 382 f.

[52] On Rabbi Zirelsohn, see *AJYB*, XXIX, 416.

[53] On the leaders of this Association, Rabbi Niemirower, see *UJE*, VIII, 217 f.; Dr. Filderman, ibid., IV, 248.

[54] On Jews in Serbia, see *AJYB*, XX, 75 ff.; on Belgrade, *UJE*, II, 151.

[55] On Bulgaria, ibid., 586.

[56] On Greece, ibid., V, 92.

[57] On Turkey, *AJYB*, XXIX, 429 ff.

[58] On Italy, see *UJE*, V, 633 ff.

[59] On Czechoslovakia, see Kreppel, pp. 345 ff., 749 ff.

[60] On child aid through Anitta Müller Cohen, see *UJE*, VIII, 34. On Seeligmann, ibid., IX, 458; on Simonsen, ibid., 549 f.; Ehrenpreis, ibid., IV, 18 f., since 1920 has published the review *Judisk Tidskrift*.

[61] There is a veil over events in the USSR which has not been lifted even after the marvellous heroism proved by the Soviet armies in the present World War. The situation of the Jews also is a puzzle. So, e. g., after 25 years of rumors of the extinction of Jewish communal life in the USSR suddenly information came about an existing organized Jewish Community in Moscow. Zionist writers who had good reasons to resent the communists' hostility against Zionism, made every effort to picture the situation in black on black and to minimize the endeavors of the Komzet (p. 553) to settle Jews on the soil. Even such a solid scholar as Jacob Lestschinsky did not remain immune from the tendency to see only the gloomy side of the development. Of historical value are but personal impressions of travelers who tried to study the situation *sine ira et studio*. Foremost among them was Boris D. Bogen, a native of Moscow, who mastered the Russian language and came in contact with different groups of the rulers and the ruled (*Born a Jew*, p. 273 ff.). Bernard Edelhertz was also a native of Russia, (*UJE*, III, 624); his *The Russian Paradox*, 1930, offers some information about the agricultural colonies. James N. Rosenberg, *On the Steppes. A Russian Diary*, 1927, and Jos. A. Rosen, *The Present Status of Russian-Jewish Agricultural Colonization*, 1926, are exclusively concerned with these. It is a pity that Dr. Rosen has not published anything on the subject since. *The Menorah Journal*, vols. X–XIII, has several articles of writers who toured USSR and discussed their impressions in different fields of life. Louis Fischer, the well-known writer (*UJE*, V, 317), who repeatedly visited Russia and pleaded for an understanding between U. S. A. and USSR, tried to explain the Jewish situation, too. Recently he summarized his impressions in the form of a discussion held in Palestine: cf. his *Men and Politics*, 1941, pp. 217–253.

[62] On the *Evsektia*, see I. Agursky, *Di yidishe komisariaten un di yidishe komunistishe sektsies*, 1928. See also Lestschinsky, in *CJR*, III, 510, 607; cf. *UJE*, III, 316 f.

[63] On *Habimah*, see ibid., V, 143 f.

[64] On Yiddish, ibid., VII, 132 f.; and on the Moscow Jewish (Yiddish) State Theater, *MJ*, XIV, 478 ff.

[65] On the Agricultural Colonies, *UJE*, III, 291.

[66] On the Agro-Joint, ibid., I, 253 ff.

[67] On the central government's attitude, see *AJYB*, XXVIII, 59 f.; statements of Kalinin, XXVIII, 77 ff.; XXIX, 65.

[68] On Biro-Bidjan, see *UJE*, II, 372 ff.

[69] The situation was completely changed through the German aggression on Russia which, first, brought numberless Jews into the army and the defense factories, and, secondly, caused numerous refugees from eastern Poland and the invaded parts of the USSR to settle in the interior regions of European and Asiatic Russia.

[70] The first one to disclose the existence of Marrano communities was Samuel Schwarz, *Os Cristãos-Novos em Portugal no século XX*, 1925. Then followed M. Ehrenpreis, *Das Land zwischen Ost und West*, 1927, and Cecil Roth, *A History of the Marranos*, 1st ed., 1932. Both of the latter told the story of de Barros Basto (*UJE*, II, 92 f.). Cf. the article "Marranos," ibid., VII, 366 ff. and the literature listed p. 369.

[71] On Lisbon, see ibid., VII, 82 f.; on Amzalak, ibid., I, 291 f.

Chapter IV

THE JEWS IN THE UNITED STATES

[1] On Louis Marshall, see *UJE*, VII, 380 ff. The quotation from Justice Benjamin Cardozo's eulogy is in *AJYB*, XXXII; on Cardozo (1870–1938) himself, see *UJE*, III, 39 ff.

[2] The quotation about the un-American spirit is from the manifesto mentioned p. 562 and printed in *AJYB*, XXIV, 333.

[3] On the Ku Klux Klan, see *UJE*, VI, 479 ff., and the literature listed there on p. 482.

[4] About the Russian émigrés, especially Boris Brasol, see H. Bernstein, *Truth*, p. xv, and *UJE*, IV, 56.

[5] Reprints of the *Protocols* appeared 1921 in Boston under the title *Protocols and World Revolution*, and in New York City under *Praemonitus Praemunitus*. Cf. *The Protocols of the Wise Men of Zion* (Curtiss, p. 108).

[6] Cf. *The Cause of the World's Unrest*, Preface.

[7] On Henry Ford's anti-Jewish adventure, see *UJE*, I, 396; IV, 96. Masserman & Baker, p. 344 ff. When Louis Marshall first called Ford to account, he received an arrogant answer, see *AJYB*, XXIII, 316 f.

In 1922–23 Burton J. Hendrick published *The Jew in America*, denouncing in particular "The Polish Jew;" among the refutations of this calumny are outstanding Max J. Kohler, *The Polish Jew in America*, and Samuel Walker McCall, *Patriotism of the American Jew*, 1924.

[8] "The 'Protocols,' Bolshevism, and the Jews," reprinted in *AJYB*, XXIII, 367–79. The protest of prominent Americans, entitled "The Peril of Racial Prejudice. A Statement to the Public," ibid., XXIV, 332 ff. John Spargo's book appeared 1921; Norman Hapgood wrote in 1923 in *Hearst's International Magazine*. For more publications of the same kind, see *UJE*, I, 397.

[9] On the Anti-Defamation League, ibid., I, 336; on the American Jewish Congress, ibid., I, 250 ff., where its publications are listed. On the *Protocols*, supra pp. 512 f.

[10] On the proposed *numerus clausus* at Harvard University, see *AJYB*, XXV, 92 ff.; XXVI, 95 ff.

[11] President Coolidge's speech of May 3, 1925, in *AJYB*, XXVIII, 87; against Klanism, ibid., XXIX, 75.

[12] Cf. Coolidge's acknowledgment of the patriotism of recent immigrants, ibid., XXVIII, 475.

[13] Henry Ford was sued for libel by Herman Bernstein, but accusations against a whole people or race were not actionable for libel. Things were different with Aaron Sapiro who sued for financial damages, see ibid., XXX, 24. The correspondence between Henry Ford and Louis Marshall, ibid., XXIX, 384 ff. Most loyally, Henry Ford who had forbidden the use of his publications for antisemitic purposes (ibid., XXXI, 346) repeated his statement in 1934 when his former publications were still being misused for anti-Jewish purposes.

[14] The details about the agitation against immigration, ibid., XXVI, 423 ff. As early as 1923 a registration of the aliens was proposed: ibid., 436. Protests and arguments against such a measure, ibid., 437 f., and XXVII, 65 f.

[15] The Emergency Committee was definitely organized on August 17, 1924: ibid., XXVI, 444. Cf. *UJE*, VII, 550, 556.

[16] The American Jewish Committee continually reported on its dealings with the competent embassies in Washington, D. C., and with the authorities of the League of Nations. The American Jewish Congress at that time worked mainly in cooperation with the *Comité des Délégations juives*. From 1931 on it urged a World Jewish Congress; at first the suggestion encountered many objections, among others from the Zionist Organization.

[17] On the Calendar Reform, see *UJE*, II, 641 f.; *AJYB*, XXXIII, 303 f.

[18] On *Shehita* in Norway, ibid., XXIX, 411, on the basis of M. Hyamson, *The Jewish Method of Slaughtering Animals from the Point of View of Humanity*, 1923. The Norwegian Parliament passed the prohibitive law in 1929: see *UJE*, VIII, 242.

[19] See Bogen, p. 268 ff.; on D. Brown's campaign, see *UJE*, II, 561.

[20] March 4, 1919, Representative Julius Kahn of California presented to President Wilson a Statement signed by 300 American Jews, against the plan for the reorganization of the Jews as a national unit. The text of this petition is printed under the title "Zionism and the Future of Palestine" in Morris Jastrow Jr., *Zionism*, p. 151 ff. This quixotic action led to nothing because it challenged what nobody had in mind. Later, April 22, 1922, Dr. D. Philipson, in a hearing before the Committee on Foreign Affairs of the House of Representatives, pleaded against consequences which were outside the intentions of the Balfour Declaration; his arguments are printed in his *Life*, p. 299 ff.

[21] On the Pittsburgh Zionist Convention of 1918 and Brandeis' social program, see De Haas, *Brandeis*, p. 95 f. On the conflict with Weizmann, ibid., p. 103 ff., and Lipsky, p. 50 f. The real background of the conflict is not yet clear.

[22] The text is in *AJYB*, XXV, 104; *RRC*, p. 31 f.

[23] On the beginning and growth of the Hebrew University, see *The Hebrew University of Jerusalem, Its History and Development*, 2d ed., 1942. The American Jewish Physicians' Committee was organized in 1921 by Dr. Nathan Ratnoff of New York, who in 1943 was still its president: see *UJE*, I, 256.

[24] On Louis Marshall's efforts, see *AJYB*, XXVIII, 25 ff.; the report of the Joint Survey Commission, ibid., XXX, 55 ff. On the meeting at Zurich in 1929, ibid., XXXII, 324, and the *Jewish Agency for Palestine's Memorandum to the Permanent Mandate's Commission*, 1929.

[25] For the organization of the Hebrew Press in 1920, see *UJE*, VI, 139; Adler, *Days*, p. 281, and Neuman, *Adler*, p. 159 f.

[26] On the Jewish Institute of Religion, see *UJE*, VI, 132 f.; the Yeshiva College, ibid., X, 595 f.

[27] On the Hebrew Union College, ibid., V, 282 f. Of the *Annual*, vol. XVII appeared in 1943. On the Jewish Theological Seminary, *UJE*, VI, 143 ff.; its publications, ibid., 146. The American Academy (ibid., I, 238) published vol. XIII of its *Proceedings* in 1943.

[28] On the present status of American Judaism, see *UJE*, VI, 239-246; *The American Jew*, ed., O. I. Janowsky, 1942. M. M. Kaplan published "A Program for the Reconstruction of Judaism" as early as August 1920, in *MJ*. On his writings and his work, see *UJE*, VI, 245, 321, and his biweekly *The Reconstructionist*.

[29] *The Menorah Movement for the Study and Advancement of Jewish Culture and Ideals: History — Purposes — Activities* was published by Henry Hurwitz and I. Leo Scharfman in 1914. The Collegiate Menorah Association was organized in a meeting, held at Chicago, Jan. 1-3, 1913: see ibid., 150 ff. *The Menorah Journal* (ibid., p. 19 f.) was first published in 1915 and started its 29th year in 1943.

[30] The quotation is from Waldo Frank, *Rediscovery of America*, p. 290.

[31] On Community Centers, see *UJE*, III, 84 ff.; VIII, 113.

[32] On Hillel Foundations, see ibid., V, 363 ff. *The Jewish Student in America: A Study made by the Research Bureau of the B. B. Hillel Foundation*, by Dr. Lee J. Levinger, 1937.

[33] On Yiddish literature and culture, see A. A. Roback; on Impressionists and Expressionists, see *UJE*, VII, 130 ff. On "New Trends in Post-War Yiddish Literature," S. Niger in *Jewish Social Studies*, I, 1939, p. 337 ff. On Goldberg's voluminous literary work, see *UJE*, V, 14.

[34] On Jews in the American press, see ibid., VIII, 454; A. S. Ochs, ibid., 280 f., *AJYB*, XXXVII, 27 ff.

[35] On Jews in American literature, see *UJE*, I, 263–270; The Theater Guild, ibid., V, 304, s. v. "Theresa Helburn;" ibid., X, 231–235, on Jews in motion pictures.

[36] On contributions to music, cf. ibid., VIII, 57 ff.; also IV, 589 ff. on G. Gershwin. Prominent in the Jewish field are Abraham Wolf Binder (ibid., II, 354); Ernest Bloch (ibid., 397 ff.); Frederick Jacobi (ibid., VI, 15 f.), Jacob Weinberg (ibid., X, 488).

[37] Alfred Stieglitz in Waldo Frank, l. c., p. 177 f. The architects and the scholars mentioned have their respective articles in *UJE*.

[38] On the Guggenheim family (now almost extinguished), see ibid., V, 116; the latest gift of Mrs. Daniel Guggenheim was an estate for a research center of the Aeronautic Sciences Institute: cf. *New York Times* of June 17, 1942.

[39] On Filene and Selling, see *UJE*, s. v. On Julius Rosenwald, see M. R. Werner, *Julius Rosenwald: The Life of a Practical Humanist*, 1939; James Weldon Johnson, *The Shining Life*, 1930. The appreciation of President Hoover is in a message sent to the American Jewish Committee. Of the immensely large number of outstanding Jewish philanthropists the following few may be mentioned: Falk — Pittsburgh; Fels — Philadelphia; George Blumenthal — N. Y. C.; I. W. Bernheim — Louisville, Ky. (now of Denver, Colo.); Jacob Epstein — Baltimore; the brothers Fleisher — Philadelphia, Pa.; Mrs. Sol Rosenbloom — Pittsburgh.

[40] On the American depression and the New Deal, see Eli Ginzberg, *The Illusion of Economic Stability*, 1939. Its effect on Jewish organizations and foundations, in *AJYB*, XXXI ff. Discrimination in employment led to the organization of a National Conference on Jewish Employment under the leadership of the IOBB. In order to promote a better understanding of the position of the Jews in the modern world the Conference on Jewish Relations was founded 1933 under the chairmanship of Prof. Morris R. Cohen. It publishes *Jewish Social Studies* (vol. VI, 1943). On its further activities, see *UJE*, III, 326. In July 1933 a Joint Consultative Council was formed of representatives of the American Jewish Committee, American Jewish Congress, and IOBB; the Jewish Labor Committee joined it in 1934. Since 1938 it has assumed the name "General Jewish Council:" see *UJE*, IV, 527 f.

Chapter V

THE JEWISH NATIONAL HOME IN PALESTINE

[1] The literature on modern Palestine is very extensive, but of course most of the books were written from subjective points of view. The most valuable authentic source material is contained in the *Reports on Palestine and Transjordan*, published by the Great Britain Colonial Office from 1920 on, and based on the annual reports of the Palestine Administration. There are the *Bulletins* and the *Reports* of the Jewish Agency for Palestine. These reports were examined and discussed by the Permanent Mandates Commission of the League of Nations. Very valuable is the *Palestine Royal Commission Report*, 1937, with its wealth of statistics, documents, maps, etc. However, this report is not unbiased. Since Lord Peel had come to the conclusion that no remedy existed for the Palestinian conflict except "Partition," he arranged and commented on facts and documents in such a way as to make any other conclusion appear impracticable.

[2] On McMahon's correspondence, see *RRC*, 17 ff.; on the Sykes-Picot agreement, ibid., 20 f.; M. Pichon's introduction to Sokolow, II, vi ff.; on the French and Italian intrigues before the Peace Commission, see Lloyd George, *Peace Memoirs*, 1162–1190. On the support of the Holy See, cf. Sokolov, l. c., 53.

[3] Emir Feisal's pledge to accept the Balfour Declaration, in *RRC*, 26 f.; disturbances in Egypt, etc., ibid., 58 ff. On the attitude of the Palestinian Arabs and the OETA, see Patterson, *Judaeans*, 241 f.

[4] On the assault on Tel Hai, see Alex Bein, in *Bitzaron*, III, 5, p. 593 ff.

[5] Sir Ronald Storrs, *Annotations*, ch. XIV, describes the dangerous situation preceding the Easter pogrom of 1920 and tries to explain the shocking events by the fact that "the Jerusalem Police Force was under the command of a junior lieutenant." Evidently it never entered his mind to ask how it could happen that at such a crucial moment no adequate precautions had been taken; the impression obtained from Patterson's narrative, l. c., p. 253 f. (whence the quotation is taken) is quite different. Even such a noble mind as Miss Henrietta Szold's could not help doubting Sir Ronald's good-will: see M. Lowenthal, *Henrietta Szold: Life and Letters*, 1942, pp. 186 f., 192, 197, 206 f. The investigation of the causes of the trouble (*RRC*, 50) did not extend to the attitude of the British administration. In June 1920 handbills with the text "Down with the Jews" were again distributed; *Szold*, ibid., p. 142.

[6] The mandate system had been tried in Egypt: see Lloyd George, l. c., 118 ff.; the distribution of mandates in the Peace Conference, ibid., 1194 ff. *A Post-War Bibliography of the Near-Eastern Mandates, 1919–1930*, was published by the American University, Beirut, 8 pts., 1932 ff.

[7] The full text of the "Mandate for Palestine" is printed in *RRC*, 34 ff., 398 ff. The sections analyzed in the text are Art. 2, 6, 7, 11, 13, 18, 22.

[8] The quotation is from Storrs, *Annotations*, p. 458. Sir Herbert's share in the preparation of the Balfour Declaration is described in his *Great Britain and Palestine*, 1935. Lord Oxford noted in his *Diaries* that as early as 1915 Sir Herbert laid before the Cabinet a "dithyrambic memorandum" urging that Great Britain should take Palestine in which Jews would in time swarm back from all parts of the globe, and in due course obtain home rule; cf. Stein, *Zionism*, 2d ed., p. 81.

[9] For the tasks and achievements of the Palestinian government according to its annual reports, see also *RRC*, 43–62.

[10] Gordon's *Collected Writings* appeared in 5 vols., Tel Aviv, 1925–29; some of his essays appeared in German translation, as *Erlösung durch Arbeit*, 1920; in English translation by Frances Burnce, *Selected Essays*, New York, 1938; cf. Hans Kohn, *L'humanisme juif*, 1931; S. Bardin, *Pioneer Youth in Palestine*, 1932; *UJE*, V, 61.

[11] On the immigration figures before 1925, see *RRC*, 46 ff. These figures do not specify the number of earlier settlers who had been evacuated during the war, and at or after its end returned to Palestine.

[12] On the Jaffa riots and the following investigation, see *RRC*, 51 f. On Brenner, see S. Spiegel, *Hebrew Reborn*, 375 ff., 465 f.; cf. *UJE*, II, 519.

[13] On the Supreme Moslem Council and Haj Amin el Husseini, see *RRC*, 52 ff., 174 ff.

[14] The statement of Winston Churchill (which was inspired by the Palestinian government) may be read in one of the numerous British *White Books*, *RRC*, 32 f. This statement was by no means more concrete than Lord Balfour's optimism, quoted by Lloyd George, p. 1137 f., or his public speech of July 1920, in *RRC*, 27.

[15] The National Party, in *RRC*, 53; their petition in *MPMC*, IV sess., p. 166.

[16] The Mandate (Cmd. 1785 of 1922), *RRC*, 32 ff.; its peculiar character is studied ibid., 37 ff., and in I. Stoyanowsky, *The Mandate for Palestine*, 1928; *UJE*, VIII, 376 ff. Col. Frederick Herman Kisch who, from 1923–1931, was a member of the Zionist Executive Committee in Jerusalem and worked as director of the political department, in his *Palestine Diary*, 1938, has some instructive notes about the attitude of certain British officials. E. g., E. T. Richmond, when he retired from Palestine Civil Service in 1924, openly attacked the Mandate as an "iniquitous document" (p. 455) and an Arab leader said of him that "he makes all cooperation with Jews impossible" (p. 34). Henrietta Szold, who certainly is not inclined to unfairness, was more than unfavorably impressed by Governor Storrs who "has been reputed an adversary of Jews and of the policies involved in the Balfour Declaration" (cf. M. Lowenthal, l. c., pp. 197, 186 f.). "How we are hated and how baselessly!" she exclaimed in 1922 when speaking of the

administration (p. 207). To be sure, one must not forget men like Sir Wyndham Deedes and his successor Sir G. Clayton who tried their best to fulfill the Mandate. Cf. Bentwich, *Wanderer*, p. 108.

[17] The "Jewish Agency for Palestine" is based on Art. 4 of the Mandate: *RRC*, 172 ff.; Bentwich, *Palestine*, 89 f.; Böhm, II, 219 ff.

[18] Weizmann's point of view is explained in the 4 vols. of his speeches, essays and letters, *Debarim*, *Neumim*, etc., 1937. Jabotinsky, who denounced Weizmann's policy as leading to the loss of Palestine, in 1923 resigned from the Zionist Executive and for a short while left the Zionist Organization. In opposition to the adopted Zionist Program he advocated mass immigration to Palestine and founded in 1925 the World Union of Zionist Revisionists (WUZR). He became the staunch leader of the opposition against admitting non-Zionists into the Jewish Agency with equal rights. Though the Zionist Congress in 1931 refused to define the aim of Zionism as a "Jewish State," he did not break away from the Organization before 1935, when he founded the New Zionist Organization (cf. *UJE*, VI, 2–4). One section of the Revisionists, however, remained within the Zionist Organization and organized, under the leadership of Meir Grossmann (ibid., V, 107 f.), the Jewish State Party. The whole movement developed into sectarianism, and Jabotinsky's incomparable gifts were wasted in utopian projects.

[19] On the *Keren Hayesod*, supra p. 571; Böhm, II, 115 ff. On the special American branch, Palestine Foundation Fund, see *UJE*, VIII, 315.

[20] The Order-in-Council is reprinted in Bentwich, *Palestine*, 318–335. The way this constitution functioned, ibid., 91 ff., 239–296.

[21] Sir Herbert surveyed the events and achievements of his administration in his *Report of the High Commissioner*, etc., *1920–25* (Col. 15), 1925. On his administration, see Bentwich, l. c., 43 ff.; Böhm, II, 133 ff., and the latter's summary of the criticism prevalent in Zionist circles, p. 383 ff.

[22] The real progress is evident from Bentwich, *Fulfilment*, p. 21 ff.; Böhm, II, 394 ff., not to speak of the numerous impressionist descriptions of occasional travelers.

[23] On the Legislative Council, see *RRC*, p. 53. *MPMC*, V sess., pp. 166 ff., 173 f. Böhm, II, 245 ff., 325.

[24] "Many are going away ... because they see no future ahead. For the moment it looks ... [bad]. Idealism is still there ... but ... organization is breaking down." So wrote Henrietta Szold in November 1920 (Lowenthal, l. c., 155 f.). A year later she was again hopeful: "the movement as a whole is a phenomenon equivalent to a miracle" (ibid., p. 165).

[25] The quotation is from H. E. Fosdick, *A Pilgrimage to Palestine*, p. 284 f. Herbert Samuel's remarks on the improvement in the *Emek* are quoted by Bentwich, *Palestine*, p. 123.

[26] *Histadrut Kelalit shel ha-Ovedim ha-Ivrim be-Eretz Yisrael* is the

full Hebrew name of the General Federation of Labor: see *UJE*, V, 384 f. All observers praise the unity of theories and deeds among the workers in the collective settlements. The saga of the *K'vutzot* was recently sung by the former High Commissioner Sir Arthur Wauchope in a paper "Communal Settlements in Palestine" which was reprinted in the *Jewish Frontier*, VIII, October 1941.

[27] On the difficulties of amalgamating the different Jewish groups, see *Szold*, l. c., pp. 150, 167.

[28] On the cultural and religious life, see Bentwich, *Fulfilment*, pp. 123 ff., 129 ff., 178 ff.; *RRC*, p. 49.

[29] On objections in Rome, see Storrs, *Annotations*, p. 508; among Arabs, see Fosdick, l. c., p. 272.

[30] All the leaders mentioned have their articles in *UJE*. On Rutenberg, see Bentwich, *Palestine*, p. 64. He proved even greater in his death than in his life. His last will showed serious apprehensions regarding the future of a disunited Jewish National Home and established a generous foundation for the promotion of Jewish unity.

[31] On the rapid growth of Tel Aviv, see *RRC*, p. 352 ff.; Bentwich, l. c., p. 118.

[32] The inspiration brought to the Diaspora is evident from all Jewish newspapers of the period as well as from the reports of many a traveler.

[33] On the opening of the Hebrew University, see *Jewish Chronicle*, April 1925; Bentwich, l. c., p. 109 ff.; id., *Fulfilment*, p. 141 ff. See also, e. g., the enthusiastic letters of Irma Lindheim, *Palestine: The Immortal Adventure*, 1928. Lord Balfour's adventures in Damascus, in Storrs, l. c., p. 506 ff.; Dugdale, *A. J. Balfour*, II, 365 ff.

[34] The so-called *Grabski Aliyah* originated from the restricting economic legislation in Poland (supra p. 534). On the depression, see *RRC*, p. 62.

[35] On Lord Plumer, see *UJE*, VIII, 554; Bentwich, *Palestine*, p. 142 ff. On the relief for unemployed, ibid., p. 162 ff. On the slow recovery, ibid., p. 179; *RRC*, p. 63.

[36] The regulation defining the Constitution of the Jewish Community, in *Report of the Administration for 1930*, p. 232 ff., see Bentwich, l. c., p. 155 f. On the *Va'ad Le'umi*, and its work for Jewish education, see *RRC*, p. 334 f.; for public health, p. 314 ff.

[37] On the meeting of the enlarged Jewish Agency in Zurich, see Bentwich, l. c., p. 182 f.; *UJE*, VI, 91.

[38] On the "Crisis of the Wailing Wall," see the very clear and dispassionate presentation in Bentwich, l. c., p. 175 ff. On the first trouble in 1928, see also *AJYB*, XXXI, 70 ff. *British White Paper* (Cmd. 3229), and *MPMC*, XV sess. (July 1929), p. 92 ff., and XVI sess. (November 1929), pp. 156 ff., 202.

[39] On Sir John Chancellor, ibid., XV sess., p. 79. The details of the incidents in the summer of 1929, ibid., XVII (extraordinary) session, held in Geneva, from June 3rd to 21st, 1930. The critical conclusions, ibid., p. 139 ff. On the riots, see Bentwich, l. c., p. 183 ff.; *RRC*,

p. 67 f.; the quotation ibid. The reaction in U. S. A., see *AJYB*, XXXII, 58 ff.; the démarche in London of the U. S. Department of State, ibid., p. 62.

[40] For the proclamation of the High Commissioner, see Bentwich, l. c., p. 188; on the B'rit Shalom, ibid., p. 194. The protests, in *AJYB*; ibid., p. 133.

[41] The Report of the "Shaw Commission" (Cmd. 3530 of 1930) in Bentwich, l. c., p. 195 ff. Extracts from it in *RRC*, p. 68 f., and in *MPMC*, of the aforementioned extraordinary session. The accompanying *White Paper*, in Cmd. 3582.

[42] Cf. *MPMC*, XX sess. (June 1931), pp. 72 ff., 77 ff. Simultaneously with Sir John Hope Simpson's Report (Cmd. 3686) a new *White Paper* (Cmd. 3692) was published which contained the ill-famed statement of policy of Prime Minister Ramsay MacDonald. Its main conclusions in *RRC*, p. 71 f.; a full discussion in Bentwich, l. c., p. 241.

[43] The catastrophic impression of this White Paper, in Kisch, *Diary*, p. 356. On Dr. Weizmann's resignation, see *AJYB*, XXXII, 24 f.; see also Adler, *Days*, 401 f. The Jewish Agency challenged "The Statistical Basis of Sir J. Hope Simpson's Statement." For Mr. MacDonald's letter, see Stein, p. 170; Bentwich, l. c., p. 225 f.

[44] The *Istiqlal* Party, in *RRC*, p. 81.

[45] A *Memorandum on the Western Wall* was published on behalf of the Jewish Agency by Dr. Cyrus Adler; cf., l. c., pp. 396, 403. The Order-in-Council on the Wailing Wall, in *Report of the Administration of Palestine for 1931*, p. 196 ff.; cf. Bentwich, l. c., p. 209 f.

[46] On further Jewish immigration, see *RRC*, p. 79; the improvement in the economic position of the Arabs and the "French-Strickland Report," ibid., p. 80 and *AJYB*, XXXV, 206.

[47] On Sir Arthur Wauchope's intentions and achievements, see *RRC*, p. 87 f.; *MPMC*, XXII sess., p. 82 ff.; Bentwich, *Wanderer*, p. 208.

[48] On the immigration of 1933 ff., in *RRC*, p. 81 f. The Revisionists' unrest and the trial connected with the Arlosoroff murder, in *AJYB*, XXXVI, 208 f. The difficulty of adjusting so many immigrants of such different backgrounds to the Palestinian life was reported by the Zionist press of those years and is still being felt today as one of the paramount problems of the *Yishub*.

[49] The rising Arab agitation, in *RRC*, p. 83 ff.; the proposal of a Legislative Council, ibid., p. 90 ff.; the Jewish protests, p. 91, and *AJYB*, XXXVIII, 354.

[50] Mussolini's intrigues in Palestine, ibid., p. 371 f.; Herbert Sidebotham, *Great Britain and Palestine*, 1937, p. 186 ff. From that period on the strategic importance of Palestine for the defense of the British Empire became more and more evident. It is significant that, when the Abyssinian crisis began, Palestinian Jews deliberated how many soldiers they were able to send to Britain's help, while the Mufti and his group sought contacts with Italian imperialism!

[51] To "The Disturbances of 1936" *RRC* dedicated a special chapter,

pp. 96–112. The "Representations Addressed to the High Commissioner by the Higher Arab Officials," ibid., p. 401 ff. The losses, ibid., p. 105 f. The deficiency of the British defense, in Bentwich, *Fulfilment*, p. 212 f.

[52] "Conclusions" of the Royal Commission, in *RRC*, p. 380 ff.; the government's "Statement of Policy" in Cmd. 5513 of 1937. The U. S. Department of State did not fail to notify London that it was entitled to be "fully informed of any proposals which may be made to the Council of the League of Nations for the modification of the Palestine Mandate" (Statement by Secretary of State Cordell Hull, reproduced in *CJR*, I, 2, p. 11). The quotation is from *MPMC*, XXXII sess., p. 233 f.

[53] The discussion in the House of Lords took place July 20–21, 1937 (*Official Report*, vol. 106, col. 599–675, 797–824); that in the Commons, July 21 (*Official Report*, col. 2235–2367); that in the *MPMC* and the League of Nations in August 1937.

[54] On the XX Zionist Congress and Meeting of the Jewish Agency (for which Cyrus Adler prepared a Memorandum: see *Days*, 425), see Bentwich, l. c., p. 218 ff.; *AJYB*, XL, 314 ff.

[55] Continuous disturbances in Palestine; Arab terror; vigorous action of the Administration, ibid., p. 325 ff.; Bentwich, p. 222 f.; Jewish leaders against Jewish terror, ibid., and *CJR*, I, 1, p. 23 f.

[56] *Report of the Partition (Woodhead) Commission, Accompanied by a New Statement of Policy*, issued November 9, 1938 (Cmd. 5893), reproduced in *CJR*, II, 1, p. 69 ff. Ibid., 76 ff., a Statement by the Jewish Agency. The criticism in the House of Commons, Nov. 24, 1938 (*Off. Rep.* 1987–2107); House of Lords on Dec. 8, 1938 (vol. III, 412 ff.).

[57] The Round Table Conference took place in London, Feb. 7–March 17, 1939 (the opening addresses, ibid., II, 2, p. 59 ff.; details, ibid., 112 ff.; II, 3, p. 122 ff.). The Conference was hardly closed when the "Immigration (Amendment) Ordinance of 1939" empowered the High Commissioner to prescribe an arbitrary maximum number of immigration certificates. The protest of the Jewish Agency, dated April 13, 1939, ibid., p. 51 ff.

[58] *British White Paper on Palestine* of May 17, 1939 (Cmd. 6019), ibid., p. 60 ff. The immediate protest of the Jewish Agency, ibid., p. 65; the discussions in the House of Commons, May 23 (*Offic. Report*, vol. 347, col. 1937–2198) and in the House of Lords, May 22 (*Off. Rep.*, vol. 113, col. 81–145). Dr. Weizmann's letter submitting a "Memorandum on the Legal Aspects of the Statement of British Policy in Palestine," ibid., II, 4, p. 70 ff. Mr. Malcolm MacDonald's Statement before the PMC, June 16, 1939, ibid., p. 85 ff., was no reply to the powerful arguments of the Agency, and the PMC referred the decision to the Council of the League (ibid., II, 5, p. 53 ff.). The British government presented a further Memorandum (ibid., 55 ff.).

[59] Resolutions of the XXI Zionist Congress, adopted August 24,

1939, which again stretched out a conciliatory hand to the Arab people, ibid., p. 60 ff.

⁶⁰ The correspondence of Dr. Weizmann and Prime Minister Chamberlain about "The War and Palestine," ibid., 62 f. Appeals of leading Jewish bodies to endorse the British war effort, ibid., II, 6, p. 52 ff. For a brief summary of what happened since the outbreak of the war, see *UJE*, VIII, 372 f. The effect of the war on Palestine's economic life up to the end of 1940, in *CJR*, III, 595 ff. On Feb. 28, 1940, a "Land Regulations Order, restricting sale of land to Jews" was published and made retroactive to May 18, 1939: ibid., 325. Ibid., 327 ff., protests of Jews and of Arabs in favor of Jews.

Chapter VI
HITLER'S TOTAL WAR AGAINST THE JEWS

¹ Publications on Hitler and Nazism, both by followers and foes, fill a library; few of them, however, are of use to the historian. Outstanding among the books on Hitler are Rudolf Olden, *Hitler*, 1935, in English translation, *Hitler the Pawn*, 1936; and Konrad Heiden, *Hitler: a Biography*, 1936; the second part of this work was translated under the title, *One Man against Europe*, 1939. Hitler's self-revelation is his book, *Mein Kampf*, 1925, first complete and unabridged, fully annotated English edition in 1939 (editorial sponsors: John Chamberlain, et al.). A sequel to *Mein Kampf* is *Adolf Hitler: My New Order*, a collection of Hitler's speeches in English translation, edited and commented on by Raoul de Roussy de Sales, 1941. The conversations which he had with prominent party members like Hermann Rauschning supplement the above (*The Revolution of Nihilism*, 1939; *Hitler Speaks*, 1939, published in 1940 under the title *Voice of Destruction*; Otto Strasser, *Hitler*, I, 1940; and Kurt Georg W. Ludeke, *I Knew Hitler*, 1937).

² Cf. *Mein Kampf*, p. 84. The obstructing influences on Hitler's political practice were reported by all observers, e. g. *Ambassador Dodd's Diaries*, p. 90 f., 323.

³ The quotation is from the letter of resignation addressed to the League of Nations by James G. McDonald, published in the American press, reproduced in *Annual Register* for 1935, II, 97 ff.; Valentin, p. 320. The same author recently revealed that Hitler quite frankly confessed to him that he considered antisemitism as a means for world conquest (*New York Times Book Review*, Nov. 29, 1942, p. 42).

⁴ On his propaganda methods Hitler wrote quite frankly in *Mein Kampf*, chapter XI, p. 846 ff. On desecrations of cemeteries, see *UJE*, III, 74; Wilhelm Michel (a Gentile), *Kampf gegen Gräber*, 1929. The desecrations stopped or took a different shape after the Nazis had come to power.

⁵ The suspension of all constitutional rights, in Heiden, p. 99 ff.;

Hitler's and Goering's ideas on justice, ibid., p. 60 f.; concentration camps, ibid., pp. 101–106. Cf. an article in the *Manchester Weekly Guardian*, 27th Sept. 1935, on Dachau.

[6] The numerous appeasing cables reproduced in the *New York Times* of March 1933 are a reflex of the terror in Germany and the resentment of the *Reichsregierung*. To be sure, no pogroms in the usual sense took place, but epidemic excesses against individual Jews and onslaughts on Jewish property. Foremost among them was the economic boycott, an old antisemitic weapon, used almost daily in one place or another after the Nazis had come to power. About the end of March, however, the party voted a *total* boycott, and the government decided to tolerate it; owing to the panic within industrial circles the boycott was limited to one day with the reservation that it could be proclaimed again if considered necessary.

[7] The cable is in *The Jews in Nazi Germany*, published by the American Jewish Committee, 1933. The official decrees and measures against the Jews, ibid., p. 1 ff.; cf. J. R. Marcus, *Rise*, p. 8 ff.; M. Lowenthal, p. 392 ff.; G. Warburg, *Six Years of Hitler*, 1939, p. 52 ff. In contrast to the Nazi lie that during the Weimar Republic Jews had swamped all positions in the Civil Service, it was officially stated in October 1937 that no more than 1,984 civil servants had been dismissed because they were Jews, i. e., that the percentage, including those who were only racial Jews, was less than negligible. The ratio of Jews was relatively large in some higher judicial and administrative positions in Prussia because the government had difficulty in finding qualified incumbents of reliable allegiance to the democratic republic.

[8] On the continuous struggle within the party, see Warburg, p. 103. On the liquidation of Jewish business enterprises, see Valentin, p. 128 ff. The mendacity of the Nazis' economic practices is thoroughly exposed in Franz L. Neumann, *Behemoth*, 1942, p. 221 ff. He calls his basic chapter: "An Economy Without Economics."

[9] The definite elimination of Jews from the academic callings, in Warburg, pp. 73, 80 f., 83. The law barring Jewish physicians from practice, in *CJR*, I, 2, pp. 15 ff.

[10] For the law, see *Jews in Nazi Germany*, p. 9 ff.; cf. Marcus, l. c., p. 10 f.; Valentin, p. 123 f.; Warburg, p. 129 ff.; E. Y. Hartshorne, *The German Universities and National Socialism*, 1937, a careful analysis of the whole situation, contains official statistics of the number of Jews dismissed from the teaching staff of the universities. They show that the figures presented by the Nazi propaganda were conscious exaggerations. Furthermore, by far the largest part of Jewish university teachers were instructors in the Faculties of Medicine and had little chance of promotion.

[11] On the burning of books and the students' resolutions concerning the publication of books, see *Jews in Nazi Germany*, p. 10; I. A. Hirschman, "The Degradation of Culture," in *Nazism: An Assault on Civilization*, ed. by Pierre van Paassen and James W. Wise, p. 88 ff.

[12] Some outstanding scientists like Prof. Planck, president of *Kaiser Wilhelm Gesellschaft*, and Dr. Eckener, the famous aviator, dared to warn Hitler of the consequences of his anti-Jewish policy but were furiously rebuked (the like happened to Frau Bertha Krupp, Sr.). One of the very few university men who voiced doubts about the fairness of the general attacks against Jews was Dr. Wolfgang Koehler, professor of psychology at Berlin University; as a result he was blackmailed and boycotted by the students. After this experience he accepted a call to Oberlin College. The quotation (p. 645) is from a speech of Dr. Walter Simons, retired president of the *Reichsgericht* ("Supreme Court") and president of the *Evangelisch-Sozialer Kongress*, who yielded his lifelong liberalism to the orders of the *Führer*. The verdict on the Nazi leaders by the famous economist Prof. Max Sering is quoted by Dodd, p. 179.

[13] The achievements of Jews in the field of German culture are summarized in Arnold Zweig, *Bilanz der deutschen Judenheit, 1933*, 1934; and A. Myerson and I. Goldberg, *The German Jew*, 1933.

[14] The appeal of M. Williams is in *Jews in Nazi Germany*, p. 16; the addresses in the U. S. Senate, June 10, 1933, ibid., 59 ff.; extracts from the debate in the British House of Commons, in Heiden, p. 65 f. President Roosevelt informed Ambassador Dodd before his departure for Berlin: "Germans are treating Jews shamefully. What we can do to moderate general persecution by unofficial and personal influence ought to be done" (*Diaries*, p. 9).

[15] The Bernheim petition (suggested by Arnold Wiener, then in Beuthen, now in Palestine) is in *AJYB*, XXXV, 74-101. The excesses in Upper Silesia in 1937, ibid., XL, 202.

[16] The numerous protests are listed ibid., XXXV, 21 ff. On the anti-Nazi boycott, see *UJE*, II, 489 f.; Dodd, *Diaries*, p. 101. It is interesting that W. Dieckhoff, later German Ambassador to Washington, advised against the test, and that Streicher and Goebbels, at that moment evidently against Hitler's intentions, started new persecutions: ibid., p. 102 f. It is significant for the abnormal situation of the Jewish people that the XVIII Zionist Congress in Karlsbad rejected the boycott against the Nazis. The main opponents were the delegates from Palestine, because the upbuilding of the country profited from the agreement with Germany.

[17] The number of Jews, who up to the end of 1933 had left Germany, was estimated by James G. McDonald, High Commissioner for Refugees (Jewish and other) coming from Germany, at 50,000: see ibid., p. 79 f.; Valentin, p. 130 f. "Minority and Refugee Questions" were discussed by the Council of the League of Nations on September 29 ff., 1933: see *AJYB*, XXXVI, 89-119. The statutes of the High Commission, ibid., p. 117 ff.; its thorny path, in Bentwich, *Wanderer*, pp. 234-262.

[18] Hyman, *25 Years*, p. 40 ff.; *AJYB*, XXXV, 60.

[19] Cf. *Das Schwarzbuch: Tatsachen und Dokumente: Die Lage der*

Juden in Deutschland 1933, herausgegeben vom Comité des Délégations juives, 1934. Cf. B. S. Deutsch, "The Disfranchisement of the Jew" and Stephen S. Wise, "The War upon World Jewry," both in *Nazism* (supra, note 11), pp. 39 ff., 202 ff.

[20] On Baeck and his associates, see Bentwich, l. c., p. 229 f., who repeatedly praises the unity and resoluteness of German Jews.

[21] On the Jewish press, see *UJE*, VIII, 439. New Jewish organizations, ibid., IV, 581 f. *Help and Reconstruction* published annual reports as long as the Nazi authorities permitted. A summary in English appeared under the title, *Jewish Constructive Work in Germany*. Most of the statements on these pages are based on personal experience.

[22] Some "signs of the Nazi blight upon Jewish life in modern Germany," in *UJE*, IV, 580. "A collection of facts and documents relating to three years' persecutions of German Jews," in *The Yellow Spot*, Knight publications, 1936, containing 48 authentic illustrations.

[23] General v. Fritsch advocated the admission of Jews to the army: cf. Fr. Oechsner, *This Is the Enemy*, 1942, p. 129. The same author reports that in a conversation with the Italian Ambassador in 1935, Adolf Hitler stated that in a decade there would be no more Jews in Germany, and in a reply shouted, "In ten years they will be gone:" ibid., p. 128.

[24] The reasons given for the Nuremberg Laws are a record of mendacity even for so brazen a liar as Hitler. The laws were published in all the newspapers of the world. For their discussion, see *UJE*, IV, 582; *AJYB*, XXXIX, 325 ff.; Warburg, p. 191 ff.

[25] Wallace R. Deuel, *People under Hitler*, 1942, has an extremely instructive chapter on "Delirium of Race," p. 181 ff. He knows of 538 trials in 1936 for race defilement and of 31 different laws regulating marriages between Jews and persons of German blood: p. 215 f. Streicher posed as educator of the German people. His qualification was proved not only through the publication of that pornographic weekly *Der Stürmer*, but even more through the books for juvenile readers which his *Stürmer Verlag* published: cf. Warburg, pp. 139 ff., 302, notes 33 and 34. Louis P. Lochner, for 14 years representative of the United Press in Berlin, expressed his *dégout* for these poisonous publications in *What about Germany*, 1941, p. 68. The sexual depravity of Julius Streicher was recently disclosed by Curt Riess in the *American Mercury*, March 1943, p. 282 ff. If but a small portion of the crimes ascribed to him is authentic, it throws considerable light on the moral standards of the Nazi party. How far their practice in the matter of sexual racial purity is from their doctrine was learned during the Second World War when Jewish girls were forced into brothels for rape by Nazi officers and soldiers.

[26] The disappointing experiences in the first attempts of the "Council," in Bentwich, l. c., p. 263 ff.

[27] Such apprehensions prevailed already in 1933. James G. Mc-

Donald "saw no enthusiasm in England and the United States to take persecuted Jews into the country." Dodd's *Diaries*, p. 79.

[28] Among the innovations of the year 1936 was the establishment in Munich of the Reich Institute for History of the New Germany which announced that it would "bring scientific clarity to bear on the racial basis of the solution of such a tremendous problem as the Jewish question." The Institute organized 12 departments for 12 sections of Jewish History; its annual meetings and its publications dealt exclusively with the Jewish question. Streicher, as a guest of honor of the Berlin University, suggested the organization at the University of a new institute devoted to raising antisemitism to a new German science. In March 1941 the Institute for Jewish Research in Frankfort was opened in the presence of many foreign guests. The Institute was endowed with several big Jewish libraries looted from occupied countries.

[29] The appointment of the Gestapo, in Heiden, p. 99 ff. On David Frankfurter, the murderer of the Nazi agent Wilhelm Gustloff in Davos, and on his trial, see *UJE*, IV, 407. The immense Nazi propaganda set loose on that occasion failed to impress the world.

[30] Some of the chicaneries, ibid., p. 582; *AJYB*, XXXVIII, 311 ff.; XL, 109 f.; 198 ff. On the IOBB, ibid., XXXIX, 224 ff., 337 f.

[31] The quotation about Austria is from Heiden, p. 261; the details were reported by the London correspondent of the *New York Times*, April 3, 1938. Cf. Warburg, p. 233 ff.; Bentwich, l. c., p. 273 ff. The Nazi district leader of Vienna bore the out and out teutonic name of Globocznik!! Cf. "Jews forced to scrub the streets," a photo reproduced in *UJE*, IV, 583. The subsequent events in Austria, *CJR*, I, 1, p. 67 ff.; *AJYB*, XL, 208 ff.

[32] The law concerning registration of Jewish property, in *CJR*, I, 1, p. 42 ff. Other chicaneries of that period, ibid., p. 65 ff.; I, 2, p. 84 ff. The law regarding Jewish given names, ibid., p. 17 ff. On the first demolitions of synagogues, cf. the series of articles published by *The Jewish Way* in the summer of 1942. On further events of 1938, see *CJR*, II, 2, p. 6 ff.

[33] The initiative of the U. S. Government, in *AJYB*, XL, 96 ff. On the Evian Conference, see Bentwich, p. 279 ff.; *AJYB*, ibid., p. 345 ff.; *CJR*, I, 1, p. 17 ff., 40 ff., 47 ff. The inferno of the refugee problem, in *AJYB*, XLI, 314 ff.

[34] For statistics of Jews in the Sudeten area, see *CJR*, I, 1, p. 57 f.; anti-Jewish measures, ibid., I, 2, p. 80 ff. Jews in the new Czechoslovakia, ibid., II, 1, p. 7 ff.

[35] Deportation of Polish Jewish citizens from Germany, ibid., II, 1, p. 66.

[36] Herschel Grynszpan's desperate act and the events which followed were reported in all the newspapers of that week. For a summary of the events see *CJR*, I, 2, p. 56a ff. The quotation is from the *Daily Telegraph*, London. For further press statements, see *New York Times*,

November 11, 1938. The barbaric method of putting fire to buildings was learned from the Ukrainian hordes in 1920–21. Eyewitnesses report that the Nazi hooligans had to be shifted from far distant places; evidently the wire-pullers were afraid that natives would shrink from such acts of vandalism.

[37] President Roosevelt's statement, first published in the daily papers, is repeated in *CJR*, ibid., p. 56d, and is reproduced in *Peace and War: U. S. Foreign Policy 1931–41*, 1942, p. 58. For further reactions, see *CJR*, ibid., 56e ff. The motion adopted by the British House of Commons, November 21, 1938, and the introductory speech of Mr. Noel Baker, ibid., II, 1, p. 33 ff.

[38] The Nazi apparatus did not function with the usual precision. The official monitors of the party, already on November 8, when vom Rath was still alive, warned that Jews would be considered as members of a hostile power. The same day synagogues in Kassel and other places of Hesse were being burnt. The exact number of synagogues burnt has so far not been revealed. The vandalism of burning and dynamiting synagogues was continued by the Nazis in Czechoslovakia and later in occupied territories, in Poland as well as in France. The British [White] *Papers concerning the Treatment of German Nationals in Germany, Presented by Secretary of State for Foreign Affairs to Parliament* (Cmd. 6120) contain the full, authentic order of police headquarters in Cologne of November 10, 1938, on how the anti-Jewish riots were to be organized. *UJE*, I, 364, has a facsimile of the orders of the police in Vienna. The White Paper contains reports of the British consuls in Cologne, Dresden, Munich, Vienna about anti-Jewish demonstrations following the death of Herr vom Rath and about the treatment of Jewish prisoners in concentration camps, partly corroborated by statements of Jewish ex-prisoners.

[39] For "Texts of the most important recent laws and decrees" in Germany, see *CJR*, II, 1, pp. 54–66; cf. II, 2, p. 6 ff. On the events of those months, ibid., II, 1, pp. 102–108; II, 2, pp. 94–98. On November 12, *The Eternal Jew*, an exhibit first shown in Munich in 1937, was opened in Berlin and made accessible to the public for two months. 1,500 anti-Jewish propaganda meetings to be held all over the country were announced November 21.

[40] The pace of emigration is evident from the official German census of 1939. The Reich, which in 1933 had numbered 599,000 Jews by religion, reduced this number to 240,000 racial Jews, i. e., including those who were half and quarter-Jews. Greater Germany numbered 330,892 racial Jews, i. e., 0.42% of the total population; 90% of all Jews were past middle age. From Austria, since the *Anschluss* up to the end of the year 1939, no less than 117,000 Jews had emigrated. On the plight of Viennese Jews, see Bentwich, l. c., p. 291 ff.

[41] On the relief work of states, organizations and individuals, ibid., 283 ff. *AJYB*, XLI, 383 ff. On refugees in France, *CJR*, III, 138 ff.; in England, ibid., II, 4, p. 22 ff. Cf. II, 5, p. 30 ff.

⁴² On the dealings of Mr. Rublee, ibid., pp. 37 ff.; Bentwich, l. c., p. 286. The proposals of the Reich as published in the *N. Y. Times*, February 14, 1939, in *CJR*, II, 2, p. 77. Whatever the bearing of the scheme and the "coordinating foundation," formed with the cooperation of the JDC and incorporated in London in 1939, might have been, conditions were changed by the political crisis which started with the occupation of Czechoslovakia, March 15, and led to the new World War, September 1. During the first two years of the war Jews who had regular visas, transport facilities, and were able to pay all dues were allowed to emigrate by way of Lisbon. A very important investigation was John Hope Simpson's *The Refugee Problem: Report of a Survey*, 1939, which brings our information down to July 1939. On the work of the JDC right after the outbreak of the war, see *CJR*, III, 227 ff.

⁴³ January 28, 1939, a conference in Paris discussed "how to combat dumping, by the Gestapo, of refugees on German steamers bound for oversea lands to which entry visas are not required for holders of German passports." The role of the Gestapo and the staffs of certain legations and consulates in this blackmailing business has not yet been ascertained, but it is certain that enormous sums were being extorted. Cuba had generously admitted refugees in 1938 and the beginning of 1939, but voided all landing permits previously issued, on May 5. Ten days later the S.S. St. Louis sailed, and the Hamburg-America Line announced that it had been assured that the landing permits would be honored. The tragic odyssey of the steamer and the efforts of the JDC to rescue the passengers, in *AJYB*, XLI, 387 ff.

⁴⁴ Cf. the chapter "Spreading the Poison," in Warburg, pp. 266–295. Ibid., 271, the main Nazi agencies for antisemitic propaganda, like the *Fichte-Bund* in Hamburg, the *Welt-Dienst* in Erfurt, and the Institute for the Study of the Jewish Question in Berlin, etc., are listed. Cf. also Curt Riess, *Totalitarian Espionage*, 1941.

⁴⁵ About the Fascists in Great Britain, see *UJE*, I, 361 f.; Canada's Fifth Column, *CJR*, III, 388 ff. On Anti-Jewish propaganda in the U. S. A., see *CJR*, II, 3, pp. 6–19; II, 4, pp. 43–57, 58–61. Cf. ibid., II, 6, p. 20 ff.; III, 370 ff. Since antisemitism had become part of the isolationists' policy, much has been written about it in popular magazines. On France, see *UJE*, I, 362 f.; IV, 379 f. A decree of the President of the Republic against religious and racial incitement of April 21, 1939, in *CJR*, II, 3, p. 67 f. To what the subversive work of the antisemitic French Fifth Column amounted was not known until after the collapse of France in 1940.

⁴⁶ On Danzig, see *CJR*, I, 2, p. 82 f.; II, 1, p. 98 f.; II, 2, p. 93; II, 3, p. 106. On Memel, see *UJE*, VII, 456. The Economic Bureau of the World Jewish Congress published in 1938 a survey, *La Situation Économique des Juifs dans le Monde: I. La Situation Économique des Minorités Juives*. Besides, the Congress published, *La Situation des Juifs en Roumanie: Pétition du Comité Executive du Congrès Juif*

Mondiale soumise au Conseil de la Société des Nations, and supplemented this petition by additional material.

[47] On Italy, see ibid., V, 636 ff.; the report on the race question, *CJR*, I, 1, p. 10 ff. The royal decrees and laws, ibid., I, 2, p. 12 f.; II, 1, pp. 77–82; II, 3, pp. 68–86. See also ibid., I, 1, p. 36 ff.; I, 2, p. 37 ff.; II, 4, p. 30 ff.; and the books reviewed in III, 105 f.

[48] On Hungary, see *UJE*, V, 501 ff.; *CJR*, I, 1, p. 32 ff. A Jewish declaration of protest, ibid., p. 26 ff. On the law of 1938, ibid., II, 3, p. 27; the law of 1939, ibid., II, 5, p. 64 ff. On Count Teleki, see Count Carlo Sforza, *The Totalitarian War and After*, p. 93.

[49] On Rumania, see *UJE*, IX, 260 ff.; *CJR*, III, p. 35 ff.; statistics, ibid., II, 5, p. 78; *AJYB*, XLI, 315 ff.

[50] On Poland, see *UJE*, VIII, 576; *CJR*, II, 1, p. 16 ff.; *AJYB*, XLI, 281 ff.

[51] On Czechoslovakia, see ibid., 268 ff.; *CJR*, I, 1, p. 7 ff.; II, 2, p. 74 ff.; II, 4, p. 108 ff.; II, 5, p. 87 f.; II, 6, p. 63 f.

BIBLIOGRAPHY*

ADLER, CYRUS, Jacob H. Schiff: His Life and Letters. 2 vols., New York, 1928.
———, "Jews in the Diplomatic Correspondence of the United States," in *PAJHS*, XV, (1906). New York, 1907.
———, and AARON M. MARGALITH, American Intercession in behalf of Jews in the Diplomatic Correspondence of the United States, 1840–1938. *PAJHS*, XXXVI, New York, 1943.
ADLER, ELKAN, London. Jewish Communities Series, Philadelphia, 1930.
AESCOLY-WEINTRAUB, A. Z., "The Falashas: A Bibliography" (Hebrew), in *K. S.*, XII (1935–36), 264 f., 370 ff., 498 ff.; XIII, 250 ff.
AGURSKY, J., The Jewish Commissariats and the Jewish Communist Sections (Yiddish). A collection of documents, 1918–21. Minsk, 1928.
AHAD HA'AM (GINZBERG, ASHER), Selected Essays. English translation by L. Simon. Philadelphia, 1912.
———, At the Crossroads (Hebrew). 4 vols., 3rd ed., Berlin, 1921.
———, Ten Essays on Zionism and Judaism. English translation by L. Simon, London, 1922.
———, Memoirs and Letters (Hebrew). Tel Aviv, 1931.
———, Letters of Ahad Ha'Am (Hebrew). 6 vols., Tel Aviv, 1923–25.
AHLWARDT, HERMANN, Neue Enthüllungen: Judenflinten. Dresden, 1892.
Allgemeine Zeitung des Judentums (Weekly), ed. by Ludwig Philippson, et al. Leipzig-Berlin, 1837–1922.
Alliance Israélite Universelle, Bulletin Mensuel de l'Alliance, etc. Paris, 1860–1913.
———, La question Juive, devant la Conférence de la Paix. Paris, 1919.
ALPERSOHN, MARCOS, Thirty Years in Argentina: Memoirs of a Jewish Colonist (Yiddish). 3 vols., Berlin, 1923–28.
American Jewish Committee, The Jews in Nazi Germany; the Factual Record of their Persecution by the National Socialists. New York, 1933.

---

*It was out of the question and unnecessary to append here a bibliography with any claim to completeness for the period with which this volume deals. Such bibliographical material may be found in vol. III of S. W. Baron's *A Social and Religious History of the Jews*, New York, 1937, and the same author's *Bibliography of Jewish Social Studies*, New York, 1941. The author of this volume decided, therefore, to attempt no more than to give the full titles of books referred to frequently in the Notes and to offer a guide to books and articles in which the reader may find a more ample discussion of any subject in which his interest was aroused [Ed.].

American Jewish Committee, The Jews in Nazi Germany. A handbook of facts regarding their present situation. New York, 1935.

American Jewish Year Book, The, ed. by Cyrus Adler, Harry Schneiderman, et al. Philadelphia, 1899–date.

AMMENDE, E., ed., Die Nationalitäten in den Staaten Europas. Sammlung von Lagenberichten hrsg. im Auftrage des Europäischen Nationalitäten-Kongress. Vienna, 1931. Ergänzungen, Vienna, 1932.

ANDREWS, FANNIE FERN, The Holy Land under Mandate. 2 vols., Boston, 1931.

AMBRUNNEN, A., Juden werden Schweizer: Dokumente zur Judenfrage in der Schweiz seit 1798. Zürich, 1935.

Antisemiten-Spiegel: die Antisemiten im Lichte des Christentums, des Rechtes und der Moral. Danzig, 1891.

ARLOSOROFF, H., Collected Writings, (Hebrew), ed. by J. Steinberg. 7 vols., Tel Aviv, 1934–35.

Baden, Gedenkbuch zum hundertundfünfundzwanzigjährigen Bestehen des Oberrats der Israeliten Badens. Frankfurt a. M., 1934.

BAECK, LEO, The Essence of Judaism (translated from Das Wesen des Judentums, 5th ed., Frankfurt, 1926). New York, 1936.

———, Wege im Judentum; Aufsätze und Reden. Berlin, 1933.

———, Aus Drei Jahrtausenden, Berlin, 1938.

BARON, S. W., The Jews in Roumania: Report submitted to the 8th Session of the American Jewish Congress. New York, 1930.

———, A Social and Religious History of the Jews. 3 vols., New York, 1937.

BAUER, J., L'Ecole Rabbinique de France (1830–1930), with a preface by Israel Lévy. Paris, 1931.

BEBEL, AUGUST, Sozialdemokratie und Antisemitismus. 2d revised ed., Berlin, 1906.

BEHR, S., Der Bevölkerungsrückgang der deutschen Juden. Frankfurt a. M. 1932.

BEIN, ALEX, Theodor Herzl: Biographie. Vienna, 1934. English edition, Philadelphia, 1940.

BEN-DAVID, E., Gli Ebrei nella vita culturale italiana (1848–1928). Citta di Castello, 1931.

BENTWICH, NORMAN, Legislation of Palestine 1918–25, compiled. 2 vols., Alexandria, 1926.

———, The Mandate's System. London, 1930.

———, England in Palestine. London, 1932.

———, Wanderer between Two Worlds. London, 1941.

BERGL, J., Geschichte der ungarischen Juden. Leipzig, 1879.

BERGMAN, HUGO, The Thinkers of This Generation (Hebrew). Tel Aviv, 1935.

BERKOWITZ, J., La Question des Israélites en Roumanie. Paris, 1923.

BERNERI, C., Le Juif antisémite. Paris, 1935.

BERNHARD, LUDWIG (LUDWIG BERNHARD ROSENBAUM), Krisis: Ein politisches Manifest. Weimar, 1932.

BERNSTEIN, F., Der Antisemitismus als Gruppenerscheinung: Versuch einer Soziologie des Judenhasses. Berlin, 1926.

BERNSTEIN, HENRY, The Truth about 'The Protocols of Zion:' a Complete Exposure. New York, 1935.
BEVAN, E. R. and SINGER, CH., The Legacy of Israel. 2d impression, Oxford, 1928.
BIALIK, CH. N., Collected Works (Hebrew). Tel Aviv, 1938.
BIELING, R., Die Juden Vornehmlich: Ein geschichtlicher Überblick über die Arbeit der Gesellschaft zur Beförderung des Christentums unter den Juden zu Berlin, 1822–1902. Berlin, 1902.
BIRNBAUM, NATHAN, Ausgewählte Schriften zur jüdischen Frage. 2 vols.. Czernowitz, 1910.
———, Im Dienste der Verheissung. Frankfurt a. M., 1927.
BLAUSTEIN, DAVID, Memoirs of, arranged by Miriam Blaustein. New York, 1913.
BLUM, J., The Jews of Baltimore: An Historical Summary of their Progress and Status as Citizens of Baltimore. Baltimore, 1910.
BOEHM, ADOLF, Die zionistische Bewegung: Eine kurze Darstellung ihrer Entwicklung. 2nd revised edition, 2 vols., Tel Aviv, 1935 ff.
BOLITHO, H., Alfred Mond, First Lord Melchett. New York, 1933.
BONNE, A., Palästina, Land und Wirtschaft. 3rd ed., Berlin, 1935.
BOROCHOV, DOV BER, Poale Zion Shriften. 2 vols., New York, 1920–28.
———, Klasse und Nation; Zur Theorie und Praxis des jüdischen Sozialismus. Berlin, 1932.
BOROVOI, S. Y., Evreiskaia zemledelcheskaia kolonizatsiia v staroi Rossii (Jewish Agricultural Colonization in Old Russia). Moscow, 1928.
BRAFMAN, J., Kniga Kahala (The Book of the Kahal). 2nd ed., 2 vols., St. Petersburg, 1882.
———, Das Buch vom Kahal auf Grund einer neuen Verdeutschung des russischen Originals. Hrsg. v. S. Passarge, 2 vols., Leipzig, 1928.
BREUER, ISAAC, Der neue Kusari: ein Weg zum Judentum. Frankfurt a. M., 1934.
———, u. ROSENHEIM, JACOB, Erez Isroel und die Orthodoxie. Frankfurt a. M., 1934.
BRUNNER, CONSTANTIN, Der Judenhass und die Juden. Berlin, 1918.
BUCHBINDER, N. A., History of the Jewish Labor Movement in Russia (Yiddish). Vilna, 1931.
BULASCHOW, D., (B. SEGEL), Bolschewismus und Judentum. Berlin, 1923.
CAHNMANN, W., Völkische Rassenlehre. Berlin, 1932.
Cause of World Unrest, The, with an introduction by (H. A. Gwynne) the editor of The Morning Post (London). New York, 1920.
CHASANOWITSCH, L., Die Krise der jüdischen Kolonisation in Argentinien und der moralische Bankrott der ICA Administration. Lemberg, 1910.
———, u. MOTZKIN, L., Die Judenfrage der Gegenwart: Dokumentensammlung. Stockholm, 1919.
CITRON, S. L., History of the "Love of Zion" Movement (Hebrew). Vol. I, Odessa, 1914.
———, A History of the Yiddish Press (Yiddish). Vol. I, Vilna, 1923.
———, A Biographical Dictionary of Zionist Leaders (Hebrew). Warsaw, 1924.

COHEN, HERMANN, Jüdische Schriften: Mit einer Einleitung von Franz Rosenzweig, hrsg. von Bruno Strauss. 3 vols., Berlin, 1924.

———, Religion der Vernunft aus den Quellen des Judentums. 2nd ed., Breslau, 1929.

COHEN, ISRAEL, The Jews in Modern Times. 2nd ed., London, 1929.

———, Vilna. Jewish Communities Series, Philadelphia, 1943.

———, The Journal of a Jewish Traveler. New York, 1925.

COHN, JOSEF, England und Palästina: Ein Beitrag zur britischen Empire-Politik (Zeitschrift für Geopolitik, Beihefte 8). Berlin, 1931.

Comité des Délégations juives, Paris. La Question des Juives allemands devant la Société des Nations. Published by the Comité, Paris, 1933.

———, Das Schwarzbuch: Tatsachen und Dokumente: Die Lage der Juden in Deutschland, 1933. Paris, 1934.

———, Dix-sept ans d'activité. Paris, 1936.

Comité pour la défense des droits des Juifs, Le IIIe Reich et les Juifs: Essai d'une documentation. Antwerp, 1933.

CORTI, COUNT EGON, The Reign of the House of Rothschild, 1830–1871 (English transl. from the German). New York, 1927.

COUDENHOVE-KALERGI, COUNT HEINRICH, Antisemitism throughout the Ages. Ed. and brought up to date by Count Richard Coudenhove-Kalergi. Authorized English transl. from the German, London, 1935.

COWEN, PHILIP, Memories of an American Jew: with an Introductory Note by Dr. A. S. W. Rosenbach. New York, 1932.

DARK, S., The Jew of To-day. London, 1933.

DAVIS, E., The History of Rodeph Shalom Congregation, Philadelphia, 1802–1926, with an Introduction by Rabbi L. Wolsey. Philadelphia, 1926.

DINABURG, BENZION, Love of Zion (Hebrew). Vol. I, Tel-Aviv, 1932.

DOUKHAN, M., ed., Laws of Palestine, 1926–31. 4 vols., Tel-Aviv, 1932–33.

———, Laws of Palestine, 1932–1933. 2 vols., Tel-Aviv, 1933–34.

DRAULT, J., (GENDROT, ALFRED), Drumont, La France juive et la Libre Parole. Paris, 1935.

DRUCK, D., Baron Edmond Rothschild: the Story of a Practical Idealist, with an Introduction by Nathan Straus. New York, 1928.

DRUMONT, E., La France juive: Essay d'histore contemporaine. 2nd ed., 2 vols., Paris, 1886.

DRUYANOV, A., Documents for the History of the "Love of Zion" and the Colonization of Palestine (Hebrew). 3 vols., Odessa-Tel-Aviv, 1910–32.

DUBNOW, S. M., History of the Jews in Russia and Poland (English transl. from the Russian). 3 vols., Philadelphia, 1916.

———, Pisma o starom i novom evreistvie (Letters on Old and Modern Judaism, 1897–1907). Revised ed., St. Petersburg, 1907. Das alte und das neue Judentum, 1926, German transl. of the first 3 Letters by E. Hurwicz.

———, Weltgeschichte des jüdischen Volkes. 10 vols., Berlin, 1925–29.

DUKER, A. G., The Situation of the Jews in Poland, with an Introductory Statement by M. R. Cohen and S. W. Baron. New York, 1936.

ECKSTEIN, ADOLF, Der Kampf der Juden um ihre Emanzipation in Bayern. Fürth, 1905.

ELBOGEN, ISMAR, Geschichte der Juden in Deutschland. Berlin, 1935.

ELZAS, BARNET, E., The Jews in South Carolina from the Earliest Times to the Present Day. Philadelphia, 1905.

EPSTEIN, Z., Mosheh Leb Lilienblum: His Views on Religion and the Jewish Renaissance in Palestine (Hebrew). Tel-Aviv, 1935.

ERIK, M. (S. MERKIN), The History of Yiddish Literature (Yiddish). Warsaw, 1928.

———, Studies in the History of the Haskalah, 1789–1881 (Yiddish). Vol. I, Minsk, 1934.

Executive Committee of the General Federation of Jewish Labor in Palestine, Documents and Essays on Jewish Labor Policy in Palestine. Tel-Aviv, 1930.

EZEKIEL, H. T., and G. LICHTENSTEIN, The History of the Jews in Richmond, Va. from 1769 to 1917. Richmond, 1917.

FAHN, R., History of Jewish National Autonomy in the Period of the West Ukrainian Republic, 1918–19 (Yiddish). Lemberg, 1933.

FAULHABER, CARDINAL MICHAEL, Judaism, Christianity and Germany (English transl. from the German). New York, 1934.

FEDER, E., Politik und Humanität: Paul Nathan: Ein Lebensbild. Berlin, 1929.

FEHST, H., Bolschewismus und Judentum: Das jüdische Element in der Führerschaft des Bolschewismus. Berlin, 1934.

FEINBERG, N. S., La Question des minorités à la Conférence de la paix de 1919–20 et l'action juive en faveur de la protection internationale des minorités. Paris, 1929.

FISHBERG, MORRIS, The Jews: A Study of Race and Environment. London, 1911.

FRANK, W., Hofprediger Adolf Stöcker und die christlich-soziale Bewegung. 2d ed., Hamburg, 1935.

FREIMANN, A. and KRACAUER, F., Frankfort. Jewish Communities Series, Philadelphia, 1929.

FREUND, ISMAR, Die Emanzipation der Juden in Preussen unter besonderer Berücksichtigung des Gesetzes vom 11. März 1812. 2 vols., Berlin, 1912.

FRIEDLÄNDER, FRITZ, Gabriel Riesser. Berlin, 1927.

FRIEDMANN, PHILIPP, Die galizischen Juden im Kampfe um ihre Gleichberechtigung (1848–1868). Frankfurt a. M., 1929.

FRISCH, EPHRAIM, A Historical Survey of Jewish Philanthrophy. New York, 1924.

GALANTÉ, A., Turcs et Juifs: Etude Historique politique. Stambul, 1933.

GEIGER, LUDWIG, Abraham Geiger: Leben und Lebenswerk. Berlin, 1910.

GELBER, N. M., Die Juden und der Polnische Aufstand von 1863. Wien, 1923.

———, Aus zwei Jahrhunderten; Beitraege zur neueren Geschichte der Juden. Wien, 1924.

GERGEL, N., The Pogroms in Ukraine, 1918–21 (Yiddish). Vilna, 1928.

———, The situation of the Jews in Russia (Yiddish). Warsaw, 1929.

GINZBERG, LOUIS, Students, Scholars and Saints. Philadelphia, 1928.

GLIKSMAN, G., L'Aspect économique et la question juive en Pologne, with prefaces by W. Oualid and L. Hersch. Paris, 1929.

GLICKSON, M., Ahad Ha'Am. his life and work (Hebrew). Jerusalem, 1927.

GOLD, H., Die Juden und Judengemeinden Mährens in Vergangenheit und Gegenwart: Ein Sammelwerk. Brünn, 1929.

———, Die Juden und die Judengemeinde Bratislawa etc. Brünn, 1932.

———, Die Juden und Judengemeinden Boehmens.... Bruenn, 1934.

GOLDBERG, M., Die Jahre 1881–82 in der Geschichte der russischen Juden. Berlin, 1934.

GOLDE, J. (or Y.), Evrei-zemladeltsi v. Krimu (Jews-Farmers in the Crimea). Moscow, 1931.

GOLDSTEIN, ISRAEL, A Century of Judaism in New York: B'nai Jeshurun 1825–1925. New York, 1930.

GOLDSTEIN, JULIUS, Rasse und Politik. 4th ed., Leipzig, 1925.

GOLDSTEIN, S. E., The League of Nations and the Grounds for Action in Behalf of the Jews of Germany. New York, 1933.

GOODHART, ARTHUR L., Poland and the Minority Races. London, [1920].

GOODMAN, PAUL AND SIMON, LEON. Zionist Thinkers and Leaders. London, 1929.

GORDON, ABRAHAM DAVID, Collected Writings (Hebrew). 5 vols., Tel-Aviv, 1925–29.

———, Erlösung durch Arbeit (Partial transl. in German). Berlin, 1920.

GORIN, B., A History of the Jewish Theater (Yiddish). 2 vols., New York, 1918.

GOTTHEIL, RICHARD J. H., Zionism. Philadelphia, 1914.

———, The Life of Gustav Gottheil: Memoir of a Priest in Israel. Williamsport, Pa., 1936.

GRAETZ, H., Geschichte der Juden. 11 vols., 1853–76.

———, History of the Jews (English transl.) 6 vols., New York, 1927.

GRAJEWSKI, P., Some Records of Jerusalem: in Memory of the First Lovers of Zion (Hebrew). Jerusalem, 1929.

GRUNWALD, MAX, Vienna. Jewish Communities Series, Philadelphia, 1936.

GUENTHER, H. F. K., Rassenkunde des jüdischen Volkes. Munich, 1930.

GUTTMANN, JULIUS, Die Philosophie des Judentums. Munich, 1933.

HAAS, JACOB DE, Theodor Herzl: A Biographical Study. Chicago, 1927.

———, Louis D. Brandeis: A Biographical Sketch. New York, 1929.

Handbuch der Judenfrage, das., Th. Fritsch, ed. 33rd ed., Leipzig, 1933.

HART, A. D., The Jew in Canada: A Complete Record of Canadian Jewry from the Days of the French Regime to the Present Time. Toronto, 1926.

HEILIKMAN, TOBIAH, History of the Social Movement among the Jews in Poland and Russia (Yiddish). Moscow, 1926.

HELLER, ABRAHAM, Die Lage der Juden in Russland von der Märzrevolution 1917 bis zur Gegenwart. Breslau, 1935.

HELLER, O., Der Untergang des Judentums: Die Judenfrage, ihre Kritik, ihre Lösung durch den Sozialismus. Vienna, 1931.

HERMONI, A., Baron Edmond Rothschild, the Father of Jewish Settlement (Hebrew). Tel-Aviv, 1935.

HERRMANN, H., Palästinakunde: Ein Hand- und Nachschlagebuch. 2d revised ed., Vienna, 1935.

HERRMANN, L., Nathan Birnbaum, sein Werk und seine Wandlung. Berlin, 1914.

———, Jubileum-buch zum 60ten geburtstag fun Noson Birnbaum (Yiddish). Warsaw, 1925.

———, A History of the Jews in South Africa from Earliest Times to 1895. 2d impression, London, 1935.

HERTZ, FREDERIC, Race and Civilization. English transl. from the German, New York, 1928.

HERZL, THEODOR, Tagebücher, 1895–1904 (ed. by Leon Kellner). 3 vols., Berlin, 1922–23.

———, Gesammelte zionistische Werke. 5 vols., Berlin, 1934.

———, A Jewish State: An attempt at a Modern Solution of the Jewish Question. English transl. by S. d'Avigdor, 2d. ed., revised with a foreword by Israel Cohen, London, 1934.

———, The Congress Addresses. English transl., New York, 1917.

HESS, MOSES, Rom and Jerusalem: A Study in Jewish Nationalism. English transl. with introduction and notes by M. Waxman, New York, 1918.

———, Jüdische Schriften. ed. by Theodor Zlocisti, Berlin, 1905.

HESSEN, JULIUS, Istoriia evreiskago naroda v rossii (A History of the Jewish People in Russia). 2 vols., Leningrad, 1925–27.

HICEM, Ten Years of Jewish Migration, 1926–36 (Yiddish). Paris, 1936.

HITLER, ADOLF, Führerzitate: Der Führer über das Judentum. Nationalsozialistische Bibliographie III, no. 12, Dec. 1938, pp. I–VI.

———, Mein Kampf. Complete and unabridged, fully annotated. Editorial Sponsors: John Chamberlain, Sidney B. Fay, et al. New York, 1939.

HOYER, K., Beiträge zur Judenfrage in Deutschland. *Deutschlands Erneuerung*, XVII–XIX.

HUGHES, I., Antisemitism (Organized Anti-Jewish Sentiment): A World Survey. Los Angeles, 1934.

HYAMSON, ALBERT, M., A History of the Jews in England. 2d ed., London, 1928.

———, Palestine, Old and New. London, 1928.

———, "British Projects for the Restoration of the Jews to Palestine," in *PAJHS*, XXVI (1918), 127–164.

ISLER, J. M., Rückkehr der Juden zur Landwirtschaft: Beitrag zur Geschichte der Landwirtschaftlichen Kolonisation der Juden in verschiedenen Ländern. Frankfurt a. M., 1929.

JABOTINSKY, VLADIMIR, The Jewish War Front. London, 1940.

———, Die jüdische Legion in Weltkrieg. Berlin, 1930.

JACOBS, JOSEPH, The Jewish Question 1875–84: A Bibliographical Hand-List. London, 1885.

———, Jewish Contributions to Civilization: An Estimate. Philadelphia, 1919.

JANOWSKY, OSCAR, I., The Jews and Minority Rights 1898–1919, with a Foreword by J. W. Mack. New York, 1933.

JESCHURIN, E. H., Vilna, a Book of Essays (Yiddish). New York, 1933.

JOSEPH, S., Jewish Immigration to the U.S. from 1881–1910. New York, 1914.
———, History of the Baron de Hirsch Fund: The Americanization of the Jewish Immigrant. Philadelphia, 1935.
Jüdisches Lexicon: Ein encyclopädisches Handbuch des jüdischen Wissens. Ed. by Georg Herlitz and Bruno Kirschner, 5 vols., Berlin, 1927–30.
KAGAN, S. R., Jewish Contributions to Medicine in America (1656–1934). Boston, 1934.
KAHN, FRITZ, Die Juden als Rasse und Kulturvolk. Berlin, 1922.
KALLEN, H. M., Judaism at Bay: Essays toward the Adjustment of Judaism to Modernity. New York, 1932.
KANTOR, I., The Jewish Population of the Ukraine (Yiddish). Kharkow, 1929.
KAPLAN, MORDECAI, M., Judaism as a Civilization: Toward a Reconstruction of American-Jewish Life. New York, 1934.
———, Judaism in Transition. New York, 1936.
KAPLUN-KOGAN, WLADIMIR W., Die jüdischen Wanderbewegungen in der neuesten Zeit. Bonn, 1919.
KAUTSKY, K., Are the Jews a Race? (English transl. from the German). 2d ed., New York, 1926.
KERLEQ, J. DE, Israël en Palestine, suivi du Mémorandum du Conseil national des Juifs à la Société des nations. Paris, 1933.
KLATZKIN, JACOB, Probleme des modernen Judentums. 2nd ed., Berlin, 1930.
KLAUSNER, JOSEF, Creators and Builders (Hebrew). 3 vols., Jerusalem, 1925–29.
———, A History of Modern Hebrew Literature (English transl. of an older, shorter work in Hebrew). London, 1932.
KLEINMANN, M., Portraits and Personalities: Essays on Modern Hebrew Literature (Hebrew). 2nd ed., Paris, 1928.
KOBER, A., Cologne. Jewish Communities Series, Philadelphia, 1940.
KOBLER, F., Juden und Judentum in deutschen Briefen aus drei Jahrhunderten. Wien, 1935.
———, Jüdische Geschichte in Briefen aus Ost und West. Wien, 1938.
KOERBER, R., PAGEL, TH. ET AL., Antisemitismus der Welt in Wort und Bild. 2nd ed., Dresden, 1935.
KOHLER, MAX J., "The Board of Delegates of American Israelites, 1859–1878," in *PAJHS*, XXIX (1925), pp. 75–135.
———, "Jews in the Anti-Slavery Movement," in *PAJHS*, V (1896), 137–155.
———, and WOLF, S., Jewish Disabilities in the Balkan States; American Contributions toward their Removal, with particular reference to the Congress of Berlin. New York, 1916.
KOHN, HANS, Martin Buber, sein Werk und seine Zeit: Ein Versuch über Religion und Politik. Hellerau, 1930.
KREPPEL, JONAS, Juden und Judentum von Heute, übersichtlich dargestellt: Ein Handbuch. Zürich, 1925.
KRETZER, P., Die beruflichen und sozialen Verhältnisse der Juden in der Sowjet Union. Berlin, 1931.
KROJANKER, GUSTAV, Juden in der deutschen Literatur: Essays über zeitgenössische Schriftsteller. Berlin, 1922.

KRUK, J., Die Rolle der auswärtigen Staaten für die Emanzipation der Juden in der Schweiz. Zürich, 1913.

LACHOWER, FEIWEL, A History of Modern Hebrew Literature (Hebrew). 4 vols., Tel-Aviv, 1928–33.

LANDAUER, E., Das geltende jüdische Minderheitenrecht: Mit besonderer Berücksichtigung Osteuropas. Leipzig, 1924.

LANGNAS, S., Jews and Academic Studies in Poland in the Years 1921–31. Lwow, 1933.

LARIN, I. (M. A. LURYE), Evrei i antisemitizm v U. S. S. R. (Jews and Antisemitism in the U. S. S. R.). Moscow, 1929.

LAZARE, BERNARD, Antisemitism, Its History and Causes (English transl.). New York, 1903.

LAZARUS, MORITZ, Ethics of Judaism (English transl. from the German). 2 vols., Philadelphia, 1900–1.

LEBLOIS, L., L'Affaire Dreyfus: l'iniquité, la réparation, les principaux faits et les principaux documents. Paris, 1929.

LÉMANN, ABBÉ J., L'Entrée des Israélites dans la société francaise et les états chrétiens d'après des documents nouveaux. 6th ed., Paris, 1886.

LESSING, THEODOR, Der jüdische Selbsthass. Berlin, 1930.

LESTSCHINSKY, JACOB, Der wirtschaftliche Zusammenbruch der Juden in Deutschland und Polen. Paris, 1936.

———, The Economic Status of the Jews in Poland (Yiddish). Berlin, 1931.

———, Between Life and Death: Ten Years of Jewish Life in Soviet Russia (Yiddish). Vilna, 1930.

LEVEN, NARCISSE, Cinquante ans d'histoire: l'Alliance israélite universelle. 2 vols., Paris, 1911–20.

LEVINGER, L. J., Antisemitism, Yesterday and Tomorrow. New York, 1936.

LEVY, B. H., Reform Judaism in America: A Study in Religious Adaptation. New York, 1933.

LEWKOWITZ, ALBERT, Das Judentum und die geistigen Strömungen des 19. Jahrhunderts. Breslau, 1935.

LEWIN, A., Kantonisten: On the Jewish *Rekrutchina* in Russia and the Period of Czar Nicholas I, 1827–56 (Yiddish). Warsaw, 1934.

LINFIELD, H. S., Jewish Migration as a Part of World Migration Movements, 1920–30. New York, 1933.

LOEB, ISIDORE, Biographie d'Albert Cohn. Paris, 1878.

LOEW, LEOPOLD, Gesammelte Schriften her. von Immanuel Loew. 5 vols., Szegedin, 1889–1900.

LOGE, CHR., Gibt es jüdische Ritualmorde? Eine Sichtung und psychologische Klärung des geschichtlichen Materials. Graz, 1934.

LONDRES, A., The Jew has Come Home. New York, 1931.

LOWENTHAL, MARVIN, The Jews of Germany: A Story of 16 Centuries. Philadelphia, 1936.

———, Letters of Henrietta Szold. New York, 1942.

LUKE, H. C. J. AND KEITH-ROACH, E., The Handbook of Palestine and Transjordan. 3rd ed., New York, 1934.

LUZZATTI, LUIGI, God in Freedom: Studies in the Relations between Church and State, with American Supplementary Chapters by William H. Taft, Irving Lehman, Louis Marshall, Max J. Kohler, Dora Askovith. New York, 1930.

MARCUS, J. R., The Rise and Destiny of the German Jew. Cincinnati, 1934.

MARGULIS, U., History of the Jews in Russia: Studies and Documents (Yiddish). Vol. I, 1772–1861. Moscow, 1930.

MARR, WILHELM, Der Sieg des Judentums über das Germanentum: Vom nichtconfessionellen Standpunkt aus betrachtet. 6th ed., Bern, 1879.

MEADE, R. D., Judah P. Benjamin. New York, 1943.

MEHNERT, K., ed., Die Soviet-Union, 1917–32: Systematische, mit Komm. versehene Bibliographie der 1917–32 in deutscher Sprache ausserhalb der Soviet-Union veröff. 1900 wichtigsten Bücher und Aufsätze. Königsberg, 1933.

MEISL, JOSEF, Heinrich Graetz: Eine Würdigung des Historikers und des Juden zu seinem 100. Geburtstage. Berlin, 1917.

———, Geschichte der Juden in Polen und Russland. 3 vols., Berlin, 1921–25.

———, Die Durchführung des Artikels 44 des Berliner Vertrages in Rumänien und die europäische Diplomatie. Berlin, 1925.

MEYER, HEINZ, Das Recht der religiösen Minderheiten in Polen. Breslau, 1932.

MEYER, R. H., Politische Gründer und die Corruption in Deutschland. Leipzig, 1877.

MIESES, M., Der Ursprung des Judenhasses. Berlin, 1923.

MILIUTIN, B., Ustroistvo i sostoianie evreiskich obschestv v Rossii (Organization and Status of the Jewish Communities in Russia). St. Petersburg, 1849–50.

Mi-yamim rishonim (A periodical for the history of Israel's renaissance). A. Druyanov, ed., Tel-Aviv, 1934–35.

MOCH, M., Le Mandat britannique en Palestine, with a preface by J. Godart. Paris, 1932.

MOMMSEN, THEODOR, Auch ein Wort über unser Judenthum. 3rd impression, Berlin, 1880; Gesammelte Schriften.

MONTEFIORE, SIR MOSES, Diaries of Sir Moses and Lady Montefiore, comprising their life and work ..... from 1812–1883. Ed. by Louis Loewe, assisted by his son. 2 vols., Chicago, 1890.

MORAIS, H. S., The Jews of Philadelphia: Their History from the Earliest Settlements to the Present Time. Philadelphia, 1894.

MOTZKIN, LEO, La Campagne antisémite en Pologne: Trouble universitaire — Question du "Numerus clausus" — Boycott économique — Attitude des tribunaux. Paris, 1932. Cahiers du Comité des délégations juives, nos. 1–4.

NARDI, N., Zionism and Education in Palestine. New York, 1934.

NAUDH, D. H. (=LOTHAR BUCHER OR H. NORDMANN), Die Juden und der deutsche Staat. 12th revised ed., Leipzig, (1877).

NORDAU, MAX, Zionism: Its History and Its Aims. Transl. from the German, London, 1905.

———, Zionistische Schriften. 2nd ed., enlarged, Berlin, 1923.

NUSSBAUM, ARTHUR, Der Polnaer Ritualmordprozess: Eine kriminalpsychologische Untersuchung auf aktenmässiger Grundlage. 2nd ed., Berlin, 1906.

OPPENHEIMER, FRANZ, Rassenprobleme. Berlin, 1930.

ORANO, PAOLO, Gli Ebrei in Italia. Rome, [1938].

OSBORNE, SIDNEY, Germany and her Jews. London, 1939.

PARKES, J. W., The Jew and His Neighbour: A Study in the Courses of Antisemitism. London, 1930.

———, The Jewish Problem in the Modern World. London, 1939.

PASMANIK, D. S., Russkaia revolutsiia i evreistvo (The Russian Revolution and Jewry). Paris, 1923.

PASSARGE, SIEGFRIED, Das Judentum als landschaftskundlich-ethnologisches Problem. Munich, 1929.

Peace Conference, The, Paris 1919: Report of the Delegation of the Jews of the British Empire on the Treaties of Versailles . . . and the Annexed Minority Treaties. Published by the Joint Foreign Committee, London, 1920.

PEARLSON, G., Twelve Centuries of Jewish Persecution . . . . . Some Account of the Different Laws und Specific Restrictions under which They Have, at Various Times, Been Placed. Hull, 1927.

PHILIPPSON, MARTIN, Neueste Geschichte des jüdischen Volkes. 3 vols., 2d ed., Frankfurt a. M., vols. I–II, 1922–30; vol. III, 1911.

PHILIPSON, DAVID, The Reform Movement in Judaism. 2nd revised ed., New York, 1931.

———, Memoirs. Cincinnati, 1941.

PINES, M. I., History of Jewish Literature to 1890 (Yiddish). Warsaw, 1911.

PINSKER, LEO, Self-Emancipation! The Only Solution of the Jewish Question. English transl. by A. L. Finkelstein, London, 1891.

———, Auto-Emancipation. Transl. from the German by D. S. Blondheim. New ed., New York, 1935.

Poale Zion. The Jews and the war; memorandum of the Jewish Socialist Labor Confederation Poale-Zion to the International Socialist Bureau . . . issued by the Poale Zion Confederation. The Hague, 1916.

POSENER, S., Adolphe Crémieux, a biography by S. Posener, translated from the French by Eugene Golob. Philadelphia, 1940.

———, Adolphe Crémieux (1796–1880) . . . Préface de M. Sylvain Lévi . . . Tome 1–2. Paris, 1933–34.

PRESS, J., Neues Palästina Handbuch: Führer durch Palästina. Vienna, 1934.

Protocole de la IIe Conférence juive mondiale. Genève, 5.–8. Septembre 1933. Geneva, 1933.

Protocole de la IIIe Conference. Genève, 20–23 août, 1934.

Protocols, The, of the Learned Elders of Zion: The Jewish Peril. 2nd ed., London, 1920.

Protokoll der Jüdischen Weltkonferenz: Genf, 14–17 August, 1932. Berlin, 1932.

Provisional Executive Committee for General Zionist Affairs, Zionism Conquers Public Opinion. Publication of the Committee, New York, 1917.

Rabin, S., L'Emigration juive de l'Europe orientale pendant les cinquante dernières années. Geneva, 1929.

Radin, Paul, The Racial Myth. New York, 1934.

Raisin, J. S., The Haskalah Movement in Russia. Philadelphia, 1915.

Reichsbund jüdischer Frontsoldaten, Die jüdischen Gefallenen des deutschen Heeres, der deutschen Marine und der deutschen Schutztruppen, 1914–1918: Ein Gedenkbuch. Berlin, 1932.

———, Gefallene deutsche Juden: Frontbriefe 1914–18. Berlin, 1935.

Reifer, Manfred, ... Ausgewählte historische schriften, dokumentensammlung. Cernauti, 1938.

Reisen, Z., Lexicon of Jewish Literature, Press and Philology (Yiddish). 2nd ed., 4 vols., Vilna, 1926–30.

Renan, Ernest, Qu'est-ce qu'une nation? Conférence Paris, 1882 (Discours et Conférences, 2d ed. pp. 277–310).

———, Le Judaisme comme race et comme religion. Conférence Paris, 1883.

Revolutsionnoe dvizhenie sredi Evreev (The Revolutionary movement among the Jews). A Collection of Essays, with a preface by S. Dimenshtein. Moscow, 1930.

Revusky, A., Jews in Palestine. New York, 1935.

Rhinewine, A., Looking Back a Century on the Centennial of Jewish Political Equality in Canada. Revised and enlarged by I. Goldstick, Toronto, 1932.

Rieger, Paul, Ein Vierteljahrhundert im Kampf um das Recht und die Zukunft der deutschen Juden: Ein Rückblick auf die Geschichte des Centralvereins deutscher Staatsbürger jüdischen Glaubens in den Jahren 1893–1918. Berlin, 1918.

Riesser, Gabriel, Gesammelte Schriften: Herausgegeben von Moritz Isler. 4 vols., Frankfurt a. M., 1867–68.

Roback, A. A., Jewish Influence in Modern Thought. Cambridge, Mass., 1935.

———, The Story of Yiddish Literature. New York, 1940.

Robinson, Jacob, Das Minoritätenproblem und seine Literatur: Kritische Einführung in die Quellen und die Literatur der Europäischen Nationalitätenfrage der Nachkriegszeit. Allgemeiner Teil, Berlin, 1928.

Roditchew, J. F. and A. Nossig, Bolschewismus und Juden. Berlin (1922).

Rohling, August, Der Talmudjude: Zur Beherzigung für Juden und Christen aller Stände. 4. Auflage mit einem Vorwort über Gottes- und Menschensatzung, über neue Rabbiner und ein Geschäftchen. Münster, 1872.

Roite Bleter (Yiddish periodical for the history of the revolutionary movement among the Jews), ed. by B. Orshanski. Vol. I, Minsk, 1929.

Rosenberg, Alfred, Die Protokolle der Weisen von Zion und die jüdische Weltpolitik. Völlig neu bearbeitet von A. Philipp, Munich, 1934.

Rosenberg, Louis, Canada's Jews; a social and economic study of the Jews in Canada. Montreal, 1939.

Rosenfeld, M., Oberrabbiner Hirsch Perez Chajes: Sein Leben und Werk. Vienna, 1933.

BIBLIOGRAPHY

ROSENFELD, S. R., Israel Salanter: his Life, his Work, and his Disciples (Hebrew). Warsaw, 1910.

ROSENHEIM, JACOB, Ohole Yaakob: Ausgewählte Aufsätze und Ansprachen. 2 vols., Frankfurt a. M., 1930.

ROSENZWEIG, FRANZ, Der Stern der Erlösung. Frankfurt a. M., 1930.

———, Zweistromland. Kleinere Schriften. Frankfurt a. M., 1926.

———, Briefe. Ed. by Edith Rosenzweig in cooperation with Ernest Simon, Berlin, 1935.

ROTH, CECIL, A History of the Marranos, Philadelphia, 1932. Revised ed., 1941.

———, The Jewish Contribution to Civilization. Cincinnati, 1941.

———, A History of the Jews in England. London, 1941.

———, Venice. Jewish Communities Series. Philadelphia, 1930.

ROTH, SANDOR, Juden im ungarischen Kulturleben in der 2. Hälfte des 19. Jahrhunderts. Berlin, 1934.

RUPPIN, ARTHUR, Soziologie der Juden, I: Die soziale Struktur der Juden; II: Der Kampf der Juden um ihre Zukunft. Berlin, 1930–31.

———, The Jews in the Modern World. Abridged English translation by L. B. Namier, London, 1934.

———, The Jewish Fate and Future. London, 1940.

———, Three Decades of Palestine. Jerusalem, 1936.

SACHAR, ABRAM LEON, Sufferance is the Badge: The Jew in the Contemporary World. New York, 1939.

SALESKI, G., Famous Musicians of a Wandering Race: Biographical Sketches of Outstanding Figures of Jewish Origin in the Musical World. New York, 1927.

SAMPTER, J. E., ed., Modern Palestine: A Symposium. 3rd revised ed., New York, 1933.

SAMUEL, SIR HERBERT, Great Britain and Palestine. Second Lucien Wolf Memorial Lecture, London, 1936.

SCHAPIRA, I., Der Antisemitismus in der französischen Literatur: Edouard Drumont und seine Quellen. Berlin, 1927.

SCHECHTER, SOLOMON, Some Aspects of Rabbinic Theology. New York, 1909.

———, Studies in Judaism. 3 vols., Philadelphia, 1896–1924.

SCHICKERT, KLAUS, Die Judenfrage in Ungarn; jüdische Assimilation und anti-semitische Bewegung im 19. und 20. Jahrhundert. Berlin [etc.], 1937.

SCHIPPER, I., A History of Jewish Theatrical Arts and Drama from the beginning to 1750 (Yiddish). 4 vols., Warsaw, 1923–28.

SCHNEIDER, H., "Grundlage einer Bibliographie der antisemitischen Literatur," in *Der Weltkampf*, Monatsschrift für die Judenfrage aller Länder, I–V (1924–28).

SCHUSTER, HANS, Die Judenfrage im Rumänien. Leipzig, 1939. [Abhandlungen des Instituts für Politik, ausländisches öffentliches Recht und Völkerrecht an der Universität Leipzig. Heft 5].

SCHWARTZ, SAMUEL, Os Cristaos Novos em Portugal no século XX, with a preface, "Pro Israel," by R. Jorge. Lisbon, 1925.

SCHWARZ, KARL, Die Juden in der Kunst. Berlin, 1928.

Segal, Simon, The New Poland and the Jews. New York, 1938.
Segel, Benjamin W., The Protocols of the Elders of Zion: The Greatest Lie in History. Authorized English Translation from the German by S. Czaczkes-Charles, with ten Letters of Endorsement from eminent German Non-Jewish Scholars, New York, 1934.
Seligmann, Cäsar, Geschichte der jüdischen Reformbewegung von Mendelssohn bis zur Gegenwart. Frankfurt a. M., 1922.
Semi-Gotha, Semigothaisches Genealogisches Taschenbuch aristokratisch-jüdischer Heiraten mit Enkel-Listen (Deszendenz-Verfolgen). Aufsammlung aller adeligen Ehen mit vollblutjüdischen und gemischtblütigen Frauen. 3rd. ed., Munich, 1914.
Semi-Kürschner oder Literarisches Lexikon der Schriftsteller, Dichter, Bankiers, Geldleute, Ärzte, Schauspieler, Künstler, Musiker, Rechtsanwälte, Revolutionäre, Frauenrechtlerinnen, Sozialdemokraten u. s. w., jüdischer Rasse und Versippung, die von 1813–1913 in Deutschland tätig oder bekannt waren.
Shatzky, J., Studies in History of the Yiddish Press in America (Yiddish). New York, 1934.
Sidebotham, Herbert, British Interests in Palestine. London, 1934.
Silbergleit, Heinrich, Die Bevölkerungs- und Berufsverhältnisse der Juden im deutschen Reich. Auf Grund von amtlichen Materialien bearbeitet. Vol. I: Freistaat Preussen. Berlin, 1930.
Simon, Ernst, Chajim Nachman Bialik; eine Einführung in sein Leben und sein Werk, mit einigen Übersetzungsproben und Gedichtanalysen. Berlin, 1935.
Simon, W., La question juive: Vue par vingt-six éminentes personalités. Paris, 1934.
Sklarz, L., Geschichte und Organisation der Ostjudenhilfe in Deutschland seit dem Jahre 1914. Rostock, 1929.
Smolenskin, Perez, Essays (Hebrew). 4 vols., Jerusalem, 1925–26.
Sokolow, Nahum, History of Zionism, 1600–1918, with an Introduction by A. J. Balfour. 2 vols., London, 1919.
Soltes, Mordecai, The Yiddish Press: an Americanizing Agency. New York, 1925.
Sombart, Werner, Die Juden und das Wirtschaftsleben. Leipzig, 1911.
———, The Jews and Modern Capitalism. English translation with notes by M. Epstein, London, 1913.
Sombart, Werner, et al., Judentaufen, with a preface by A. Landsberger. Munich, 1912.
———, Der moderne Kapitalismus: Historisch-systematische Darstellung des gesamt-europäischen Wirtschaftslebens von seinen Anfängen bis zur Gegenwart. 3rd ed., 3 vols., Munich, 1921–1927.
Sosis, I., The History of the Jewish Social Currents in Russia during the 19th Century (Yiddish). Minsk, 1929.
Spiegel, Shalom, Hebrew Reborn, New York, 1930.
Stein, Leonard, Zionism. 2nd ed., London, 1934.
Steinberg, I., Als ich Volkskommissar war. Munich, 1929.

STILLSCHWEIG, KURT, Die Juden Osteuropas in den minderheitenverträgen. Berlin [c.1936].

STOYANOVSKY, J., The Mandate for Palestine: A Contribution to the Theory and Practise of International Mandate. London, 1928.

STRACK, HERMANN LEBRECHT, The Jew and Human Sacrifice (Human Blood and Jewish Ritual): an Historical and Sociological Inquiry (English transl. from 8th German edition). New York, 1909.

STRAUS, OSCAR S., Under Four Administrations. Boston, 1922.

STRONG, DONALD S., Organized anti-Semitism in America; the rise of group prejudice during the decade 1930–40. Washington, D. C., [c. 1941].

TAGER, A. B., The Decay of Czarism: The Beilis Trial (English translation from the Russian). Philadelphia, 1935.

TARTAKOWER, A., A History of the Jewish Labor Movement (Hebrew). 3 vols., Warsaw, 1929–31.

THOMPSON, F., America's Jew-deal. Woodhaven, N. Y., 1935.

TIETZE, HANS, Die Juden Wiens; Geschichte, Wirtschaft, Kultur. Leipzig 1933.

TOUSSENEL, A., Les Juifs rois de l'époque: Histoire de la féodalité financière. Paris, 1845.

TRAUB, M., Jüdische Wanderbewegungen vor und nach dem Weltkriege. Berlin, 1930.

TSCHERIKOVER, E., "The Beginnings of the Jewish Socialist Movement," in *YIVO Historishe Shriften*, I (1929), pp. 469–594.

ULLMANN, S., Histoire des Juifs en Belgique jusqu'au 19e siècle, 1700–1830. The Hague, 1934.

Union of American Hebrew Congregations, Reform Judaism in the Large Cities: A Survey. New York, 1931.

VALENTIN, HUGO, Judarnas historia i Sverige (A History of the Jews in Sweden). Stockholm, 1924.

———, Antisemitism, Historically and Critically examined. English translation from the Swedish, New York, 1936.

VAN PAASSEN, P., AND J. W. WISE, ed., Nazism: An Assault on Civilization, with a Preface by R. F. Wagner. New York, 1934.

———, The Forgotten Ally. New York, 1943.

VICTOR, W., Die Emanzipation der Juden in Schleswig-Holstein. Wandsbeck, 1913.

VOGELSTEIN, HERMANN, Rome. Jewish Communities Series, Philadelphia, 1941.

WACHSTEIN, BERNHARD, Diskussionsschriften über die Judenfrage: das neue Gesicht des Antisemitismus. Vienna, 1933.

WALDSTEIN, A. S., The Evolution of Modern Hebrew Literature. New York, 1916.

WALKER-SMITH, D., Lord Reading and His Cases: The Study of a Great Career. London, 1934.

WAWRZINEK, K., Die Entstehung der deutschen Antisemitenpartei (1873–90). Historische Studien, Heft 168. Berlin, 1927.

WAXMAN, MEYER, A History of Jewish Literature. Vol. 4, New York, 1939.

WEICHSELBAUM, W., Der Rechtsschutz der Juden in Deutsch-Oberschlesien nach dem Genfer Abkommen von 1922. Dresden, 1935.

WEINRYB, B., Das Wirtschaftsleben der Juden in Russland und Polen von der 1. polnischen Teilung bis zum Tode Alexanders II (1772–1881). Breslau, 1934.

WIENER, L., A History of Yiddish Literature in the Nineteenth Century. New York, 1899.

WIENER, MAX, Jüdische Religion im Zeitalter der Emanzipation. Berlin, 1933.

WIERNIK, PETER, History of the Jews in America from the Period of the Discovery of the New World to the Present Time. 2nd revised ed., New York, 1931.

WIRTH, LOUIS, The Ghetto. Chicago, 1928.

WISCHNITZER, MARK, Die Juden in der Welt: Gegenwart und Geschichte des Judentums in allen Ländern. Berlin, 1935.

WITTKE, CARL, We Who Built America: The Saga of the Immigrant. New York, 1940.

WOLF, LUCIEN, Notes on the Diplomatic History of the Jewish Question: With Texts of Protocols, Treaty Stipulations and Other Public Acts and Official Documents. London, 1919.

WOLF, SIMON, The American Jew as Patriot, Soldier and Citizen. Philadelphia, 1895.

———, The Presidents I Have Known. Washington, 1918.

YACHINSON, J., Social-Economic Life of the Jews in Russia during the 19th Century; a collection of sources from memoirs and belles lettres (Yiddish). Kharkov, 1929.

Yearbook of the Central Conference of American Rabbis. I ff., 1890 ff.

ZANGWILL, ISRAEL, The Voice of Jerusalem: A Collection of Essays. New York, 1921.

Zeitschrift für Demographie und Statistik der Juden, ed. by A. Ruppin, et al. 16 vols., Berlin, 1905–1920; 3 vols., Berlin, 1924–26.

Zeitschrift für die Geschichte der Juden in Deutschland, ed. by Ludwig Geiger. 5 vols., Braunschweig 1892–97; ed. by I. Elbogen, A. Freimann, M. Freudenthal, 7 vols., 1929–1937.

ZIELENZIGER, KURT, Juden in der deutschen Wirtschaft. Berlin, 1930.

ZINBERG, I., A History of Jewish Literature in Europe (Yiddish). 7 vols., Vilna, 1929–36.

ZLOCISTI, THEODOR, Moses Hess, der Vorkämpfer des Sozialismus und Zionismus, 1812–1875: Eine Biographie. 2nd revised ed., 1921.

ZOLLSCHAN, IGNATZ, Das Rassenproblem, unter besonderer Berücksichtigung der theoretischen Grundlagen der jüdischen Rassenfrage. 4th ed., Vienna, 1920.

ZWEIG, ARNOLD, Caliban, oder Politik und Leidenschaft. Berlin, 1927.

———, Bilanz der deutschen Judenheit 1933: Ein Versuch. Amsterdam, 1934.

ZYLBERCWAJG, Z., AND J. MESTEL, ed., Lexicon of the Yiddish Theater (Yiddish). 2 vols., New York and Warsaw, 1931–34.

INDEX

INDEX

Aargau, Switzerland, 32
Abel, Bavarian minister, 11
Abrahams, Israel, 196, 315, 319
Abramowitch, Jacob, *see* Mendele Mocher Seforim
Academy for Adult Education, New York, 579
Acco, Galilee, 300
Addis Ababa, teachers' seminary in, 420
"An Address to their Fellow Citizens by American Jewish Organizations," 562
Adelaide, Australia, 137
Adler, Cyrus, 347, 352, 434, 443 f., 733, 738, 761
Adler, Dankmar, 340
Adler, Felix, 340
Adler, Hermann, 281, 318
Adler, Jacob P., 448
Adler, Nathan, 39
Adler, Salo, 410
Adler, Samuel, 129
Adler, Sarah, 448
Adler, Victor, 707
Aegean Islands, 670
Africa, West, 135
Africa, South, 134, 320
Agriculture, 50, 87, 229, 250, 258 f., 269, 323, 334, 552 f., 695
Agro-Joint, *see* American Jewish Joint Agricultural Corporation
Agudat Yisrael, 422, 464, 505, 528, 538 f., 616
Aguilar, Grace, 102
Agunot, 460
Ahad Ha'am, 196, 263 ff., 286, 297, 318, 375, 407, 577, 610, 722, 724
Ahavat Hesed Congregation, New York, 343

Ahavat Zion v'Yerushalaim, Mapu, 108
Ahiasaf, Warsaw publishing house, 270
Ahlwardt, Hermann, 165
Akademie für die Wissenschaft des Judentums, Germany, 519
'*Al Parashat Derachim*, Ahad Ha'am, 270
Albania, 563
Albany, N. Y., 128
Alcoholic beverage trade, 42, 220, 356, 370
Aleichem, Shalom (Rabinovich), 375, 407
Aleppo, 80, 253
Alexander I, Czar, 43
Alexander II, Czar, 57 f., 109, 200
Alexander III, Czar, 205, 371
Alexander, Samuel, 701
Algeciras, Conference of, 438
Algiers, 35, 186
Alien Act, England, 314
Alien Immigration Royal Commission, 313
Allenby, General, 479, 482
Allgemeine Zeitung des Judentums, 103
Alliance, N. J., 334
Alliance Israélite Universelle, 34 f., 61 f., 72, 75, 87, 95, 117, 151, 176, 226, 233, 250, 359, 397, 412, 419, 504 f., 522, 544, 692, 693
Alsace-Lorraine, xxvi, 17, 32, 35, 181, 226, 516, 522
Altman, Benjamin, 340
Altneuland, Herzl, 277
AmBidjan, 555
Amalgamated Clothing Workers of America, 447

American Academy for Jewish Research, 576
American Chamber of Commerce, 585
American Committee on the Rights of Religious Minorities, 562
American Hebrew, periodical, 332
American Israelite, periodical, 126
American Jewish Committee, 367, 412, 433 f., 466, 505, 562 f., 741, 750, 753
American Jewish Congress, 505, 562 f., 646, 673, 750, 753
American Jewish Historical Society, 347
American Jewish Joint Agricultural Corporation, 552
American Jewish Physicians Committee, 572
American Jewish Year Book, 347
American Joint Distribution Committee for the Relief of Jewish War Sufferers, *see* Joint Distribution Committee
American Relief Administration, 500, 548
American Society for Jewish Farmers' Settlement in Russia, 553 f.
American Zionist Federation, 466
American Zion Medical Unit, 483
Amicis, Edmondo de, 76
Amzalak, Moses Bensabbat, 558
An-ski, playwright, 550
Anatolian Railway, 363
Anglo-Jewish Association, 72, 309, 477
Anglo-Jewish Conjoint Committee, 367
Anglo-Jewish Historical Exhibition, 195, 316
Anti-Defamation League, I. O. B. B., 563
Antijuif, L', newspaper, 189
Antilles, 132
Anti-Nazi League to Champion Human Rights, United States, 646
Antisemitic League, 355, 360
Antisemitism, 141, 145, 150, 171, 196, 200, 424, 456

Antokolski, Mark, 86, 89
Apologetik des Judentums, Güdemann, 418
Arabs, 249, 269, 479, 513, 590, 596, 627, 632
Archives Israelites de France, periodical, 103
Argentina, 229, 234 f., 276, 342, 427, 582, 656
Arlosoroff, Chaim, 760
Armenians, 730
Art, 89, 166, 522, 583
Art, "Jewish," 288
Artisans, *see* Occupations, Trades
Asch, Sholem, 407, 448, 677
Assembly, German National of 1848, 5
Asser, T. M. C., 88
Assimilation, 93
Associations Cultuelles, France, 418
Association for Czech-Jewish Understanding, 172
Association for Jewish History and Literature, Berlin, 195
Association of National German Jews, 516
Association of Rumanian Jews, 543
Association for Warding Off Antisemitism, Germany, 164
Asson, Michelangelo, 88
Atlantic Charter, 635
Auerbach, Berthold, 102, 151, 696, 706, 711
Augsburg Synod, 696
Australia, 137 f., 320
Austria, xxx, 17 f., 24, 168, 366, 369, 658
Auto-Emancipation: Admonition to his Brethren by a Russian Jew, Pinsker, 256
Avukah, Zionist student organization, 579
Awake, My People, Gordon, 109
Ayit Zabua, Mapu, 108
d'Azeglio, Massimo and Roberto, 29

INDEX

BACHER, WILHELM, 195
Baden, xxix f., 10
Baden, Grand Duke of, 280
Baeck, Leo, 522, 648, 650, 711
Baerwald, Hermann, 410
Bagdad, 80, 632
Baginsky, Adolf, 736
Bahr, Hermann, 274
Baldwin, Edward C., 579
Baldwin, Lord, 667
Balfour, A. J., 314, 473, 477, 570, 589, 613
Balfour Declaration, 473 ff.
Balkans, 66 f., 411, 438, 539
Ballarat, Australia, 138
Ballin, Albert, 166
Balta, Podolia, 203 f.
Baltic Provinces, 217
Baltimore, Md., 129, 324, 349
Bamberger, Ludwig, 6, 15, 706
Banking, *see* Finance
Barbados, 132
Barberton, Transvaal, 137
Bari radio, 628
Barnato, Barney, 320
Barnay, Ludwig, 90
Baron de Hirsch Foundation, 176, 230
Baron de Hirsch Fund, 336, 369
Baron de Hirsch Institute, Montreal, 323
Barondess, Joseph, 433
Barros Basto, Arturo Carlos de, 557 ff.
Barth, Jacob, 195
Basle, 32, 295
Basle Program, Zionist, 284 f.
Bauernfeld, 21
Baumann, Isaak, 137
Bavaria, xxxii, 11, 191, 489
Beaconsfield, Earl of, 142
Beer Sheba, 479
Beilis, Menahem Mendel, 402 ff.
Beirut, 632
Beit, Alfred, 320
Belasco, David, 340
Belgium, 36, 669
Belloc, Hilaire, 514
Ben Gorion (M. J. Berdiczewski), 375

Ben Yehudah, Eliezer, 254, 305, 608
Bender, Alfred P., 322
Benderly, Samson, 441
Benedict XIV, Pope, 741
Benedikt, M., 708
Beni-Israel, 80
Benjamin, Judah P., 119
Benjamin the Second, 77, 698
Bensaude, Joaquin, 558
Berdichev, 497
Berdyczewski, Micha Joseph (Ben Gorion), 375
Bergmann, Hugo, 522
Bergson, Henri, 414
Bergtheil, Jonas, 135
Berkowitz, Henry, 348
Berlad, Rumania, 362
Berlin, 82, 144, 161, 410 f., 520, 648
Berlin Convention of 1878, 73
Berlin Reform Congregation, xxxix, 102
Berlin, Naftali Z. J., 107
Berliner, Abraham, 195
Berliner, Emil, 340
Berliner Volkszeitung, 102
Bernays, Isaac, xxxvi
Bernays, Jacob, 97
Berne, Switzerland, 32
Bernstein, Eduard, 408
Bernstein, Herman, 563, 753
Bertillon, in Dreyfus case, 185
Bessarabetz, Kishinev newspaper, 379, 383
Bessarabia, 73, 361, 387, 393, 539
Bezalel School, Jerusalem, 305
Bialik, Chaim Nachman, 104, 375 f., 381, 385, 407, 610, 613
Bialystok, 305, 392, 398 f.
Bible, 194, 280, 580
Bible translations, 101, 347, 445, 521 f., 543, 691
Bible View of Slavery, M. J. Raphall, 118
Bien, Julius, 700
BILU (*Beth Ja'acob Lechu Uenelcha*), 255 f., 263
Binder, A. W., 755

Bingham, New York Police Commissioner, 738
Birnbaum, Nathan, 278, 368
Biro-Bidjan, 554 f.
Bismarck, Otto von, 8, 14 f., 72, 85, 92, 142, 160 f., 687, 704
Black Hundred, Russia, 371, 391, 402, 470
Blaine, James G., 689, 692
Blaser, I., 406
Blau, Julius, 410
Blaustein, David, 430, 730
Bleichröder, Gerson von, 85, 192, 706
Bloch, Abraham, 460
Bloch, Ernest, 755
Bloch, Joseph Loeb, 406
Bloch, Joseph Samuel, 153 f., 170, 175, 190
Blockade running, Civil War, 119
Bloemfontain, Orange Free State, 137
Blood accusation, *see* Ritual murder charge
Bloomgarden, Solomon (*Yehoash*), 448
B'nai Jeshurun congregation, Cincinnati, 125
B'nai Jeshurun congregation, New York, 122
B'ne Mosheh, fraternal order, 266 f.
Board of Delegates of American Israelites, New York, 117, 120, 126, 131, 692, 693, 694, 698
Board of Deputies of British Jews, 477
Board of Deputies of Transvaal and Natal, 322
Boas, A. T., 138
Boas, Franz, 584
Bodenheimer, Max I., 282
Bodensee, 191
Boer War, 313
Boers, 137, 321
Bogdanowicz, General, 396
Bogen, Boris D., 751
Bohemia, 172, 546
Bolshevism, 471; in Hungary, 490; "Jewish," 511 f.
Bombay, 80
Book burning, Germany, 643

Bordeaux, 186
Börne, Ludwig, xxxiii
Bosnia, 366
Boyars, 356
Boycott, of Jews in Germany, 639; against Nazis, 646
Brafmann, Jacob, 62
Brahm, Otto, 166
Brainin, Reuben, 375
Brandeis, Louis D., 447, 475, 570 f., 603
Brandes, Georg, 741
Bratianu, 68
"Braude" schools, 537
Brazil, 134, 427, 582, 656
Breitner, Hugo, 524
Brenner, Joseph Hayyim, 596
Breslauer, Bernhard, 421
Brest-Litovsk, peace of, 487
B'rit Shalom, 760
"Britons," antisemitic organization, 566
Brill, Yehiel, 254
Brod, Max, 522
Brody, 225, 255, 264
Brown, David A., 569 f.
Bródy, Sándor, 709
Browning, Robert, 226
Brunner, Sebastian, 703
Brünn, 82
Brunswick, xl
Brussels Conference on Rumanian Jews (1872), 72
Brzezany, 454
Buber, Martin, 288, 521 f., 650, 737, 741
Bucharest, 70, 367, 438
Bucharin, Soviet leader, 512
Buchenwald, concentration camp, 638
Budapest, 83, 157, 180, 273, 363, 490
Buenos Aires, 342, 427
Bukovina, 368, 422, 461 f., 539
Bulgaria, 67, 367, 543
Bülow, Bernhard von, 289
"Bund," General Jewish Workers' Union of Lithuania, Poland, and Russia, 373 f., 376, 398, 464, 538 f.

INDEX

Bund der Landwirte, antisemitic peasant party, 165
Burgenland, 660
Buschoff, accused of ritual murder, 165
Butler, General B. F., 119 f., 700

CAHAN, ABRAHAM, 339
Cairo, 294
Calendar reform, 568
Cambridge, England, 352
Camp of National Unification, Poland, 673
Canada, 133, 323 ff., 427, 694
"Cantonists," boys conscripted in Russia, 45
Cantor, Bernard, 501
Cape Colony, 135
Cape Town, 135, 321 f.
Cardozo, Benjamin N., 560
Carmel, N. J., 334
Carol, King of Rumania, 363, 672
Carp, Peter, 68 f., 362
Carpathians, 546
Cassuto, Umberto, 545
Cassel Consistory, xxxv
Casualties, World War I, 459 f.
Catholic, positions on Jewish questions, 143, 152, 164, 180, 314, 414, 423, 533, 590, 645, 670, 695
"Catholic Israel," expression of Schechter, 352, 441
Catholic Peoples' Party, Hungary, 181
Cavaignac, French minister of war, 188
Cavour, Camillo, 30
Centers, Jewish community houses, 579
Central British Fund for German Jewry, 647
Central Committee for Relief and Reconstruction, Germany, 649
Central Conference of American Rabbis, 283, 345, 348
Central Institute for Adult Education, Germany, 650

Ceylon, 80
Chagall, Marc, 522
Chaizes, Adolf, 19
Chajes, Hirsch Perez, 523
Chamber of Cultural Affairs, Nazi, 644
Chamberlain, Houston S., 167, 514, 637
Chamberlain, Joseph, 294
Chancellor, Sir John, 618
Chaplains, Jewish, 741
Charleston, S. C., 121, 349
Chasanowitz, Joseph, 305
Chernigov, 201
Chicago, 348, 429, 575, 585
Chief rabbinate, London, 131
China, 513
Christian oath, 13, 38, 133
Christian Social Party, Austria, 144, 148, 168, 170
"Christian State," xxxii, 150, 401
Christopher Columbus and the Participation of the Jews in the Spanish and Portuguese Discoveries, Kayserling, 347
Churchill, Winston, 597 f., 635
Ciceruacchio, Italian popular leader, 29
Cincinnati, Ohio, 124
Civil War, American, 118 f.
Civilization, Judaism as a, 576 f.
Clemenceau, Georges, 189, 509, 710
Clermont-Tonnere, xxvi
"Cliveden Set," in English policy, 634
Clothing industry, 430, 447, 569
Cochin, 80
Cohen, Anitta Müller, 547, 751
Cohen, Henry, 302
Cohen, Hermann, 415 f., 418, 737, 741
Cohen, Levi A., 694
Cohen, Lionel Louis, 39
Cohen, Mendes, 340
Cohen, Morris R., 755
Cohn, Albert, 249 f.
Cohn-Oppenheim, Baroness Julie von, 409

Collective communes (*k'vuzot*), Palestine, 607
Collegio Rabbinico Italiano, 419, 545
Cologne, 82
Colonial Bank, 288
Colonial Office, London, 301
Colonies, Palestine, 304
Columbia University, 576
Columbian Exposition, Chicago, 347
Comité des Délégations Juive auprès de la Conférence de la Paix, 504 f., 522
Commerce, *see* Finance
Commission to Investigate Immigration in Europe, United States, 335
Commission for Resolving the Jewish Problem, Russia, 216
Committee for Defense Against Antisemitic Attacks, Germany, 196
Commonweal, Catholic periodical, 645
Communism in Germany, 487 f.
Compendium of Jewish Ethics, 692
Confederacy, United States, 119
Conference on Jewish Relations, 755
Confiscations, Nazi, 660
Congress, United States, 123
Congress of Berlin, 67, 72, 360, 365
Congress of Vienna, xxxi
Congresses, Zionist, 295; Sixth, 295; Seventh, 301; Eighth, 304; Eleventh, 307; Eighteenth, 764; Nineteenth, 616; Twentieth, 631
Conscription, military in Russia, 57
Consistories, Jewish in France, 418
Constantinople, 255
Convention between the United Kingdom and the United States Respecting the Rights ... in Palestine, 571
Conversion, to Christianity, xxxv, 77, 95, 110, 162, 167, 190, 219, 425, 492, 671, 674, 707, 708; to Judaism, 689
Coolidge, Calvin, 564
Copenhagen, 476; Zionist Manifesto of, 1918, 504
Cornell University, 384
Corpus Tannaiticum, 417

Correspondence de l'Est, periodical, 280
Council of American Jewish Student Affairs, 580
Cracow, 83, 178
Creagh, Father, 314
Credit Union Association, Filene foundation, 585
Crémieux, Adolph, 34, 69, 151, 689
Crémieux Decree for Algerian Jews, 35 f., 689
Cresson, Warder, 719
Crimea, agricultural settlement in, 552
Cuba, 342, 668, 768
Cultural Union of German Jews, under Nazis, 651
Curaçao, 132
Cuza, A. C., 541 f.
Cyprus, 362
Czechoslovakia, 172, 495, 525 f., 546 f., 662, 673
Czernowitz, 368, 540

DACHAU, concentration camp, 638
Damascus, 613
Daniel Deronda, Eliot, 252, 279
Danzig, 669
Darwin, Charles, 226
D'Avigdor, E. H., 263
Davis, Jefferson, 119
Dawison, Bogumil, 90
Dead Sea, potash works at, 625
Dearborn Independent, Ford publication, 561, 563 f.
Defense Organization, after Kishinev, 386
Deganyah, Palestine, 595
Délégation du Gouvernement de la Défense Nationale, 35
Delitzsch, Franz, 152 f.
Denikin, General, 496, 499
Denmark, 36, 547
De Pass, family, 135
Depression, in Palestine, 1926, 614; in United States, 1929, 586 f.
Derishat Zion, Kalischer, 250
Deroulède, anti-Dreyfus, 189

INDEX

de Sola, Abraham, 133
Dessau, 410
Detroit, 565
Deutsch-Israelitischer Gemeindebund, 410, 696
Deutsche Schriften, de Laguarde, 163
Devil's Island, 185
Dialogue aux Enfers entre Machiavel et Montesquieu...., source for *Protocols*, 513
Dick, Eisik Meir, 112
Dickmann, Enrique, 342
Dingaan, African king, 135
Dismissals, Nazi, of Jews, 641 f.
Disraeli, Benjamin, 72, 85, 142
Dittel, Leopold von, 88
Divorce, 319
Dizengoff, Meier, 611
Dmowski, Román, 735
Dóczi, Lajos, 709
Dodd, William E., 642, 646, 764
Dohm, Christian Wilhelm, xxix
Domicile, right of, 213, 216, 388
Dress, 48, 56
Dreyfus, Alfred, 181 ff., 274
Dropsie College for Hebrew and Cognate Learning, 444 f.
Drumont, Edouard, 182, 187
Dubnow, Simon M., 390, 407
Dubrovin, Russian antisemite, 400
Dühring, Eugen, 145
Duma, Russian assembly, 393, 398 ff.
Dumas, Alexandre, 35
Dünaburg, yeshibah at, 530
Dybuk, An-ski, 550
Dyte, Charles, 138

EAST SIDE, New York City, 238, 429
Easter, 355, 379
École Rabbinique, Metz, 100
Eder, M. D., 743
Education, xxxv, xxxvii, 52, 54, 69, 95, 99 f., 104 f., 110, 121, 177, 193, 195, 241, 247, 305, 317, 337, 348, 358, 406, 430, 441, 524, 528, 530, 534, 537, 540, 545, 579, 649

Educational Alliance, New York City, 337, 430
Eiss, Ritter von, 708
Egypt, 294
Ehrenkranz, Wolf, 112
Ehrenpreis, Marcus, 288, 547
Einhorn, David, 118, 125, 129
Einstein, Albert, 521 f., 571, 652
Eisner, Kurt, 488
Ekatrinoslav, 201, 231, 393
Elections, 369, 529, 533
Eliezer ben Yehudah, *see* Ben Yehudah
Eliot, George (Mary Ann Evans), 252, 287, 696
Elisavethgrad, 201
Elstätter, Moritz, 686
Emek Jezreel, 606
Emergency Committee on Jewish Refugees, United States, 567 f.
Emigdirect, United Committee for Jewish Emigration, 502
Employment difficulties, United States, 587
Encyclopedia, Jewish, 316, 350 f.
Engel, Joseph, 89
England, 37 f., 228, 309 ff., 522 f.
English Zionist Federation, 477
Enquiry on the Jewish Question, Bahr, 274
Epidemics, 469
Epstein, Jacob, 131, 459
Epstein, Moses Mordechai, 406
Esterhazy, Dreyfus case, 183, 188
Estonia, 529
Ethical Culture Society, 340, 445
Ethical monotheism, 415
Ethics of Judaism, Lazarus, 199
Ethiopia, 419 f., 546
Ettinger, Salomo, 112
Evans-Gordon, Sir W., 313
Eveline de Rothschild School for Girls, Palestine, 249
Evian Conference, on refugees, 662
Expulsions, Russian, 213 f.
Ezekiel, Moses, 119

FAIRCHILD, LUCIUS, 694
Faitlovich, Jacques, 419
Falashas, Ethiopia, 419 f.
Falastin, Arab newspaper, 619
Fascism, 544, 739
Fastov, violence at, 499
Federal Council of Churches of Christ in America, Boston convention of 1920, 562
Federation of American Zionists, 349
Feisal, Emir, 590
Felsenthal, Bernhard, 118
Felshtin, Ukraine, 497
Fenchel, Julius, 192
Ferdinand, prince of Bulgaria, 281
Festival, celebrations in Palestine, 608
Filene, Edward A., 585
Finance, xxvi, 85, 91, 144, 166, 182, 409, 518, 524, 569
Finland, 217
Finzi, Giuseppe, 688
First Fruits of the West, periodical, 132
Fischer, Bishop of Cologne, 165
Fischhof, Adolf, 18, 20
Fiume, 544
Fleg, Edmond, 418, 522
Flexner, Abraham, 584
Flexner, Simon, 584
Folkists, Yiddish, 581
Ford, Henry, 561, 565
Foster, J. W., 336, 691, 714
Foundations of the Nineteenth Century, Chamberlain, 167
Fourier, F. M. C., 709
France, 181 f., 418, 522, 589, 669
France Juive, La, Drumont, 182
France n'est pas Juive, La, anonymous, 182
Francis Joseph I, 21, 24, 30, 169
Frank, Waldo, 577
Frankel, Benjamin M., 580
Frankel, Lee K., 572
Frankel, Zacharias, xxxix, 97, 696
Frankfort on the Main, 250, 410, 422, 650; conference at, xl
Frankfurter, David, 766

Frankl, Ludwig August, 19, 249
Frankl, Pinkus F., 195
Franklin, Benjamin, 705
Frederick the Great, xxix
Frederick III, 160
Frederick William IV, 14
Free Association for the Interests of Orthodox Judaism, Germany, 420
Free Synagogue, New York, 443, 574
Freemasons, 512
French National Assembly, on Human Rights, xxvi
French Revolution, 709
Freud, Sigmund, 521
Freudenthal, Jacob, 195
Freytag, Gustav, 190
Friedlaender, Israel, 501
Friedenwald, Aaron, 720; Harry, 349
Friedmann, Meir, 196
Friedmann, lawyer at Tisza Eszlar, 158
Frischman, David, 375
Fritsch, Theodor, 566
Frug, Simon Samuel, 404
Frumkin, I. D., 251
Fuchs, Eugen, 712, 736, 741
Fürth, 12

GALATZ, violence in, 71
Galicia, 41, 173 f., 369, 371, 422, 461 f., 527
Galilee, 249, 300
Gallipoli, 458
Galveston, Texas, 302, 428
Gambetta, Leon, 182
Gambia, 135
Gans, Eduard, xxxvii
Garibaldi, Giuseppe, 31
Gaster, Moses, 315, 360, 474
Gaza, 479
Geiger, Abraham, xxxviii, 88, 98, 575, 690, 701; Ludwig, 736
General Jewish Council, 755
General Jewish Workers' Union of Lithuania, Poland, and Russia, *see* Bund

INDEX

General Safety Organization, Russia, 383
Geneva, 32
Genizah, of Cairo, 315
Gerer Rebbe, 538
Germany, 160 ff., 516 ff., 636 ff.
Germania Judaica, 417
Gershwin, George, 755
Gerstein, J., 691
Gesellschaft zur Förderung der Wissenschaft des Judentums, 417
Gestapo, 657
Ghetto, Rome, 30
Gibraltar, 75, 558
Gimbel, Adam, 698 f.
Ginzberg, Asher, 264
Ginzberg, Louis, 576
Ginze Schechter, 575
Gladstone, W. E., 142
Gniewosz, Polish deputy, 175
Gobineau, Arthur de, 167, 514
Godefroi, M. H., 36
Goebbels, Joseph, 636, 651, 657, 762–769 passim
Goering, Hermann, 638, 659
Goga-Cuza, Rumanian statesman, 672
Goldberg, Isaac, 582
Goldberger, Ludwig Max, 412, 736
Goldfaden, Abraham, 112
Goldmark, Karl, 19 f.
Goldschmidt, M. A., 696
Goldschmidt, Levin, 88
Goldsmid, Col. A. E. W., 263
Goldsmid, Sir Francis, 38, 132, 693
Golem, Leivick, 582
Gompers, Samuel, 317, 339
Gompertz, Th., 708
Gonse, General, 185
Gopishitza, Kiev, 264
Gordin, Jacob, 449
Gordon, Aaron David, 595
Gordon, David, 260
Gordon, J. L., 60, 109, 111
Gorion, Ben (Berdyczewski), 375
Gorki, Maxim, 381
Gorodsenski, Chaim Oser, 537
Gortschakov, Prince, 72

Gottlober, A. B., 112, 698
Grabski, Polish minister, 534, 759
Graetz, H., xl, 97, 101, 190, 250, 261, 316, 347, 349
Grant, U. S., 72, 119
Gratz, Rebecca, 122
Graves, Philipp, 563, 747
Graz, 660
Greece, 366, 543 f.
Grey, Sir Edward, 367
Grigoriev, Ukrainian leader, 498
Grodno, 406
Grossmann, Meir, 758
Grosswardein, 440, 442
Grundriss einer Gesamtwissenschaft des Judentums, 417
Grünhut, K. S., 708
Grynszpan, Herschl, 663
Güdemann, Moritz, 196, 281, 418
Guérin, Jules, 148, 188
Guggenheim, Daniel, 584
Guggenheim, Meyer, 584
Guggenheim, Simon, 584
Guggenheim Foundation, 584
Guild Hall Meeting, London, on Jewish suffering, 218
Günzburg, Baron Horace, 222
Günzburg, Mordecai Aron, 107
Gurland, Jonah Hayyim, 691
Gustloff, Wilhelm, 766
Guttmann, Jacob, 195, 417

HAAS, LUDWIG, 464
Haase, Hugo, 487
Habimah, theatrical company, 550
Hadassah, 483, 572, 579, 599
Haganah, Palestine self-defense, 633
Hague, 304
Haham Bashi, chief rabbi's title in Turkey, 544
Haidamaks, Poland, 496
Haifa, 246, 611, 615, 620, 625
Haj Amin Effendi el Husseini, 597 ff.; *see* Mufti
Ha-Lapid, Portuguese periodical, 557
Halévi, Joseph, 419
Halevy, J. F. F., 89

Haller, General, 495
Hallgarten, Charles L., 410
Halphon, Samuel, 427
Halukkah, Palestinian charity, 246, 250 f., 261
Ha-Maggid, Hoveve Zion periodical, 260
Ha-Matmid, Bialik, 104
Hamburg, synagogue in, xxxvi
Hamilton, Canada, 134
Hanover, xxxvi, 16
Ha-Po'el ha-Tza'ir, workers' youth organization, 539
Harbin, 404
Hardenberg, Prince Karl August, xxx
Harkavy, Abraham, 691
Harrison, Benjamin, 230 f.
Hart, Ezekiel, 133
Hartmann, Moritz, 5, 17
Harvard University, 446, 564, 575, 668
Ha-Shahar, periodical, 222
Ha-Shiloah, periodical, 270, 407, 721
Hasidim and Mitnaggedim, 96
Haskalah, movement, 104
Hatikvah, by Imber, 270
Hauran, 263
Hay, John, 363 f.
Haynau, General, 27
Hebrew, 254, 270, 297, 305, 307, 366, 368, 371, 375, 515, 546, 549, 608, 706, 724
Hebrew Immigrants Aid Societies, United States, 328, 502
Hebrew Presses, United States, 573
Hebrew Teachers' Seminary, Palestine, 611
Hebrew Technical Institute, New York, 333
Hebrew Theological College, Chicago, 575
Hebrew Union College, Cincinnati, 127, 442, 575
Hebrew University, Jerusalem, 307, 483 f., 572, 612, 630
Hebron, 246, 619
Hechler, William H., 280

Hedjaz, 480
He-Halutz, pioneer movement, 539, 595
Heilprin, Michael, 118, 330, 333
Heine, Heinrich, xxxiii, xxxv f.
Henri, Lt. Col., 183, 188
Henry Street Settlement, New York City, 340
Hertz, J. H., 322, 523
Hertz, Wilhelm, 736
Herz, Jacob, 88
Herzl, Theodor, 273 ff., 300, 384, 478, 602, 733
Herzl Gymnasium, Jaffa, 305
Hess, Moses, 94, 279
Hesse-Cassel, xxxvi, 16, 136
Heydenfeldt, Solomon, 699
HICEM, immigrant aid, 522
Hildesheimer, Esriel, 28, 99, 250, 575
Hildesheimer, Hirsch, 190
Hilfsverein der deutschen Juden, Berlin, 302, 305 ff., 411 f., 423, 468
Hillel Foundation, American universities, 580 f.
Hillman, Sidney, 447
Hilsner, Leopold, 173
Hilton-Seligman incident, 699
Himmler, Heinrich, 636, 657
Hindenburg, General Paul von, 487, 636, 641
Hirsch, Aron, 736
Hirsch, family of Halberstadt, 249
Hirsch, Clara Bischoffsheim de, 178, 232, 237
Hirsch, Emil G., 348
Hirsch, Baron Maurice de, 84, 176, 232 f., 334, 721, 725
Hirsch, Otto, 650
Hirsch, Samson Raphael, xxxvii, 96, 99, 222, 420
Hirsch, Samuel, 129
Histadrut ha-'Ovedim, Palestine labor organization, 606
Historical Poetry of the Ancient Hebrews, Heilprin, 331
History of Jewish Literature, Karpeles, 196

History of a Lie, Bernstein, 563
History of Zionism, Sokolov, 473
Hitler, Adolf, 145, 171, 510, 518, 633, 635, 707
Hochschule für die Wissenschaft des Judentums, Berlin, 98
Hoffmann, David, 191, 195
Hohenzollern, Carol von, 70 f.
Hohenzollern, Karl Anton von, 91
Holdheim, Samuel, xxxix
Holland, 36, 547, 669
Holleschau, Moravia, 495
Hollywood, California, 583
Holy Synod, Russia, 378, 387
Homel, violence at, 386
Hoover, Herbert C., 500, 548, 586
Horovitz, Marcus, 410
Horowitz, Louis J., 584
Horwitz, Maximilian, 712
Horthy, Admiral, 490
Hoveve Zion, lovers of Zion, 259, 260 ff., 265, 283, 304, 348, 611
Hubermann, Bronislaw, 630
Hübsch, Adolph, 130
Hugo, Victor, 717
Hull, Cordell, 761
Humboldt, Alexander von, 89
Hungarian Autonomous Orthodox Confession, 420
Hungary, 27, 41, 156, 179, 489, 491 f., 671
Hurwitz, Henry, 446
Hydroelectric development, Palestine, 611

ICA, *see* Jewish Colonization Association
ICOR, association for assisting agriculturists in Russia, 555
Ignatiev, Count, 205 ff., 227
Illinois, University of, 580
Imber, N. H., 270
Immigration, 361, 369, 428, 502, 528; to England, 310 ff.; to Palestine, 246, 268, 508; illicit, 624, 633; from Germany, 626; to United States, 62, 64, 178, 225, 229 f., 326 ff., 361, 369, 428, 528, 692; *see* Argentine, Australia, Canada, South Africa
Immigration Resting Committee, United States, 435
Immigration restrictions, United States, 566 f.
Imperial Airways, Palestine, 625
Imredy, Baron, 672
Independent Order B'nai B'rith, 122, 192, 328, 384, 412, 433, 501, 519, 562 f., 580, 657
India, 625
Industrial Removing Committee, United States, 428
Institut du Droit International, 88
Institute for Higher Jewish Studies, St. Petersburg, 406
Institute for Jewish Research, 766
Institute for the Promotion of Jewish Literature, 101
Institution Israélite pour Instruction et Travail, Palestine, 249
Interfaith cooperation, 65
Intermarriage, xxviii, 92, 445, 520, 556
International Anti-Jewish Congress, Dresden 1882, 149
International Chamber of Commerce, United States, 585
"The International Jew," *Dearborn Independent*, 561
Irkutsk, 405
Isaac, Nathaniel, 134
Isaac, Rabbi of Wolozhin, 53, 105
Isaacs, M. S., 120, 700
Isaacs, Rufus, 320
Isaacs, Samuel M., 123
Isabella of Spain, 36
Ispahan, 78 f.
Israel, Berthold, 736
Israelit, Mainz periodical, 103
Israelite, American periodical, 125
Israelitische Allianz, Vienna, 176, 193, 363
Israelitische Landeskanzlei, Hungary, 28
Israelitische Landessekretariat, Hungary, 28

Israelitischer Verein zur Kolonisierung in Palästina, Frankfort a. M., 250
Israels, Josef, 89
Istiqlal, Arab party, 624
Istituto Rabbinico, Padua, 97
Istóczy, Victor von, 149, 179
Italy, 367 f., 418 f., 544 f., 590, 669
Ivanhoe, Scott, 122

JABOTINSKY, VLADIMIR, 459, 591, 602, 758
J'Accuse, Zola, 186
Jacobs, Joseph, 315, 351, 694, 701, 714
Jacobs, Simeon, 136
Jacobson, Israel, xxxv f.
Jacoby, Frederick, 755
Jacoby, Johann, 685
Jacques, Heinrich, 23
Jaffa, 246, 249, 269, 304, 461, 595 f., 630
Jamaica, 132
Japan, 377, 388, 513
Jassy, Rumania, 70, 366, 541 f.
Jastrow, Marcus, 130
Jastrow, Moritz, 65
Jellinek, Adolf, 101, 176, 712
Jellinek, Hermann, 21
Jericho, 480
Jerusalem, 245, 248, 251, 480, 591, 611, 619
Jessel, Sir George, 88
The Jew and American Ideals, Spargo, 563
Jewish Agency, The, 570 ff., 592, 599, 601, 614, 623
Jewish Board of Guardians, England, 310
Jewish Chautauqua Society, United States, 348
Jewish Chronicle, London, 103, 275, 315
Jewish Colonial Trust, 296
Jewish Colonization Association, 235 f., 304, 323, 342, 359, 369, 372, 406, 412, 427, 468, 502, 511, 522, 546, 554, 732

Jewish Daily Forward, New York City, 339
Jewish Encyclopedia, 350 f.
Jewish Faith, Aguilar, 103
Jewish Farm School, New Jersey, 338
Jewish Free School, London, 317
Jewish Historical Society, England, 316
Jewish Institute of Religion, New York, 574
Jewish Legion, Palestine, 459, 481, 635
Jewish National Fund, 296; see Keren Hayesod
Jewish National Library, Jerusalem, 305
"Jewish" press, 22, 91, 141
Jewish Publication Society of America, 347, 573
Jewish Quarterly Review, Philadelphia, 316
Jewish Relief Committee, United States, 230
Jewish Scientific Institute of Leningrad, 550
Jewish Scientific Institute in Wilna, 537
Jewish Social Studies, 755
Jewish Theological Seminary of America, 345, 352, 441 f., 575
Jewish Theological Seminary at Breslau, 97
Jewish Welfare Board, United States, 469
Jewish World Relief Conference, Carlsbad 1920, 502
The Jews, Belloc, 514
Jews' badge, Germany, 643
Jews' College, London, 39, 99 f.
Jews' "Days," Germany, 413
Jews' oath, 366
Joel, M., Breslau, 101
Joffe, Adolf, 487
Johannesburg, South Africa, 322
Joint Distribution Committee, 467, 500, 502, 516, 528, 546 ff., 552, 569 ff., 647 ff., 768

INDEX

Joint Palestine Survey Commission, 614
Joly, Maurice, 513
Journalism, Jews in, 90; see Periodicals
Judaism as a civilization, see Reconstructionism
"Judapest," 181
Jude, Der, 741
Judeans, military troop, 459
Judenstaat, Der, Herzl, 273, 275 ff., 348
Jüdische Presse, Berlin, 190
Jüdische Rundschau, Berlin, 648
Jugoslavia, 543
Justschinski, Andrei, 402

KADIMAH, Viennese student organization, 191
Kahal, in Russia, 47 f., 51, 94
Kahal, Book of the, 62
Kahan, Israel Meir, 537
Kahan, Jacob, 537
Kahn, Julius, 341, 754
Kahn, Zadoc, 101, 194, 259
Kaiser, German in Palestine, 289
Kalandia, Palestine, 619
Kalinin, Soviet leader, 512
Kalisch, Bertha, 448
Kalischer, Z. H., 250
Kamenetz Podolsk, 229
Kamenev, Soviet leader, 512
Kansas City, 429
Kaplan, Dora, 472
Kaplan, Mordecai M., 576 ff.
Karbatchev, St. Petersburg lawyer, 383
Karlsruhe, xxxvi, 10, 280
Karolyi, Count Michael, 489
Karpeles, Gustav, 195
Kassor, John A., 693
Kattowitz, 260, 422
Kaufmann, David, 196
Kayserling, Meyer, 347
Kehillah, New York, 439 f.
Kellner, Leon, 282
Kemal Pasha, 460 f.

Kempster, W., 230 f.
Keren Hayesod, Palestine foundation fund, 571, 603
Keren Kayemet, Palestine fund, 595, 611
Kerensky government, Russia, 471
Kharkov, 255, 299
Kherson, 50, 201, 393
Kiev, 49, 201, 214, 393, 550
Kimberley, South Africa, 136 f.
Kingston, Jamaica, 132
Kirschstein, Sally, 575
Kiryat Anavim, Palestine, 606
Kisch, Frederick Herman, 757
Kishinev, 53, 292, 298, 314, 377 f., 411, 432, 540
Kissilev, Count, 49, 58
Kisz, József, 709
Kittsee, Hungary, 95
Klatzkin, Eliahu, 537
Klausner, Joseph, 407, 721
Kluger, Salomo, 100
K'nesset Yisrael, Palestine assembly, 615
Knights Templar of Württemberg, 251
Kobrin, Leon, 448 f.
Kohler, Kaufmann, 343 f., 418, 442
Kohn, Pinchas, 464
Kohut, Alexander, 343; Memorial Foundation, 576
Kolchak, General, 499
Kompert, Leopold, 102, 696
KOMZET, Russian commission for settling Jews, 552, 554
Konitz, West Prussia, 167, 198
Kook, A. J., 609 f.
Korolenko, V. G., 216
Korrespondenzblatt, Berlin, 414
Kossuth, Louis, 25
Kovno, 221
Kramstück, Emil, 65
Krauskopf, Joseph, 347
Kreuzzeitung (*Neue Preussische Zeitung*), 13
Krivoye Osero, violence at, 499
Ku Klux Klan, 560, 566

Kuhn, Loeb and Co., 331
Kulturbund Deutscher Juden, under Nazis, 651
Kun, Bela, 489
Kuranda, Ignatz, 5, 21
K'vutzot, Palestinian communes, 607

La Juive, Halévy, 89
Labor movement and unions, 239, 311 f., 317, 339, 373, 433, 446 f., 581, 587, 606, 725, 726; *see* Bund
Laguarde, Paul de, 163
Lambsdorf, Count, 397
Lämel, Elise Herz von, 249, 305
Lämel School, Palestine, 249, 305
Land laws, Russia, 211
Landau, J. L., 322
Landau, Leopold, 736
Landau, R. S., 278
Landauer, Gustav, 488
Landesverbände, German Jewish state associations, 519
Landesrabbinerschule, Budapest, 97
Landsberg, Otto, 487
Landsmannschaften, New York, 439
Language war, 724; *see* Hebrew
Lansdowne, Lord, 294
Lasalle, Ferdinand, 14
Lasker, Eduard, 15, 192, 703
Latour, Count, 19
Latvia, 525, 529
Law, position of Jewish, xxviii
Lazare, Bernard, 710
Lazarus, Emma, 252, 332
Lazarus, Moritz, 14, 97, 191 f., 199 f., 686
League of Antisemites, 144
League for Attainment of Equal Rights for the Jewish People in Russia, 390
League of British Jews, 477
League of Nations, 484, 568, 599, 631, 645, 661
Lebensohn, A. B., 108
Lebensohn, M. J., 108
Lecky, quoted, 115
Leeds, 240, 311

Leeser, Isaac, 123 f., 128
Legislative Council, Palestine, 604, 627
Lehren des Judentums, Die, 414
Leipzig, 566; synod at, in 1869, 97
Leitmeritz, Bishop of, 582
Leivick, H., 582
Leman, Abbé J., 703
Lemberg, 83, 493, 532
Lenin, Nicolai, 472, 512
Lessing, G. E., xxvi, 271
Lestschinsky, Jacob, 751
Levendal, Baron, 383
Levi, Aaron, 138
Levi, J. I. (Montefiore), 138
Levi, Leo N., 384
Levin, Shmarya, 474 f.
Levine-Niessen, Eugen, 488
Levinson, Isaac Baer, 52
Levy, Barnett, 138
Levy, Israel, 195
Lewanda, J. L., 692
Liberal Jewish Synagogue, London, 319
Liberal Jewish Union, England, 319
Liberman, Hyman, 321
Libermann, Aaron S., 726
Liberty Bell, Philadelphia, 115
Libin, Zvi, 448
Libre Parole, antisemitic French paper, 183
Libya, 670
Lida, 406, 493
Lieberman, Max, 166
Ligue Nationale Antisémite en France, 183
Lilienblum, M. L., 109, 222, 407
Lilienthal, Max, in Russia, 53 f., 105 f.; in the United States, 125, 127
Limerick, Ireland, 314
Lincoln, Abraham, 119 f.
Linz, 660
Lionel de Rothschild School, Palestine, 249
Lipkin, Israel, 105
Lisbon, 557 f.
Lithuania, 53, 321, 464, 468 f., 530

INDEX

Littauer, Nathan, 575
Liubawich, 406
Lloyd George, David, 470, 592, 742
Lo zeh ha-Derech, Ahad Ha'am, 264
Lodz, 532
Loeb, Isidore, 195
Loew, Leopold, 28
Loewy, Maurice, 181
London, 240, 295, 311; Guild Hall Meeting, 207; Lord Mayor's Memorandum of 1899, 217; ritual reform in, xxxvii, 319
Longfellow, H. W., 582, 694
Los Angeles, 429
Louisiana, 341
Louisville, Ky., 31
Löwenfeld, Raphael, 712
Lublin, 532
Lucca, Pauline, 90
Ludendorff, General, 463, 487, 511, 518, 565
Lueger, Karl, 18, 170, 181
Luftmensch, 214, 296
Luxemburg, Rosa, 488
Luzzatto, S. D., 94
Luzzatti, Luigi, 419, 741
Lynar, Prince of, xxxii
Lyons, 186

MAATSCHAPPIJ TOT NYT VAN ISRAELITEN IN NEDERLAND, 36
Macaulay, T. B., xxxiv, 514; his *Civil Disabilities of the Jews*, 38
Maccabeans, The, English society, 281
Maccabean, American periodical, 349
MacDonald, Ramsay, 623
Mack, Julian W., 505
Madrid, 36; conference of 1880, 76 f.
Magnes, J. L., 432, 440, 443, 468, 572
Magyarization, 24, 28, 181
Maine, U. S. S., 341
Malvano, Graziadio, 419
Manchester, 240, 318
Mandate, Palestinian, 571, 591, 599, 622, 630; Arabs' protest, 605; Permanent Commission, 622

Mandelkern, Solomon, 691
Mandelstamm, Benj., 691
Mandelstamm, Max, 302
Manifesto, Russian, of October 1905, 393
Mannheimer, Noah, 19 f.
Manning, Cardinal, 220
Mansion House Committee, London, 226, 330
Mapu, Abraham, 108
Maretzki, L., 711
Margolin, A. D., 735
Margulies, Samuel H., 419
Marix, Adolph, 341
Marr, Wilhelm, 149, 702
Marranos, 103; in Portugal, 556 ff.
Marshall, Louis, 355, 433 f., 437, 505, 559, 565 f., 572 f., 735
Marx, Alexander, 575
Marx, Karl, 241, 408
Masaryk, T. G., 173, 495
Maskilim, Russia, 104
May Laws, Russia, 210 f., 265, 336
Mayer, Sigmund, 688
McDonald, James G., 762, 764, 765 f.
McGill University, 133
McMahon, Sir Henry, 589
McMichael, Sir Harold Alfred, 633
Mecklenburg-Schwerin, 10, 16
Mekor Hayyim Synagogue, Oporto, 558
Mehemed Ali, 248
Mein Kampf, Hitler, 637
Meisels, Dov Baer, 20, 65 f.
Melchett, Lord, 572, 623
Memel, 669
Mendele Mocher Seforim (Jacob Abramowich), 61, 112, 375, 407, 698
Mendelssohn, Moses, xxvi, xxxiv, 222, 522
Mendes, H. Pereira, 350
Menorah Association, 446, 577
Menorah Journal, New York, 446, 754
Merano, 544
Mesopotamia, 80

804 A CENTURY OF JEWISH LIFE

Metropolitan Museum, New York, 340
Metternich, 17
Metz, École Rabbinique, 100
Mexico, 582
Meyer, Adolph, 341
Meyerbeer, Giacomo, 89, 142
Michelson, Alfred A., 431
Mikveh Israel, Palestine agricultural school, 250
Mikveh Israel, colony, 259
Mikveh Israel, congregation, of Philadelphia, 123
Military service, xxix, 26, 44 f., 56, 69, 119, 172, 361, 389, 430, 455, 457, 459, 481, 635
Mill, John Stuart, 265
Miller Foundation, Columbia University, 576
Miller, Henry, 339
Millon, Ben Jehudah, 305
Minhag America, prayer book, 129
Minority rights, 502 f., 506, 525
Minsk, 550
Mirror of Antisemites, German liberal publication, 164
Mission doctrine, 130
Missionary activity, Christian, 30 f., 136, 247, 419
Mizrahi Federation, 287, 305, 538
Mogador, 75
Mohilever, Samuel, 223, 254, 259, 284
Moldavia, 68, 73, 365
Mommsen, Theodor, 706
Monash, Sir John, 455
Monatsschrift für Geschichte und Wissenschaft des Judentums, 417
Mond, Sir Alfred, 572
Mongols, 365
Montagu, Lily H., 319
Montagu Samuel, 263
Montefiore, Australia, 137
Montefiore, Claude G., 315, 319, 523
Montefiore, Jacob, 137
Montefiore, Joseph Barrow, 137
Montefiore, Sir Moses, 31, 48 ff., 54, 60 f., 75 f., 79, 237, 245, 247 ff., 251, 315
Montreal, 77, 133 f., 324
Morais, Sabato, 118, 127, 343
Morales, C. M., 132
Moravia, 546
Morgenstern, Julian, 575
Morgenthau, Henry, 461, 466
Morocco, 75, 438, 558
Mortara, Edgar, 30 f.
Mortara, Lodovico, 545
Moscow, 218
Mosenthal, family, 136
Moses, Adolf, 31
Mosesville, Argentina, 229
Moslem-Christian Union, Palestine, 605, 613
Mosque of Al Aksa, 616 f.
Mossinsohn, Benzion, 305
Mossul, 80; pipe-line, 625
Motion picture industry, 583
Motzkin, Leon, 715
Moza, Palestine, 619
Mufti, Haj Amin, 597 f., 617, 621, 632, 760
Mühsam, Erich, 488
Müller, Anita, 524
Munich, 283, 488, 661
Munkascz, 546
Muravyev, Nicolai, 66, 693
Musar literature, 105
Museum of Jewish Ceremonial Objects, New York, 575
Music, Jews in, 583, 756; Society of Jewish, St. Petersburg, 612
Mussolini, Benito, 544, 609, 678
Myers, Asher L., 315

NABLUS, 620
Nancy, France, 186
Nantes, France, 186
Napoleon III, 30, 66, 71, 119, 513
Natal, 134 f.
Nathan and Lina Straus Health Center, Palestine, 599
Nathan, Ernesto, 419
Nathan, Matthew, 309

INDEX

Nathan, M. N., 132
Nathan, Paul, 391, 411, 712, 724
Nathansohn, J. S., 100
National Christian Defense League, Rumania, 541
National Committee of German Jews, under Nazis, 650 f.
National Conference on Jewish Employment, 755
National Council of Jewish Women, United States, 348
National Rumanian Christian Students Union, 541
Nationalism, European, 143
Nationalism, Jewish, 198, 222, 257, 265 f., 271 f., 370
Nazism, 513, 517 f., 636 ff., 692, 707
Nazr ed-Din, Shah, 79
Near East, 411
Nebi Musa, riots at Jerusalem, 591
Needle trades, New York, 239, 446 f.
Negroes, 586
Neidhard, Col., 395
Netter, Charles, 226, 250, 259
Neue Freie Presse, Vienna, 273
Neue jüdische Monatshefte, 741
Neumann, I., 708
Neurath, Baron von, 636
Neustettin, 161
New Deal, United States, 588
New Economic Policy, Russia, 551
New Orleans, La., 121, 429
New South Wales, 137
New York City, 124, 238, 240, 326, 333, 337, 340, 429 f., 439, 568
New York Times, 430
Newlinsky, Baron von, 280
Newport, R. I., xxvi, 121
Nicholas I, Czar, 43
Nicholas II, Czar, 371 ff., 393
Niemirower, Rabbi of Jassy, 366
Nietzsche, 414
Nihilists, Russian, 206
Nikolaev, 49
Nilus, Sergei, 512
Nisselovitch, Duma deputy, 402
Nissim b. Shelomo, 694

Nobel, N. A., 749
Nobel Prize Winners, 431, 521
Nöldecke, Theodor, 418
Non-Partisan Conference of American Jews to Consider Palestinian Problems, 572
Nordau, Max, 282, 284, 295, 297, 424
Norden, Benjamin, 136
Norway, 37, 568, 669
Novoye Vremya, official Russian newspaper, 210
Numerus clausus, xxxii, 215, 402, 492, 535, 540, 564, 642
Nuremberg, 12, 638, 653
Nuremberg Laws, 1935, 654 ff.

O'CONNELL, WILLIAM CARDINAL, 562
The Occident and American Jewish Advocate, periodical, 123 f.
Occupations and Trades, 61, 142, 206, 311, 338, 357, 359, 372 f., 426, 430, 526, 551; see Professions
Occupation Enemy Territory Administration (OETA), Palestine, 482 f., 590
Ochs, Adolph S., 430
Odd Fellows, fraternal order, 192
Odenwald, 10 f.
Odessa, 53, 63, 265, 395, 406 f., 552
Odessa Committee, Society for Supporting Jewish Agriculturists and Artisans in Syria and Palestine, 262
Oetvoes, Hungarian minister, 28
OETA, see Occupation Enemy Territory Administration
Offenbach, J., 89
Oko, A. S., 575
Olat Tamid, prayer book, 129
Oliphant, Laurence, 253, 255, 270
On the Anarchists, Lambsdorff, 397
'Oneg Shabbat, institution of, 610
Onody, Geza von, 149
Oporto, Portugal, 557
Oppenheim, family, 84
Oppert, Jules, 181
Orange Free State, 136
Oranienburg, concentration camp, 638

Organ, in synagogue service, 97, 129
Orléanists, French, 188
Ormsby-Gore, Major (Lord Hankey), 743
Orschansky, Ilya, 110
ORT, 522, 528, 552, 554
Orthodoxy, new, 99; *see* Agudat Israel; Mizrahi
OSE, *see* Society for the Protection of Health etc.
Ostelbien, 161
Ottolenghi, General Giuseppe, 419
Ottoman Empire, *see* Turkey
Ovrush, Ukraine, 497
OZET, 552

PADEREWSKI, IGNACE J., 492, 509
Paedagogium, Vienna, 524
Pahlen, Count von, 216
Pale of Settlement, 43, 58, 210, 231, 402
Palestine, 245, 276, 361, 412, 460 f., 521, 570, 589 ff., 604; British administration of, 594 f.; Commission, 306; Development Co., 304; effect of World War on, 635; Foundation Fund, *see* Keren ha-Yesod; *see also* Mandate; Office, 304; Philharmonic Orchestra, 630; projected partition, Peel report, 631, 634; *see, inter al.*, Ahad Ha'am, Herzl, Hoveve Zion, Zionism
Pallière, Aimé, 418, 515, 522
Panama Canal Scandal, 709
Panona mines, 135
Panslavism, 200
Pappenheim, Bertha, 410
Paris, 82, 515, 522; Conference of 1858, 69
Passover, 379, 608
Passports, U. S., in Russia, 435 f.
Patterson, Lt. Col. J. H., 458 f., 481, 591
Peabody, George, 177
Peace Conference, World War I, 504, 589
Peddling, 116, 357

Peel, Earl William Robert, 630 f.
Peixotto, B. F., 72, 122
Pereire, family, 85
Perez, Judah Leib, 375, 407
Periodicals, Jewish, xxxiv, 102 f., 123 f., 125 f., 132, 190, 275, 282, 315, 332, 339, 342, 349, 414, 446, 543, 557, 648
Perlmann, Eliezer, 254
Permanent Mandates Commission, League of Nations, 601
Persia, 77 f.
Pest, Hungary, 25
Petaḥ Tikvah, Palestine, 251 f., 258
Petlura, S. V., 473, 496 f.
Philadelphia, 122, 240, 324, 343, 429, 444
Philanthropy, 91, 94, 121, 193, 237, 324, 409 f., 467, 519, 569, 585 f.
Philharmonic Orchestra, Palestine, 630
Philippines, 342
Philippson, Martin, 95, 410, 413, 417
Philippson, Ludwig, xl, 13, 101, 103, 687
Philipson, David, 754
Philosemitism, 150
Physique, 430
PICA, 595
Pichon, French foreign minister, 589
Picot, Georges, 589
Picquart, General, 185, 188
Pilichowski, Leopold, 612
Pilsudski, Marshal, 534
Pines, J. M., 251
Pinner, Adolf, 736
Pinner, Moritz, 118
Pinsk, 493; "Pinsk versus Washington," 571
Pinsker, Leo, 256 f., 260 f., 279
Pinski, David, 449
Pirbright, Lord, 309
Pissarev, Russian rationalist, 264
Pissarro, Camillo, 89
Pittsburgh, Conference of 1885, 344; Zionist Program of 1918, 570
Pius IX, 29, 141
Pius X, 293

INDEX

Pius XII, 32
Plehve, Wencelas von, 292, 299, 377, 384, 387, 393
Plotke, Julius, 410
Plumer, Lord, 614 f.
Po'ale Zion, Palestine workers' organization, 370, 374, 581
Pobiedonostzev, K. P., 208, 216, 219, 377
Podolia, 393
Poe, E. A., 582
Pogroms, Russian, 161, 202 f., 376 ff., 713 f.; technique of, 394 ff.; German, 663 f.
Poincaré, Raymond, 518
Poland, 9, 64, 213, 404, 468 f., 492 f., 496, 507 f., 525 f., 532 f., 662, 673; under German rule, 676 f.
Poliakoff, family, 84
Polna, 173
Population shifts, 82; *see* Immigration
Poltava, 201, 393
Polyakof, Jacob, 227
Poor Jews' Temporary Shelter, London, 310
Port Arthur, 388
Portland, Oregon, 585
Portugal, 556
Posen, xxxi, 82
Poverty, 61, 516, 533
Poznanski, G., 349
Poznanski, Samuel A., 537
Prague, 520, 546, 747; University of, 152
Press, Jews in, 90, 103, 537, 755; *see* Periodicals; under Nazis, 649
Pressburg, 25, 82, 95
Pretoria, 137
Preuss, Hugo, 487
Prim, General, 36
Proceedings of American Academy for Jewish Research, 576
Professions, 88, 162, 172, 180, 340, 358, 368, 413, 532, 535, 643; *see* Occupations
Profiteers, World War I, 515
Prosnitz, 82

Protestantism, 117, 686
Protocols of the Elders of Zion, 376 ff., 397, 512 f., 560 f., 563, 619, 637, 734
Prostitution, 219, 427
Publishers, United States, 582
Puritanism, in American tradition, 115

QUEBEC, 134
Queensland, 138
Quota laws, United States, 567

RABBI ISAAC ELCHANAN YESHIVA, New York, 574
Rabbinical Assembly of America, 444
Rabbinical Seminary, Budapest, 191
Rabbinical Seminary for Orthodox Judaism ("Hildesheimer's"), Berlin, 99
Rabbinowitz, Ossip, 110, 696
Rabinovitch, Sholom, 407
Rabinowitz, Joel, 136
Rachel, Elisa Felix, 90
Racism, 145, 167, 365, 514, 560, 637, 669
Radek, Soviet leader, 512
Radetzky, 17
Rafah, 479
Railroad development, 84, 232, 331, 340
Ramsgate, 260
Raphall, M. J., 118, 123
Rasryaden law, Russia, 56
Rath, Ernst vom, 663 f., 767
Rathenau, Emil, 166
Rathenau, Walter, 518, 744
Ratnoff, Nathan, 754
Reading, Lord, 320
Real estate development, 84, 239, 569
Reconstruction, Civil War, 125
Reconstructionist movement, 576 f.
Red Cross, 340
Reform, ritual, 28, 64, 96 f., 128 f., 132, 319, 418, 421; *see* Theology
Refugees problem, 501, 567 f., 647, 662, 667
Régis, Max, 186 f.

Reich Institute for History of the New Germany, 766
Reichstag, German, 165
Reichsrat, *see* Austria
Reichsvertretung der deutschen Juden, German Jewish national committee under Nazis, 650
Reifmann, Jacob, 692
Reines, I. J., 223, 287, 406
Religion, 93, 121, 136, 138; and *see* Reform, Secularization
Religion of Revelation, Steinheim, 96
Religion der Vernunft aus den Quellen des Judentums, Cohen, 416 ff.
Remak, Robert, 88
Renan, Ernest, 702
Rennes, France, 189
Restrictions on Immigration, United States, 335; England, 294
Reuter's, news agency, 90
Revel, Bernard, 574
Revisionism, 758
Revisionists, Palestine, 625, 758, 760
Revolution of 1848, Berlin, 6
Revolution of 1905, Russia, 392 f.
Revolutionaries, Jewish, 220, 486, 692
Rhodes, 545
Rhodes, Cecil, 320
Richards, Bernard G., 746
Richmond, E. T., 757
Richmond, Va., 123
Richtlinien zu einem Programm für das liberale Judentum, Program for liberal Judaism, Seligmann, 421 f.
Riess, Peter A., 89
Riesser, Gabriel, xxxiii, 5, 14, 88, 198, 685
Riga, 53, 530
Rio de Janeiro, 427
Rishon le-Zion, Palestine, 258
Risorgimento, Italian, 29
Ritual murder charge, 152 f., 155, 158, 165, 168, 170, 172 f., 355, 379, 402 ff., 708
Rodeph Shalom congregation, Philadelphia, 122
Rohling, August, 152 f., 183

Roosevelt, F. D., 662, 664, 667, 764
Roosevelt, Theodore, 341, 363, 383, 431, 436
Rosebery, Lord, 263
Rosen, Joseph A., 552
Rosenberg, Arthur, 637
Rosenberg, James N., 553
Rosenbloom, Sol, 572
Rosenfeld, Morris, 329
Rosenhayn, N. J., 334
Rosenheim, Jacob, 422
Rosenthal, Harry, 726
Rosenwald, Julius, 469, 553, 585 f., 741
Rosenzweig, Franz, 521
Rosh Pinah, Palestine, 258
Rothschild, House of, 84 f., 248 f., 716, 721
Rothschild, Lord, 363
Rothschild, Baron Edmond de, 259 f., 304, 418 f.
Rothschild, Lord Lionel Walter, 363, 477
Rothschild, Baron Meier Carl von, 11
Rothschild, Nathaniel, 38, 726
Rothschild, Nathaniel Meyer, 309
Royal Alien Immigration Commission, 294
Royal Commission, Palestine, 630
Royal Fusiliers, 459
Rublee, W., 668, 768
Rülf, Isaac, 250
Rumania, 41, 68, 70 ff., 355 ff., 362 f., 367, 507, 525 ff., 539 ff., 672 f.
Rumbold, Sir Horace, 744
Ruppin, Arthur, 304
Russia, 41 ff., 200 ff., 371 ff., 469 ff., 547 ff.; New Economic Policy, 551; revolution of 1917, 469 ff.
Russian Emigrants Relief Fund, United States, 225, 327
Russian Treaty, abrogation of, 692
Russification, 59, 200 f.
Russo-Japanese War, 388
Rutenberg, Pinchas, 611, 615, 759; power station, 625
Ruthenia, 174, 368

INDEX

SABBATH, observance, neglect, disabilities, 13, 98, 366, 507 f., 568, 608; *see* Sunday laws
Sabsovich, N., 338
Sacerdote, Angelo, 544
Sachs, Michael, xxxix, 6
Sachse-Weimar, xxxvi
Sadagora, Galicia, 264
Safed, 246, 258, 620
St. Louis, Mo., 429
"St. Louis," S. S., 668
St. Petersburg, 381, 406
Salanter, R., 105
Salomons, David, 38
Saloniki, 366, 507, 543
Salvendi, Adolf, 250
Samuel, Lord Herbert, 320, 592 f., 596 ff., 742
Samuel, Sir Stuart, 744
San Francisco, 429
San Remo, 592
Sanhedrin, Napoleon's, xxvii f.
São Paulo, 427
Sapiro, Aron, 565
Sassoon, family, 80
Savannah, Ga., 121
Saxony, 16
Schacht, Hjalmar, 636
Schapira, Hermann, 296
Schapiro, Raphael, 406
Schechter, Solomon, 196, 199, 315, 353, 441 f., 575; *Ginze Schechter*, 575
Schereschewski, I., 692
Scheurer-Kestner, senator, 710
Schiff Classics, 445
Schiff, Jacob H., 302, 306, 331, 334, 352, 363, 433, 436, 741
Schlachta, Polish, 175, 178, 494
Schleswig-Holstein, 16
Schneerson, Sholom Baer, 406
Schneider, Ernest, 148, 170
Schneur, Zalman, 407
Schnirer, Dr., 289
Scholars and scholarship, Jewish, 195, 444, 519, 576
Schönerer, Georg von, 637, 707

Schorr, Moses, 537
Schreiber, A. S. B., 100
Schulmann, K., 107
Schultheiss, U. S. Commissioner of Immigration, 335
Schurman, Jacob Gould, 384
Schwartzbard, Shalom, 498, 739
Schwarz, Samuel, 556, 752
Schwarzfeld, Elias, 360
Schweitzer, Ritter von, 708
Scott, Sir Walter, 122
Second Balkan War, 367
Secularization, 111, 373, 420 f., 548 f., 577 f., 609
Sejm, Polish, 531, 533
Seligman, E. R. A., 431
Seligman, James, 699
Seligmann, Cäsar, 421
Seligman, Jesse, 698
Seligsohn, Julius, 650
Selling, Ben, 585
Semi-Gotha, 424
Semi-Kirschner, 424
Senator, Hermann, 736
Simosenko, Petlura leader, 497
Serbia, 67, 250, 367, 543
Sergius, Grand Duke, 377, 389
Serkele, Ettinger, 112
Sermons, publication of, 101
Shah of Persia, in London, 79
Shaikev-Shomer, 112
Shanghai, 656
Shaw, Sir Walter, 621
Shearith Israel congregation, Montreal, 133
Shehitah, 191 f., 198, 318, 414, 568, 652
Shekel, 285
Shemitta, 262
Sheriff of Mecca, 589
Shiites, in Persia, 77
Shiraz, 77 ff.
Siberia, 217
Silesia, 546
Silvester, J. J., 89
Simon, H. V., 736
Simon, James, 411

Simon, Jules, 35
Simonsen, David, 547
Simpson, Sir John Hope, 622 f., 768
Sinai congregation, Baltimore, 125
Sinai Peninsula, 294
Sinclair, Upton, 515
Singer, Isidore, 350, 712
Singer, Simeon, 319
Sirach, Book of, 315
Sketches from Half Asia, Franzos, 102
Skop, Simon, 406
Skwira, Ukraine, 264
Slavery, views on American, 118
Sliosberg, H., 739, 740, 741
Slobodka, yeshibah at, 406
Slovakia, 546
Smith, C. E., 727
Smolenskin, Perez, 222, 279
Social Democrats, 164
Socialism, 339, 371, 373, 374, 408, 447
Sociéte des Études Juives, Paris, 194
Society for Diffusion of Culture among Jews, Russia, 60, 62, 111, 222
Society of Jewish Music, St. Petersburg, 612
Society for the Prevention of Immigration of Destitute Aliens, England, 228, 311
Society for the Protection of the Health of the Jews (OSE), Russian, 501, 522
Society for Supporting Jewish Agriculturists and Artisans in Palestine and Syria, 262
Sofer, Moses, 24, 93
Sokolov, Nahum, 473, 509, 589
Solel Boneh, building construction firm, Palestine, 595
Solis-Cohen, Solomon, 352
Solomons, family, 133
Solomons, Adolphus S., 340
Solymosi, Esther, 155 f.
Sombart, Werner, 424
Sonnenthal, Adolf, 90
Sonntagsblaetter, Vienna, 19

Southern states, United States, 303, 328
Spain, 36, 543
Spanish-American War, 341
Spargo, John, 563
Spektor, Isaac Elhanan, 221, 714
Spencer, Herbert, 265
Spire, Andre, 522
Stalin, Joseph, 512
Stanislavsky, Russian theatrical producer, 550
Star of David, 284
Staub, Hermann, 736
Steinamanger, Austria, 25
Steinberg, Judah, 691
Steinschneider, Moritz, 102, 702
Steinthal, N., 191, 195
Stern der Erlösung, Rosenzweig, 521
Stern, Adolf, 730
Stern, Moritz A., 88
Stern, Sigismund, xxxviii
Stieglitz, Alfred, 583 f.
Stöcker, Adolf, 144, 160 f., 164, 179
Stojalowski, Father, 178
Stolypin, Russian minister of interior, 398 ff.
Storrs, Sir Ronald, 743
Straucher, Benno, 368
Straus, Nathan, 340, 563
Straus, Oscar S., 334, 341, 347, 363
Streicher, Julius, 636, 763, 764, 765
Strike, Arab in Palestine, 628 f.
Struck, Hermann, 464, 741
Students, activities and organizations, 163, 191, 194, 445 f., 536, 541, 579 f., 712
Sturdza, Rumanian minister, 365
Stürmer, Der, Nazi periodical, 655
Stybel, Abraham, 537
Sudeten, 172, 662
Südfeld, Gabriel, 282
Sue, Eugene, 107
Suez, 85
Sultan, 280, 288, 290
Sulzberger, Mayer, 334, 346, 350, 352, 433
Sunday laws, 198, 210, 319, 414, 532

INDEX

Sunday School, Philadelphia, 121
Sunday services, *see* Reform
Supreme Moslem Council, 597
Sutro, A. H. J., 341
Suttner, Bertha von, 722, 730
Swartopol, 49
Sweatshops, 239, 328
Sweden, 37, 547
Switzerland, 32 f., 547, 698
Sydney, Australia, 137
Sykes, Sir Mark, 589, 742
Sylva, Carmen, 358
Synagogues, organization of, 94; burning in Germany, 661, 664, 767
Syria, 80, 245, 589
Szamuelly, Tibor, 490
Szold, Benjamin, 129 f.
Szold, Henrietta, 570, 626, 756, 757, 758

TAAFFE, EDUARD F. J., Count von, 168
Taft, William Howard, 332, 437, 562
Tahkemoni school, Palestine, 305
Talmud, 152, 182, 191, 222; forged citations from, xxx, 170
Talmudjude, Der, Rohling, 152
Talpiot, Palestine, 619
Tangiers, 557
Tarbut, Polish Hebrew cultural organization, 536
Tartu (Dorpat), 529
Tauria, Russian province, 393
Tchaka, African king, 134 f.
Tchernigov, 393
Teachers' training schools, United States, 445
Technicum, school at Haifa, 306 f., 411
Teheran, 632
Tel Aviv, 305, 461, 611, 614, 620, 630
Tel Hai, 590
Teleki, Count Paul, 672
Telschi, yeshibah at, 406
Tennyson, Alfred, 226
Terrorists, Russian, 206
Tetuan, 75

Teudah b'Yisrael, Levinsohn, 52
Theater, 90, 112, 138, 375, 448, 537, 550, 582 f., 607
Theology, xxxvi, xxxviii; *see, inter al.,* Cohen, Kaplan, Schechter, Seligmann, Wise
Tiberias, 246, 611
Tietz, Oskar, 736
Tiktin, Solomon, 574
Tikvath Israel congregation, Capetown, 136
Tillet, Ben, 725
Timendorfer, Berthold, 412
Tisza, Kolomon, 180
Tisza-Eszlar, ritual murder charge, 149, 155, 157, 180
Toller, Ernst, 488
Tolstoi, Count D. A., 207
Tolstoi, Count Leo, 208, 378
Toronto, 134, 324
Toscanini, Arturo, 630
Touro, Judah, 121, 249
Trades, 50, 59, 83, 86, 214 f., 217, 239, 328; *see* Occupations, Professions
Transjordania, 263, 592
Translations, Bible and prayer book, 123; into Hebrew, 108; into Yiddish, 448
Transvaal, 137, 322
Transylvania, 539
Traube, Ludwig, 88
Travels and Adventures in Eastern Africa, N. Isaac, 135
Treaty, of Lausanne, 544; U. S.-Russian, abrogated, 438; Versailles, 502 f.
Treitschke, Heinrich von, 162, 191
Trepov, General, 388, 396
Trieste, 544
Tripoli, 367
Trotzky, Leon, 472, 512
Trumpeldor, Joseph, 458, 590
Tschernichowski, Saul, 407
Tschernowitz, Chaim, 406
Turin, 82
Tyler, John, 114 f.

Turkey, 245, 253, 261, 263, 291, 363, 412, 478, 544
Twentieth Century Fund, United States, 585

Uganda, 294 f., 297 f., 301, 314
Ukraine, 472 f., 496 f., 552
Um-esh Shert, 481
Uman, 53
Unger, Jos., 688
Union of American Judaic Congregations, 125
Union of American Hebrew Congregations, 126, 433
Union of British Fascists, 668
Union of Jewish Literary Societies, England, 316
Union of Jewish Women, England, 316
Union of Liberal Rabbis, Germany, 421
Union Libérale Juive, France, 418
Union of Orthodox Jewish Congregations in the United States and Canada, 349
Union Prayer Book, 345
Union of the Russian People, 400
Union of South Africa, 321
Union Universelle de la Jeunesse Juive, 515
Unions, trade, *see* Labor movement and unions
United Committee for Jewish Emigration, 502
United Hebrew Trades, 339
United Jewish Charities, United States, 333
United States, 33, 114 ff., 559 ff., 761; and defense of Jewish rights, 72, 687, 689, 693 f.
United Synagogue of America, 443 f.
United Synagogue, England, 39, 94, 319
Univers Israelite, Paris, 103
Universitaet, Die, Frankl, 19
University, of Brussels, 413; Budapest, 157; German, 685; Hebrew, 483 f.; Illinois, 579 f.; Manchester, 473; Oregon, 585
Ussischkin, M. M., 268, 304, 611, 631, 723, 743
Uvaroff, Russian minister, 52, 690

Va'ad ha-Lashon, Palestine, 305
Va'ad Le-Umi, Palestine, 610, 615, 634
Va'ad ha-Zirim, Palestine, 482 f.
Vachtangoff, Soviet leader, 550
Valentin, Gabriel Gustav, 32, 88
Vambéry, Armin, 290
Vancouver, B. C., 324
Vaszony, Wilhelm, 491
Vatican, 281
Veit, Moritz, 5
Veneziani, Immanuel, 233
Verband der deutschen Juden, Germany, 413 f.
Verein Jüdischer Studenten, Germany, 194
Verein für Kultur und Wissenschaft der Juden, xxxvii
Vereinigung für das liberale Judentum, 421
Versailles Treaty, 502 f.
Viadrina, Breslau students' association, 193
Viborg Manifesto, of liberal Russians, 399
Victor Emmanuel III, 293
Victoria, Canada, 134
Victoria, Queen, 38, 309
Vienna, 82, 153, 169, 193, 273, 520, 523
Vinaver, Duma deputy, 391
Vladivostok, 404
Vogelstein, Heinemann, 421, 696
Volunteers, in Civil War, 119; and *see* Military service
"Vulcan," S. S., 468

Wagener, Hermann, 13
Wagner, Richard, 141, 167
Wailing Wall, Jerusalem, 246, 616 ff., 625

INDEX

Wakfs, Palestine, 592
Wald, Lillian D., 340
Waldeck-Rousseau, 189
Wales, South, 320
Wallachia, 68
Walley, Count Arco, 488
Wanderers, The, British group, 195, 315
Warburg, Felix M., 467, 572 f., 623
Warburg, Max M., 744
Warburg, Otto, 306
Warsaw, 207, 404, 407, 494, 532
Warschawski, family, 84
Washington, George, xxvi, 117
Wassermann, Jakob, 521
Wassermann, Oskar, 572
Watchord, Robert, 730
Wattenberg, Philip, 572
Wauchope, Sir Arthur, 625
Weber, J. C., 230
Weimar Republic, Germany, 487, 517, 520, 652
Weinberg, Jacob, 755
Weinstein, Bernhard, 339
Weiss, Isaac H., 196
Weizmann, Chaim, 473 ff., 482, 571, 602, 613, 616, 623, 631, 762
Wellhausen, Julius, 418
Die Welt, Zionist weekly, 282 f.
Weltsch, Siegfried, 522
Wergeland, Henrik, 37
Wessely, N. H., 52
West, United States, 328
West Indies, 131, 134
West London Synagogue, 319
White, Arnold, 234, 717 f., 723, 725
White, Henry, 438
White Paper, British on Palestine, 623, 760, 761
Whitechapel, London, 238
Whitman, Walt, 582
Wielopolski, Marquis, 65
William I, Germany, 160, 164
William II, Germany, 167, 280, 383
Villiams, Michael, 645
Villstaetter, Richard, 521

Wilna, 49, 54 f., 60, 104, 407, 493 f., 531 f., 693
Wilson, Woodrow, 475 f., 477 f., 506, 562, 566, 754
Windisch-Graetz, Prince, 20, 127
Winnipeg, 324
Winternitz, W., 708
Wise, I. M., 124, 343, 346, 348, 442
Wise, S. S., 349, 443, 505, 563, 574
Wissotzki, Moscow philanthropist, 306
Witte, Count Sergei, 208, 220, 292, 377, 390, 392, 397, 400, 436
Wolf, Lucien, 302, 315, 714
Wolf, Simon, 126 f., 336
Wolff's, news agency, 90
Wolffsohn, David, 282, 301, 306
Wolozhyn, yeshibah at, 53, 105, 406
Woodbine, N. J., 337
Workmen's Circle, New York, 581
World Council for German Jewry, London, 656
World Jewish Congress, 753
World Union for Progressive Judaism, England, 523
World Union of Zionist Revisionists, 758
World War I, 453 ff.
World War II, 675 ff.
Worms, family, 80
Worms, Henry de, 309
Wrangel, General, 499
Wright, P., 744
Württemberg, xxxii, 10
Würzburg, 650

XANTEN, 165

YALE UNIVERSITY, 576
Yanuskevich, Russian general, 740
Yearbook, of Association for Jewish History and Literature, 195
Yehoash (Bloomgarden), 448
Yehuda, Eliezer ben, 305
Yellin, David, 610
Yemen, 303
Yeshiva College, New York, 574

Yeshibah Markazit 'Olamit, Palestine, 609
Yeshibot, 100, 221, 406, 530
Yewreiskaya Enciclopedia, 406 f.
Yewreiskaya Starina, St. Petersburg, 407
Yiddish, 113, 241, 321, 324, 339, 368, 371 ff., 447 f., 531 f., 536, 550 f., 555, 581; translations from and into, 582
Yiddish Art Theater, 538, 582
Der Yiddishe Fonograf, Buenos Aires, 342
Yildiz Kiosk, 290
Young Men's and Young Women's Hebrew Associations, 122, 579
Young Men's Hebrew Benevolent Society, Montreal, 134, 323
Young Turks, 303, 366
Youth '*Aliyah*, to Palestine, 626
Youth movement, 515; *see* Students

ZANGWILL, ISRAEL, 92, 94, 98, 198, 241, 302, 314 f., 347, 559, 696, 733
Zbaszyn, Poland, 663
Zeisler, Fanny Bloomfield, 340
Zemach, Nahum, 550

Zentralverein deutscher Staatsbürger jüdischen Glaubens, 196 f.
Zhitomir, 54 f., 214, 391, 497
Zhyd, 377
Zichron Ja'acob, Palestine, 258
Zinoviev, Soviet leader, 512
Zion Mule Corps, 458
Zione Zion, Zionist group, 304
Zionism, 179, 273 ff., 281 ff., 348, 374, 404, 419, 422 f., 443, 524, 538 f., 570 ff., 733; *see*, *inter al.*, Ahad Ha'am, Herzl, Weizmann
Zionist Commission, British, 1918, 482 f.
Zionist Congresses, *see* Congresses
Zionist declarations, Copenhagen Manifesto of 1918, 504; Pittsburgh Program, 570
Zionist Organization, 571, 592 f., 601, 753
Zirelsohn, Rabbi of Kishinev, 542
Zola, Emile, 186 f.
Zulus, 134
Zunz, Leopold, xxxvii, 6, 102
Zurich, 573
Zweig, Arnold, 464, 741

296
E37 Elbogen.
Century of Jewish life.

Date Due		
B7226	24 Mar '56	
6493	19 Nov '56	
2956	19 Dec '56	
4	2 Jan '57	
3693	26 Jan '57	
7746	9 Mar '57	
9807	13 Dec	
X1487	3 Jul '61	
A10786	4 May '79	
MAR 2 5	1981	
JAN 27	1995	
2 22		

PRINTED IN U.S.A.